W9-AFB-606

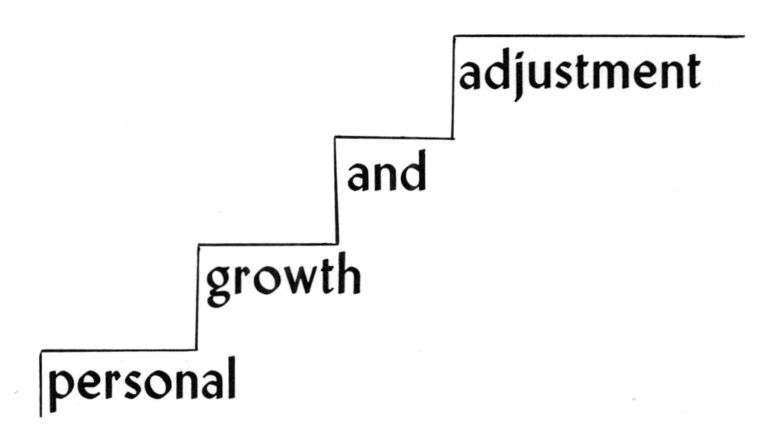
adjustment
and
growth
personal

Guy L. Roberts
PENNSYLVANIA STATE UNIVERSITY

personal growth and adjustment

holbrook press, inc.
boston

470 Atlantic Avenue
Boston, Mass. 02210

Library of Congress Catalog Card Number: 68:18056

Printed in the United States of America

preface

In writing this book, I have found it difficult to decide what information to omit, because of the rapid accumulation of knowledge, changing emphases, aroused public interest, and rapid expansion of mental health facilities. A closely related problem was the task of balancing old and fundamentally sound information with new and promising but not yet proven material. How could this be done and keep the book to a usable size?

By drawing upon several years of experience teaching "mental hygiene" and many more years of working in liaison with a variety of mental health agencies, I have done my best to attain this balance and to balance my own point of view with that of others. Thus I have quoted widely to maintain the eclecticism that a useful textbook should have. However, knowing that most teachers are highly individualistic, I expect that some will wonder why I omitted this and belabored that. Ample material is presented for these teachers to deemphasize certain topics and to expand upon others, in accord with their individual teaching philosophy and method.

This book is designed for under-graduate college students who may have had little previous work in psychology and for adults in Continuing Education. I have tried to avoid being overly technical and involving the student in the more abstruse theories, while presenting material advanced enough to be challenging. My primary purpose is to provide material that will be most helpful to the reader in guiding his own personal growth or that of those with whom he is associated. In view of the great public concern with mental health, my second objective is to provide sufficient coverage of mental illness and recovery, and to acquaint the student with the disciplines and institutions that effect recovery.

I have organized my material around the central thesis that structure determines capacity, capacity modified by evaluation determines need, and need being satisfied or frustrated determines mental health or illness (wholesome or disordered growth and adjustment). The theme moves from the nature or structure of personality and the self through needs and values to the satisfying and frustrating environment—detours through the defenses, disorders, and restoration of those whose development is disrupted—then proceeds with the major self-actualization areas.

I have presented as a second thesis what I call the new synthesis in behavior dynamics. The older psychology looked chiefly to man's biological nature, the instincts, for his dynamics—*the thesis*. The swing later was to society or the cultural environment, making the stimulus situation the locus of dynamics—*the antithesis*. I have moved to the position of the self (whole person in the role of acting agent) as true locus of behavior dynamics—*the synthesis*. These theses and my manner of treatment are somewhat new, and will probably create some controversy which should provide the student with the challenge to confirm or contradict.

Emphasis has been given to an interdisciplinary approach in relation to personal growth and mental health. Psychiatrists, other mental hygienists, and particularly the new researchers in human potentials development, are compelling us to take this broader approach. All of the empirical knowledge that scientific psychology can provide is essential in the prevention and treatment of mental illness and in guiding personal growth. But alone this is not enough. We must draw from other disciplines, and this I have done.

In the preparation of this manuscript I acknowledge and express my gratitude to my several colleagues who read parts of the manuscript and made many helpful suggestions: R. E. Brown, Henry Durand, Leon Gorlow, Dale Harris, Robert Horn, Raymond Hummel, Florence Johnson, Richard Lundy, Frank Melone, Peter Steese, and Hugh Urban. I owe much to my wife, Stella, who did much of the preliminary typing and helped extensively with the proofreading. I am also indebted to the many publishers and authors who freely permitted me to quote them.

Guy L. Roberts

contents

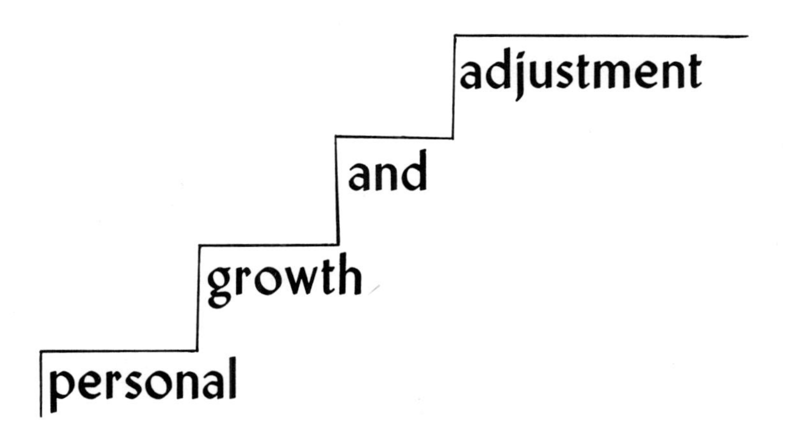
adjustment
and
growth
personal

1

Man Studies Himself

People are funny. Interesting. Complex. Difficult. Puzzling. Man may love or hate himself and trust or fear himself. He may love or hate his neighbor and trust or fear his neighbor. But he is always interested in himself and his neighbor. Man is his own chief enigma. The body cannot lift itself by the boot straps. The eye cannot see itself. Why, then, should we expect that the mind is capable of comprehending itself?

Man has done well in gaining knowledge of and power over the outer world with the marvelous instrument he calls the "mind." With this instrument and his modern scientific method of using it, knowledge of the world is burgeoning at such a rate that book publishing has become one of the giant industries, and textbooks are getting thicker with every new edition. New courses are being added to the school curricula; education has become a lifetime activity.

THE DILEMMA

Modern man excels with power over his world. He has broken both the sound and gravity barrier. The most distant point on earth is but a few hours away, the moon but a few days, and other planets but a few weeks. In opening the nucleus of the atom, man has given himself such power as staggers the imagination—power to create or to destroy. New materials and new products have made this the gadget age, with comforts and conveniences undreamed of until well into this century. He is on the threshold of a breakthrough in synthetic foods and new modes of food production, second only to the jump in power output as a consequence of atomic fission. Modern man will be ready to provide for himself a life of comfort, ease, and affluence when he can stop warring and use his technical knowledge and power creatively in a peaceful economy.

UNBALANCED ACHIEVEMENT

Modern man has acquired knowledge of his physical nature and power to control it. He is living longer, and his children are growing taller. His wonder drugs are greatly reducing suffering and eliminating many illnesses. Personal hygiene and beauty aids run even ahead of health; and they add special touches of grace to life that crowns affluence and good health. Man stands at another threshold. He is at the verge of creating living organisms in the laboratory which he may use to combat infectious organisms. He is also on the verge of breaking the genetic barrier by altering the gene and producing the characteristics he desires in plants and animals in his offspring. Man stands equipped for all this, for a vast organic world made to his own specifications, but he has not been able to come to terms with himself and his neighbor.

The ancient Hebrew scriptures state that when God created the world, He pronounced it good. Then He made man heir of the world, saying, "Be fruitful and multiply, and fill the earth and subdue it; and have dominion over the fish of the sea and over the birds of the air and over every living thing that moves upon the earth."[1] In this century, man has leaped far ahead in his control over every living creature in this world, except himself and his neighbor. He has built a society and culture somewhat as illustrated in Figure 1. His scientific method has been highly successful in working with the mineral world; his material

[1] *Genesis* 1:28, 29

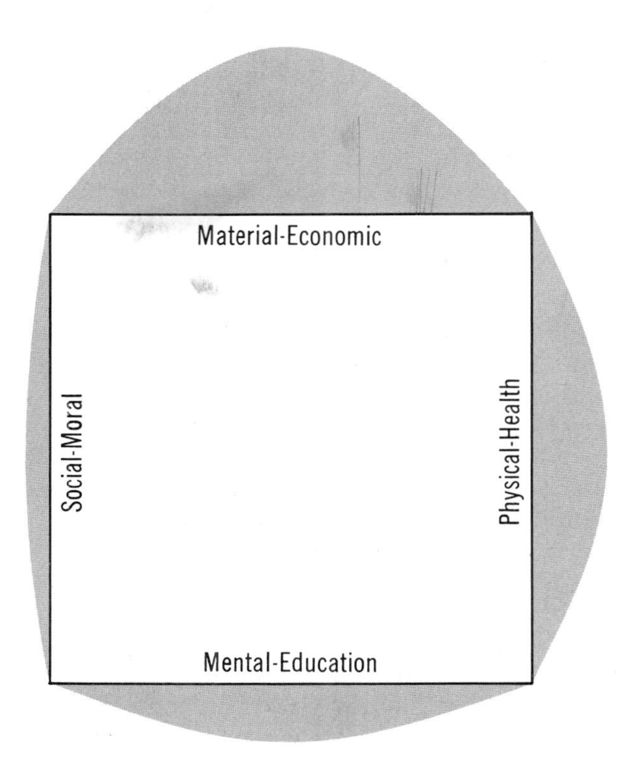

Figure 1.

interests have become disproportionate. The scientific method has been effective in the organic realm and much progress has been made in the spheres of health and physical well-being; yet this is far short of his material progress. His techniques have not been as effective in the intellectual and cultural sphere. There has been progress, but the lag is greater than in the physical. In deeper involvement with his neighbor—in the realm of true self-knowledge and self-control; of character, morals, and interpersonal relationships; in understanding and actualizing his own potential—creative and creator man has made some progress, however little. He has created a lopsided culture which bulges too much on one side and is almost flat on the other. His society is not rolling smoothly, and he is not functioning smoothly within himself.

Twentieth-century man is aware of his dilemma in a general way. He knows that much is wrong with his society and himself, but knowledge of his own being, and its application in controlled behavior, is not yet adequate. He is afraid.

PROXIMITY TENSION

Man is not ready for the responsibility in using the power which he already possesses and the power he will attain. He is under great stress; he feels inadequate. Life has become a threat rather than a challenge. Likewise, there is the stress of too many people with too many problems. Since geographical barriers have been eliminated with rapid transportation and instant communication, the whole world has become his neighborhood. Yet it is a neighborhood of strangers, with neighbors whom he does not understand, does not trust and can not love. He is constantly bombarded with their problems; he hears their cries and curses, feels their hate and fears, and knows that in some way his well-being has become entangled with theirs. Yet, he can do little about it but feel the frustration and threat, and turn the resulting hostility and anxiety against himself.

TRANSIENT SOCIETY

Man is on the move. His is an intermingling society, and cultural mixing is the order of the day. He has been fighting and traveling all over the world. Boundaries that formerly separated people into ethnic groups—nationalities, races, and religions—have been trod over if not trampled down. The folkways, mores, morals, creeds and ideologies that gave identity and stability to distinct societies have become so intermingled that modern man is left in the state of *anomie*. He lacks a dependable creed or philosophy of life or value system, necessary for security and direction. He lacks faith in God, in the old moral codes, in himself, and in other people. His life lacks meaning and purpose. He sees no worthy goal. He is confused, anxious, angry, sick. He has burst too suddenly from parochialism to cosmopolitanism, from community man to world citizen.

EXCESS STIMULATION

Modern man is over-stimulated. Numerous experiments demonstrate that prolonged under- and over-stimulation impair both physiological and mental processes. Either will cause the endocrine glands and nervous systems to deviate from their normal range. Constantly surrounded by people, telephones, the roar and click of industrial and office machinery and signal systems, the nervous system of today's man is bombarded incessantly. He can not escape it when he goes home. His or his neighbor's yard is filled with noisy children. The roar of traffic is at his door. His wife and/or his daughter is on the phone. His older boy is listening to a ball game on the radio, while his younger boy is enjoying a shooting-westerner on TV. Modern man needs quiet, experiences frustration, suppresses his anger, and becomes sick.

It would be difficult to exaggerate the stress to which modern man has subjected himself. It is the stress of frustration and threat: from too great responsibility for his knowledge and experience; from confusion of values and loss of goals; from over stimulation and lack of rest; from too rapid change. He has built an unbalanced, disproportionate social culture; and he is not sure whether he can correct his handiwork before it falls apart.

KNOW THYSELF

Why, then, should man be so interested in acquiring more complete knowledge of himself? He needs to understand himself better, in order to direct his potential capacities into more effective channels, and to express his own potential. It is only by expressing his potential capacity as fully as he can that higher potential is attained, while unused potential capacity deteriorates and is ultimately lost. Full-functioning, healthy-minded individuals create the healthy community which, in turn, produces more effective persons. Man helps to direct his own evolution. Man has an innate curiosity, an inherent drive to explore and to know all things, including himself, the most complex.

In this course you will be studying the nature and potential capacity of man; the nature of the self (yourself); man's motives and needs, his value-goals; the enhancing and inhibiting environmental forces; his defenses; his mental illnesses and disorders; his cure by individual and community treatment; and his high-level achievement in personal, social, and vocational living. It will be emphasized repeatedly that man's primary concern is not only the prevention of mental illness and adequate adjustment to present-day social-economic requirements. Rather, it is the fulfillment of potential in a pattern of life which may not be well-adjusted to the present culture-society but may be adjusted to one of the future.

> The class may profitably spend a few minutes discussing the stress factor in modern life, citing local examples. Someone may present briefly the essence of Dr. Selye's theory regarding stress and illness. See his *Stress of Life.*

OUR STATE OF MENTAL HEALTH

While I was walking behind three business men on their way to lunch, I overheard one of them inform the others of the many tranquilizers he had been taking. He climaxed with the remark, "but I'm going on bourbon tonight." I have mentioned that our generation may become known as the gadget age. Perhaps, more appropriately, it may be designated the tranquilizer era. Pharmaceutical firms have hit the jackpot in these recent years with analgesics and tranquilizers; and people are turning to their "bourbon" in ever increasing numbers. They smoke too much in spite of the doctor's warning. They seek release in gambling, in sexual promiscuity, in "pot" or LSD, and other excitement. But none of these so-called "liberators" provides lasting satisfaction.

INEFFECTIVE LIVING

This trend is the result of the unhappiness and ineffective life of modern man. Unhappiness and ineffectiveness are not synonymous nor conterminous with mental health, but they are correlates. Man senses this relationship but is not sure of its nature. He wants to be happy and effective, but he does not know how. He is fairly accomplished in his vocational achievement but not without much inner tension. He is not sufficiently effective in his interpersonal relationships and in his own inner personal growth and fulfillment. He lacks adequate knowledge of himself and his fellowmen.

Many of his friends and neighbors are worse off. Many are not mentally ill, but neither are they healthy. They increasingly depend on alcohol and/or drugs, from sleeping pills to morphine. Their families may be psychologically or legally torn apart by excessive conflict and divorce, their children may turn to delinquency and his neighbors to crime. Others, less openly hostile, may become afflicted with a variety of psychosomatic disorders and/or neurotic syndromes.* Few receive psychiatric treatment and very few report to mental hospitals. Consequently, reliable statistics are sparse. Common observation and numerous spot-checks indicate rather convincingly that the percentage of mentally ill people has been rising in this country such that some writers have characterized ours as a neurotic generation. Socially or personally crippling compulsive behavior, psychosomatic disorders, and the neuroses are forms of mental illness, if not the most severe, and they involve a large portion of the total population.

Of delinquency, Dorothy Rogers[2] says: "During a period when the population of children aged 10 to 17 increased to 19 percent, juvenile delinquency rates doubled. Furthermore, between 1948 and 1955, the number of juvenile court cases increased by 70 percent, which is four times greater than the rate of child population growth. . . ." (521). Statistics compiled by the FBI indicate that the juvenile crime index in 1960 was over three

* This will be discussed thoroughly in Chapter 8.

[2] Dorothy Rogers, *The Psychology of Adolescence* (New York: Appleton-Century-Crofts, 1962).

times as great as in 1940 and more than twice that of 1950, while the juvenile population increase was approximately one-third. Latest releases show the trend still increasing.

THE MENTALLY ILL

We find more reliable statistics for the more serious forms of mental illness, the psychoses. Psychotics are persons who are so ineffective at work and in their relationships with others that they cannot meet the minimum of acceptability. Most become family or community charges and are persuaded to accept psychiatric treatment or to be committed to mental hospitals. The numbers of such cases treated in hospitals, outpatient clinics or as private psychiatric patients have increased greatly during the past half century. At mid-century approximately 700,000 mental patients could have been found in hospitals on any one day, with perhaps twice as many needing treatment. Or, to state it differently, on any given day nearly one-half of all hospital beds were occupied by mental patients.

This does not imply that at mid-century an equal number of physically ill and mentally ill patients were being treated in any given year. Neither does it imply that the increase in actual incidence of serious mental illness has been as great as the increase in cases treated. Added facilities for treatment, greater emphasis on proper treatment, and a changing attitude on the part of the public toward mental illness account largely for increased numbers accepting or being committed for treatment. A much higher percentage of the mentally ill is now receiving psychiatric treatment than in former generations, yet many mentally ill persons are still going untreated. However, the probable fact remains that the population ratio succumbing to mental illness has been steadily rising throughout the century.

The *1967 Fact Sheet* published by the National Association for Mental Health states: "At least one person in every ten—19,000,000 in all—has some form of mental or emotional illness (from mild to severe) that needs psychiatric treatment. . . .

"The latest figures show that over 1,500,000 persons are on the books of public and private mental hospitals, psychiatric services of general hospitals, and Veterans Administration psychiatric facilities. . . .

"Currently about 800,000 persons are admitted during the year to public and private mental hospitals and the psychiatric services of general hospitals. Of these, nearly 300,000 have already been hospitalized one or more times. . . .

"Mental illness occurs at all ages, including childhood. It is estimated that there are more than half a million mentally ill children in the United States classified as psychotic or borderline cases. Most of these children are suffering from the psychiatric disorder known as childhood schizophrenia.

"Only a very small percentage of the total are receiving any kind of psychiatric treatment."

Table 1 shows the increase in the number of cases admitted to mental hospitals for treatment; because of better treatment there is a decrease in the number who remain there to die and in the total number resident at any one time. Table 2 illustrates the need and treatment inadequacies for our emotionally disturbed children. Conditions are similar in most states.

TABLE 1. PATIENTS IN PUBLIC MENTAL HOSPITALS

Item	*Actual 1960*	*Estimate 1961*	*Percentage Increase*
First admission	137,853	144,372	4.7
Re-admissions	96,989	108,743	10.8
Net releases	191,755	215,566	12.3
Deaths in Hospitals	49,774	46,975	5.6
Resident patients	535,269	527,945	1.4

Source: Facts on mental health and mental illness. U.S. Department of Health, Education and Welfare. Public Health Service. Publication No. 543, 1962.

STRESS

Increase in mental illness is due primarily to the increased stresses of modern life. Where the potential exists, it is the crisis that brings on the full-blown neurosis or psychotic break. The

TABLE 2. PENNSYLVANIA'S EMOTIONALLY DISTURBED CHILDREN 1963–64 SURVEY

Conditions needing special professional treatment	*Number and Percentage*	*Treatment for disturbed children*	*Counties with none*
Early symptoms of general emotional disturbances	195,827 7.3%	Community psychiatric clinics	70%
Seriously immature: extreme infantile behavior	74,022 2.8%	Gen. Hospital clinics	75%
Over-controlled: excessive and persistent anxiety	41,124 1.5%	Day care centers	80%
Under-controlled: impulsive hyperactivity	80,681 3.0%	Residential or hospital treatment services	60%

Adapted from a 1965 publication of Pennsylvania Mental Health, Inc.

personal factors (the inner dynamics) exist previous to the break, but the sudden increase of stress, frustration, and threat breaks through the defenses and behavior runs amuck.

For example, the first few weeks in school for the young child, college or military service for the youth, marriage or a new and responsible occupation for the adult, may be a crisis of events of greatly increased stress that breaks through defenses and brings out uncontrollable and ineffectual patterns of response. There are few psychotic breaks during the elementary school years, but the prepsychotic dynamics are at work even then, and neurotic school children are plentiful. Schizophrenia shows up frequently in high school and is a common illness of college years. It is estimated that ten percent of college students have emotional problems of sufficient pain and complexity to warrant personal counseling and five percent so serious as to need psychotherapy or hospitalization. These figures are approximately the same for the general population. The greater stress of college life is compensated by the generally greater character strength of college students.

CULTURAL IMBALANCE

The second factor that accounts for the high frequency of mental illness is a deficiency in our total educational system. Modern man has developed an unbalanced social culture which places an unbalanced emphasis on the development of its young members. The emphasis, and thus stimuli, are disproportionate and are not conducive to the full development of selfhood—to even maturation and balanced, harmonious functioning of the mental processes. Much emphasis has been placed on and much progress has been made in the intellectual, the academic and technical, and the physical development of children and youth. Little has been done to guide the child in the growth of a strong self—in building an adequate value system which includes a high value placed on himself, an adequate self-image, making it possible for him to identify deeply with others, thus finding identity and security.*

Two great wars have dramatically revealed this defect in the training of our children. The many young men who "cracked up" under the stress of combat conditions and many who are being rejected by the Selective Service because of potential mental illness have been a shocking revelation to both educators and the public. Much talk has been focused on the problem, but little progress toward correcting it has been made. This is one area where our knowledge is shallow and our achievement short.

Two cases of "disturbed" children taken from my files may illustrate this problem.

Susan J., age 9 and in third grade, was referred for psychological evaluation because of erratic academic performance and erratic temper displays. She talks freely and enjoys conversation when she can direct it or keep it in certain areas. At other times she becomes evasive, anxious or hostile. The Wechsler revealed

* The implications of this statement will unfold in the next four chapters.

average intelligence with depressed verbal performance in certain categories. She also produced a sparsity of verbal material relative to certain pictures of the Children's Apperceptive Test (CAT), areas in which she would not project. These suggest anxieties springing from deeply repressed material relating to certain experiences.

Her mother was a patient in a mental hospital at the time of Susan's birth and totally rejected the child. At the age of three Susan's father gave her to her paternal grandmother. The grandmother, widowed and uneducated, has done her best but cannot provide a normal home of mother-daughter relationship. Her maternal grandmother also has shown evidence of psychotic behavior. Certain genetic factors may predispose to instability or mental illness. As perceptive as children are, the rejection and mistreatment of early childhood are highly traumatic.

This child has the intellectual capacity and general personality traits for a well-adjusted and happy life. It appears necessary that she should have psychotherapy of sufficient duration to establish empathy and uncover, if existent, suspected repressed material to help the child build sufficient ego-strength (self-sufficiency—sense of worth) in order to withstand the stresses of adult life. Without this there is a high potential for future mental illness. With proper treatment there need not be any such development.

Jennie T., age 7, had just finished first grade and was referred for evaluation because of extreme insecurity, particularly in not doing her school work without the presence of the teacher.

All of her symptoms center around deep fear. She constantly checks to see if her mother is near. When sent to bed she returns to the head of the stairs repeatedly and calls down. When scolded or spanked, she shows hostility, stomps, and bites herself. She constantly interrupts when her mother is talking to a neighbor. She had few children to play with until after four years of age and does not play well with children. She is highly ego-centric.

She had feeding difficulties from birth, was in the hospital two weeks at the age of four months, twice between 1½ and 2 years of age, and again at 4½. She also had a severe case of measles. Medical examination (ages 4 to 5), including head X-ray, EEG, and spinal tap, revealed no organic damage. Mental tests showed low-normal intelligence which probably was depressed by her extreme anxiety.

Jennie was a sickly child, pampered in early childhood, became very dependent, matured slowly, and felt very insecure. Her life was threatened more at age four, at which time a younger sister was born and occupied much of her mother's attention. The second child was healthy and appeared to be more competent. Relatives compared the two—Jennie unfavorably, who was already low in self-sufficiency. Life became too threatening. Great fear engulfed her, manifesting itself in many ways. Panic-engendered hostility showed some ego-strength.

She needs prolonged psychotherapy to help her work out her fears and develop a new sense of worth and self-sufficiency. The parents and teachers should consult with the therapist frequently in order to cooperate adequately.

Similar conditions persist at the college age such that a girl may commit suicide because she is rejected by a certain sorority.

COST

Not least in our concern is great cost of our failure. The annual care and treatment of the mentally ill and the criminal runs well into the billions. The loss of their usefulness in economic and cultural production costs us much more. The cost in suffering, to them and to their families, is greatest of all.

HOPE

The situation is improving. Problems must exist and be recognized before they can be solved. Psychology is well on its way toward a rediscovery of the self and its vast potential—a self that can mobilize its resources and act determinatively and creatively on its environment. Twentieth-century man is becoming more confident that he can solve the problem. Education and religion, medical science and social science are combining their resources in growth-oriented, self-actualizing programs to help build strong character and full selfhood, not merely to overcome illness and adjust to the present level. It is a bare beginning, but it has begun. Sutherland and Smith[3] state:

> The emotional climate of our day is still a composite of alarm, hostility, and "the more gentle emotions." But our fear is beginning to give faint evidence of a return to what is reasonable and protective. Man will survive if he will only give himself time to further his use of love, basic trust, confidence, and the compassion of tolerance. These he may gain through new understanding of himself and his fellows, and by putting into practice his basic morality, of the essential dignity of all men. (p. 14).

Man is gaining faith in himself as a feeling, reasoning entity. Man is beginning to have greater trust in his fellowmen as he learns to be more sure of himself. Man is gaining confidence in his ability to control his ingenious inventions for the survival and well-being of all men.

SCIENCE IN PSYCHOLOGY AND MENTAL HYGIENE

Man always has been interested in his own and his neighbor's behavior, particularly in its unusual modes of expression. And man's interpretation of and efforts to regulate (influence) his and his neighbor's behavior always have been determined by his prior assumptions and his frame of reference. Primitive man assumed the reality of a multiplicity of spirits both benign and malignant that could be induced by certain rituals to work good or evil in his or his neighbor's life. To this end he practiced magic (his method), both white and black. There was no distinction between science and religion. Both science and religion, as modern man's two basic approaches to reality, evolved from spiritism as the basic assumption and magic as the basic method. Because the present trend is toward a broad interdisciplinary approach to mental health and personal growth, it seems appropriate at

[3] Robert I. Sutherland and Bert Kruger Smith, *Understanding Mental Health* (Princeton, N.J.: D. Van Nostrand Co., Inc., 1965). Used with permission.

this time to take a look at the common origin and basic differences of these two disciplines.

EMERGENCE OF RELIGION AND SCIENCE

On the religious side, spirits gave way to a hierarchy of gods and goddesses and to a higher order of ritual with some true worship characteristics. However, these deities and their activities were, in the main, the personification and dramatization of natural forces and their relationships. Man's worship and his relationship to his deities were more naturalistic than moralistic. On the scientific side, spiritism gave way slowly to naturalism as a basic assumption and to magic as a method, to such pseudo-sciences as palmistry, astrology, and alchemy. The distinction between the two approaches was not complete but beginning to take form.

SUBJECTIVE APPROACH

Religion finally emerged (in the West) as a highly or deeply subjective approach to reality, built chiefly around the response-pillars of love and faith and based on the assumption of God as Supreme Being or Absolute Person—the source of man's unique attributes and the goal of his ultimate attainment, the actualization of his potentials. "God is" became the primary theorem in the Judeo-Christian religion; and its first corollary, "He rewards those who diligently seek him." In other words, the existence of God and man's experience of God became the supreme realities of the religiously oriented person. His worship developed into a system (ritualistic or non-ritualistic) by which he attempted to enhance his faith and love and establish empathy with his God. He claimed to find in this empathic relationship a dynamic that enlarged his faith and love, gave a sense of eternal security, enhanced his sense of worth and selfhood, and conduced more healthful living, mental and physical. (When I use the term religion, it will be somewhat in the above sense, i.e., not associated with any organization or establishment, yet not so broad as to include a system of values and subjective "beliefs" that deny absolute Being generally termed God.)

OBJECTIVE APPROACH

Science emerged as the thoroughly objective approach to reality based on the assumption of a highly structured, orderly universe of natural forces bearing distinctive cause-and-effect relationships that can be observed, measured, described systematically and, with this knowledge, controlled. The distinction between the religious and scientific approaches became more apparent.

Other disciplines, especially other social sciences, have a stake in mental hygiene, but it is basically a field of applied science.

SCIENTIFIC METHOD

Key to the scientific method is the word *objective*—that which can be confirmed by others, not markedly influenced by individual uniqueness. It is empirical—the gathering of facts by sensory awareness with or without instrumental aid. The attitude of the scientist is cautious, even skeptical; he demands observable proof, verifiable by others. He is slow to reach a conclusion and does not assume to reach absolute truth or complete knowledge. He strives for greater and greater discriminations of facts in order to make truer and truer generalizations, and more precise descriptions of relationships, to gain greater and greater control over causative forces and their consequences.

The scientific method as applied to any field of inquiry has been variously described in terms of four to six steps. Assuming that a general problem has been cognized and formulated, the scientist: (1) gathers additional specific data by systematic observation and investigation. (2) With these data systematically arranged and studied, he constructs a tentative theory or hypothesis to explain relationships. The hypothesis may be broken down into two or more related hypotheses for testing, if he can use the experimental method, and is usually stated as a prediction to be proved right or wrong. (3) He tests the hypothesis by new observations and by comparisons with similar studies of others. Where possible, experimental studies are preferred at this step. (4) The new data are treated (statistically if appropriate) in systematic order, and a generalization made. The final treatment of data and generalization may be considered separate steps; generalizations are refined from many repetitions of the process before acceptance as natural law. Replicate! Replicate! Replicate! is the watchword of science. Having formulated its guiding principle or theory, science is then concerned with its application in prediction and control.

For the student or class with a special interest in the development of the scientific method in psychology, Dyal (1962, Chapter 1) gives a good selection of articles, 5 through 9.

PSYCHOLOGY AND MENTAL HEALTH

Ancient men were astute observers of human nature and behavior. Chinese and Greek philosophers and Hebrew and Hindu writers of their sacred books made some very profound and discerning statements about man and his behavior. But it was not scientific and not objectively verifiable. Overlooking earlier embryonic traces, the scientific study of human behavior began in the nineteenth century. The French doctor, Philippe Pinel, fought long and hard for the humane treatment of insane people, insisting that they were not evil creatures but sick people whose symptoms sprang from natural causes subject to scientific study and treatment.

The big impetus to the scientific study and treatment of problem behavior came late in that century with the work of Sigmund Freud, and of his disciples. His theories and method will be presented later. This, however, was looked upon as a specialization within the field of medicine. Scientific psychology was born about the same time in the German universities, springing largely from the experimental work of Wundt and his associates.

Slowly during the early twentieth century, scientific psychology and psychoanalysis joined forces in the study of deviant behavior, the ill and maladjusted. A large variety of research methods and techniques developed which are now grouped into two broad categories and designated as the clinical method and the experimental method.

CLINICAL METHOD

The clinical method studies the individual in his social environment and probes for the dynamic factors and their interrelationships which combine to cause the behavior symptoms. It is longitudinal since it traces the origin and development of the dynamic factors from infancy. This method utilizes the history of significant experiences throughout the life of the individual. The case history and the interview are the principle techniques employed. Psychological tests are frequently but not always used. The two cases previously cited are examples. This method requires the study of one person at a time and extensive time for each. It is limited to a relatively small number of cases. Over a long period of time, however, and with numerous clinicians engaged in similar research, common dynamic factors associated with similar symptoms can be observed in a sufficient number of cases to form fairly valid generalizations.

EXPERIMENTAL METHOD

The most significant characteristics of the experimental method are objectivity and control. A hundred experimenters may follow the same experimental techniques and get similar results. The situation is set up and the factors controlled, except the one variable being studied. The normal procedure is to use two matched groups of subjects—the control group and the experimental group so that the response of the two groups relative to the one variable being studied can be compared statistically. For instance, two groups of evenly matched children may be placed in a simulated classroom situation and assigned a specific learning task such as learning vocabulary or working arithmetic problems. The control group works under normal supervision but the experimental group is harassed with frequent critical, negative and threatening remarks. Their performance is then compared.

Animals such as rats, dogs, and monkeys are frequently used to study behavior problems for two major reasons: (1) It is easier to control the various factors involved and thus get more specific results; and (2) the animals may be subjected to experimental conditions that are too dangerous or painful for people. To illustrate this method, rats may be stimulated by electric shock to learn a certain response that would eliminate the painful shock. Then the learning situation is made too difficult for the rat's intellectual capacity. Faced with constant threat and his own inadequacy, the rat's fear mounts and develops into multiple symptoms of a full-blown neurosis.

Most of the major concepts related to personality adjustment and mental hygiene were derived from clinical work. Its deficiencies lie in the relatively small number of cases, the lack of systematic and controlled procedure, and in its subjectivity. Personal bias tends to influence findings since the observer projects into the observed behavior some of his own prejudice, thus tending to find what he is looking for. The experimental method, superior in these, may be criticized on the basis that it deals chiefly with the simple, superficial, and atomistic aspects of human behavior. It cannot adequately come to grips with the deeper dynamic factors and describe their patterned interrelationships. Its subjects are most often studied in a contrived, artificial environment instead of under natural circumstances. Based on the past century of research, it appears that the clinical method yields the deeper insights necessary for basic theories, while the experimental method is needed for correction and refinment. They are complementary and should be mutually supportive and if the findings of either should contradict the other, the whole problem should be researched more extensively by both.

WHAT IS MENTAL HYGIENE?

First, what is mental hygiene? It is chiefly a field of applied psychology; but it borrows from other sciences, philosophy, and religion. It is also a term commonly used but so ambiguous in meaning that the behavioral sciences are seeking a more satisfactory term.

Mental hygiene is concerned with the whole person, because the whole person is involved in healthful or unhealthful performance. Its concern is focused specifically on the person's realistic, effective mental processes and their expression in self-satisfying, efficient work and interpersonal relationships. It is a field of work employing persons of various disciplines in the promotion of mental health by research, prevention and treatment of the ill, and promotion of healthful living.

CHANGING CONCEPTS

The public attitude toward mental illness has changed greatly during this century. Persons so afflicted are not now known as the insane, the crazy, the mad, the demon possessed; they are *sick* people. The particular syndrome of their condition includes more, or to a more serious degree, malfunctioning mental processes than in the more common organic illnesses. The pattern of disordered physiological and mental processes involved is more heavily weighted on the mental side. This change of attitude is rooted in the past century, begun chiefly by the French psychiatrist, Philippe Pinel, and given a big thrust by Freud. Early in this century, Clifford Beers became mentally ill and a patient in several institutions for the "insane." Over a period of several years, he fought his way back to health—with the help of parts of his treatment and in spite of other parts of it. Later he wrote the book, *The Mind That Found Itself*, which was a biography of this period of his life and a revealing account of mental illness from the patient's point of view. It was sensational and became the fuse that ignited a powder barrel of discontent that had been building up. The mental hygiene movement was launched. With greater understanding, the public attitude began to change rapidly while treatment changed more slowly.

Interest may be kindled and additional information given by a report on the history of the mental health movement. Another student may give a short report on Beers' book.

The mid-twentieth century has introduced another change in attitude or point of view. Ask almost anyone to define good health (physical or mental) and he generally will mention various symptoms of illness which the healthy person does not have. In other words, the prevailing attitude has been that health is the state of absence of illness—a negative approach. This attitude still exists in the minds of the majority. But thinking is taking a more positive turn among those who are active in the field of mental health. Health is now being seen as something positive and more than an absence of illness (physical or mental). A person may be in either of three health states: sick, not-sick-not-healthy, or healthy. The symptoms of illness may be removed, so that a person is no longer ill, yet he is not in a healthy condition—health having characteristics over and above the mere absence of illness.

Abraham Maslow, one of the chief instigators of this point of view, has said in effect that it is one task to make the sick person "not-sick" and quite another to make the "not-sick" person truly healthy. In other words, certain traits are common to both illness and health, the difference being a matter of their degree of functioning. Other traits are operative in states of illness, while nonexistent (operatively, at least) in health; and vice versa.

With respect to the term mental health, two factors stand out: (1) it is firmly established in the thoughts and speech of the general public and specialists in the field, and (2) it is ambiguous with no exact or clearly definitive meaning.

Marie Jahoda[4] (Chapter II) discusses certain unsuitable criteria or conceptualizations of mental health: (1) *The Absence of Mental Disease,* (2) *Normalcy,* and (3) *Various States of Well-Being.* The first ignores wide differences in health potential and functioning forces between two people equally free from symptoms of mental illness. The second is complicated by the social or cultural determination of what is "normal" and that majority responses may include "many things we hesitate to call mentally healthy." The third is so highly subjective, and thus variable, it is most difficult to measure and describe definitively. Yet it is a widely used criterion. She quotes Karl Menninger[5] as saying

[4] Marie Jahoda, *Current Concepts of Positive Mental Health* (New York: Basic Books, Inc., 1958). Used with permission.

[5] From *The Human Mind,* (Third Edition) (New York: Alfred A. Knopf, 1945).

"Let us define mental health as the adjustment of human beings to the world and to each other with a maximum of effectiveness and happiness"; and she refers to W. W. Boehm[6] who wrote: "Mental health is a condition and level of social functioning which is socially acceptable and personally satisfying."

CONCEPTUAL CATEGORIES

Having made a very extensive survey of the relevant literature, Jahoda describes "six major categories of concepts" that emerged, saying:

> 1. There are several proposals suggesting that indicators of positive mental health should be sought in the attitudes of an individual toward his own self. . . .
> 2. Another group of criteria designates the individual's style and degree of growth, development, or self-actualization. . . .
> 3. Various proposals place the emphasis on a central synthesizing psychological function, incorporating some of the suggested criteria defined in (1) and (2) above. This function will here be called integration.
> 4. Autonomy singles out the individual's degree of independence from social influences as most revealing of the state of his mental health.
> 5. A number of proposals suggest that mental health is manifested in the adequacy of an individual's perception of reality.
> 6. Finally, there are suggestions that environmental mastery be regarded as a criterion for mental health. (p. 23).

Looking more closely at the last three, we see in No. 4 the individual who is relatively free from anxious dependency and free to set his own course. He is under no compulsion to "keep up with the Joneses." He is motivated toward growth, full self-development and creative living regardless of any moderate threat his action may entail. He is his own man, neither rebellious nor submissive, but interdependent. In No. 5 we again see the

[6] From "The Role of Psychiatric Social Work in Mental Health," In A.M. Rose (ed) *Mental Health and Mental Disorder* (New York: W. W. Norton & Company, Inc., 1955).

anxiety-free individual with self-confidence who is able to face reality squarely and see things as they are. He is free of "selective perception" and does not need to suppress or repress elements in the situation he fears facing. He has greater appreciation and better judgment with full perception. In No. 6 we see the growth motive finding expression in productive, satisfying work and social relations. Not inhibited by anxiety, he is free to release more energy in effective performance. He can act on the environment as well as merely react to it. His life is much more than adjustment. It is growth toward fulfillment even though it may mean social or environmental conflict.

CRITERIA

Schneiders[7] (pp. 49–53) presents the following criteria of mental health:

1. The Criterion of Mental Efficiency.
2. Control and Integration of Thought and Conflict.
3. Integration of Motives and Control of Conflict and Frustration.
4. Positive, Healthy Feelings and Emotions.
5. Tranquility or Peace of Mind.
6. Healthy Attitudes.
7. Healthy Self-Concept.
8. Adequate Ego-identity.
9. Adequate Relation to Reality.

Sutherland and Smith (1965, p. 39) set up the following as criteria of healthy adult personality:

1. On the one hand, he works for human betterment but, on the the other hand, accepts most people and situations, especially minor situations, as he finds them. . . .
2. He feels himself a part of a group, especially of society as a whole, and derives his satisfaction in life more through the contributions he makes to others than through selfish, self-centered gain or pleasure.

[7] Alexander A. Schneiders, *Personality Dynamics and Mental Health* (New York: Holt, Rinehart and Winston, Inc., 1965). Reprinted by permission of the publishers.

3. He is aware of his relation to the universe. He is interested in religious values. . . .
4. He has a reasonable amount of self-confidence. This does not mean overconfidence. But he knows his own abilities and limitations and therefore can meet life successfully.
5. His personality is integrated. He is not torn by internal conflict—one part of him fighting against another part of him. He is characterized by a pattern of sound, consistent values. . . .
6. He approaches problems realistically and constructively. He does not evade problems and confuse his evasion with solution. . . .
7. He has a forward look. He looks to the future, not to the past. His life is not dull or empty or boring because he has live and growing interests. He does not rest on the oars of previous achievement. . . .

Older textbooks in mental hygiene dealt almost entirely with mental illnesses—their causes, consequences, and cures. Now the swing is toward the positive, describing mental and social health. Jourard[8] illustrates this newer emphasis. In *Personal Adjustment*, the whole first chapter is given to definitions of healthy personality. He states in summary:

> . . . Mental health, or personality health, as it will be called throughout this volume, refers to ways of behaving that are valued, for good reasons, by personality hygienists in our culture.
> . . . The psychiatrist compares the behavior of people with his concepts of "mental illness." If a person's behavior resembles the behavior expected in mental disease, then the person is so labelled. If his behavior does not resemble that of the "mentally ill," then he is adjudged "normal." The clinical psychologist uses various tests as a means of refining and making more objective the impressions of the psychiatrist. The personality hygienist makes explicit a concept of personality health, and compares the behavior which he observes in a given person with this concept of health. If there is overlap, then the person is adjudged healthy. If not, a detailed list of deviations from health is prepared. These deviations are called symptoms. (pp. 19–20).

[8] Reprinted with permission of the Macmillan Company from *Personal Adjustment* by Sidney M. Jourard. © The Macmillan Company, 1958.

FUNCTIONS

Klein (1956), on the other hand, states the function of mental hygiene as both prophylactic and meliorative. That is, one major function is to prevent mental illness and the other is to effect a cure. This is true, but the emphasis is largely on the negative side—preventing the not-sick from becoming sick and making the sick not-sick. It does not place sufficient emphasis on a third major function of mental hygiene, making the not-sick truly healthy, i.e., attaining the fullest possible self-actualization.

I have tried to give adequate emphasis to all three of these major functions. Central emphasis is placed on the healthy self, functioning wholesomely in its mental processes and interpersonal activities. Equal emphasis is then given to how people become mentally and socially "ill" or maladaptive, how this may be prevented, and how they are restored to health.

APPROACHES TO MENTAL HYGIENE

There are numerous schools of thought in psychology. There are not only different branches of psychology but also different points of view, different approaches to problems, and different interpretations of findings within the same branch. This alone is sufficient evidence that psychology is not an exact science and has not yet attained full objectivity. This situation is especially notable in the allied fields: psychology of personality, psychology of adjustment, and mental hygiene.

The psychoanalytic school begun by Freud, but which since has branched out into several varieties and adaptations, is the chief theoretical source or frame of reference of many psychiatrists and clinical psychologists even though they have moved far from Freud in specific theories and methods. Their approach is more from the point of view of the inner dynamics than specific behavior traits, of the whole person and his uniqueness rather than amassing atomistic facts about the many and drawing universal generalizations. They think primarily of strengthening the ego,* which will then regulate behavior more effectively, rather than diagnosing specific behavior traits that impair behavior, then by operant conditioning* change these trait responses to more adequate ones.

Behaviorism, not begun but made popular by J. B. Watson, provides the other chief frame of reference. Few, if any, of the present-day behavioristic school would agree with Watson's extreme position, and many have borrowed from other sources. But this term more or less defines the position of a large number of psychologists whose thinking is farthest removed from the psychoanalytic. Their approach generally follows the "rather than" phrases in the above paragraph. It is the most specifically objective and "scientific" psychological approach.

The datum of behaviorism is behavior—all responses of man and animal. These are measurable, largely controllable, and may be predictable. Subjective states are either ignored (in actual work) or dealt with merely as inferences and are of secondary concern. The human organism has very few, very simple, and very diffused response tendencies at birth. Through the mechanism of conditioning, the repertoire of responses is greatly enlarged. By conditioned discrimination and generalization specific responses are learned and clustered into habits which are personality traits and which may be adjustively efficient or inefficient. More of the behavioristic and the psychoanalytic approaches will be presented as our study progresses.

A newer "school" of psychologists, which is increasing in popularity and gaining in recognition, may be characterized chiefly as having a common frame of reference in philosophical existentialism. This is a rather nebulous and non-systematic philosophy and incorporates a variety of specific points of view. Likewise, psychologists who lean toward existentialism differ in some of their theories and methods, but there are enough common elements to group them together. Self Psychologists, Phenomenologists, and Existential Psychologists are among the titles being used for designation; but their variations and changing emphases are at present a little too great for close categorization. Subjective experience, values, and the self-image are emphasized more by these psychologists. These "approaches,"

* These concepts will be discussed later.

however, do not exist as strictly separate points of view. There are all the intermediate positions. Behavior therapists are in general agreement on many factors, particularly the principles of learning and the role of learning in behavior.

A number of existentialism-oriented psychologists have formed the American Association for Humanistic Psychology. Their objective is to correct or supplement some of the deficiencies of the behavioristic and psychoanalytic schools. In his introduction, Severin[9] writes:

> Humanistic psychology is a new movement sometimes referred to as a "third force" between behaviorism and psychoanalysis. It aims to introduce a new orientation to psychology rather than a new psychology. Through constructive criticism and research it hopes to bring psychology of every theoretical complexion into closer contact with out every-day perceptions of man. (p. XV).

The *Articles of Association* of the American Association for Humanistic Psychology[10] defines its role as follows:

> Humanistic psychology is primarily an orientation toward the whole of psychology rather than a distinct area or school. It stands for respect for the worth of persons, respect for differences of approach, open-mindedness as to acceptable methods, and interest in exploration of new aspects of human behavior. As a "third force" in contemporary psychology it is concerned with topics having little place in existing theories and systems: e.g., love, creativity, self, growth, organism, basic need-gratification, self-actualization, higher values, being, becoming, spontaneity, play, humor, affection, naturalness, responsibility, meaning, fair play, transcendental experience, peak experience, courage, and related concepts.

My position is somewhere in the broad range of this new "school." Existentialism, phenomenology, and the self, and how they relate to mental health, will unfold in the subsequent chapters as a reflection of this point of view. Other theoretical

---

[9] Frank T. Severin, *Humanistic Viewpoints in Psychology* (New York: McGraw-Hill Book Co., 1965). Used with permission.

[10] From A. J. Sutich. AAHP—Articles of Association, Palo Alto, California: August 28, 1963 (Mimeographed Paper).

positions are also presented, with supporting research, in the effort to be reasonably eclectic.

> A short description of existentialism and Phenomenology would be helpful at this point, presented as a student report to the class, with followup discussion. See: Caruso, 1964; May, 1961; Kaufman, 1956; Macnab, 1966; Olson, 1962; Van-Kaam, 1966.

LOOKING AHEAD

This first chapter has been largely introductory and in part a preview of the developments ahead. The topics and concepts introduced here will reappear in one or another of the chapters that follow. We will study the structure of personality and the human capacity (potential) for living. From capacity, need is derived; and it is self-need. Frustrated need produces hostility and fear, which, if mishandled or too great, leads to behavior disorders. If not too great and handled effectively, the end is health and growth. Since many people move in either of these directions, you will study the causes, prevention, and cures of mental illness and maladjustment, and you will get acquainted with the community organizations which are most actively involved with mental health. You will then study the characteristics of mental health as revealed in one's intellectual and emotional life, his vocation, and his social relations (including love and sex). Scientific verification of basic principles will be given where available, but you will not be studying an exact science. As Klein[11] has said:

> In many respects the practice of mental hygiene is more of an art than a science. A vast portion of this art rests on the foundation of critical common sense, thoughtful clinical observation, and much preoccupation with the troubles of per-

[11] D. B. Klein, *Mental Hygiene* (New York: Holt, Rinehart and Winston, Inc., 1956). Reprinted by permission of the publishers.

turbed people. The psychiatrist, the psychoanalyst, and the clinical psychologist have all contributed to the mental hygiene movement. However, specialists of this sort do the bulk of their professional work in the consulting room and not in the laboratory. As the product of this work we get a case history rather than an experiment. This means that experimental support for mental hygiene teachings is available for only a limited number of such teachings.

Taken by and large, in other words, the kind of science underlying the doctrines and theories of mental hygiene is still at the descriptive and empirical level. By this it is meant that it is based on a more or less systematic ordering of the fruits of clinical observation. It is rooted in experience, but not the **controlled** experience of the laboratory. Even that phase of it which we have called prophylactic mental hygiene—the phase concerned with **preventing** mental breakdown—does not rest on secure experimental foundations. (p. 21).

. . . . .

Many of the key concepts of psychopathology do not lend themselves to experimental elaboration. As the authors[12] of a recent text point out, "the traditional experimental approach has developed few techniques which are appropriate to the study of significant variables in behavior pathology." Accordingly, to the extent that mental hygiene is concerned with the prevention of behavior pathology just to that extent are there almost no experimentally established principles or "laws" of mental hygiene. (p. 22).

Having read this introductory chapter and in looking ahead at the main content of the course, the student may feel somewhat as suggested by Thomas Parsons[13] who discussed the problems of recognition and restoration of mental health in a society replete with pathological elements and stated the dilemma in this paradoxical form:

But why is mentally hygienic living a desirable goal? And once reached, how can it be a durable one? For if, we are

---

[12] Margaret A. and N. Cameron, *Behavior Pathology* (Boston: Houghton-Mifflin Co., 1951), p. 19.

[13] "A Mental Health Paradox," *University of Michigan School of Education Bulletin,* 1956, 27, pp. 73–76. Also in Hountras (ed) *Mental Hygiene* (Columbus: Charles E. Merrill Books, Inc., 1961), pp. 12–15. Used with permission of author and publisher.

> told, the normal modes of contemporary living are not entirely hygienic—and if hygienic living therefore involves abnormal behavior—what profit can there be in thus marching out of step with the rest of society? Won't such nonconforming behavior be observed and chastised? And won't the mentally healthy person thus be impelled to return to the unhealthy norm?

Parsons acknowledges this as a partial truth and observes that the primary concern is not the specific response or behavior pattern, but rather its how and why, i.e., "what it looks like to the individual"; and he concludes: "Hygienic living may not, therefore, be characterized by 'abnormal' or 'normal' specific behavior patterns. Consequently, it is not susceptible to popular discrimination, chastisement, and pressure to reform. Rather, it differs from the 'pathic norm' precisely because it is flexible, more adaptable to an ever-changing environment; and it therefore provides the individual with greater survival value in any kind of social environment."

SUMMARY

Mid-twentieth century man finds himself in a dilemma. His knowledge and control of things, physical forces, have far exceeded his knowledge and control of himself. He has developed a highly unbalanced culture, bulging far out on the material progress side and almost flat on the social-spiritual side. This unbalanced culture, in turn, has been producing unbalanced, tension-beset, mentally disordered individuals to an alarming extent. Mental illness, crime, divorce, and general social-economic discord have seemingly been increasing by a ratio far in excess of population growth. This was especially noted in juvenile delinquency, which in two decades more than trebled in ratio, and in the gigantic increase in the use of analgesics and tranquilizers of many varieties.

Today there are straws in the wind that give rise to hope, that suggest a solution to the dilemma is in the making. Mental health has become a major national concern, with community resources being fully mobilized. Psychology, which has been largely of conflicting psychologies, is now showing signs of the "we" experience—of sufficient maturity for cooperation within its various "schools" and with other social sciences and religion. These disciplines are beginning to make progress in their comprehension of human nature, by working together to discover its high potential and need, its value-goals and frustrations, and how to guide its growth toward fulfillment.

The new concept of mental health is something other than absence of major symptoms of mental illness or merely normal adjustment to and ability to cope with the environment. We are now thinking in terms of a high-level healthy-mindedness or psychosocial attainment which is reflected in relatively uninhibited growth, toward the full actualization of potential capacity for personal, interpersonal, and vocational living. *To be* is becoming of greater consequence than *to do*. It is recognized that what one becomes is largely influenced by what he does, but the obverse is now being seen as the primary relationship. One's quality of performance, his doing, is more truly a consequence of his being, the kind of a person he is. Thus, mental hygiene is seen as a system of procedures designed to aid the individual in the development of full selfhood, of becoming the most complete person his potentiality permits.

GLOSSARY

Anomie. A general state of confused or lack of values and goals.

Empathy. A subjective mental state of shared feelings, tensions, etc., as client and therapist experiencing the same general thoughts and feelings beyond those verbally expressed, a knowing not clearly structured—or the one may duplicate the subjective state of the other by vividly projecting himself into the other's "mental shoes."

Existentialism. A philosophical frame of reference that starts on the base line of being (existence) and experience, of which rational thinking is only a part. Thus, it finds validity in elements of experience beyond the strictly logical, emphasizing "will," "values," etc.

Insane. A legal term (not medical) that designates an individual as being in a temporary or permanent mental condition incapable of assuming responsibility for his conduct.

Neurosis. A milder form of "mental illness" or behavior disorder with much anxiety and inner tension, accompanied by varying defensive and ineffective response patterns without incapacitating the individual.

Phenomenology. A psychological point of view that approaches the study of behavior from the position of the behaver, describing the phenomena of experience as the subject perceives them.

Project (ion). To attribute one's own ideas, attitudes, impulses, etc. to others.

Prophylactic. Pertaining to the prevention of a condition.

Psychosis. A major mental disorder characterized by erratic and inappropriate responses, disorientation, and defective cognition.

Psychosomatic. A type of illness in which the organic or physiological impairment is chiefly caused by a psychologic tension.

Psychotherapy. The treatment of psychological disorders, chiefly in person to person conversation.

REFERENCES AND SUGGESTED READINGS

BENNETT, EDWARD, *The Search for Emotional Security*, New York: The Ronald Press Company, 1959.

BEERS, CLIFFORD W., *A Mind That Found Itself*, New York: Doubleday & Company, Inc., 1908.

DYAL, JAMES A., *Readings in Psychology: Understanding Human Behavior*, New York: McGraw-Hill Book Co., 1962.

HOUNTRAS, PETER T. (ed), *Mental Hygiene*, Columbus: Charles E. Merrill Books, Inc., 1961.

JAHODA, MARIE, *Current Concepts of Positive Mental Health*, New York: Basic Books, Inc., 1958.

JOURARD, SIDNEY M., *Personal Adjustment*, New York: The Macmillan Company, 1958.

KLEIN, D. B., *Mental Hygiene*, New York: Holt, Rinehart and Winston, Inc., 1956.

LINTON, RALPH, *Culture and Mental Disorders*, Springfield, Ill.: Charles C. Thomas, Publisher, 1956.

MASLOW, ABRAHAM H., *Toward a Psychology of Being*, Princeton, N.J.: D. Van Nostrand Co., Inc., 1962.

MENNINGER, K. A., *The Human Mind*, New York: Alfred A. Knopf, Inc., 1945.

ROGERS, DOROTHY, *The Psychology of Adolescence*, New York: Appleton-Century-Crofts, Inc., 1962.

SCHNEIDERS, ALEXANDER A., *Personality Dynamics and Mental Health*, New York: Holt, Rinehart and Winston, 1965.

SELYE, HANS, *The Stress of Life*, New York: McGraw-Hill Book Co., 1956.

SEVERIN, FRANK T., *Humanistic Viewpoints in Psychology*, New York: McGraw-Hill Book Co., 1965.
STROTHERS, CHARLES R., (ed), *Psychology and Mental Health*, Washington, D.C.: American Psychological Association, 1955.
SUTHERLAND, ROBERT I. and BERT KRUGER SMITH, *Understanding Mental Health*, Princeton, N.J.: D. Van Nostrand Co., Inc., 1965.

2

The Mind and Personality: Human Potential

In this chapter we turn from the general mental health situation and general approach to more specific methods of self-study and see what man has discovered about himself—his structure and capacity to behave as a man, fully and healthfully. We will look at him as object and energy system, as an instrument for structuring patterns of behavior. In Chapter 3 we will see him as subject, as self, as an acting behaver. Behavior depends on need, need on capacity, and capacity on structure. This chapter presents in brief outline the structure and capacity of man, in mental processes and personality, with some hint at his high potential and full humanness. It will be a short review and will assume that you already have some basic knowledge of human biology.

BEHAVIOR REGULATORS

Behavior is integrated and purposeful action in varying degree, and that degree is a correlate of mental health. Integration is attained chiefly by the muscle-skeleton system, the nervous system, and the system of endocrine glands, with the help of the blood stream. The nervous and endocrine systems are of the greatest significance.

PHYSICAL ATTRIBUTES

The matter of color and physical appearance is not without significance. In looking at ourselves and others, we see marked differences in color of hair and skin, ranging from albino white to coal black. Some attempt has been made to type people according to the color of their hair, but it has not been very meaningful. We seldom accept some people and reject others on the basis of hair color, even though some gentlemen may prefer blondes. But people are evaluated highly or lowly, accepted or rejected, integrated or segregated, on the basis of skin color. This, in turn, has a vital effect on the self-image, social adjustment, and mental health. Since the hair is little more than elongated epidermal cells and its pigmentation is of the same general nature as that of the skin, one may wonder why we place so much more emphasis on one than on the other. But we do, and thus we make a mental health problem out of skin color.

Next to skin color, bodily form is the most observable mark of distinction among people. Later in this chapter, attempts will be made to classify people into personality types based on bodily build. At this point, I wish merely to call attention to the significance of bodily form in relation to mental health. Fat and skinny children are more frequently the objects of ridicule and criticism than medium build children. Build, along with other factors, is important in social adjustment and mental health. The muscular child is likely to become a good athlete, be well received by others, and have a high opinion of himself. These factors are conducive to his mental health. In other words, muscle and mental health are interrelated. Personality development is in part a function of bodily form and condition, the degree depending largely on the value the particular sub-culture or community places on physical appearance and athletic skill.

CONTROL SYSTEMS

The infinite variety of human responses, the high level of skillful performance and interpersonal relations, the fine discrimination and richness of appreciation are functons of the brain—particularly the cerebrum which truly may be said to be *man's brain*, the center of conscious experience and voluntary control. The more basic and vital processes are regulated chiefly by the older brain structure and the autonomic and endocrine systems. The manner in which these systems go into correlated action with each other and with the cerebrum in emergency or unusual situations is extremely complex and not yet fully understood by professionals in those fields of study. The beginning student of mental health and personal growth should familiarize himself with the principal elements of these regulating systems and their basic functions.

Most behavior, including personality traits, is learned. The Pavlov-type experiment demonstrates learning at the lowest and most basic dimension. It shows how new and varied responses at the automatic, glandular, and reflex level is attained and this is basic to the new conditioned reflex therapy. The Skinner-type operant or instrumental conditioning experiment demonstrates the next higher dimension of learned behavior which involves more directly the cerebrum and responses largely controlled by the experimental subject. This is basic to the relatively new behavior or conditioned response therapy. These therapies will be described later.

> To refresh the memory of the class, one student may give a short report on the chief divisions and functions of the brain, autonomic nervous system, and endocrine system, observing Figures 2, 3 and 4. Another student may describe briefly Pavlov's and Skinner's original conditioning experiments. Any good textbook in Introductory Psychology will provide sufficient information for these reports. Also see Appendix.

PSYCHOMETRY

Chapter 1 makes reference to man's scientific study of himself and various techniques of intelligence testing, personality appraisal, and the discipline of psychometrics. Many tests have been

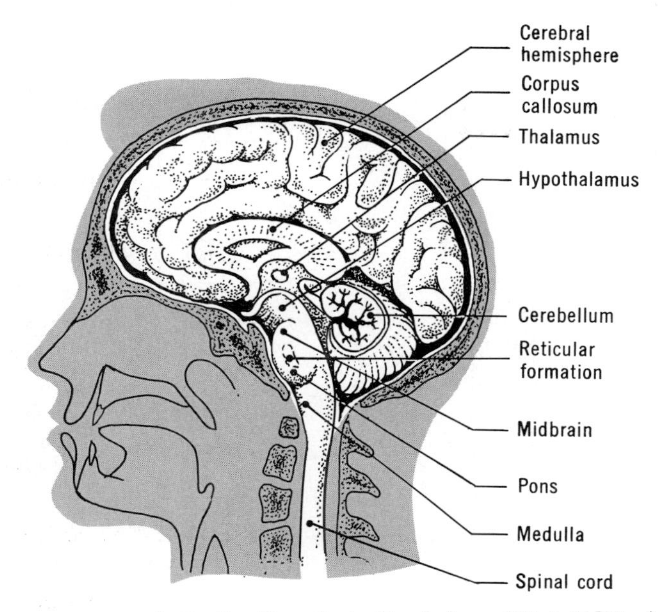

Source: Howard H. Kendler, *Basic Psychology* (First Edition), p. 94. Copyright © 1963 by Meredith Publishing Company. Reproduced by permission of Appleton-Century-Crofts.

Figure 2. A vertical section of the human brain in its position in the skull.

developed for research instruments and for diagnosis purposes. Intelligence testing and I.Q. test development have become one of the most extensive areas of educational and experimental psychology. Intelligence, as general aptitude, is conceived by some psychologists and educators as a major aspect of personality. Others hesitate to so categorize it and draw a distinction between basic mental processes and the more directly observable and overt behavior patterns. Regardless of one's point of view, mental processes have a direct bearing on personality structure; yet there are certain basic distinctions between intelligence and personality and between intelligence testing and personality appraisal. Difference among people in intelligence is more a matter of degree than of kind, even though the tests are so designed as to allow for different types of intelligence, e.g., the so-called general and

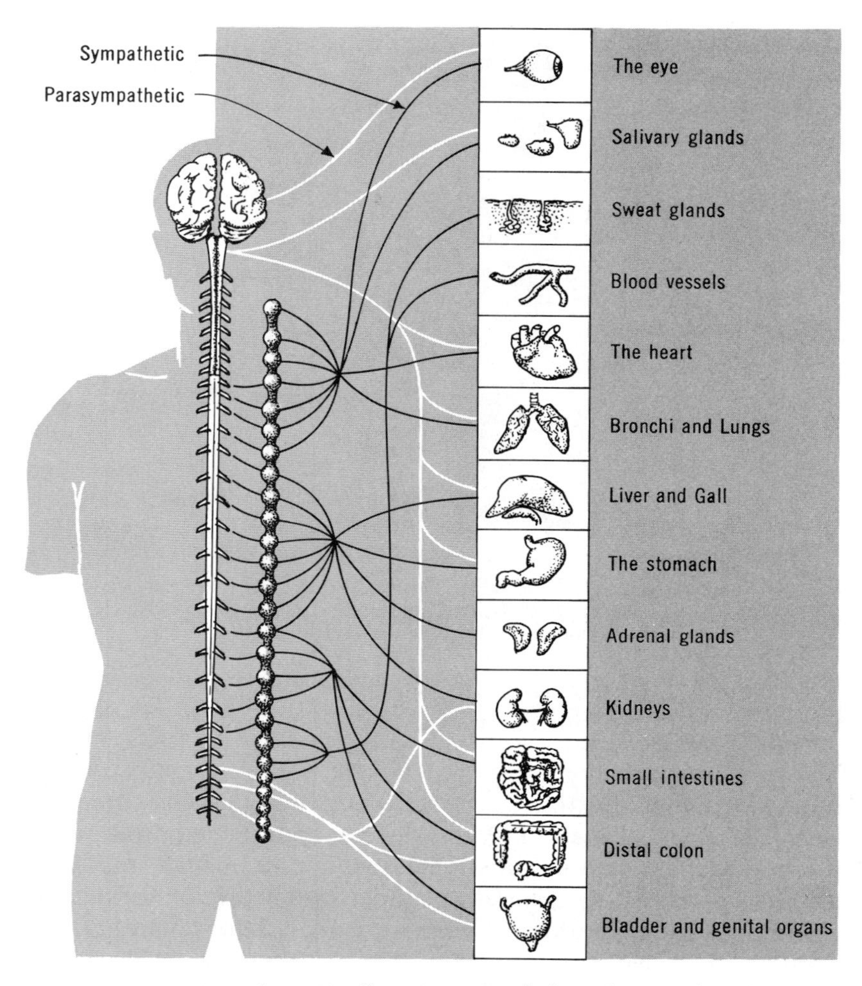

Source: Howard H. Kendler, *Basic Psychology* (First Edition), p. 98. Copyright © 1963 by Meredith Publishing Company. Reproduced by permission of Appleton-Century-Crofts.

Figure 3. A schematic representation of the autonomic nervous system. The black lines represent the parasympathetic and the white lines the sympathetic division of the autonomic nervous system.

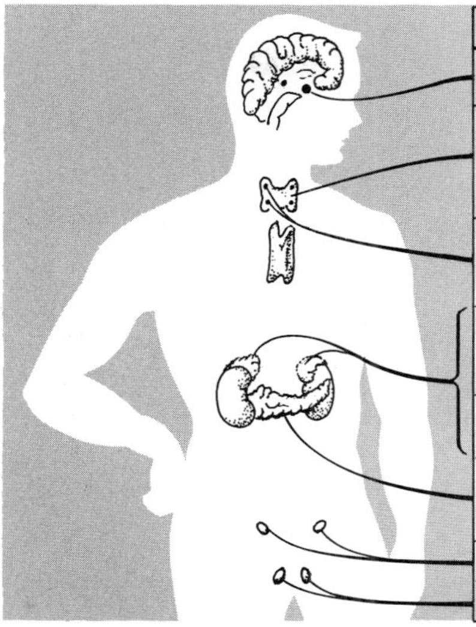

Gland	Oversecretion	Undersecretion
Pituitary	Early—giantism Late—acromegaly	Dwarfism
Thyroid	High BMR Basal metabolism Exophthalmia Loss of weight	Low BMR Cretin-ism Simple goiter Obesity
Parathyroids	Muscle spasms Tetany	Softened bones and teeth; Excretory loss
Adrenal cortex	Sexual precocity Male character-istics in female	Addison's disease
Adrenal medulla	Irritability Hyperactivity	Passivity
Pancreas	Low blood sugar Starvation of cells, especially neurons	Diabetis mellitis
Ovaries—(F)	Sexual precocity	Sterility
Testes—(M)	Sexual precocity	Infantilism

Source: F. H. Sanford, ***Psychology: A Scientific Study of Man*** (2nd ed), 1965, p. 80. © 1961, 1965 by Wadsworth Publishing Company, Inc., Belmont, California. Reproduced by permission of the publisher.

Figure 4. Endocrine system.

specific factors. The problem of uniqueness is less critical in testing intelligence, therefore it is easier to score the individual against universal standards and to establish valid norms.

The uniqueness of each person and his personality poses a difficult problem in the development of valid personality tests, since no two individuals have the same genetic endowment, nor do they develop under exactly the same environmental influences. There are many common elements in both the biological and cultural influences and therefore many mutual personality characteristics. As tests improve, knowledge grows and as knowledge grows, the tests are improved. Regardless of the difficulties involved and the imperfection of these instruments, they are growing in number and effectiveness. Psychometrics has become a major activity of the mental health clinic and the school. As research tools, they help the psychologist gain insight into the significant characteristics of man in order to formulate general principles or theories of personality. As diagnostic tools, they help the therapist and educator determine the most suitable treatment and training for the individual or group with which they are concerned.

If a test is to be useful, it must withstand the threefold test to which tests are subjected—*validity*, *reliability*, and *practicability*. Validity means that the test actually measures what it was designed to measure. If it is an interest test, then differences in scores on the test should be indices of real interest differences. Reliability means that the same test, or an equivalent form, will yield closely comparable results when given to the same person or group on different occasions separated by a reasonable period of time. If a test is practical, the information it yields is worth the expenditure of time and money.

CLINICAL TESTS

The psychological clinic and laboratory use mostly interest finders, intelligence tests, and a variety of instruments to reveal and assess personality traits or characteristics. Among the interest finders, the Kuder Vocational Preference Scale and the Strong Vocational Interest Blank are most widely used. The Kuder is a little more popular at the high school age level and the Strong for college and adult age levels. They are similar, and both are scaled to compare the subjects pattern of interests with a large population of persons who are happily and successfully engaged in the various occupations for which they are scaled.

Intelligence tests of the group type are too numerous for discussion here. Many are used frequently in the school room and experimental laboratory. The clinic uses chiefly individual tests of which the Wechsler Intelligence Scale for Children (WISC) and Wechsler Adult Intelligence Scale (WAIS) are perhaps the most popular. The Wechsler is composed of 11 subtests (10 for children). Usually all are given but one or more may be omitted. Six of the subtests require the normal use of language and are scored to give a verbal I.Q. The other five require little language ability and are scaled to give a performance I.Q. The total is then scaled to give the full-scale I.Q. This enables the clinician to give both an extensive and definitive description of the subject's intelligence capabilities. The Stanford-Binet is another individual test of intelligence used in clinics but is more popular in schools.

It depends on verbal achievement to a greater degree and correlates more highly with academic aptitude than other types of intelligence.

The most popular clinical tests for diagnosing personality disorders is the Rorschach Ink-blot Test. The subject being tested is given consecutively 10 cards. On each one is an irregular design formed from a large ink-blot. He describes what he sees in each figure, having projected into it certain characteristics of his own unique conceptual and emotional pattern, part of which is not consciously known to the subject. Thus, it is known as a projective test. The scoring procedure is quite complicated, and requires an experienced clinical psychologist who can describe certain deviate conceptual and emotional patterns which may help in psychotherapy.

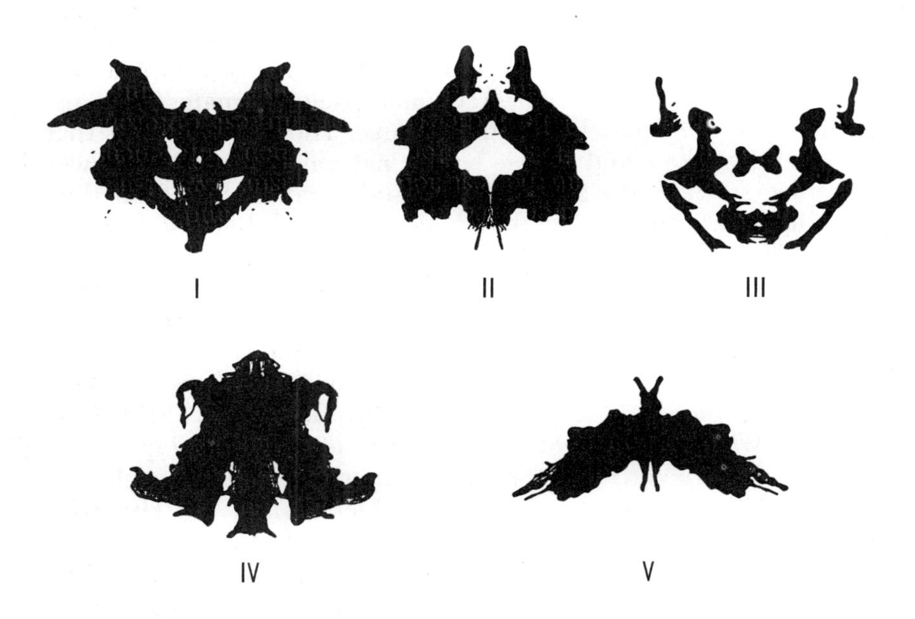

Figure 5. The first inkblots on the Rorschach.

The Thematic Apperception Test (TAT), and its counterpart for children, the CAT, are similar in principle. They use ambiguous pictures instead of ink-blots, about which the subject tells stories. Therefore he projects into the activities and relationships he describes, some of his own emotional problems that may be largely unknown to him. The Sentence Completion test is another projective test of a different sort whereby two or three words of each of a number of sentences are given and the subject completes the sentence. Certain conceptual and emotional difficulties are indicated by the completed sentences.

The chief defects of these tests, except the last, are that they are expensive and time consuming and limit the number of subjects that can be tested. They are also partly subjective and even the experienced administrator may project some of his own bias into his interpretation of responses. Their chief value lies in their ability to help bring out into the open for clearer description, hidden (unconscious) mental conditions. The many personality inventory type tests are easier to administer, more objective, and less expensive. They are used widely in schools and research to rate and classify traits of less seriously disturbed or crippled personalities—where little repressed (unconscious) material is suspected. And they may be given to groups. Their chief fault is that they can be faked, and people have a natural tendency to answer in terms of what may seem more desirable rather than how they actually feel. Projective tests may also be faked, but not as easily nor extensively. In cases of more serious emotional disturbances, the projective test is generally preferred but the inventory types serve well as diagnostic instruments for more normal persons.

These tests are usually composed of questions (100-500) which the subjects answer in terms of "T" or "F" or "yes", "no", or "?". The Minnesota Multiphasic Personality Inventory (MMPI) is the most widely used for diagnostic purposes. It is a long questionnaire of the True or False type and purports to measure such syndromes as: (1) Hypochondriasis; (2) Depression; (3) Hysteria; (4) Psychopathic Deviation; (5) Masculinity-Femininity; (6) Paranoia; (7) Psychasthenia; (8) Schizophrenia and (9) Hypomania. (See Figures 5 and 6). The vertical columns marked Hs to Ma (Figure 6) are the above syndromes. The normal range of scores are found between 30 and 70.

Several tests are designed to measure a single trait along a scale from one extreme to the other, e.g., introversion-extroversion, ascendance-submission, etc. The Q-Sort, a self-image test has gained in popularity with some clinicians. The subject is given a

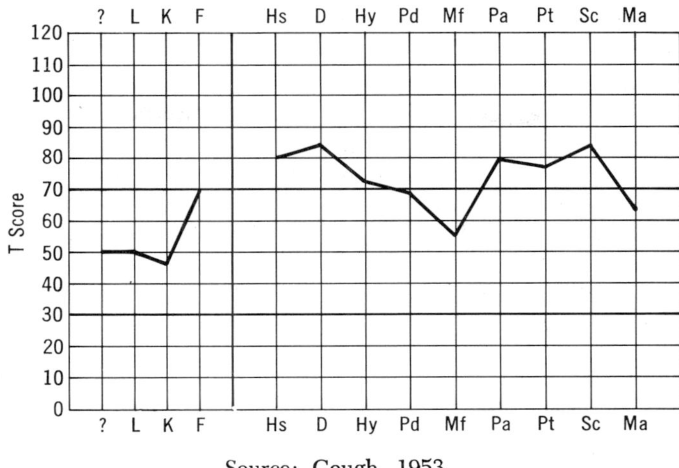

Source: Gough, 1953.

Figure 6. A typical psychotic profile on the Minnesota multiphasic personality inventory.

set of cards on each of which is written a personality trait; the number may range from 70 to more than 200. He sorts the cards and arranges them in usually seven or nine columns. At one end are the cards bearing the traits he judges to be most characteristic of himself and those next most like him in the second column. At the other end are the trait-cards least like, etc., moving toward the middle with the trait-cards that are just so-so, not much like nor much unlike. This test helps the person become better acquainted with himself, and helps the counselor learn what his client really thinks of himself. Psychotherapists sometimes use this test at the beginning of treatment and again after several weeks to note the change in one's self-evaluation.

SPECIAL DIAGNOSTIC TESTS

Sundberg and Tyler[1] list and describe briefly (pp. 502–507) 50 tests commonly used for diagnostic and research purposes by

[1] Norman D. Sundberg and Leona E. Tyler, *Clinical Psychology* (New York: Appleton-Century-Crofts, 1962). Used with permission.

clinicians. A few of these were mentioned in Chapter 1. Some others are:

1. *Author Point Scale of Performance Tests.* A collection of performance tests including formboards, mazes, block designs, etc. . . . (Ages 4½ to Adult)
2. *Draw-a-man* (Goodenough). An old and simple procedure for obtaining a rough estimate of intelligence by scoring a child's drawing for details, proportion, etc. (Ages 5 to 15). . . .
3. *Porteus Maze Test.* A series of printed labyrinths on which the subject draws his way from the starting place to the exit. . . . A useful clinical tool found to be effective in cases of brain damage and delinquency (Ages 3 to Adult).
4. *Goldstein-Scheerer Tests of Abstract and Concrete Thinking.* A series of clinical techniques for testing a patient's ability to conceptualize, including sorting of objects and copying of designs. . . .
5. *Visual-Motor Gestalt Test* (Bender-Gestalt). The subject's task on this test is simply to copy nine designs as they are presented one at a time. The brief and nonthreatening task is used to reveal perceptual distortion suggesting brain damage, developmental retardation, and personality characteristics. . . .
6. *Adjustment Inventory* (Bell). . . . Developed by internal consistency methods to cover adjustment in four areas: home, health, social, and emotional. (Grades 9–16 and Adults)
7. *California Test of Personality.* . . . One of the very few tests of personality for elementary grades. Provides 15 scores on such topics as self-reliance, feeling of belonging, and family relations (Group test; Kindergarten to Adult).
8. *Edwards Personal Preference Schedule* (EPPS). . . . Provides 15 scores of the subject's reports on his "needs" such as achievement, intraception, dominance, abasement, and aggression (individual or group; college and adult).
9. *Personality Inventory* (Bernreuter). An older test, . . . Provides 6 scores; neurotic tendency, self-sufficiency, introversion-extroversion, dominance-submission, confidence, and sociability (Individual or Group; Grades 9–16 and Adult).
10. *The Blacky Pictures.* A series of 12 cartoon drawings designed to elicit material related to psychosexual development as hypothesized by psychoanalytic theory. . . . (Ages 5 and over).
11. *Rosenzweig Picture-Frustration Study* (P-F). A set of cartoons presenting frustrating situations in response to which

the subject must write what the frustrated character would say (Individual or Group; children and adult forms.)

12. *Vineland Social Maturity Scale.* Uses the reports of an informant being interviewed by the clinician regarding the observed behavior of the patient or client in the areas of locomotion, communication, socialization and occupation (Birth to Adult).

With these and many other similar instruments, the psychologist attempts to understand more clearly and describe man's mental processes and personality traits and thus, his potential and actual performance levels—his personal growth and mental health status.

THE MIND

The phrase "mental health" implies a "mind" that is in a state of good health. Mind, however, is not generally thought of as an entity but as a class or type of processes associated with the brain. It is a class of mental processes (action), therefore the person, by means of the brain, is in a state of *mentation*, is acting mentally. It is yet to be scientifically demonstrated whether this activity is the energy discharge of brain neurons in chain action or whether this brain cell action is merely the physiological correlate of something else. The matter is still in the speculative stage, but regardless of the exact nature of "mind," the realistic, reliable, efficient operation of these processes are the marks of mental health. Therefore the student of mental hygiene should have some knowledge of their nature. Two aspects of "mind" are presented here. The description is suggestive rather than comprehensive.

INTELLECTUAL PROCESSES

"Intelligence" and "the intellect" are nouns used to designate a variety of processes involving brain action. They include perceiving (cognizing and recognizing), conceptualizing, thinking, and evaluating and judging. These are not discrete activities but are overlapping and more or less sequential. From a pattern of stimuli that is exciting action in afferent nerves leading to the brain, a group of brain cells becomes more highly activated than the surrounding cells to give a mental reproduction—a perception, cognition, idea. The person may be aware by recall or recognition that this same and closely related pattern of cells was previously activated, thus he conceptualized this as a member of a related group. This activated pattern of brain cells (idea or concept) may initiate a chain reaction in closely associated neurons, following lines of least resistance—these lines determined by residual chemical differences at the synapses from previous associated activation. This effortless activity may be designated reverie thinking or free association. It may be imagining or remembering.

The thinking person may also exert effort and direct attention, increasing resistance at certain synapses and decreasing it at others, thus guiding the chain of association either in recall or imagination. This would be critical or reflective thinking. Foreign substances, such as chemicals or toxins produced by infectious organisms, may so change the chemical condition at the synapses that normal association cannot take place, thus blocking or distorting percepts, concepts, recall and imaginative thinking. Strong and prolonged emotional disturbances, especially fear, may do the same. This malfunctioning would be mental illness—abnormal, irrational, distorted, ineffective intellective processes. The above is an oversimplified theoretical construction that has not been experimentally confirmed.

Various estimates of the number of brain cells have been given. Seven or eight billion may be a fair estimate of the number in the cerebrum. By way of comparison, there are only 26 letters in our alphabet. If over a million different words can be made from those 26 letters being arrranged in different patterns, how many ideas (concepts) could be formed with seven or eight billion brain cells? Assuming that each brain cell may not function as independently as a letter of the alphabet but, rather, in small clusters, there would still be a half-billion to a billion cell clusters; and the number of possible ideas is astronomical. This is offered for speculative purposes only, to suggest the untapped human mental potential. At the present time we have no scientific evidence of the exact relation of brain cell quantity to conceptual capacity.

In mental hygiene we are concerned with man's potential and with growth toward its actualization. Man has the potential intellectual capacity to grasp every fact, every time-space relationship in this vast universe, but he has far to go in actualizing this potential before bringing all things under his control, especially himself. His potential capacity for discrimination, appreciation, and evaluation is just as great and far from being actualized. When these potentials are actualized, man's life will be infinitely richer and more satisfying. Mental hygiene is concerned with speeding man's growth toward full actualization. Although he has not yet attained the functional capacity, man now has almost infinite structural capacity to perceive, compare, and associate facts into patterns, to abstract qualities, evaluate things relative to each other, and to evaluate situations in relationship to himself. The intellective functioning of the brain is all of this, and more. Evaluation leads to the second aspect of mentation, *emotion.*

EMOTIONAL BEHAVIOR

I have never developed the art of memorizing material to a high degree and have not practiced it extensively. One of the few things I memorized as a college student was the definition of emotion. My old professor required it of every student. "Emotion is a complex state of consciousness of high affective coloring, appearing under sudden stress of a rapidly developing situation, to which situation adequate adjustment is temporarily blocked . . ." It was a half page in length and I could recite it "by heart," never sure that I knew what it meant nor what it meant to the professor who assigned it.

Because it is so difficult to conceptualize and define, not being an entity or even a process but a quality of mentation with its physiological correlates, most psychologists have turned to the phrase "emotional behavior." They can observe and describe changes in physical behavior and in many physiological processes when a person (or animal) becomes highly agitated. This is especially true of the experimentally or behavioristically oriented psychologist who thinks of emotion as certain describable behavior characteristics. Psychologists of a different orientation may consider these as being merely the physical and physiological correlates of emotion which is primarily the color tone of consciousness, noticeable in the higher intensities of consciousness.

The analogy of photography in grays (black and white) and in color may be used to illustrate intellective processes that are detached from *self* and relatively free of affective color (emotion) and those in which self becomes central, the process becoming more intense and affectively colored. Suppose you are at a zoo watching a big Bengal tiger in his cage and idly reflecting on various aspects of jungle life. The thinking is primarily objective with little self-involvement or affective color. Then, suddenly the beast lurches against the cage door; it swings open, and he leaps out. There is no barrier between you and him. Just as suddenly, self becomes central in your thinking. It becomes subjective, centered on the subject, *you.* It is evaluative. You are evaluating yourself in relation to the tiger and he to you. You picture yourself greatly threatened and very inadequate. You experience strong fear—the affective color of your more intense state of consciousness, your conceptualizing.

The thinking (intellective activity) becomes subjective and evaluative in any situation where self becomes central in one's thinking. Self and the thing or situation are being evaluated relative to each other. If the evaluation is favorable to self, the emotional tone is pleasant, positive; if unfavorable to self, the emotional tone is unpleasant, a negative emotion. The strength or intensity of the emotion depends on the degree of the evaluation—whether mildly or strongly favorable or unfavorable. Therefore, intellective activity phases into the emotional as it becomes subjectively evaluative. *This is the primary aspect of emotion.* It is the color tone of concepts involving self; it is a qualitative characteristic of intellective activity, of evaluative cognition, not something else. However, its existence in higher degree greatly alters behavior, so we study its secondary aspect as observed in the physical and physiological changes.

To visualize this more clearly, let us return to the caged tiger in the zoo and turn back to the schematic drawing of the brain (page 37). While the tiger is caged, your thinking is objective and not very intense, but when he leaps out in front of you, he suddenly becomes a threat, and you suddenly evaluate yourself (your situation) accordingly. The instant impulse to flee is inhibited because your child or other children are present.

Action is momentarily blocked. The threat is great, the stimulus is powerful, the situation is incongruous. Many more cerebral neurons are discharging. Mental activity is very intense. While Mr. Tiger was caged, this neural activity was relatively mild and confined to the cerebrum. Now it spills over into the *thalamus* and midbrain. Reticular formation produces a high state of arousal as the *autonomic nervous system* and *endocrine glands* go into emergency operation. These, working through the *hypothalamus* and *medulla*, regulate the visceral functions such as metabolism, temperature, breathing, heartbeat, etc., preparing for emergency action. The cerebellum receives constant, almost instantaneous, feedback and directs the body to flee. This would normally occur, but you, having attained a high system of values, inhibit the impulse if there are others who require your help.

This illustration gives a general picture of the processes involved. Many details are not known, although a mass of factual information is available. These processes occur in a matter of seconds or fractions of a second. The person in this state is aware of his own bodily tensions, perspiring and prickly skin, rapid heartbeat and breathing, queasy stomach feelings, and inner warmth. These can also be observed, measured, and described by another person. This is generally described as *emotional behavior*. A comparable description can be made of positive (enjoyable) emotional behavior such as a participant winning a highly valued award or a lover with his beloved, except that the physiological correlates are not as specific nor as easily measured.

Emotion, then, is primarily the color tone (affect) of *evaluative cognition*, arising when self well-being is involved. The nature and strength of the evaluation determines the nature and strength of the emotion. Secondarily, it is the unusual (emergency) physiological processes described above, or, perhaps more truly, the experiencing of these.

The student who is conversant with experimental psychology may recall studies of the emotional responses of animals, the cat in particular, that have had a large portion of the brain cortex removed. How does one explain the emotional reaction of the decorticate cat if evaluative cognition is essential to the arousal of emotion? We are concerned here with human emotion and emotional behavior, and a decorticate man would not live, much less respond with emotion. In quadrupeds, the old brain areas, especially the cerebellum, play a much greater role in behavior control. Cognition is awareness, but not necessarily conscious. In emergency situations, even in man, the cerebellum receives feedback and signals response before the cortex is able to function. When the organism is experiencing serious threat, evaluative cognition is handled by means of the cerebellum. It is automatic and unconscious.

The importance of these physiological processes is not deprecated because they are the secondary aspects of emotion. They are essential to emergency behavior and heightened experience, and they are what the aroused person is most aware of. I am merely suggesting that basic to these, a normal prerequisite, is the mental process of evaluation which sets the arousal mechanism and endocrine system to action. Under abnormal conditions—imbibed drugs or toxins from infection—the process may be reversed, the physiological change seemingly causes the change in effect. As in any mentation, the physiological and mental processes are inseparable—correlates of each other.

> For a significant study of the physiology of fear and anger with implications for chemotherapy, see Funkenstein (1955) in *Scientific American*, 192; 74–80 or Dyal 1955. It is excellent on clinical and laboratory methods and may be used later in Chapters 8 and 10.

Since the movement is from structure to capacity, to need, to satisfaction, to adequate adjustment and mental health, it becomes the mental hygientist's duty to concern himself with the structures and processes involved in man's great intellectual and emotional capacities. From these spring the primary needs most directly related to his mental health. From these he sees their relative degree of satisfaction, and constructs characteristic patterns of adjustive behavior. These structural patterns give rise to secondary needs that are partially satisfied or frustrated and become significant for mental health. We turn now to man's behavior structures. Personality traits are behavior structures which are developed to satisfy needs and which, having become stable structures, need expression.

THE PERSONALITY

DEFINITION

It is even more difficult to define *personality* than it was to define emotion. Personality is a popular term that may have one meaning to the users, but does not mean exactly the same thing to any other two people. Allport (1937) devotes a whole chapter to some fifty different definitions, offers his own, and admits that none is satisfactory. Hall and Lindzey[2] place the many popular meanings under two headings.

> The first usage equates the term to social skill or adroitness. An individual's personality is assessed by the effectiveness with which he is able to elicit positive reactions from a variety of persons under different circumstances. It is in this sense that the schools which specialize in glamorizing the American female intend the term when they refer to courses in "personality training." . . . The second usage considers the personality of the individual to inhere in the most outstanding or salient impression which he creates in others. A person may thus be said to have an "aggressive personality" or a "submissive personality" or a "fearful personality." (pp. 7, 8).

These authors continue their discussion of types or categories of definitions (there are so many they require classification), then state that "the way in which a given individual will define personality will depend completely upon his particular theoretical preference." Admitting to its probable unsatisfactoriness, they say: "Personality consists concretely of a set of values or descriptive terms which are used to describe the individual being studied according to the variables or dimensions which occupy a central position within the particular theory utilized."

Some have defined personality simply as a person's characteristic pattern of response, or, the sort of a person one is. The trait theorist and behavioristic psychologists generally think of personality in terms of specific traits and patterned clusters of

---

[2] C.S. Hall and G. Lindzey, *Theories of Personality* (New York: John Wiley & Sons, Inc., 1957). Used with permission.

traits commonly expressed by people. Those oriented more toward a dynamic or self or phenomenological approach may include in personality the dynamic processes involved in establishing and maintaining the individual's private world.

When you think of the personality of another person, you form a very broad concept, or a chain of concepts, that includes many acts, statements, mannerisms, etc., as you have observed and responded to them on numerous occasions. When you think of yourself as a person, you think in terms of wholeness, of an acting subject. But when you think about your personality, you think in terms of frequent and varied responses from others and the *behavior you displayed to evoke* these responses—in short, how you affected them. Therefore, when thinking of personality, you are thinking of the other person, or yourself, as an object-stimulus. You give an evaluative description which is a generalization and condensation.

The psychologist does about the same, except that with the aid of tests and interviews he observes many more characteristics; but he makes an evaluative description of the other person, who, by his varied responses, is a complex object-stimulus. May we not say, then, that *personality is the object-side of a person acting in a multiplicity of variable and fixed patterns as a complex stimulus which evokes evaluative responses by others?* This is in keeping with the origin of the term, the *persona* or mask worn by the ancient actor in order to portray different roles of different characters. He was the object-stimulus in a multiplicity of roles arousing evaluative responses from the audience.

Sawrey and Telford[3] (p. 303) describe personality in terms of "both a stimulus and a response aspect," the characteristic ways the person affects others and the way others affect him. I feel that these are merely the two phases or cycles of the person as object-stimulus. The person as acting subject develops certain types of behavior to evoke a desired response. Then, according to the other's response, he responds in certain characteristic ways to extend or modify the other person's continuing responses.

It is a common expression that "personality does not develop in a social vacuum." Its development is chiefly a consequence of

[3] James M. Sawrey and Charles W. Telford, *Psychology of Adjustment* (Second Edition). Copyright © 1967 by Allyn and Bacon, Inc., 1967.

interpersonal relationships and the roles one plays. It would seem appropriate and reasonably definitive to refer to personality *as the total behavior traits and styles of response designed, consciously and unconsciously, to evoke desired responses from other people*—the objective side of the person in his many facets acting as a stimulus.

Since no definition or short description of personality can encompass what it means to all people, I do not present this as being wholly satisfactory or complete. It is a point of view and a practical working description. It incorporates not only the individual's overt behavior but also the basic fixed motives, attitudes, defenses, etc., which, largely if not fully, are also structured by a self to aid in the establishment of satisfactory relationships.

DEVELOPING PERSONALITY THEORY

An individual's behavior in any given situation springs from two sources: (1) the external stimuli, i.e., the elements in the stimulus situation, and (2) the inner development and disposition of the person—self and his attitudes, habits, evaluative cognition, degree of selective perception, etc. A difficult homework assignment may evoke in one child three hours of zestful study and complete unawareness of the noise and fun outside. In another child it may evoke an evasion of the library, defensive forgetting,* a feigned or felt illness, or playing hookey. In a hard-fought football game an exceptionally hard tackle or accidental foul may cause one player to rise up cursing and punching, while another would extend an open hand with a "good work" or "good try." The individual's reaction depends in large measure on how he perceives and evaluates, which, in turn, is largely a consequence of his inherited tendencies and previous conditioning. I shall deal with the *self factor* in the next chapter. These inner attitudes, dispositions or attributes become tendencies, characteristics and generalized modes of response by which personality is described. Each individual develops his own particular style of behavior.

By direct observation and the help of instruments (tests), the scientific psychologist studies the typical or generalized ex-

* A form of repression, discussed in Chapter 7.

ternal responses of different individuals and makes inferences relative to the inner attitudes, etc., that are assumed to be the determinants or correlates. He uses the concepts of structure and process. A school system is a structure. The interaction within the classroom is a learning process. The more or less fixed patterns of mental response, physical habits, and interpersonal relations are personality structures. Interplay between the person and his environment stimulates temporary internal actions which are termed mental and physiological processes—personality processes in that they are altered or conditioned by the personality structures. Personality processes and structures are interdependent since structures condition the responses and structures develop and change (usually slowly) as a consequence of the processes.

Theories of personality are based on both observation and inference. Certain processes and mental structures cannot be observed and measured directly. One can observe and measure a student's performance on an I.Q. test, but the quality and potential and type of mental processes involved can only be inferred. This is the dilemma of scientific psychology in its study of personality. It cannot, as of now, describe empirically and validate objectively all that goes into personality. Because empirical facts are very incomplete and much has to be drawn from inference, there is no one general or basic theory of personality but several theories. To describe these would require a large volume, of which there are several. Pertaining to this matter, Lazarus[4] writes:

> It is often distressing to the beginning student to discover all the diverse ways there are of conceptualizing personality. The myriad of theoretical systems is so confusing that he is frustrated in his desire to have simple, authoritative statements about the structure and dynamics of personality. This multiplicity of theories reflects two things—first, the great richness and complexity of personality, and second, the early stage the science of personality is still in.
>
> The science of personality as a self-conscious discipline is a very new one, having got under way shortly before the turn of the century. Yet learned men have speculated about such matters for thousands of years, and their ideas make up

[4] Richard S. Lazarus, *Personality and Adjustment*. Reprinted by permission of Prentice-Hall, Inc., Englewood Cliffs, N.J., © 1963.

> part of the philosophical background for modern theoretical systems. . . .
>
> . . . If we knew enough and had a sufficiently comprehensive conceptual framework, those theories that were less adequate would be discarded. And even though scientific theories are always being revised or replaced, the presence of so many side by side, suggests inadequacies in their present formulation and in the available evidence with which to evaluate them. Yet they remain active because, in spite of many similarities among them, each contributes something that the others do not. The great challenge to the personality theorist is to advance us beyond our present limited confines with respect to both conceptualizations and relevant empirical data. (pp. 51, 52).

While we wait for this development, we are confronted with the problems of personality growth and disorders, and with the interplay of personalities in our interpersonal relations. We can profit from the much that is true, although unvalidated, in several theories and from the insights of keen observers and profound thinkers in other disciplines.

PERSONALITY STRUCTURE

In Chapter 1, typical schools of psychological thought and approaches to mental hygiene were presented briefly. Out of these have evolved the various theories of personality development and structure already alluded to. My concepts, along with certain variations, will unfold as the course progresses. The purpose here is to call attention to the structuring of personality and to show its bearing on mental health.

At birth the infant enters a world that is detached from himself and within which he must learn to live. He comes endowed with certain capacities and needs. From his first day onward he meets both satisfaction and frustration of these needs. Soon he learns to distinguish self from the not-self and to form attitudes about each and their relationship to one another. Backed by these basic attitudes toward self and not-self, he develops more or less fixed, characteristic, types of responses designed to secure more satisfaction of need and less frustration and its consequences. Each child in maturing develops his own style of life, a complex system of responses, characteristic ways of behaving. His personality is developed to impress the not-self world and evoke desired response, thus the objective aspects of person as object-stimulus. What he thinks of himself, how he thinks he impresses others and judges their impressions of him, in short his personality, has a vital bearing on his mental health.

Argyris[5] in his discussion of personality development and organization, says: "... Since the human personality is a developing organism, one way to become more precise is to define the basic growth or development trends 'inherent' in it (so long as it remains in the same culture). One can logically assume that, at any given moment in time, the human personality will be predisposed to find expression for these development trends. Such an assumption implies another, namely, that there are basic development trends characteristic of a relatively large majority of the population being considered . . . This does not preclude the possibility that each individual can express these basic characteristics in his own idiosyncratic manner." He continues:

> So much for the logic behind the developmental trends listed below. It is assumed that human beings in our culture:
> 1. Tend to develop from a state of passivity as infants to a state of increasing activity as adults. . . .
> 2. Tend to develop from a state of dependence upon others as infants to a state of relative independence as adults. Relative independence is the ability to "stand on one's own two feet" and simultaneously to acknowledge healthy dependencies. . . .
> 3. Tend to develop from being capable of behaving only in a few ways as an infant, to being capable of behaving in many different ways as an adult.
> 4. Tend to develop from erratic, shallow, casual, quickly-dropped interests as an infant to having deeper interests as an adult. The mature state is characterized by an endless series of challenges, where the reward comes from doing something for its own sake. . . .
> 5. Tend to develop from having a short time perspective (i.e., the present largely determines behavior) as an infant to a much longer time perspective as an adult. . . .
> 6. Tend to develop from being in a subordinate position in

[5] Chris Argyris, *Personality and Organization* (New York: Harper & Row, 1957). By permission of Harper & Row, Publishers.

the family and society as an infant to aspiring to occupy an equal and/or superordinate position relative to their peers. 7. Tend to develop from a lack of awareness of self as an infant to an awareness of and control over self as an adult. The adult who tends to experience adequate and successful control over his own behavior tends to develop a sense of integrity and feelings of self-worth. . . . (pp. 49, 50).

PERSONALITY TYPES

A commonly expressed formula, used especially by social psychologists, goes something like this: each person is like no other person; each person is like some other persons; each person is like all other persons. It is true that no two children enter life with the same endowments (identical twins excepted) and no two grow up in identical environments (no exception). Thus there are ways in which no two are alike. But some are more alike than others. From the earliest time that man began to study himself seriously, he saw these patterned similarities and differences and has attempted to categorize people into personality types. These have been of much interest in theory, some value in study, but of little validity and practical significance.

William Sheldon's physical typing—endomorphic (fat), mesomorphic (muscular), and ectomorphic (thin)—has aroused considerable interest. These body-types, according to Sheldon, spring from variations in the cells—unbalanced cells cause imbalance in bodily development and in social adjustment.

Sheldon found certain irregularities among people relative to his three basic types, i.e., a person may have a torso of one type and legs of another. Physiques of these irregular types are called dysplastic. Sheldon claimed that he could distinguish 70 types of constitutional build. He typed personalities under the three basic categories: (1) viscerotonic (sociable, amiable, complacent, relaxed, comfort-loving, etc.) associated with endomorphic build; (2) somatotonic (adventurous, assertive, energetic, dominating, direct, etc.) associated with mesomorphic build; and (3) cerebrotonic (restrained, intense, inhibited, secretive, etc.) associated with ectomorphism. Concerning Sheldon's work, Allport[6] says:

[6] Gordon W. Allport, *Pattern and Growth in Personality* (New York: Holt & Co., 1961).

> To conclude, we cannot doubt the fact that bodily constitution and temperament have some close relationship. They are paired raw materials from which we fashion, in part, our personalities through learning. The sciences of genetics, of biochemistry, and of anthropological and psychological measurement have not advanced enough to tell us precisely what parallels do exist. Yet the doctrine of somatotypes in relation to temperament gives us a promising, if still imperfect, guide. (p. 63).

TABLE 3. EXAMPLES FROM JUNG OF INTROVERT AND MATERNAL NEED

	Thinking	*Feeling*	*Sensation*	*Intuition*
Introvert	A philosopher like Kant	Seen mainly in women who express their confidences in diaries and secret poetry	An oil painter like Renoir	A mystical dreamer—may be an artist or an unappreciated "genius"
Extrovert	A scientist like Charles Darwin	Fashion-conscious people interested in social causes and cultural affairs—especially common in women	An outgoing seeker of "sense" experience, as a gourmet or an art lover	A promoter who has a keen nose for new enterprises showing promise for development

Source. C. G. Jung: *Psychological Types*, Pantheon, New York, 1959. Adapted.

Of greater interest is Jung's introvert-extrovert typing, with thinking-feeling and sensation-intuition subtypes, thus eight basic psychological types (see Table 3). Of some interest and clinical possibility is the typing proposed by Spranger (1928) and used by

Allport, Vernon, and Lindzey (1959) in their Study of Values. Six types are defined: (1) the *theoretical* man, (2) the *economic* man, (3) the *esthetic* man, (4) the *social* man, (5) the *political* man, and (6) the *religious* man.

> Rather than give excess space here to this interesting topic of typing personalities, I would suggest that it be covered by a student in a special classroom report if class time permits. There is much resource material, including Suggested Readings at the end of this chapter.

Freud described personality types, or dominant traits, as consequences of crisis stages in development: oral, anal, phallic, latent and pubic or genital. Problems or difficulties in passing through these critical developmental periods would tend to fix certain types of responses which would continue as dominant personality traits—the first three being the most important. He structured personality around the id, ego, and super-ego. Dr. William C. Menninger,[7] a modified Freudian, describes these three structures:

> The Id, which is the sum total of the personality at birth, is primitive and exists entirely in the unconscious. By primitive we mean that it is animal-like, uncivilized, uncultured. It is the "id" in all of us that accounts for the demanding, selfish, inconsiderate part of all of us. If one were to verbalize its continuous theme song, it would be "it wants."
>
> At birth there is no Ego. As the personality develops, that conscious portion of ourselves (although part of it remains unconscious) that acts as an intermediary between the Id and the external world is called the Ego. In it resides our storehouse of knowledge and the intellectual capacities to choose and to judge and to think. Its theme song, both to the Id and to the world, is "I will" or "I will not."
>
> The Super-ego is a third portion of the personality that grows with us. It is our internal policeman; it functions as the

[7] Menninger, William C., *Psychiatry, Its Evolution and Present Status,* Copyright 1948 by Cornell University. Used with permission of Cornell University Press. Also in *Personality Dynamics and Effective Behavior* by James C. Coleman. Copyright © 1960 by Scott, Foresman and Company.

> judge and the critic; it embraces what we call conscience. The phrase which characterizes its advice to the Ego is "you must not." (p. 443).

PERSONALITY TRAITS

Most theorists of personality development and structure center on traits, with their variation and patterns, and on the deeper dynamic forces (need, motives, etc.). The theoretical nature and arrangement of these vary considerably, in accordance with their authors' varying frames of reference. Whatever interpretation we may give, each person develops characteristic response structures, which in turn have a capacity for exercise and thus a need for expression. These secondary or acquired needs, even as primary needs, may be satisfied or frustrated; therefore, personality structure and mental health are correlated.

Based on the dictum that no two people are alike and on the fact that it is impossible to compare one whole person with another whole person, psychologists analyze behavior into specific ways in which people differ, thus the properties of persons. They have different characteristic responses and typically express the same responses to a different degree. These responses can be measured and compared and personality described in terms of these traits, showing in what ways and to what extent one person differs from another or any individual from established norms. A trait may be a narrow and specific habitual response or a broad general typical response. Psychologists differ considerably in their naming and classifying of traits; some distinguish between character and personality traits, while others do not. In the former case, character is thought of more as the deeper dimension of basic attitudes and mental characteristics and personality as the more external physical and social patterns of response. But these distinctions are never finely drawn, since intellectual capacities and qualities are usually included in personality traits.

Using ratings made by observers, questionnaires answered by the individuals themselves, and objective tests, Cattell subjected the data to the complex statistical treatment called factor analysis. Common or overlapping elements were thus determined and personality traits thus classified as surface and source traits.

TABLE 4. ILLUSTRATIVE SOURCE AND SURFACE TRAITS

Source	*Surface*
A. AFFECTOTHYMIA vs. SIZOTHYMIA	Good-natured vs. critical, grasping Attentive to people vs. cool, aloof Trustful vs. suspicious Adaptable vs. rigid
C. EGO STRENGTH vs. EMOTIONALITY AND NEUROTICISM	Mature vs. unable to tolerate frustration Steady, persistent vs. changeable Realistic about problems vs. evasive, avoids decisions Absence of neurotic fatigue vs. neurotically fatigued
E. DOMINANCE vs. SUBMISSIVENESS	Self-assertive, confident vs. submissive, unsure Boastful, conceited vs. modest, retiring Aggressive, pugnacious vs. complaisant Vigorous, forceful vs. meek, quiet
F. SURGENCY vs. DESURGENCY	Cheerful, joyous vs. depressed, pessimistic Sociable, responsive vs. seclusive, retiring Energetic vs. subdued, languid Humorous, witty vs. dull, phlegmatic

From Cattell (1965, 1966), pp. 66, 73, 90, 92. Adapted from longer list. Copyright © Raymond B. Cattell, *The Scientific Study of Personality*. Penguin Books, Ltd., 1965 and Chicago: Aldine Publishing Company, 1966.

Because of close parallel (not identical) between my approach and that of Andras Angyal to the study of personality and because of its close relationship to the need-value presentation in Chapters 4 and 5, I shall present Angyal's "model for a formation of a theory of personality." He sees personality as a unified dynamic organization, a patterned process of living. He says:[8]

[8] In C. Moustakas (ed) *The Self* (New York: Harper & Row, Publisher, Inc., 1956). Used with permission.

> The over-all pattern of personality function can be described from two different vantage points. Viewed from one of these vantage points, the human being seems to be striving basically to assert and to expand his self-determination. He is an autonomous being, a self-governing entity that asserts itself actively instead of reacting passively like a physical body to the impacts of the surrounding world. This tendency—which I have termed "the trend toward increased autonomy"—expresses itself in spontaneity, self-assertiveness, striving for freedom and for mastery. In an objective fashion this tendency can be described as follows: the human being is an autonomous unity that, acting upon the surrounding world, molds and modifies it. . . .
>
> Seen from another vantage point, human life reveals a very different basic pattern from the one described above. From this point of view, the person appears to seek a place for himself in a larger unit of which he strives to become a part . . . he seems rather to strive to surrender himself willingly, to seek a home for himself in and to become an organic part of something that he conceives as greater than himself. . . .
>
> These two tendencies of the human being, the tendency to increase his self-determination in his expanding personal world, and the tendency to surrender himself willingly to a superordinate whole, can be summed up by saying that the human being comports himself *as if he were a whole of an intermediate order*. . . . The human being is both a *unifier*, an organizer of his immediate personal world, and a *participant* in what he conceives as the superordinate whole to which he belongs (pp. 44–46).

He justifies his model for the study of personality—its functional pattern of self-determination and self-surrender—on the basis of its practicality, particularly with relation to mental health. He says:

> I suggest the following thesis: The backbone of neurosis consists in a disturbance of two basic tendencies that we have assumed as forming the over-all pattern of personality functioning. The two cardinal disturbances on which the neurosis rests consist, first in the person's loss of mastery over his own fate, and second, what is rather generally accepted as a basic factor in the neuroses, namely anxiety. Loss of mastery is another expression for the impairment of the capacity for

> self-determination; anxiety, as we will try to show, is related to the impairment of the capacity for self-surrender and the capacity for love . . . (p. 50).

Angyal defends his thesis with sound principles and examples, then concludes:

> Summing up this sketch of the origin of the neuroses, we have assumed that certain traumatizing experiences create in the child a derogatory picture, a feeling of the worthlessness of his self. This feeling of worthlessness has two components: first, the feeling that one is inadequate, too weak to cope with the environment; and second, the feeling that one is unloved and unworthy of love. These then lead to an impairment of the person's self-determination on the one hand, and to anxiety with the loss of capacity to love on the other. . . . (p. 55).

After mulling over a dozen or more "theories of personality" one may share the feeling of Ferber:[9]

> New theories are being constructed and older ones revised, the better to incorporate and account for new findings. It is in the very nature of behavior theoretical formulations that they be modified on the basis of empirical facts. Since the empirical facts of psychology include those relating to individual differences, one may anticipate that as behavior theories become more precise and more comprehensive, they will encompass more and more phenomena now referred to under the rubric of "personality." *I, for one, look forward to the day, which I do not expect to see myself, when personality theories are regarded as historical curiosities.* (p. 37).

Whatever psychologists decide to incorporate in the term "personality," it is behavior; and behavior is objective—the structured activities and relationships of the person. This is the rightful sphere of experimental psychology and a behavioristic approach, becoming more and more definitive in its description and reliable in its correlate, causal and predictive findings. Generalizations from these findings would seem adequate to describe personality structure.

---

[9] In Philip Worchel and Donn Byrne, *Personality Change* (New York: John Wiley & Sons, Inc., 1964.) Used with permission.

GENERAL SUMMARY

Since personality theories are many and varied, they are grouped into classes of which the following is typical: *type, trait, developmental, dynamic,* and *self.* The first two have been described adequately for our purpose, and they are fairly specific while the other three are less specific and more complex in their interrelationships and overlapping elements. For instance, the basic psychoanalytic interpretation of personality is together *type, developmental,* and *dynamic.* Fixation at the strongly emphasized developmental stages determine the types, and the consequential dynamic forces are continually stressed.

Developmental. Emphasis is placed on the developmental history of the child. Biological potentialities are thought of as fixing more or less definite limits within which personality development takes place. Much attention is given to continuity of development and how response patterns formed at one stage influence the next and succeeding ones. Learning and role theories of personality come under the developmental type. Common to the psychoanalytic and learning theories is the tendency to explain present conditions in terms of past influences. Difference lies chiefly in that learning theorists place less stress on psychosexual dynamics, using a broader repertoire of primary and acquired drives, and emphasizing reward and punishment factors in conditioning habitual responses. Role theorists may be thought of as subsidiary learning theorists who find and emphasize the moulding influence of the specific role the family and other primary groups thrust upon the individual—his relative position in the group. The significance of developmental theories may be seen in the wide use of the case history in the diagnosis and treatment of personality disorders.

Dynamic. These theorists observe personality more from the viewpoint of interacting forces, e.g., attitudes, motives, drives, etc., and relative degrees of stability and equilibrium. The psychoanalytic id, ego, and superego have been described. The learning and role theorists stress the interaction and conflict among habits and role behavior determined by the various positions the individual occupies in his society. Developmental influences are taken more or less for granted in the formation of personality structures, but greater concern is with inferring the nature of these structures from observation (in natural settings when possible), psychological tests, and interviews.

Self Theory. This vague and nondiscrete class of theories includes much that is emphasized in the other theory types. Greater emphasis is placed on a unifying principle or entity, on functional wholeness, on the holistic character of personality and behavior in general. This is thought to be necessary for an adequate understanding of self-identity and experiential continuity. Thus *self* is posited as a principle or a conceptual construct or even an entity, an acting agent. The next chapter will be given to this subject.

> The student who may wish to pursue the study further, and perhaps report to the class may find excellent material in *Theories of Personality: Primary Sources and Research*, by Lindzey and Hall (eds), (1965) and *Concepts of Personality*, by Wepman and Heine (eds), (1963) or *An Introduction to Personality*, by Byrne (1966), plus References at end of this chapter.
> To see more clearly how the various theories are supplementary, or even complementary, rather than contradictory, a student may report on *Letters to Jenny*, by Allport (1965).

MAN'S GENETIC ENDOWMENT

That all men are created equal may be true, or a valid principle, in a political and religious sense—all to be given equal opportunity and receive equal consideration—but it is not true biologically. Even in the above sense, its validity is relative to differences in genetic endowment. It is generally accepted as true that men are not born with equal genetic endowments, that their organic structure varies in many details, and that these variations determine differences in functional capacity. The ancestral genes set certain limitations of capacity to function, thus scope and direction of need-drive.

THE INSTRUMENTS OF HEREDITY

The gene is the carrier of inherited (genetic) traits. It is estimated that there are many hundreds of these very complex molecules in each of the twenty-three chromosomes found in the sperm and in the ovule. When sperm and ovum combine to form the cells of a new body, each cell contains 46, or 23 pairs of chromosomes and many thousands of genes. In rare developmental abnormalities, as Klinefelter syndrome in males, there are 47 chromosomes and in the female, Turner's syndrome, 45 chromosomes—an excess or deficiency of one female sex chromosome. As far as is known, the pairing of chromosomes and arrangement of genes is a matter of chance. The possible variations are so infinitely great that, except for identical twins, no two people inherit the same pattern of genes. Thus, siblings may vary rather widely in genetic endowment and resemble different ancestors. Two cousins may resemble each other more than two siblings and, occasionally, a distant relative more than one of the immediate family. Within his inherited structure resides man's behavior or achievement potential. His environment has most to do with the degree to which it is actualized.

INHERITED CHARACTERISTICS

What do people inherit? It is not known exactly; but not as much as once was thought. The degree to which character, sociability, ambition, crime, mental illness, etc. are determined genetically is generally thought not to be as great as was believed in the past. The exact characteristics and degree of each is yet to be learned. A general rule-of-thumb statement might be that physical structure and consequential physiological processes are to a large degree matters of inheritance. The degree to which behavior, symptoms of illness, is causally related to these would define its genetic origin. The biologically-oriented psychologist generally sees more of this relationship; the sociologically-oriented psychologist sees less. The general nature and degree of inherited characteristics may be classified as follows:

1. *Bodily Characteristics.* Size, shape, strength, pigmentation, etc. are largely determined by the genes. These have little direct bearing on character, health and good social adjustment. They may have a major indirect relationship, e.g., the value placed on athletics by certain communities, the rejection based on skin color, and the teasing of "red-heads" or "fatties" too much. In such cases the environment is the primary factor, not the physique.

2. *Vigor and Resistance.* Babies from birth show marked differences in their amount of movement, expenditure of energy, and resistance to physical and psychological upsets. Unless altered by an unusual environment, these characteristics generally hold through life. They directly affect adjustment and health but in widely varying degree.

3. *Reflex Action.* The speed of the nerve impulse, synaptic facility, and nerve-muscle coordination are, in part, genetically determined. Athletic and musical skills may be partly determined by these and, in turn, affect social adjustment and mental health.

4. *Intelligence.* Whatever intelligence may be, it includes the capacity to learn, to adjust, and the intellective functions described above. These are, in part if not wholly, functions of brain structure and physiology which are inherited. While the ability to make a certain score on an intelligence test may depend considerably on the cultural environment, the genes mark limits and variations in facility.

5. *Sensitivity.* From very early infancy children show marked differences to sensory stimulation. Some children react to colors more quickly, are more easily disturbed by sounds, and show greater response to skin stimuli. Such children may be more nervous and excitable than the average, have less frustration tolerance, and thus become more susceptible to functional disorders.

6. *Temperament.* This may be a catch-all and certainly includes some elements of the above factors. But there are certain distinctive characteristics of people that seem to adhere from earliest infancy, e.g., their prevailing moods (lethargic, phlegmatic, excitable, etc.). These appear to be genetically determined in large measure, and it may be due to inherent structural and functional differences in the older brain parts and/or the endocrine system.

These are not discrete categories nor do they include all in man that is influenced by heredity. The point of interest is not so much what in man's behavior is determined by heredity but to what extent, and to what extent can it be modified. Man's great potential lies in his relative freedom from biological determinism. The scope and variety of his response potential is not fixed by genetic determinants to a degree that is closely comparable with his next highest kin. He stands in a category that includes no other—co-creator as well as creature—with the potential capacity to learn all and control all. In his full humanness he is unique.

INTELLIGENCE

Behavior scientists and mental hygienists are interested primarily in the extent genetic factors determine the degree of intelligence and susceptibility to mental illness. The individual with low intelligence will probably have greater adjustment difficulties and lower frustration tolerance, thus be more prone to psychosocial disorders. If we can discover the degree to which the major types of mental illness are inherited, we may be able to infer that mental health factors are equally genetic. Two types of studies have been most fruitful in both these areas: (1) comparing children's biological parents and foster parents and (2) comparing siblings—identical twins with fraternal twins and non-twin siblings and identical twins reared apart.

Independent studies at Stanford University (Burk, 1928),[10]

[10] From B.S. Burk, "The Relative Influence of Nature and Nurture upon Mental Development . . ." 27th Yearbook, Part I, *Nat. Soc. Stu. of Educ.* Chicago: Univ. of Chicago Press, 1928.

and the Universities of Minnesota (Leahy, 1935)[11] and Iowa (Skodak and Skeels, 1949)[12] compared the I.Q.'s of children (adopted during the first few months of life) with the I.Q.'s of their biological parents and with their adoptive parents, several years after adoption. In general, the correlation between the I.Q.'s of the children was higher than would have been predicted from hereditary backgrounds, but the composite findings of the three studies indicated clearly that a higher correlation exists between I.Q.'s of children and biological parents than between the same children and the adoptive parents who reared them. The conclusion is that intelligence (as measured by tests—I.Q. scores) is a function of both genetic factors and cultural influences. In comparative studies of siblings, identical twins correlate significantly more highly in I.Q. scores, whether reared together or apart (by adoption in different homes), than do fraternal or non-twins. And while identical twins reared in widely different educational environments show a growing gap in I.Q. ratings, they remain more similar than do other siblings, thus confirming the above conclusion.

Another, and currently more popular, approach to heredity and intelligence is the comparative study of intelligence test scores of children (especially, but also adults) from different cultural environments: lower socioeconomic class children compared with middle class children; Negroes who moved from the rural South to the industrial North compared with Negroes born and reared in the North; and children whose I.Q.'s were similar at age 6 or 7 compared after several years when reared with widely different cultural advantages. The indications are clear that the social culture—the education-oriented home and good schools—produces marked increases of mean scores on intelligence tests.

The problem of appraising the relative effect of heredity and culture hinges on two factors: (1) tests only measure performance from which the quality of intellectual functioning is inferred; thus the question of whether the higher test scores demonstrate increased intelligence or merely increased skill in

---

[11] From A. M. Leahy, "Nature-Nurture and Intelligence." *Genet. Psychol. Monogr.*, 17:235–308,1935.

[12] From M. Skodak and H. M. Skeels, "A Final Follow-up of One Hundred Adopted Children." *J. Gener. Psychol.*, 75:3–19, 1949.

the use of intelligence through much practice; and (2) the various concepts of intelligence, and they vary widely. It is most difficult to determine to what extent anything is inherited or socially determined when we do not know, or can not agree on, what that element is. At present, we must assume that the various mental processes that are, in part, determined by brain structure and physiological processes are largely influenced by genetic factors. Evidence appears to warrant the further assumption that these structures and processes are not rigidly fixed and their functional capacity can be significantly increased by cultural stimuli and one's attitudes, motives, etc. However attained, by family genes or community culture, the mental capacity of the individual determines a major area of his needs which, if satisfied, is conducive to mental health or, if frustrated, may conduce serious psychosocial disorders.

Personality. The role heredity plays as a determinant of personality is well summarized by McKeachie and Doyle:[13]

> Among lower animals, characteristics analogous to human personality characteristics are inherited. For example, in a classic experiment, Stone (1932) demonstrated that rats could be bred for wildness, establishing strains with clear-cut differences in this characteristic. Everyone is familiar with the temperamental differences between different kinds of dogs, such as the difference between collies and terriers. Well-controlled studies show that these inherited differences affect dog behavior in a variety of ways (Scott, 1958). (p. 92).

The degree to which temperamental differences in man are influenced by heredity is still unknown. One of the major problems in studying such differences is that of obtaining adequate measures of personality characteristics. Many investigators have carried out twin studies using questionnaires and other measures to assess personality characteristics. The similarity between identical twins is greater than that of fraternal twins on questionnaire measures of extroversion and activity. Even though the environment of identical twins may be more similar than that of fraternal, it is probable that this greater similarity of identical twins is partly the result of their hereditary identity.

---

[13] W.J. McKeachie and Charlotte L. Doyle, *Psychology* (Reading, Mass.: Addison-Wesley Publishing Co., Inc., 1966.

As an example of a recent study of heredity and personality, I cite the study by Scarr of Harvard[14] of "Genetic Factors in Activity Motivation." She compared 61 pairs of identical and fraternal twins between the ages of 6 and 10, with ratings on (1) reaction time; (2) number of activities; (3) percentage of active games; (4) anxiety; and (5) patience. She used ratings of activity by mothers of the children, the children's choices of activity games, and measures of time required for various performances—making choices, etc. She states:

> Identical twins had higher intraclass correlations for all five measures of preferred reaction time. . . . The intraclass coefficients for total different activities were considerably higher for MZ (identical) than for DZ (fraternal) twins. The heritability estimate was 40 percent suggesting that variation in the number of activities in which a child engaged was determined, in part, by genetic factors. The particular kinds of games, such as active or sedentary ones, however, were not affected at all by genetics. . . . Ratings of anxiety, and its correlates, by the mothers indicated that individual differences in anxiety have a firm genetic basis. . . .

In short, Scarr found significant evidence of genetic factors in all five of the above (possibly excepting No. 5), especially the anxiety and patience-impatience factors and cited other studies with similar findings, concluding: "The results of this study suggest that several empirically defined aspects of activity motivation have moderate heritability. Better measures of different populations will further define the genetic contribution to activity motivation."

> A sound principle in behavioral science is that the structure (thus capacity and need) and behavior of the organism depend on a continual interaction of inherited characteristics with pre- and postnatal environmental factors. For supporting scientific evidence of this see, Dyal, Chapter 2, selections 10 and 11 by Montagu and Gesell.

---

[14] Sandra Scarr, "Genetic Factors in Activity Motivation," *Child Development* (The Society for Research in Child Development, Inc., 1966) 37, pp. 663–673. Used with permission.

WHAT IS MAN'S POTENTIAL?

In structure resides capacity—its limits and limitless potential. The structure of the human body, the hand, the brain, the mental processes, the interpersonal relationships give promise of near infinitude. It was previously mentioned that the cerebrum has some 8 billion cells, sufficient to conceptualize every time-space relationship, every objective fact in the universe. William James is often quoted as saying that the average person uses no more than ten percent of his brain capacity, which is probably a very conservative statement. Russian psychologists have been engaged in extensive research into the human mental potential and agree fully with James. They have stated that the average man is capable of learning 40 or more languages and mastering the courses of a dozen or more majors in college.

One of the most exciting and promising endeavors in this field of investigation is the Human Potentialities Research Project at the University of Utah under the direction of Dr. Herbert A. Otto.[15] The general purpose of the project is to explore some of the dimensions of individual and family potential, develop a theoretical framework of these strengths and resources, and the factors inimical to their development, and to devise methods and instruments to help make better use of their potential.

In the pilot projects being conducted, Otto's groups are concerned with the social milieu as a conducing and inhibiting influence on both social and mental potential development, the interpersonal encounter being the major medium for personality development and growth. Experimental activity centers on means by which individuals can get the greatest possible growth stimulation from their social milieu and reforms in the milieu to enable it to contribute more, saying: "Undoubtedly man's institutions are functioning at a fraction of their potential." The question they ask of each social institution is: "To what extent does the function of the institution foster the realization of human potential?" And they add: "The newly emerging concept of human potentialities re-emphasizes the individual's uniqueness

---

[15] From Herbert A. Otto, *Explorations in Human Potentialities,* 1966. Courtesy of Charles C. Thomas, Publisher.

and adds new dignity and respect to our understanding of the person, *for each member of society, regardless of his status, is seen as having a prodigious potential which we have not yet learned to unfold. . . .* It therefore becomes a most pressing task to humanize and modify social institutions so that they will function in consonance with man's deepest aspirations, aims and goals. . . . Man's social potential remains largely untapped: "We have not as yet developed both the art and science of institutional regeneration." (pp. 410, 411).

Self-knowledge, acceptance and confidence are keys to the release and development of man's potential, these researchers are demonstrating. Yet, they say, much of man's exploration of his own inner world, and add:

> Usually, it is only when a person is in the process of breakdown that treatment and increased self-knowledge is sought from the psychologist or social worker. To maximize the psychological health of all people, these disciplines need to shift much of the emphasis from the treatment of personality pathology to helping the so-called healthy and well-functioning citizen to mobilize his potential, which includes helping him to achieve gains in self-understanding and self-knowledge. *Programs which focus on the development of the human potential are of the very essence of prevention.* Mass treatment of psychological breakdown is best achieved by fostering psychological health. . . . (p. 411).

Otto and his associates are discovering some of the ways our social milieu and personal attitudes inhibit the creative expression of our human potential. They state some of their expectations from the ongoing unfolding of man's psychological potential, of which the following is a part:

a. An extension of the ability to communicate, and the communication system. . . .
b. The development and amplification of sensory modalities and their transformation into new means of communication.
c. The availability of vast masses of stored data (most material in the brain's memory banks appear to be in a type of dead storage) for problem-solving of life-coping purposes.
d. A very marked increase in the range of affective functioning and experiencing. . . .

e. A greatly expanded understanding of the relationship of motivation (including unconscious motivation) to the realization of individual potential. . . .
f. An enlarged understanding of the role played by man's values and life-goals in relation to the unfolding of his possibilities. . . .
g. The development of a vastly increased interoceptive and proprioceptive awareness. . . .

Finally, we can anticipate that the findings from research in human potentialities will lead to the emergence of a new (psychological) image of man—a revised and enlarged perception of himself and his relation to all which surrounds him. (pp. 413, 414).

More will be quoted from Otto, Maslow, and others on the human potential. Our main thesis centers on capacity, need-goal, satisfaction or frustration, mental health or illness, and personal growth.

SUMMARY

If healthy-mindedness means growth toward the fullest possible expression of one's potential capacity, knowledge of the human structure and consequential capacity are essential prerequisites. While there is a paucity of reliable knowledge of how to guide personal growth toward fulfillment, we have learned much about man's physical and personality structure. His erect posture, hand structure, and great brain development provide the potential for the fine arts and tremendous physical skills. Reared in a community where high value is placed on these, the child who is innately or by accident deficient in this capacity is confronted with a serious problem of acceptance, esteem, and mental health.

The unique complexity of the human cerebrum with its 8 billion or more cells and open synaptic connections permits an infinite variety of associations and factual concepts, sufficient in potential for the learning of all time-space relations (objective data) in this physical universe. We are just beginning to learn how emotional stress, especially fear, and certain chemicals effect blockings or ease of transmission at the synapses. We now stand at the threshold of a new era of enhanced learning, recall, and creative mentation, and in the clearing away delusion and other cognitive disorders. Likewise, the equally complex structure and integrated functioning of the older brain parts, autonomic nervous system, and endocrine glands equip man for the emergencies of a complex civilization.

Personality has been defined, described, and its elements categorized in various ways because, in their refined specificity, man's responses can be numbered in both observed and inferred ways. How these are studied largely determines how they are grouped into dynamic systems and/or specific and general traits. My belief is that the individual may organize and express on any given occasion any combination of his many thousands of response possibilities, thus presenting a facet of his "personality," which is himself as object-stimulus at that moment, designed to evoke a desired response by other persons. Thus, personality is an interpersonal development and dynamic rather than static. The autonomous, truly healthy-minded person has a flexible complex personality which is capable of forming many richly satisfying interpersonal relationships. The insecure, defensive person has a more rigid personality (his responses mostly habitual or compulsive) which has less capacity for social adjustment and satisfying relationships.

Man's physical structure is largely inherited and his physiological and mental processes are partly determined by the genes. These tend to fix certain limitations on his potential capacity for adjustment and facilitates the psychosocial development of others. But in this, man is relatively free from organic determinism and thus his choice and cultural environment are the more determinative, except in the most extreme cases. And, except for these most serious defectives, the undeveloped intellectual, social, and spiritual potentialities are at least ten times greater than any but the few have dreamed of. During this decade a few very significant pilot projects have been in operation, designed to help clarify and develop man's so great potentiality.

GLOSSARY

Correlates. The relationship between two or more variables such as height and age of children or social-economic status and delinquency. As age increases ordinarily so does height (positive correlation) and as the social-economic status rises, delinquency tends to decrease (negative correlation).

Genetic. Pertaining to the genes—to inherited characteristics.

Idiosyncratic. Pertaining to the study of particular and significant individual characteristics rather than general traits.

Metabolism. The aggregate of all chemical processes constantly taking place in a living organism—both the conversion of nutritive materials into protoplasm (anabolism) and its breaking down to release energy for vital processes (catabolism).

Nomothetic. Pertaining to the study of particular and significant individual characteristics rather than general traits.

Rubric (izing). A division, group, or category, e.g., some psychologists resist being rubricized, placed in a definite "school."

Selective Perception. Responding to and thus aware of certain elements of the stimulus situation while ignoring (unconsciously, undeliberately) other elements—thus a distorted or unrealistic perception.

Syndrome. An aggregate or pattern of symptoms indicating the presence and general nature of an illness.

Trauma (tizing). An organic or psychologic injury due to shock or severe stress, e.g., certain childhood experiences of severe rejection, fright, or guilt may be traumatizing.

REFERENCES AND SUGGESTED READINGS

ALLPORT, GORDON W., *Personality*, New York: Holt, Rinehart and Winston, Inc., 1937.

ALLPORT, GORDON W., *Pattern and Growth in Personality*, New York: Holt, Rinehart and Winston, Inc., 1961.

ANGYAL, A., *Neuroses and Treatment; A Holistic Theory*, New York: John Wiley & Sons, Inc., 1965.

ARGYRIS, CHRIS, *Personality and Organization*, New York: Harper & Row, 1957.

CATTELL, R. B., *Description and Measurement of Personality*, Yonkers, New York: World Book Company, 1946.

CATTELL, R. B., *The Scientific Analysis of Personality*, Chicago: Aldine Publishing Co., 1966.

COLEMAN, JAMES C., *Personality Dynamics and Effective Behavior*, Chicago: Scott, Foresman and Company, 1960.

DREGER, RALPH W., *Fundamentals of Personality*, Philadelphia: J. B. Lippincott Co., 1962.

DYAL, JAMES A. (ed), *Readings in Psychology: Understanding Human Behavior*, New York: McGraw-Hill Book Co., 1962 (several articles).

HALL, C. S. and G. LINDZEY, *Theories of Personality*, New York: John Wiley & Sons, Inc., 1957.

HILGARD, ERNEST R., *Introduction to Psychology,* New York: Harcourt, Brace and World, 1962.

JUNG, C. J., *Psychological Types,* New York: Pantheon Books, Inc., 1959.

KUNKLE, FRITZ, *My Dear Ego,* Boston: Pilgrim Press, 1947.

LAZARUS, RICHARD S., *Personality and Adjustment,* Englewood Cliffs, N.J.: Prentice-Hall, Inc., 1963.

MC KEACHIE, W. J. and CHARLOTTE L. DOYLE, *Psychology,* Reading, Mass.: Addison Wesley Pub. Co., 1966.

MOUSTAKAS, C. (ed), *The Self,* New York: Harper & Row, 1956 (esp. articles by Allport, Angyal, Lecky, and Jung).

OTTO, HERBERT A., *Exploration in Human Potentialities,* Springfield, Ill.: Charles C. Thomas, 1966.

SAWREY, JAMES M. and CHARLES W. TELFORD, *Psychology of Adjustment,* Boston: Allyn and Bacon, Inc., 1967.

SEVERIN, FRANK T. (ed), *Humanistic Viewpoints in Psychology,* New York: McGraw-Hill Book Co., 1965 (several articles).

SHELDON, W. H., STEVENS, S. S. and W. B. TUCKER, *The Varieties of Human Physique,* New York: Harper & Row, 1940.

SNYGG, D. and A. W. COOMBS, *Individual Behavior,* New York: Harper & Row, 1959.

SUNDBERG, NORMAN D. and LEONA E. TYLER, *Clinical Psychology,* New York: Appleton-Century-Crofts, 1962.

3

The Self and its Image

Self-awareness, self-identity, self-acceptance, self-respect, self-satisfaction—these are the core conditions of mental health. To come to terms with ourselves is basic to our mental health. To come to terms with the selves of our neighbors is basic to a healthy society. We have learned much about our bodies during several centuries of scientific study; and we have accumulated a considerable amount of reliable information about our mental processes during nearly a century of scientific psychology. These mental and physical processes combine to comprise the objective side of our nature; this is the legitimate field of scientific investigation. For this it designed its methods and instruments. But what do we know about the self, the *we* as subjects who are aware, who do the accepting, who become satisfied? When our bodily structures become deficient and malfunctioning we are "ill" and seek medical treatment. This could be termed objective illness. But when *self* becomes deficient, weak, malfunctioning, we know very little about what to do and next to nothing about why we do it. This illness, commonly called mental, could be termed subjective illness—the malfunctioning subject. Our primary public health problem may well be to gain greater insight into the nature of the *self* and how it functions via the brain and other organs. Our primary concern may be the development of a healthy self which, in turn, can develop its effective mental processes.

WHY THIS CONCERN WITH SELF

I stated in Chapter 1 that my frame of reference best fits into that of the new humanistic movement in psychology which is often referred to as a "third force" with respect for different approaches and utilizing the insights and techniques of the major "schools." In other words, it is a synthesizing movement in psychology. I believe it is essential that we study man as a reacting object for clarification and more definitive description of specific behavior traits and their immediate antecedents. It is equally important to study man as a choosing, acting subject: a dynamic self. If, in this discussion of the self, I appear to belabor certain points, it is due to language deficiency and to the fact that little scientific study of the self has been made—thus the scarcity of factual information. In mental health or psychosocial development the issue is whether the disordered personality is to be "healed" (readjusted) by others or whether the self is to grow into wholeness and the ability to readjust its own behavior—whether merely environmental adjustment or adjustment plus growth and fulfillment. Though no sharp distinction between adjustment and growth is warranted, the former is a prerequisite to the latter; adjustive behavior can be explained or described more fully by the objective behavioristic approach than can growth or self-actualizing behavior. In the latter, good adjustment may be deliberately rejected to make way for future growth in self-hood, the *adequate* explanation of which requires insight into the self as the initiating, acting agent.

Early psychologists sought the source of behavior dynamics in man's biological nature via the instincts—the *thesis*. Later psychologists turned to society, endowing the stimulus situation with motivational power—the *antithesis*. Today, many psychologists are finding neither of these positions fully satisfactory and are turning to the self for the source of behavior dynamics—the *synthesis*. It is a synthesis in that the self is inherent in person and genetically determined.

The development of the self, its strength and quality, is largely conditioned by the social environment. But man, the person, has the unique capacity to dissociate himself (transcend), in varying degrees, from the deterministic forces of both his biological inheritance and social conditioning and *himself* choose between alternatives, becoming the initiator and director of his own behavior. Thus, the motivational energy which is rooted in the biologic and social is synthesized in the self and may be surcharged and redirected as self evaluates the situation.

BACK TO WHOLENESS

In his opening chapter, "Humanistic Psychology," Severin (1965, p. 16) makes this concluding remark: "If I see it correctly, we are leaving the stage of preoccupation with part functions and getting back to what psychology seemed to most of us to mean when we first entered the field. We are returning to what psychology still seems to mean to the average, intelligent layman, that is, the functioning and experience of a whole human being." In the same book, Gordon Allport explains this same trend in terms of the following:

> Without the coordinating concept of *person* (or some equivalent, such as *self* or *ego*), it is impossible to account for the interaction of psychological processes. . . .
>
> The organization of thought or behavior can have no significance unless viewed as taking place within a definite framework. Psychological states do not organize themselves or lead independent existences. Their arrangement merely constitutes part of a larger arrangement—the personal life.
>
> Such concepts as *function, adaption, use* have no significance without reference to the person. If an adjustment takes place, it must be an adjustment *of* something, *for* something. Again, the person is central.
>
> All the evidence—introspective and otherwise—that forces psychology to take account of the *self* is here relevant. The very elusiveness of the self—James says that to grasp it fully in consciousness is like trying to step on one's own shadow—proves that it is the ground of all experience. Although seldom salient itself, it provides the platform for all other experience.
>
> We cannot talk about strata of personality or of propriate, as distinguished from peripheral, states without implying that a superior totality includes both. (p. 39).

Human behavior, whether irrational and ineffectual or realistic and self-satisfying, has meaning only as given by the self;

since it is motivated either to defend or to fulfill the self. We have learned much about personality from psychoanalytic and behavioristic psychology. However, a more adequate knowledge of the self, elusive as it may be, is our key to the meaningfulness of "healthy" and "unhealthy" behavior. Since self has successfully eluded the experimentalist, there are little empirical findings available. Whether by scientist, philosopher, or theologian, the approach is chiefly inferential, speculative, theoretical—the awareness largely experiential.

THE AMBIGUITY OF THE "SELF"

Psychology has been defined, perhaps facetiously, as "common sense reduced to terms." Terms, however, the matter of *semantics*, is one of psychology's chief enigmas. The jargon of psychology has grown to such proportions in recent decades, and so often lacks specific concrete referents, that psychologists themselves find it very difficult to understand each other, particularly among psychologists of different frames of reference.

Among these many terms, few are used with greater variance and confusion than the word *self*. Self is a word of very ancient lineage. And, until psychology took it over, there was no problem with its meaning. Everybody used the word, and knew what it meant. We psychologists confuse the meaning. The layman still knows what he means when he speaks of *myself, self-control, self-conscious* or *self-concern,* and so does the person with whom he is conversing. These terms have a *common sense* meaning because they stem from *common experience*. We psychologists in trying to objectify, analyze, abstract, and reduce to terms have complicated the meaning of the word.

AS PSYCHOLOGISTS SEE THE SELF

Kendler, in his *Basic Psychology,*[1] assumes to give a general view held by many when he states: "Although, we are all aware that as a child matures he is forming judgments about others, we

[1] H.H. Kendler, *Basic Psychology* (New York: Appleton-Century-Crofts, 1963). Used with permission.

forget that he is also learning attitudes toward himself. The concept of *the self* refers to these attitudes. . . . He perceives his mother as kind and gentle and his father as strong and competent. It is a truism to add that how he perceives himself becomes *his self*." (p. 459).

Hilgard,[2] says: ". . . many psychologists accept a distinction between two aspects of the self—one inferred by an external observer, one of which the subject himself is aware. The inferred self, that is, the personality structure that represents the core of decision-making, planning, and defensiveness, can be understood by an external observer. This aspect of the self is commonly called the ego, the term being borrowed from Freud, though not adhering precisely to the Freudian definition. The ego is, then, a construction from behavior, an inference that can be made by competent and informed observers. The word *self* can then be reserved for the self of which the subject is aware (sometimes called the phenomenal self), the self of self-perception." (p. 491).

Inference and perception are mental constructs, images, not entities. Thus, in either case as in Kendler's statement, there is no distinction between *self* and *self-image*. Coleman writes (1960, p. 63): "In introducing the concept of self as the third major determinant of man's development, we must be careful to avoid the idea of some "little man" sitting up in the brain deciding how we should behave. When psychologists refer to 'self' they are thinking in terms of a *conceptual* structure rather than a physical one. Like gravity, the self cannot be observed directly but is inferred from various phenomena which can be observed and which seem to operate according to some unifying principle. The self, in other words, is not a mystical entity but a useful and seemingly necessary construct for explaining many aspects of individual behavior." Coleman then speaks of two aspects of self-perception, that of being different from other individuals which he calls *"self as object,"* by which he means self-image, and *"self as process,"* i.e. "knower, striver, and doer." Coleman appears closer to the true nature of the self, but the confusion is in not distinguishing between "doer," which is subject, and "process," which is the action of a doer, the verb.

---

[2] Ernest R. Hilgard, *Introduction to Psychology* (New York: Harcourt, Brace & World, 1962). Used with permission.

A SUMMARY OF VIEWS

Hall and Lindzey have written one of the most comprehensive surveys of personality theories available (1957, 1961). Nearly all of the theorists quoted by these authors attempt to describe the self. Let us now examine their summary statement, before we make our own observations:

> The term self as used in modern psychology has come to have two distinct meanings. On the one hand it is defined as the person's attitudes and feelings about himself, and on the other hand it is regarded as a group of psychological processes which govern behavior and adjustment. The first meaning may be called the *self-as-object* definition since it denotes the person's attitudes, feelings, perceptions, and evaluations of himself as an object. In this sense, the self is what a person thinks of himself. The second meaning may be called the *self-as-process* definition. The self is a doer, in the sense that it consists of an active group of processes such as thinking, remembering, and perceiving.
>
> The two conceptions of the self are so distinctly different that it would be better to have separate terms for them. Some writers have adopted the convention of using the term *ego* when they wish to refer to the group of psychological processes, and to reserve the term *self* for the person's system of conception of himself. However, this convention is not universally followed. Sometimes the term *self* and *ego* are employed in just the opposite sense from the one given above, or sometimes one of them, either the ego or the self, is used to designate both the process and the object that is perceived.
>
> It should be pointed out and clearly understood that no modern theory of the self holds that there is a psychic agent or "inner manikin" which regulates man's actions. The self, whether it be conceived as object or as process or both, is not an homunculus or "man within the breast" or soul; rather, it refers to the object of psychological processes or to those processes themselves, and these processes are assumed to be governed by the principle of causality. In other words, the self is not a metaphysical or religious concept; it is a concept that falls within the domain of a scientific psychology. Self theory represents a serious attempt to account for certain phenomena and to conceptualize one's observations of certain aspects of

> behavior. In referring to the self as a doer, we do not wish to imply that it is anything other than a name for a group of processes. (p. 468).

Kendler says one's *concept* of himself becomes *his* self. Coleman says that psychologists think of the self as a conceptual structure with two subdivisions: (1) concept based on observation of one's behavior ("object") and (2) concept based on awareness of oneself as doer or the doing ("process"). And Hall and Lindzey conclude that psychologists have two distinct meanings for the term *self*: (1) one's perceptions and evaluations of himself as an object—his physical structure and external behavior—and (2) self as "an active group of processes such as thinking, remembering, and perceiving." They call this "a doer" and "self-as-process," then add that self as a doer means only "a name for a group of processes."

We may conclude, after careful examination, that there is no basic difference between these two so-called "distinct meanings." Process is activity, e.g., a gland secreting hormones, brain cells generating electrochemical energy, a person perceiving, thinking, evaluating, not *something* that exists. The process is the secreting, the generating, the thinking and evaluating. A mental image or concept is not some*thing* that exists, but rather the process of perceiving, conceptualizing, thinking. In order to remain completely scientific, psychologists can explain only the objective behavior, which can be observed and measured, and certain mental processes (activities) which may be inferred from the behavior. They can not reach and describe the subject that does the thinking, remembering, and evaluating and thus can not explain or describe the self. Thus, as both Coleman and Hall and Lindzey conclude, current psychology speaks in terms of *object-self* and *process-self*. But, as defined, these are merely different processes—mental activities, not the acting subject.

THE PRIMARY PROBLEM

Scientific psychologists observe overt behavior and from that infer certain basic or core mental processes, and abstract from these a concept we call "self." Some call it the core personality organization; others, the core mental processes by which personality organization is maintained. Mental processes, core or peripheral, are periodic activities, not something that exists. Thus, the self of you, or you as self, would exist only periodically—a very evanescent self.

The primary question before us appears to be this: When we use the term *self*, shall we refer only to a certain type of mental process or shall we refer to the "I" and the "you" which exist as entities, permanent, as acting subjects (not verbs), which form the concepts and direct the processes? I believe this is what the term has meant to laymen throughout the centuries. Therefore it would seem more appropriate and practical if we in psychology should hold to this age-old meaning, enlarge our research methods, and learn to describe or define *self* more accurately in operational terms. We should establish a new term to express the concept of "core mental processes" or "core of personality organization," something a little broader or more basic than is generally meant by ego.

Man naturally expresses himself as subject (acting agent, initiator), as verb (processes and activities), and as object (bodily and behavior structures). Perhaps that is why his basic unit of communication, the sentence, was given that structure. By our limited objective methods we can describe man as object and as verb, with some inference, but we have not yet learned to observe and describe him as subject. Some will argue that it is not necessary to posit a doer to describe the doing. However, for adequate understanding and control of action or process, knowledge of the subject-agent that initiates and directs the action would seem to be necessary. In mental health and personal growth, we are concerned with cause and control, with the behaver and the behavior. Because we have not yet learned how scientifically to describe man as subject, we continue to confuse the thinker with the thinking, the actor with the action, verb with subject; and *mental processes* become the *self*. Note that the individual does not speak (nor experience) in terms of "*my self*" but, rather, "*myself*"—not "my self did this" but "I myself did this." I and myself are the same. *Self* does not belong to the objective case nor to the possessive case. It is nominative. Self, as experienced by people generally, is the behaver, the subject-agent.

The alternative posited by many psychologists is to choose between the self as certain core mental processes synonymous with or closely related to the psychoanalytic ego or as a "little man," a mystical being within one, serving one, a "homunculus." Perhaps there is another alternative. It seems unrealistic to attribute functions to a core of mental processes which only an entity, a subject-agent, can perform; and it is equally unrealistic to think in terms of a ghostly something-or-other that is *in* a person or *belongs to* a person. Rather, *may self be understood as the person in his subject role, doer, expressing his life by means of mental processes and structured physical organs and behavior patterns?* Myself is I—not something that is in me, belongs to me, or serves me.

My position relative to "self" is not as much at variance from that of the majority of psychologists as the above may seem to imply, but I want to keep intact the basic meaning of a word of long and universal usage. I accept the concept or principle of basic, near-fixed, core mental processes and personality traits around which one's characteristic behavior traits are organized; but this should be given a name other than self. I am also trying to avoid attributing to processes, activities, and instruments (verbs and objects) the dynamic, instigating, causative powers that only a subject-agent possesses; and with this I am trying to push our investigation into a new dimension of personhood, the study of human nature.

Scientists operate on the basis of certain basic assumptions, e.g., the universe is orderly, lawful, and knowledge of it can be systematized. In view of the age-long common experience of oneself, it would seem to be appropriate for us as psychologists and students of psychology to approach the study of human nature with the basic assumption of the existent self, the given, the person as subject, the "I am." From this base we could slowly expand our techniques until we truly come to grips with the self (ourselves) in communicable, validated experience. This is a psychological frontier. Until it has been conquered, we will need the help of other disciplines to better understand ourselves and to better regulate our lives.

SUBJECTIVE VALIDATION

The answer to this dilemma may be found in extensive researching the experience of empathy and returning to the use of trained, clinically directed introspection. The latter is a technique of self-reporting that was popular in early psychology, but which has been virtually discarded. Empathy is a term that rapidly attained popular usage and took on too many interpretations. The therapist-client relationship developed it to include the subject-subject rather than subject-object type of knowing, which most psychotherapists have experienced in their intimate problem-sharing with their clients. Awareness moves from conceptualizing, which is objective, through intuiting, which is half-and-half, to an empathic, nonstructured, nonsensory awareness, which is subjective but valid. It might be more meaningful to think of awareness as a structure-nonstructure continuum rather than a dichotomy or a three phase process. Awareness may be in the form of a clear-cut image or concept of a fully structured object or relationship. Again, in moments of silent communion with a person with whom one is deeply identified, there is an awareness at the level of the self and its qualities that are fully subjective and very real but which are not structured images and cannot be objectively described. Between these are all degrees of overlap and combinations. Figure 7 may help clarify this if we keep in mind that it is necessary to resort to analogy or other figurative expression when trying to communicate that which is nonconceptual or not clearly conceptual.

Subject	*Verb*	*Object*	
John	talks	to Jim	(Subject-object relationship)
John and Jim share			(Subject-subject relationship)

Figure 7.

When the interpersonal relationship reaches the state of deep acceptance and trust (empathic oneness), there is a mutual awareness of each other as experiencing subjects (not objects). There is also a knowledge of each other's attitudes, with occasional awareness of each other's thoughts. This is nonstructured mentation. I have experienced this on numerous occasions with certain clients and with my wife. I have talked with others whose experiences have been similar. This is also how one truly experiences himself—I knowing myself (not *my* self). It is self experiencing itself in immediate subjective awareness. And it is a normal experience—not in the sense of the usual or statistical norm, but in the sense of being a natural characteristic of the human potential. These are the awarenesses, the cognitive realizations, of those lucid moments when man is most himself. It reaches beyond the mental construct we term concept. And it is basic to one's sense of his own identity, continuity, and stability in a world of change.

Abraham Maslow's work with high self-actualizing people and his findings and inferences in relation to B-cognition (cognition of being) may well be the opening wedge that will lead to a break-through to subjective validation of self as acting agent. These high self-actualizers Maslow studied show an intuitive, subjective quality of awareness well above that of the average person. If several small groups of such persons were brought together once or twice a week for several months to explore their potentialities, practice forming close identity and empathic relations, and with this practice introspection, checking their awareness with each other, the findings may meet the standards of scientific requirements. Of B-cognition, Maslow says in effect:[3]

In B-cognition there is the tendency to experience the object in its wholeness and uniqueness, detached from any possible usefulness and relatedness, perhaps somewhat as the mother may perceive her baby, and is exclusively attended to. Since the object (or person) is not seen in its relevance or utility, it is experienced more truly in accord with its own nature, free of "selective perception," and, according to Maslow, "repeated *B-cognizing* seems to make the *perception richer.*" (p. 72). He states:

> My findings indicate that in the normal perceptions of self-actualizing people and in the more occasional peak experiences of average people, *perceptions can be relatively ego-transcending, self-forgetful, egoless.* It can be unmotivated, impersonal, desireless, unselfish, not *needing*, detached. . . . *The peak-experience is felt as a self-validating, self-justifying moment which carries its own intrinsic value with it.* That is to say, it is an end in itself, what we may call an end-experience rather than a means-experience. . . . *In all the common peak-experiences which I have studied, there is a very characteristic*

[3] A. Maslow, *Toward A Psychology of Being* (Princeton, N.J.: D. Van Nostrand Co., Inc., 1962). Used with permission.

> *disorientation in time and space.* It would be accurate to say that in these moments the person is outside of time and space subjectively. . . . (74, 75).
>
> *Peak experiences are from this point of view more absolute and less relative.* Not only are they timeless and spaceless in the senses which I have indicated above, not only are they detached from the ground and perceived more in themselves, not only are they unmotivated and detached from the interests of man, but they are also perceived and reacted to as if they were in themselves, "out there," as if they were perceptions of a reality independent of man and persisting beyond his life. . . .
>
> Ordinary cognition is a very active process. It is characteristically a kind of shaping and selection by the beholder. . . . *B-cognition is much more passive and receptive than active,* although, of course, it never can be completely so. . . . (pp. 80, 81).

Clark Moustakas, staff psychotherapist at the Merril-Pamer School, says (1956, Chapter 1):

> True experience may be understood through empathy in communal living or in self-expression or utterance. But it cannot be communicated. To communicate the self is to abstract from it, speak of its aspects or parts and thus do violence to it. Communication represents or symbolizes the self. It distinguishes, compares, and characterizes. Communication is used to influence and often to change. Communication requires explanation, analysis, description, and clarification. . . . Self-expression is not persuasive and is without special purpose or function. The self is undifferentiated in time and space. It is being, becoming, moving, undivided from the world of nature or the social world.
>
> True growth, actualization of one's potential, occurs in a setting where the person is felt and experienced as sheer personal being. In such an atmosphere the person is free to explore his capacities and to discover for himself meanings and values of life consistent with the self.
>
> In spite of all the advances in tests and measurements and in analyzing human behavior, understanding the person from his point of view, in the light of his own unique experience, is the most real way of knowing him. More and more we are realizing that the self-expression of the individual in true experience is complete in itself. . . .

FROM PSYCHOLOGY TO PHILOSOPHY

I wish to make clear at this point that we have moved outside the sphere of orthodox or scientific psychology and into the sphere of philosophy and/or the metapsychology as proposed by Maslow. As a philosophical frame of reference, existentialism puts structured, rational, conceptual thinking within and a part of experience. It also lays the ground work for such a metapsychology or for social scientists, philosophers, and religionists to combine their disciplines in a more comprehensive knowledge of man. Many psychotherapists and mental hygienists have recognized the need for this more comprehensive *knowing*. We need to develop better terms in order to validate and describe subjective awareness.

LOGICAL VALIDATION

The philosopher in his speculative approach to reality is able to move one step beyond the empirical scientist. Castell[4] states, with neither objective validation nor invalidation, that "a self is an object" (i.e., entity) but the type of object one does not reason about but with, that not only reacts but acts—that is, self is the kind of object that is also a subject, most objects not being subjects. He distinguishes between the natures of the two and rules out theories of self as material object and sensible object.

> We deal with so many objects that are not subjects and deal with them so successfully, that we fall into the habit of treating objects that are subjects as though they were not subjects. This is excusable but not reasonable. If we treat an object that is not a subject as though it were, we would personify it, and our discourse becomes metaphorical. But by parity of reasoning, if we treat an object that is a subject as though it were not, we would "thingify" it, and our discourse becomes

[4] Reprinted with permission of The Macmillan Company from *The Self in Philosophy* by Alburey Castell. Copyright © Alburey Castell, 1965.

> metaphorical. In both cases the metaphor is easily gotten rid of. (p. 57).
>
> I see no promise in discourse about the self that begins with the claim that the self is a material object or process, a sensible object or process, or an activity. These will not get us where, in the end, we have to go. On the other hand, I see some promise in the claim that the self is a subject and an agent, although I am aware that what a subject is, and what an agent is, remains far from clear and distinct. I would, however, conclude with a caveat: in seeking to make these notions clear and distinct, we must not beg the whole question by presupposing that the modes of clarity and distinctness appropriate to objects, processes, and activities are definitive for entities that are neither objects nor processes nor activities. If that point is conceded, then time spent trying to say what the self is not, is not time wasted. (p. 59).

Castell attempts a logical validation of his theory by demonstrating self to be an identity or continuant and that activity is not a continuant but is transient. Then he argues:

> This is to say that a self has qualities but is not those qualities, not any one of them and not all of them taken together. Further, a self stands in relations, but is not those relations; performs activities, but is not those activities; has experiences, but is not those experiences; lives through events that happened to it, but is not those events; undergoes change, but is not those changes. The objection has been raised that this makes the self obscure, even mysterious. That is as may be. It is not impossible that the self *is* obscure, even mysterious. Emerson may not have been misled when he said, "In mystery the soul abides." I have asked myself repeatedly whether I *am* the qualities that from time to time characterizes me; whether I *am* the relations I stand in; whether I *am* the activities I perform. . . . If I am asked what qualities I have, there is, at any one time, an answer; for example: sad, slow-witted, jealous, puzzled, hungry, hopeful, ambitious, bored. But if I am asked whether I *am* those qualities, either the question is not clear, or the answer is "NO." (pp. 56–60).

I am trying to establish the point that, while mental hygiene is basically a field of applied psychology, it involves the whole person in dynamic operation; and the whole person involves more than present-day orthodox or scientific psychology is able to

h. When a person is mentally ill, he is malfunctioning ut his being—the self, the mental processes, and the ity traits. To understand him fully and cope with him ely, we in mental hygiene or clinical psychology need a broader base of operation than we have at the present time. *We are not calling for less science but more, and more than science.*

RECAPITULATION

Self is person acting in his wholeness as subject, the locus of behavior dynamics, from which springs the power to act. Self is not the brain nor in the brain; not the physiological processes of the brain nor their mental correlates. These are parts, mechanisms and processes—material that can be abstracted and conceptualized. It is not those regulating processes often called *ego;* for these, although relatively stable, are mental processes. Self (whole person, subject-agent) may be acting through or via id impulses, ego conflict, and superego restraint at the same time—these being parts, instrumental processes, not dynamic sources.

Since science must be cautious, many behavioral scientists are disturbed by the danger of personifying or hypostatizing abstract qualities when self is thus interpreted. This would be legitimate if self were posited as a part of the person, a homunculus or its counterpart. But, lacking a clear formulation of self as agent, we are in danger of hypostatizing ego and superego. Thus, we attribute to a system of mental processes, the power of action which only a subject-agent can possess. We are doing just this when we speak of the ego or id or superego as *doing* this, that, or the other. They are not the doers, but are mental instruments.

The above discussion may appear to be quite abstruse to the reader. The self *is* elusive. But for self-control, self-evaluation, and self-respect, all so closely related to mental health, a working knowledge of the self is pertinent. Self-understanding would seem to imply understanding the *self,* drawing from all available sources.

We have taken this detour into philosophy and skirted the fringe of religion to apprehend (we can not comprehend) the self and to grasp something of its nature and potentiality. "Mental" is a class of processes, transient activities, which can neither be sick nor well, but may be ineffective or effective. We shall examine briefly how the self experiences, its reaching out in self-expression, its confrontation with outer reality. In this is need; and in its satisfaction or frustration is health or illness.

PERSONALITY AND NEED AS FUNCTIONS OF SELF

Self initiates, acts, is constantly reaching out to apprehend, to cope with, and to find means of developing and expressing its potential. The consequences of these probing trial activities are evaluated and the most significant retained to color the growing self-attitude and the quality of the growing self. Thus each new experience is colored by and evaluated in a frame of reference of a self conditioned by all preceding experience. As certain repeated acts and responses become helpful in protecting self and/or leading to actualization, they become established as a unit-pattern or trait with meaning to the self in accordance with its strength quality and whole reservoir of experience. Just what action-elements go into these traits is determined by self's appraisal of the situation and of itself—by one's self-image or self-attitude. Personality traits may be thought of as functions of the self-attitude or a consequence of it, and they, in turn, influence it, depending on their relative success as behavior structures. As the person approaches maturity, he develops many specific attitudes toward himself based on appraisals of his performance in various situations. Each is more or less firmly established and functions to produce a typical response in that situation, the personality trait. Specific self-attitudes cluster or generalize into broader patterns or types and, in many, may generalize into an over-all self-attitude or image.

These established response structures carry their own need of expression. Need is inherent in structure. Thus, each personality trait (each symptom in illness) has function, purpose, goal. Self created it to serve a purpose; these are the secondary needs of the person, and they are many. Their degree of satisfaction is directly associated with mental health. Being acquired needs and goal-directed, with a function, there is resistance to change, even if toward improvement.

This structure-function principle is widely applied in sociology toward institutions and individuals. Now it is finding a prominent place in psychology. For example, in adolescence high value is placed on physical traits that contribute to athletic prowess and personal attraction. The individual who lacks these may develop compensating behavior—intellectual, moral, etc.—to which he gives excess value, thus compensating the value of the trait he prized, but lacked. Therefore, self creates a behavior structure with a strong need-function, to maintain its own sense of worth.

> Interest might be added to the study of this unit if three students conduct a panel discussion of the self, and present different points of view challenging or supporting the position of this chapter. Suggested Readings at the end of the chapter will supply ample material.

SELF-AWARENESS AND THE SELF-IMAGE

It has not been possible to discuss the self without frequent references to the self-image, and allusions to its meaning. Becoming aware of himself, forming concepts about himself, and developing attitudes toward himself are among the most significant features of child development. The course of this development is traced largely by inference with very little experimental evidence. However, there is general agreement among psychologists on this matter, with varying emphasis on stages and influences.

DEVELOPING A SELF-IMAGE

The neonate in entering a new world is suddenly met with a flood of new stimuli—some pleasant, some painful. He soon learns that crying gets response. He explores his body and other objects, watches his mother come and go, and soon experiences differentiation or separateness. He can throw the bright toy from his crib but not the soft wiggly foot. In his own self-initiated but often random actions, he gets different responses. He soon learns to direct his actions toward anticipated and desired responses. The degree of his success accounts for the quality of his self-image in the earliest stages. If he gets the response he needs and desires, he values his action more highly and begins to feel his worth. Frustrated and deprived, he deprecates his performance and feels of little worth. "If I were of greater worth, I would be loved more and treated better," the very young child *thinks-feels* in diffused non- or part-conceptual awareness. When he learns to use language, concepts are more clearly formulated relative to himself and others—"yours," "mine," etc. The words and voice tone used by others in the family when speaking to or about him provide affective colors for the mental picture of himself, and what he takes to be their concept of him becomes, in a large measure, his. Of course, he may misinterpret or exaggerate their opinions and form a distorted image that may last for years. As he grows older he may in large measure correct that faulty image by a more realistic evaluation of his own performance or he may go through life looking at himself through astigmatic perceptive lenses.

Growth does not take place evenly through childhood. There are short periods when the social environment is more than normally demanding; when the child's growing adjustment responses are tested most severely; or when the child is most zestful in asserting himself. These periods are most consequential in self-image formation, giving some credence to the psychoanalytic typing—oral, anal, phallic, etc.,—but perhaps not as much as the true Freudians stress. Other episodic periods may be added. Over-shadowing tones cast upon the self-image at one or two of these periods may tend to hinder it for the remainder of his life. The depth and frequency of one's involvement with others and their significance to him determines the degree his self-image is affected by their responses. There is also that inherent factor of temperament that partly determines how a child is affected by others in his opinion of himself. Allowing for considerable individual variations, the tendency is for the child to evaluate himself as others do. He loves himself as he has been loved. Then, in turn, he loves others as himself. Concepts of the real-self, imagined-self, or feared-self and of the ideal-self may be carried side by side, giving rise to confused patterns of behavior.

DIFFERENT SELVES OR SELF-IMAGES

Those of us who do not distinguish between self and self-image, who use the term self to designate a pattern of mental concepts relative to the self, speak of various selves e.g., social-self, family-self, professional-self, etc. We fail to distinguish between the terms *ideal-self* and *ideal-self-image.* Our concern is with the formation of the latter and its relation to mental health.

The two approaches toward an understanding of another person, an image of his personality or self, have been presented: the objective method of observing and measuring (with tests) personality traits and inferring certain characteristics of the self; and the empathic way of immediate awareness. The self may assess and evaluate itself by the same two polar approaches. The self that can identify deeply with itself may be said to have a high (or deep) degree of empathy with itself; it knows itself in a nonsensory, nonconceptual manner. It can assess its action-reaction patterns, its traits, place relative value on them and still maintain a unified or generalized and stable image of and attitude toward itself. This is more likely to be the healthy, stable self.

Other selves, especially those deprived of love, trust, acceptance, etc., become weaker selves which are less able to attain self-identity and self-empathy and to truly know themselves. They can only draw inferences about themselves based on their perception of how others evaluate them, later supplemented in varying degree by their evaluation of their own behavior traits. These may be highly distorted by *selective* perception, thus, the person creates a faulty self-image and an unrealistic or inappropriate self-attitude. We may call this the *feared-self-image,* the kind of self he is afraid he is. To compensate for this, in fantasy experiences he creates a system of adequate and worthy traits and develops an *ideal-self-image*—the image of the kind of person he would like to be. These two images may be in wide contrast. There may be more than two images but less clearly defined and separated. Lacking a true knowledge of himself and functioning from the viewpoint of conflicting self-images, he acquires spurious or pseudo needs; values and goals become confused and behavior unsatisfactory.

Let us keep in mind that these are structures, and structures function in needs. Such selves are generally weak and are inadequate in self-identity and self-knowledge. There is one self; but lacking strength and integration, it forms various self-images. These contrasting and confused self-images as conceptual structures lead to conflicting and confused need-drives toward confused goals. Therefore, these persons become behavior problems and, often, mentally ill. The extreme of this is seen in the condition designated as multiple personality. More often they are the neurotic, the confused, dependent, insecure, lonely-in-a-crowd people who, like Willy Loman in Arthur Miller's *Death of a Salesman,* don't know who they are.

Karen Horney[5] discusses the *ideal-image* quite lucidly, particularly in relation to neurotic personalities who "repress" certain awarenesses and create self-images which are more acceptable.

> . . . Conscious or unconscious, the image is always in large degree removed from reality, though the influence it exerts on the person's life is very real indeed. What is more, it is always flattering in character, as illustrated by a cartoon in the *New Yorker* in which a large middle-aged woman sees herself in the mirror a slender young girl. The particular features of the image vary and are determined by the structure of the personality: beauty may be held to be outstanding, or power, intelligence, genius, saintliness, honesty, or what you will. . . . (p. 96).
>
> In all its essentials the idealized image is an unconscious phenomenon. Although his self-inflation may be most obvious even to an untrained observer, the neurotic is not aware that he is idealizing himself. Nor does he know what a bizarre conglomeration of characters is assembled there. . . . (p. 97).
>
> In contrast to authentic ideals, the idealized image has a static quality. It is not a goal toward whose attainment he

[5] Karen Horney, *Our Inner Conflicts* (New York: W. W. Norton & Company, Inc., 1945), Chapter 6. Used with permission.

> strives but a fixed idea which he worships. Ideals have a dynamic quality; they arouse an incentive to approximate them; they are an indispensable and invaluable force for growth and development. The idealized image is a decided hindrance to growth because it either denies shortcomings or merely condemns them. . . . (p. 98).

Horney discusses the various functions of the idealized image. It is a substitute for realistic self-confidence, aids a person in comparing himself with others, gives a sort of vicarious purpose to his life, glosses over one's faults and weaknesses, and "represents a kind of artistic creation in which opposites appear reconciled or in which, at any rate, they no longer appear as conflicts to the individual himself." (p. 104). She describes one of her clients whose unrealistic behavior had resulted in serious conflicts:

> In his idealized image he was the knight in shining armor, the crusader with wide and unfailing vision, ever pursuing the right. . . . He was honest without being hypocritical. Women loved him and he could be a great lover but was not tied to any woman. Here the same goal is achieved as in other instances: the elements of the basic conflict are blended.
>
> The idealized image is thus an attempt at solving the basic conflict, an attempt of at least as great importance as the others I have described. It has the enormous subjective value of serving as a binder, of holding together a divided individual, and although it exists only in the person's mind, it exerts a decisive influence on his relations with others. (p. 108).

We may challenge the appropriateness of the term, self-image. The image or concept is a mental structure formed in response to structured things, relationships, etc. Self as person in his subject-wholeness is not structured in parts and cannot be truly imaged. But the child can form an image of his behavior and appraise its effectiveness or accept the appraisal given to it by others, therefore he actually forms a *personality-image*. From this he may infer certain qualities of self-hood and evaluate self as being worthy or unworthy, capable or inept, and have positive or negative feelings toward himself. This might be termed *self-attitude*.

A student may wish to report on Karen Horney's explanation of the *real self* and *idealized self.* See either Horney (1945) or Horney (1950).

FORMING SELF ATTITUDES

Whether or not the individual accepts himself depends on his self-attitude. Jersild[6] (p. 21) states: "Self-acceptance is an essential condition of mental health. Acceptance of self is the healthy counterpart of an unhealthy state of self-rejection. Self-acceptance is not the same as smugness, or conceit, or the illusion of being perfect."

As previously stated there is virtually no empirical data on the self by which any theory can be validated. On the "self-image," or self-attitude as I prefer, there is much too little. One of the most significant studies is Jersild's (1952). After carefully explaining the purpose of his study, Jersild obtained compositions from approximately a thousand elementary school children, about sixteen hundred junior and senior high school pupils, and two hundred college students. Anonymity was assured, and the group wrote on the topics, "What I Like About Myself" and "What I Dislike About Myself." Some of the pupils were from parochial schools and a few were Negroes. They covered a wide and fairly representative socioeconomic range. The study included a large sample of personal interviews, some group discussions, and certain other subsidiary features.

From careful analysis of the thousands of responses, they were grouped into several main categories and subcategories. Jersild discusses his findings under these categories which may be designated as dimensions of experience:*

1. Personality, Character, Inner Resources
2. Self-control

---

[6] Reprinted with the permission of the publisher from Arthur T. Jersild, *In Search of Self* (New York: Teachers College Press, 1952). Copyright 1952 by Teachers College, Columbia University.

* Chapter Headings from Jersild, *In Search of Self.*

3. Social Attitudes and Relatedness to Others
4. Relationships with the Opposite Sex
5. Intellectual Abilities
6. Home and Family
7. Physical Characteristics
8. Clothing and Grooming
9. Special Talents, Sports, Recreation, Health
10. Religion
11. "Just Me, Myself"

Self-attitudes are formed on the basis of one's performance in these categories or dimensions of experience. Self is adjudged to be worthy or unworthy by inference based on one's own or others' appraisal of his performance in these. That so many answers came under the last category lends some support to my contention that the individual has an innate subjective awareness of *self* as being *himself* in wholeness, defying analysis and clear conceptualization. I like or dislike *myself,* not *my self.* This is something different from I like my body, or my intellect, or my personality.

Categories 1 and 3 above received the greatest number of responses indicating that these are the most significant determiners of self-attitude. These two are closely related in that one's personality and character are most often evaluated in terms of social attitudes and relationships. As a general interpretation, Jersild says:

> . . . Self-evaluation in terms of personality and character, and social attitudes and relationships did receive considerably more attention from the older people than from the younger ones, and there was more mention among the younger people of such matters as friendly and disagreeable experiences at home.
>
> But apart from certain quite clearly age-linked responses, an outstanding characteristic of the results is that most of the categories of self-description prominent at any one age level are also prominent at other levels. This is especially true of categories that involve feelings or attitudes with regard to one's own character traits, emotional tendencies, or feelings involved in relationships with people. There are matters pertaining to self-evaluation that seem to have a more or less common meaning and to represent a common understanding at all age levels in the population in this study. . . . (pp. 29, 30).

> The class may find it interesting if a student reports on a few detailed findings under several of these categories; also with that, a report on the role of the school in self-evaluation which is presented by Jersild. This could be used again in Chapter 6.

POTENTIAL UNLIMITED

LOVE AND FAITH

It seems appropriate to devote ourselves to an examination of love and faith in our last topic on the self and its potential. These capacities are unique in man and give rise to his most unique and important needs. Their roots may have sprung from his animal forebears, but their development and expression in man carries a quality of otherness or transcendence. I have mentioned the discovery of love by psychiatrists as being a very significant prophylactic and ameliorative agent in mental hygiene, but they have not yet discovered the role of faith in this field of need. The two are so closely related in function that this must be developed for further knowledge. These are experiential capacities of the self which may be structured in social behavior and which are evident in the empathic relationship of mutual knowing, trusting, and sharing. When structured as mental processes and social behavior these capacities become attitudes and character or personality traits. But first they are capacities of a self that is an experiencing subject.

These attributes will be discussed more fully in Chapters 13 and 14 where high level healthy-mindedness in personal and social living is presented. Only the briefest preview is given here because they are both capacities and needs which can be adequately understood only as characteristics of the subject-self. They are essential to adequate growth of the self and may be expressed adequately only by the strong, adequate self. *Faith* is not an irrational, uncritical, credulous type of belief. It is the outreach of the self in the *affirming, apprehending, experiencing* of oneself, others, and life. Thus it is a natural *cognitive* process. It is a state of self that is relatively free from doubt and inner tension, thus unity and strength. It affirms life and self and thus is the key to self-acceptance and acceptance of others.

Love is more *conative* in nature, with or without the *affective* element. Love is a generous *goodwill* (willing good) attitude that may be expressed toward all people. Toward some people, love involves deep identity, sharing, the growth of affection. Faith affirms and love identifies in experiential sequence. Faith and love are the special self-capacities of man which make possible his dissociation from and transcendence of his genetic and cultural determinants and by which he may identify with and find his ultimate meaning in a humanity that transcends the physical and temporal.

OUR POTENTIAL

We have tried in this chapter to show that man's natural capacity for living, for experiencing, is much beyond our present level of knowledge and much greater than the opportunity we provide for its growth and expression. How great the need, how great the frustration, and how they are handled set the stage for mental health or illness.

Maslow (1962, Chap. 8), in his discussion of B-cognition (awareness of one's own state of being), reveals the anxiety and reluctance of people in coming to terms with themselves at the depth of their self-hood. Otto and his associates are demonstrating in their experimental groups the inhibiting tendencies of the individual, the family, and other social institutions that prevent full self-awareness and the expression of his so very great potential. Rollo May[7] uses the biblical story of Adam, the Greek myths of Prometheus and Orestes, and Dostoevski's story of the Inquisitor to show that through the centuries, truly perceptive men have seen the great anxiety and resistance men have always experienced when they became cognizant of their unique potentiality and its obligatory demands. It is the capacity to dissociate himself from the world of the animal and physical nature, to transcend it, and to stand alone as representative of a new order. It is the capacity to establish values, to build, to change, to

[7] Rollo May, *Man's Search For Himself* (New York: W .W. Norton & Company, Inc., 1953), Chapter 6. Used with permission.

create—alone or in league with a higher order, the gods, or God—to stand with or against his culture. Man's ability to respond is so great that he fears his responsibility. Perhaps this partly explains why we psychologists have been so slow in coming to terms with the self, why we have encapsulated it as merely a mental construct, a core of mental processes, determined and controllable, safe. It is in a free, substantive, subject-self that the unique and unrealized human potential lies. It is in such a self that we find the true locus of behavior dynamics. As self grows on and on toward fullness of selfhood, more and more of man's vast mental potential will be released and directed by it toward the creation of a richer life.

SUMMARY

The condition and functional quality of the self is the key to mental health. Among psychologists there is much confusion in the meaning given to this term. Hall and Lindzey (1961), after a study of many interpretations, state that the term has come to have two distinct meanings: self-as-object (one's feelings, perceptions, and attitudes toward himself) and self-as-process (such as thing, remembering, and perceiving). Careful analysis would reveal no basic difference between these. The problem seems to be whether to have the term self mean a certain type of mental image or process or restore its meaning to that which is in keeping with common usage—self as acting subject that produces the processes and images.

It is suggested that a major reason for the confusion is that we as scientific psychologists with our limited objective approach, limit our findings. We can observe and describe only the *objective* and *verbal* aspects of the total person—his structured behavior and certain mental processes which culminate in the observed behavior. But we can not, by our present methods, validate our subjective experiences of the self, which is the person functioning in his role as subject, the initiator, and director of action. The self is of the *nominative* case, not the *objective* nor the *possessive*. It is *myself, yourself,* not *my* self or *your* self. The challenge appears to be for psychology to enlarge its methods and discover means of validating subjective awareness of the self (subject-agent). In the meantime, psychologists may look to philosophy and theology for additional insight into the self as subject, validated logically on the basis of continuity and commonality of empathic awareness. Castell particularly emphasized that "I" and what "I perform," on the basis of continuity of existence, cannot be the same.

It is argued that the individual knows himself better than anyone else can know him and that much of that knowledge (cognition) is subjective and noncommunicable, cannot be structured into clear concepts and verbal symbols, and that the fullest understanding of another self is in close empathic relation—self experiencing self in nonstructured, nonverbal communication. But this subjective or empathic knowing is not entirely different than the objective. Rather, they represent the extremities of a cognitive continuum with between stages.

The growing self deprived of adequate trust and love remains weak and is prone to selective perception, thus forming faulty concepts of his own abilities, character or personality. Being weak and self-distrustful, he is deficient in self-empathy, true self-awareness, and continues with his distorted *feared-self-image* which is generally of low quality and for which he compensates by constructing an *ideal-self-image,* both being unrealistic. Guided by these, which are truly personality or character-images rather than self-images, he is likely to develop psychosocial disorders.

Faith and love are presented as, first, capacities, then needs and basic attitudes of the self as experiencing subject and unique in man—adequate in the strong, healthy self and inadequate in the weak, immature self.

Finally, I suggested that man's potential capacity for transcendent and creative living is so great he fears the responsibility it entails, and thus he represses awareness of his high potentiality.

GLOSSARY

Becoming. A term widely used in existential philosophy denoting that no person is in a state of absolute being, has not attained perfect or complete self-hood, but all are in a state of becoming.

Cognition(ive). The processes involved in knowing, becoming aware, such as perceiving, conceptualizing, thinking, remembering, etc.

Conate(ive). The processes of willing, striving, expressing endeavor—closely related to, but not synonymous with, motive and drive.

Entity. Something that actually exists in and of itself—in contrast to an abstraction.

Homunculus. Derived from "small man," midget or dwarf—and from the concept of a minute body contained in the spermatozoon or ovum.

Process. An operation, activity, movement such as glandular secretions, various mental activities, or continuing growth.

Proprium(iate). Those mental processes that relate most closely to the self or one's image of himself—that especially influence or help defend one's self-image or self-attitude—those which have special subjective significance, that give special unity and distinctiveness to personality.

REFERENCES AND SUGGESTED READINGS

ALLPORT, GORDON W., *Becoming,* New Haven: Yale University Press, 1955.

CARUSO, IGOR, *Existential Psychology,* New York: Herder and Herder, Inc., 1964.

CASTELL, ALBUREY, *The Self in Philosophy,* New York: The Macmillan Company, 1965.

COLEMAN, JAMES C., *Personality Dynamics and Effective Behavior,* New York: Scott, Foresman & Company, 1960.

HALL, CALVIN S. and GARDNER LINDZEY, *Theories of Personality,* New York: John Wiley & Sons, Inc., 1957.

HILGARD, ERNEST R., *Introduction to Psychology,* New York: Harcourt, Brace & World, Inc., 1962.

HORNEY, KAREN, *Neuroses and Human Growth,* New York: W. W. Norton & Company, Inc., 1950.

———, *Our Inner Conflicts,* New York: W. W. Norton & Company, Inc., 1945.

JERSILD, ARTHUR T., *In Search of Self,* New York: Bureau of Publications, T.C., Columbia University, 1952.

KENDLER, H. H., *Basic Psychology,* New York: Appleton-Century-Crofts, 1963.

MASLOW, A., *Toward a Psychology of Being,* Princeton, N.J.: D. Van Nostrand Co., Inc., 1952.

MAY, ROLLO, *Man's Search for Himself,* New York: W. W. Norton & Company, Inc., 1953.

MOUSTAKAS, CLARK (ed), *The Self,* New York: Harper & Row, 1956.

ROGERS, CARL R., *On Becoming a Person,* Boston: Houghton Mifflin Company, 1961.

SEVERIN, FRANK T., *Humanistic Viewpoints in Psychology,* New York: McGraw-Hill Book Co., 1965.

4 | The Dynamics of Behavior

Animals appear to be puzzled at times, but the questioning of life reaches a unique development in man; it is a unique characteristic of his unique capacity for life. The asking begins early in life and ends only at death. "Why? Why? Why?" is the ceaseless challenge of the very young child to virtually every parental command or request. And there is no end to our questioning the behavior of ourselves. Why is one child so tender and considerate, while his playmate delights in torturing a pet animal? Why does one mother drown her crying baby, while another literally wears herself out to provide a good education for her child? Why does one youth beat a helpless old man to death "for kicks," while another youth volunteers for a special military mission that means almost certain death? Why does an individual behave on one occasion in such a manner as to experience a state of exaltation, then again in a manner that causes him to toss in bed most of the night in self-condemnation and remorse? Why are some people compulsive conformists and others rebels? Some cautious, others daring? Why are some people honest and others dishonest? Some virtuous and others sensualists? There seems to be no limit of questions. Perhaps it is because man's potentiality is limitless.

Modern day psychologists are becoming aware of man's higher potentialities, and are finding it necessary to make a more penetrating and realistic examination of man's needs, goals, and motivation. I shall review only a few of the most pertinent interpretations to point out the chief contrasting views and refer the student to more comprehensive surveys. My purpose is to probe into the nature of motives, so that each of you may investigate your own motives more deeply.

THEORIES OF MOTIVATION

With the question *Why?* we move from man's nature, structure and capacity, to the dynamics of his behavior, the well-spring of action, the release and direction of the energy that activates him. Motivation is the term used to designate these generalized concepts, and few topics have been more discussed and written about by mid-twentieth century psychologists. Motivation springs from the same Latin root as the infinitive *to move,* it refers to that which tends to produce or modify action—to instigate, energize, sustain, direct and halt. The motivated person (or animal) is in a state of action or readiness to act, as viewed outwardly. Inwardly, he is already in a state of heightened physiological and psychological activity.

INSTINCT THEORY

Earlier psychologists explained motivation in terms of "instincts." People collect things because of a "hoarding instinct." They form groups because of the "herding instinct." Later psychologists have largely discarded the term for various reasons: instinct does not explain but merely renames, i.e., circular thinking; psychologists and laymen discovered more and more "instincts" to account for the various patterns of behavior; instinct as defined, is a structured pattern of response mechanisms that are inherent in the organism. Experimental psychology has demonstrated that few such structures exist in the human neonate. It is probable that the human infant comes into the world with certain sets, dispositions or tendencies to form certain response patterns, but virtually all of his behavior patterns are learned. Thus, the term *instinctoid tendency* is sometimes used to designate this root condition. Need and drive are its current replacements, and will be presented later. William McDougall's *hormic* theory[1] was the widely accepted explanation of motivated behavior early in this century. McDougall enlarged upon William James' 28 instincts,[2] arranged them into a neat system, and ascribed a specific emotion to each. These were held to be the innate mental driving forces which instigated adjustive or need-satisfying behavior.

PSYCHOANALYTIC THEORY

Sigmund Freud, who pioneered psychoanalysis, reduced the dynamic instincts to one, later adding another. His *Eros* (sex or life) instinct and *Thanatos* (death) instinct which ruled psychoanalytic thinking until recently, is slowly being replaced by the preferred terminology of sex-drive and aggression-drive which culminate in creative and/or destructive behavior. These aroused forces are then given direction by (or through) the competing (or interacting) mental constructs called id, ego, and super-ego, in accordance with the pleasure and reality principles. (See Chapter 2).

> As a continuation, or follow-up, of the report on the psychoanalytic theory of personality suggested in Chapter 2, a student may present a report to the class on the psychoanalytic theory of behavior dynamics. An excellent condensed treatment may be found in Louis P. Thorpe, *The Psychology of Mental Health,* Chapter 2, 1960.

The direction aspect of motivation has been explained by both the psychoanalysts and behaviorists in terms of hedonism. In Freudianism it was the pleasure principle, gratifying primitive desires, modified as reality dictated but still pleasure as permitted. In behaviorism it was pleasure that gave direction to behavior,

[1] William McDougall, *Outline of Psychology* (New York: Charles Scribner's Sons, 1923), pp. 135–265.

[2] William James, *Principles of Psychology* (Briefer Course) (New York: Henry Holt & Co., Inc., 1892), p. 403.

but pleasure was described in terms of tension reduction, e.g., hunger is experienced as organic tension and eating reduces the tension to give pleasure.

The survival of Freudian doctrine and symbols suggests that Freud comprehended many truths in human behavior, but was hampered by nineteenth century scientism, and limited knowledge of the thought structures or language adequate for communication. Therefore, he resorted to somewhat mythological terminology. Most behaviorists and nonpsychoanalytic clinical psychologists have discarded most of the Freudian terms and greatly modified many of his theoretical assumptions. This departure is based chiefly on the following criticism: (1) His observations and inferences were based on sick (abnormal) rather than healthy (normal) people. (2) They were based on too few cases to be highly valid. (3) His cases were selected from a limited social class, geographical area, and historical period, thus it was not a universal and valid sample. (4) His inferences were fashioned too much by an inadequate nineteenth century biological frame of reference and ignorance of sociology. (5) He tended toward oversimplification of behavior complexities and to force "facts" to fit his theories. (6) His enlarged and somewhat unusual meaning given to the word sex and exaggerated emphasis on sexuality as the primary motivation. This last point is incorporated in other theories but carries its own special significance.

Many variations of the psychoanalytic and other "instinct" or biologic-rooted theories of motivation took form, slowly moving from a biophysical to a biosocial point of view. Karen Horney and Harry S. Sullivan, Neo-Freudians, played major roles in this movement focusing on interpersonal relationships as the motivator of character or personality structure and finding serious disturbances in human relationships the chief cause of neuroses.

ALLPORT'S THEORY

In Moustakas (1956, Ch. 3), G. W. Allport discusses the trend in motivational theory.[3] He reviews the current tendency

[3] Dr. Allport has been a prolific writer and speaker on this subject, and his ideas may be found in numerous articles and books.

to overemphasize unconscious motivation and dependency on projective techniques to reveal these and cites experimental evidence to show that, while this may be necessary in neurotic cases, normal fairly well-adjusted people are fully conscious of their significant motives and can be trusted to reveal them in direct tests and interviews, and the trend is to trust people's insights relative to themselves. In normal people the tension reduction goal is not given much credence as a dynamic factor in any but the lowest levels of need-satisfaction, the organic.

> Before such an adequate conceptualization can be achieved there is one current dogma in motivational theory that demands re-examination. I refer to the oft-encountered statement that all motives aim at "the reduction of tensions." This doctrine—found in instinctivism, psychoanalysis, and stimulus-response psychology—operates to keep us on a primitive level of theorizing. We cannot, of course, deny that basic drives seem to seek "reduction of tension." Oxygen need, hunger, thirst, elimination are examples. But these drives are not a trustworthy model for all normal adult motivation. Goldstein remarks that patients who seek only tension reduction are clearly pathological. . . . Normal people, by contrast, are dominated by their "preferred patterns" of self-actualization. Their psychogenic interests are modes of sustaining and directing tension rather than escaping it.
>
> We should, I think, agree with Goldstein that tension reduction is not an adequate statement of the functioning of natural psychogenic motives. At the time of his inauguration as president of Harvard, James Bryant Conant remarked that he was undertaking his duties "with a heavy heart but gladly." He knew he would reduce no tension by committing himself to the new job. . . . Striving for equilibrium, "tension reduction," "death wish," seem trivial and erroneous representations of normal adult motivation. . . . (pp. 40, 41).

And in his own *Personality and Social Encounter*[4] Allport says: "To sum up: We need in our motivational theory to make a sharper distinction between infantilisms and motivation that is strictly contemporary and at age."

---

[4] G.W. Allport, *Personality and Social Encounter* (Boston: Beacon Press, 1964), p. 105.

INTRINSIC MOTIVATION

J. McV. Hunt[5] describes what he calls "The Traditional Dominant Conceptual Scheme," then develops his own "intrinsic motivation" concept, i.e., motivation inherent in the process of cognition. He raises eight questions that motivation theories have tried to answer, then he shows their shortcomings and what his theory has to offer in answering each question. Of these eight, I will quote only two:

> First, according to this dominant conceptual scheme, organisms are instigated to act by strong and painful stimuli; by such homeostatic needs as hunger and thirst, by sex, or by innocuous stimuli which have been associated with (conditioned to emotional responses evoked by) the strong painful stimuli or the homeostatic needs and sex. . . .
>
> Second, this traditionally dominant conception has found the determinants of the vigor of activity in the intensity of painful stimulation, or in the degree of homeostatic need, or in the intensity of the emotional responses that were originally part of the total response to such stimulation but which have come via conditioning to be evoked by originally innocuous stimuli. . . .

Hunt cites numerous experimental studies to sustain his criticism of these "dominant" concepts: "This paper has reviewed the evidence, coming largely since World War II, which shows that play, manipulation, exploration, spontaneous alternation in mazes, and concern with novel stimuli all occur in the absence of homeostatic need and painful stimulation. Moreover, painful stimulation, homeostatic need, or innocuous stimuli which have been associated with them, tend, if anything, to inhibit these various forms of behavior. These suggest that there must be another kind of motivation, one inherent in information processing and action." (p. 93).

[5] *Motivation and Social Interaction—Cognitive Determinants,* edited by O.J. Harvey (New York: The Ronald Press, 1963). Copyright © 1963 by The Ronald Press. (Especially Chapter 3 by J. McV. Hunt).

A STATE OF THE SELF

We shall limit the discussion of Hunt's "intrinsic motivation" theory to his interpretation of arousal, the instigation question, which is basic to the others and based on extensive research (Hebb, 1949, 1955; Hunt, 1960; Miller, Galanter, and Pribram, 1960; Taylor, 1960; and others in Harvey, 1963). Anatomical and physiological research during the 1950–60 decade has demonstrated the insufficiency of the old stimulus-response (S-R formula), whereby afferent nerves carry the stimulus impulse to the association area of the brain cortex and from thence over efferent nerves to the appropriate acting organs. This oversimplified concept has been replaced by what these investigators call the "feedback loop" through which central processes can regulate "receptor input." Thus, arousal is not a simple function of the reflex arc under strong stimulation, but is regulated by this central feedback operation between the cerebral cortex and sensory areas on the one hand and the thalamus, hypothalamus, and reticular formation of the brain stem on the other (see Figure 2). This feedback is part of the cognitive process. Based on previous experience and what is expected or acceptable, if the feedback on the stimulus situation is congruous (in harmony with the expected and acceptable), the afferent impulse will be weak and will produce little or no instigation of action. If the feedback on the stimulus situation is adjudged incongruous (unexpected, unaccustomed, unacceptable), the afferent impulse is heightened and arousal is experienced. A mother may sleep through the roar of outside street traffic, but if her baby in the adjoining room should cry with a less intense sound stimulus, she would be aroused immediately to action.

I agree wholeheartedly with Hunt, Harvey, and Schroder in their inferences about motivation. Moving from the experimental end of the continuum, they have approached a self-psychology and have demonstrated the invaluable contributions of experimental psychology to human behavior. They have demonstrated the necessity of inserting the O-variable (e.g., the organism acting as mediator between stimulus and response) into the S-R formula. They have gone as far as the scientific psychologist (by present scientific methods) can go in coming to terms with the self and in placing the self in the O-variable position as mediator. As scientists they are limited by structure and structured concepts and thus are unable to reach the self, the whole person as subject, as acting agent. Therefore, they attribute motivation to the self, a true self-function, but describe the self as a system of cognitive processes which are really activities of the self; and thus motivation is equated with the cognitive processes, not being able to scientifically differentiate between the cognitive processes and the self that instigates the cognitive processes.

Although these psychologists have not been able to explain the essential nature of motivation as a state or condition within the self (only the metaphysicist or metapsychologist with subjective validation criteria may do this), they have done an excellent job in describing the mechanics of motivation, an example of the true and valuable role of experimental psychology. Their findings open the door to the validation of the newer theory of behavior dynamics (motive) resident in the self, which is the new synthesis of the older biologic and social origins.

My position is that the substantive self as subject-agent is this mediator; the self, evaluating the incongruence or unusualness of the stimulus situation, is aroused to heightened mental activity with affective overtones (emotion). The vigor and direction of the activity is a consequence of self's continuing evaluation and re-evaluation in terms of an anticipated and desired goal—whether to approach or avoid, whether to sustain or eliminate the stimulus situation. Likewise, it is self that can possess a value hierarchy by which choice of response is made and carried out via its learned (habitual) mechanism when found effectual and by re-evaluation and redirecting when old forms are ineffectual—the "goal" or "aim" being maintenance and enhancement of self, not pleasure nor tension reduction.

Hunt's "intrinsic motivation" theory is sound; but the "motivation" is an intrinsic qualitative state of the self, of which the central feedback operation is a function. Scientific description can account for only the anatomical mechanisms and physiological processes by means of which arousal is achieved and need-drive operates. Self and its qualitative state of readiness to act remain in the unexplored frontiers of science.

MOTIVE, THE WHY OF BEHAVIOR

Cofer and Appley have produced a classic volume on Motivation.[6] They ask (p. 9) "Why is the Motivation Construct Used?" The answer is succinctly given in one sentence: "So far, it is clear that the motivation construct must have been developed to correspond to certain properties of behavior—properties for which other constructs are presumed not to be sufficient." (p. 10). They continue: "It is often said that all behavior is motivated and that behavior serves the organism's needs. . . ." They raise a question with regard to the last statement and discuss these properties of behavior which make theories of motivation necessary, then state in summary:

> . . . There are a number of more specific aspects of behavior which have seemed to theorists to be uniquely motivational, however, theorists do not agree as to which ones are crucial, and these differences will be further analysed in this book. At the moment we must be content with the statement that any one or any combination of the following points about behavior may lead to the postulation of a motivational process; that behavior occurs at all, that a variety of responses is facilitated by some operation (like deprivation of food), that responses vary in vigor, that behavior has direction, that certain kinds of subsequent event may strengthen (and other kinds may weaken) a behaviored sequence. The reader may ask of each theory whether it purports to deal with these points, whether it is adequate to do so. . . . (p. 13).

The above authors define certain issues that are relevant to the problem of motivation as being:

1. *Emphasis on innate or acquired processes in behavior.*
2. *Conscious and unconscious factors in behavior.*
3. *Is behavior primary or is it instrumental?*
4. *Is organismic functioning conservative or growth-oriented?*
5. *The nature of human nature.* (pp. 14, 15).

---

[6] C.N. Cofer and M.H. Appley, *Motivation: Theory and Research* (New York: John Wiley & Sons, Inc., 1964). Used with permission.

HUMAN NATURE

Let us reverse the order of these points and make a careful study of the last item mentioned, for it is basic to all other issues raised in both quotes and to any satisfactory understanding of motivation. For this we need the assistance of philosophy. It is an old discipline, long engaged in studying "the nature of human nature," and more at home in the *why* of human behavior. Science is more concerned with the *how* of behavior; it describes. The why and how cannot be fully separated; nor can philosophy and science be separated.

Max Scheler,[7] said to be one of the most brilliant thinkers of this century, deals specifically with "the nature of human nature," with man's unique capacities. He describes five psychic levels in the "biopsychological" world from the simplest vital impulses and sensitivity of the lowest forms of life to the "spirit" nature of man. Man shares the first four psychic stages with the lower orders of life (plant and animal kingdoms), but stands alone and unique at the fifth or spirit level. These five levels parallel closely my five structure-capacity-need levels as presented later in this chapter.

Scheler sets "spirit," the highest psychic order, against "life," the four lower psychic orders, which we may refer to as "natural life." He says that it is only man as a spirit being who can dissociate himself from nature and objectify and abstract it. The animal is so fully a part of nature he cannot do this. Thus man can free himself from the dominant control of these natural forces (biologic determinism) and transcend them. He argues, however, that life (lower order of nature) and spirit are complementary rather than antagonistic and that by suppressing or repressing the lower order impulses or drives, energy is diverted to the higher level, becoming the means of altruistic motives, etc. Thus Scheler establishes a rational (philosophical) basis for the locus of motivation in the autonomous self. As a spiritual being, Scheler argues, man may attain his "existential liberation" from

[7] Max Scheler, *Man's Place in Nature* (Trans. H. Meyerhuff). Reprinted by permission of the Beacon Press; copyright © 1961 by Beacon Press.

the organic world and its drives and from environment, maintaining an openness to the world.

Viktor Frankl, psychiatrist-philosopher, discovered this same capacity to transcend environmental determinism, this "nature of human nature," in the crucible of the most compelling circumstances. He says:[8]

> We who lived in concentration camps can remember the men who walked through the huts comforting others, giving away their last piece of bread. They may have been few in number, but they offer sufficient proof that everything can be taken from a man but one thing; the last of the human freedoms—to choose one's own way. (p. 65).

Later Frankl says:[9]

> There are two specifically human phenomena by which existence is characterized. The first is constituted by man's capacity for *self-detachment*. Another capacity of man is that for *self-transcendence*. In fact, it is a constitutive characteristic of being human that it always points, and is directed to something other than self. This self-transcending quality of human existence is ignored and neglected by those motivation theories which are based on the homeostasis principle. . . . (p. 97).

To recapitulate, Scheler and Frankl see in the nature of man the power to dissociate himself from both his biologic and social matrices, choose from among alternatives, and initiate and direct his own behavior. If these men are realistic in their assessment of human nature (capacity), then we may turn to the self, person in his wholeness as subject-agent, for the locus of motivation. Hunt and his associates, with other experimentalists, provide valuable information on how motivation operates, the mechanics of arousal, direction, and reduction of coping behavior. Biologic urges and social pressures alone cannot account for human behavior. Unless the dynamics of behavior is in the self, how can we account for self-discipline, self-directed growth and creative

---

[8] Viktor E. Frankl, *Man's Search For Meaning* (Boston: Beacon Press, 1962). Reprinted by permission of the Beacon Press; copyright © 1959, 1962 by Viktor Frankl.

[9] Viktor E. Frankl, "Self Transcendence as a Human Phenomenon," *Journal of Humanistic Psychology,* Fall 1966, pp. 97–106. Used with permission.

achievement? How else can we expect the "mentally ill," the maladjusted, the psychosocially crippled individual to arouse himself and to assume responsibility for correcting his own behavior and attain wholeness?

WHAT IS MOTIVATION?

Difficulties with the instinct theories of motivation were mentioned; and the *need* and *drive* concepts have been substituted. Sometimes these terms are used synonymously and often with different connotations. Frequently they are used interchangeably with motivation. Until more exact definitions are given to these terms, I will assign them the following meaning and relationship: motivation = need → drive → goal.

By the nature of his structure and self-being, man has certain capacities and a multitude of potentials. Capacity to function carries with it the need to function. And need is experienced as drive toward a goal. Motive is this *need-drive-goal* set of the self which may be dormant as a state of readiness or aroused in directed behavior. For example, a child who has learned to fear dogs, and evaluated them as being dangerous, may be playing in his room and if suddenly a dog outside the window barks loudly, the child runs screaming to his mother. The fixed state of readiness was permanently present, a qualitative state of self based on self's former evaluation of dogs, but was aroused only when the dog barked.

When I use the term drive, I think in terms of the self, which engenders action toward an anticipated goal after an evaluation of the stimulus situation. The potential energy of the need state or disposition becomes kinetic. The permanent need disposition, resident in potential capacity, then becomes a unit experience of need-drive-goal. In normal (and much abnormal) complex human behavior, self is not a reacting object. It holds its reacting objective mechanisms in abeyance until the situation is evaluated, then acts upon the situation. Thus, *drive* is the potential difference between the "push" of capacity-need and the "pull" of evaluated goal, the pull of anticipation.

MOTIVE SUBJECTIVELY EXPERIENCED

One may analyze the findings of a hundred experimental studies, and he would learn a vast array of facts and inferences *about* motivation. The facts *are* very helpful, and the inferences *may* be, in education and in mental hygiene, but taken alone, they simply are not enough. Working as a psychotherapist with one's client, wrestling with a highly significant behavior problem, each highly motivated and sharing in deep empathic relation, each motivated, thinking, subject-self experiences the other in immediate awareness. It is a subject-subject cognitive experience and thus the two experience each other's motives as quality states of the self. It is then that one *knows* what motivation *is* experientially. In full clarity of awareness such empathic cognitive experiences are relatively rare; but as more vaguely experienced, they are fairly commonplace. Let one hundred therapists who have had at least one or two such occurrences, relate his own experience to the others. Though each would describe it differently, using different figurative and analogic language, each will know the nature of the other's experience and its meaning. Thus, these experiences are subjectively validated to a degree equivalent to .05 level of statistical significance.*

FREEDOM AND DETERMINISM

Since motivation is posited as the answer to the Why? of behavior, it involves the problem of freedom vs. determinism. When one approaches human behavior from the objective side of the continuum, he observes structured patterns of response and sees only an organism responding to stimuli, thus determined behavior. Although he is never sure that the responses are completely determined by the stimulus situation, he infers as much, on the basis of what he can observe and measure. But when one experiences the behaving subject from the subjective side of the con-

* A term used by statisticians to denote a fairly high degree of reliability or validity, not explainable by chance.

tinuum, he is cognitive of a free, holistic, nonstructured self as acting subject, a macrocosm, unique, and of the nature of the absolute rather than the relative. In the self's acting on his environment, there is freedom, choice, and alternatives. To the degree that there is structure and differentiation, there is relativity and determinism, because these are structured conceptualizations of structured behavior, of which we are more sharply aware because of their definitiveness. Structure implies parts in relation to each other and to the whole. Subjective experience, however, is on the side of wholeness and freedom, and man is intuitively aware of them within himself and in the other person when the two are in empathic relation.

Since human nature is structured on a multidimensional scale (approximating Scheler's five levels), and man is unique in his capacity to transcend the physical order, motivation has to be scaled at each of these dimensions. New elements or factors are involved at each higher dimension of behavior. While normal behavior is generally holistic and there is constant interaction at different levels, certain behavior sequences are cued, instigated, and directed chiefly from the base of one or another level: organic and reflexive, overt physical activity, intellectual, social, or spiritual. At the lower dimensions, behavior is largely stimulus reaction and tension reducing, and is adequately explained by inferences from animal experimentation. Moving up the scale to intellectual, social, and "moral" or "spiritual" behavior, there is more insight, evaluation, and subject choice. In man, all of this is involved. Therefore, to answer the why of human behavior and cover the issues raised by Cofer and Appley, it seems necessary to interpret motivation along the lines presented above.

EXPERIMENTAL STUDY

Hundreds of experimental studies have been made with animals to try to determine the general nature and relative strength of such "drives" as hunger, sex, fear, etc. The inferences drawn from these provide satisfactory descriptions and explanations of behavior motivation at the lower dimensions, which includes most animal and some human behavior. The work of

Atkinson and McClelland[10] over a period of several years, with various associates, is outstanding. Their basic work was with hunger as a primary motive, in which they developed their technique based on perceptual and fantasy responses to pictures—a projective technique.

U.S. Navy personnel were used as test subjects. They were deprived of food for different intervals of time: one-, four-, and 16-hour periods. They were then shown a set of six pictures and asked to write stories about them, centering around several standard questions. The scoring system was based on responses relative to food deprivation: +1 or +2 was given to responses that showed a moderate or large increase from a short to long period of deprivation; −1 or −2 was given to those responses that decreased with longer periods of hunger. No score was given to responses that did not change. By this technique they demonstrated that motivation or need-drive influences one's fantasy and can be determined to a relatively satisfactory degree by the themes they apperceive in ambiguous pictures—what they project into the picture.

In their more significant work, the experimental study of the achievement motive, McClelland et al[11] conducted a large number of tests, mostly with college students. The subjects were given various test assignments to perform under various conditions of encouragement and frustration. For stimulus pictures, the Murray Thematic Apperception Test was used. This test shows how individuals with different personalities and family relationships perform under various conditions. The findings have contributed much to our knowledge of the background circumstances which foster the growth of high or low achievement motivation.

> The work of these men is of great significance and if class time permits, a 15 or 20 minute report by a competent student would be very worthwhile. Detailed reports can be found in several psychological journals, books on motivation and the footnote references.

---

[10] J.W. Atkinson and D.C. McClelland, "The Projective Expression of Needs: . . ." *J. Exp. Psychol.* 38: 643–658. Also in J.W. Atkinson (ed), *Motives in Fantasy, Action and Society* (New York: D. Van Nostrand, 1958), pp. 288–305.

[11] D.C. McClelland et al, *The Achievement Motive* (New York: Appleton-Century-Crofts, 1953).

NEED CATEGORIES

To be objective one must differentiate, discriminate, abstract, and generalize; therefore, observe the specific and categorize. The objective students of motivation have found a vast variety of categories since there are almost as many needs as acts. These can be studied from several points of view.

One of the early classifications, popularly used for many years, is Thomas' four basic "wishes":[12] *security, recognition, response from others,* and *new experience.* Needs (or drives) are commonly classified as *primary* and *secondary,* the former derived from the inherent structure of the organism and the latter learned or acquired. Others group them into *bodily* (or physiological) *psychological,* and *social.* Murray[13] developed a more complex and practical classification that could be used as a basis for diagnostic testing. He delineates 13 "viscerogenic" and 28 "psychogenic" needs. The former are physiological processes associated with *lacks, distentions,* and *harms* (three subdivisions). Typical of the psychogenic are: acquisition, conservation, orderliness; superiority, recognition, aggression, abasement; affiliation, nurturance.

Hilgard (1962) prefers to study them as *survival motives, social motives,* and *ego-integrative motives.* Raths[14] lists eight basic needs for children: (1) Need for belonging; (2) need for achievement; (3) need for freedom from fear; (4) need for love and affection; (5) need for freedom from guilt; (6) need for sharing; (7) need for understanding and knowledge and (8) need for economic security.

DEFICIENCY VERSUS GROWTH

Abraham Maslow has been deeply involved with the more profound experiences of man, and he classified and reclassified

[12] W.I. Thomas and F. Znaniecki, *The Polish Peasant in Europe and America,* (Boston: Mt. Vernon Press, 1919).

[13] N.A. Murray et al, *Explorations in Personality* (New York: Oxford Press, 1938).

[14] Reprinted with permission of The Macmillan Company from *Mental Hygiene for Teachers* by Lester and Alice Crow. © The Macmillan Company, 1963.

the needs he observes. He states[15] that needs arrange themselves in a hierarchy, from the most basic biological requirements to the most complete self-actualization. He has suggested five categories or dimensions:

(1) body needs
(2) safety needs
(3) love and belonging needs
(4) security, adequacy, and esteem needs, and
(5) self-fulfillment.

Later (1962) he describes needs in terms of *deficiency motivation* and *growth motivation.* Hierarchies exist in these two hemispheres, but Maslow makes no sharp classification. Rather he describes them operationally. Deficiency motivation is directed toward supplying the need-deficiencies that maintain life, health, and self-stability. These are means-needs, not goal-needs. With health secured, the "not sick" organism may go on toward full self-hood, the end- or goal-needs. He speaks of neuroses as deficiency diseases: "Most neuroses involved, along with other complex determinants, ungratified wishes for safety, for belongingness and identification, for close love relationships and for respect and prestige." (p. 19). Then he adds:

> In recent years more and more psychologists have found themselves compelled to postulate some tendency to growth or self-perfection to supplement the concepts of equilibrium, homeostasis, tension-reduction, defense and other conserving motivations. . . . (p. 21).
>
> So far as motivational status is concerned, healthy people have sufficiently gratified their basic needs for safety, belongingness, love, respect and self-esteem so that they are motivated primarily by trends to self-actualization (defined as ongoing actualization of potentials, capacities and talents, as fulfillment of mission, or call, fate, destiny, or vocation), as a fuller knowledge of, and acceptance of, the person's own intrinsic nature. . . . (p. 23).
>
> The multitude of idiosyncratic motives which come under the head of "self-actualization" can hardly be listed since each person has different talents, capacities, potentialities. But some characteristics are general to all of them. And one is

[15] A. Maslow, *Motivation and Personality* (New York: Harper & Row, 1954).

> that these impulses are desired and welcomed, are enjoyable and pleasant, that the person wants more of them rather than less, and that if they constitute tensions, they are pleasurable tensions. The creator ordinarily welcomes his creative impulses, the talented person enjoys using and expanding his talents.
>
> It is simply inaccurate to speak in such instances of tension-reduction, implying thereby the getting rid of an annoying state. For these states are not annoying. (p. 27).

Maslow's theory of a D-cognition and B-cognition, mentioned in the preceding chapter, was derived from his motivation studies. The person, who through childhood, was deprived of many basic needs—particularly acceptance, love and general security—tends to exaggerate the value of those need-gratifications. He becomes dependency motivated and in a manner somewhat like selective perception, his cognitive processes tend to focus on his deficiences and what is necessary for security. He tends to see and evaluate people and situations in terms of their capacity to gratify his deficiency needs, not cognitive of himself or others in terms of his or their own being and non-utilitarian worth. The individual, whose basic need-gratifications were amply provided through childhood, while valuing them no less, has sufficient confidence to more or less take for granted that he will not be denied these. Therefore he becomes motivated more toward growth, high achievement and self-fulfillment. His cognitive processes focus more freely and truly upon his own state of being or that of the other person, on the intrinsic worth of people. Being devoid of utilitarian motivation and dependency need, self and other-person-awareness are more acute and realistic.

The following discussion of needs will reveal more of Maslow's contrasts between deficiency and growth needs.

> Members of the class may profitably read Buhler's "Basic Tendencies" report at this point, relating them to Murray's and Maslow's needs, perhaps giving additional study to Murray's method of classifying. For Buhler, see Appendix. Also, in Dyal (1962), selections 14, 15 and 16, the interested student will find valuable articles illustrative of the experimental and clinical ap-

proaches to motivation. The first, by Neal Miller, presents several interesting experimental studies which indicate *motivation mechanisms.* The other two, by Maslow, present the necessary complementary approach to the deeper nature of motive.

HUMAN NEED: ITS NATURE AND PATTERN

Self-actualization has been advocated by many professional psychologists and laymen as the supreme life motive, the over-all need-drive-goal of human life. A self is striving for its fulfillment, maturation, and the fruition of its potential capacities to function as subject, agent, entity. Only this can strive—not an image nor a group of cognitive processes. These are the striving, the acting, the functions of the striver. Neither can tissue (nerve or muscle) strive nor become actualized; they merely react, convey, provide the mechanism for the action and full realization of the self which senses, responds, initiates, directs or experiences. It is the subject-agent—the you, the I; not a part of you or me, which strives, and is motivated.

NEED INHERENT IN SELF

It is the self that experiences need, experiences it as a tension within the self and a drive with direction tendency toward a general or specific goal. Strong stimuli, incongruity in the stimulus situation, unusual biochemical activity, and "feedback" or communication between the old brain structures and cerebral cortex, as Hunt established—all these are the mechanisms by which need is experienced in the self. It is the self evaluating the situation, in relationship to self-growth or well-being, which puts one in a state of readiness to act. Hunt and his associates, tie motivation to cognition and they describe the mechanics of it as the best that experimental evidence permits. Cognition of things, events, relationships unrelated (relatively) to self does not give a sense of need and does not motivate. But when cognizance of the thing, event, or situation in relationship to self takes place, need-tension is experienced with the drive to avoid or approach. This is evaluative cognition that carries affect. Emotion is the affect tone accompanying evaluative cognition, a part of the need experience. This evaluating may be conscious or unconscious, usually the former but often the latter, particularly at the age-old "vital process" level, the bottom category of Figure 8. We shall attempt to clarify the above in the following pages.

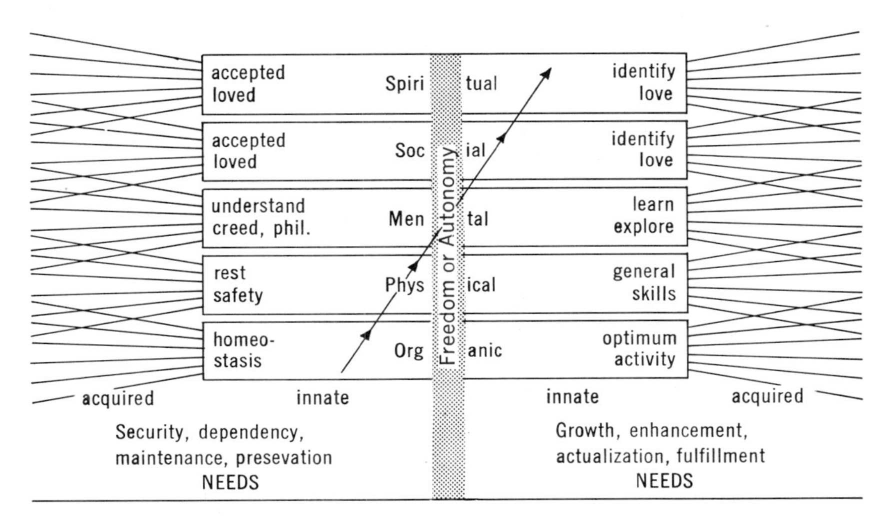

Figure 8. Need dimension, directions and growth line.

I have attempted in Figure 8 to present my own scheme of the need pattern and basis for classifying needs. It is based on the postulate that need is a function of capacity (potential) which, in turn, is resident in structure. Reading from bottom to top are the dimensions of human structure and capacity. Man is of the same substance as all other living creatures and, except for minor detail, has the same organic structure, physiological processes, and biochemical needs. Having a physical body with various appendages and organs, he has the capacity and need for many and varied bodily activities, and in these is very much like higher animals. He has sensory apparatus, a brain, and a very complex nervous system, structures by which he (the self) may perceive, conceptualize, abstract, evaluate, appreciate, reproduce sensory images (imagination) and reflect on these, and to contemplate on that which cannot be imaged. His is a mental capacity with a new element based on a new dimension in the human structure and capacity. He has an innate need-drive to learn at different dimensions. He has the sex structure to unite the body with another and the capacity to identify and communicate with others—to share in the process of life. Therefore, he has certain basic social needs. In these, dimensions 3 and 4, he is also like the higher animals but has risen so far above them that in their expression, he is in many ways virtually unique.

Here science and scientific psychology stop. (Thus the double line). The objective method, which is limited to structure and structured activity, cannot proceed beyond this point. This is the dimension of religion, of metaphysics, and possibly of a metapsychology which may develop. But it is a dimension of reality and of human experience and need. It is the realm of the self, of the absolute, of holism, of spirit, of nonstructured cognizance, of peak experiences. It is very much involved with mental health as many psychiatrists and psychotherapists have recently learned. Physicists, years ago, became aware of this boundary beyond which their science could not take them, and accepted its reality; many stood in awe and reverence. Psychologists, their science not nearly as mature, have been more reluctant to give credence to that realm of experiential reality beyond the scope of their scientific reach. Many scientists, including psychologists, are men of religion (and/or of metaphysics) who recognize the reality of that realm and try to relate to it as persons, even though they cannot do so as scientists. There is a growing alignment in recent years of religion and psychiatry which will be described in a later chapter.

This does not imply that behavioral science is not concerned with needs and experiences that center in this fifth dimension. It merely suggests that we are unable to measure and objectively describe and validate these experiences. Also, it does not suggest that religion is limited to this dimension; but rather that religion finds its basis in this area and did not exist until life evolved to this point. There is interactivity among the behavior responses at all of these levels and mixed need patterns. And each higher dimension incorporates elements of all that is lower. To satisfy physical needs, organic processes are involved. Intellectual need satisfactions utilize both physical performance and organic activity; and so with the social and spiritual dimensions.

NEED-DRIVE IS TWO-DIRECTIONAL

Turning to the two hemispheres in Figure 8, we have a schematic representation of need-drive direction. In the sense of needs which are inherent in the human structure and characteristic of all people, the above five classes could be designated primary needs, and the hundreds or thousands of acquired need-capacities that spring from them, secondary. In a functional sense the needs on the right may be called primary and those on the left, secondary. This would be realistic since the primary functions are directed toward self-actualization along those various routes. They may be called goal needs, growth needs, enhancement needs, productive needs, or any of a half dozen other designations. Some have referred to the need of achievement in this positive sense, but "achievement" may apply equally to the left side. One may achieve safety from injury by withdrawal from activity, physical or social. In the left hemisphere, then, would be the secondary needs in that protection and maintenance are means to an end; are secondary to the purpose of production. One repairs and maintains machinery in order for it to produce, and likewise the body and mind must do so. These, then, may also be designated security needs, dependency needs, maintenance needs, preservation needs or deprivation needs.

The lines that diverge from each of these five dimensional categories and criss-cross each other indicate the acquired personality or character structures, habitual patterns of response, that carry their capacity-needs. These are multitudinous and vary with each individual. Becoming established patterns of behavior with functional capacity and set (need), they may function autonomously, independent of any original primary need source, as Allport postulates. To make the figure truly apt, the diverging lines would have to bend around from both sides and criss-cross each other. Needs of both kinds are found in everyone, and the balance may be about equal or weighted heavily in one direction or the other. From the innumerable specific need-drives that motivate man's thousands of behavior patterns, Murray has derived his types of needs, each of which is a compound or mixture rather than an element.

If we accept self-actualization as the one supreme, all-encompassing motive (need-drive-goal), we may see it, by analogy, as a giant cable made of five strands, each of which is composed of many wires, and with these latter varying from person to person. From infancy to maturity, the direction of normal or healthful motivation and growth is from lower left to upper right. In early childhood the organic and physical needs are predominant, and dependency, security, etc., are of primary concern. With growth and maturity the mental, social, and spiritual become paramount, and growth is in the direction of production and self-actualization.

To move from the dependency, security-dominant need side to the productive, self-actualization side brings into operation the freedom or autonomy need. This becomes a primary need in moving from childhood to maturity and from a neurotic or sick orientation to healthful productivity. The problem is found in education and psychotherapy as well as in politics. An immature person or society values security more than fulfillment in productivity and will not fight for the freedom that is necessary for the latter. The mature person or society will sacrifice security for the freedom that is prerequisite to self-actualization.

In this schematic representation of needs, Angyal's model for personality study may be seen more clearly (Chapter 2), his two-directional orientation of personality growth toward self-determination and self-surrender. In seeking and satisfying the need categories to the right, man builds an autonomous, self-determining, self-actualizing personality. In striving to gratify the need categories to the left, he builds self-surrender and dependency behavior patterns. Serious frustration and deprivation of these strivings culminate in a low self-evaluation, anxiety, and neurosis. All this will be amply treated in Chapter 6.

Organic Needs. The term physiological or biochemical may be used to designate this category. Included are those basics needed by the organism for survival and normal functioning of the various organs. Stimuli are needed since man has a highly structured sensory-cognitive system. Oxygen, water, and certain food chemicals are needed for body maintenance and activity, and with these the needs of elimination of waste products. When these needed products are supplied within the normal range of acceptance, tolerance, or utilization by the particular system involved, the processes generally operate unconsciously with no aroused state in the organism as a whole. But when the situation becomes such that the supply is deficient (or in some types, excess), tensions are increased beyond the acceptance or tolerance range and the organism as a whole is aroused to action in order to correct the situation. The mechanics of this were described earlier in the chapter as explained by Hunt and others—"feedback" or communication between the lower and higher brain structures. Self evaluates the situation as threatening or as unusual and sets in operation (arouses) the whole emergency system for correction.

A separate chapter would be needed to fully explain and illustrate each of these five need categories. Only one or two needs in each can be presented with references to experimental studies and more elaborate discussion. Many experimental studies have been made on the food need (hunger drive) and in recent years several significant studies deal with excess and deficient sensory stimulation.

> At this point, if time and class interest permits, a student may present a report on the nature and operation of certain other needs, especially sensory stimuli, with supporting experimental studies. See Suggested Readings at end of chapter for resources.

Hunger. The food need is experienced as a hunger drive, directed toward obtaining certain products for ingestion that will satisfy this need. In the lower forms of animal life the patterns of response are largely determined (fixed) by established instinctual mechanisms. In man, the modes of response are open. Therefore, we no longer speak of a food-getting instinct; instead, a food need and hunger drive. Many studies of the food-need arousal have been made, but few have studied its counterpart, the need to regurgitate unacceptable products. Some have traced the hunger arousal to contractions of the walls of the stomach when depletion reaches a certain point. Verification of this theory is largely based on having experimental subjects swallow rubber balloons when their stomachs are relatively empty. The balloons are then inflated and stomach contractions recorded via a pressure tube, stylus, and drum combination. During this procedure the subject presses a key when he feels hunger pangs, recording on the drum the points at which hunger is apparent. Three contrary facts are: (1) the subject's attitude or anticipation alters his physiological responses; (2) hunger is also experienced when the stomach is removed; and (3) hunger is also felt when the sensory nerves from stomach to brain have been cut.

Sugar content of the blood is widely held as a stimulus factor. By injecting glucose into the blood stream of a hungry animal or person, the effect in reducing the drive to obtain food or feeling of hunger can be observed. Undoubtedly it is, or may be, a part of the stimulus situation, but only a part. Neural factors are also involved in hunger. Cofer and Appley (1964) state:

> . . . Techniques of stimulating points in the hypothalamus, electrically or chemically, have been utilized in uncovering the role of this area of the brain in hunger.
>
> Hetherington and Ranson (1940) demonstrated that obesity could be produced in animals by causing hypothalamic lesions. . . . Brobeck, Tepperman, and Long (1943) showed that this obesity arose because of overeating (hyperphagia), and then Anand and Brobeck (1951) made electrolytic lesions in various hypothalamic regions of rats and cats and found that cessation of eating, even in hyperphagic animals, was produced by bilateral lesions in the lateral regions of the hypothalamus. . . . (p. 217).

In a summary statement these authors say:

> The evidence reviewed concerning the role of neural factors in hunger rather strikingly suggests that there are two hypothalamic centers important in the control of hunger. One, in the lateral hypothalamus, appears to be an eating center, since its stimulation induces eating and other drive-like aspects of behavior, and since its destruction renders animals aphagic (the role of dehydration in this aphagia may be important). The other center, located in the ventromedial hypothalamus, may be an inhibitory or satiety center, since appetite-depressing drugs increase its activity, and since its destruction is

> associated with the development of hyperphagia and obesity. . . .
>
> Recent theory would suggest that these hypothalamic centers are probably responsive either to changes in the blood constitution or to changes in body temperature, or to both, and several authors (e.g. Janowitz, 1961) stress multiple controlling factors. . . . Both the onset and the termination of stomach contractions and of other peripheral factors of hunger may well be controlled by impulses arising in the hypothalamic centers, and these centers may also be controlled in their activity by impulses arising from contractions, distension, smelling and tasting food, as well as chewing and swallowing it. . . . (p. 227).

These many experimental studies provide valuable information about the multiple stimuli factors involved in the arousal and inhibition of the hunger drive and about the mechanics of the process; and they confirm the theories of Harvey, Hunt, et al with respect to motivation being associated with cognitive processes where incongruities exist in the stimulus situation and feedback between the cerebral cortex and hypothalamus occurs. It is the self, however, that experiences need for food and is aroused to a state of conscious hunger via these media, based on how self evaluates the incongruity of the stimulus situation. It is self, operating by means of these same brain, nerve, and endocrine gland mechanisms, that sets in action the emergency (usually emotionally toned) behavior that may be necessary to supply the needed product. Self experiences need as hunger drive on the basis of its evaluation of the stimulus situation, and directs food-getting activities in accord with its chiefly learned value system.

Animals have an instinctual or unlearned value system by which they select specific foods to satisfy specific food needs. This selectivity by means of learned values is much more pronounced in humans. Where selection of goods is involved, and particularly choice of eating procedure, it is generally a sound inference that the whole organism is engaged in a cognitive-evaluative process and experiences need-drive-goal as a unitary motivated act. Let this example suffice.

Imagine yourself in a closed room engaged in study or a game of chess. You have not eaten for several hours and are not sufficiently conscious of stomach warnings to be aroused. Suddenly the door opens and a friend walks in with a fresh, hot hamburger. Suddenly, you consciously experience food need and hunger drive, with the impulse to leap up and snatch it from his hand or rush to the nearby snack shop for one. Blood condition, stomach contractions, odor and sight combine to provide the stimulus incongruence. Reticular formation area and parts of the hypothalamus are specific mechanisms involved in the arousal. But you, the self that is you, evaluating your bodily condition and the desirability of the hamburger, produce the food-need experience with hunger drive. Again, with you in an identical condition, this friend walks in with a Limburger cheese sandwich. You happen to detest both the odor and taste of Limburger. There is little sense of hunger and no drive to appropriate that sandwich.

A man may choose to remain hungry rather than to eat in an unsanitary restaurant or to die in a jungle rather than resort to cannibalism. His evaluation of the situation has much to do with his conscious experience of hunger and virtually all to do with its direction in appropriate action. In states of ecstasy and deep grief, hunger is not experienced even when one is deprived of food for many hours. A child may wither and die from undernourishment when he is in a prolonged state of sorrow, anxiety, or disappointment from a deep sense of rejection, without experiencing (consciously) food-need and hunger.

The thirst need may be explained in a very similar manner. The human sex drive has been discussed as an organic need-drive; it belongs in the social need category, for it functions in the preservation and qualitative growth of society.

Physical Need. The bodily structure is designed for locomotion and physical manipulation. Growth of muscles and development of manipulative skills requires physical action. Muscles and skills, once developed, will atrophy unless exercised. The baby squirms, wiggles, and kicks. Young children spontaneously engage in play filled with bustling activity. Youth engages in strenuous, and dangerous sports, for sheer fun or for the social value (status symbol) placed upon such skills. The professional athlete and other public entertainers, e.g., circus performers, find not only monetary reward and social status but also a sense of fulfillment, self-actualization. This is especially true of the artist, musician, and skilled craftsman. In all these higher forms of expression, the social, mental, and physical need-drives are interrelated. The need for such activities and the arousal and sustaining of activity is experienced in and determined by the self in cognitive evaluation of one's own capacity and the social significance of the skill. The evaluation and need-experience of infants are largely unconscious; the drive is directed simply toward physical growth.

The situation is very similar in regards to the protective, security side of the need hemisphere. Toxic factors and other stimuli provide a spread of stimulus incongruence beyond the tolerance range. Certain mechanisms in the older brain areas, in communication with the cerebral cortex, provide the channels. But self, in evaluative cognizance of the situation relative to its well-being, experiences the need for rest or sleep and unconsciously self sets in motion the mechanisms for reducing activity. If an outside stimulus is perceived and evaluated as a threat, a high state of consciousness is involved with strong affective overtones (emotion). Neural activity in the brain is more intense, the discharge spills over into the autonomic system and emergency behavior is directed toward removal of or from the danger. Self evaluates the situation and directs and sustains the need-drive and brings it to a state of cessation when the situation is reevaluated as normal.

Two boys may have equal physical capacity to perform at football. One declines to participate because he evaluates it as too great a threat to his well-being. The other engages in it at every opportunity, regardless of the risk of injury, since he places a greater value on the activity and its social consequences than on the danger. We can safely conject that motivation to physical activity springs from the self in cognitive evaluation.

At these two lower levels, tension reduction and homeostasis are drive goals, but they account for only one side. Optimum glandular secretion and nerve or muscle tension may well be the drive goal for emergency conflict or escape, for the enjoyable excitement of sports, for high aesthetic appreciation, and for the ecstasy that is in certain peak experiences.

Mental Needs. Among the more interesting experiments in comparative psychology are those that demonstrate the investigatory responses (curiosity) of animals. Monkeys seem especially interested in taking things apart with no extrinsic reward given. Butler's 1954 report states:[16]

> Harry F. Harlow and his associates at the University of Wisconsin were the first to investigate manipulatory behavior in monkeys. Their experiments were designed to determine whether monkeys can learn how to solve a mechanical puzzle with no reward other than the working of it. . . . The monkeys went on disassembling it repeatedly for ten hours, at which time the experimenters, rather than the subjects, had had enough.
>
> These experiments yielded two important findings: that the opportunity to manipulate objects is reward enough to motivate monkeys to learn, and that an external stimulus, like an internal, biological one, can evoke a drive. The curiosity motives apparently are initiated by external stimuli.

I would add only that a more accurate and realistic interpretation is: the curiosity motive is initiated by the monkey-as-subject evaluating the stimulus situation relative to his mental capacity-need.

Rats, well trained to follow a definite course to obtain their food reward, when given the opportunity have paused or taken a different course to explore a novel figure. Piaget[17] describes the curiosity or investigatory behavior of children from five months to one year of age. Every parent knows how young children like to take objects apart and try to put them back together again. It is a common experience to watch the cat explore new surroundings; and every farmer knows that cows, when placed in a new pasture, will explore the area before settling down to graze. Animals and man have the capacity for cognizance and therefore the need to learn.

A child will seek information and learn if he is given interesting stimuli in natural environment, laboratory, museum, or books. The mental activity itself is its own reward. In the growth-motivated person self automatically evaluates the importance of more knowledge and greater powers of discrimination in the attain-

---

[10] From Robert A. Butler, "Curiosity in Monkeys." Copyright © February 1954 by *Scientific American, Inc.*, Vol. 190, No. 2, pp. 70–75. All rights reserved.

[17] J. Piaget, *The Origins of Intelligence in Children* (New York: International Universities Press, 1952).

ment of self-actualization. Since one must choose his learning areas, self makes its evaluations and motivates the learning activities in selected directions. One person may place such low value on academic learning that he never attends school or drops out at the earliest opportunity. Another may evaluate it so highly that he will sacrifice his health and economic needs to obtain as much education as possible. Still another may pursue his learning and the promulgation of "truth" as he sees it, to the point where he is banished from his community or nation or even killed by the ruling powers. The motivation to learn is a set condition or state within the self, a need-capacity, experienced as curiosity with an investigative or learning drive that knows no limits when evaluated sufficiently high by the self.

On the dependency side of the need hemisphere (Figure 8), we find knowledge or understanding to be a security or preservation need. The young child needs to know how his parents will probably respond to him in anticipated situations in order to feel secure. Inconsistency on the part of parents poses a threat to the child which tends toward permanent insecurity and anxiety. The parent who brags about the child on one occasion and slaps him down at another time in response to a similar performance is a stimulus situation of such incongruity that it exceeds the child's normal acceptance or tolerance range. It is evaluatively cognized by the self as threatening; emergency escape mechanisms go into operation. Since the child is dependent on the parent for his very existence, there is no escape, and permanent threat and anxiety are the results. At the adult level, a creed or philosophy of life is needed for protection against the threat of life or to gain the security of group acceptance. Many people shun new learning out of fear that it will destroy their protective creed or philosophy; therefore, security-motivated people cease to grow and fall far short of self-actualization. Their fixed creed or philosophy is outgrown and they become insecure and prone to neurosis.

Further consequence of the expression of mental needs will be discussed later. The point I am trying to make here is that the value placed on certain knowledge (parent's action, a religious creed or doctrine, etc.) by the self, determines its experience of learning need and the drive toward acquiring the necessary knowledge formulas to give security. The insecure child places too much value on fixed formulas which appear to be safe beliefs;

he is afraid to venture after new truths, and thereby suppresses his curiosity or exploratory drive.

Social Needs. Consequences of these need-drives in their frustration or satisfaction and their relation to mental and social health will be presented later. Our purpose, at the present time, is to try to interpret their general nature. Social need is like other basic needs. It is experienced in the self, as a function of its capacity to identify with other selves in shared and mutually enriching activities. It is the capacity for empathy, for love. This need-capacity has its roots in organic sex, and many psychologists still try to explain the sexual behavior and needs of humans in terms of sex as an organic or physiological need, in the same category with the food need and hunger drive. They draw their inferences largely from experiments with animals.

The gonads, as endocrine glands, operate as mechanisms to supply the organic and physical sex characteristics. But all of this is automatic and unconscious and is not a part of what is designated as sexual behavior. The various processes involved with reproduction, e.g., sight, odor, hormones, etc., compose the stimulus situation which is somewhat comparable to the hunger drive. In the case of hunger, it is the self, evaluating the stimulus situation in relation to self well-being, that causes the experience of the sex need-drive. Since reproduction is the basic social function, sex behavior falls in the social need category.

The secretion of hormones, as in the estrus period, is a major factor in the sex arousal of the female quadruped. But it is a somewhat less dominant factor in female primates (sub-human) and a very minor determinant in woman. Likewise, the removal of the ovaries at the quadruped level virtually eliminates sex desire and response; but not as much at the primate level and hardly at all at the human level. It is similar with the male. The castrated male rat shows some sex drive and capacity to function sexually; the monkey shows more; and when man is castrated he may experience sex drive and engage in intercourse for years, although slow diminution generally follows.

The higher in the scale of life, the less the sex drive or need is of an organic nature. At the animal level arousal is, in the main, instinctually controlled and periodic (female); and in the male, by fixed stimuli. The drive is toward reproduction only.

At the human level the organic factors are of little consequence and the biological (instinctual) controls are off. Man is free to engage in sexual intercourse daily or never. In either case it will have little consequence on his physical well-being (hardly so in the case of food). And the need-drive is directed toward much broader social ends than merely reproduction.

In man, the sex need-drive (desire) is experienced chiefly as a consequence of cognitive evaluation. Object or fantasy perception, physical contact (caresses, etc.) form the stimulus situation. Arousal is a consequence of self's evaluation of the anticipated relationship. "It is all in the mind," is a common expression with much truth in it; as is, also, "keep your mind out of the gutter." If sexual intercourse is taboo in one's value system, the above stimuli will have little arousal effect. It is a well known fact that even in the act of heavy petting or intercourse, a sudden qualm of conscience, a doubt or disturbing thought, or a feeling of anxiety may deaden the response immediately.

Contrary to what many people think, Hollywood and a flood of fiction writers not-with-standing, sexual intercourse and social need are not synonymous. Nor would the majority of social scientists, philosophers, and nonprofessional students of human relationships agree with the Freudian view of sex as the all-encompassing social need. The love capacity in its early evolution may have been rooted in sex; but at the human level it has emerged into a full-blown need in its own right, transcending sex rather than a sublimation of sex. Love is what people need, not sex; although sex may become a channel for expressing love. Two selves need to identify with each other at a deeper dimension than merely the physical level. This may be experienced with or without sexual intercourse. Love is essential to self-actualization, to the growth and health of subject-self. Consciously or unconsciously, self is cognizant of this, evaluates it most highly, and experiences the need to love and be loved. At this level, physiological correlates and brain-neural mechanisms play a very ill-defined and nebulous role. Experimental controls are virtually impossible to establish, and laboratory conditions cannot be made to adequately simulate real life situations. It is a most difficult area for scientific psychology.

On the preservation-dependency side, the need to be accepted and loved is vital. Children become sickly, die or become weak, insecure, stunted selves when totally or seriously deprived of love and acceptance. Self evaluates, as of vital importance, the acts of being accepted and loved, and of being able to identify, self-to-self, with another significant person. They are necessary for self-identity and self-worth.

Spiritual Needs. We must move out of the realm of scientific psychology to confront man at this dimension of his capacity. Again I remind the student that need is a function of capacity, is resident in capacity; it is capacity striving to be expressed, dormant until aroused. To be more exact, capacity (potential) can not strive; only the self strives; capacity only marks the bounds. Neither can "mind" or emotion or muscle strive. They are merely the instruments of striving, marking limits. What are man's limits of striving, of knowing, of experiencing? Only these limit his need.

One might turn to a score or more of eminent theologians for their views of man's highest capacity and most profound need. But as a mental hygienist, I prefer to work from the point of view of the behavioral scientist who has found the problem of man beyond the scope of his scientific method and whose concern has moved him into and through phenomenology into self-psychology, there to stand looking at what is beyond, and wondering. There are many of these students of human nature who have spent two or three decades grappling with the thorniest problems of human behavior. These pragmatic realists have exhausted the resources of orthodox psychology and psychotherapy and are cautiously probing for something more.

The very astute thinker, Scheler, feels that man can transcend the physical order, detach himself, and live by his spiritual potential. To detach oneself is to become disengaged, and dis-identified. To become dis-identified (a sort of voluntary excommunication) with one order and not to identify with another, leaves the self with no identity—insecure, lonely, anxious. Psychiatrists and psychotherapists of the status of Viktor Frankl, Rollo May, and Jung, have found much of this insecurity and anxiety in the problems of their patients. The struggle of Kierkegaard to resolve that type of anxiety in his own life gave existentialism to the modern world.

Existentialism divides itself very roughly into two divisions: (1) the humanistic nonreligious; and (2) the humanistic religious. Both are humanistically oriented, concerned with human resources and potentiality. The difference lies in where the bounds of that potentiality are. Does it rise into that fifth dimension of spirit which Scheler posits? Or do his potentialities limit his experiences to the four lower orders encompassed by higher animals as well as man, the physical and the structured? If Scheler and the many religion-oriented existentialists and scientists, are correct, then the universe in which spiritual man lives, which gave birth to him, is also a universe of spirit as well as one of matter and energy. In such case, man's deepest need is to achieve identification with this eternal realm of reality. These are some of the questions being raised and ideas being posited by the persons who are struggling with the problem of man, with problem people, trying to set man back on the road to full selfhood.

In Chapter 3, I presented love as a unique capacity-need of the healthy, autonomous, transcendent self, and of the nature of good-will. As a capacity-need, it is a motive, attitude, set or readiness of self to evaluate and act in terms of its highest good, its full actualization. Perhaps it would be appropriate to supplement this statement with the observation that the permanent motivation toward self-fulfillment (dominant and supreme in high self-actualizers) is *love*—deep self-identity, self-acceptance and a willing of one's good. To balance the one-sidedness of this and for full psycho-*social* development, one must love his neighbor as himself and identify deeply with others. This double-barreled motive provides the drive that carries the individual and society upward toward ultimate fulfillment. Psychiatrists and other behavioral scientists are just now discovering the importance of this theory. Thus, one of their primary concerns is to help their patients or clients regain or attain this ability and dominant motive.

MOTIVATION AND LEARNING

The "Law of Readiness" is an old formulation of a mental state essential to learning, which means that the animal or child must be motivated in order to learn. Many schools admit children to the first grade on the basis of a reading readiness test. As previously stated and illustrated, the urge or drive of curiosity and exploration is inherent within intellectual capacity itself. Thus, there is a natural intrinsic motivation to learn—a primary need for intellectual growth and self-fulfillment. Self automatically evaluates these activities highly, just as it values food and physical exercise. Other learning is induced by extrinsic rewards—the "Law of Reinforcement"—verified by hundreds of experiments with animals and children. It is the central factor operant conditioning.

> An experiment was conducted with 78 students and 78 psychiatric patients as subjects. They were given several cards on each of which was printed six pronouns and a verb and asked to compose sentences using one pronoun and the verb on each. When subjects used "I" or "we," the response was reinforced by giving cigarettes or candy, poker chips, or by the experimenters saying "Good." Cigarettes or candy and the verbal approval were effective conditioners with both groups. The poker chips were not.[18]

This illustrates the important fact that extrinsic rewards are motivating only to the degree that they are valued, which also is learned. Approval, however, seems to be intrinsic as a motivator, springing from an inherent capacity and need. This is suggested by the following:

> Eighteen of twenty-one three-month-old infants were taught to vocalize more freely by the experimenter bending over their cribs, smiling, making pleasant "tch, tch" sounds, and touching the baby's abdomen. The experimenter followed with two days of silent, expressionless treatment (extinction days) and the vocalizing decreased greatly.[19]

It seems a plausible interpretation that at this early age there is an inherent capacity for the self to reach out for acceptance, approval, and social intercourse; and thus the intrinsic motivation to learn the necessary action (personality traits) to attain this. Whether the child learns adjustive, creative, self-actualization behavior or defensive, reality-escaping, growth-thwarting traits, depends to a large degree on the value he learns to place on things, on responses of others, and on his own action by which he attempts to maintain or improve his position.

---

[18] From A.H. Buss et al, "Verbal Conditioning and Extinction with Verbal and Nonverbal Reinforcers." *J. Exp. Psychol.* 56:139–145 (1958).

[19] From Harriet Rheingold et al, "Social Conditioning of Vocalizations in the Infant." *J. Comp. Physiol. Psychol.,* 52:68–73 (1959).

SUMMARY

What a person is able to do is one thing. What he will do or why he does it is something else. Early psychologists attributed motivation to instinct, and they "discovered" many. Freud reduced them to two: Eros and Thanatos (sex or life and death). Later psychologists discarded the concept of instincts and spoke in terms of needs and drives. When need is aroused, the drive is experienced as tension, which directs responses toward a goal that reduces tension, i.e., gives pleasure. More recent clinical observations seem to support the position of many psychologists that this is only one aspect of motivation, reflected at the lower levels of behavior, and that man in his high-level activities seeks goals that increase and prolong tension.

My position has been that motivation = need → drive → goal. It exists as an unconscious, quiescent need-state of the self, a readiness, until it is aroused. It is experienced as a drive toward a goal that is valued proportionately to the importance of the need and the degree it is thought to satisfy. Therefore, in its arousal and direction, motivated behavior is a consequence of evaluative cognition.

Needs are as varied as personality traits and, like personality traits, they are classified in various ways, with general agreement that there are a few innate or primary needs and many acquired or secondary needs. My scheme presents five primary (universal) needs based on the concept of the human structure and potential capacity and theory that need is a function of capacity. In ascending order, these are: organic, physical, mental, social and spiritual. These also may be expressed as dependency, deficiency, wanting-to-possess needs or as growth, self-actualizing, expending-oneself needs. From various combinations of primary need-elements, hundreds or thousands of acquired needs may develop.

Organic Needs. In these the evaluative cognition of unacceptable organic conditions is largely unconscious and the processes automatic, but calls for consciously directed behavior in some. Action may be directed toward the restoration homeostasis or maximum organic functions to prepare for emergencies.

Physical Needs. These are expressed chiefly in conscious behavior, until thoroughly habitualized, which may be directed toward protection against disease, injury, and death or toward developing athletic skills, craftsmanship, etc., even though these may invite injury—the action based on evaluation relative to self.

Mental Needs. Man has the capacity to learn and based on his evaluation of the importance to the self of knowledge, truth, and creativity, the curiosity-exploratory drive may direct behavior toward merely acquiring certain expected education with ethnocentric attitudes and a popular creed to insure acceptance; or he may be "driven" toward the search for truth and creation of theories whether it brings public adulation or ostracism—even martyrdom.

Social Needs. Sex is classed as a social need because its chief roles are to maintain society and to enrich social relations (the family relationship). Its arousal and control are chiefly matters of evaluative cognition—how it is evaluated in relation to self. But love is the most essential social need, both to receive and to express love, and behavior is directed unceasingly, in both these directions.

Spiritual Needs. This moves out of the sphere of psychology and is largely an extension of man's social need—the need to worship, to identify with the eternal, to receive and express divine love. The experience of receiving divine love gives a sense of eternal security and of expressing divinely enhanced love, a sense of eternal fulfillment—the highest self-actualization.

All human motivation is directed toward the maintenance and enhancement of the total person, the behavior pattern changing from moment to moment as self evaluates the changing situation in relation to personal well-being. This supreme motive is *love.*

GLOSSARY

Cathexis. The directing or fixing of psychic energy upon an object or persons—its goal—investing something with significance, valuing.

Hedonism (istic). The theory or doctrine that pleasure is the normal or natural goal of endeavor, the goal of motivated behavior.

Holistic. A systematic study of the whole configuration; the view of man as a unified psychobiologic organism functioning as a whole.

Homeostasis. The body's automatic effort to maintain a constant, normal state of the blood stream—or more broadly, a general state of equilibrium among the vital processes.

Hormic theory. The view that organic phenomena are largely determined by purposive factors (e.g., native dispositions, urges, etc.) which transcend the purely physical. From *horme* (Gr.), an urge to action.

Incongruence. Elements or aspects of a situation not normally or properly belonging together—inconsistent with what is judged to be suitable or acceptable—out of place, inappropriate.

Psychogenic. The psychological origin; illnesses or other disturbances originating in the psychological functioning of the individual.

REFERENCES AND SUGGESTED READINGS

ATKINSON, J. W., *An Introduction to Motivation,* Princeton, N.J.: D. Van Nostrand Co., Inc., 1964.

CARROLL, HERBERT A., *Mental Hygiene,* Englewood Cliffs, N.J.: Prentice-Hall, Inc., 1964.

CROW, LESTER and ALICE CROW, *Mental Hygiene for Teachers,* New York: The Macmillan Company, 1963.

FRANKL, VIKTOR E., *Man's Search for Meaning,* Boston: Beacon Press, 1962.

———, "Self-Transcendence as a Human Phenomenon," *Humanistic Psychology,* Fall, 1966, pp. 97–106.

HALL, JOHN F., *Psychology of Motivation,* Philadelphia: J. B. Lippincott Co., 1961.

HILGARD, ERNEST R., *Introduction to Psychology,* New York: Harcourt, Brace, and World, Inc., 1962.

MASLOW, A., *Motivation and Personality,* New York: Harper & Row, 1954.

———, *Toward a Psychology of Being,* Princeton, New Jersey: D. Van Nostrand Co., Inc., 1962.

MC CLELLAND, D. C. et al, *The Achievement Motive,* New York: Apple-ton-Century-Crofts, 1953.

MOUSTAKAS, CLARK (ed), *The Self,* New York: Harper & Row, 1956.

PIAGET, J., *The Origins of Intelligence in Children,* New York: Int. Univer. Press, 1952.

ROGERS, CARL R., "The Characteristics of a Helping Relationship," *Personnel and Guidance Journal.* 37, 6–16, 1958.

SCHELER, MAX, *Man's Place in Nature* (Transl., H. Meyerhoff), Boston: Beacon Press, 1961.

SCHNEIDERS, A. A., *Personality Dynamics and Mental Hygiene,* New York: Holt, Rinehart and Winston, Inc., 1965.

SNYGG, D. and A. W. COMBS, *Individual Behavior,* New York: Harper & Row, 1959.

5 | Values and Goals

> Preparatory to starting this chapter the class or a selected group of students may take the Allport et al *Study of Values* test (self-administering) or make a list of their values (free choices in various situations) and categorize these. The first session may begin with a 15 to 20 minute discussion of these.

Lewis Mumford said:[1] "Without food, man can survive for barely thirty days; without water, for little more than three days; without air hardly for more than three minutes; but without hope he might destroy himself in an even shorter time." This observation is a reminder of the vital significance of goals and values, the something in life which is worth striving for, and the loss of which is a major factor not only in suicide but in most mental illness. We have been looking at motivation from the need end; now we turn to the goal end. When experiencing need, self is aroused to action; and action is directed toward an anticipated goal. Motivation is the push of need and the pull of the valued goal. When goals are blurred and confused, psychosocial disorders develop.

Viktor Frankl, after suffering physical torture and every personal indignity in a World War II concentration camp and after

[1] Lewis Mumford, *Conduct of Life* (New York: Harcourt and Brace, 1951), p. 30.

several years of psychiatric practice, was so convinced of this truth that he developed a new method of treating his neurotic patients which he called *logotherapy.* He combined psychology, philosophy, and religion in psychiatric interviews to help his patients attain or *regain meaning and purpose in life and for their lives,* based on a reorganized and effective system of values. Mental health and the value system are inextricably interwoven, and to cope with values requires an interdisciplinary approach.

SCIENCE'S CONCERN WITH VALUES

Social scientists have been split in their attitudes toward values as a subject for scientific inquiry. The extreme behaviorists argue that values are matters of subjective experience, therefore are not proper subject matter for a thoroughly objective discipline. They feel that science deals with statistical probabilities and measurable quantities on the assumption of causal determinism and relativism, and that value systems generally imply freedom and some absolutes and lend themselves poorly to quantitative treatment. Not all behaviorists object to the study of values; some object merely to the unscientific way with which they are treated. Other sociologists and psychologists argue that values are facts of human experience and are determinants of human behavior. Therefore, they are not only legitimate data of any truly human science, but are essential, and the scientific method must be enlarged to encompass them. Thus, the problem of values has become the special concern of those most concerned with behavior problems, with the behaver, not just behavior in the abstract.

Dr. Ija Korner (in Otto, 1966, Chapter 6) refers to values as the Hydra monster that perpetuates itself in spite of science's efforts to destroy it, and in spite of its being "ignored, declared unnecessary, unscientific, metaphysical, renamed, redefined, reassigned, in the hope that somehow it would go away and cease to plague the fields." (p. 63). He wonders why the "value issue" is so indestructible and finds the answer that people continue, century after century, to do things, "not because they are useful, economical, rational, intelligent, beautiful, etc., but because they are 'important' . . ." to the person who experiences human worth,

and certain things (behaviors) contribute to that worth regardless of expediency or utilitarian considerations. Korner adds:

> With measurement far away, the discussion of values demands the courage of *speculation.* Values must be assumed to exist, and their hierarchical order must be at least postulated. Only if this is done can the long, tedious process of testing, verification and rejection commence. (p. 66).
>
> This task of the behavioral scientist will be difficult to achieve, and he will approach it full of ambivalence and reluctance. He will need to learn more about the nature, the operations, the manipulations of value systems because they underlie the structure of all rational thinking; they are the hidden activators of behavior. Eventually the behavior scientist may encounter the *basic values.* It is hoped that he will be able to meet this supreme challenge. (p. 78).

In Crisis. Again we turn to Frankl (1962) and his concentration camp experiences for the survival value of values—for meaning and purpose based on high values.

> Any attempt at fighting the camp's psychopathological influence on the prisoner by psychotherapeutic or psychohygienic methods had to aim at giving him inner strength by pointing out to him a future goal to which he could look forward. Instinctively some of the prisoners attempted to find one on their own. It is a peculiarity of man that he can only live by looking to the future. . . .
>
> I became disgusted with the state of affairs which compelled me, daily and hourly, to think of only such trivial things. I forced my thoughts to turn to another subject. Suddenly I saw myself standing on the platform of a well-lit, warm and pleasant lecture room. In front of me sat an attentive audience on comfortable upholstered seats. I was giving a lecture on the psychology of the concentration camp! All that oppressed at that moment became objective, seen and described from the remote viewpoint of science. By this method I succeeded somehow in rising above the situation, above the sufferings of the moment. . . .
>
> As we said before, any attempt to restore a man's inner strength in the camp had first to succeed in showing him some future goal. . . . Whenever there was an opportunity for it, one had to give them a why—an aim—for their lives, in order to strengthen them to bear the terrible how of their existence.

> Woe to him who saw no more sense in his life, no aim, no purpose, and therefore no point in carrying on. He was soon lost. . . . (p. 76).

Large scale confirmation of the importance of meaning and purpose (value-goals) has been obtained from the responses of prisoners of war. The eminent neurologist, Harold G. Wolff wrote:[2]

> . . . Thus, of approximately 6,000 United States prisoners of war captured by the North Koreans, about one-third died. Medical observers reported that the cause of death in many instances was ill-defined, and was referred to by them as "give-up-itis." Occurring as it did in a setting of serious demoralization, humiliation, despair and deprivation of human support and affection, the prisoner became apathetic, listless, neither ate nor drank, helped himself in no way, stared into space and finally died.
>
> In short, prolonged circumstances which are perceived as dangerous, as lonely, as hopeless, may drain a man of hope and of his health; but he is capable of enduring incredible burdens and taking cruel punishment when he has self-esteem, hope, purpose, and belief in his fellows.

NEUROSIS AND VALUE

Another psychiatrist, Igor Caruso[3] describes neurosis as "life heresies," i.e., faulty beliefs about life, a faulty value system:

> We have, then, reached the following conclusion concerning the phenomenology of neurosis: the neurotic punishes himself for a guilt which he has carefully repressed into his unconscious, and in order to be able to explain his guilt feelings, he searches for a scapegoat. . . .
>
> The misplacement of guilt feelings, and their simultaneous punishment, implies a wrong evaluation either of the cause of guilt or of the punisher. There must have been an over-valuation either of the existential significance of the repressed

[2] Harold G. Wolff, "A Scientific Report on What Hope Does for Man," *Saturday Review*, January 5, 1957, pp. 44–45. Reprinted by permission.

[3] Igor Caruso, *Existential Psychology* (New York: Herder & Herder, Inc., 1964). Used with permission.

periences approximate so closely the absolute values given by religion that they may be assumed to be near-absolute values, safe guides for the general population. Furthermore, man discovers his values as intrinsic characteristics of his inherent or basic needs in their hierarchic relationship. (The goal aspect of these needs as I have decribed them.) But man also creates values by the free choices he makes among alternative ways of gratifying these needs. The "sick," deprived, dependency-oriented person usually chooses lower order need-gratification, while the autonomous, growth-oriented, self-actualizer usually chooses higher-order need fulfillment. These differences can be observed and described objectively.

Maslow discussed the role of psychotherapy (and psychoanalysis) in "uncovering" certain values, then stated: "indeed, I think it possible that we may soon even *define* therapy as a search for values, because ultimately the search for identity is, in essence, the search for one's own intrinsic, authentic values. . . ." (p. 166).

PSYCHOLOGY AND CHOICE

An article by Nicholas Hobbs[4] brings to a sharp focus the limited, but valuable, contribution scientific psychology is making to the process of choice (value) and the nature of its shortcomings. Scientific psychology deals with value in terms of its operational expression in choice in any given circumstance, since in any given situation there is a hierarchy of probabilities that the individual will respond in certain specific ways based on past experience, e.g., learning, as he has been conditioned by the past. Hobbs discusses certain variant positions of psychologists relative to choice and determinism, describes behavior as interaction, saying, "Man remakes the world, and the world remakes man in an ongoing process," then says:

> The extent to which psychological science can contribute to this process of interaction valid observations about the nature

[4] Nicholas Hobbs, "Science and Ethical Behavior," *The American Psychologist, 14,* No. 5 (May 1959), pp. 217–225. Used with permission. Also in Coleman (1960, pp. 531–533).

of man, to this extent psychology can make a contribution to ethical behavior and then, secondarily, to ethical theory itself by supplying the philosopher with more data to work into his ethical systems.

Psychology may also increase the probability of the occurrence of ethically good responses by freeing a person to act on ethically good hypotheses that he already has but cannot use. . . . A common expression of this dilemma may be seen in the plight of the person who cannot risk loving for fear of getting hurt. There is the intriguing possibility that man may already know all that he needs to know to achieve fullest self realization for himself and others. A simple factoring out of the common elements in the major revealed or intuitive and rationally developed ethical systems of the world might yield 90 percent of the ethical ideas that are important to have. . . .

. . . If psychology can make widely available to people, the results of a number of verified "if—then" statements about behavior of people in relationship one with the other, the required consequences will be an improvement in ethical choices, if the description of the process of choice, given earlier, is accurate . . . by adding to the response repertory of the individual a number of alternative ways of behaving.

ESTABLISHING NORMS

In his article, Hobbs has singled out the practical and very important services of scientific psychology relative to behavior improvement: (1) "clarifying the process of decision making"; (2) "divesting repressed responses" (clinical); (3) and "adding to the reponse repertory"—as stated above. By the most exacting work, the experimentalist can trace the physiological processes that correlate with these complex mental processes, their mechanics, and thus provide facts that will help to correct theories. To factor out common elements of ethical systems would, in all probability, be a practical contribution to social psychology and mental hygiene. The answer Maslow and many clinicians might make to this suggestion is that statistical norms and mass patterns may not be quite sufficient for self-actualization, even though these norms may be normal ideals. Instead, Maslow would factor out the elements expressed in the high choices of high self-actualizers.

A sound interdisciplinary approach is necessary to discover, factor out, and define in operational terms, the values (i.e., free choices) of people who seemingly have attained the highest levels of living. The age-long insights of the philosopher and theologian, relative to universal ethics and morality, warrant careful consideration, but they need the testing of the clinician and experimentalist for practical implementation. In this area both the anthropologist and the sociologist can lend a helpful hand since the values are expressed and the choices are made in a society with cultural roots and in proximity with other societies.

The deficiency of the behavioristic approach alone is brought sharply to focus in the statement: "He makes the response, *or better*, the response *is made*." Having no self, as doer, they must of necessity attribute functions *of the self* to *the function itself*. There is no behaver with a system of values that govern his responses and who assumes responsibility for his responses. There is only response—no acting agent, just reaction—predictable on the basis of external determinative forces. The delinquent or the neurotic cannot be held responsible for his own actions. He has a scapegoat. We are all familiar with the saying: "there are no delinquent children, only delinquent parents." The realities of mental hygiene appear to be driving more and more psychologists to a realistic grappling with the self which creates values, sets goals, and assumes responsibility. It is most elusive, and we have far to go before becoming sharply definitive in its characterization.

WHAT ARE VALUES?

Brewster Smith[5] sets for himself the task of establishing some order in the chaos of confused meanings ascribed to the term *values*. He speaks of his own previous studies and others: "Subsequent concern with the concept of mental health convinced me that this embarrassingly unsatisfactory term barely conceals an al-

[5] In Robert W. White (ed), *The Study of Lives,* Chapter 14.

most pure value problem." He mentions that only a few major empirical studies have been made and these started from different preconceptions, thus decreasing their value. He suggests that: "At present, one may hope that a tentative armchair analysis will be fruitful." Then he presents his approach to the problem.

> To be useful in the study of lives, a conception of values should include in its reference at least some of the important human phenomena that one encounters when one sees people valuing, caring, committing themselves, judging as better or worse. A meaning should be found, if the term is to be at all serviceable, that falls within the vaguely bounded area of discourse evoked by such situations. And further, the use of a special term, rather than others more firmly grounded in general psychological theories not specifically human in reference, will be most clearly justified if it refers to distinctively human phenomena within this broader area—phenomena, that is, that are not exhausted by more general terms like motive, incentive, and valence, which apply equally at human and infrahuman levels. (pp. 326, 327).

Smith then suggests starting with the general conception which, "it seems to me, is that of selective behavior—in which a person chooses, rejects, takes interest in, approves, disapproves—with respect to a physical, social, or ideal object." He notes "the major cleavage in the use of the term value divides those who focus on the person and his dispositions, on the one hand, and those who apply the term to properties of the object of choice, on the other." He adds: "Theorists concerned with personological problems have sometimes applied the term to classifications of the objects or goals of behavior," but that: "More characteristically, however, students of personality have understandably been preoccupied with dispositions of the person, and when they have used the term value, they have had some class of evaluative attitude in mind." (pp. 328, 329). Then he states: "My starting point will be the definition given by Clyde Kluckhohn, which has had considerable currency":

> A value is a conception, explicit or implicit, distinctive of an individual or characteristic of a group, of the desirable which influences the selection from available modes, means, and ends of action. (p. 331).

I would start with Kluckhohn's definition but would make a slight revision in order to present the element of subjectivity and evaluation as a self-function—self in process of evaluative cognition, involving somewhat broader and less clearly structured awareness than a "conception." Now let us continue with our "armchair analysis," hoping that it will help to reduce the ambiguity of the term "value" and add some insight into its nature at the human level.

THE EVALUATING SELF

I have interpreted the self as being the subject aspect of the total person and its being of the nature of a whole—not structured into parts. Therefore, it cannot be easily conceptualized and what is commonly referred to as the self-image is the image or concept that one has of his personality, the objective side of the person. But there can be true self-awareness by subjective cognition. The self that is mature, autonomous, confident, trusting, free of defenses, may experience itself in the act of experiencing, and most surely in deep empathic relation with another self in a deeply significant and shared experience such as the peak experiences of client and therapist or of two people in love. Because these peak empathic experiences are significant, each person experiences the other as an evaluating self in evaluative cognition, not only cognizant of an event but also of its meaning to the self for good or bad. In this empathic relation, value is experienced as inherent in and a condition of the other self, the *intrinsic* value Maslow was dealing with rationally.

INTRINSIC AND PROJECTED VALUE

When experienced subjectively in empathic cognition, value and need are experienced together as a state or quality of the self. The need is inherent in both the capacity to function and the internalized value system. *Together, what one is capable of doing and what he has evaluated as worth doing determine need.* The feeling of need is aroused by incongruity in the stimulus situation evaluated as going beyond the accustomed, tolerated, or acceptable; then an imaged goal is created and evaluated in contrast with the situation. The values placed on these goals (evaluated-ends) are the *created* values Maslow mentioned. With repetition, the intrinsic value that is projected with the need-drive to the goal becomes fixed on it as created value and carries value conferred upon it by self from its store of intrinsic value. Intrinsic value of (or inherent in) self is experienced subjectively. Projected or conferred value is inferred from one's behavior as objectively observed by the free choices he makes.

The storage battery may be used for analogous comparison. The positive and negative plates stand side by side in the charged battery, dormant till aroused by closing the switch. Self forms an image of a situation and evaluates it negatively. It immediately imagines a remedial situation, which is evaluated positively. The potential difference between the positive and negative evaluations determines the arousal drive as the charge on the battery plates determines the current strength. This points to a very crucial matter in mental health. Based upon this innate, intrinsic need-value condition, as described above, self is cognizant of the goal (thing, person, situation, behavior) to be attained for satisfaction. This cognizance of awareness may or may not be fully conceptualized and conscious. But due to past conditioning and secondary value formation by internalization of family and/or community value-goals, these secondary (acquired) need-value states become superimposed upon the other. Then when aroused in a given situation, this acquired value system overshadows the true-to-self value system and places value or worth on goals incongruent with the true or basic needs of the person. In other words, need-drives based on acquired, conferred value-goals are incongruent with need-drives based on real capacity and its intrinsic value. Inner tension and conflict is the consequence, a dissonance within the self, a weakened self, and ineffectual, unsatisfying living, mental illness or less than adequate mental health.

EVALUATION OF SELF

Self evaluates its own behavior and basic mental processes (concepts, attitudes, motives, etc.) in the same manner as it evaluates others. This is the manner in which one develops a generalized image of his own personality, his character, his worth as a person. He has attributed value to himself and if this image is negative or of low worth, it is painful to behold. The tendency is to suppress it and to create in its stead an imagined ideal self. There is cognitive dissonance* with relationship to self; this is a tension and weakness within the self. In case of the strong, sound, healthy self with a fairly well integrated personality, this disparity is not very great and the images are not widely different, the *ought* just sufficiently above the *is* for the cognitive dissonance to arouse normal motivation toward realistic improvement. In case of the weaker self with an unrealistic negative self or personality-evaluation, anxiety distorts further evaluation, the idealized image is unrealistically high, and motivation is toward fantasy achievement instead of real. One's value system is determinative in self-evaluation. It governs the relationship between the *is* and the *ought*, thus having a vital bearing on motivation, social adjustment, and mental health.

The classical soliloquy of Hamlet, "*To be or not to be?*" may be restated as the universal question: *To be or to do?* Being and doing are closely interrelated. The quality of one's being is in part determined by his doings, and the quality of his doings (performance) is a product of his state of being. But *being* should hold the prime position. Doing values are relative. *Being values* are of the nature of universals, and are intrinsic.

One may observe his performance objectively as he would another's, thus forming an evaluative concept (image) of *his personality* and an attitude toward himself—projecting or conferring self-value. To the degree that a person is autonomous and self-empathic, he may become subjectively aware of himself and experience his own intrinsic value. Scientific psychology has been largely limited to the former approach, leaving the latter for philosophy and religion to validate. Because of our cultural emphasis on the empirical and pragmatic, we have neglected to develop the latter and are seriously deficient in its operation, in true self-identity and self-awareness. Therefore, we find the incongruity between the objective personality-image and projected self-value and the subjective, vaguely apprehend intrinsic value of

* See Glossary.

self. The correction of this incongruity of self-evaluation and the resulting intrapersonal conflict is a major problem in mental hygiene.

It may be noted here that in the broad field of dissonance study, experimental psychology is making valuable contributions to the understanding of the mechanics of need-goals and evaluation. Deeper insight comes via the idiographic work of the clinician, as the therapist in deep empathy with his client experiencing in immediate awareness the state of dissonance and the conflicting need-value struggle within the self of his client. By bringing together the findings of both clinical and experimental psychology, truer and more definitive descriptions of these conditions and processes can be given.

To test the hypothesis that better-adjusted children will be able to accept more damaging statements about themselves than will the poorer-adjusted children, Taylor and Combs[6] made the following study of 205 sixth-grade children. Using the California Test of Personality, Elementary Form A, the children were divided into two groups, better- and poorer-adjusted, based on test scores. Then they prepared a list of twenty statements that were "probably true" of all children, yet damaging to self if admitted. Some of the statements were:

1. I sometimes disobey my parents.
2. I sometimes say bad words or swear.
3. I sometimes copy or cheat on schoolwork.
4. I sometimes am rude to older people.

Normal precautions were taken to get honest answers, but by an obscured code they could tell which set of answers came from each group. Based on the mean scores of the two groups, their hypothesis was confirmed. The better-adjusted admitted significantly higher numbers of self-derogatory acts.

While this was a crude experiment, it is one of several studies which indicate a high positive correlation between healthy, well-adjusted persons and persons with realistic self-awareness, self-evaluation, self-acceptance, and distinction between the *is* and *ought*. In the future we may be able to verify the hypothesis that the more healthy-minded or better-adjusted place primary value

[6] From Charles Taylor and Arthur W. Combs, "Self-Acceptance and Adjustment." *J. of Consult. Psychol.*, 16:89–91 (1952).

on *being* over *doing* and thus can better accept minor behavior faults.

VALUE CLASSIFICATION AND PERSONALITY

In the study of values we encounter the same problem found in the study of personality and motivation (need states or dispositions). Objective study requires discrimination, specification, abstraction, and classification. Motivation and value are two sides of the same coin: motivation experienced as *need-drive-goal* and value as both *intrinsic* and, when projected to certain means and ends, as *created* values. In other words, motivation is a latent state of self and until aroused, is experienced subjectively and conjointly with intrinsic worth. Then, when aroused and expressed as a need-drive toward a goal, it is experienced as behavior with conferred value. These determine behavior traits and patterns, i.e., personality. There are as many values as there are personality or behavior traits, for each is directed toward a goal that has conferred or created value; and every individual has his own unique style of life, his response patterns and value system. Understanding requires generalizing specifics into categories, so we classify values that are supposed to be common to all, but which never carry the same weight in any two persons. Cultures, subcultures, communities, families and individuals attribute different value-weight to various goals (relationships, performance, etc.), thus our variant and often conflicting "values," conflicting behavior tendencies determined by incongruent values, or incongruence within the value system.

VALUE AND PERSONALITY

Allport has given much time to the study of values and, with Vernon and Lindzey, developed an inventory type test to measure the predominant values that govern choices. In their *Manual for the Study of Values,*[7] these authors state that the classification

[7] G.W. Allport, Philip Vernon and Gardner Lindzey, *Study of Values* (Third Edition) (Boston: Houghton Mifflin Co., 1951, 1960).

was based on Edward Spranger's *Types of Men*. The types of men, personality types, are consequences of their characteristic value systems, their need-value hierarchies. These are: (1) the theoretical; (2) the economic; (3) the aesthetic; (4) the social; (5) the political; and (6) the religious. In some people the value system is heavily weighted in one or another of these directions. In others, there may be balanced harmony or conflict.

> In selecting his six types, Spranger may be said to hold a flattering view of human nature. He does not allow for formless or valueless personalities, nor for those who follow an expedient or hedonistic philosophy of life. The neglect of sheerly sensuous values is a special weakness in his typology. His attempt to reduce hedonistic choices partly to economic and partly to aesthetic values seems unconvincing. . . . (p. 3).

Again Allport writes:[8]

> The healthy adult, we know, develops under the influence of value schemata whose fulfillment he regards as desirable even though it may never be completely attained. In agreement with such schemata he selects his perceptions, consults his conscience, inhibits irrelevant or contrary lines of conduct, drops and forms subsystems of habits according as they are dissonant or harmonious with his commitments. In short, in proportion as active schemata for conduct develop, they exert a dynamic influence upon specific choices. . . .
>
> Few, if any, of our value-orientations hold the prospect of complete fulfillment. Does any worker for the United Nations, however ardent, really expect a peaceful family of nations in his lifetime? Does the devotee of democracy expect to see his ideal fully realized? The devoutly religious person, however keen his hunger for God, knows that in this world his hunger will not be completely satisfied. Yet all such goals, unattainable as they are, exert a present dynamic effect upon daily conduct, and in so doing direct the course of becoming. How wrong we have been in viewing the process of growth as a reaction to past and present stimuli; neglecting the dynamics of futurity: of orientation, intention, and valuation. (pp. 75, 76).

[8] G.W. Allport, *Becoming* (New Haven: Yale University Press, 1955). Used with permission.

VALUE DISCREPANCY AND CONFLICT

Other categories and schemata have been devised, but the above examples should suffice to make the point clear. I would use the same schema to classify values as for needs. (Chapter 4). They are experienced together with need felt as the situation is evaluated and value ascribed as the behavior satisfies the need. Sometimes value incongruence and conflict result from having accepted the incongruent values of different significant persons or groups in the same developmental period, e.g., church youth fellowship and college or high school fraternity. They may also result from different values that are dominant at different stages in growth, the earlier not having been adequately displaced. Coleman (1960, pp. 302, 303), discusses "conceived" vs. "operative" values and states:

> Sometimes the discrepancy between an individual's conceived and operative values indicates an alarming schism between his "idealized" and "real" self. The business man who professes to accept the golden rule but violates even the most basic business ethics, the woman who extols selfless mother love but governs her child with refined cruelty, and the politician who speaks of freedom but denies fellow citizens the right to vote are only very obvious examples of an all too common phenomenon. Sometimes a person holds dual standards without realizing it, sometimes knowingly from a conviction that the end justifies the means. . . .
>
> We have already commented on the havoc created in our own day by the crumbling of our traditional picture of the universe and, with it, many of our most basic values. As physical and philosophical boundaries fade before the advances of science and technology, men have become less sure of their role in the universe and more uncertain of their ability to guide their own destiny. Some people cling rigidly to the values of an earlier and more stable period, only to find themselves continually at odds with a changing world; others, no more wisely, discount *all* traditional values because *some* have proved invalid; still others pay lip service to traditional values but have little faith in them as practical guides. Symptoms of confusion and insecurity are seen in the increasing incidence of mental illness in the United States and our often deplored trend toward conformity.

TABLE 5. SOME VALUE CONFLICTS IN AMERICAN SOCIETY

Initiative vs. Passivity	Belief in the value and effectiveness of individual initiative conflicts with the tendency to wait passively for a lucky break or to automatic advancement through seniority.
Liberty vs. Conformity	Belief in the value of the individual and the importance of freedom of conscience conflicts with admiration for efficient mass organization in which the individual must subordinate his goals to those of the group.
Responsibility vs. Determinism	Belief in the moral responsibility of the individual for his own acts conflicts with the tendency to seek out causes over which the individual has no control.
Equal Opportunity vs. Pull	Belief in equal opportunity for all conflicts with the readiness to take advantage of personal influence and special privilege in order to move ahead.
Brotherly Love vs. Competition	Belief in responsibility for one's fellow man conflicts with the determination to look out for one's own interest in any competition ("Good guys finish last").
Social Equality vs. Success	Belief in the ideal of social equality conflicts with the determination to achieve financial success and acquire the various symbols of higher social status (expensive home, car, clothes. exclusive neighborhood, schools, clubs, etc.).
Saving vs. Spending	Belief in the virtue of thrift, both for the individual and the nation, conflicts with the individual drive to display success symbols and a national economy based on increasing consumption.
Simplicity vs. Show	Belief in the virtue of humility and lack of ostentation conflicts with admiration for visible proof of financial success.
Playing Safe vs. Taking Risks	Belief in the virtue of responsibility and conservatism for bold gambles for high stakes.

Source: J. Coleman, *Personality Dynamics and Effective Behavior,* Chicago: Scott, Foresman, 1960, p. 301. (Adapted from Kapar Naegele, an unpublished Values Study Project, Harvard University, 1949.)

Due to such wide-spread intermingling of cultures and sub-cultures, many people are in such a state of value confusion (anomie) that they try to assume all three positions mentioned above.

Table 5 shows some typical value conflicts. The reader may easily think of several others, e.g., civil rights vs. property rights. The reconciliation of such conflicts or incongruences in the value system becomes the chief social and personal problem. The net result is the degree of social and personal stability achieved.

To clarify our individual and group goals, we need a well-defined and coherent system of values. Table 5 is a summary of one attempt to identify some current conflicts in American values.

THE ADEQUATE VALUE SYSTEM

Much of the value confusion described above is due to the fact that many people have turned to science for the *whys* of life as well as for the *whats* and *hows*. We have described the important role of scientific psychology in this matter and its limitations. Science can describe and help clarify values, but it cannot yet confirm or validate them. Social scientists, in their cross-cultural studies, have singled out and described the folkways and mores of people of different cultures, their values relative to time, place, and ethnic development, with the assumption that what may be good for one may not be so for another. They tend to avoid universals and ignore the reality of absolute values. They have made *folkways* and *mores* virtually synonymous with morals. It may be said of modern man, as was once said of the ancient Israelites, "Every man does what is right in his own sight." Expediency too often overrules great moral imperatives and the welter of relative values finds no consistency or order from lacking anchorage in absolutes.

SCIENCE AND RELIGION COMPLEMENTARY

If one's value system is to be a valid and reliable guide to the patterning of behavior that leads through a wilderness of continuous choice and change, it would seem that relative values should be ordered around a framework of absolutes and choices of expediency fall into their proper hierarchic position in relation to the great universal moral imperatives. For these, man has been accustomed to turn to his religion. Their validation is a matter of faith: faith as was presented in Chapter 3—not as credulity, i.e., uncritical mental assent, but as a cognitive process or capacity that is not dependent on sensory structure, the subjective knowing by immediate awareness when two selves are in empathic oneness. The ancient prophet and modern mystic testify to such empathic union with God, the Absolute Self, and translate experienced absolute values to the masses who lack the degree of faith-perceptiveness and have lower faith-cognition quotients. The spiritually less gifted man may accept these faith-derived values credulously and feel secure, as long as circumstances permit, or he may test them through the years of living and thus experience the greater satisfaction and sense of fulfillment they give. As a person of relatively adequate faith in self and others and thus free of inner defenses, and while in a state of empathic self-awareness or empathic relation with another self, one may experience the validity of absolute values and universal moral imperatives. At the self dimension, man is of the nature of the absolute and mankind universally is alike, with like needs and like values.

This has been religion's approach to values. In those areas of common humanness wherein "each person is like every other person," universal needs and moral values prevail. What is best for one is best for all. In those areas where we differ, needs and values are relative. An expanded science may well describe traits that are common to all mankind as well as the universal human needs and absolute values. This would seem to be a plausible future expectation, but one not yet attained.

There seems to be a growing feeling that at the present time, when science is making such rapid progress in its sphere, man's great need is not for less religion, but for more realistic and effective religion, and that they (science and religion) are complementary approaches to reality and have complementary roles in mental hygiene. With more adequate science and more adequate religion working together as complementary approaches to reality, more adequate knowledge of human nature and its *values* may be obtained with the anchorage of relative values in a hierarchical pattern relative to absolute or universal value (moral imperatives). With this would follow deeper insights into frustration of value-needs, existential anxiety, and the source-roots of much psychosocial disturbance.

Coleman (1960) in his discussion of this theme says:

> In organizing his universe into a meaningful pattern and developing a system of values, man can turn to three chief sources of understanding: (1) *science,* which can help man better to understand himself and the universe in which he lives; (2) *experience,* which relates, both for the group and the individual, the consequences of various types of behavior in terms of need-satisfaction, happiness, and fulfillment; and (3) *belief,* which gives subjective validity to religious and ethical concepts about the meaning and proper conduct of human life. No one of these sources seems sufficient in itself, nor is any of them infallible. (p. 303).
>
> . . . Although theologians have used logic, reason, and historical arguments to help prove the existence of God and the validity of their beliefs, the "proof" of religious truth must rest finally on faith. People who have received strength and comfort from their religion have an unshakable belief in their God; but the correctness of their belief can never, by argument alone, be made convincing to anyone who has not shared a similar experience. . . . (p. 306).

ABSOLUTE VALUES

A value system, with its many relatives organized around a few absolutes and its moral imperatives above its expediency choices in hierarchical order, possesses the inner consistency and flexibility necessary for both stability and growth. In the flux of changing experience and constant choice, the specific value-judgments need to change along with their relative importance. The value system changes with experience. Since self remains self, with its true self-identity, through the years of personality growth and change, so the core of the value system based on absolutes remains steadfast in all the re-evaluations and the necessary changes in relative values that growing experience demands.

Man evaluates various aspects of the world of objective reality in relationship to himself, to see what these may contribute to his well-being. Therefore he projects, confers, and creates value, all of which is relative. He is able to do this because intrinsic value is characteristic of the universe that gave him birth and the life of which he is a part; and it is characteristic of him as the highest creation of his world. It is a universe of spirit as he, the self, is a creature of spirit and a creator of value. This is the argument of many religious existentialists. Bertocci and Millard[9] seem to be arguing from this position when they state:

> In bare terms, the ethical realist holds that if there is no value already in the universe, be it in God, in a Platonic realm of Ideas, or man as the kind of being he is, then no values can "rub off" on man because of anything he may like or want. . . . Unless a man became aware of values as standards by which he is to guide and transform his nature, not only will he have no moral sign posts to guide him, but he will never know when or to what extent his being has been fulfilled. For "fulfilled" is a value term. Psychological health has no meaning if we look only into man and neglect the values by which man's health is to be evaluated. . . .
>
> . . . Man is the kind of being who can fulfill himself not solely by consulting his interests, wants, and capacities, as he interacts with his environment, but by heeding the claims of rights and values whose worth does not depend upon man's knowing them or wanting them. Nor can man ever realize himself in his world without heeding the imperatives of his moral consciousness. (pp. 256, 257, 259).

CRITERIA

Lehner and Kube[10] give six criteria for rating values, thus determining their relative position in one's value hierarchy.

---

[9] Peter A. Bertocci and Richard Millard, *Personality and the Good* (New York: David McKay Co., 1963). Used with permission.

[10] George F. Lehner and Ella Kube, *The Dynamics of Personal Adjustment* (Second Edition) © 1964. Reprinted by permission of Prentice-Hall, Inc., Englewood Cliffs, N.J.

1. *Inclusiveness.* A value that affects all men rather than some is, other things being equal, superior. For example, freedom for all is of greater value than freedom for only a few persons.
2. *Permanence.* A value that lasts is higher than a temporary one.
3. *Irrevocability.* A value that is not replaceable or readily created by human effort is higher than one that can be produced easily. For example, the books of brilliant thinkers and the paintings of gifted artists are of more worth than mediocre products.
4. *Congruency.* A value that harmonizes with a person's total pattern of beliefs is superior to one that is inconsistent with the entire structure of integrated behavior.
5. *Cognitive Completeness.* A value that is based on full information and broad experience is higher than one resting on partial and fragmentary knowledge.
6. *Survival.* A value that contributes to the maintenance of the individual or the human race is superior to one that leads to the extinction of either.

In summary, it appears that an adequate value system would, (1) show little incongruity between one's subjectively experienced intrinsic values and objectively formulated (learned) values conferred on certain goals (things, activities or relationships). (2) Growth and self-actualization values should stand above dependency or maintenance values. (3) Relative values should be ordered in relation to each other and relative to absolute or universal values, with a few great moral imperatives ruling over the many expediences. (4) The hierarchic structure should rise in ascending order from material values to physical, mental, social and spiritual as appears to be in accord with the evolutionary development of human uniqueness. Since these need-value levels are interrelated and deeply entwined in most of our secondary or learned need-values, the problem of ordering is complex and difficult. (5) We should have a set of guiding principles or criteria by which we structure our system. The principles and criteria given by Bertocci and Millard and Lehner and Kube may serve this purpose.

VALUES AND CHARACTER

Character is another ambiguous word with a long history of common usage which the behavorial sciences adopted but have been unable to define concisely. Some psychologists use it almost synonymously with personality, while others confine its use to the more basic traits and the attitudes that determine one's more significant behavior which is judged by society as being acceptable or unacceptable. *Character* is most commonly used to identify the behavior which is more specifically morally tinged and value oriented. My definition of a person of strong character is one who has developed a strong, healthy self which is relatively free to choose among alternatives and to direct his behavior in accord with a well-organized value system, in which higher order values most always take precedence over those lower in the hierarchy.

EXPERIMENTAL STUDIES

During the post World War I period, character education became a major interest of educators and psychologists. It had been generally assumed that religious education had strong character building effect. Judges frequently made church-school attendance one of the conditions of probation for juvenile offenders. Then behavioral scientists began to challenge the assumption, claiming it to be unsupported by empirical evidence. Numerous character studies were launched. Hightower,[11] in his University of Iowa character studies, found no significant relationship between biblical knowledge and conduct. Using a 70-item test, Hill[12] compared the ethical knowledge of 517 delinquent boys to that of more than 1000 high school students and 148 adults, and found very little difference between the scores of the offenders

---

[11] Pleasant R. Hightower, "Biblical Information in Relation to Character and Conduct," *University of Iowa Studies in Character,* Vol. III, No. 2, Iowa City: University of Iowa Press, 1930.

[12] George E. Hill, "The Ethical Knowledge of Delinquent and Non-delinquent Boys," in *Journal of Soc. Psychology,* Vol. 6, No. 1 (Feb. 1935), 107–114.

and the school group. The validity of these studies was seriously challenged, largely on the basis that they merely compared knowledge differences and that factual knowledge is a minor element of character.

The classic of the era was the series of studies directed by Hartshorn and May.[13] Their major problems were to define character in operational terms and to devise tests that would evoke true character responses or responses from which character traits could be inferred. On the assumption that the ability to foresee and evaluate consequences were essential elements in character development, they developed two tests: (1) Short statements of specific acts were made, to which the children replied with as many consequences as they could imagine (good and bad). (2) A multiple choice test, composed of brief descriptions of several situations, each followed with a few possible alternate responses. The children were told to check the sentence which expressed the best possible solution to the problem.

Next they developed a *provocations test* in which certain acts were stated, such as lying, stealing, etc. under various circumstances. The children's responses as to when or under what circumstances these acts were justifiable were elicited. Finally, they developed certain *conduct tests* to measure patterns of conduct: *deception, co-operation, inhibition,* and *persistence.* The first of these four has received the most publicity.

These investigators used approved methods of test construction and their tests had a fairly high validity but the findings were many and varied, with too many contingencies to present here. They revealed many factors which relate to character development. One finding that attracted considerable attention was what they called "the specificity of moral conduct." People are not apt to be honest in general and under all circumstances, but are honest sometimes, with some people, and under certain conditions. Their conduct tests demonstrated fairly well that most people, school age at least, do not have a well organized value system in hierarchical arrangement under an over-all group of universal values.

My study of delinquency included an intensive study of the religious attitudes and opinions of delinquent adolescents. Find-

---

[13] Hugh Hartshorn and M.A. May, *Studies in Deceit* (New York: The Macmillan Company, 1928).

ings indicated that they believed as strongly in religion and the church, but they were perhaps a little more orthodox than the general adolescent population. The majority of the delinquents and one parent if not both, were affiliated with a church. But I also found that the majority of delinquents had discontinued Sunday school. The church affiliation of their parents, in most cases, was rather tenuous, or the affiliation was with an extremist group whose social ethic was at wide variance with the community at large. One 16-year-old delinquent boy expressed rather lucidly what others felt but could not verbalize their feelings as well. He said: "I want to go straight; I want to do right. I want to be a Christian and think I am, but I keep messing up and don't know why."

IDENTIFICATION AND MORAL DEVELOPMENT

Other delinquent studies in addition to my own, seem to show that most of these behavior-problem young people believed sincerely in "religion" (its moral codes), but theirs was largely a religion of ideas, accepting "right" opinions, often naive and sometimes contradictory. They were not identified deeply with a "mother" church nor any primary group or significant individuals who seriously tried and partly succeeded in living up to the implications of their religion. They were little involved at the self dimension. Since many of them lived behind their defenses from middle childhood, their distrust prevented them from achieving any depth of identity. They were unable to attain the more immediate subjective awareness and empathic response to the intrinsic values experienced in relationship to these significant people. The character problems of these young people were a consequence of both types of value conflict described earlier in this chapter. The values formed at one stage of development, which were immature and inadequate, were not "outgrown" and continued to conflict with those of a later and more mature stage. In addition to this was the conflict between the divergent values held by different primary groups with which the individual is affiliated. These conflicts are not limited to delinquents but always create behavior problems of varying severity and strain, and may even break one's character structure.

In his study of moral development, Kohlberg[14] distinguished six types that characterize children from ages 7 to 16, which he describes as follows, with illustrative behavior:

Level I. Premoral.
Stage 1, Punishment and obedience orientation: Obeys rules in order to avoid punishment.
Stage 2, Naive instrumental hedonism: Conforms to obtain rewards, to have favors returned.

Level II. Morality of conventional role-conformity.
Stage 3, "Good-boy" morality of maintaining good relations, approval of others: Conforms to avoid disapproval, dislike by others.
Stage 4, Authority maintaining morality: Conforms to avoid censure by legitimate authorities with resultant guilt.

Level III. Morality of self-accepted moral principles.
Stage 5, Morality of contract, of individual rights, and democratically accepted law: Conforms to maintain the respect of the impartial spectator judging in terms of community welfare.
Stage 6, Morality of individual principles of conscience: Conforms to avoid self-condemnation.

At age seven nearly all statements are at Level I, moving progressively upward with most 16-year-old responses in Levels II and III. The rise in moral level may be interpreted as due to both maturational factors and social learning, with growing capacity to evaluate and with the internalization of value judgments from identifying with significant persons and primary groups. Adults may be found at each of these levels, and their mental-social health is in part a consequence.

Related to Kohlberg's findings is a rather ingenious experimental study of the development of conscience in preschool children, conducted by Sears, Ran, and Alpert.[15] The children were confronted with five situations that called for resistance to temptation after the experimenter left the room: (1) eating appetizing candy; (2) violating rules of a ring-toss game; (3)

---

[14] From L. Kohlberg, "The Development of Children's Orientations Toward a Moral Order: I. Sequence in the Development of Moral Thought." *Vita Humana,* 6:11–33 (1963). Used with permission.

[15] Material summarized from R.R. Sears, L. Ran, and R. Alpert, *Identification and Child Rearing.* Stanford, Calif.: Stanford Univ. Press, 1965. Used with permission.

playing with a forbidden toy; (4) a "quoting rules" drama in which the child is expected to urge another to obey the restrictive rules; and (5) the child left alone to watch over a caged hamster and prevent its escape. In the last instance, the experimenter trips a switch that allows the hamster to drop to the floor through a false bottom and hide if the child fails in vigilance, the child soon finding the animal and feeling better.

With the exception of the candy test, there was general consistency among the "resistance to temptation" indicators, forming a composite resistance score and demonstrating that some children are generally more resistant to temptation than others. It also indicated that girls were more resistant than boys and that in this limited age range of 20 months, the older children showed more capacity for resistance than the younger.

CONSCIENCE AND GUILT

Since man has the capacity to evaluate, he appraises his behavior and experiences an affect that is spoken of as conscience. Conscience has been given much attention as a subject of psychological study.

THE SUPEREGO

Psychoanalysts use the Freudian personality constructs as a guide, and the term conscience as a synonym of the superego; or, to be specific, conscience is the dominant function of the superego. As presented in Chapter 2, the *id* represents the child's natural, biological urges, the aggressive and erotic drives, bent on gratification in accord with the *pleasure principle,* undisciplined and unsocialized. The process of social adaptation results in the growth of the *ego,* a system of mental processes structured to control the id impulses and regulate behavior in accord with the realities of one's environment. The superego develops along with the ego—partly conscious, but largely unconscious—as a special mental construct for inhibiting the id drives and condemning the ego if it fails to control the id. Therefore, superego may be on the side of ego in controlling id or against ego if the latter is lax in its work. Superego is generally thought of as being negative and critical. In some cases superego may be too weak for its voice to be heard, but it is still in general known as bad conscience.

How does the superego develop? The generally accepted explanation is that it is the "introjected" voice of authority which begins with the parent's commands, restricts the child's impulsive behavior, and extends to other authoritative significant persons. The young child enjoys masturbating. It is a pleasant sensation, an id gratification. But momma sees. Momma's sharp command and sharper smack on the hand are painful and frustrating. The child is angry, and strikes back, but he receives a sharper rebuke, both verbal and physical. He can't win. Dependency-need demands conformity. The child identifies with the parent, and the external "No" is internalized, mostly as an unconscious process, and operates as the restrictive "voice of conscience." In other words, it is the opposite of the paranoia's *projecting* his inner condemnatory voice outward to others and hearing criticism or threats from their lips which, in reality, are not there. The psychoanalytic view is that conscience is not an innate or inherent force that would normally develop within the individual, but is a social introjection which originates in society.

Traditionally, most psychologists have explained conscience in a similar manner without equating it with the hypothetical superego. It is the consequence of conditioned learning (operant conditioning), with punishment the conditioner that inhibits the unacceptable act and parental pleasure or acceptance the reward that reinforces the tendency to inhibit. This process becomes generalized as the child grows older, from both the response and stimulus ends. The command voices of a number of authoritative figures merge into one, and certain patterns of behavior become inhibited by these generalized "voices"; or, if failing to inhibit, they produce feelings of guilt.

As the child matures, he learns to evaluate his own behavior and himself, and he is forced to choose which of two or more "command voices" (value guides) he will obey. His childhood "conscience" becomes modified. Sometimes, in poorly integrated personalities, two or more "consciences" form that may be contradictory and in conflict. The widely different ethics or moral codes of two significant persons or groups may become internalized concurrently. Quite often one of these is kept repressed most of the time and operates subconsciously, with partial conscious awareness under certain circumstances. The degree or scope of conscience changes from the interjected values of others to one's own evaluations and varies widely with his degree of maturity. The immature, dependency, security motivated person, regardless of age, is ruled or tormented by a conscience that is predominantly the "voice" of parent, church, or society. The mature, autonomous, growth motivated person will have remolded his earlier "consciences" extensively by his own freedom and capacity to evaluate independently. In addition to this growing degree of maturity and autonomy, the conscience affect—the guilt-anxiety-dread feeling—moves from physical-punishment-directed to social-directed, and to self, e.g., having to live with oneself while self-judged as being unworthy. Allport (1955, p. 73) says:

> The theory I am here suggesting holds that the must-consciousness precedes the ought-consciousness, but that in the course of transformation three important changes occur. (1) External sanctions give way to internal—a change adequately accounted for by the processes of identification and introjection familiar in Freudian and behavioral theory. (2) Experiences of prohibition, fear, and "must" give way to experiences of preference, self-respect, and "ought." This shift becomes possible in proportion as the self-image and value-systems of the individual develop. (3) Specific habits of obedience give way to generic self-guidance, that is to say, to broad schemata of values that confer direction upon conduct.

I believe that conscience is the mental process of self-evaluation. It is experienced consciously in the mixed affect tone of remorse-anxiety-dread when self or its behavior is adjudged unworthy, but is experienced as an affect tone of well-being, happiness, or joy when self is adjudged worthy. Somehow we have not stressed the positive side very much in comparison with the negative. Perhaps we experience the negative side much more. Therefore, conscience is as innate as cognition. A person may evaluate the behavior of a bully or vicious dog as being a threat to himself and thus experience fear. He may likewise evaluate his own behavior at a given instance, in relation to his capacity or opportunity, as being unworthy with the negative feelings mentioned above. Even though it derives from self's innate capacity to evaluate itself and its behavior, learning is essential to its growth and operation; and the conditions of that learning determine in large measure the degree to which it becomes one's own balanced, effective, self-developed guide or remains, as from early childhood, the introjected "musts" of the outside world. I believe that the psychological trend is swinging in this direction in the interpretation of conscience.

SIN VS. SICKNESS

At the 1959 Convention of the American Psychological Association, O. H. Mowrer astonished many of the delegates in his presentation of a paper titled, "The Role of the Concept of Sin in Psychotherapy."[16] He revealed certain weaknesses of current psychoanalytic theory and therapeutic practice, saying:

> Therefore, in light of the total situation, I see no alternative but to turn again to the old, painful, but also promising possibility that man is pre-eminently a *social* creature and that he lives or dies, psychologically and personally, as a function of the openness, community relatedness, and integrity which by good action he attains and by evil action destroys. (p. 44).

Because of the wide interest aroused by the paper, Mowrer wrote a supplement to it arguing to the effect that sin is a strong term denoting strength of action and responsibility of choice. Sickness, on the other hand, is a sort of palliative term, and to call maladaptive behavior "sickness" is a partial denial of responsibility, evasive at least, and a failure to come to grips with the real issues involved—that a *man* should be man enough to recognize and admit that when his life becomes all fouled up, he is at fault somewhere, has made wrong choices, been led by wrong values. He says (1961): "In becoming amoral, ethically neutral, and "free," we have cut the very roots of our being; lost

[16] O.H. Mowrer, *The Crisis in Psychiatry and Religion,* (Princeton, N.J.: D. Van Nostrand Co., Inc., 1961). Used with permission.

our deepest sense of selfhood and identity; . . . In reaction to the state of near-limbo into which we have drifted, we have become suddenly aware, once again, of the problem of *values* and of their centrality in the human enterprise. . . ."

He deals with guilt as a *real* determinative factor in much, if not all, mental illness, citing several cases, then states:

> And so might one continue, indefinitely, to mobilize evidence that sin and emotional sickness are no strangers to one another and that it is only by flagrant disregard of the clinical facts that one can imagine that neurotic and functionally psychotic individuals have been too thoroughly socialized and are the victims of an unduly severe, oppressive morality. Therefore, although it is realized that the evidence cited will probably not be sufficient to convince anyone holding a strongly contrary view, it will be accepted here as typical of a much larger body of facts which justify further consideration of the view that mental illness is a social and moral illness and, in the final analysis, capable of remediation only along social and moral lines. (p. 91).

While Mowrer does not give a specific definition of sin, his case examples portray what it apparently means to him. My impression is that it is in keeping with the ancient biblical connotation, *to miss the mark*. By a person's choices, his distorted or inadequate system of values, his life moves off on a tangent and misses its true goal, thus failure in self-actualization. And Bertocci and Millard (1963, p. 19) would seem to agree with Mowrer's central thesis. They say: "Mental health, in the last analysis, has no standards or norms of its own that are independent of what we are now calling the moral order of life."

Guilt is the tonal affect the voice of conscience carries when self is deeply disturbed by its own behavior. It is mixed emotion and painful, composed of or associated with remorse, anxiety, and dread. It is more than mere dissatisfaction. Circumstances (external factors) often prevent a person from performing to the level of his capacity and he experiences dissatisfaction. If he has an alibi, he does not condemn himself. Each man has his value system, his code of ethics and his standards. When he violates one of these values because of his own weakness, he himself evaluates his performance relative to his self-expectations and adjudges himself as being unworthy. He feels ashamed, remorseful, and anxious in varying degrees.

Normal, realistic guilt is an essential quality of experience. It is that qualitative state of consciousness by which a person is acutely aware of his failures. Therefore, it is an essential aid to self-reform, self-discipline, self-improvement. It is the "inner voice" calling for growth of selfhood, self-fulfillment, actualization of one's potential for being. An excessive, unrealistic, morbid guilt is a crippling factor and is a basic symptom of much mental illness. It is the voice that is telling one his value system is wrong, that his standards of judgment need to be overhauled. In fact, a high degree of realistic, appropriate guilt is found in much mental illness. Here it is the behavior that continues to be unworthy, inappropriate; and the "voice" keeps crying out against it. In either case, the problem is not merely the removal of the guilt symptom; psychotherapy often has been "guilty" of this mistake. The problem of therapy is to use these guilt-feelings to bring the person into full awareness of the faulty value system in the one case and the faulty behavior in the other.

To help a person achieve a basic reorientation of his inner life which is essential to restore mental health is a most difficult task, since there is strong resistance. The *wise* use of guilt is very helpful, if not necessary, in accomplishing this. In religion this has always been done, but not always wisely. In the past psychotherapy, particularly psychoanalysis, has been less wise in trying to eliminate the guilt without correcting the faulty behavior.

CONSCIENCE IS UNIQUE IN MAN

Several years ago Mowrer conducted a series of experiments with rats to see if they could develop a sort of ethical sense, e.g., evaluate the present in relationship to the future. Pellets of food were dropped in front of the hungry animals. If they sought the food immediately, they received an electric shock, but if they would wait a few seconds there was no harm. Even this rudimentary ethical choice was beyond them. The stronger ones seized the food regardless of consequences like irresponsible delinquents, while the weaker ones withdrew in equally irresponsible neurotic syndromes.

Apparently man alone adjudges the quality of his behavior, establishes value-goals, and transcends the immediate present and biological compulsion. Man not only *can* make value choices, he *must* do so. His own personal integration, his direction of the life processes and his control of the universe depend on this. It is an awesome responsibility which he shuns. Lacking absolute knowledge, he sometimes makes wrong choices and suffers guilt pangs. To avoid this he rationalizes and evades the responsibility of moral choice, which produces greater guilt. This negative voice of conscience, guilt, is man's guide to responsible living, to overcoming his anxiety and reluctance to accept his ability and opportunity. The positive voice of conscience is joy and peace—a "well done, good and faithful servant"—that wells up from within when man rises to the challenge and achieves in high proportion to his potential. The animal experiences pain and pleasure but no guilt or joy. These are for man. And the ratio of guilt to joy bears heavily on his state of mental health.

SUMMARY

When experiencing need, self is aroused in action toward a goal that is value-conferred. Confused values give rise to psychosocial disorders. This is of great consequence since mental health and the value system are inextricably interwoven. Since freedom of choice, responsibility, and the sense of wrong (sin and guilt) are so closely associated with mental illness, Mowrer has appealed for "consideration of the view that mental illness is a social and moral illness and, in the final analysis, capable of remediation only along social and moral lines."

Social scientists, in order to remain objective, have been reluctant to make a place for values in disciplines. Their persistence as regulators of behavior and determiners of health has become so evidenced in recent years, especially in great crisis, that behavior scientists are coming to see values as not only legitimate but essential data. Maslow thinks that therapy may be defined in terms of a search for values and that a system of universal values, sufficient behavior guides, can be scientifically determined by studying the free choices of high self-actualizers in their many varieties of behavior. Hobbs suggests various ways psychology can (and will) contribute to ethical behavior and that, "A simple factoring out of the common elements of the major . . .

ethical systems of the world might yield 90 percent of the ethical ideas that are important to have."

Intrinsic value, inherent in the self, is largely a matter of subjective experience, i.e., empathic cognition. It is experienced in conjunction with latent motivation or need as two sides of the same coin. When self is aroused in need-drive-goal behavior, value is experienced as being projected to the behavior-goal as conferred value. Self evaluates in accord with its intrinsic value and inherent need. Superimposed upon one's true-to-self values are the values acquired from other significant people by introjection. This is conducive to inner conflict and psychosocial disorders. Value systems are as individual and varied as are personality patterns. Personality traits are goal-value oriented, and the conferred value of the goal is a personal variable. A reliable and effectual value system is one in which these relative values are organized into a hierarchy with a more or less fixed relation to certain universal values. Until psychology can produce definitive descriptions and objective validation of universal values, as suggested by Maslow and Hobbs, we look to religious experience and rational philosophy for their validity.

Conscience is seen as a derivation of evaluative cognition and thus inherent. It is evaluative self-awareness carrying the affect tone of guilt if negative or happiness (joy or general well-being) if positive. In operation it is greatly modified by family and community introjected values, e.g., the Freudian superego. Normal guilt is essential to motivation and growth. Pathological guilt requires psychotherapy and the reorganization of the value system.

GLOSSARY

Cognitive dissonance. Dissonance originally meant a discordant mingling of sounds, clashing tones that are disharmonious. Psychologists apply the term to other sensations than sound and more specifically to the mental processes involved in gaining knowledge, becoming aware, i.e., cognition. Thus cognitive dissonance is a discordant, disharmonious and incongruent group of perceptions involved in the broader process of cognition. As commonly used, it is the existing mental state when new perceptions are incongruous with old assumptions.

Idiographic. The mode of personality study that emphasizes the unique aspects of the individual as contrasted with emphasis on common traits and statistical norms.

Introjection. The incorporation of values of another person or group into one's own value system (ego structure as some use this term), usually as a part of the process of identifying with them and not generally a conscious deliberate imitation.

Operational. Pertaining to action. To avoid a common confusion of defining abstractions in terms of other abstractions with no concrete referents, psychologists try to define or describe concepts in terms of the actions they encompass.

Organicism. The theory that living processes derive from all the organs of the body (organism) acting as a whole—an integrated system.

Solipsist(ism). Holding that the self is the only truly existent thing and that all reality is subjective.

Telism. A term derived from teleology which Dr. Sinnott used to designate a philosophy of goals—to account for purposiveness in life.

Vitalism. The philosophical doctrine, popularized by Bergson, that life and its phenomena spring from a hypothetical vital force.

REFERENCES AND SUGGESTED READINGS

ALLPORT, G. W., PHILIP VERNON and GARDNER LINDZEY, *Study of Values,* Boston: Houghton Mifflin Company, 1951, 1960.

———, *Becoming,* New Haven: Yale University Press, 1955.

BERTOCCI, PETER A. and RICHARD M. MILLARD, *Personality and the Good,* New York: David McKay Co., Inc., 1963.

CARUSO, IGOR, *Existential Psychology,* New York: Herder and Herder, Inc., 1964.

COLEMAN, JAMES C., *Personality Dynamics and Effective Behavior,* Chicago: Scott, Foresman & Company, 1960.

FRANKL, VIKTOR, *Man's Search for Meaning,* Boston: Beacon Press, 1962.

———, *The Doctor and The Soul,* New York: Alfred A. Knopf, Inc., 1955.

FROMM, ERICH, *Man for Himself,* New York: Holt, Rinehart and Winston, 1947.

HARTSHORN, HUGH and M. A. MAY, *Studies in Deceit,* New York: The Macmillan Company, 1928.

HOBBS, NICHOLAS, "Science and Ethical Behavior," *The American Psychologist.* May 1959, 14, No. 5, 217–225.

MASLOW, A., *Toward a Psychology of Being,* New York: D. Van Nostrand Co., Inc., 1962.

MOWRER, O. H., *The Crisis in Psychiatry and Religion,* Princeton, New Jersey: D. Van Nostrand Co., Inc., 1961.

OTTO, HERBERT A. (ed), *Explorations in Human Potentialities,* Springfield, Ill.: Charles C. Thomas, Publisher, 1966. (Chapter 6 by Ija Korner).

ROBERTS, GUY L., *Where Delinquency Begins,* Richmond: John Knox Press, 1958.

SINNOTT, EDMUND, *Biology of the Spirit,* New York: The Viking Press, 1955.

WOLFF, HAROLD G., "A Scientific Report on What Hope Does for Man," *Saturday Review.* (1957), 11:44–45.

6 | The Satisfying and Frustrating Environment

There is much truth in the adage, "Personality does not grow in a social vacuum." Tarzan is a noble fiction character, but he is *fiction*. Society is the mother of the individual personality as truly as the individual woman is the biological mother of her child. The quality of the social culture, the character of the interpersonal and person-group relationships determine the quality of the growing personality. However, biological fathers are a necessary part of the reproduction process, and there is a father factor involved in the birth and growth of personality. We may identify this with the inherent self, the behaver.

SOCIETY SUPPLIES AND DENIES

Adjustment and self-development begin when the neonate makes his advent into the world of society—from the pleasant, sheltered, homeostatic position in the womb—as both actor and reactor. His first experience is *frustration*. He needs oxygen; his lungs do not work; he squirms and wiggles; the doctor (society) administers the proverbial smack on the buttocks; shock therapy is effective; the infant inhales; then yells. Within one minute from birth he has experienced need and frustration and has acted and reacted; he has suffered pain. He has experienced, nonconceptually, two new capacities—freedom of movement and the ability to make a noise. So it goes through life. Whether society continues to cooperate by supplying basic needs and opportunities to develop innate capacities or whether it withholds these in too great frustration sets the pattern and direction of personality growth.

Maslow (1962, Chapter 4) describes the environmental conditions that are conducive for spontaneous, expressive, growth-oriented behavior, which will keep the child reaching out to the environment in wonder and interest, not crippled by fear but feeling safe and accepted, experiencing delight "fortuitously encountered" or "offered to him by helpers," going on to more complex, richer experiences and accomplishments that give him feelings of capability, mastery, self-trust, and self-esteem. It is society that provides all the child's safety needs and permits him to retain the subjective experiences of delight and boredom as *the* criteria of the correct choice for him.

> In this process the environment (parents, therapists, teachers) is important in various ways, even though the ultimate choice must be made by the child:
>
> a. it can gratify his basic needs for safety, belongingness, love and respect, so that he can feel unthreatened, autonomous, interested and spontaneous and thus dare to choose the unknown;
>
> b. it can help by making the growth choice positively attractive and less dangerous, and by making the regressive choice less attractive and more costly. (p. 56).

ENVIRONMENTAL DEPRIVATION

In direct contrast to this is the frustrating environment that stifles spontaneity and creativeness and orients the person toward deficiency-concern, defensiveness, dependency and security.

Sensory Deprivation Research has clearly indicated the disorganizing effects on the personality and mental processes when the experimental subjects were cut off from minimum stimulation needs. The child who lives in a home and community that provide a wide variety of enriched stimulus situations is in a situation which is conducive to his growth, productivity and self-actualization. The home and community that are deficient in cultural stimulation are a depriving and frustrating environment inimical to growth and fulfillment. The main part of this chapter will be devoted to these positive and negative influences and relationships. But, first, let us examine the general nature and immediate effects of frustration.

WHAT IS FRUSTRATION?

CRITERIA

Schneiders (1965) presents three criteria of an acceptable definition: "First of all, frustration applies to the blocking or hindrance of behavior as well as motivation or mental activity. . . . Second, an acceptable definition of frustration should be predicated on a clear distinction between subjective and objective frustration. . . . Third, it is important to note that the character of frustration and its subsequent effects on adjustment vary considerably with the kind of motivation or response involved and with the psychological context in which it occurs. . . . In the light of these considerations, and for the special purpose of adjustment psychology, frustration may be defined as the subjective reaction to the blocking or hindrance of significant behavior or motivation that leads to interference with adequate and effective adjustment." (p. 178).

The term, as currently used, incorporates the above definition. Schneider's definition is quite satisfactory in its context from the adjustment psychology point of view. The psychologist concerned with growth, creative production, and self-actualization would find it deficient, for these involve behavior and a type of motivation different from merely the adjustive.

Instead of criteria let us look at a number of factors that are to be considered before attempting to give a definition or concise description of frustration. First, there is need or desire, behavior directed toward a value-goal. Second, the behavior is blocked or impeded, thwarted. Third, this impediment or thwarting factor may be something in the external environment or a condition within the individual. Fourth, it may be an obstacle that exists as an opposition or it may be a deficiency. Fifth, there is an inner emotional (affective) state. There is little disagreement relative to the first, third, and fourth of these factors. Some, however, think of frustration more in terms of the situation that blocks behavior and arouses the accompanying emotions. Others refer to this as the *thwarting* situation and use *frustration* to connote the inner state—feeling frustrated.

THE DEFINITION

My approach is from the self—myself, yourself; the I, the you, the acting, experiencing subject. The self is aroused to experience need and to initiate action toward a desired goal determined by self's evaluation. Self experiences a barrier which is thwarting. And self experiences a conscious state or affect that may be termed annoyance, anger, or fear (anxiety), depending on the nature and meaning of the need-value. Therefore it is need or self-in-need that is frustrated, and the frustration experience may involve all five of the above factors. I would define frustration as *any combination of factors in the outer environment or physical and mental structure of the person that tend to thwart him in achieving either his maintenance (security) need-goals or growth and self-actualization and which is experienced as annoyance, anger or fear.* It involves both the situation that is experienced and the quality of the experience. One does not exist without the other.

STRESS FACTOR

There is stress, since need is thwarted and value-goal resisted. The strength of the need-drive and the stress depends on the attributed value, plus the strength of the thwarting factors. This, in turn, determines the intensity of consciousness and the affect tone. If a sudden, unexpected snow storm becomes an impediment to attending a political rally that one did not value very highly, one does not experience much stress nor will he expend much effort to get there; and the affect tone will be no more than a mild annoyance. But if this same storm came at a time when his wife had just burned herself very badly and perhaps her life depended on reaching the hospital very soon, the thwarting storm would be met with great stress, effort to overcome, and emotional tones of mingled anger and fear. The situation would be threatening.

In mild frustration, the thwarting of lesser need-satisfaction, the affect tone is *annoyance*. In greater frustration, the thwarting of basic needs, the normal affect is *anger*. One's basic rights are blocked and he resents it hotly when he judges the situation as surmountable. But if much is at stake, frustration is prolonged, and he feels unable to surmount it, then it becomes a threat and *fear* is the normal affect. The manner in which a person handles his frustration—the hostility and anxiety he engenders—becomes a major factor in mental health. The stronger the self, the greater is one's frustration tolerance and the greater the stress he can take without succumbing to excess hostility or fear.

FRUSTRATION TOLERANCE

The amount of frustration (stress) tolerance varies greatly among individuals. It may be partly due to genetic differences in temperament, but is generally conceded to depend mostly on childhood conditioning. The home and community climate that is conducive to full growth, autonomy, and maturity of selfhood, "ego-strength," produces an individual with high stress tolerance. He can work under prolonged pressure, take ordinary thwartings, and face the problems of life as challenges instead of threats. Only the big frustrations and threats arouse him to anger and fear, and these do not occur frequently. The child who is reared in a climate of neglect, distrust, and deprivation of basic needs remains insecure, dependent, distrusting and suspicious, and so marginally adjusted he gives way under the ordinary or slightly extraordinary stresses of life. This difference was clearly revealed under war conditions. The most stable character structure would finally give way to week after week of constant physical stress, inadequate sleep, and ceaseless danger. Battle fatigue and battle neurosis would finally develop. In far too many cases the "crack-up" came early in combat experience or even before going into combat. Therefore, we approach the stress problem in mental hygiene from the basis of the strength of the person and the severity of the stress. Coleman (1960, p. 163) summarizes the latter, as it is experienced:

1. The longer the stress situation continues.
2. The more important the need being frustrated or the more difficult the demands of a situation.
3. The larger the number of frustrations or pressures.
4. The stronger the opposing forces in a conflict and the more equal they are in strength.
5. The closer one gets to a goal in an approach-avoidance conflict and the greater the relative strength of the avoidance gradient.
6. The more unfamiliar and unexpected the problem.
7. The less competent one feels (rightly or wrongly) to cope with the stress situation.
8. The more threatening and ego-involving the problem seems to the individual.
9. The less tolerance the individual has for the problems of a given magnitude or type.

CONFLICT AND AGGRESSION

Closely associated with frustration are the experiences of conflict and aggression. The frustrated person tends to act aggressively to eliminate or surmount the thwarting forces. Whether the aggression is hostile or friendly (motivated by ill-will or good-will) depends on how self evaluates the situation. For example, at a football game, the ball-carrier charges the line with all the aggressive energy he can muster, but is either thrown back for a loss or makes a very slight gain. The situation is frustrating. That desired goal-line is not being reached. But there is little or no hostility or anger, no desire to hurt the opponent, but a friendly aggressiveness directed at overcoming the thwarting opposition. The pattern of values associated with the game—good sportsmanship and the rules of the game—keeps aggressive conflict on a friendly basis.

Then an opposing player breaks a rule, displaying poor sportsmanship, and attempts to injure the ball-carrier after he is tackled. The behavior is immediately evaluated as unjust, wrong, and hostility is aroused. The same ball-carrier may be hit just as hard and shaken as badly by two different tacklers, but whether he comes up with a smile and "good work, pal!" or with blazing eyes and profane words depends on his evaluation of the tactics. In other words, conflict and aggression go with frustration, and whether it is friendly or hostile has a direct relationship with mental and social health.

CONFLICT AND VALUES

When the frustration is bound up within the person himself—one need or desire (valued goal) thwarting another—he experiences inner conflict. Also, as in the previous example, whether he can laugh off the conflict with a true sense of humor and keep the self-directed aggression friendly, or whether there is self-directed hostility, depends on his value system—how he evaluates himself, the opposing goals, and the relationship of these to himself. A teenage boy may be in a quandary over a choice between two girls he would like to date on a certain occasion. He might think that either would accept, but he can not decide which he would prefer. He evaluates them equally as date-partners, but he can not have both for the same evening. After a reasonable amount of aggressive mental conflict, one boy may toss a coin and laugh it off. Another may become impotent with self-directed rage. Mental-social health is involved in the latter.

This type of conflict is known as *approach-approach* conflict where equal positive value is ascribed to both goals. A similar experience of inner conflict occurs when two situations are given about equal negative value. The person involved would like to avoid both, but he can not. He must choose. He is a good baseball player and a good musician. He does not care for baseball and wishes to avoid a place on the team, fearing a hand injury that would interfere with a musical career. His school mates place a high value on baseball and insist that he play, accusing him of being disloyal if he does not. He wishes to avoid their enmity and rejection. The need to avoid physical injury and social injury are in conflict—*avoidance-avoidance* conflict. The above situation may also be used to illustrate the third type, *approach-avoidance* conflict. This student may evaluate baseball highly and want to play, but he also judges it as being dangerous, since it would perhaps result in broken fingers which would ruin his musical career, and this he wishes (needs) to avoid. The same situation may be evaluated both positively and negatively.

Every person has experienced these dilemmas. If too frequently, it indicates an inadequate and immature value system. A practical, realistic hierarchical arrangement has not become established. If self is weak, the vacillation and inner conflict is great; and hostility is usually directed against the self or projected to others. Children are immature and have not developed adequate value systems. They are more apt to have such conflict and need help from their environment in dealing with it.

Frustration is a field that has been researched extensively with many experimental studies reported. Both animals and humans are used as experimental subjects, and many thwarting devices are employed. Food may be taken from a hungry animal or baby soon after it starts eating. Under painful stimulus the animal may have to make too fine a discrimination or solve too complex a problem in order to escape. Students may be given problems that are too complex, may have their scores falsified, or may be annoyed or harshly condemned for minor failures. Or, as in Masserman's work with cats and monkeys, a noxious element was associated with the food reward to produce severe approach-avoidance conflict. His cats received an electric shock or blast of air when they were about to take the food after learning to operate the mechanism that made it available. His monkeys found a small toy snake in their food box.

A student may wish to report on three or four studies of the above type. See (1) Masserman, J. H., *Behavior and Neurosis,* 1943; (2) Marquis, D. R., "A Study of Frustration in New Born Infants," *J. Exp. Psychol.,* 1943, **32,** 123–138; (3) Sears, R. R., "Initiation of the Repression Sequence by Experienced Failure," *J. Exp. Psychol.,* 1937, **26,** 570–580; (4) Adams, C. R., "Individual Differences in Behavior Resulting from Experimentally Induced Frustration." *J. Psychol.,* 1940, **10,** 157–176; (5) Zander, A. F., "A Study of Experimental Frustration." *Psychol. Monogr.,* 1944, **56,** No. 256. Many others are available.

THE HOME ENVIRONMENT

A child is born into a family. It is my point of view that this human neonate is born a subject-self with object-body and the mental potential for growth-guidance and self-actualization. I have briefly described the neonate's active-reactive behavior in gratifying his first need, oxygen.

Within two or three hours this young self experiences hunger, the need for nourishment. It is an unconscious, nonconceptual cognitive evaluation of the bodily stimuli, but self is aroused and goes into action with sucking mouth movements, random bodily movements, and sounds. The food is not offered immediately. The infant suffers some frustration and stress; he strives, and the sounds take on a tone of distress. Mother provides the food. He learns how to act to control a part of his environment by his striving.

MATERNAL NEED

And mother supplies his other needs. Her soft voice, softer breast and caressing hands provide sound and tactile stimuli that are needed. Soon the touch and the sound become more than sensory stimuli and are experienced as acceptance and love, providing a sense of security and worth. Bright pictures and toys are given to him that stimulate discriminatory responses, growth in perception, and satisfaction. He is played with, talked and sung to, and read to. While some frustration is permitted, and necessary, his basic maintenance-security needs are provided for and given satisfaction. He feels secure and competent; self grows strong, the self-image (personality-image) becomes positive. He has little fear and much faith; little hostility and much freedom to love. He can move toward autonomy, growth-motivation, creative productivity, fulfillment. This is the growth-conducing home environment. It is the family that supplies comfort, pleasure, faith and love; and it supplies a wealth of enriching stimuli and challenge during early childhood.

In a summary statement Harry and Margaret Harlow say:[1]

[1] Harry F. and Margaret K. Harlow, "The Effects of Rearing Conditions on Behavior," *Bulletin of the Menninger Clinic,* 1962 26, 213–224. Reprinted in the *International Journal of Psychiatry,* Vol. No. 1, pp. 43–50 (January 1965). Used with permission.

"Infant rhesus monkeys have been reared, starting on the first day of life, in a variety of situations: partial isolation, either in individual bare wire cages in a colony room for two years or longer, or in individual wire cages with access to one or two mother surrogates for at least the first six months; and in situations with real or surrogate mothers for at least the first six months; and in situations with real or surrogate mothers plus contact with other infants for the first year or two of life.

Total isolation for two years resulted in failure to display social or sexual behavior in the next two years, spent in a joint living cage. Results on six months of such isolation are still being gathered and suggest severe, but not complete, social deficits. Only mild effects have been observed thus far in monkeys isolated through the first 80 days of life. . . ."

> A student report on Harlow's classic experiments with baby monkeys would be appropriate at this point. See *Amer. Psychol.* 13:675–685, 1958, Dyal, 1962, Ch. 4, or any of several other sources.

FRUSTRATING FAMILIES

Not all children are so fortunate as to have a home environment conducive to growth. Statistical reports from several child welfare agencies indicate that at mid-century more than 2 million children under 18 were living with neither parent and nearly 4 million with only one parent, their families broken by death, divorce, or desertion. In many public school rooms more than half of the children report only one parent or a step parent. Added to this are the several million mothers of young children who from necessity or a distorted sense of value are employed outside the home for too many hours to give their children the necessary care. Often it is the fatherless home where the mother must spend so much time away from the home, leaving the children virtually parentless. We also have other millions of children in poverty homes, in the slums or on the ever-moving trucks of migrant workers. In all these we find the frustrating family environments.

For a balanced view, perhaps, it should be noted that while the above conditions are real and create real problems, a moderate amount of frustration is unavoidable and helpful for growth and that only a minority of children are seriously affected by mothers employed outside the home. Also, the quality of the mother-child relationship is the important factor, not the number of hours they spend together.

DENIAL OF LOVE

The greatest frustration, it seems, is to be deprived of adequate love in early childhood. The divorced or widowed mother, who must engage in full-time outside employment and then return home for several hours of house work, does not have the time to express adequate love and share enough of herself with her children, no matter how devoted she may be. The frustrated, deprived child is angry but can not express it directly; it becomes displaced, turned against the community in delinquency or against the self in neurosis. The prolonged frustration becomes a threat to the child's security with the resulting anxiety.

But it is not only the broken home that is frustrating in this respect. Both parents may be living together but without togetherness. They may not be mature enough for the responsibilities of marriage, may be ill-matched, and may be so involved with their own ego problems, defenses, and spouse conflicts they can not express an adequate love for their children. I recently was involved with such a mother in conversation. She was bemoaning her teenage daughter's delinquent behavior. "I can't understand how Julie could have done such things. I gave her everything she ever asked for." Subconsciously, the mother sensed that *things* were a substitute for the true *affection* she was unable to give. The daughter was not mistaken. She was deprived of adequate love, and experienced prolonged frustration that posed a constant threat. She took *things* and *sex* as substitutes for the love that she was denied. The cases of Susan and Jennie in Chapter 1 may be reread as illustrations of the effects of frustrating family conditions. These are the severely deprived. Most children are tough enough to withstand a moderate amount.

Young children totally deprived of love may actually die. This occurred frequently earlier in this century before medical science had discovered the close correlation between love and health. Babies, less than a year of age, confined in hospitals for several weeks with little or no mother visitation, slowly withered away and died while receiving what appeared to be completely adequate medical and dietary care. The doctors soon learned that these babies were dying from love starvation. Then they prescribed TLC (tender loving care). Nurses were instructed to serve as surrogate mothers, and the natural mothers, if available, were encouraged to spend as much time as possible with their infants while in the hospital.

PERMANENT INJURY

Serious and prolonged love deprivation, as in the older type foundling homes, frequently resulted in a condition often termed infantile autism. This is a condition of extreme self-centeredness and often with seriously depressed mental functioning. Other investigators question the relevancy of "autism" as a descriptive term for these effects but generally agree on the depressing and stunting effects of such deprivation. Many studies have been made of institutionalized children (at an early age) who were thus deprived of adequate love. (See Goldfarb, 1945; Spitz, 1949 or any good textbook in child psychology for additional information.) Kaplan[2] summarized several of these.

> The Goldfarb study throws some light on what to expect in later years from children who survive the effects of emotional impoverishment in infancy. This investigator followed two groups of children through their early school years and in some cases through adolescence. One group had been in an orphanage from the earliest months of life to about the age of three years, at which time they were transferred to foster homes. The other group, used as a control, consisted of children who had been brought up in foster homes from the beginning.
>
> The orphanage children had the best of physical care but no opportunity to relate themselves to anyone who would give them warm physical affection. They were cared for by a succession of nurses who had little time for emotional comforting.

[2] From Louis Kaplan, *Mental Health and Human Relations in Education* Copyright © 1959 by Louis Kaplan. Reprinted by permission of Harper & Row, Publishers.

The children in foster homes had adequate psychological satisfactions in a loving environment. They developed more or less normally. The orphanage children, however, showed distinct symptoms of personality difficulties, prominent among which were these:

1. They were unmanageable and unresponsive to normal motivation. They would wander off aimlessly from the school grounds and come home hours later than expected. This behavior persisted despite the warnings and punishments administered by the foster parents.
2. They had a history of extremely difficult behavior. In school they disregarded rules, accepted academic failure in a complacent manner; they were destructive, stubborn, given to severe temper outbursts, provoked fights frequently, and could not get along with other children.
3. Although these children had an insatiable appetite for love they did not know how to accept it. They were emotionally isolated and cold toward people, even those who tried to be affectionate toward them.

In general, Goldfarb concluded, these children even through adolescence showed characteristics similar in many respects to the personality structure found in children who had sustained severe head injuries early in life. They presented a picture of warped personalities who viewed the world as a cold hostile place, who could form no genuine attachments to people, and who displayed retaliatory, aggressive behavior. (pp. 118–122).

Experimental psychologists find much to criticize in most studies of deprivation (both general stimulus and mothering) based largely on a lack of control over stimulus factors, too little account of the time factor or periodicity, sometimes a naive concept of physiology, and generally deducing too much from their data. Therefore, a considerable amount of doubt has been cast on the validity of these studies. Stone discusses these criticisms in some detail, admits their scientific defects, but sees in much of this criticism an example of "throwing out the baby with the bath water." He says:[3]

---

[3] From L. Joseph Stone, "A Critique of Studies of Child Isolation," *Child Development*, 1954, *25*, 9–20. Used with permission.

> Admittedly, a major flaw in the work of what one may allude to as the "psychodynamic wing" of child psychology has been the paucity of experimental evidence, the argument from clinical instances, and the great willingness of its proponents, nonetheless, to offer suggestions regarding the desirable emotional climate for child care. Actually the basis for such advice has, I think, been sounder than its critics recognize. For one thing, this is primarily a medically or psychiatrically or clinically oriented group, and it has been less concerned with marshalling and citing the evidence that a well-trained psychologist can bear. . . .
>
> What is clear, then, is that our experimental task is to address ourselves to detailing and specifying precisely what is *adequate social stimulation* and in what respects it is adequate. Spitz, for one, has made a beginning at partialing out the time factor to show that neglect is most dangerous in the last quarter of the first year. . . .

THE CHILD-PARENT RELATIONSHIP

Parents who are mature, free of defensiveness and are able to express affection richly with understanding and confidence, generally will develop the quality of relationships with their children that conduces autonomy, growth, and full self-realization. Those who fail seriously in providing this climate of confidence, mutual understanding, and warm emotional support create a frustrating relationship that engenders hostility, anxiety, and defensiveness which inhibit growth and fulfillment. The files of every child guidance clinic are filled with case reports of children with records of school failure, speech defects, truancy, stealing, property damage, sexual delinquencies and various neurotic symptoms that spring from unwholesome, dissatisfying child-parent relationships.

Rejection. The institutional studies cited above reveal the crippling effect of parent-deprivation (rejection), but a child may experience rejection when living with his parents. All interpersonal relationships are complex, and motives or attitudes are mixed. The parent's attitude toward the child may be characterized by the approach-avoidance type of conflict; thus the behavior is contradictory and confusing, with rejection accompanied by over-protection or indulgence, or alternating between domination and compliance. The attitude may also be one of extreme unconcern, with harsh punishment or abandonment. Whatever form it takes, children are highly perceptive and suffer the ill effects of frustrated love-need. While rejection and love-deprivation are not necessarily synonymous, the child who "feels" rejected usually experiences it as love deficiency. Rejection in the home is rarely so complete as to cause the child to die, as in the hospital cases, but is frequently a root cause of delinquency, general social maladjustment, neurosis, and in the more serious cases, autism and psychosis.

The weak child (poorly developed self) tends to experience rejection as a threat, is dominated by anxiety, becomes submissive and is often withdrawn or overly attentive in trying to garner a crumb of affection. Rejection is stifling to growth and may lead to serious mental illness. Such a child represses the hostility which the frustrated need would normally arouse by means of the greater anxiety that is experienced. He turns the hostility against himself and becomes mentally ill. The stronger child (self) is more prone to experience the frustration of rejection as a wrong, an injustice, the denial of a basic right; and thus the feeling of resentment will remain dominant. This type more often becomes the bully, the delinquent, the social rebel. His hostility is expressed outwardly, not against himself, but displaced to others. No two develop identical patterns of response. The degree of rejection, how early it is experienced; how prolonged it is; the inherent temperament of the child, and a host of intervening factors alter the outcome. It is always frustrating; it hurts and inevitably hinders psychosocial development.

Overprotection. On the part of the parent, overprotection may reflect a subconscious compensation for rejection, or it may be an expression of true love and concern but deficient in faith or trust—the inadequate love of an immature parent who lacks self-confidence and the courage of responsible parenthood and who may possess a strong sentimental trait or a compulsive need to dominate as a compensatory defense against feelings of inadequacy. Such a parent is overly solicitous, sees danger too often, tries to protect against imaginary harm, urges too many precautions, and displays many other modes of distrust. This creates exaggerated anxiety in the child; tends toward an "inferiority complex," prevents normal social maturation and thus impedes growth toward creative productivity and self-actualization. Te be trusted is an essential part of being accepted and loved. Therefore, a basic need is thwarted and frustration is experienced. Not being trusted, the child doesn't trust himself. He feels, vaguely perceives, that something is basically wrong with him or he would be trusted more. He feels unworthy, weak, is generally docile and subservient. Since he is weak, the normal feelings of hostility that accompany frustration are blocked from expression by the greater anxiety. He is generally ineffectual, does not give adequate development to and expression of his potentiality.

Some are not as weak if the overprotection did not begin quite as soon in life or if it were accompanied by other factors. The child may then revolt against it, usually by some rash, overcompensatory behavior. The hostility toward the frustrating parent partly breaks through and is expressed indirectly (displaced). Earl typifies such a child. I met him in a school for delinquent boys.

Earl's father died when he was at the age when a boy turns from his mother to establish a closer identification with his father. They were an average middle class family and he was an only child. The mother returned to live with her parents so that they could take care of Earl while she was at work. Her unmarried sister, a teacher, also lived with her parents. After three years passed, Earl's grandfather died, and Earl was left to the care of three overly-protective women. He became the "Little Lord Fauntleroy" of the community. When the neighborhood boys were playing football on the vacant lot, Earl had to practice his music. When the other boys went swimming in the creek by the railroad, he had to stay home, and make excuses. The boys gave him a rough time. Added to the frustration of not being trusted (truly accepted) by his family was that of not being accepted by his peers.

The whole neighborhood was shocked when the police discovered that it was Earl who, with another boy, broke into the neighborhood store and ransacked the place. "Not Earl! It just couldn't be, such nice people." The judge placed Earl on probation. He was watched over even more closely. Within less than a year it happened again. This time, he broke into a building with a younger boy, and lit a fire inside the building. He really did not intend to burn the building down; he just started a fire in the waste paper basket to impress his younger companion. But he could not extinguish the blaze, and by the time the firemen did, the damage was about $75,000. This time Earl was sent away, a 14-year-old delinquent chiefly as a result of overprotection.[4] (pp. 36, 37).

Domination and Overindulgence. The overly protective parent may be either dominating or overindulgent. The effects on the child of the openly dominating parent is much as described above. Sometimes a new element of frustration is added when the dominating parent is pushing the child toward an achievement level beyond his natural capacity or toward a career for which he has no inclination. It may be that the frustrated parent is seeking vicarious satisfaction through the child's achievement. The sweetly dominating, "dear mom" type is usually more crippling than the parent who is overtly domineering. In the latter case, the child is freer to admit to himself his resentment and, if or when strong enough, express the hostility. The former, however, is hard to resist. At the first signs of resistance, she assumes the martyr role. "My whole life is devoted to you. I make every sacrifice for your good. It will break my heart if . . ." So it goes; and rising rebellion is smothered by guilt feelings. Mom wins and rules.

Overindulgence, which is often associated with being overly permissive, reflects the same lack of confidence in the child and prevents the growth of self-confidence. It also reflects a weakness and irresponsibility on the part of the parent, an assuaging of guilt from lack of realistic love. The child is doubly frustrated in not being trusted and in not getting the guidance and protection his security demands or given the responsibility his growth demands. "If they loved me, they would give me more guidance and make me do what is best for me," the child feels without clear conceptualization. He grows up with little true self-confidence, is undisciplined, socially maladjusted and spoiled.

---

[4] From *Where Delinquency Begins*, Guy L. Roberts, Richmond: John Knox Press, 1958. Used with permission.

DISCIPLINE

Child-parent relations come to a focus on the problem of discipline, a parental control system designed, supposedly, for the welfare of the child. The question becomes: Is it satisfying or frustrating? With the increase in juvenile delinquency, it has become a topic of much discussion, although it was never a neglected one. Many are calling for a return to the "old fashioned" firmness and the return of father as "head of the house." One commentator suggested that the increase in delinquency was due chiefly to the invention of the safety razor and electric shaver, and that a father can not raise a boy without a razor strap.

Psychologists of the past generation have been accused of over-emphasizing freedom from restraint and permissiveness, thus creating in parents a fear of responsibility, a fear that they might frustrate, inhibit, cause "a complex." It took only one generation to reveal that too much permissiveness and freedom are frustrating and anxiety-producing. Children are immature and insecure. They need psychological and social protection as well as physical protection, and they realize this even when fighting for freedom. They need direction towards healthy behavior from their parents. If it is not provided, the children become frustrated.

It has been said that all-out permissiveness is not discipline; too much is poor discipline. But what about the opposite: harsh discipline? Many studies have been made of physical punishment as a means of controlling behavior (Hollenberg and Sperry, 1950; Sears et al, 1957). The general conclusion is that it serves only to inhibit undesired responses (often temporarily) but does not contribute to the formation of desired traits. In fact, it may hinder this in that it is hostility-producing with a tendency to set the child in opposition to the goals of the punisher. The weak child tends to become fear-ridden, cowed, subservient, with repressed hostility, and is afraid to take responsibility or show initiative. The child who is a little stronger may alternate between this type of behavior and temper tantrums, as well as extreme stubbornness. The still stronger child tends to nurse his hostility and displace it outwardly on society whenever the occasions arise.

DISPLACED HOSTILITY

Bob was a good-looking, medium-sized, but muscular Negro boy, surly and noncommunicative until rapport was established. His father had a good position and provided adequately for the family's material needs. He was an active churchman as well as a stern disciplinarian. He beat Bob frequently and harshly, and Bob beat up the neighbor children and was frequently "in trouble at school." Bob was compelled to attend church regularly until in his early teens when he refused and punishment was to no avail. He broke several windows in a neighbor's home out of revenge, since the boy there had previously played a trick on him. Then he ran away, but was picked up by the police three days later. He was placed on probation under his father's custody and was again severely beaten. Three months later he was accused of sexual improprieties with a girl and writing an obscene note to a teacher. The latter he denied; and he claimed that the girl "was willing." He was committed to a correctional institution, a tough and embittered boy. His fighting, destruction of property, and sex aggression were expressions of displaced hostility. (Roberts, 1958, pp. 17–20 condensed).

How much hostility is engendered by harsh physical punishment and how harmful the effect depends largely on the child's awareness of the parent's motives; whether he perceives rejection, an irrational sadism, or merely a misplaced and unreasonable but true concern. How seriously crippling the effect is, whether it tends to cause delinquency or the other character disorders described in Chapter 9, or any of a variety of neurotic or psychotic syndromes, depends on a variety of additional factors. Some of these factors are: the age of the child, how much rejection is perceived in it by the child, genetic temperamental traits, the supply or lack of other-than-parental supports, etc. Delinquency has been mentioned several times as a common manifestation of the effects of inadequate child-parent relations, but any variety of psychosocial disorder may spring partly from this. The delinquent population includes a variety of persons with neuroses and other psychosocial disorders. The majority of children will withstand faulty discipline and much love deficiency, permit their wounds to heal, and become normal, useful citizens.

Inconsistency. Erratic and inconsistent discipline perhaps does the most harm, especially with younger children. It is essential to the security of a child that he know what to expect of his parents. For a child to be laughed at or bragged about for something "cute" on one occasion, then later to be punished severely for virtually the same thing is very confusing to a child. If this is extensive, it produces hostility and anxiety. Usually, such parents have a very inadequate value system and tend to frustrate the child's efforts to arrive at a reliable set of value-guides.

RESEARCH REPORTS

Child psychologists, Mussen, Conger and Kagan, relate the following about frustrating child-parent relations:[5]

Maternal acceptance is a necessary prerequisite for the effective socialization of the child. Lack of acceptance frustrates the child's needs for love and increases his resistance to adopting the rules of the society in which he lives. Thus, one of the most frequent consequences of maternal rejection is a pattern of aggressive and social behavior.

Symonds compared the personality characteristics and social adjustment of 31 rejected and 31 accepted children. . . . The two groups were carefully matched in sex, age, school grade, socio-economic background, and intellectual level. . . .

Children in the accepted group showed more socially acceptable behavior and appeared more cooperative, friendly, honest, emotionally stable, deliberate, and cheerful. Children in the rejected group, on the other hand, were more often rated as emotionally unstable, restless, overactive, and given to attention-getting behavior. In general, they were more resentful of authority, including their parents, and more rebellious against society's rules and regulations. They manifested pronounced delinquent trends, frequent lying, truanting, running away from home, stealing and quarrelling. (p. 393).

It may be inferred that in unhappy, tense homes characterized by marital discord, children endure many upsets and frus-

[5] Condensation of pp. 393–399 and p. 216 of *Child Development and Personality* by H.M. Mussen, J.J. Conger and J. Kagan. Copyright © 1956 by Harper & Row, Publishers Incorporated. Used with permission.

trations, but few satisfying experiences. In many cases, their needs are probably satisfied only through such extreme behavior as violent aggression, complete submission, or neurotic symptoms. Under the circumstances, immature, socially maladaptive behavior is directly rewarded and learned. Also, insofar as these children identify with their parents, they probably adopt some of these adults' maladaptive and socially inadequate behavior. . . . (p. 397).

A second class of maternal behavior, which is relatively independent of maternal acceptance, involves the degree of restrictiveness and control the mother imposes upon her child's behavior. An overly restrictive mother frustrates her child's desire for autonomous action and, for that reason, is apt to generate hostility in her child. Second, curbing the child's freedom may lead him to develop feelings of inadequacy. . . . Excessive restriction might be expected to lead to timidity and shyness in the child. (p. 398).

Using techniques similar to those employed in his study of acceptance and rejection, Symonds (1939) compared the consequences of parental domination or submission upon children's personality structures. The children of "dominating parents" tended to be polite, inhibited, careful, dependable, but submissive, docile, shy, and self-conscious. As might be anticipated, they had greater difficulty in self-expression, and suffered more from feelings of inferiority, insecurity, and bewilderment than children who had more freedom.

Children of "submissive parents," on the other hand, were rated as more disobedient, irresponsible, stubborn, rebellious against authority, and antagonistic; however, they were seen as self-confident and spontaneous in forming friendships outside the family. . . . (p. 399).

FIRM BUT FAIR

I have summarized my views on discipline and child-parent relationship in a previous publication (Roberts, 1958, pp. 40, 41):

> We parents need not know all the answers pertaining to our children and their problems. If that were necessary, we would all be in despair. These youngsters of ours are resilient and can take a lot of our imperfections. . . .

There is an old adage that has a lot of truth in it—allowing for oversimplification, of course; "Give them plenty of food and plenty of love and don't worry. . . ." And we can give them love. If we are at all mature in our own emotional responses, we can keep our anxieties and our marital conflicts under moderate control so that love, confidence, and optimism are the prevailing moods.

Love means discipline—firmness as well as tenderness. Extreme laxness and apparent indifference to conduct make for insecurity and lack of confidence and self-control on the part of the child. "Thou shalt" and "Thou shalt not" have a place in the family relationship. There ought to be a few definite "musts" and "must nots" clearly understood by the child, interpreted insofar as possible in terms of his understanding and experience, and enforced kindly but firmly. There are certain moral imperatives that five thousand years of human history have proved valuable. These should be accepted by us parents and lived to the best of our ability, and no doubts should be left in the minds of our children regarding what we expect of them on these points.

But between these pillars of do's and don'ts, there are vast areas of conduct where relativity and change prevail. With justice and mercy, fairness, kindness, and good sportsmanship, our guiding rule, problems in these fields should be worked out on an individual, give-and-take basis.

We can make our kids feel needed and wanted and important in our family organization by giving them specific responsibilities, working with them, and bringing them into the discussion of family problems. . . . This is the democratic family relationship advocated by most authorities on family life.

A class report and discussion on autocratic vs. democratic discipline and child-training might prove interesting at this point. See especially, Fels Research Institute studies; also other references at the end of this chapter.

IDENTIFICATION PROBLEMS

Much more space is required to cover in sufficient detail the beneficial and harmful effects of child-parent or intrafamily relationships—presence or absence of the father, age position of child in the family, sibling rivalry, etc. One of the major ill effects of the frustrating child-parent relationship is the matter of child identifying with parent. The child's identification becomes abnormal if the parents' behavior is extreme. This may be in either the direction of gross subservience with a restrictive, coercive conscience or a negative identification that sets the child against whatever the parent stood for, the good qualities as well as the evil. To play his role effectively in society and in marriage, the child needs to be able to identify satisfactorily with parents who are playing those roles well. It has been pointed out (Chapter 5) how the child's value system and conscience formation are influenced by parental identity. Children are likely to feel insecure and have some difficulty making adequate social adjustments, if they do not have positive identification with the parents.

THE SCHOOL ENVIRONMENT

The first five years of a child's life are the most crucial in the structuring of his personality. These are the pre-school years during which the child's environment consists chiefly of his family. A few near neighbors and more distant (geographic) relatives provide some social stimulation, plus the T.V., but the family is the dominant formative agency during these years, and for several years after. Furthermore, what the family influences have done to the child during these first five years alters greatly his responses to the stimulus situations in the new school environment. The child is subjected to new situations in the school environment and formative forces that have a marked effect on personality development and changes for good or ill.

The school is a social agency. Its primary function is to equip the new generation for effective roles in society. The term *education* is virtually synonymous with *socialization*. Not all of this socializing process is carried on in the classroom. Much of it is on the playground in a variety of peer group activities. In all of these, there may be factors conducive to growth and mental-social health and factors that are frustrating. It may be stated that the influence of the school is second only to the home as a conditioning influence during childhood.

A STRANGE FAMILY

Two new groups of social stimulus objects are thrust upon the child when he begins school: teachers and peers. These become to a large degree parent surrogates and sibling surrogates. It is an enlarged, extended family with different attitudes, expectations, and demands. New patterns of response must be made. The acceptance or rejection and praise or blame the child receives in this new environment may be based on a different value system than he learned at home. There is more and greater competition, and he must now earn praise and acceptance by new and strange performances. Frustration and stress are experienced by all pupils, with much more for some than others.

CLASS DIFFERENCES

The school is a middle class institution built around middle class traditions and values and operated by middle class teachers. Most Americans are middle class. Thus, we should, perhaps, designate the school as middle class. Many studies have been made which indicate clearly that children from middle class, majority culture homes adjust to school more readily, and experience less frustration, than do children from the lower social-economic brackets and ethnic minority groups. Children from the so-called "lower class" families have developed a different value system, especially as reflected in emphasis on "book learning" and certain types of socially approved (school approved) behavior. Child training practices are somewhat different, with larger numbers of parents tending toward the extremes of harsh or permissive discipline and more children bringing with them to school their hostilities, suspicions, and anxieties. These homes also generally offer fewer cultural advantages: books, magazines, travel and exploration, the better types of public entertainment. Thus their children enter school with a poorer foundation. Finally, while authentic information is spotty on this point, it is generally accepted that children from these homes are a little lower in general intelligence.

In sum, then, by motivation, by certain emotional and social behavior patterns, by pre-school educational opportunities, and by intelligence, children from the lower classes are less adequately prepared for entrance to school and thus find it a more frustrating experience. Note: this is a *general tendency*, a matter of statistical norm. The differences are not so very great, and there is wide overlap. Also, these distinctions are lessening as class distinctions grow less marked and as the schools are deliberately striving to accommodate all.

PROBLEMS BROUGHT TO SCHOOL

Children from all social strata bring their physical, mental, and social handicaps, their personality problems, with them into the school environment. Here, they are confronted with different conduct standards and greater performance requirements to receive approval and acceptance. The cruel jibes of thoughtless children, the hostility and anxieties of the less adequate children, tend to increase and patterns of over-compensating aggressiveness or withdrawal already begun are enhanced. The enlarged demands of the environment produce greater thwarting and deeper experiences of frustration. Withdrawal and aggressive tendencies established in the early school years are likely to continue into adulthood as shown by the Fels Research Institute studies (Kagan and Moss, 1962). The better adjusted children will be able to accept these new demands as a challenge and take them in stride.

The teacher has been mentioned as parent surrogate. His (her) attitudes, skills, and character determine, above all else, whether or not the school environment is conducive to growth and self-actualization or is frustrating, and whether the failures of the home are, in part, aggravated or corrected. The pupil-teacher relationship could be discussed under each of the above types as was the child-parent relationship, and with similar consequences but to a lesser degree. Some teachers are cold, rejecting, autocratic, and harsh; and their influence is frustrating and hurtful, but the majority are not. The warm, affectionate, sympathetic, understanding teacher who maintains in the classroom a democratic, friendly, and confident climate can do much to offset damages begun in the home.

The function of the school is to socialize, and education is a process of growth. In fact, the school may be defined as an agency designed to provide the resources, activities, and guidance necessary to help each child discover and actualize his potentials. It presents the child with a planned environment with most of the activities controlled, not rigidly, but a sort of regulated permissiveness. The school makes available a multitude of stimulus situations for enriched response. It provides challenge, choice, and a permissive climate, as well as chosen guided activities. Planned environment enhances the development of potential. It provides enriched situations and a variety of opportunities for achievement with the experience of success. In the ideal situation it conduces self-understanding, self-acceptance, and self-actualization, as well as growth and mental-social health. Functionally, it is moving steadily toward that ideal.

BASIC PERSONALITY COMPONENTS

Erik Erikson[6] has elaborated and refined the stages of personality development posited by Freud (oral, anal, etc.). He describes these as consisting of eight critical periods during which his eight basic components of personality are structured for good or ill, effective or ineffective. Only the first four basic components will be presented and their special relation to the early childhood, family and school enviroment.

1. Erikson's first component of a "healthy personality" is *basic trust.* The latter part of the first year and early second is the critical period. The quality of the mother's physical care, particularly feeding and weaning, is largely determinative—things given and/or withheld without the child experiencing too much uncertainty, deprivation, feelings of being abandoned, basic distrust. He learns to trust his ability to get and to get others to do.

[6] Erik H. Erikson, *Childhood and Society* (W.W. Norton & Company, Inc., 1950). Used with permission.

2. His second, and growing out of the first, component is *autonomy vs. shame*. This develops chiefly during the second year and is associated particularly with muscular growth and bowel control, the anal period of retention and elimination, self-control vs. parental domination. Here is where love that is firm and fair, directive and supportive needs to find expression, so that self-control can be attained without loss of self-esteem. Mishandled, the developmental tendency may be toward regression, or a willful hostility with "dirty" word or action tendencies, or a pseudoautonomy that is really a denial of the need or value of identification and interdependency.

3. Next comes *initiative vs. guilt*. Having attained a fair degree of autonomy, with language and locomotion ability, the child is ready to find out what kind of a person he is. It is the period of exploration, self-assertiveness, play, which may include his or his playmate's body as well as other things. How he is helped to experience success or failure, worth or unworth (guilt) is critical to his development. Self-confidence, initiative and creativity may be enhanced or permanently inhibited at this time—roughly ages three to five.

4. Then comes the development of *industry vs. inferiority*, the free expenditure vs. unconscious inhibition of productive energy. These are the early school years with alternation of play and work, of working alone at a task and turning to parent or teacher for support. How parents and teachers cope with the child has a special bearing on whether he becomes security- or growth-motivated, whether a confident industriousness or inhibiting inferiority.

It is quite apparent that these stages are not sharply discrete, but phase from one to the other. If the home and school provide the satisfying, growth conducing climate that will carry the child successfully through these stages, only under the most adverse circumstances will he later develop any serious psychosocial disorder. The other four basic personality components—identity vs. role diffusion, intimacy vs. isolation, generativity vs. ego-stagnation, and integrity vs. despair—will be presented in their relation to self-actualization (Chapter 13).

FROM FAMILY AND SCHOOL TO COMMUNITY

The community at large begins to play a larger role in determining the child's behavior as he grows into middle childhood and adolescence. More and more he turns to the community for his value-goals and for the satisfaction of his needs. He turns from the school playground to the larger community sports to satisfy physical needs and to its various cultural offerings for intellectual and emotional stimulation and exploration. His growing social needs demand acceptance and love, both passive and active, in relationships with others beyond the family and school. His growing capacities require expression in activities beyond the home and local school if they are to continue in growth. Therefore, he turns to the larger community, and he experiences the satisfactions conducing growth and fulfillment, or frustration.

CULTURAL DEPRIVATION

Many communities provide the means for satisfying these needs of many of their young people. Others are deficient in these growth-enriching stimulus situations, and many of our youth either can not afford the cost of participation or have not developed a value system that includes these basic growth-need satisfiers. Thus, these young people experience the frustration of basic mental-social needs and live culturally-stunted lives. Some, seeing these opportunities extended to others while denied to them, turn their resentment into hostile action against the community and are numbered among our delinquents. They organize their own peer groups (gangs) and attempt to work out their own need-satisfaction to compensate for their deprivation according to their distorted value system. (This alone is no sufficient cause of delinquency, but is only one of several factors.) The stunting, crippling effect of the deprived frustrating community can be seen most clearly by a thoughtful look at the Negro problem. The same factors and effects are found in varying degrees in any socially-economically depressed area where there appear greater degrees of rejection and deprivation. One of the most comprehensive studies and reports, of this problem was by Karon (1958). He attempted to test somewhat more scientifically than most studies the relation of cultural deprivation to psycho-social disorders.

SEGREGATION AND DEPRIVATION

As an essential step in any truly scientific study, Karon examined the findings of related studies before beginning his. Most of these relate to the depressed intellectual and emotional functioning of Negroes reared in culturally deprived communities and homes. Typical among the effects of discrimination found in these studies reviewed by Karon were: low self-esteem; fear manifested in self-abnegation, caution and apologetic behavior; unrealistically high aspirations which are frustrated, leading to apathy, hedonism, or a life of crime; anger inhibited by anxiety manifested in behavior that is ingratiating but removed and distrustful; a denial or repression of anger, leading to passivity, resignation, even good humor and affability; displaced hostility manifested in much fighting among themselves; the expenditure of much psychic energy containing their hostility, resulting in weak affect and low motivation.[7]

In conducting his very extensive study, Karon[8] used the Tompkins-Horn Picture Arrangements Test (PAT), a projective test that can be used with groups, and scored objectively, originally derived from the TAT protocols and based on a similar rationale. Thus Karon made a comparative study of several hundred carefully selected representative cases of whites and Negroes, the latter included both southern and northern. In the pilot study, comparing Negroes and whites, eleven discriminatory personality characteristics were significant: "The feeling that people are going out of their way to make trouble for you (high general aggressive press), not 'recognizing' situations involving anger (the four denials of aggression),* strong but

[7] From previous studies by A. Kardiner and L. Ovesey, *The March of Oppression* (New York: Norton, 1951). Reviewed by Karon.

[8] B.P. Karon, *The Negro Personality* (New York: Springer Publishing Company, Inc., 1958). Used with permission.

* This refers to four different types of aspects of aggression-denial as measured by different test scales.

consciously suppressed anger (delayed and negativistic aggression), deadened emotions (weak affect), emotions which change rapidly to their opposites (labile affect), conflicting work motivation, continuing to work only under the promptings of another person and not because of one's own inner standards (externalized work motivation), and avoiding close contact between men." (p. 162).

To determine the degree to which these differences are due to caste and the living conditions attributable to it (social rejection), extensive testing and statistical analysis were made. Significant findings were found in seven of these: "the feeling that people are going out of their way to make trouble for you, the four denials of aggression, labile affect, and externalized work motivation" (p. 164). Karon says:

> In this experiment, where the southern sample is drawn from an area of markedly severe caste sanctions, the use of denial with respect to every aspect of aggression measured by the test is even more striking than before. The difference reaches far beyond the one percent level of significance** for all of these types of denial, except the denial of aggression, which reached the two percent level.*** Thus, the ideas of someone being angry at him, of a physical fight, of the subject's being angry when someone else is angry at him, or of his becoming angry even when no one is around are all so frightening that the unconscious defense mechanism of denial is aroused, and he just does not recognize the threatening situations. . . . (p. 166).

He states that weak affect was significant at the five percent level (statistically acceptable but low), but the other two of the seven did not quite reach this significance level due to small numbers. He felt that they are significant in the life situation. Relative to weak affect, he says: "The importance of this difference in personality functioning should not be underestimated. A person who cannot feel emotions is a psychological cripple who lives, at most, half a life." (p. 168). And he adds:

> These findings seem to confirm the widely held belief among social scientists that the most serious emotional problems of the Negro concern the handling of aggression. . . .

** Relatively high relationship, small chance of coincidence alone.
*** A low but significant relationship.

> It is striking that, with the exception of labile affect, all of these characteristics are indicators of pathology, that is, they indicate disturbed individuals. . . . (pp. 172, 173).

In varying degrees, these findings apply to all minority groups, the socially rejected, and all who are deprived of family concern and a true sense of worth.

A child is born into the world with certain potential capacities which in some cases, may be quite low but in most is quite great, and so great, in fact, that we are just now beginning to comprehend how far short we have been in realizing the abundant mental-social spiritual life that is within our reach. The home, school, and community at large make up the social milieu in which these potentials grow into actuality. The quality of this milieu, how conducive it is to growth and how frustrating, determines in large measure to what degree this high potential is actualized in abundant living. Being human, a person, the child is not entirely molded by these forces. Neither the thesis of biologic determinism nor the antithesis of social-cultural determinism can fully account for his development. Inherent in self, whole person in the role of subject, is the capacity to withhold reaction, evaluate, choose, and act on his environment. This is the new synthesis, the locus of behavior dynamics in the self, which, when better understood, will help us to see more clearly why there is such great variation in the conditioning effect of the home, school, and community on our children.

SPIRITUAL FRUSTRATION AND CREATIVITY

We should call attention to one other point. If man is a transcendent being with spiritual capacities (as suggested by Scheler, Frankl, Sinnott, and many other scientist-philosophers, as well as theologians) and if man can by faith and love attain a sense of eternal security and fellowship and therein experience universal values and enlargement of self-hood as millions of religiously oriented people testify, then if the family and community do not provide adequate facilities for the development of this potential, may not this deficiency be experienced as the great frustration of one's supreme need?

It is the growing emphasis of many in the behavioral sciences that man is a subject who acts on his environment to mold and re-create it. He does this to the degree that he is mature, autonomous, and growth-oriented. The degree of maturation is a matter of self-development. The *self* is stunted in a depriving social milieu or matures normally in a growth-conducing, need-satisfying milieu. The mature self acts with appropriate emotional behavior. Each generation changes its cultural environment which, in turn, makes changes in the next generation. Thus man participates in his own evolutionary development.

Mature self-hood, creativity, transcendence, love and faith that overcome destructive hostility and fear—all of these high level personal attributes seem to relate closely to man's spiritual nature. There is no scientific proof nor objective validation of this. However, as we work from the "sick" to the "not sick" and from the "not sick" to high level healthy mindedness, there is growing clinical evidence that strongly suggests this relation. As potential development projects increase and become more refined, further evidence seems likely. Spirit is free, the source of creative action. Matter is determined, it can only react.

But, as Herbert Otto and other potentialities researchers suggest, only a very small fraction of the creative potential of the total population ever finds expression, thus confirming the general observations presented above. His findings also indicate that a negative environment is not the entire, if even the major, cause of this failure. Otto says:

> To return briefly to the puzzling question, "Why does man continue to want to make better use of his potentialities and yet is unable to do so"? The fear-guilt-anxiety cycle, the pathogenic social vectors and other hypotheses mentioned previously are only a part of the picture. Much more remains to be discovered and verified. For example, any change or the prospect of change engenders resistance in most people; moreover, most individuals seem to lack a positive self-concept of their potential. To gain something better, something has to be given up; old ideas, the shells of values, etc. Growth and the actualization of potential also mean renunciation, discipline, commitment and responsibility as well as change in life style. Finally, for man to be fully involved in the continuous act of self-creation he must have both the

> *vision* of his potentials and the *courage* to realize his possibilities. . . . (1966, p. 423).

In his potentialities research he has found a significant place for man's spiritual potential and its development relative to the above. After pointing to a major weakness of organized religion, he says:

> From another perspective, man's spiritual concerns and values can be experienced by him as a source of strength, inspiration and aspiration. Man's interpretation of his *relatedness* to the universe, to all things, to life and living (and, in turn, the process of building and forming such a relatedness) can be a source of fulfillment and a means of constant growth and development throughout the life cycle. Man's spiritual potential can serve as a matrix for constant growth. . . . (1966, p. 415).

Otto is optimistic and is devoting his full time in work directed toward that end. The broader aspects of this problem and the nature of this end will be covered in later chapters. But first we turn to the next phase in the development (or deterioration) of those who suffer too much frustration of need-drive—their defense mechanisms.

SUMMARY

Society is the mother of personality, molding its embryonic growth largely by supplying and denying the individual's basic needs. Frustration and satisfaction of need (oxygen) and social interaction begin at birth and continue until death. Only as maintenance needs are satisfied and frustration kept moderate is the child free to turn toward growth and self-actualization. In spite of, or perhaps because of, its common and wide usage, the term "fustration" has been variously defined. I interpret it as any combination of outer or inner factors that tend to thwart a person's need-goal responses and the accompanying experience of annoyance, anger, or fear.

The normal effect of frustration is a state of tension (stress) and aggressive action. Whether the aggression is friendly or hostile depends on evaluation of oneself and the situation relative to self. When there is choice between alternative goal-actions, each of which is evaluated as beneficial, the stress is approach-approach conflict; when each is adjudged harmful, it is avoidance-avoidance conflict; and when the same goal seems to be about equally harmful and beneficial, it is approach-avoidance conflict. If these types of conflict are very frequent, it denotes confused values—an inadequate hierarchical organization of values that may result in various psychosocial disorders.

Children frequently experience frustration of their acceptance, love, and trust needs in the home environment, with strong approach-avoidance conflict and stunting of self-growth. Parental rejection may be harsh and domineering, an attitude of indifference, or in the guise of over-indulgence and protectiveness, or a combination of these. In either case it is a denial of adequate love and trust. The child's natural aggressive response may be expressed in open rebellion and overt denial of the parent and his values, displaced against others at school or in the neighborhood, or anxiety—repressed and directed against himself. The consequences may be any of several varieties of psychosocial disorders. Parents who create a home climate of love and trust, a democratic parent-child relationship, and who are both firm and fair in discipline, satisfy both the dependency and growth needs of their children.

Entering school the child brings to the new situation his facility or difficulty of identification and adjustment and finds an enlarged and more demanding environment, with new values and expectations. The teacher becomes the parent surrogate and the peer group becomes an extended family of siblings. The greater facilities of the school may be used to help each child experience successful performance and a sense of worth or by permitting too much competition increase the sense of failure and lack of worth, with anxiety withdrawal, inappropriate compensatory behavior, etc. And of greater importance, by understanding and warm acceptance, the teacher may help the child identify with her and correct some of the damage from the inadequate parent-child relationship. Or the teacher may be as rejecting as many parents are, thus aggravating the problems of the disturbed child.

With increasing age the child turns to the community beyond the immediate neighborhood for dates, recreation and other cultural satisfactions. He needs more money and freedom, but also more understanding and guidance. Those from culturally deprived homes and neighborhoods, and love- and trust-deprived families, are confronted with greater than ordinary need and temptation and usually have lower frustration tolerance. Among these is found the greatest incidence of various psychosocial disorders.

But the individual person in his self-role as subject, is not entirely a product of his environment. He may act on it creatively or destructively. Much promise is seen in certain recent pilot projects in human potentiality development—group effort in discovering, accepting, and utilizing community resources to develop a more complete and satisfying life.

GLOSSARY

Autism. Extremely self-centered, inordinately subjective.
Pathogenic. Productive of or giving origin to disease (mental or physical).
Protocol. The preliminary draft of an official document, a report, as the results of a test or group of tests by a clinical psychologist.
Rationale. The logical basis of something, underlying theories.
Surrogate. A substitute; one who plays the role of another.

REFERENCES AND SUGGESTED READINGS

COLEMAN, JAMES C., *Personality Dynamics and Effective Behavior,* Chicago: Scott, Foresman & Company, 1960.
CROW, LESTER and ALICE CROW, *Mental Hygiene for Teachers,* New York: The Macmillan Company, 1963.
DYAL, JAMES A., *Readings in Psychology: Understanding Human Behavior,* New York: McGraw-Hill Book Co., 1962.
ERIKSON, ERIK H., *Childhood and Society,* New York: W. W. Norton & Co., 1950.
GESELL, A. et al, *The First Five Years of Life,* New York: Harper, 1960.
GOLDFARB, W., "Psychological Privation in Infancy and Subsequent Adjustment," *American Journal of Orthopsychiatry,* 15:247–255 (April 1945).
———, "Variations in Adolescent Adjustment of Institutionally Reared Children," *American Journal of Orthopsychiatry,* 17:449–457 (1947).
GRIFFIN, G. A. and H. F. HARLOW, "Effects of Three Months of Total Social Deprivation on Social Adjustment and Learning in the Rhesus Monkey," *Child Development,* 37, 3, 533–547 (Sept. 1966).
HOLLENBERG, E., and M. SPERRY, "Some Antecedents of Aggression and Effects of Frustration on Doll Play," *Personality,* 1, 32–43 (1950).
KAGAN, J. and H. A. MOSS, *Birth to Maturity,* New York: John Wiley & Sons, Inc., 1962.

KAPLAN, LOUIS, *Mental Health and Human Relations in Education,* New York: Harper & Row, 1959.

KARON, B. P., *The Negro Personality,* New York: Springer Publishing Co., Inc., 1958.

MASLOW, A., *Toward a Psychology of Being,* Princeton, N.J.: D. Van Nostrand Co., Inc., 1962.

MASSERMAN, J. H., *Behavior and Neurosis,* Chicago: Univ. of Chicago Press, 1943.

MUSSEN, H. M., J. J. CONGER and J. KAGAN, *Child Development and Personality,* New York: Harper & Row, 1963.

OTTO, HERBERT A. (ed), *Explorations in Human Potentialities,* Springfield, Ill.: Charles C. Thomas, Publisher, 1966.

REDYL, F. and D. WINEMAN, *Children Who Hate,* Glencoe, Ill.: The Free Press, 1951.

ROBERTS, GUY L., *Where Delinquency Begins,* Richmond: John Knox Press, 1958.

SCHNEIDERS, A. A., *Personality Dynamics and Mental Health,* New York: Holt, Rinehart and Winston, Inc., 1965.

SCHWARTZ, E. E. (ed), *Children and Youth at the Midcentury: A Chart Book.* Midcentury White House Conference on Children and Youth, National Publishing Co., 1950.

SEARS, R. R. et al, *Patterns of Child Rearing,* Evanston, Ill.: Row, Peterson, 1957.

SEGEL, D., *Frustration in Adolescent Youth,* Washington: U.S. Office of Educ. Bull. No. 1, 1951.

SHAFFER, L. F., and E. J. SHOBEN, JR., *The Psychology of Adjustment,* Boston: Houghton Mifflin Company, 1956.

SPITZ, R. A., "The Role of Ecological Factors in Emotional Development in Infancy," *Child Development,* 20: 145–155 (September 1949).

SYMONDS, P. M., *The Dynamics of Parent-Child Relationships,* New York: T. C. Columbia University Bureau of Publications, 1949.

WINNICOTT, D. W., *The Maturational Process and the Facilitating Environment,* New York: International Universities Press, Inc., 1965.

7 | Defensive Adjustment

In this phase of our study, I have moved from the dynamics into the patterns of behavior. I wish to establish certain broad principles of behavior to help us in our study of human behavior from the viewpoint of mental hygiene.

GENERAL PRINCIPLES OF BEHAVIOR

IT IS HOLISTIC

First, behavior is normally holistic. When self is aroused to action by a stimulus situation (cognitive incongruity), the whole organism is "set" for cooperative action as self-directs, including the brain and nervous system, and endocrine system. Self is set (state of readiness) to direct responses in accordance with need-value experience toward protective-maintenance-security goals or growth-enhancement-actualization goals. The self must be strong and healthful with a wholesome, well organized, realistic value system if the behavior is to be as stated. With this dynamic strength, realistic evaluations of the situation and self-potential and appropriate responses are made.

Holistic, integrated behavior means selective responses. Some neuron paths, glands, and muscle tissue are more highly activated while others are reduced in action. Self as an evaluating, directing agent increases or decreases resistance at synapses while anticipating possible consequences (mental trial and error with success as a goal). Certain stimuli elements are admitted, others blocked; certain response tendencies are reinforced, others inhibited.

For instance, the college student may be seated at his desk engaged in concentrated study. Self facilitates word and diagram perception and responses associated with these, because of the value placed on the completion of the task. Conversation in the adjoining room and normal traffic sounds are unheard. The endocrine system is in a relatively homeostatic state; all is inwardly calm. This equilibrium is disturbed when a fire truck with clanging gongs and open sirens roars by or comes to a halt nearby. Suddenly, there is a new state of arousal, of stimulus evaluation, the stimulus situation is incongruent with accepted study conditions, and other perceptive and response patterns are activated while the former ones are inhibited. The student has been behaving as an organized whole, regulating stimulus reception (selective perception) and responses in accord with valued goals and congruence of situations. The degree of activity of the many subsystems varies widely and almost constantly, but as a cooperating whole, as directed by a healthy self with a wholesome value system.

Angyal,[1] one of the leading proponents of the holistic approach, defines life as a *process of self-expansion* which is to a large extent *self-governing* and which functions as a whole, as *unitas multiplex.* He says: "There are wholes in which all the significant positions of the system are occupied in perfect accordance with the system principle; and there are wholes in which only a limited number of positions are occupied in this way, while other members are out of position. . . ." (p. 47). Later he adds: "The holistic approach postulates that man is to be understood not in terms of specific functions or traits, but in terms of the broad system principles which organize these traits into a hierarchy of systems and subsystems. According to my particular conception, personality viewed in its broad outline is a *dualistic organization;* any personal trait can function as a part

[1] Andras Angyal (E. Haufmann, ed), *Neurosis and Treatment: A Holistic Theory* (New York: John Wiley & Sons, Inc., 1965). Used with permission.

of the organization of health or of that of neurosis. Viewed in greater detail, it is also a *pluralistic organization*; each concrete item can function as a part of a number of subsystems of the two major organizations. . . ." (p. 203).

The defense mechanisms are subsystems by which the threatened person (as self) attempts to maintain wholeness on the side of healthful organization. If these fail, then the system may shift and become a neurotic organization, still whole but disordered and inefficient.

CONSCIOUS OR UNCONSCIOUS

Second, behavior may be either conscious or unconscious. Behavior is interpreted as including the responses of the whole organism and of its various subsystems. Many of the vital organs function for the most part at an entirely unconscious level, since direction of their activity is handled by or *through* the older lower brain structures, the person never having been conscious of these. Other activities are learned in early infancy before sufficient maturation for mental concepts and verbal expression (structuring). These may continue to be reactivated periodically and unconsciously, since they have never been structured into conscious concepts.

Certain activities consciously learned and repeated so frequently become automatic and unconscious and their direction has been relegated to the lower brain centers. Much of our routine performance is of this nature, but one may become conscious of these at anytime they may become a response part of an incongruous stimulus situation. There is no set or fixed resistance to being conscious of them; it is just a matter of convenience and efficiency, when self is able to focus effort on whatever it momentarily evaluates as being the most significant. Finally, there are those types of mental activities (memories, desires, attitudes) that are so painful and threatening to self that a strong, fixed, relatively permanent resistance to their becoming conscious is established. This is the so-called "repression"; it is a fixed selective perception and selective recall.

The first three types of unconscious behavior are normal and are a necessary part of growth and effective living. It is the latter that is especially significant to ineffectual behavior and the defense mechanisms we are about to study. The child who has been too seriously deprived of basic security-maintenance needs, places too great value on these and is prone to establish fixed resistance to elements in the stimulus situation (inadequate perception), elements of himself (inadequate self-image), and recall of hurtful, threatening former experiences (inadequate use of experience). These add up to an inadequate value system and therefore inadequate behavior control, which introduces another basic principle.

EVALUATING COGNITION

Third, behavior is a consequence of how a situation is perceived and how it is evaluated. These two processes are not entirely discrete: one phases into the other. Perception is more dependent on maturation, and the evaluation of what is perceived is more a matter of learning, but both depend on the strength of the self. Two people may be observing the same object or situation. One may perceive it as a threat, the other as an interesting challenge. The greatly deprived or anxiety-ridden person is prone to faulty, distorted perception of the situation and himself (his abilities), and his evaluations of each are unrealistic. His need-goal evaluation is also distorted, unrealistic, and his directed responses are unsatisfactory. This increases his insecurity, lack of confidence, still more selective perception and unrealistic evaluation; it is a vicious circle. Such a self is weak and has a confused, ineffectual value system. The dynamics of the self—the power of self-initiated, self-directed action—is at low ebb. Environmental determinism is dominant. This person becomes protection-security motivated, builds defense patterns of response that generally impede growth and productivity. Furthermore, the weak self as an ineffectual director of behavior and, with a confused value system, builds or permits to develop certain protective behavior patterns that do not coordinate well with each other. They function semi-autonomously and often at variance, creating inner tensions and stress, and further cripple his performance. Behavior is no longer truly holistic. The ultimate is reached in either a psychotic break or a "multiple personality." The various "defense mechanisms" are designed to help maintain stability and systematic wholeness.

FRUSTRATION TOLERANCE

A fourth principle may be stated in terms of behavior as a consequence of frustration tolerance or stress tolerance. Frustration tolerance has been presented. The child who grew up in a climate of acceptance, love, and support and where his whole basic maintenance needs were amply supplied, becomes confident, autonomous, and production motivated. His strength of selfhood and self-confidence enables him to meet frustrating situations as challenges, with perhaps some momentary feelings of annoyance or irritation but with little anger or hostility. He can face prolonged or severe frustration with little anxiety. In other words, it takes big frustrations and big threats to arouse anger and fear in the "big" (mature, strong, confident) person. These do not occur often. Therefore, his behavior is relatively free of these and of protective defenses. His anger may be great at such times but is of short duration. The opposite is true of the child whose environment did not provide adequate basic need gratification, leaving him weak and dependent, with a low sense of worth and capability. He experiences frequent feelings of anxiety and hostility and permanent defenses are established as a protection against threats which are more or less permanent.

THE INFERIORITY COMPLEX

These principles do not exhaust the possible listing, but serve our present purpose which is to provide insight into adjustment by defense. Together they suggest the personality type or condition which is most prone to defensive adjustment—the *inferiority complex.* Adler is generally credited with giving this concept to modern psychology. His view differed sharply with Freud's sex drive as the predominant motivation factor, putting in its place the drive for high achievement or *dominance.* Lacking or fearing the lack of capacity for dominant achievement, the person develops feelings of inferiority and a pattern of compensatory behavior. He can hide from awareness of (repress) these feelings but they remain as an inferiority complex. Every child tends to compare his performance with that of his parents or older siblings and thus experiences inferiority if he does not compare favorably. In order to compensate, he strives in various ways to gain dominance and eliminate the painful feelings of inferiority. If his social environment is satisfactory, he learns that he is accepted and loved and his basic needs are gratified without his being dominated. He can identify with love and cooperate with others as an effective member of society. However, inferiority feelings become a fixed complex because the social environment is seldom fully satisfactory, those ideal satisfactions are not always attained and the compensatory drive to dominate becomes fixed. On the other hand, if the person experiences little or no success in his compensatory behavior, and is surpassed on all sides, he becomes more painfully aware of his inferiority, usually exaggerates it, and becomes excessively submissive.

THE ADLERIAN VIEW

Alfred Adler, who emphasizes holistic, goal-directed behavior based on evaluation of self and circumstances, speaks as follows:[2]

> Let me, by a slight suggestion, prove and yet soften down these heretical propositions:* more important than tendencies, objective experience and milieu is *the subjective evaluation*, an evaluation which stands furthermore in a certain, often strange, relation to realities. Out of this evaluation, however, which generally results in the development of a permanent mood *of the nature of a feeling of inferiority* there arises, depending upon the unconscious technique of our thought-apparatus, an imagined goal, an attempt at a planned final compensation and a life-plan. . . .
>
> A thorough-going study has taught us that we can best

[2] Alfred Adler, *Theory and Practice of Individual Psychology*, 1964. Used with permission of Humanities Press, Inc., and Routledge & Kegan Paul Ltd.

* He was a heretic from the viewpoint of orthodox psychoanalysis.

> understand the manifold and diverse movements of the psyche as soon as our *most general presupposition,* that the psyche has as its objective the goal of superiority, is recognized. . . .
>
> This goal of complete superiority, with its strange appearance at times, does not come from the world of reality. Inherently, we must place it under "fictions" and "imagination." . . . Whoever takes this goal of godlikeness seriously or literally, will soon be compelled to flee from real life and compromise, by seeking life within life; if fortunate in art, but more generally in pietism, neurosis or crime. . . . (1963, pp. 6, 7 and 8).

I would substitute *self* for *psyche* and give credence to much in Adler's basic theory. In it he establishes a basis for much of our *defensive* approach to life.

The inferiority complex, or psychic inferiority, may be defined as a negative and depressing attitude toward the self that stems from real and/or imagined deficiencies and which is usually or largely unconscious. The four principles described above in their negative aspects characterize the behavior of the person with strong psychic inferiority. His behavior patterns are not holistic and well integrated but frequently piece-meal and contradictory. Or his behavior becomes organized into a distorted unrealistic whole. There are too many fixed unconscious elements in his motivation, which produce selective perception and repression. His perceptions and evaluations are often distorted and unrealistic and are way out of proportion. Consciously or subconsciously he senses his inadequacy, and tends to anticipate frustration and exaggerate its significance. He experiences it unrealistically as unjust and threatening; therefore his behavior is colored with too much hostility and anxiety and hemmed in with defensiveness. He has low frustration tolerance. He is most likely to develop one or more "defense mechanisms" as protection against the feeling of inferiority or anticipated failure.

> The class may profit from a short discussion of the basic causes of inferiority feelings or the more permanent psychic inferiority; physical and mental deficiencies, moral turpitude of parents, childhood rearing, poverty, etc. The discussion may follow a report by a student.

PRODUCTION OR MAINTENANCE GOALS

The person who has developed under favorable circumstances—who is autonomous, confident, and growth motivated—continues to strive for excellence of performance in his own mental processes, in productive work, and in his interpersonal relations. Once in a while, he experiences some opposition and frustration. He pushes ahead relentlessly overcoming them by frontal tactics as long as they succeed, by an indirect approach if the frontal attack does not work, and sometimes by temporary withdrawal (retreat). The compromise and changing tactics, however, usually relate to means of achievement and not to end-goals. The withdrawal is a retreat to reappraise the situation, re-examine one's resources, obtain more information and allies, if necessary, then continue the struggle under more favorable conditions. Such a person is free to admit temporary defeat and inadequacy without any fixed feelings of inferiority. He can appraise or evaluate the situation, himself and his personal resources, and the desired goal in a realistic frame of reference. Thus, the tentative goal will be a stage in the attainment of the ultimate goal—excellence in personal responses, work performance, and interpersonal relations. He is not under a "perfectionist compulsion" and can accept relative failure where circumstances are relatively adverse.

The defensive, security motivated person, when faced with obstacles and experiencing frustration, tends to forget excellence and seeks only mediocre performance which is accompanied by protection. His goal is maintenance rather than continued growth and fulfillment. He is prone to avoid frontal attack. His compromises are likely to involve major end-goals, thus basic values, rather than means to these ends. His withdrawal (retreat) is usually permanent. He gives up the struggle and accepts a less adequate, less satisfying substitute. His behavior is chiefly adaptive, adjustive, coping and protective, rather than venturesome, creative, and productive. Defensive mechanisms develop. Under the stress of adult responsibilities, these defense devices are seldom fully protective but are under threat of failing. The behavior of such a person carries an excess of defensive anger, anxiety, and guilt. This type of person is generally touchy and hypercritical, apathetic, or morbid and depressed.

THE DEFENSE MECHANISMS

The classification of responses has always been a difficult task. The same problem prevails with respect to personality traits, needs, symptoms of illness and for these so-called "defense mechanisms," which are, in reality, personality or character traits, i.e., characteristic forms of behavior. The term is one of common usage but ambiguous meaning. The response patterns that compose each are complex, and there is wide overlap of elements. Whatever their nature and number, they are unconsciously and indeliberately (relatively so) formed as protective devices. They protect self from experiencing anticipated failure and rejection at the sacrifice of satisfying productivity. They protect self from full awareness of its own real or imagined deficiencies, and they may protect self from awareness of external threats. They are low-order adjustive patterns that distort awareness of reality and the real self, therefore, they hamper growth toward self-actualization.

Crow and Crow (1963, p. 121) state: "The normal individual is usually able, through the exercise of socially accepted means, to achieve his goals in his struggle for existence and for the satisfaction of other wants and urges. The habit patterns thus established attain for him not only individual satisfaction but also the approval of his fellows. However, if individual limitations or the forces of his environment interfere with the normal achievement of his goals, the individual is compelled by the strength of his inner drives to develop socially less desirable and individually less healthful behavior patterns. . . ." They refer to these behavior patterns as "defense mechanisms" and as "mechanisms of adjustment" and list twenty of these; going a little beyond most listings.

Introjection	Malingering	Idealization
Compensation	Egocentrism	Conversion
Displacement	Attention-getting	Withdrawing
Identification	Criticism	Negativism
Rationalization	Sympathy	Retrogression
Projection	Daydreaming and fantasy	Repression
Sublimation		Neurotic behavior

I will use a slightly different listing and order of arrangement, beginning with the three R's: repression, reaction formation, and rationalization.

DELUDING REACTIONS

Repression. The term "repression" was introduced by Freud, and made popular by the psychoanalysts. It explained the process of forced forgetting of thoughts, feelings, desires, and memories "repressed into the unconscious." It functions to protect the person's self-image. The person given to repression becomes unable to recognize painful and guilt-producing memories or attitudes and desires that run contrary to his consciously accepted image of himself. Certain topics not only are not talked about, they are not thought about and are kept blocked off from the focal point of attention. Some people are more prone to employ this type of reaction than are others. These are usually persons who are suggestible, and easily hypnotized. The process is akin to autosuggestion since hypnosis and/or free association are agents in the restoration of cognition. It may also occur spontaneously, when the repressing anxiety is reduced.

A typical Freudian illustration might be like this: A young child, having been severely condemned by his parents for masturbating and warned of dire consequences if it is continued, is caught in the act by an older sibling. The older child also condemns the guilty one and threatens to tell the parents. The child is in a state of terror—fear of parental punishment or utter rejection and some other vague, general or divine punishment coupled with guilt from having disobeyed the parents and having engaged in an evil act. The recall is so painful and threatening to self (Ego, the Freudians would say), and incongruous with his desired opinion of himself, it is "repressed," i.e., blocked from recall. Years later, conversation may lead to experiences of such similar nature that the normal person would recall the experience, but the above mentioned person would feel only a vague anxiety and inner tension.

The term has been broadened to include most deep and prolonged forgetting (motivated forgetting) and rejection of clear awareness of unworthy attitudes. It is one of the most basic of the defense mechanisms and operates in most forms of mental illness and much abnormal behavior. In some cases of unhappy childhood, the person can recall virtually nothing during that period or prior to entering school. It is especially related to phobias and amnesia but is characteristic of virtually all mental illness.

Normal forgetting is essential to concentrated conscious effort. In concentrated thinking, the focal point of attention is being self-directed in narrow channels of cortical activity. Resistance is established in the surrounding neurons to keep out interfering percepts. When the problem is solved or deliberately set aside, that specific need subsides and the surrounding resistance zones relax. Attention (conscious awareness) then may wander into any of those other areas of cortical activity that the momentary stimulus cues may determine. Recall is the reactivating of a cortical area under appropriate stimulus and its again becoming the focal area of attention. Resistance to recall may be set up momentarily when two competing concepts momentarily block each other, but it relaxes normally when the immediate need or conflict passes.

Repression is a purposive fixed forgetting, an inability to recall, because the need is permanent. Since recall would be painful and guilt-producing, and shatter one's self-regard, the resistance lines around that particular cortical area are permanent. The focal point of attention cannot enter, even though it may be partially aroused by an element in the stimulus situation similar to the original situation. In the latter case, one experiences some anxiety and tension but not the memory of the original experience nor the full force of its hurt. Person as subject (self) exerts the resistance for self-protection. When the person is strong, confident and no longer afraid, self can permit the resistance to relax.

Rationalization. It is assumed that when a person performs any act or engages in any pattern of behavior, he has a motive, a purpose or a reason for doing it. One generally does a particular act because he wants to do it. But motives, needs, and desires are complex, and usually more than one is involved in any complex action.

aspects of the same general or core mechanism. Each of these prevents awareness of certain aspects of reality and thus tends to delude a person as to his past experience, attitudes, etc. Repression is also found where there is rationalization and/or reaction-formation. Rationalization and reaction-formation are aids that keep the person from becoming aware of the repressed processes. They afford an acceptable explanation of behavior which is partly motivated by the subconscious factors. They are similar in character, but reaction-formation is a little stronger and a more aggressive mode of behavior and is more directly opposed to the repressed material. Negativism may be associated with these three as being a mode of expression of reaction-formation. Negativism is normal in early childhood, at about 2½ to 3 years of age, when the child begins to assert himself against parental domination. Normally, it is outgrown.

Let us now examine the basic needs the three R's help to gratify; what is being protected? The growing self needs acceptance, approval, and love from others and himself. If a child grows up in a family and community environment which seriously deprives him of these, the child places an exaggerated value on their gratification. He also feels himself to be of low worth or else he would have been more amply supplied with these, and places a high value on being accepted, approved, and loved. He fears that he is unworthy and cannot achieve them. These three mechanisms help him to select what he perceives, what he remembers, and what constitutes his conscious desires, etc. He protects self from the painful awareness of some of the social- and self-rejection and from motives and actions which might increase them. They are maladjustive because they distort reality and realistic evaluations (judgments) and tend toward confusion, with greater uncertainty and insecurity, and a tightening up of defensive behavior with its inhibitions and rigidity.

SUBSTITUTIVE MECHANISMS

Next are a group of substitutive mechanisms which help the weak self in its coping with reality but which may become hampering when too rigidly adhered to. Conscious, deliberate substitution is a necessary action in the give-and-take of normal living. The college student finds one curriculum or career choice too difficult or too expensive and deliberately makes a substitution with a rational and practical choice. The legislator trying to get a bill passed may have to accept substitutions at certain points. Democracy could not otherwise function. These are fully conscious, deliberate, and temporary. Other substitutive mechanisms are more fixed and permanent and, while they may function consciously, are not developed with the same deliberate and conscious choice.

Compensation. The term "compensation" implies exchange. One exchanges his labor for money. One is injured by a careless driver and receives compensation. The college student who is very much interested in athletics finds himself unable to make the varsity, and feels that he will not be able to make it as a professional, so he turns to a major in physical education and trains other boys. He is more or less consciously deliberate in this change of goal. Partly, he just drifts in that direction. He derives a satisfaction from helping the athletic development of other boys. Thus, there is no sharp distinction between normal substitution and compensation. Also there may be, and often is, an element of rationalization involved. The disappointed athlete may convince himself that he actually prefers teaching.

The behavior that is designated as overcompensation involves a different type of substitution. The goal remains of the same nature, but extra special effort is substituted for normal effort to attain the goal and a higher goal is reached than otherwise expected. Demosthenes, by unusual (abnormal) effort, overcame his speech defect, not only learned to speak distinctly but also became a renowned orator. Glen Cunningham, whose legs were so badly burned that he was told he would never be able to walk, learned to walk, to run, and became a champion miler—by supernormal effort. Adler presents overcompensation as a standard procedure by which the not-too-weak person overcomes or succeeds in spite of his inferiority complex.

Sublimation. The term "sublimation" is a form of substitution of one goal, aim in life, or career for another; and it affords compensation for that which is missed in the other. It differs in degree of deliberate consciousness in its development and in quality of its expression, and is largely unconscious in its inception and development. Therefore, it is a more fixed and permanent characteristic of behavior. The crippled, unattractive youth sets a high value on romantic love but is largely deprived of it. He grows into manhood and writes romantic poetry finding a certain degree of vicarious satisfaction in that sublimated expression. The young woman who sets high value on marriage and motherhood is, by circumstances, compelled to remain unwed. She becomes a teacher or social worker and finds a certain amount of love satisfaction in this sublimated mode of expression. The choice to write romantic poetry or to become a teacher is not deliberately made with this motive in mind. Thus, it is not a conscious or deliberate substitution. It is generally considered to be of positive individual and social value as an adjustive mechanism. There is some satisfying expression of love, or Freudian libido, and it is directed to socially beneficial ends.

Fantasy. Daydreaming is a universal experience. For the normal, well-adjusted person, it is a wholesome form of relaxation, a "getting away from it all." We watch a TV western or a soap opera, read a Pacific Islands travelogue or a Lil' Abner or Steve Canyon "Comic," or we just sit back and give imagination a free rein. We escape the humdrum and regimented activities of real world responsibilities and satisfy neglected need-drives (desires) with fantasy goals. But we do not let these moments of day dreaming become habitual and time-consuming substitutes for real-life achievement.

For many people, fantasy becomes a chief occupation. The disappointed wife with a low sense of adequacy spends most of the day watching TV "soap operas" or reading the romance magazines. She fantasies herself in these roles and achieves some small measure of vicarious satisfaction. The physical weakling gains his satisfaction by becoming, in fantasy, an all-star athlete. Thus, it is maladaptive in that so much time and mental energy are given over to the process that it interferes with more substantial achievement, the real life improvement which anyone could make. In the more serious cases, we have the pathological liar and paranoid personality. In the latter, the fantasies are fully believed to be real.

One of my former clients was a young man who had gotten into trouble by impersonating an air force officer. He gained admission to the Officers' Club and became the toast of the group until the hoax was uncovered. Previous diagnosis designated him as a pathological liar. His parents were divorced before he was 10 and he was placed in the custody of his mother. He showed artistic talent during the teen years and wanted to make a career in art. His mother had other ideas. She was ambitious, materialistic, and domineering. She had a good position with a large company. She was determined to make a successful businessman of him. He was not strong enough to openly oppose her, and he had identified sufficiently to accept her high value of social status that money provided, but he loved art and hated all that he knew about business. He finally left home, joined the air force, reached only the rating of corporal, "washed out" and was discharged, then drifted about the country for a few years, feeding his ego with fantasied successes. Then, he hit upon the idea of using these fantasy attainments as a substitute for real achievements in order to feed his body and gain sporadic social status. This was termed pathological lying and impersonation—serious maladjustment.

Regression. A more serious form of substitution, unconsciously established, is the mechanism termed "regression." Like fantasy, it is a retreat from the reality of temporary failure, a loss of confidence. Regression is the substituting of a lower-order, more infantile mode of action, and a retreat into the past. The five-year-old who has been the center of attention, suddenly finds himself seemingly replaced by a new baby. His mother who had been so attentive to him previously, now gives nearly all of her attention to the newcomer, his rival. Since he was pampered and over-protected, he lacks self-confidence but tries a few random devices to regain his position. These not being very successful, he panics and retreats, substituting more infantile patterns of response, such as thumb-sucking, bed-wetting or pants-soiling. He receives some attention, if not approval. The college student, finding the curriculum insurmountable, returns home to accept parental support and whatever local job may be available that provides minimum need-satisfaction and permits him to remain at home, thereby regressing to an early adolescent level. The adult, finding the responsibilities of life too harsh, begins to show psychotic symptoms of inappropriate behavior and slowly or rapidly regresses back, back, and back to infantile dependency and institutional care.

Angyal says: "The phenomena of aggression fall into two groups: passive setback and strategic retreat. A passive setback is analogous to the situation of a man swimming against the current. His activity aims at progression in a given direction but it is impeded by the force of the stream. The resulting movement depends on the relative strength of the two components, but even if the man is carried backward we still can say that his tendency is to move upstream. The tendency of the organism is toward increased autonomy, even if strong heteronomous influences result in a decrease of autonomy. Similarly, in the case of strategic retreat the goal itself remains "progressive." Regression may occur when a situation becomes untenable at a complex level, and the person retreats to a more primitive and familiar one to gather his forces for a new advance. . . ." (1965, p. 7).

COMMON FEATURES

These four mechanisms, as more or less fixed and subconsciously formed mental processes, serve the purpose of protecting the self from the more painful perceptions of serious failure, and protect self-esteem. Every child needs to experience some success in his strivings, achieve his need-goals to a reasonable degree, or he suffers a deep sense of inferiority. The child who is reared in an environment of frustration and deprival and fails so often to achieve satisfaction, views himself as being incompetent, inferior, of little worth, and anticipates continued failure. As a self, he is weak and has a low frustration tolerance; thus, he tends to withdraw from stressful demands, and to experience further failure and greater unworth. This unending cycle would destroy all sense of worth if he were not able to partially hide this fear and feeling of incompetence behind these defenses, gaining partial achievement and recognition. They are similar in nature and function but differ in degree and detail.

Denial of Reality. This is somtimes mentioned as a defense mechanism. If we choose to designate it as such, it should be seen as a narrower mental process and as an element of nearly all of the above, especially the first three. *Malingering,* is also designated as a defense mechanism by some psychologists. The infantryman, starting on an all-day 25-mile march, falls by the roadside after about five miles and can not go on. His platoon officer curses, calls him a faker, a "goldbricker." He actually fantasies a pain or dizziness and rationalizes his failure. The feared failure he anticipated built up to the point where this mechanism went into operation and protected him from the hurt of real failure. Therefore, it is a mixture of fantasy, regression, and rationalization.

INTERPERSONAL PROTECTIVE PROCESSES

Identification. This mechanism has been discussed as a normal process in child development since it relates especially to one's acquiring basic traits from his parents and other significant people. When growth and maturation are adequate, the autonomous individual revises his value system in the light of his own insights and as an independent, self-confident capacity to evaluate objects and situations. The deprived person who is low in self-sufficiency and is security-motivated continues in adult life to identify himself with significant persons and organizations and to *internalize* their values and achievements, their prestige, and experience these as his own. Therefore, we find that the student joins the prestige fraternity or sorority; the local ward politician attaches himself to the governor and speaks often of "my friend, Gov. so-and-so." The parent who did not complete his education, pushes his son or daughter through college and graduate school and into the profession he (or she) dreamed of. He then proudly refers to my son (daughter) the doctor, the lawyer. It illustrates the old adage: "A good offense is the best defense." Self is enhanced vicariously by being identified with the successful; thus it is protected against the pain of its own otherwise perceived failure. Identification is often affiliated with fantasy, e.g., when the reader of a novel or viewer of a movie identifies with the hero or heroine. This may be a normal and temporary process or a fixed mechanism, depending on degree and duration.

Introjection. This mechanism is much akin to, if not the same mental process as, "identification." More specifically, it is the internalizing process of acquiring values or attitudes from others with whom one has identified, while identification refers more specifically to accepting another's behavior. They are at least complementary processes. The term is used most often to designate the unconscious (largely) acquisition of a new code of values and their motivated behavior that are antagonistic to the previously established values and habits. For example, the teenager joins a neighborhood gang and *introjects* their values which are in opposition with his former values and with those of his family. Many inmates of war prisons and concentration camps "introjected" the attitudes and imitated the practices of their guards, often to the extent of victimizing their own companions. This mechanism serves the need of temporary protection or status, but generally contributes to social and mental maladjustment in the long run.

Projection. This mechanism incorporates elements of the three R's which we have discussed. One could, with much truth, say that it is a special form of the expression of repression, rationalization and reaction-formation. It is self-deceiving and reality-rejecting, but it meets the need of self-esteem by protecting the individual from the painful awareness of his own unworthy feelings and desires or inadequacies that caused his failure. The chronic gossip and compulsive reformer see "serious" sexual improprieties and dishonesty in others. One is able to keep such impulses "repressed" within himself by exposing and combating these fantasied evils. In the most severe cases, the individual actually hears his inner voice of self-accusation coming from the lips of real or fantasied persons, and becomes a victim of hallucinations and delusions of persecution.

In cases of delusions of grandeur, the need of a sense of worth is so very great and realistically hopeless that the individual projects an idealized self-image. He hears himself proclaimed a Messiah or a Napoleon or a man of destiny charged with saving the nation. These psychotic symptoms may be termed abnormal projection and may occur after normal projection breaks down.

Projection is not always related to the negative traits nor is it always defensive. We tend, in varying degrees, to perceive others as we are. If we are generally happy, friendly or honest, we are inclined to see a little more of these traits in other people than really exist. This may be due in part to a simple lack of information, but not altogether. We are prone to project elements of our character to others and perceive it as characteristic of them.

Shapiro[3] discusses projection as a special characteristic of the paranoid, defining it as "the attribution to external figures of motivations, drives, or other tensions that are repudiated and intolerable in oneself." (p. 68). He adds that projection is not limited to the paranoid but in a general sense is more or less universal, saying: "Perhaps, any kind of empathic error or distortion—the way people often 'understand' their pets, for instance—can be regarded as a reflection of this tendency. Possibly, one could also include the tendency of the person in love to endow the object of that love with undeserved characteristics or the tendency of people who feel frightened or small to endow their enemies with greater size or more power than is actually warranted." On the defensive function of projection, he says:

> For example, it may be said that projection accomplishes an advantageous transformation of such an internal threat as that created by the pressure of an intolerable impulse into a more manageable external threat. . . . (p. 69). Projection, unlike these other sorts of reality impairment, does not involve a breakdown of cognition and a withdrawal of attention from the external world. On the contrary, it occurs in the act of cognition and with keen attention to the external world. Thus, projection is generally faithful to and does not distort apparent reality, nor does it usually include perceptual distortion. Projection distorts the significance of apparent reality; it is an autistic interpretative distortion of external reality. . . . (p. 70).

Displacement. The offended worker whose boss cussed him for a triviality cannot express his hostility directly at his boss out of fear of losing his job, but when he arrives home, he cusses his wife or slaps Junior down for some equally trivial matter. He has displaced his hostility from his boss to his wife or son. Or the college professor leaves home feeling very angry at his wife but has suppressed its expression. An hour or two later he bawls out a student for some trivial omission. As a defense mechanism the displacement is largely unconscious, else it would not serve its purpose; it would arouse guilty feelings. Other strong emotions

---

[3] From *Neurotic Styles* by David Shapiro, Basic Books, Inc., New York, 1965. Used with permission.

and symbolic meanings may be displaced in their many expressions, as fear in a phobia. It is like the substitutive mechanisms on the one hand and projection on the other. Displacement is a temporary protection of self-esteem but tends toward the impairment of interpersonal relationships which, in turn, may undermine self-esteem.

The classical experimental demonstration of displaced aggression was made by Neal Miller.[4] A white rat in a box with a grid floor learns to strike another rat by operant conditioning, the aggressive act being rewarded by terminating the electric shock when it makes the aggressive response. Next, instead of a second rat the experimenter placed a white doll of similar height in the box. Then when given the shock, the rat immediately attacked the doll. Thus, aggression is transferred (displaced) from an inaccessible (psychologically or physically) to an accessible object. Miller interprets this in terms of stimulus generalization, an established reaction directed to a new stimulus that has some elements in common with the original stimulus. Whether the rat was angry with the doll and thus "displacing" hostility or had merely learned an act to gain quick relief from pain was not clearly revealed.

Several experiments have been made with children and college students in controlled situations, e.g., classroom or laboratory. After a period of repeated subjection to insult, annoyance and thwarting, the subjects were released for play or given test activities and their aggressive responses observed relative to that of control groups. Significant increases of aggressive acts were noted in the experimental groups. (Sears et al, 1953; Ferson, 1958).

> For student reports and special discussion, as time permits, the following studies are suggested: (1) Brody, M. W. and Mahoney, V. P., "Introjection, Identification, and Incorporation," *Inter. J. Psychoanal.*, 1964, **46**, 57–63. (2) Goldin, P. C., "Experimental Investigation of Selective Memory and the Concept of Repression and Defense,"

---

[4] N.E. Miller, "Theory and experiment relating psychoanalytic displacement to stimulus-response generalization," *J. Abnorm. Soc. Psychol.*, 48:155–178 (1948).

J. Abnorm. Soc. Psychol., 1964, **69**, 365–380. (3) Haan, Norma, "Coping and Defense Mechanisms Related to Personality Inventories," *J. Consult. Psychol.*, 1965, **29**, 373–378. (4) Kagan, J., "The Concept of Identification," *Psychol. Review*, 1958, **65**, 296–305. (5) Murstein, Bernard I. and Pryer, Ronald S., "The Concept of Projection: a Review," *Psychol. Bull.*, 1959, **56**, 353–374.

CLARIFICATION NEEDED

There are several other mechanisms but to me they are ambiguous and are less specifically associated with maladaptive behavior. Those mentioned are sufficient to illustrate the variety of fixed behavior patterns that many deprived, security-motivated individuals use to achieve a precarious and partial satisfaction of basic needs. They are adjustive, coping devices which are inadequate for satisfying living but which are clung to desperately by inadequate people. They are not discrete traits that are clearly definitive, and any categorization is rather arbitrary. They are complex, strongly habitual mental processes with numerous overlapping elements. Scientific psychology could perform a much needed service by conducting a massive experimental program with statistical treatment of data by factor analysis to more clearly delineate the specific response elements of each and cluster these into operational patterns as they normally function. This would enhance our understanding of these very significant forms of behavior and advance the work in mental health.

SOME POSITIVE VALUES

It should be kept in mind that everyone has defense mechanisms of one type or another. No matter how autonomous and growth-motivated one may be, he has a reputation, a social position, a character structure to protect. Therefore, some mental energy must be diverted to the maintenance of one's defenses. They may serve a creative or growth purpose when not too severely imposing. The normal person with his normal defenses has an anxiety freedom that permits him to tackle new problems and explore new possibilities, new roles and modes of adjustment or productivity. Sublimation-motivated productivity, e.g., the romantic poet, and reactive-formation instigated social reform are quite often beneficial. Without these mechanisms they would not have occurred, and the person who performs good work is helped to some degree, regardless of the motive. The line between suppression-repression is rather ambiguous and often the supressed-repressed attitudes, desires, fears, etc., die or weaken to ineffectiveness, leaving a sounder and more positive character structure. Rationalized behavior often becomes realistically reasoned behavior since the repressed motives weaken and the rationalized or introjected desires are more fully internalized.

In general, these structures as found in their established patterns, tend to inhibit growth and productivity, fix character structure at an ineffectual level and arrest self-actualization. The rigidity and compulsiveness of such defense-oriented behavior prevent one's rolling with the punches of life. He can not adapt with changing conditions and demands, thus increasing tension and anxiety and a tightening of defenses until something cracks. The distortions of reality and self-deceptiveness that characterize much of his work cause confused and unrealistic coping efforts. Finally, even though protection against self-awareness is the central function of some of these mechanisms, it never is complete. There are those quiet moments of self-confrontation when the individual is vaguely aware of his own evasions, escape efforts and betrayal of growth responsibility. Then he is miserable; his self-esteem hits bottom.

Joy is that affective state experienced by the person who is aware of high-level performance, of living up to his responsibilities, actualizing his potentialities to a relatively high degree, participating in life abundantly, and hearing the commendation of the inner voice saying, "Well done, good and faithful servant." The fear-ridden self who lives behind a rigid system of defenses does not experience this. In those occasional lucid moments the voice that speaks to him is the voice of anxiety and guilt and misery. It is a threat of self-deterioration and self-extinction. The very weak and inadequate self, who is caught in the avoidance-avoidance conflict between this terrifying inner voice of self-condemnation and the equally terrifying threat of reality demands, regresses to the helpless state of insanity when his normal defenses break down.

We must remember that when we are thinking about these defensive mental processes (mechanisms or character traits), we should keep in mind the fact that they are not defenses against frustration *per se* but against danger or threat, whether real or imaginary and clearly or vaguely perceived. Prolonged frustration often becomes a threat, resulting in anxiety. Therefore, the defenses temporarily reduce anxiety but do not solve the original conflict.

ADJUSTIVE RANGE

To illustrate the wide range and variety of adjustive reactions in a given situation, ranging all the way from the most practical and approved to that which is definitely psychotic and socially maladaptive, Sawrey and Telford (1967, pp. 22–24) give the following hypothetical case:

> A young married woman with a strong maternal motive finds that she is apparently incapable of bearing children. This threatens her concept of herself as wife and potential mother. She becomes anxious, and in order to reduce her anxiety and to resist a change in her self-concept, she may react to the frustrating situation in one or more of the following ways:
>
> *Direct Overt Attack*
>
> (1) Have a thorough examination and diagnosis by a competent physician.
> (2) Prevail upon her husband to have an examination for possible sterility.
> (3) Follow through prescribed surgical, medical, or behavioral procedures recommended.
>
> *Socially Acceptable Substitute Reactions (Compensatory Activities)*
>
> Either in place of the above or after failure of it to remedy the situation she may:
>
> (1) Adopt children.
> (2) Become a children's nurse, pediatrician, or teacher.
> (3) Adopt and keep pets or establish a veterinary hospital.
> (4) Join or found an antivivisection society or society for the prevention of cruelty to animals.
>
> *Borderline Defensive Reactions*
>
> (1) Insist upon the blessings of childlessness (rationalization).
> (2) Place the blame for her sterility upon her own parents' neglect of her in childhood (projection).

(3) Revert to the behavior of a young adolescent (regression).
(4) Resort to daydreams in which the children in the neighborhood become her own (fantasy).
(5) Develop an aversion to children (reaction formation).

Socially Unacceptable Overt Reactions (Compensatory Reactions)

(1) Indulge in sexual promiscuity.
(2) Contract multiple marriages.
(3) Engage in anxiety-driven social or economic aggresisveness.
(4) Resort to alcoholism or drug addiction.

Socially and Personally Handicapping Psychosomatic and Neurotic Adjustment Patterns

(1) Display a functional amenorrhea (abnormal cessation of menstruation).
(2) Suffer from "morning sickness" without pregnancy.
(3) Experience "pseudo-pregnancy" distortion of the abdomen and other signs of pregnancy without actual pregnancy.)

Psychotic (Mentally Ill) Patterns of Adjustment (Delusions)

(1) Experience delusions of persecution concerning the seductive behavior of men.
(2) Have delusions of being drugged and raped.
(3) Believe that she will give birth to a Messiah.
(4) Experience delusions of motherhood.

LEARNED EMOTIONS AND DEFENSES

A brief working description of emotion was given in Chapter 2. Since mental health, social adjustment and the defensive behavior structures described are so intimately related to emotional expression, especially fear and anger, it seems appropriate to examine them as determiners of defensive behavior. Defense is against threat of injury as was previously stated. Psychologists have found it difficult to conceptualize emotion *per se* and generally prefer the descriptive term "emotional behavior." The question before us is this: Is emotion of such a nature that it can be designated as the motivator, the causer of certain behaviors, or is it merely a qualitative state of the mental and physiological processes involved in certain behaviors? There is a fundamental difference. The position one takes would alter the manner of his approach to the problem of controlling or regulating emotional behavior, whether to confront emotions directly as causers or to ignore the affect tone and confront whatever causes the inappropriate emotional behavior.

The layman has no doubts. Emotion causes people to do unusual things. John Doe killed his wife because he was in a rage. His anger caused him to kill her. Most psychologists have certain doubts, yet we discuss emotions as drives, as determiners of human behavior, while at the same time describing them as qualitative states, as accompaniments. A majority of psychologists cannot be entirely wrong. There must be some reality to this concept, but there is confusion as to which we should keep trying to dispel since complex behavior is confusing. Let us re-examine motivation and emotion in their interrelationship, both stemming from the same root.

I have stated that motivation is the state of readiness, the disposition of self to respond when aroused. New behavior is necessary because self is aroused by the adjudged incongruities of the stimulus situation, and evaluates the situation in relation to self (self in relation to it). This motivated response is experienced as a need-drive-goal response, a unified experience in which the need and goal are the inseparable push and pull of the response, with self pushing toward an anticipated goal and attracted by the value of that goal. The drive is the desire or interest. It is either strong or weak in proportion to the evaluation. If the situation is adjudged highly threatening and self is adjudged greatly inadequate, the need is strongly experienced and the goal strongly desired. The response is highly motivated, with an intense state of consciousness and neural discharge that carries a high degree of negative affect termed fear. If the situation changed slightly and self is adjudged as being adequate, the affect tone changes to anger or resentment, correlated with certain changes in the physiological accompaniments that occur.

THE SELF CAUSES, INITIATES

Emotion is not something that can drive a person to do something; neither is it, in normal behavior, a goal toward which behavior is directed. Self is the mover, the motivater, the driver, the causer and a needed-desired situational change is the goal. Emotion is the affect tone of the motivated behavior, the need awareness, and its function is of the nature of a means. Its utility is in the constant "feedback" and re-evaluation required in emergency adjustive behavior or new creative responses. John Doe did not kill his wife because he was angry. Anger was not the something that *caused* the killing action. John Doe as self, evaluated the adulterous behavior of his wife as being of such thwarting and injustice (wrong) to his own self-hood that *he* chose to kill her; he was in a high state of anger at the time. The anger was a correlate, not a cause. It was the quality state of his evaluative cognition. One might argue, if he had not been so very angry, he would not have killed her. This is probably true; but the reduced drive to kill her would not have been caused by the reduced anger. Rather, had John Doe taken more time to think, he probably would have re-evaluated the situation as not being so terribly disastrous and would have chosen a different response accompanied by somewhat less resentment. Often defense mechanisms are built to protect self from the threat of its own hostile impulses, when it lacks the strength and frustration tolerance necessary for rational reappraisal and behavior control.

The soldier does not flee the battlefield because of his great fear. He flees because he (the self of him) has evaluated the situation as being a threat to his existence and flight appears to be the only recourse. The great fear is the highly colored qualitative state of his intense consciousness of the situation. In what sense, then, can it be said that fear, or its more diffused counterpart anxiety, may be a drive, a determiner of behavior?

In normal behavior, the person does not act in a certain way to remove a fear. Fear reduction is not the goal that may induce a behavior response. The action is directed toward removing the threatening object or changing the dangerous situation. But in abnormal or deviant behavior like the neurotic, the situation is somewhat different.

We will see, in the following chapters, how anxiety is the predominant factor in neuroses. Anxiety is fear that springs from a more generalized and prolonged threatening situation that is ill-defined. Such as, the threat of general responsibility or vaguely conceived eternal punishment, or a fear reaction that has become detached from its original cause (by repression) but is aroused by some corresponding element of the current situation which was a part of the old threat. The neurotic person periodically experiences waves of terrific fear (anxiety) without being able to recognize the source of the threat or danger. The goal may become that of eliminating the fear that is so distressing. In abnormal behavior, the fear may be designated as the cause of the specific action. It is perverted or abnormal behavior (motivation) because a means has been changed into an end.

FEAR AS THE THREAT

To designate fear as a drive or its removal as a goal is not concise thinking even in neurotic cases. The actual mental process is this: The irrational fear and impulse toward inappropriate behavior are evaluated as posing a threat to the self or to one's state of mind or social status and thus he strives to eliminate it. He is afraid of this strange fear and what he might do. Therefore, even in abnormal behavior the principle still holds: fear is the affective coloring of the intensive state of consciousness when self adjudges (evaluates) itself as being threatened and being inadequate to cope with the danger. The following case may illustrate.

Mrs. B had been suffering a state of "general anxiety neurosis." She was in her late thirties, and as a child she had been reared in a deprived home and community situation, but after her marriage, she was quite comfortably situated and securely established. She was a member of the Country Club set, active in golfing and bridge. Frequently, while on the golf course or at a bridge table, among friends who were having a lovely time, a tidal wave of fear would sweep over or through her with such intensity that she literally became ill. On some occasions she could hardly restrain herself from knocking everything from the table and rushing screaming from the room. She had a great fear of these fear-experiences.

In this case, the abnormal (neurotic) fear-experience was the incongruous stimulus situation which she evaluated as being a great threat to her sanity and social status, and she evaluated herself as being inadequate to cope with it. She experienced a normal fear of this abnormal fear reaction. She was afraid that she might become insane or that she might leap up screaming and disgrace herself. Her earlier unrealistic thoughts, desires and memories, were repressed, and composed the real threat since they were blocked from conscious awareness. She was not able to recognize them, and recalled only the strong affect. The fear response was consciously experienced by her as painfully threatening. In such cases, the abnormal fear response could be termed a motivating factor but not a drive. The need, as experienced, is to eliminate the abnormal fear, and this the goal. The true need, however, is to remove or change the unrealistic and inappropriate thoughts, judgments, evaluations, etc. of which the neurotic is unaware.

Is all of this merely a play on words, a problem of semantics, difficulty in communication because our terms lack precision? Partly. But a fundamental issue is also involved. If fear is actually a force that can cause a neurotic syndrome, then our primary objective, as psychotherapists, would be to remove the fear symptom. The purpose of therapy is to remove causes of affliction. If the fear (emotion) is merely an accompaniment, the affect tone of evaluative thinking and highly motivated behavior, then our therapeutic objective should be to correct the faulty thinking, concepts and evaluations of both the stimulus situation and the self which responds to the situation. The process of evaluating and the system of values may need revision.

LEARNING PROCEDURES

Adequate, effective coping behavior is learned. The mechanisms I have described above are learned, and the neurotic symptoms I shall be describing are also learned. Values are learned; and fears and angers are learned. How? Only the most condensed report can be given here. I shall assume that you have some knowledge of Pavlovian classical conditioning and Skinnerian operant (instrumental) conditioning, or will turn to any textbook in Introductory Psychology for a quick background. (See also Appendix.)

To learn a new response, depending on its complexity, there are:

1. A cue, a stimulus situation, cognitive incongruence. Consciously or unconsciously there is organismic awareness.

2. A motive, need, state of readiness, based on potential capacity.

3. Frustration, old responses inadequate, a new pattern necessary.

4. An anticipated or imagined goal, a condition or situation sought. Whether this would apply at the lowest learning level of simple reflexive action is conjectural.

5. A repertoire of general or random movements, a trial and error-success series of responses. With primates and children beyond the first few months of age, deliberate imitation and a sort of mental trial-and-error become operative and thus reduces the generalized movements.

6. Reinforcement and extinction. As with No. 5, with certain types of learning by higher animals and children, no extrinsic rewards or punishments are necessary for reinforcement or extinction. The experience of success itself reinforces the response and facilitates its continued use, while the experience of failure is frustrating and sets up an inhibiting resistance that tends to extinguish faulty movements. Thus, in motivated learning where need is being experienced and self is cognizant, imaginatively, of a satisfying goal, responses perceived as leading toward that goal carry their own reward and are reinforced while those specific responses perceived as not leading toward the goal are frustrating and resistance is imposed that tends toward extinction. In other words, in meaningful, goal-directed learning, there is constant feedback and re-evaluation of relative success. This feedback process, in which emotion finds its function, accounts for reinforcement and extinction.

7. Repetition or practice. In the classical conditioning of sensory-motor type reactions, many reinforced repetitions are required to establish (learn) the association. In the more complex learned responses of the animal, of the operant conditioning type, several but not as many reinforced trials are necessary. In many cases of learned response at the human level, it is a one-only situation. This suggests that at the higher levels, a self with insight is the learner and director of the learning process. When self places high value on the response, evaluates it as being of great significance to self, one-trial successful response is all that is required. It is learned.

Whether the individual learns a wide repertoire of effective coping responses and creative behavior or a rigid system of defense mechanisms and/or neurotic syndromes is determined in large measure by his previously learned fear responses. To surrender these mechanisms and syndromes, it is helpful to understand the nature of the underlying fear reactions and how they are learned.

CONDITIONING AND EVALUATION

N. E. Miller[5] conducted extensive experiments with rats, conditioning them to fear. A rat was placed in the left compartment of a two-compartment box with no escape, except through a trap door into the second compartment. In the first compartment, and first phase of the experiment, the rat received electric shocks repeatedly with the escape door securely fastened. It reacted with all the typical fear responses of jumping, squealing, defecating, and trying to escape, until it learned the escape route into the second compartment where it received no shocks. After several repetitions, the rat was thoroughly conditioned (learned) to express fear. Then (second phase of the test) with the electrical device removed, the rat was "motivated by fear" to learn to escape into the right compartment. The fear conditioned rat was placed repeatedly in the left compartment and continued to show fear-agitation for several hundred trials (trial numbers varying with different rats) before the response became extinguished. The test was repeated with numerous rats with the same general results, illustrating learning by operant conditioning. We shall examine it a little more closely.

Had the experimenter removed the upper cerebral cortex of the rat, it would have taken many repetitions of the electric shock in association with the inner left compartment before the rat would have evinced the physiological fear reactions. These occurred almost from the beginning, showing that the rat itself had sufficient mental ability to evaluate that compartment as being a great threat to him.

The rat learned to adjudge the compartment as a threat and to evaluate it as extremely detrimental. The fear was the affective

[5] N.E. Miller, "Studies of fear as an acquirable drive: fear as motivation and fear reduction as reinforcement in the learning of new responses," *J. Exper. Psychol.,* 38:89–101 (1948).

quality of his mental state. Since the rat had no knowledge of electricity, it took many repeated exposures to the formerly hurtful compartment before he learned to re-evaluate it as no longer a threat. He learned to recognize and to re-evaluate the situation in relation to himself. When this was done, the affect tone changed, slowly died away and was extinguished.

Man, with his greater insight and knowledge, would immediately have perceived that the electric device had been removed and on the first occasion would have re-evaluated the situation as no longer a threat. His fear response would have ceased very soon. When a person acquires a new fear, he has learned to evaluate a new situation, such as a real or imagined relationship as being a threat of such magnitude that he is unable to cope with it. The anxiety-ridden, neurotic individual has learned in the past to perceive much of life's realities. The reason it is so hard for him to eliminate his irrational fears is that the faulty evaluative concepts are repressed and blocked from consciousness. Therefore, he cannot learn to re-evaluate the situation in relation to self. The fear, as the color tone of the repressed mental activity, may show through the repressive resistance barrier and be experienced just as the color of an object may show through translucent glass without the object itself being visible.

Fear is like any emotion. It is experienced both as the affect quality of consciousness and as excessive physiological processes and it may be aroused by either the self in evaluative cognition or by a physical stimulus. Extinction may be produced at the reflex level by conditioning or at the cognitive level by re-evaluation.

EMOTIONS GENERALIZED IN ATTITUDES

Fear and anger (any emotion) are not drives that determine any particular action by a person. Instead, they are accompaniments that function in feedback and thus aid in the constant re-evaluation. In cases of persons reared in a social environment that is so frustrating and threatening that they experience anger and fear almost constantly, these emotions become generalized as basic attitudes and dispositions of the self. We may draw a distinction between attitudes and motives but to no practical purpose relative to the way they operate in adjustive or productive behavior. At our level of concern they are virtually synonymous. Under these conditions of learned evaluation of life in general, we have millions of people whose predominant attitudes (motives) are cautious and distrustful, suspicious and resentful. Of such people it may be said that their behavior is fear and hate determined. The proportion and nature of these determine their defense patterns.

On the other hand, those persons who are reared in a social climate of acceptance, approval, and love, with their basic needs well provided, experience much happiness and general positive affect. (These emotions are not as well defined as are the negative ones.) These positive emotions also become generalized and become basic attitudes and dispositions of the self, motivating behavior in general toward trustful involvement and deep empathic relations of goodwill and sincere concern. The behavior of these people may be said to be determined largely by faith and love; it is free of defense and spontaneous. However, it is self, motivated by fear or hate or faith or love, that determines behavior.

These are the "big four" determiners of human behavior attitudes which give quality and direction to human behavior. They are mixed and competing in all of us, and they are colored by other attitudes. Love may be more pronounced than faith or faith than love, but these usually serve together as inseparable partners. We have the creative, productive person where these are dominant. On the other side, anxiety (generalized fear) may be more pronounced than hate or vice versa, but these usually work together. We have the ineffective and maladaptive, the mentally and socially ill where they predominate. Karl Menninger's popular book, *Love Against Hate* could be revised to include faith against fear.

SUMMARY

Certain general principles of behavior were presented as: (1) It is normally holistic and integrated, with responses selected by self and directed toward satisfying goals in accord with the established value system. (2) It may be conscious or unconscious, with some forms never having been under conscious controls (vital processes and preconceptual responses) and others formed consciously but relegated to unconscious control centers (habits). (3) It is determined by evaluative cognition of which selective perception, selective recall, etc. are examples. The weaker the self, the more faulty the cognition and ineffective the behavior (a greater need for defense). (4) It is determined by the degree of frustration tolerance, thus the degree and frequency of hostility, anger, etc.—again, the need of defenses.

The inferiority complex or psychic inferiority was presented as a general condition that necessitates defensive behavior devices. Certain frequently mentioned defense mechanisms are interrelated character or personality traits with overlapping elements designed to protect the self from real or imagined threat and deprivation. Thus, they are adjustive but generally restricting and maintenance-oriented more than growth. There is a variation of patterns of defensive behavior with each individual, in accordance with what he has learned to value most in relation to self, thus need the most, and what his feared weaknesses are. Those described were: repression, rationalization, reaction-formation, compensation, sublimation, fantasy, regression, identification, introjection, projection, and displacement.

Emotion was re-examined in its relation to motivation and defensive behavior, not as a causer but as affective accompaniment. Self causes on the basis of need and goal values, which includes one's defenses. A strong emotion like fear or rage may be said to indirectly cause a certain response when the anticipated fear or rage-action itself is evaluated as being a threat. Self evaluates an anticipated situation which causes the response, the developing of defenses. How behavior is learned (including defenses) was presented as occurring at different levels from conditioned reflexes requiring many repetitions to one-shot insight learning where self evaluates and provides its own reinforcement or extinction in the process of evaluation.

GLOSSARY

Amnesia. A temporary loss of identity. The individual may go for days, months, or several years unable to recall any of his life previous to the onset, a sort of total repression.

Hallucination. A sensory perception without a basis in objective reality. A mental image projected outwardly and "seen" as an object.

Heteronomous. Subject to the rule or authority of others, as opposed to autonomy. The voluntary merging into group interdependence.

Internalization. The relatively unconscious mental process by which one person appropriates the values, attitudes, etc. of another person or group.

Phobia. A strong irrational and inappropriate fear of some object or situation that normally would not evoke a fear reaction. These will be discussed in the next chapter.

Suggestible. Yielding (mentally); uncritical assent. Responsive to ideas or suggestions of others; easily hypnotized.

Typology. A set or listing of types; categorization.

REFERENCES AND SUGGESTED READINGS

ADLER, ALFRED, *Individual Psychology,* Patterson, N.J.: Littlefield, Adams & Company, 1963.

ANGYAL, ANDRAS (E. Haufmann, ed), *Neurosis and Treatment: A Holistic Theory,* New York: John Wiley & Sons, Inc., 1965.

BUS, ARNOLD H., *The Psychology of Aggression,* New York: John Wiley & Sons, Inc., 1961.

CROW, LESTER and ALICE CROW, *Mental Hygiene for Teachers,* New York: The Macmillan Company, 1963.

MENNINGER, KARL, *Love Against Hate,* New York: Harcourt, Brace & World, Inc., 1942.

MILLER, N. E., "Fear as Motivation and Fear-reduction as Reinforcement. . ." *J. Exper. Psychol.,* (1948) 38, 89–101.

———, "Theory and Experiment Relating Psychoanalytic Displacement to Stimulus-Response Generalization," *J. Abnormal Social Psychol.,* (1948) 43, 155–178.

SAWREY, JAMES M. and CHARLES W. TELFORD, *Psychology of Adjustment,* Boston: Allyn and Bacon, Inc., 1967.

SHAPIRO, DAVID, *Neurotic Styles,* New York: Basic Books, Inc., 1965.

8

Psychotic and Neurotic Behavior

Fascinating and mysterious have been the sudden or rapid changes in behavior which characterized so many people through the centuries. These changes separate them from virtually all normal social relationships and from communication and understanding. Quiet men suddenly ran amuck, became violent and dangerous. Outgoing, friendly people became surly, suspicious or withdrawn recluses. Honest, reputable persons began to weave fanciful stories about themselves, hearing voices, seeing things that did not exist. Their fellowmen could not understand them, stood in awe of them, or feared and persecuted them.

THE PSYCHOSES

Such people, in primitive times, were thought to be those who had been forsaken by the gods, or were victims of their wrath, for having failed to observe some obligatory ritual or an established taboo.[1] Unprotected by the gods, they became possessed by demons. Later in history, they were thought to be in league with the devil or bewitched. They were criminals against God and man, strange creatures to be feared and despised, to be per-

[1] From S. L. Rogers, "Attitudes Toward Insanity in Primitive Cultures," *Ciba Symposia* 9, pp. 602–608, (1947).

secuted or chained in prisons for protection. They had betrayed and thus abrogated their humanity. Still later, they became the mad, the crazy, the insane, objects of disgust and shame to be hidden away from their respectable families. Finally, the attention of science was focused upon them with its naturalistic approach, and they were seen as *pathos*—pathetic, sick, suffering illness of the psyche. Today, some are questioning whether these aberrant behaviors should be termed illnesses.

AS THEY SEE THEMSELVES

Dr. Carney Landis[2] gives some vivid and insightful accounts of the psychotic break as described by the patients themselves.

> I went out of my head and wrote to my sister that I was crazy. The voices told me that I was and that they were going to kill me. The devil offered me unlimited power if I would do his bidding. He said he would give me half of hell to rule over when I died. He would under no condition let me go to heaven because I knew too much about him and would put him out of business. I was supposed to rule the world and wipe out civilization. There was a new force by which the mind of man could be controlled. It came from another planet and it manifested itself through me. (p. 12).
>
> I seem shut into myself, withdrawn from real contact with the outer world as also from contact with God; the sun does not really shine, the trees and fields are not really green; I am shut in with my thoughts, always of a depressing and melancholy nature. The sense of isolation, of being cut off from God, one's fellows and the world, seems to me to be the paramount feature underlying the whole state. . . .
>
> Moral tension returns in full force. I am haunted by a sense of guilt; my conscience gives me no rest, even when there do not seem to be any particularly grievous sins upon it. Whatever I am doing, I feel I ought to be doing something else. I worry perpetually about my past sins and failures; not for a moment can I forget the mess I seem to have made of

[2] Carney Landis (Fred A. Mettlee, ed), *Varieties of Psychopathological Experience* (New York: Holt, Rinehart and Winston, 1964). Reprinted by permission of Holt, Rinehart and Winston, Inc. Originally from *Wisdom, Madness and Folly* by J. Custance. Reprinted by permission of Farrar, Straus & Giroux, Inc.

> my life. However I may pray for and think of forgiveness, no forgiveness comes. Eventually the terrors of Hell approach. . . . (p. 4).
>
> I knew definitely that the figure in the mirror was mad. I was mad. I have never learned words with which to describe the sensations accompanying that realization. I seemed dual; struggling against the truth, crying out against fate, pleading, praying; and at the same time, cool and almost surgical in my analysis of the situation. I probed to find the cause; I reckoned the factor of fatigue, long continued fever, strain, tension; I checked my recent behavior and the accompanying drives and emotions. Yes, that explained it all. I was mad. Again I looked at the mirrored figure. It seemed all eyes. I called it by name. "Do you know," I said, "do you know that you are insane? Do you know what that means? Do you know they won't trust you anymore? They can't. You may not work in the fall. You will disappoint them all. Do you know what it is like to be mad? That *thing* will get stronger and stronger. Some day it will *be* you. . . . Everyone will know soon. They will shut you up. . . . Do you know it's *you* that's mad, you, and not anyone you are reading about? . . . Yes, I know; I know; . . . I know it's me that's mad." (p. 19).

Of these and several others, Landis says: "Essentially, each patient is trying to say, 'Something new, different, terrifying and indescribable is happening or has happened to my mind. Things seem unreal and indescribable; I can't control them; they frighten me; something makes me do things that I don't want to do but I can't help myself; new feelings, ideas and thoughts come to my mind; I don't really know how to tell you what it's like.'

"After surveying many autobiographical descriptions, I conclude from the reports of the subjective experience that two major considerations occupy the patient's mind at the onset of the psychopathological experience; first, the realization of the loss of adequate self-control, and second, the attempts, usually not too successful, to explain these experiences to himself." (p. 42).

The central schizophrenic problem as Boisen[3] sees it is "an intolerable loss of self-respect." Former defenses broken, schizophrenia becomes a way of life—a way of saving self from a sense

[3] Anton T. Boisen, *Out of the Depths* (New York: Harper & Brothers, 1960).

of utter annihilation, the greatest of experiential anxieties. It takes three forms, Boisen thinks, comparable to what is commonly described as *paranoiac*, *catatonic*, and *simple* schizophrenia.

SYMPTOM CATEGORIES

Paranoiac. The characteristic symptoms are delusions, usually of persecution or grandeur, but sometimes jealous and erotic. These are frequently accompanied by fantasies of some national catastrophe or world cataclysm with oneself as a conquering hero or savior. Furtive, eccentric, and irrational behavior of various types accompany these delusions and fantasies. The mechanisms of projection and fantasy have reached their ultimate development in one's effort to protect the self from its own terribly painful self-condemnation. The "idealized" self, which is poles apart from the "feared" self that is too painfully worthless to behold, becomes the real self in delusional awareness; a fantasied world-stage replaces the too frustrating real world which is totally rejected. By becoming a persecuted person, the self is given a sense of worth, of the significance of his mission. The torturing voice of conscience is evaded by perceiving these pernicious, inhuman motives and traits in others.

The onset of paranoiac reactions may be gradual, sudden, or make their open appearance rather suddenly but following a period of incubation. Cameron[4] lists the following precipitating factors that especially favor paranoiac reactions.

(1) Anything that confirms the chronic expectation of receiving sadistic treatment, and therefore increases a readiness to retaliate.
(2) Anything that increases suspicion and distrust, thereby confirming a lifelong expectation of deception and betrayal.
(3) Whatever increases vigilance and at the same time tends to isolate a person from social interchange with others.
(4) Anything that increases envy and jealousy, thereby arousing resentment, hatred, and a sense of inferiority.
(5) Whatever lowers self-esteem, thus encouraging superego attack, and necessitating vigorous denial and projection.

[4] Norman Cameron, *Personality Development and Psychopathology* (Boston: Houghton Mifflin Co., 1963). Used with permission.

(6) Anything that stimulates a person to see his own defects in others, thus increasing his anxiety, and demanding more denial and projective discharge to overcome it.
(7) Situations combining idleness with isolation, which leave a person free to ruminate over probable meanings and motivations, when he has less than average chance for valid social reality testing. . . . (p. 481).

Catatonic. This state is sometimes designated as "the living dead," based on the common symptom of stupor, sometimes flaccid but usually rigid with clenched hands, closed eyes, closed mouth, seeing nothing, hearing nothing (?), saying nothing, recognizing no one, responding neither to hunger, toilet habits, nor even to drugs except in unusual dosage. They are fed by spoon or intravenously, diapered and changed like an infant, and remain like a statue in whatever position they are placed. They are the ultimate in regression.

Not all are immobile to that degree, however, and most do not remain in the stuporous state. They frequently move slowly into a state of catatonic excitement and manifest intense activity such as throwing and breaking things. They become noisy and aggressive, agitated and very anxious. Thus, the basic syndrome is psychomotor abnormality and great fear. Nurses have stated that they have never seen eyes that expressed so much fright as those of the catatonic when he is coming out of the stupor. During the transition period hallucinations are common, and often add to the anxiety, since the visions are often terrifying. Some are unconscious of their surroundings during extreme stupor or do not remember it later. Others are aware of what is going on but cannot respond. It is not a conscious, deliberate negativism.

The weak self with shattered confidence, fear-ridden and with the most despairing sense of unworth, finds life so horribly threatening that it negates the whole of reality and regresses to the state of helpless infancy for protection. "Take care of me, love me, prove my worth" is the unconscious cry of their tortured souls. It requires a lot of proving before they are convinced. The onset is usually more sudden than with most schizophrenics and prognosis of recovery is a little better.

Hebephrenic. The term "hebephrenic" literally means "the mind of youth." The characteristic symptoms of these patients reflect the extreme silliness and emotionality of early adolescence.

Their emotional responses are excessive and inappropriate and their behavior is disorganized. They may giggle and laugh or cry over nothing or anything. The silliness is also revealed in mannerisms, bizarre speech and gestures. They are often given to stereotype phrases and ritualistic acts, and the coining of new and usually inappropriate words (neologisms). They, too, have hallucinations and delusions but not of the same nature as the paranoid. They are more weird and bizarre and have less of the persecution or grandeur aspects. They often experience a deep sense of loss and weep accordingly without knowing the reason.

The onset is usually gradual, unless triggered by a crisis experience, such as an unusual loss, hurt or disappointment. The prognosis of recovery is poor. They are, perhaps, the most difficult type to cure. Regression is slower and may be in stages, the most noticeable being at the early adolescent period. The hebephrenic may become more and more preoccupied with his private world of fantasy, withdraw more deeply into himself, and regress to the point of virtual inaccessibility.

Simple. This type is marked by fewer of the bizarre, dramatic symptoms. Such persons may go on for years functioning at a minimum of occupational and social acceptability. There is a gradual regression or deterioration of mental processes, loss of interest and ambition (or repression of), concern for personal appearance, and moral values, and perhaps social withdrawal and general apathy. The layman may not see these as signs of mental illness and call such a person lazy, untidy, queer, eccentric, stubborn, etc. If symptoms begin early in life, the child may be diagnosed as mentally retarded. Some hoboes, hermits, "skid row" bums, and prostitutes are of the simple schizophrenic type.

Onset is slow, and so is recovery. They protect themselves against feared failure by not trying.

Undifferentiated. There are the acute and chronic undifferentiated types. These manifest a variety of symptoms so well mixed they do not fit into either of the above types, any more one than another. In fact, many cases first diagnosed as one or another of the above types may change symptoms and later be diagnosed differently.

Schizophrenia is a broad category of many specific types or patterns of mental malfunction and of varying degrees of regression. Of 1000 cases, no two are alike. They are the disorganized personalities and distorted or deranged mental processes of a very weak self. The stresses of life can not be faced, since the self is too weak and afraid to maintain an integrated, rational structure of mental processes and well-organized and controlled social-physical behavior. Activities are reorganized into a schizophrenic way of life.

CHARACTERISTIC REACTIONS

Cameron (1963, p. 584) says: "*Schizophrenic reactions are regressive attempts to escape tension and anxiety by abandoning realistic interpersonal object relations and constructing delusions and hallucinations.*" He adds:

> Schizophrenic reactions can be considered adaptive in the limited sense that regression and withdrawal may protect a person from a frightening social reality. Withdrawal has the virtue of reducing the complexity and the pressure of external reality; but it leaves the patient helpless. Delusions and hallucinations are adaptive, if they provide satisfactory substitutes for whatever the patient has lost in his object relations. The advantages of such adaptive attempts are lost if the schizophrenic patient, when he regresses and withdraws into fantasy, finds himself either in an objectless world, which in itself is frightening, or encounters the kinds of primitive experiences that normal adults meet in dreams. Since the schizophrenic person is not asleep he cannot escape from desolate or frightening fantasies by waking up. (P. 585).

Stern[5] says: "The group of pathological reactions included under the collective label of schizophrenia contains those forms of mental disorder which most closely resemble the popular image of insanity. One finds here scary, weird, uncanny phenomena—such things as hallucinations, delusions, catatonic immobility, and fits of raving madness—phenomena which seem to be located at the most extreme limit of mental alienation . . . the schizophrenic is quite literally unhinged, alienated, divorced from

---

[5] Paul J. Stern, *The Abnormal Person and His World* (Princeton, N.J.: D. Van Nostrand Co., Inc., 1964). Used with permission.

the world of generally accepted reality. The whole structure of meaning of his existence is shattered, and he seems to dwell in a transmogrified, irrational, idiosyncratic world. . . ." (pp. 167–168).

From the above types we can garner the chief characteristics of schizophrenia: deterioration of conduct and personal habits, disturbed perception (hallucination), disorganized and delusional thinking, behavior extremes from apathy to violence, displaced and inappropriate affect from flat no-feeling to emotional peaks, and tendencies toward seclusiveness. Their thinking is rich in archaic symbolism and often has the special concreteness of childhood. Abstract ideas are perceived in hallucination as things.

Arieti[6] says: "For example, a patient who, before the onset of the psychosis, had a very low opinion of himself, especially on account of his homosexual desires, now has an olfactory hallucination. He smells an awful odor emanating from his body. Here again we have a perceptualization of the feelings he has toward himself: he is a rotten character, he stinks." (p. 476).

Beck[7] discusses schizophrenia in terms of five *basic processes* which are generally permanent, although fluid, and the means by which the schizophrenic achieves adaptation. He postulates that all mental disorders are adaptive and directed toward survival. They are the logical responses to the *unreal* world that the schizophrenic has created, having found the *real* world too difficult to face. Beck says: "Schizophrenia is, then, a seemingly intelligent solution of the problems presented to an individual by his phenomena, i.e., by the appearances in his awareness. This philosophic orientation ignores external realities. . . . His emotioned-toned phenomena—or 'appearances,' i.e., understanding—do not form linkage with the emotional phenomena of the outside world. . . . In sum, the schizophrenic's phenomenological world, his picture of reality, is incomplete. Hence, the disaster which schizophrenia is. The patient is adapting (a) to inner data, to appearances which he has (b) substituted for external ones. It is a maladjustive adaptation."

---

[6] S. Arieti (ed), *American Handbook of Psychiatry*, Vol. 1, pp. 455–507 (1959).

[7] Samuel J. Beck, *Psychological Processes in the Schizophrenic Adaptation* (New York: Grune and Stratton, 1965) pp. 5, 29. Used by permission of author and publisher.

From several hundred clinically observed symptomatic responses, 170 characteristic symptoms of schizophrenia in general were derived by condensation. These symptoms, in turn, were subjected to factor analysis and the five basic processes determined. The procedure parallels Catell's treatment of personality traits, producing his surface and core traits (Chapter 2). The symptoms change from time to time in the behavior of the individual and varies among patients. But the processes are permanent patterns or styles of behavior. These basic processes are manifested by each patient through his various and changing symptoms at different adjustive-maladjustive levels. They are:

I. The defenses: A, Constrictive; B, Pathogenic; C, Adjustive.
II. Intellectual functioning: A, Orderly; B, Disrupted.
III. Fantasy activity: A, Autistic; B, Regressive; C, Little or none; D, Potentially creative.
IV. Emotional state: A, Lability; B, Fixed tone; C, Controlled release.
V. Social adaptation: A, Self-absorbed; B, Self-deprived; C, Restitutional; D, Constructive life objectives.

(Beck's work is continuing and is deserving of additional study and discussion.)

PARANOIA REACTION

Paranoia is a psychotic structure with the rigidly defensive and delusion of persecution symptoms found in the paranoiac schizophrenic, but he is not a schizophrenic. He is stronger at the center of his being (the self) and seldom or never "breaks" under the normal stresses of life. He projects his inner self-condemnation to others, to the degree that he actually hears people plot against him. He can organize a number of unrelated and insignificant facts into a rational and air-tight logical conviction that a jealous relative, or boss, or the communists are plotting to do him harm. Although he is rather rigid in his ways and poorly adaptive, he can play his family and occupational roles sufficiently to get by. His delusions are so logical and convincing that people go on believing him for a long time. When his stories become too extreme and unrealistic or his neighbors get contrary evidence, they may merely consider him eccentric or a liar. However, he is too sincere to be considered a liar for long, so he is "well, just a little off," or perhaps a "crank."

This person may be intelligent and educated and show no characteristics of insanity other than his delusions. But he builds much of his life around these, goes out and gathers information to sustain them, and, if he is a strong person, he may fight his persecutor or persecutors. He may be dangerous, since he can kill from a sense of duty or self-defense. If he is a weaker character, he may resort to escape, become a drifter, and move from job to job. He is usually suspicious, on guard, misinterprets what is said, writes warning letters to newspapers, and is frequently involved in lawsuits. His is the type of projection described by Shapiro in Chapter 7. Meanings are distorted. He is not as weak as the schizophrenic in self-development, has less fear, does not regress as does a schizophrenic; but he has a deep sense of guilt or worthlessness that is repressed and projected to the degree of delusions.

MANIC-DEPRESSIVE PSYCHOSIS

This is a mental or behavior disorder characterized by various deviant moods. It is affect psychosis, extreme emotional behavior change. The intense emotional states may impair sound judgment and "common sense" behavior, but there are not the intellectual disruption, strong hallucinations, delusions, and general personality disorganization found in schizophrenia. It is usually slow in development and often appears without a precipitating crisis experience. Manic-depressive states are generally less malignant and regression less complete than in schizophrenia. However, there are several common symptoms and transitional forms that make diagnosis difficult. Some psychiatrists say that in some cases, the manic-depressive state deteriorates into schizophrenia. This is a disputed point and diagnosis is not of highest validity. The type form is cyclic as shown in Figure 9, the cyclic changes occurring anywhere from a period of a few days to several weeks. In some, the manic phase is followed by little depression, while

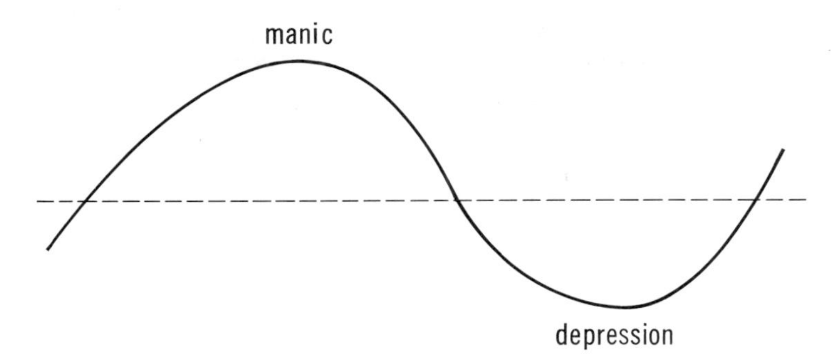

Figure 9.

others are prone to depression only, going from normalcy to depression and back to normalcy, without reaching the manic peak.

Manic Reaction. This is the state of high excitement, euphoria, elation. Tremendous amounts of energy are consumed by the manic driven person who is on the go 20 of the 24-hour day. The world is wonderful and he, the manic, most wonderful of all. He effervesces enthusiasm and self-confidence. His thoughts runs away with him, and most communication is a one-way street. His thinking is apt to be shallow and his wit less sharp than he thinks. In conversation, his mania may appear to be megalomania as he parades himself and his plans, and in this state there may occur mild delusions of grandeur and even hallucinations. He is seldom dangerous to others but may be to himself by his reckless tendencies and incoordination due to excitability and nervous exhaustion.

Cameron says (1963, p. 559): "There is little of adaptive value in mania. Regression is too deep, reality testing too severely impaired. The manic patient is like an over-excited child who is unable to quiet down and unable to make use of his environment in adult ways. He behaves as though there were every reason for his being madly playful and aggressively, insistently self-assertive. His expansive and often silly talk, his often dangerous lack of consideration for others, his inability to run his own life and cope with his own daily needs—all these seem to the patient right and normal.

"The only sense in which mania can be considered adaptive is that it does *deny a reality* which is too painful to be faced, a reality which would justify a psychotic depression in anyone with such a personality organization. In this sense, the manic reaction can be considered as a defense against psychotic depression, as a refusal or inability to accept the intolerably painful truths of a reality situation. . . ."

His break with reality is not of a deep nature and he finally burns himself out. The mask of self-deception, denial of reality, high fantasy, and selective perception (perception of self and the outer world) wears thin, the decline begins.

Depressive Reaction. Sadness, dejection, and black gloom characterize this phase of the cycle when it reaches bottom. The patient is listless, seclusive, withdrawn, neglectful of personal appearance, has no energy for anything. There is a depressed flow of neural energy. He is gloomy, despondent, apprehensive, guilt-laden, and self-condemnatory, worthy of death; and he is in danger of suicide. When this occurs, however, it usually is just before he reaches the lowest ebb or when he starts back up again. Perhaps he lacks even the energy for self-destruction at the lowest point. This sometimes becomes a point of depressive stupor.

Both the manic and depressive phases of the cycle are subdivided, each into four subtypes, given here in reverse order of intensity: hypomania, acute mania, hypermania, and delusional mania; simple depression, marked depression, stuporous depression, and delusional depression. There are wide variations among patients and a minority follow the balanced cyclic phases.

Involutional Melancholia. Authorities differ as to whether this depressive state of sadness, apprehension, and self-condemnation warrants separate classification or whether it should be designated as psychotic depression appearing during the involutional period of menopause in women and its counterpart in men. Hypochrondriacal symptoms are often prevalent with delusionary convictions of incurable disease or abnormal bodily changes. The age of the patient may account for this characteristic, health anxiety generally being greater at this period. Involutional melancholy is generally classed as a functional disorder, but undoubtedly there are certain physiological factors involved.

ORGANIC OR STRUCTURAL PSYCHOSIS

Mental processes are correlates of both the self (subject) and certain nerve structures. Any organic factors that may impair brain or nerve structure and their physiological processes will affect the mental processes. Since this is the sphere of medical science rather than mental hygiene, I shall list only a few of these types: (1) Brain trauma; (2) infection of brain or nerve tissue (syphilitic spirochetes); (3) alcoholic psychosis or delirium tremens; (4) convulsive disorders (epilepsy); (5) circulatory disturbances such as cerebral embolism and arteriosclerosis; (6) metabolic disturbances such as cretinism; and (7) Huntington's chorea, nerve impairment due chiefly to heredity.

I suggest that we think of the mentally defective individual in this category. Brain function as an organic process is involved and treatment is chiefly medical or a matter of special education to help the individual make the fullest possible use of his limited capacity. There is a functional depression of intellectual and emotional responses due to severe stimulus and love deprivation in early childhood, which is difficult to distinguish from innate defectiveness. This is a common symptom of the mental illnesses of children.

> The class may profit from reports by two students on these two topics. Most of the references listed at the end of the chapter will provide ample material: Cameron, Stern, Klein, etc.

ETIOLOGY OF PSYCHOTIC BEHAVIOR

What causes a person to "lose his mind," to "go crazy," to develop a syndrome of psychotic reactions? The doctor, the psychologist, and the layman have found this to be a fascinating as well as a puzzling question. To find the answer has been placed high among the objectives of both clinical and experimental psychology and medical science. The problem has been solved only in part. The nature-nurture, heredity-environment controversy persists. Observation and theory have not yet been adequately verified by empirical evidence, The biologically-oriented continue to emphasize genetic factors, while the sociologically-oriented find sufficient cause in the early environmental conditioning. In the organic types the etiology is relatively clear, and it is relatively physical. Our concern is chiefly with the so-called "functional" types.

HEREDITY

Nonscientific observers believe that "insanity runs in families," therefore it is inherited. Laws to permit sterilization of both the feeble minded and the mentally ill have been strongly advocated and have been based on this assumption and a desire to elevate the human race. In 1934, the American Neurological Association (ANA) appointed a committee to make a comprehensive study of factors bearing on inheritance of mental illness and related conditions. Their report (1936) included the following four propositions (Klein, 1956, p. 221):

1. Hereditary factors seem to play an important part in the etiology of schizophrenic disorders.
2. These hereditary factors are often not sufficient to produce a psychosis.
3. The hereditary factors are not to be regarded as "highly specific" in the causation of schizophrenia. If they were, then whenever one member of a pair of identical or monozygotic twins suffers from schizophrenia, one would expect the other twin to be a victim of the same disease. Studies of mental disorders among twins fail to confirm this expectation. There is a higher rate of incidence among identical than among fraternal twins, but the degree of correspondence in the former group is far from perfect. . . .
4. There are cases of schizophrenia in which no hereditary factor can be demonstrated to play a part; hence it is concluded that such factors are "not essential in the etiology of so-called schizophrenic psychoses.

Three decades of additional research have added little to these findings. Evidence supports the position that genetic factors are involved in schizophrenia but are not alone sufficient to account for all cases. It does not indicate whether these are major or minor determiners nor the manner nor degree of their causality. But researchers continue their work and our knowledge grows. Twins are popular experimental subjects.

Kallman's extensive researching of this question is widely quoted.[8] He studied 953 pairs of twins in psychiatric hospitals and came to the conclusion that the probability of the identical twin of a schizophrenic patient developing schizophrenia is about five times as great as for the fraternal twin (84.2 percent and 16.4 percent respectively). These findings were widely heralded until searching criticism revealed flaws in his methods and counter arguments were presented[9] to the effect that Kallman's study did not eliminate the environmental factor—that identical twins have a unique relationship and environment which are also more nearly identical than in cases of fraternal twins. Identical twins identify more closely with each other than do other siblings. Thus, each feels more strongly the other's frustrations, anxieties, etc., and each would be more greatly influenced by the other's situation.

The issue remains undecided, but methods of study are improving.

PHYSIOLOGICAL AND BIOCHEMICAL FACTORS

While geneticists have been concerned with hereditary factors, medical research has been expending much time and effort trying to identify correlative and possible causitive factors in the anatomy, physiology, and biochemistry of the body, particularly cell metabolism and the endocrine system. Some correlates were established and much interest was aroused only to find, by more extensive study, that little or no causal relationship could be established. It was found that the tranquilizer *Reserpine* tended

[8] F.J. Kallman, *Heredity in Health and Mental Disorder* (New York: W.W. Norton & Company, Inc., 1953).

[9] From D. Jackson, *The Etiology of Schizophrenia* (New York: Basic Books), 1960.

to reduce serotonin concentration in the brain and that irregularities in serotonin concentration are associated with certain schizophrenic reactions. The experimental use of hallucinogenic drugs, such as lysergic acid, to artificially induce psychotic-like mental states and, with this, the study of brain chemistry have given some hope for establishing a physiological etiological base for mental illnesses hitherto termed functional.

Biochemical differences between schizophrenics and mentally healthy persons have been established. Whether these physiological and biochemical differences were genetically determined and are thus causal factors or if they developed along with, and a part of, the schizophrenic syndrome as a consequence of other causal factors has not been determined.

THE PROCESS-REACTIVE THEORY

Various investigators felt that the research findings suggest that the broad category of illnesses termed schizophrenia should be divided into two subdivisions—genetic and physiological factors seemed to appear in some cases and not in others. The division was made on the basis of developmental and precipitating (onset) differences. Chronic cases of gradual deterioration and symptomatic unfolding which was relatively independent of a crisis situation were labeled *process* cases. Those in which the patient had succeeded in living a fairly normal life behind his defenses, until they gave way and the schizophrenic syndrome appeared rather suddenly, were labeled *reactive* cases.

The former was assumed to indicate a higher prevalence of genetic factors in its etiology and the latter virtually none. Some studies have indicated that there are certain biochemical differences between the two (not yet conclusive), and extensive Rorschach testing has revealed significant differences between the two groups (as diagnosed) relative to the quality of their fantasies, habits of thinking, ideational and emotional control, etc. The Rorschach protocols revealed that the *process* cases manifested stronger, more marked pyschotic traits; and case histories showed that these cases had a more difficult childhood environment and displayed greater difficulties in adjusting throughout their childhood years.

CAUSES NOT YET KNOWN

The nature-nurture question still remains unanswered. There are too many variations of reactive patterns and degrees of intensity among schizophrenics to permit a simple clear-cut answer. The greater and more prolonged childhood stress and anxiety of the process-type cases, may account for the physiological as well as the psychological differences, rather than these being the consequence of differences in heredity. It may not. Consensus still favors the general answer that there are certain inherited tendencies of increased probability that under similarly adverse conditions some persons will develop schizophrenic reactions; but early childhood environment carries the greater weight. What has been said for schizophrenia generally holds for the manic-depressive type, except that evidence seems to point a little more clearly toward definite but minor genetic causal factors. Stern (1964, pp. 185, 186) says:

> If one attempts to extract a solid core of established fact from the voluminous literature on somatic factors in schizophrenia, one is left with preciously little. Manfred Bleuler,[10] in reviewing the literature, could discover only one incontrovertible finding, namely, that the range of variability of somatic indexes is somewhat greater with schizophrenics than with normals. Bleuler pointed out that even if dependable biological correlates of schizophrenia were to be found they might be consequences, rather than causes, of the disturbed emotionality. No empirical finding by itself can prove that the organic realm is more basic than the psychic one. At best, one can hope to establish a more or less precise correspondence between emotional and bodily states. . . .
>
> Bellak,[11] equally dissatisfied with the existing etiological theories, proposed to think in terms of a "psychosomatic multifunctional origin" of schizophrenia. But his formula is too general to be of much use. While conceding some etiological significance to organic factors, he tends to assign greater causal weight to psychological factors. . . . (p. 60).

---

[10] From M. Bleuler, "Forschungen und Begriffswandlungen in der Schizophrenielehre," *Fortschr. Neurol. Psychiat.*, 9/10, 385–452.

[11] From L. Bellak (ed), Schizophrenia: *A Review of the Syndrome* (New York: Logos Press, 1958).

FAMILY NURTURE

The early home environment provides information about the most crucial etiological factors. You may wish to review the frustrating family and child-parent relationships described in Chapter 6. Mussen, Conger, and Kagan (1963, p. 210), after reviewing several studies of mother-child relationships during the second year of age relative to the child's autonomy and positive self-image, make some generalizations:

> . . . Regardless of the sample of mothers used or the psychologist doing the assessment, two basic dimensions of maternal behaviors seem to be particularly important in describing the mother-child interaction. These are *hostility* versus *love,* and *overcontrol* versus the granting of autonomy. These two dimensions may be combined in different ways; that is, a loving mother can be controlling and restrictive, or she can give her child freedom of action, and allow him to explore his world and set his own limits. Similarly, a rejecting mother can either restrict the child's activity or she can be indifferent and let him do as he wishes. Four general categories of maternal behavior can be distinguished; loving and restrictive, loving and permissive, rejecting and restricting, and, finally, rejecting but permissive.
>
> Perhaps the happiest combination of parental attitudes is that of acceptance and moderate autonomy. These attitudes should lead to self-confidence and effective socialization. The most deleterious combination appears to be rejection and severe restriction. This set of maternal attitudes may result in seriously disturbed functioning in later childhood and adolescence.

We may add that rejection and restriction may be direct and harsh or more subdued and in the guise of over-protection. Either way, it robs the child of his chance to develop a strong autonomous self. His feelings of weakness, inadequacy, and unworth grow with the years. His defenses grow until they break under the pressure of reality or reach psychotic dimensions. Often, it is found that the mother's own childhood deprivation caused her to establish a pattern in which she sought to derive from the child what she had failed to get from her mother; and the need of the mother to feel in some way superior was obtained at the expense of the child. The tap root of psychotic reactions undoubtedly extends into this type of frustrating and anxiety-producing child-mother relationship; the total etiological pattern broadens to include the family. Many studies of the "schizophrenic" mother have been made, resulting in a stereotype image of her as a cold, rejecting, dominating creature. More adequate study is altering this picture and relieving her of some of the responsibility.

TOTAL FAMILY RESEARCH

A recent emphasis in research is the study of the whole family constellation. This is a relatively new field of investigation and much is yet to be learned. In virtually all cases studied, the marital relationships of the parents were pathological. Both were found to be immature, their identity shallow, and each assumed a rather rigid role that filled a deep unconscious need. More often than not, the wife assumed the dominant role. To permit this rather unstable pattern to continue, the child heeds the inarticulate demands to remain passively submissive in a continuing infantilism, ruling as he may from a position of weakness. Under the later stresses of life, he regresses to this pattern. Stern says (1964, p. 177):

> The role of the father in this sort of family constellation is that of the peripherally attached family member, whose nearness or distance from the child is controlled by the mother. At times, with the express permission of the mother, he can be intimate with the child. His own pathology does not permit him to rebel decisively against the monopolistic position of the mother, and thus to establish a more direct relationship to the child.
>
> The family constellation just described is unlikely to be the only one which can predispose to the development of schizophrenia in the child, and it is too schematic. Nevertheless, it points up the decisive observation of various investigators that the pathology of the marriage relationship itself and the individual pathologies of both partners constitute the preschizophrenic milieu which corrodes the developing personality of the child. . . .

THE ONSET

Our etiological probing has led us to the home where the parents have certain pathological traits but not to the dimension of the psychotic member, and where the husband-wife relationship and child-parent relationship are pathological and have been (usually) for two or three generations. To what degree the genes carry this pathology remains unanswered. Now let us turn from origin to onset. Children "nurtured" in such a family environment may find certain stress situations intolerable which the "normal" child could bear. Cameron (1963, p. 481) states five such precipitating conditions:

(1) *Loss or threatened loss of a major source of gratification,* which deprives a person of his accustomed emotional outlets.
(2) *Loss or threatened loss of basic security,* which reduces or eliminates a person's available emotional support.
(3) *An upsurge of erotic or hostile drive,* which either finds no adequate discharge or leads to unacceptable behavior.
(4) *A sudden increase in guilt,* because of superego reaction or because of the accusatory attitudes of other persons.
(5) *Reduced general effectiveness of the defense organization,* because of any one of a number of circumstances, internal as well as external.

Studies of the etiology and onset of schizophrenia as cited clearly portray the role relationships that are conducive to schizophrenic reactions. The role relations of the parents to the siblings, to each other, and to their respective parents provide a three-generation constellation that is conducive to mental health or illness, to psychosocial development or disorder. Ambivalent parental attitudes that evoke role conflict in the child are especially crippling. The child soon learns his role in the family constellation. The child whose role is most self-depreciating and ambivalent is the one most likely to "learn" a schizophrenic role. Another child in the same family, but learning to play a different role, will develop a different character structure.

THE NEUROSES

What is the difference between a psychosis and a neurosis? between psychotic and neurotic adjustments? Both terms designate broad categories of abnormal, deviant, maladaptive behavior. Neurotic symptoms are so commonplace, that the milder forms of neuroses may well be the normal condition. This is verified by the large use of tranquilizers. There is no discernible boundary between the so-called normal person and the neurotic; the border between the neuroses and psychoses is very ragged and ill-defined. The recent trend is away from this distinction toward a more definitive description of various more-or-less fixed behavior patterns (reaction types) that cut across the neuroses-psychoses boundary, some of these reactions being characteristic of both and some very largely limited to one or the other. Relative to certain traits or symptoms, they overlap widely with the psychotic manifestations the more severe; while in other characteristic symptoms they differ widely.

Cameron (1963) discussed behavior disorders under a number of headings without making a sharp distinction between the neuroses and psychoses. These were: Anxiety reactions, Phobic reactions, Conversion reactions, Dissociative reactions, Obsessive Compulsive reactions, Neurotic depressive reactions, Paranoid reactions, Psychotic depressive reactions, Mania and Manic-Depressive cycles, Schizophrenic reactions, and Involutional psychotic reactions.

The first six disorders would be designated as the neuroses and the last five, the psychoses. Some of these reaction patterns run through both groups. In both divisions the anxiety-fear response is paramount, there is much repression, also depression; and several of the same defense mechanisms are employed but varying in degree. This is an area for research; and experimental psychology could launch a vast program of observation, measurement, and statistical analysis of the many "neurotic" and "psychotic" symptoms and reclassify them somewhat as Cattell and associates did with personality traits (Chapter 2). After all, these are personality traits.

In Table 6, the differences are outlined as generally observed,

TABLE 6. COMPARISON OF NEUROTIC AND PSYCHOTIC DISORDERS IN TERMS OF PRIMARY CHARACTERISTICS

Neuroses	*Psychoses*
Reactions less severe	Reactions much more severe and disturbing; disruptive in character
Less pervasive, involving only several areas of personality	Extremely pervasive; tend to involve the whole personality
Fairly good contact with reality	Generally poor contact with reality; may involve total abandonment of reality
Emotions fairly flexible; little impoverishment	Considerable emotional debilitation; often seriously diminished or abolished altogether
No intellectual deterioration; some impairment	Often serious intellectual deterioration or impairment
Generally fairly good insight; capacity to be objective regarding self	Generally lacking in insight; little understanding of difficulty
Not incapacitated; able to live in society	Incapacitated; often dangerous to self and society
Seldom require hospitalization	Require hospitalization

Source: A.A. Schneiders, *Personal Dynamics and Mental Health* (New York: Holt, Rinehart and Winston, Inc., 1965, p. 308. Reprinted by permission of the publishers.

but let us not assume that those distinctions are sharply defined or that accurate diagnosis can always be made.

We also find variations of classification according to the various types of neurotic disorders. Cameron's six types of reactions given above were assumed to cover the neuroses basically. In Table 7, the classifications of four other authors are listed. Carroll's was taken from the official nomenclature of the American Psychological Association, 1952.

Virtually all neurotic disorders, reactive syndromes, are designed to aid the individual in coping with anxiety and leave him with sufficient resources to make at least a minimum adjustment

TABLE 7. PSYCHONEUROTIC DISORDERS

Carroll (1964, p. 217)	*Stern (1964, p. 53)*	*Schneiders (1965, p. 315)*	*Thorpe (1960, p. 142)*
Anxiety reaction	Psychoneuroses	Simple neurotic symptoms	Neurasthenia
Dissociative reaction	Traumatic neuroses	Anxiety neurosis and psychomotor disturbances	Psychasthenia: phobias, obsessions and compulsions
Conversion reaction	Anxiety states	Obsessive-compulsive reactions	Hysteria
Phobic reaction	Phobias	Organ neuroses (psychosomatics)	Anxiety neurosis
Obsessive compulsive reaction	Hysterias; Conversion and dissociative	Neurasthenia and hypochondria	Hypochondria
Depressive reaction	Obsessive-compulsive conditions	Hysteria (conversion)	Traumatic neurosis
Psychoneurotic reaction, other			Operational fatigue

to reality. They are all anxiety states, with the particular defenses against. The neurotic is a person of weakened self who finds his former defense system inadequate. He has reorganized his basic responses into a distorted holistic system directed toward coping with the unrealistic and ambiguous threat of life with its accompanying anxiety. Having lost "sight" of any real objective threat, he focuses on the anxiety itself and its anticipated consequence as the "real" threat. Therefore, he is organized to cope with unreality in a real world. I shall describe each type very briefly, then give a more general description and interpretation.

ANXIETY NEUROSIS

The individual lives in a permanent state of anxiety and vague dread. He is at low ebb most of the time but frequently breaks into a virtual state of panic under a variety of conditions and circumstances. (Case mentioned in Chapter 7). The victim cannot pin it down to a particular stimulus situation, as with the phobias, nor does he have a specific defense that keeps him unconscious of the anxiety most of the time. It is always present in varying degrees of intensity; and it is often referred to as "free-floating" or diffuse anxiety.

There is general apprehension and indecision, a vague fear of making a mistake without knowing why. Basically, the neurotic lacks self-confidence and having these irrational fears adds to it. He needs help in making decisions and often resents the help offered. He needs help to keep occupied and entertained in order to forget the anxiety associated with his work, but resents that dependency; he soon tires, from his work and from the inner tension, adding still more to his low opinion of himself. He is likely to be touchy and fussy. His old defense has worn very thin. He is like a turtle without its shell. He suffers the subjective pain of the hidden threat; but the pain of that feared condition might be greater if he had to face it. Perhaps absorption with the anxiety may help mask the real or imagined condition of threat. He frequently sinks into depression since he gets tired of defending himself against some vague unknown. He may have forebodings of death, insanity, some malignant disease, of being shunned by friends, etc.

PHOBIAS

The term "phobia" means fear. But as presently used, it is an irrational and inappropriate fear. The sufferer of phobia is expressing too much affect in a situation that should warrant very little, if any. It may be designated as a displaced fear, dissociated from the original threat and fixed on something else. However, this something else is in some way symbolic of the original threatening thing or situation; or some element in the new fear-arousing situation is like one in the original and thus can trigger the fear without the individual recognizing the original. He is free of anxiety as long as he stays away from his specific phobia stimulus. Thus, his anxiety is bound to a surrogate and he is protected against the original threat.

There are several phobias of which the most common are:

1. *Acrophobia*—fear of high places
2. *Agoraphobia*—fear of open places
3. *Algophobia*—fear of pain
4. *Astraphobia*—fear of storms or thunder and lightening
5. *Claustrophobia*—fear of closed or narrow places
6. *Mysophobia*—fear of contamination
7. *Nyctophobia*—fear of darkness
8. *Toxophobia*—fear of being poisoned
9. *Zoophobia*—fear of animals

Characteristics. Thorpe (1960, p. 144) states six factors concerning phobias from the psychoanalytic point of view: (1) they act as a defense against the threat of psychological pain; (2) they mask a problem or conflict which the individual is afraid to recognize; (3) they usually date from an intensely unpleasant experience which occurred in childhood or adolescence; (4) feelings of guilt and shame are of major significance in etiology; (5) feelings of inferiority and insecurity frequently contribute to their development; and (6) a phobia which originated as a fear-reaction in a specific situation may spread to a broad class of objects.[12]

The psychoanalysts generally interpret phobia as a masking of repressed id impulses which are feared and that it most frequently appears during adolescence from anxiety over sex drives. This may be true, but phobias are not limited to such repressed "wishes," and, like allergies, phobic fears may shift from one object to another.

CONVERSION (HYSTERIA)

Conversion was formerly designated as *hysteria* or *conversion hysteria.* This striking reaction is the unconscious transformation of a neurotic anxiety-conflict into, or transferred to, a physical symptom. Classic examples are the many cases of "shell shock" that received much attention during World War I. Week after week in combat, facing constant threat and experiencing

[12] From Otto Fenichel, "Remarks on the Common Phobias," *Psychoanalytic Quarterly.* (1944), 13:313–326. [As quoted by Thorpe, 1960, p. 144.] Used with permission.

ceaseless fear, which becomes generalized to a permanent anxiety state, the soldier nurses fantasy wishes of desertion. It would be just as dangerous for him to desert, and would carry an element of guilt. The avoidance-avoidance conflict becomes unbearable until, in a state of near exhaustion or in close proximity with an exploding shell, he loses his sight or an arm becomes paralyzed. The torturing mental conflict is transferred, *converted*, to nerve-muscle conflict in eyes or arms. He can now escape the threat of battle and his fear, and at the same time do it in a manner to "save face" and escape guilt. It is an unconscious process or it would not serve its protecting role. It is functional, with no tissue impairment of the bodily organs, and the symptom can be removed by hypnosis or hypnotic drugs.

The condition is not limited to military life nor is it a modern phenomenon. Cases have been described in literature through the centuries. It became a subject of special interest to the nineteenth century French psychiatrists, Charcot and Janet, and to Freud and his disciples, and to the whole field of psychiatry during World War I. The type of person most susceptible is one who is generally anxious, insecure and responsive to suggestion. If one is faced with a very threatening situation which cannot be escaped without equal threat (divorce, leaving one's profession, family disgrace) and perhaps shame—also somewhat self-centered and angry at the imagined injustice of it—the intolerable mental conflict which paralyzes decisive action becomes symbolically expressed in physical paralysis. Usually there is the admixture of fear, anger, and guilt which are masked. It is better to be crippled than dead, disgraced, and self-hating.

Using body symbolism in thought and speech is commonplace. Perhaps the conversion-type neurotic is more prone to this type of expression, as children are. We speak of blind rage and being paralyzed by fear, and we frequently close our eyes and stop our ears against sights and sounds which we wish to escape. The conversion-hysteric reaction is the unconscious fixation of these gestures as a protective mechanism.

DISSOCIATION REACTION

Hysteria. This term, as defined by early psychiatry, is given physical expression by *conversion;* its mental counterpart is termed *dissociation.* It is a special type of repression by which a whole vast area of mental processes are cut off, so that the focal point of attention (consciousness) cannot cross that resistance line established in a large path of brain neurons. A large area of one's life that was filled with anxiety-guilt-resentment conflict (as above) is cut off from memory and the suffering is eased. In its simpler forms are narcolepsy, an unnatural functional "sleeping sickness" as an escape mechanism; *somnambulism,* sleepwalking; and the *fugue,* which is a short-term forgetting of one's identity and former associations. We shall confine our discussion to its more dramatic and prolonged forms of expression, *amnesia* and *multiple personality.*

Amnesia. The soldier, as described, while in a self-hypnotic trance-like state may wander from his unit, acquire civilian clothes and a new name, and take up a new existence in some other part of the country or world. He functions normally in this new role, but cannot remember his former life, its associations, or how he made the transition. It is as though he were born into a new world in full adulthood. His somnambulistic and fugue state was of a more serious nature, a deeper dissociation, from which he did not "awake" in a few days. The amnesiac sufferer also may have been a highly respected clergyman, whose ministry had subjected him to excessive stress with considerable anxiety and suppressed resentment. Coupled with this, perhaps, is an incompatible marriage or family tension. He longs to escape it all, but this wish is guilt-producing since it would be a moral wrong and social disgrace to divorce his wife and leave the ministry. The intolerable avoidance-avoidance conflict continues until a minor incident triggers the split. Dissociation occurs. He escapes the threatening situation and the anxiety-guilt pain, but at a great price.

Multiple Personality. This neurotic state is of the same general nature as amnesia with the exception that it may be compared to a vertical, rather than horizontal split. Instead of a past episode or period of life being dissociated, two or more aspects of one's current living become separated. Under certain stimulus conditions, the center of gravity of one's conscious direction may shift from one to the other in a matter of several hours or days. When the shift is made from one role and personality type to the other, neither subself is conscious of the other and its mode of life. This phenomenon may be compared to multiple birth where the newly fused reproductive cells divide into two or more embryos instead of forming one.

Early in life, when self is in bud and the child is living in a state of anxiety and struggling with two conflicting need-desires, he constructs two self-images which are somewhat contradictory and of near equal significance. Identification is made with one image at times, and then with the other in child play and fantasy. As the child grows toward maturity and faces the realities of adult responsibility, a fissure (figuratively speaking) forms deep within the self, and divides it into twin subselves, one usually being dominant and more socially acceptable. When the life stress becomes exhausting, carrying considerable anxiety and resentment (often suppressed) and some degree of guilty conscience, one wishes to escape from it all. The center of conscious control shifts to the hitherto recessive subself and it (he) directs behavior in line with its self-image and personality structure. Twin (triplet or quadruplet) selves, self-images, and personality structures occupy and alternately operate within one total person. He has become a compound subject and has structured a dual personality. The dissociation and shift serves the same purpose as in amnesia, to escape without guilt.

> At this point a student report and class discussion based on *The Three Faces of Eve* (Thigpen and Cleckley, 1957) and/or Morton Prince's classic case (1920), would add interest.

OBSESSIVE-COMPULSIVE REACTION

All normal people have obsessive thoughts from time to time and may have mildly compulsive action tendencies. The two are frequently associated together, although they operate more or less independently. For instance, if a woman is a compulsive house-cleaner, she may have obsessive thoughts of contamination. Common to normal people is the experience of a certain tune continually "popping into mind." Perhaps the name of a friend one has not recalled for months that, for no known reason, keeps coming back to consciousness though dismissed again and again. There is also the woman who nearly everytime she leaves the house for even a short trip returns from the car two or three times to make sure the electric iron or gas heater is turned off.

Normal Obsessions. All of these examples may fall well within the range of normal experience and should be of no great concern. In fact, certain obsessive thoughts and compulsive tendencies may become positive factors in a worthy ambition.* When these intruding thoughts become too frequent and compelling, and virtually dominate consciousness and interfere with sound judgment, peace of mind, and normal performance, they have attained neurotic proportion and serve a protective purpose. These obsessions are many and varied and include a mother's thoughts of harming her child, persistent thoughts and half-convictions that one has cancer, incessant thoughts of having committed the "unpardonable sin," etc. The compulsive, ritualistic acts are as varied. They cause the afflicted person no little anxiety about himself, lowering his self-esteem, making him disgusted with himself, and interfere with his efficient social and intellectual performance. Other thoughts or fears relative to his character or worth as a human being are repressed. They may serve as the partial and symbolic expression of, or masks to cover, deeper guilt and self-condemnation. They may also be projected to another person, since one is obsessed with the thoughts of his wrong-doing.

The psychological factors involved in the obsessive-compulsive reactions (their psychogenesis) are complex and not fully understood. In general, such persons outwardly reflect high ideals and social conscience, concern for others, freedom from hostility and rancor, excessive orderliness and cleanliness that often becomes a fetish, and extreme rigidity that may appear as stubborness. They experience the same high degree of insecurity and anxiety like most neurotics do, but their defensive compulsions serve as a mask. The element of difference that may account for

* Note Lloyd Douglas, *The Magnificent Obsession* (Boston: Houghton Mifflin, 1929).

their defense taking this particular form is the large admixture of guilt which the compulsive act symbolizes and helps to repress. Extreme anger and fear of its expression may also be a factor. The classic literary example is that of Lady Macbeth trying to cleanse her hands in her sleep, symbolic of her guilt. Carroll (1964, p. 233) cites an example of compulsive reaction in a 10-year-old boy.

Larry had several compulsive forms of behavior. While working on arithmetic problems he was compelled to fill in, very carefully, all numbers which had closed loops or circles, that is, 0, 6, 8, and 9. It is significant that he was accelerated one year in school, even though his intelligence was at the low normal level. Whenever he turned in papers in the classroom, he felt forced to return to the teacher's desk and tap the papers at least once. There were also compulsive behavior patterns at home. When getting dressed in the morning he had to put on his shoes three times. He could never go downstairs without going back up and down again. Certain objects in his room had to be lined up in perfect order.

Larry had many anxieties that were only partially relieved by his neurotic escape. He was afraid to be alone in his room, especially at night. He was very concerned about dying and at times was sure that someone would break into the house and take him away and kill him. Much of the time he was just anxious without knowing what he was anxious about.

In the course of the interviews, Larry began to talk more and more about his severely retarded sister, who was three years younger than he. In the past he had wanted her to play with him, but she was incapable of doing so. His mother had tried to explain the situation to him, but he failed to understand. At times, after his parents had retired, he would get up, take his sister from her bed, and try to force her to play games. Occasionally, he hurt her unintentionally, causing her to cry out. Once the mother heard the cries and punished the boy, who not only felt guilty but also was sure that he had inflicted serious harm on the little girl.

Eventually the parents decided to have their daughter institutionalized. Larry was overwhelmed by the decision, largely because he was convinced that he was to blame for her present condition. After a few months at the state institution, the girl died. Larry was sure that she had been killed and at the same time was not certain that she had died at all. This doubt was intensified when his parents refused to let him go to the funeral.

The boy's guilt-laden associations with his retarded sister were the principal cause of his anxiety and of the obsessive-compulsive reactions that represented an attempt to escape from the anxiety. When his experiences, many of which had been repressed, were fully expressed and understood, Larry began to improve.

Of the neurotic reaction types discussed above, psychoanalysts consider the obsessive-compulsives the most deep-seated, complex, and difficult. They generally attribute its etiology to the unresolved Oedipal conflict as the general pathogenic factor and the anal period in psycho-sexual development as the more specific factor. These are associated with rigidity and, more especially, uncleanness. The rigid ritualistic reactions protect against consciousness of moral depravity and uncleanness.

Variety. Among the more common compulsions of public and clinical concern are: *dipsomania,* compulsive drinking; *kleptomania,* compulsive stealing; and *pyromania,* the fire-bug impulse.

> There are many other compulsions which you may be able to name. I shall leave it to student interest to read the descriptions of certain other behavior syndromes that may be classified with the neuroses: hypochondriasis, neurasthenia (general fatigue), scrupulosity, accident proneness, and the "traumatic neurosis," (fixed emotional disturbances that follow a specific traumatic experience). The class may also name a score or more of specific neurotic traits found in the behavior of otherwise thoroughly normal people.

THE NEUROTIC PERSONALITY

The normal person often makes a typically neurotic response, but he does not develop a fixed syndrome of such traits that plays a continual defensive role and continually reduces his performance efficiency. The latter belongs to the neurotic personality. Anxiety is the chief characteristic of the neurotic personality, and is the keystone of neurosis. Anxiety has a direct relationship to health. This fact has been known from the time of the ancient Greek physicians; the great medieval Muslim doctor, Avicenna, was very much concerned with this relationship.

EXISTENTIAL ANXIETY

Freud and present day clinical psychologists have interpreted anxiety as generalized fear. Fear which is detached from its original object by repression or from having suffered fear so frequently that it spread to life in general. Since the invasion of psychology by existentialism, the anxiety-fear relationship has been reversed. These existentialists would say that anxiety is primary in the life of primitive man and the infant. It occurs as a feeling of dread from the threat of existence, and from the total strange world and vaguely sensed responsibility. As the child matures (and primitive man began his cultural growth) the specific fears of specific object-situations develop by discriminative concept formation. I would agree with this general position as being both philosophically and psychologically sound. But relative to most neurotic behavior, the anxiety encountered is generalized from a multiplicity of childhood fears. In the most extreme cases, and perhaps more so in the psychoses, the anxiety that was generalized from specific fears became associated or merged with the residual primitive or primordial anxiety that preceded discriminative conceptualization and specific fear. The student may pursue this argument on his own as he may be inclined.

The key insight that should be established is that anxiety is restricting. It is derived from the Latin *angustus* and *ango*, meaning narrow, constricted; to bind, throttle, strangle. That is what it does to the personality. It is *self* in a state of anxiety that throttles itself, constricts its activity, represses and inhibits. Thus, self has little dynamics for the initiating and directing of action against frustration. The child who matures in the frustrating family situation described in Chapter 6, has a self that fails to mature adequately, is self-restricted, weak, with feelings of inferiority or lack of worth. This becomes a vicious circle—fear and low worth, restricted response, less effective achievement, greater sense of unworth. This makes repression and one or another of the more specific defense mechanisms necessary. Therefore, repression becomes the second most significant personality characteristic.

DISTORTED AWARENESS

Repression is necessary to protect the person from the painful self-image which is distorted and much worse than he actually is. Other defenses help maintain repression, and the defenses could not develop without repression, which distorts reality. The mental processes are reciprocal. Repression means selective perception of the external world, selective perception of self, and selective perception of the past (what is recalled). If one is unable to recall the old threats, they cannot be re-evaluated nor the fear unlearned. Therefore, it is a process of restricted awareness, experience, and achievement. One part of his aggressiveness is used to maintain his defenses and the other part goes into productive work. He may be compared to a six-cylinder engine with two cylinders cross-wired. They fire against each other. The engine will pull the automobile, but it is weak and there is much inner heat and tension.

What has been said above has been applied to the psychotic personality as well. The difference is basically a matter of time and degree, with perhaps slightly less inherited proneness, a temperamental difference. The family environment is a little worse, more frustrating and crippling, and the crippling forces begin to work earlier in the life of the psychotic. The stifling of self-growth begins in the first or second year in the psychotic's life. Thus, self is weaker, self-contempt greater, and self-protective mechanisms need to be stronger and so much so that they become utterly unrealistic or crumble. The neurotic's, being less so, may be maintained through life, merely reducing efficiency. Or, he may make a shift of balance in his defense system to strengthen it at the expense of efficient living.

IMMATURITY

Next we find immaturity as a prominent characteristic of neurotics. The above mentioned deprivations and restrictiveness prevent full maturation. With immaturity there usually follows frustration-intolerance and anger (resentment), a touchiness and sensitivity to criticism, and a fear and shunning of responsibility, not trusting their abilities and judgments. In conjunction with these, there often is manifested an overly self-centeredness that is sometimes a morbid self-concern, self-pity, and neurotic guilt. Neurotics generally lack a wholesome sense of humor, and are emotionally unstable. In each, the self is weak and feels its incompetence.

Neurotics vary as all human beings do. The relative strength and interrelationship of the above characteristics varies widely from one to another. It is this relative strength and relationship, in addition to the environmental factors, which determines the type of defense mechanism and neurotic syndrome that develops. The various neurotic syndromes may shift with the shifting sands of circumstances. If not given adequate treatment, the general anxiety patient may become phobic or a hypochondriac. If the phobic patient has his central symptom removed without a full cure, he may develop another phobia or an obsessive-compulsive reaction.

White[13] says of the neurosis:

> The trouble starts with what we have called the neurotic nucleus, a process by which anxiety, typically in childhood, is subjected to such radical defenses that a new evaluation of the danger cannot be made. The trouble continues with the formation of overdriven strivings, tendencies that are exaggerated in the effort to maintain security. Overdriven strivings are likely to conflict with each other and with other tendencies in the personality, a situation that we have called neurotic conflict. Integrative efforts continue, however, and the person steadily builds for himself a protective organization, becoming a full-fledged neurotic personality. At any point along the way the situation may get out of hand: anxiety may increase, and the defenses may become more desperate. The person feels much worse, and it is usually at such a point that symptom formation occurs. We shall refer to this as *neurotic breakdown.* In the older terminology, it is at this point that the person starts to be sick and to "have" a neurosis. In our present understanding, the neurotic breakdown is a sort of climax that occurs when the protective structure is seriously threatened

[13] Robert W. White, *The Abnormal Personality.* Copyright © 1964 The Ronald Press Company, New York.

and can no longer be maintained intact. Neurotic breakdown occurs only on the basis of an already existing neurotic personality. (p. 241).

MENTAL ILLNESS IN CHILDHOOD AND OLD AGE

THE DISTURBED CHILD

Psychiatrists did not begin to give serious thought to basic differences between adult and child psychoses until almost the middle of this century. Since then, childhood schizophrenia has been recognized as fairly commonplace and different in some ways from adult schizophrenia. There is an increasing tendency to speak in terms of "childhood schizophrenias" because of variety and instability of symptoms and difficulty in establishing a typology. Some of the symptoms closely resemble mental retardation, dullness, and apathy; these children formerly were diagnosed as being mentally defective or brain damaged.

Specific symptoms do not differ very much from those found among the four types of schizophrenia. Patterns differ, and they are not as fixed. They also shift more frequently; and classification or typing is more difficult. This may be due to the fact that young children have not developed a clear sense of reality in relation to the outer world nor do they have an established self-image. Therefore, whatever hallucinations and delusions they may suffer are not of as definite a pattern nor are they of fixed persistence. Since children have not lived for several years behind the protective walls of a rigid defense system, the psychotic patterns are not as systematically organized.

In very recent years a concerted attempt has been made to place schizophrenic children into one of two categories: *primary infantile autism* and *symbolic infantile psychosis.* The former is extremely withdrawn, self-centered, given to morbid self-absorption, and virtually unresponsive to his mother. The latter clings to his mother, demands attention and affection, talks frequently and manifests outwardly much more fear and anger. A sizable number of other seriously disturbed children display mixtures of both types.

In relation to etiology, little can be added to the discussion earlier in this chapter. The same indication of genetic, physiological or biochemical, and psychosocial (family constellation) factors are involved. Two distinctions may be suggested: (1) The fact that symptoms begin to show up within a few weeks or months after birth, as in some cases of autism, would seem to indicate that genetic and/or physiological factors play a proportionately larger causative role, and (2) that the child is forced into a severely self-debilitating role at an earlier age than in the case of adult schizophrenics. In either case, the child has not been able to grow in sufficient self-strength to develop a system of defenses that would carry him through childhood.

Children also suffer neuroses. But these are less distinctly marked than the more serious disturbances of psychoses. Any attempt at classification is futile. These are merely emotionally disturbed children of a wide variety and degree, and are nervous, anxious, confused, unhappy, and inefficient. Little more can be said of those called psychotic, except that they are a little more so. Irving Berlin, child psychiatrist says:[14]

> To the child psychiatrist, a three or four year old child who is isolated and self-absorbed, who does not speak except to make eerie noises, rocks constantly, twirls objects in front of his eyes, laughs or cries without apparent stimulus, has sudden temper outbursts with destructive and assaultive rages, and appears otherwise to be in a world of his own—such a child would fit the diagnostic category of childhood schizophrenia.
>
> I saw such a four year old child last year. We made the diagnosis of childhood schizophrenia after two day's observation. In two weeks there were marked shifts toward improvement, and in three months this youngster was well. What we had seen was a case of very severe social and psychologic deprivation. The child responded to individual attention of nurses in every activity on the ward, in the play yard, and on many outings. . . .

So it is with most. The symptoms are flexible, the defenses less rigid, and response more sure. Given the right treatment, prognosis is good.

---

[14] From Irving Berlin, "The Emotional and Learning Problems of the Socially and Culturally Deprived Child," *Mental Hygiene*, 50: 340–349 (1966). Used with permission.

IN OLD AGE

Relative to the mental illnesses of our older people, even less distinctions can be made than between childhood and adult disorders. The ratio of those so afflicted is little different than of the general adult population. A greater ratio of older people suffer mental disorders from organic and physiological impairment: hardening of arteries in the brain, slight hemorrhages in the brain, endocrine disorders, etc. As stated earlier in this chapter, these are organic illnesses and are in the sphere of medical science. They also present social problems.

The functional psychoses are a little less prevalent beyond the age of 65, and their nature would warrant no special discussion. The fact that a person has withstood the stresses of life until that age indicates a stronger than average self and character structure. A high percentage of the weak have broken before reaching that age. Counteracting this is the loss of interest in life—motivation, meaning and purpose—that often follows retirement, the decrease in social activities, and watching one's friends die.

But this is not sufficient to cause many cases of psychosis or serious neurosis. It may tend to increase "crankiness," eccentricity, depression, etc. Most characteristics of old age would be the increase of mild neurosis and neurotic symptoms held by ordinarily normal people.

DEPRESSION AND SUICIDE

We turn now from anxiety and the neurotic personality to a frequent consequential state of anxiety and its companion emotions. It is the "dog house" state of existence into which certain neurotic and psychotic personalities slip from time to time and remain for short or long duration.

NEUROTIC DEPRESSION

Depression is sometimes described as an emotion and is related to grief. They are related in that both are responses to loss and the suffering it entails. Grief, however, is more specifically an emotion, the affect tone of the suffering when one is acutely experiencing loss. The depression usually follows as an emotional compound or admixture, when the grief mixes or fuses with the anxiety, anger, and guilt that are readily aroused in the neurotic person along with the grief. Thus, normal healing of grief is prevented. Depression is more of the nature of mood and attitude than it is of a specific emotion.

Earlier is this chapter I spoke of several neurotic responses frequently made by normal people, but that they were not parts of an established pattern or syndrome. The same may be said of depression. Normal adolescents have their depressed moods frequently, but not quite as frequently, as adults. There is also the mood state termed *reactive depression* that frequently follows loss of a dearly loved one or one's job. The grief mixes with the related emotions for a time, but the sufferer usually shakes it off and recovery is spontaneous with the assistance of friends and family. This is a borderline normal-neurotic type of depression.

In the full-scale neurotic depression, the afflicted not only experiences the grief of an outer loss, but also suffers intensely a loss of self-hood, of worth, of hope, of meaning and purpose. Sometimes a succession of small losses that are so insignificant the individual hardly remembers them, may lead to an onset of the depression, with the anxiety, resentment and guilt (usually repressed) being ever present. More often, the sufferer is so strongly identified with the lost object (person, job, or money) and so dependent upon it that when it goes, it appears to be the end of his private world. He loses his hope, confidence, worth, and life's meaning and purpose. He is lost in pessimism, despair, and dejection, given to unpleasant forebodings and ruminations, bemoaning his utter incapacity and worthlessness. It truly is a state of depression since both mental and physiological processes are restricted; mental and physical performances are depressed. Somatic manifestations sometimes occur and forebodings become fixed upon these, producing hypochondriasis. Quite often, the obsessive-compulsive syndrome develops to ease the depression, each being, in part, a defense against the anxiety-anger-guilt compound.

Depression serves a purpose as a neurotic syndrome. Stern (1964, p. 167) says: "From a functional point of view, the behavior of the depressive can be interpreted as a desperate, pathetic appeal for crumbs of love, an appeal which because of its desperately uncertain, beseeching note is often self-defeating." Nevertheless, it is used as a means of soliciting support, succorance, and reassurance. Out of sympathy or pity, someone will respond with help, giving support, comfort, and reassurance. "You are not nearly as bad as you think you are. With this little bit of help, everything is going to be okay." And it provides a partial release from inner stress by expressing some of his guilt and hostility in the disguised form of self-deprecation. Thus, he keeps a hold on reality and avoids a psychotic break.

The Freudians speak of depression in terms of the conflict between a harsh, critical super-ego and a weak ego, the latter having failed to handle id impulses. It exemplifies regression to the oral stage of dependency, of clinging compliance to get its needs supplied. If these needs are supplied and ego support given, regression (to oral stage) is only partial, and fair contact with reality is maintained. If not supplied, and friends and relatives turn away in disgust (equivalent to utter rejection in early childhood), regression may become complete and reach a deeper level of oral dependency, therefore becoming psychotic depression. Defenses crumble with hope, and ego structure is shattered, i.e., self is depressed to a state of impotence and its power to regulate behavior is lost.

SUICIDE

Twenty thousand or more deaths in the United States each year are self-inflicted, and this does not include many others that go down in vital statistics as accidental, but which may have been unconscious suicides. Some authorities have placed it as the tenth ranking cause of death and higher than that among youth. Suicide is more prevalent among men than women, among single than married, and among whites than Negroes. The prevalence also varies widely with subcultures. Yet, in spite of its great prevalence and centuries of concern, it is still poorly understood, since only he who commits suicide can fully understand what the experience of death means to him, and after suicide has taken place, he is not available for interview. The central question is: Is suicide due to an inner state or to outer conditions?

Rational. In various pagan societies, especially ancient Rome, suicide was accepted as an honorable withdrawal from the scene of conflict. The Roman noble considered it an honor to be given the alternative of "opening his veins" rather than being executed. For the Japanese nobleman, *harakiri* is an honorable mode of demise. Not only the *kamikaze* pilot but also many other military men have volunteered for suicidal missions. Buddhist monks have chosen immolation to dramatize an ideal. And millions of martyrs have chosen death (at the hands of another) in preference to compromise, an act very close to suicide.

One may argue abnormal emotional states in all these cases; but evidence is insufficient to warrant the inference of mental illness or that these were not people of sound minds making rational choices based on their value system. In some cases, the motive was to escape an intolerable and insurmountable situation; in others to transcend it; and in still others to make a sacrifice play that would contribute to ultimate victory. It would seem to warrant designating all these rational and voluntary suicide, as against compulsive, regardless of emotional overtones.

In the Judeo-Christian tradition, suicide generally has been interpreted as murder, a cardinal sin, and one that is unforgivable since the dead person can not repent. Some dispute this view on the grounds that if the Judeo-Christian belief in the continuation of life is valid, one can not absolutely rule out the possibility of forgiveness beyond the grave. However, in the Western world, suicide is generally held to be not only sinful but also unlawful. The suicidal person is not given public execution nor is his carcass incarcerated in a prison, but the unsuccessful would-be suicide may be subject to prosecution.

Illness. With the modern advance in medical science, particularly psychiatry, suicide became classified as an illness, and the termination of neurotic or psychotic depression. Regardless of the suicidal note that described the circumstances which caused John Doe to take his own life, the wise only shook their heads and declared that he was mentally ill and was rationalizing. This may be true, in many cases and to a large degree, but not entirely.

Karl Menninger's three basic factors in suicide have been widely quoted, namely, that the suicidal person has a desire to kill, a desire to be killed, and a desire to die.[15] Generally, those who attempt suicide and fail have the first two desires but not the third, therefore they subconsciously thwart themselves. These desires develop from years of frustration and immature, petulant anger, the anger (hostility) blocked by anxiety, and consequently acutely experienced weakness and unworth producing guilt and self-hate, all festering into depression, mental illness, suicidal tendencies.

My position is that suicide is the resultant of three basic forces: (1) the thwarting unacceptable environmental situation; (2) the strength and health of the individual self; and (3) the value system that gives meaning and purpose to the individual. The relative strength of these forces determines whether or not suicide is the result, and if so, whether the motive is to escape, transcend, or to make a sacrifice play for the sake of future progress. There is this environmental impasse, a real-world situation unacceptable and seemingly insurmountable in all cases of suicide. Whether or not it appears insurmountable, or the degree to which it is unacceptable, is partly determined by the healthy strength of the self (ego-strength).

The ideals, religious convictions, and system of values by which the individual directs his life, determine in large measure how he will act when confronted with the insurmountable. Certain depressive reactions are apparent in nearly all cases of suicide, but in some of these it is no more than that which is characteristic of normal people under abnormal conditions. However, in the large majority, the established depressive syndrome appears to have been operating at either the neurotic or psychotic levels. It seems unfair to attribute all cases of suicide to mental illness. There is a trend toward designating neurotic and psychotic syndromes as adjustive attempts, often termed maladjustive by "normal" people. It may be preferable to define suicide as a type of adaptive behavior by which the individual attempts to escape, transcend, or through sacrifice ultimately overcome an intolerable situation. That description might, however, define all "illness." Again, it is a problem of semantics.

---

[15] Karl Menninger, *Man Against Himself* (New York: Harcourt, Brace & Co., 1956). Used with permission.

Warning. All statements about suicide need to be qualified. I feel that *generally* the psychotic-depressive suicide proceeds quietly on his course with little or no previous warning. Likewise, the rational suicide may or may not state his interest in advance. But the neurotic-depressive, composing from sixty to seventy percent of the total suicides and attempted suicides, usually communicates his suicidal ruminations a number of times before the event. Since he has not made the break with reality, as in the case of the psychotic, his is that desperate appeal for help and a "crumb of love," acceptance and support. If his pathetic appeal, made verbally or by the "half-hearted" suicide attempt, wins sympathy, acceptance, and help, his purpose has been attained and he will choose life, not death. If not, then he may in despair regress more deeply and make the suicidal escape. Statistics indicate that more than two-thirds of those who commit suicide have previously stated this intention. They also reveal that the majority who have made such statements of intention, do not carry out the intent. These apparently receive the desired support and hang on.

Help. Suicide is closely allied with depression and usually follows the experiencing of great loss and despair. Most incidents can be prevented if the would-be victim finds a friend or is with another person and gains support. The nonprofessional therapist can prevent most of these suicides. The psychotic depressive, of course, is beyond the depth of the layman, but these are in the minority. The "nonsick," rational contemplator of suicide may be granted the right to carry out his decision, especially if the "sacrifice hit" motive is prevalent. Or the empathic friend may, by logical argument and a re-evaluation of facts, convince him to choose an alternate course. The central problem falls on the neurotic depressive, the majority type. The intelligent, concerned layman can establish an accepting, empathic relationship with the neurotic depressives and lend the necessary support to help them over the crisis. Referral to a professional source may then follow to help them grow stronger selves and reconstruct more adequate personalities.

This position seems to be supported by Kobler and Stotland who made an intensive study of suicidal patients in a private psychiatric hospital, during a short period of high incidence. They state their orientation as "psychosocial, field-theoretical, or transactional, (p. VII) and stress both environmental and intrapsychic factors. Following a detailed discussion of several cases, they say:[16]

> We have theorized that in order for an actual suicide to take place, certain conditions must prevail in the "field." An individual comes to feel that his future is devoid of hope; he, or someone else, brings the alternative of suicide into his "field." He attempts to communicate his conviction of hopelessness to others, in an effort to gain their assurance that some hope still exists for him. The character of the response at this point is crucial in determining whether or not suicide will take place. For actual suicide to occur, a necessary (though not sufficient) aspect of the field is a response characterized by helplessness and hopelessness. The helpless-hopeless response usually is communicated through an implicit or explicit expectation that the troubled person will kill himself.
>
> . . . Each of the cases substantiates the appropriateness of our theory: the responses of all the emotionally significant people to the cries for help be decisive in each situation. Those who committed suicide found their worlds pervaded by anxiety about suicide, and by helplessness; no person in the immediate environment was hopeful and confident immediately prior to the suicide. The facts indicate that suicide did not take place—although it was possible—until the individual's aloneness was absolute, until all possible roads to hope were closed. (p. 252).

For a stimulating student report and class discussion, I suggest *Suicide and the Soul* by James Hillman, Director of Studies of the Jung Institute in Zurich. The point of view is psychoanalytic but somewhat unique. Dr. Hillman says, "*the issue is not for or against suicide, but what it means in the psyche.*" And he claims that the analyst is the one who is in the best position to understand this.

---

[16] Reprinted with permission of the Macmillan Company from *The End of Hope* by A.L. Kobler and E. Stotland. © The Macmillan Company, 1964.

SUMMARY

The evolution of the public attitude toward psychosocial disorders was from being "demon possessed" to "bewitched" to the "mad" and "insane" and finally to the "ill." Some would prefer dropping the term "illness" and refer to the neuroses and psychoses as "behavior disorders," except, of course, those that derive from organic malfunction. Anton Boisen, a former psychotic patient, describes the schizophrenias as "ways of life." Psychiatrists generally classify the schizophrenias as: paranoic, catatonic, hebephrenic, and simple. But many patients cannot be diagnosed as specifically one type or the other. Symptoms cross lines. Dr. Cameron observes that the schizophrenic reactions are adaptive to the degree that they provide substitutes for the escaped reality.

Next in frequency and interest among the functional psychoses are the manic-depressives. Most of these are cyclic, swinging from a high state of euphoria and excessive activity to the gloom of deep depression and withdrawal. But the mood swing is variable in pattern and in the duration of the moods.

In spite of extensive research, much remains to be learned about the specific causes (etiology) of the psychoses. There is evidence that genetic factors make some people more susceptible than others, and it seems to vary considerably with the type and in the process more than the reactive types of schizophrenia. Certain endocrine and brain chemistry differences between certain psychotics and normals have been noted. But whether these factors are causative or merely correlates has not been clearly determined. Early childhood conditioning in a family constellation that prevents normal identification with the parents and growth of autonomy is believed to be the major etiological situation in most cases.

The boundary that separates the neuroses from the psychoses is not as firmly drawn as formerly. Anxiety (fear) is the principle factor in both. In neuroses there is less regression, better contact with reality, less disorganization of the mental processes, and the ability to sustain oneself in moderately normal living but with inefficiency and much mental misery. They, too, cannot be classified into discrete types, for symptoms often change. But they are generally classified relative to the most prominent symptom cluster: anxiety reactions, phobic reactions, obsessive-compulsive reactions, dissociation reactions, conversion reactions, etc. Their causes may be similar to that of the psychoses except that the genetic factor is less obvious and the family stunting was not as severe nor started as early. Self became stronger but not fully mature nor free of its childhood insecurities.

Depression is seen in its normal, neurotic, and psychotic dimensions. It is described as a mood of which the basic element is grief compounded with anxiety, anger, and guilt in varying amounts. Neurotic and psychotic depression frequently terminates in suicide. The former often communicates his suicidal interests, while the latter seldom does. If those who do hint or openly speak of their intentions are given the support and help they need, most could be prevented from taking the desperate fatal step.

GLOSSARY

Delusion. A persistent false belief; a fixed opinion not based on facts; faulty interpretation of facts or deriving unwarranted meanings.

Euphoria. An emotional state of high exaltation and well-being with exaggerated buoyancy and vigor.

Hallucination. A sensory perception that has no external stimulus; a mental image projected outward and seen as an object.

Idiosyncratic. Pertaining to habits, traits, modes of expression, etc. peculiar to an individual. An individualistic approach.

Labile. Unstable, changing, liable to lapses.

Narcolepsy. Uncontrollable, compulsive sleeping attacks, a psychologically caused "sleeping sickness."

Prognosis. A prediction as to the likelihood of recovery or the probable outcome of a disease.

Protocol. Preliminary draft of official documents. The official report of test results in psychometry.

Scrupulosity. Exaggerated concern or conscientiousness about one's behavior being right; a compulsive doing right and/or being good.

Somnambulism. The act of walking about while asleep.

Symbiotic. Pertains to living together as algae or fungi with the host plant; the foetus-mother relationship, or the extremely close interdependent relationship between mother and infant.

Transmogrified. Something converted or transformed into a different shape.

Typology. The study of types; or a set or listing of types.

Zygotic. Pertaining to a new organism developed from the union of two gametes. Thus, monozygotic twins are two organisms from the same united gametes, while dizygotic twins develop each from a different pair.

REFERENCES AND SUGGESTED READINGS

ARIETI, S. (ed), *American Handbook of Psychiatry,* Vol. 1, pp. 455–507, (1959).

BECK, SAMUEL J., *Psychological Processes in the Schizophrenic Adaptation,* New York: Grune & Stratton, Inc., 1965.

BELLAK, L. (ed), *Schizophrenia: A Review of the Syndrome,* New York: Logos Press, 1958.

BERLIN, IRVING, "The Emotional and Learning Problems of the Socially and Culturally Deprived Child," *Mental Hygiene* (1966) 50: 340–349.

BOISEN, ANTON T., *Out of the Depths,* New York: Harper & Brothers, 1960.

CAMERON, NORMAN, *Personality Development and Psychopathology,* Boston: Houghton Mifflin Company, 1963.

CAPLAN, GERALD, *Emotional Problems of Early Childhood,* New York: Basic Books, Inc., 1955.

CARROLL, HERBERT, *Mental Hygiene,* Englewood Cliffs, N.J.: Prentice-Hall, Inc., 1964.

FREUD, ANNA, *Normality and Pathology in Childhood,* New York: International Universities Press, 1965.

HILLMAN, JAMES, *Suicide and the Soul,* New York: Harper & Row, 1964.

KALLMAN, F. J., *Heredity in Health and Mental Disorder,* New York: W. W. Norton and Company, 1953.

KLEIN, D. B., *Mental Hygiene,* New York: Holt, Rinehart and Winston, Inc., 1956.

KOBLER, ARTHUR L. and EZRA STOTLAND, *The End of Hope,* Glencoe, Ill.: The Free Press, 1964.

LANDIS, CARNEY, METTLER, FRED A. (ed), *Varieties of Psychopathological Experience,* New York: Holt, Rinehart and Winston, 1964.

MENNINGER, KARL, *Man Against Himself,* New York: Harcourt, Brace & Co., 1956.

MILT, HARRY, *Serious Mental Illness in Children,* (Public Affairs Pamphlet No. 352) New York: Public Affairs Committee, Inc., 1963.

MUSSEN, H. M., J. J. CONGER, and J. KAGAN, *Child Development and Personality,* New York: Harper & Row, 1963.

PRINCE, MORTON, *The Unconscious,* New York: The Macmillan Company, 1920.

SCHNEIDERS, A. A., *Personal Dynamics and Mental Health,* New York: Holt, Rinehart and Winston, Inc., 1965.

STERN, PAUL J., *The Abnormal Person and His World*, Princeton, N.J.: D. Van Nostrand Co., Inc., 1964.

TAYLOR, W. S. and M. F. MARTIN, "Multiple Personality," *J. Abnormal and Soc. Psychol.*, XXXIX, 281–300 (1944).

THIGPEN, CORBET H. and HENRY M. CLECKLEY, *The Three Faces of Eve*, New York: McGraw-Hill Book Company, Inc., 1957.

THORPE, LOUIS, *The Psychology of Mental Health*, New York: The Ronald Press Company, 1960.

TOMAN, WALTER, *Family Constellation*, New York: Springer Publishing Company, Inc., 1961.

WHITE, ROBERT W., *The Abnormal Personality*, New York: The Ronald Press Company, 1964.

Menninger (1938 and 1956) describes it as inward-directed hostility, a sort of "man against himself" conflict, which is a partial or long-drawn suicide. And Boss (in Stern, 1964, p. 118) shows how minority groups, particularly the Negro, suffer from hypertension to a greater degree, because of the greater social pressure they are under and their inferior social position makes greater suppression (and semirepression) necessary. He speaks of the hypertensive as one who is "walled in alive" and in whom the "stream of life is dammed up behind a thick facade of self-control, amiability, and propriety." After reviewing Boss and several others, Stern makes the summary statement: "On closer inspection, Boss's formulations are not radically different from those of the psychoanalysts, even though the language differs. Boss stresses the etiological importance of the same factors which Alexander, Menninger, Reiser, Binger, Dunbar, and others have emphasized—perfectionism, obsessiveness, repressed anger, general paralysis of self-expression—and his hypotheses suffer from the same shortcomings as theirs: a lack of precision. . . . The parallel between the calcification of the blood vessels and the existential "being walled in" of the hypertensive is certainly suggestive; whether it is more remains to be seen."

OUTER AND INNER SKIN DISORDERS

The skin is a marvelously complex organ—so tough and tender, so exposed to the harsh environmental forces and of such intimate relation to the self (one's appearance), and with so many tiny glands. It is subject to many illnesses that it has become a major area of specialization in medical science. Contact allergens cause some skin disturbances, but psychologic factors appear to be of greater consequence. Prolonged emotional stress may well be the important factor in causing the skin to be sensitive to allergens. Prolonged frustration and inner tension are associated with at least several types of skin rash or lesion. The specific episodes often occur in connection with a somewhat more than usual emotional situation. It is as though the suppressed-repressed anger pops out through the skin. Some theorists of the psychoanalytic school associate itching with libidinal drives and scratching with self-directed hostility. The libidinal anger is not being directed freely against others, and the taloned hands that normally would rip at the other person now rip one's own skin. Empirical facts are insufficient, and theories are generally inadequate. Frustration, anger, and its suppressed-repressed blocking are involved, with the habit springing from childhood.

We now turn to the gastrointestinal disorders and overlook differences in descriptive terminology as much as possible. There is general agreement that the typical ulcerative patient is outwardly calm and methodical, thoroughly conscientious and ambitious, but must push himself all the time to over-compensate for his strong dependency-security needs. With these dependency needs which he is fighting (consciously or unconsciously) to overcome, he is permanently tense and angry at himself because of his dependency and deficiency in true self-confidence. Being ambitious, he pushes hard to succeed in order to prove himself and, therefore, he faces much frustration and generates anger. Much of his anger is suppressed because he is afraid that he will offend his business associates or other people with whom he is in contact. He is almost always angry; the acidic digestive (peptic) fluids are being secreted continuously. When the stomach is relatively empty and a lesion has formed that exposes the unprotected tissue of the stomach wall, the peptic fluids literally digest a part of the stomach wall.

There are fewer findings about the psychologic aspects of colitis than about ulcers. The basic factors of colitis and ulcers are similar. Cases of either suffer much inner tension between the dual dependency-autonomy and succorance-productive achievement needs. The consequence is frustration and anger, and the latter is blocked from adequate expression. The studies of ulcer patients usually show that they are stronger in their achievement drive and are more prone to anger which activates the stomach fluids. In cases of colitis, however, the patients are more dependent and succorance-motivated. Anxiety is predominant over the anger, and keeps it more fully repressed. Colitis patients are usually quite sensitive to loss and suffer a greater sense of sorrow or grief. These emotions tend to depress stomach action, but do not cause peptic ulcers. Instead they set up destructive action in the wall of the intestines.

To succinctly summarize the distinction between the two, one may say that the ulcer patient is running mad and the colitis patient is running sad, and a little afraid.

ASTHMA, THE MYSTERY AFFLICTION

It was stated above that a bronchial asthmatic attack may be triggered either by breathing an allergen or by an emotional disturbance. Various laboratory experiments have demonstrated that attacks may be precipitated by simulated objects and situations, plastic toys that resemble the offending object, etc. Dekkar and Groen,* Bastiaans and Groen* describe asthmatic patients as generally being persons who are overly rigid, with much inner emotional stress of which they are only partly conscious, and that their excess emotion is not discharged adequately through normal channels, but after build-ups is discharged by the asthmatic attack. In a sense, the victim is literally choking with rage. Miller and Baruch* trace the etiology to the mother-child relationship and find in most cases cold or rejecting mothers who had difficulty expressing love. Having reviewed numerous studies, Cameron (1963, p. 693, 694) writes:

> It is generally agreed that asthmatic attacks with psychosomatic components are found in persons with strong but repressed dependency needs, especially needs for protection. There is the familiar emotional ambivalence, with destructive wishes toward a loved person. Different persons build up different patterns of defense against their conflicts. . . .
>
> The asthmatic attack has been interpreted as a *suppressed cry for help* from a mother figure, when the patient faces loss of separation. The patient can express his dependency only in an infantile way. Asthmatic persons often report difficulty in crying, and relief from asthma when they have *learned to cry.* Attacks in psychosomatic patients are also relieved sometimes by *confession,* if they have had conscious or unconscious feelings of guilt over their hostility, and fears of losing the love they need. Patients who discover that they are accepted, in spite of real or fantasied "badness" often experience relief.
>
> Some clinicians maintain that the dependency needs of asthmatic patients are inordinate because these were not met in childhood. Some feel that allergic children have been unusually sensitive from birth so that they raise difficulties in early mother-child relationships and precipitate mutual frus-

* Discussed in Stern, 1964., pp. 119–121.

> tration. Some of the mothers studied had obviously not solved their own dependency conflicts. They often showed their ambivalence by first holding their child so close as almost to choke it, and then pushing it away in a gesture of rejection. . . . Knapp and Nemetz (1957) made an intensive study of 40 asthmatic patients relative to their neurotic tendencies and found a very high correlation between the extent of pulmonary disability and degree of neuroticism. In the later study (1960) they found not so much suppression of the crying response as conflict over expressing any strong feeling, and they observed strong moods of sorrow and depression.

GENERAL PSYCHOSOMATIC CHARACTERISTICS

One emphasis which has been made at various points in this book is that of human individuality, the uniqueness of the self and its personality. No two psychotics, neurotics, or psychosomatics are alike in their specific etiologies or syndromes. But any systematic study requires categorizing and generalizing. We now look for the commonalities of psychosomatics and their relation to the neuroses. After making allowances for individual variability and various terms used to describe similar traits or characteristics, we find a striking core of common characteristics running through the chief psychosomatic disorders.

In general, these patients come from the same type of home environment that produces neurotics. The exception is that the deprivation of acceptance and love, and thus prolonged dependency-succorance needs, are not quite as strong. Self is a little stronger and has less anxiety and repression. There is, in varying degrees of consciousness, an awareness of anxiety and dependency desires, and self tries to overcompensate by ambition and success motivation. However, it is a dual motivation with permanent inner tension and outer calm. Their behavior is more than normally rigid and they lack freedom to express emotions normally. Being less than fully mature, autonomous, and self-confident, these persons are a little more sensitive and less frustration tolerant than the normal person, thus almost constantly in a state of anger. Because they learned to suppress their hostility in childhood, the habit continues and their anger is kept suppressed (perhaps in some degree repressed) until the stress brings illness. The colitis and asthmatic cases generally show a little more dependency, sadness, anxiety, and repression of their anger. However, the anger is a factor and often they are angry at themselves for being so dependent and anxious.

Thus, psychosomatics stand astride that broad boundary between normals and neurotics—some, in most personality traits, being as normal as anyone and some being well among the more serious neurotics. They resemble both the obsessive-compulsive personalities and the hysteria conversion type. However, there is not nearly the degree of unconscious purposive defense nor symbolic representation, but perhaps some degree of these. Becoming ill does relieve a person of the severe frustration; and it is more self-satisfying (face-saving) to fail from illness rather than from lack of ability. It also gratifies the need of dependency and succorance. But it is highly questionable whether there is any significant degree of unconscious purposeness in this. Psychoanalytic theorists are in agreement that it seems more plausible to attribute the illness to the natural stress effect, its location depending chiefly on inherent or developmental susceptibility of one organ or another.

Stern's (1964, p. 127) general conclusions on this problem are stated as follows:

> If we return now to the question of the etiology of psychosomatic disorders, we find that many workers, reviewing the research data presently available, have revised earlier formulas. The one-sided psychogenic or somatogenic emphases which prevailed during the 1940's are no longer much in vogue. The present trend is to think of psychosomatic syndromes as complexly determined by a multiplicity of conditions, both organic and psychic, with no factor by itself sufficient to "cause" a given disease. This conceptual marriage of heterogeneous psychic and organic factors may be philosophic suspect. . . , but it seems to reflect best the present state of our empirical knowledge. The following conditions are widely held to determine the onset of psychosomatic disorders:
>
> 1. A vulnerable or sensitized organ or organ system ("somatic compliance");
> 2. The presence of some illness involving the organ system in a relative ("psychic exposure");
> 3. The symbolic meaning to the patient of a given organ system;
> 4. Overall psychic vulnerability ("readiness to regress");
> 5. The nature and severity of the situational stress.

It seems to me that the present impasse confronting scientific medicine and psychology, with relation to the "cause" in psychosomatics, is closely related to the psychological impasse discussed in Chapter 3, which was relative to *self* as acting subject and the *self-image* as mental process or activity, of the nature of verb. When one engages in the philosophical discussion of mind controlling the body and body controlling the mind, with one causing the other to act in any given way, he is talking about interrelated processes which are correlative but not causal. They are mental and physiological, therefore actions, of the nature of verb, not acting subject. Cause is found in subject, the acting agent.

These processes may be well integrated or badly disorganized, functioning cooperatively or antagonistically. Self as subject, when acting upon its environment as object, functions through its mental and physiological processes, with constant "feed-back" through the lower brain structures. The "cause," then, of psychosomatic illness may be found in a weak self that is unable to maintain well integrated mental and physiological processes directed toward harmonious and realistic goals. The dominant motives are about equally balanced between the security-maintenance and growth-actualization sides of our need schema. (p. 125). Competing or antagonistic processes result, with weakened organic resistance, e.g., Dr. Selye's stress theory. The other (somatic) cause then may be found in invading organisms that, as agents, act destructively on the weakened bodily organs. The patient is then organically ill.

> Since allergies are so commonplace, it may be of benefit and interest if each member of the class would interview his family doctor and a few friends to determine local incidence. Report these statistics to the class and follow with a discussion of the probable degree to which allergies may be attributed to genetic factors, air pollution, and emotional stress.

CHARACTER DISORDERS

Since the term "character" expresses an ill-defined concept, the meaning of character disorders or character neuroses is rather ambiguous. Persons included in this category generally reveal personality structures of a neurotic nature. Their patterns of neurotic responses, however, effect a disorganization of basic attitudes and values, thus "character" deterioration, and hurtful interpersonal relationships which may or may not be unlawful. Many such persons are also to be found among the psychosomatics.

ALCOHOLISM

In past generations, the alcoholic was characterized as a "bum," a plain "drunk," an offender to be jailed, a creature to be despised by the "respectable" community and alternately pitied and hated by his family. Modern science speaks of him as being a sick person. The official position of medical science and most psychologists is that alcoholism is a disease. Some are challenging this position, but the problem reverts to semantics. How wide is the range of concepts that can be symbolized by one word? Should the term "illness" (or "disease") be limited to organic dysfunction, or shall it be broadened to incorporate the psychoses, neuroses, the psychopath and delinquent, and virtually every type of maladaptive behavior of an organic, mental, and social nature?

If the neuroses are to be classified as illnesses, then alcoholism must be included; for most alcoholics are neurotic persons. There is no distinct border line between normal and neurotic personalities; and there is none between the normal drinker of alcoholic beverages and the alcoholic, the compulsive drinker, or, one may say, the neurotic drinker. Various estimates of the number of such drinkers in the United States runs from five to eight million. Most of these are listed as "problem drinkers," of whom 20 to 25 percent are the true addicts. This last group comprises the more serious neurotics with quite a few psychotics among them. Of all patients entering mental hospitals for the first time, during the 1950's, about 18,000 each year were alcohol-psychotics. They are problem drinkers, in that the economic loss to the country is several billion dollars a year and the hurt to themselves and their families is beyond calculation.

Even though there is no sharp line of demarcation, certain criteria have been suggested by which to determine the degree or stage of alcoholism: (1) the regularity of the drinking spree—periodic, whether closely or widely spaced; (2) drinking alone; (3) drinking early in the morning; (4) feeling the need for drink at definite times; (5) a tense, restless, anxious feeling if the drink is not available; (6) drinking enough to interfere with one's work and family relations; (7) occasional memory lapses and blackouts.

Neurotics. Alcoholics are basically neurotics; but some are psychotics and psychosomatics. In reference to character or personality structure, they cover a wide number of the categories under which these have been discussed, and the etiology is the same as for these. One is not dealing merely with a disease nor one type of person, but with a large variety of personality types, dynamic factors, and contributing circumstances. Psychoanalysts characterize them as being oral dependency types. Like all serious neurotics and psychotics, they are immature and have suffered the deprivation of satisfactory child-parent relations. They have become defeated, frustrated, or confused by the old anxiety-anger-guilt complex. They have resorted to alcohol as a tranquilizer to ease this inner tension and conflict. Alcoholism is the consequence of a self-administered and unsuccessful treatment of a neurosis; the side effects are disastrous. Extensive studies by H. A. Witkin et al[3] found a widely variant symptomatological picture among alcoholics, but springing from a basic character disorder that included such traits as being excessively *dependent, depressed, hostile, sexually immature,* and *schizoid.*

Treatment. Medical treatment is a necessary part of the program for the correction of these side effects. Liver malfunctioning may need to be corrected and general health restored, the patient having suffered malnutrition, avitaminosis, and disturbances in hormone production. The aversion treatment is a popular "cure," used widely for many years. It is based on conditioning, the repeated application of pain or discomfort to ex-

[3] H.A. Witkin et al, *Personality Through Perception* (New York: Harper & Row, 1954).

tinguish the undesired response. Antabus (disulfiram) was, until recently, popularly used for this purpose. When it was taken shortly before drinking, it caused physical discomfort and anxiety. Temposil (citrated calcium carbimide) has come into more popular use in recent years. Tranquilizers and/or antidepressants are also used to relieve the inner stress and thus reduce the "need" of alcohol. Results of all these have shown only limited value.

> For new techniques of aversion conditioning, the student is referred to Franks (1964, Chapter 13 and 14). Also see Appendix.

Alcoholics Anonymous has become a popular and relatively effective organization for the treating of the alcoholic. It does not assume to "cure" alcoholism but helps to keep the alcoholic sober. The procedure may be called a social-spiritual method. AA helps meet the alcoholic's basic needs in three ways: (1) it gives him understanding, acceptance, and love; (2) it gives nurturance and succorance, a lot of attention and care; (3) it provides a spiritual stimulus, growth in faith—faith in God, in self, and in life generally developing together. When the alcoholic joins an AA chapter he is pledged to take certain steps: admit his inability to handle alcohol, believe in a higher power, turn his life over to God as understood, make a searching self-inventory, confess the nature of his wrongs, ask and expect help from God, list all people harmed and make amends, if possible, and continue taking personal inventory and seeking Divine aid.

Religious Need. Clinebell[4] postulates that the alcoholic is seeking in alcohol the satisfaction of transcendent needs which only religion can give.

> Alcoholism is a tragic response to areas of tragedy in our culture. The insecurity and emotional malnutrition bred by an anxious, puritanical, competitive society has resulted in many damaged orphans of the spirit. These are people who,

[4] Howard J. Clinebell, Jr., *Understanding and Counseling the Alcoholic* (Nashville: Abingdon Press, 1956), Chapter 6. Used with permission.

because of their fears and inner conflicts, are cut off from satisfying, fulfilling fellowship with other human beings. Alcohol has always had something to offer these, the weary, the anxious, the lonely, the spirtual wanderers. It offers the illusion of unity with one's fellows, temporary deadening of anxiety, and the quieting of inner conflict. Its relief is temporary and illusory, but available to many who have found no other. . . . (p. 146).

In his general summary, Clinebell states certain specific ways religion can help the alcoholic:

1. A religious solution can provide the individual with a *sense of superhuman help,* not only in meeting the specific problem of alcoholism, but in bearing the general frustrations, disappointments, drudgery, and interpersonal friction which contribute to the etiology of alcoholism. . . .
2. A religious approach can provide the alcoholic with a *feeling of being accepted by life. . . .*
3. A religious approach can provide the alcoholic with a means of handling his *ultimate anxiety. . . .*
4. An effective religious approach can help the individual to discover a purpose in living by establishing his personality on the foundation of *a meaningful philosophy of life. . . .*
5. A religious orientation can provide a group approach to alcoholism with a *unifying commitment to a group-transcending value. . . .* (pp. 150, 151, 154).

Dr. Giorgio Lolli[5] says:

Total Personality. There is practically no case of alcoholic addiction isolated from other neurotic disorders or bodily illnesses. Alcohol addiction can be set apart from an intricate personality frame for descriptive purposes only and because an understanding of what is and what is not addictive is prerequisite to prognosis and treatment. This knowledge permits an evaluation, in a given patient, of how addictive and other reaction patterns interact. . . . (p. 307). . . . A study of the individual when intoxicated gives clues to a better understanding of his sober personality. It is this return of the repressed, the release of primitive drives, which sets the addictive drinker

[5] In Gardner Murphy and Arthur J. Bachrach, *An Outline of Abnormal Psychology* (Revised Edition) (New York: The Modern Library, Random House, 1954). Used with permission. Also in the *Quarterly Journal of Studies on Alcohol,* Vol. 10, 1949.

> at odds with the world. If the workings of civilization consist in taming the beast in man, the workings of addictive drinking are characterized by the reverse process with resulting asocial or antisocial behavior. (p. 310).

Since the complexity of the factors in alcoholism is so great and the personality types so varied, total community resources are needed in its treatment: social and economic support, medical aid and psychotherapy, and the self-enhancing work of a vital religious faith.

DRUG ADDICTION

The illicit traffic in narcotics is a major social problem, and the addictive use of narcotics is a major contribution to crime and character decay. The confirmed addict will stoop to almost any crime or immorality to obtain his favorite drug. The etiology and general personality structure of drug addicts are very much the same as in alcoholics. The addiction is more serious and more difficult to overcome because of the much greater physiological effects. Addiction to alcohol is almost entirely psychological, while narcotic drugs of the opium class (codeine, heroin, dilantin, metapon) effect physiological changes that make their denial very painful. The barbiturates and such stimulants as cocaine, mescaline, benzedrine, and marijuana are less physiological in their addictive hold. Treatment should be along the lines suggested above for alcoholism, with the exception that prolonged hospitalization and medical treatment are generally essential. A few recoveries by psychotherapy alone have been reported. And a few reportedly have made recovery by the aid of religion alone. Conditioned reflex therapy also offers promise. (See Chapter 10 and Appendix).

SEXUAL DEVIATES

Overt homosexuality, genital exhibitionism, voyeurism, fetishism, transvestism, and sadomasochism* fall into this category.

* See Glossary for meaning of these terms.

Cameron (1963, p. 660) defines these as *"patterns of sex behavior which do not culminate in heterosexual intercourse when this outcome is permissible and objectively possible."* We shall pass by all of these except homosexuality and examine it briefly.

The Kinsey reports[6] revealed such a high incidence of homosexuality that some people, including psychologists argued that it ought not be designated sexual deviation. But the large majority who reported homosexual tendencies to Kinsey interviewers had not expressed the tendency overtly since youth, and then rarely, or else were bisexual and maintained fairly normal heterosexual relations. In other words, most of the respondents in the Kinsey study were not exclusively nor predominantly homosexuals. The number of these is hard to come by, since people are reluctant to report practices that are both illegal and generally looked upon with contempt.

Causes. Why are some people homosexuals? That is another question about human character and behavior that has no satisfactory answer. There were the popular physical and physiological explanations. "Hermaphrodite" became an epithet of contempt. But true hermaphroditism, dual genitalia, is extremely rare. As to the physiological, both men and women secrete both testosterone and estrogen, the balance being more or less heavily toward one or the other; but no scientific evidence is yet available that indicates any significant relationship between homosexuality and sex hormone balance.

Cameron states (1963, p. 665):

> The complexity of the childhood interrelationships can be illustrated by the way in which opposite conditions seem to produce similar deviations. Thus, *if a boy fears his father so much that he cannot identify with him, he may also not dare to love his mother or any other woman. On the other hand, if it is his mother who seems dangerous and frightening to a boy, he may renounce all women as too frightening. In both instances the outcome may be homosexuality.*

---

[6] Alfred C. Kinsey, *Sexual Behavior in the Human Male,* (Phila.: Saunders, 1948).
Alfred C. Kinsey, *Sexual Behavior in the Human Female,* (Phila.: Saunders, 1953).

Bieber et al[7] have given a very comprehensive report on both etiology and treatment, based on prolonged clinical work with 106 homosexuals. The large majority of these cases came out of a family configuration where the mother was dominatingly possessive, seductive (sometimes of a hysteroid type) with the child and dominant toward the husband. The father played a minimum role and was submissive, indifferent, or rejecting. In either case, the child could not identify adequately with the father and frequently had an ambivalent attitude toward the mother.

General Factors. At the present time, we do not have a complete understanding of its causes, but certain general conditions may be observed as contributing toward homosexual tendencies. (1) Unsatisfactory identity with one's parents especially in middle and late childhood. (2) Social-circumstantial factors which center around intimacies in the family. (3) Late childhood sexual play habits that tend to form abnormally strong attachments to peers of the same sex. (4) Fear of heterosexual relations created by faulty sex education, more often in the mother-to-daughter relation. There is some evidence pointing toward a sort of reaction-formation type of rejection of normal social mores or values and with this the lack of an adequate capacity for normal love. This last, of course, may be a consequence of the others; or it may be even more basic and contribute to them.

Homosexuality is usually built into one's character structure relatively early and has become accepted by him. Most do not admit it as a problem nor do they want or seek help. Some seek psychotherapeutic help with associated problems and may change their sexual patterns with the broader reconstruction of behavior patterns. For the true homosexual, prolonged psychotherapy is required and results have been modest. Conditioned reflex treatment offers some promise.

> Sexual behavior is generally an interesting topic of discussion. The class may benefit if each member will list a few criteria and/or specific behavior responses that differentiate "normal"

[7] I. Bieber et al, *Homosexuality: A Psychoanalytic Study of Male Homosexuals* (New York: Basic Books, Inc., 1962).

and "deviant" sex experience. Is it a matter of what is common or uncommon (statistics) or can it be established on the basis of personal and social benefit or detriment?

THE PSYCHOPATH

The term "psychopath" is still popular with the public but is not an adequate term in professional circles. As a category of human personality types or behavior disorders, it is ambiguous. Any one of the especially troublesome, irritating, and puzzling sociopaths who can not be classified specifically, may be safely called a psychopath, since no one can prove that he is not one. There are many trait names that are ascribed to the "psychopath." Most are epithets of an uncomplimentary nature, and they overlap widely in meaning.

Traits. The psychopath is egocentric and irresponsible. He lives for himself, expediency being his highest value. He lacks or is deficient in conscience (weak super-ego, if Freudian) and thus in a value system. He may resort to crime or immorality if it serves his immediate interest, whether for financial gain, pleasure, or even curiosity. He is seldom rash, is cool and collected, and can lie convincingly for fun or gain. He will sign a contract, business deal or marriage, with little intention of honoring it. If his intention is sincere at the time, it may change the next day or next month. He knows (intellectually) the rules of society and may pay them lip-service. He can and may confess and repent convincingly when it serves his purpose. He may be cruel and sadistic, disobedient and incorrigible, or he may be pleasant, affable, and cooperative.

The psychopath is not neurotic in the normal sense of the term. His traits are disorganized, impulsive, aberrant and are not a system of symptoms (syndrome) serving a special need, or at least they are not as apparent. On the surface, he is virtually devoid of the anxiety-anger-guilt complex that is so characteristic of the neuroses. But on closer examination, this may be mere appearance. Deeper knowledge may reveal more deeply repressed anxiety and possibly its companions, hostility and guilt. The hypothetical psychopath does not exist. There are persons with various combinations and varying degrees of the above traits—persons more or less psychopathic.

Causes. As to etiology, only a very little is known. "He was born that way" is the old and easy explanation. Some children from birth are intellectually deficient, likewise, some children are emotionally deficient and incapable of deep and meaningful interpersonal relations. This theory has not held up well in the face of empirical evidence, although, it is highly probable that genetic factors play a minor role. Recent efforts have been made to link psychopathic traits with organic brain conditions, based on observations of several cases which from brain infection or damage developed certain psychopathic traits. Much more research will be required to validate this assumption or reveal the degree of its causality.

At the present time the most plausible theory is that the psychopathic character develops as a consequence of failure during the child's early socializing experiences. This begins, usually, during the third year when self has developed considerable strength and has become self-assertive; it is the "no" phase in the child's life. At this point and through the preschool years, the parents need to supply much acceptance and love to reward the child sufficiently for him to relinquish his egocentric desires. If supplied, the child identifies, internalizes their values, and is socialized. If the child lacks this love-reward, the future psychopath does not identify and accept parental values but follows his own whimsical way. He differs from most neurotics who spring from similar situations, in that his self is a little tougher and he develops a different defense. He rationalizes away the value of love and acceptance, of deep interpersonal involvement, and goes blithely along without them. He is neither anxious, angry, nor guilty about interpersonal relations. Nothing is that important to him. The values by which most of us live, which spring from and find their functional significance in deep and meaningful interpersonal involvement, do not affect him. His character from childhood has been constructed around the unreal rationalization that such relationships are of no value and by adulthood, he is virtually incapable of such.

A Case. A former client of mine who had been previously diagnosed at a psychiatric clinic as a psychopath, again began consultation at his young wife's insistence. They were separated at the time, but both seemed to want to salvage the marriage against the urgings of her parents and the advice of the psychiatrist. We managed to establish rapport and, after several interviews, some degree of empathy (deep empathy not being possible with the psychopath). Tom's childhood fit the above description rather closely. His unconscious rationalization of his childhood deprivation was too deeply established to be shaken by logic or rational interpretation, and empathy was too shallow for subjective dynamics to be effective. His wife belonged to a church whose minister was young, personable, and well versed in basic psychology. We solicited his help and, at his request, two other lay couples took a special interest in Tom. Tom took the course of instruction, was inducted into the church, and became active in the young adult fellowship. The Church slowly became a mother surrogate who accepted and loved him. Its mystical ritual and symbolism slowly pentrated the defense that was impervious to normal psychotherapy.

His was no radical conversion, and the situation was shaky for a long time. But Tom slowly improved and the marriage was holding after three years. He may have been described as a middle-of-the-road psychopath. The more hardened variety may not have responded to the above approach. For most thorough going psychopaths, prognosis of basic change through psychotherapy is poor. They do not care enough to seek help and will not, or cannot, identify sufficiently with the therapist to effect a "cure." However, they are not hopeless. Tom's case is not presented as a typical mode of treatment but merely to suggest that in many cases the psychopath's rigid defense against interpersonal involvement and concern can be "dissolved away" by some form of parent surrogate, individual or institutional, if and when we learn better how to instigate such relationship.

THE JUVENILE DELINQUENT

Fear (anxiety) is the predominant factor in the fear-hostility-guilt complex that determines the basic mood and attitude of psychotic and neurotic patients. The psychosomatic patient has a balance which is more nearly equal. In the so-called "character neuroses" there is too much variation to make a generalization, except that the true psychopath has repressed both his fear and anger so deeply that neither is openly manifested to a significant degree. In delinquency, the hostility (anger) factor is dominant in the anxiety-hostility-guilt complex that sets the basic attitude of these psychosocial problem cases. All in all, the fear-anger-guilt complex is dominant over the faith-love-self-satisfaction complex.

Some authorities have stated that delinquents are troubled with less anxiety than normal adolescents. I have not found it so in my work or studies. The anxiety is suppressed or repressed more fully in the majority of cases and may not manifest itself as clearly, but consciously or unconsciously, delinquents generally experience more anxiety than normals. The majority of cases show that hostile aggressiveness appears to be dominant over the anxiety factor, but often this is an effort at over-compensation, or a defense against anxiety. A sizable minority of delinquents are overtly dependent, anxiety-dominated clingers who feel so rejected and inadequate that they turn to the delinquent gang for acceptance and identity. They are "used" by the tougher members. Many of these may be designated as neurotic delinquents. We also have psychopathic delinquents, sex deviate delinquents, alcoholic and dope addictive delinquents, and the various compulsive-reaction types (kleptomania, etc.). There are many types of delinquents. Some writers combine addictive drinkers and dopesters, sex deviates, psychopaths and delinquents into one group and call them sociopaths. I prefer the term *psychosocial deviates.*

Delinquency is a legal term and is defined differently in the statutes of different states. Accurate statistics are hard to obtain and its exact nature is hard to ascertain. However, it is behavior unacceptable to society and has increased rapidly during the past two decades, running from approximately 200,000 in 1940, about 1 percent of the adolescent population, to nearly 500,000 in the mid 1960's about 2 percent of the adolescent population. These are annual figures of juvenile court cases. One would multiply these figures by 6 or 7 to get the total number and percentage of juveniles involved in delinquent behavior, and this would allow for repeaters.

THE WHAT AND WHY OF DELINQUENCY

I shall begin with a summary statement, then examine parts in greater detail. Cole[8] says:

> Although there are some exceptions, delinquent adolescents tend to share certain distinctive traits. They often show an average or slightly below-average intelligence, they are markedly over-active, they are retarded educationally far beyond the degree one might expect from their slight mental retardation, they dislike the traditional school, and they are not content with modes of emotional expression that are accepted as norms by their age-mates. They often show a high degree of hositility, aggressiveness, and suspicion. Their typical escape from their frustrations consists in making an attack upon their environment. Their homes may be undesirable places in which to raise children, usually for reasons having little to do with economic impoverishment. The homes most commonly fail to give the delinquent or predelinquent child the needed support, even though other siblings find the homes supportive enough for their needs. In some cases, the neighborhood may accept and even encourage delinquent behavior as a means of achieving status for both juveniles and adults. The varied frustrations that find expression in antisocial reactions may come from the general social background, the familial structure, internal pressures within the individual, or from any combination of these factors. Overindulgence, undercontrol, or sheer indifference on the part of the parents may contribute to the individual's delinquency. It is probable that the emergence of full-scale delinquency depends upon the way in which the potentially determining factors come together in a particular case and the reactions of family, friends, school, and neighborhood to the first manifestations of maladjustment or delinquency. (p. 448).

Health. There is little difference between the delinquent and nondelinquent population relative to general health and physical strength. That little difference seems to be on the delinquency side, except skin conditions and certain other psy-

[8] Luella Cole (with Irma Hall), *Adolescent Psychology,* (New York: Holt, Rinehart and Winston, Inc., 1964). Reprinted by permission of the publishers.

chosomatic disorders to which the delinquent is more prone, and is an indicator of more inner conflict.

Mental Traits. The mean scores of delinquents on intelligence tests run several points (10 to 12) lower than those for nondelinquents. Tests such as the Wechsler which have both a verbal and performance I.Q. score, show little difference in the performance score and much difference in the verbal. This difference is due more to lack of interest and general academic retardation than to actual intellectual retardation. The general consensus is that delinquents are slightly less intelligent than nondelinquents. Delinquents show less mature emotional behavior, which means that the self is less mature and thus the environment appears more frustrating and threatening. The delinquent has less frustration-tolerance and expresses more anger (hostility) and anxiety; the former is predominant in the majority of cases. He has a less mature, less adequate, and more confused value system, based on the type and degree of identifications he makes.

Heredity. Since most delinquents come from the lower social-economic class, it may be assumed that their parents are a little lower in intelligence than middle and upper class adults and thus their small intellectual deficiency is due largely to heredity. Incidences of mental defectiveness, epilepsy, and certain forms of insanity are a little higher among the parents of delinquents. Certain temperamental traits, energeticness, etc., that contribute to a delinquency proneness, may also be inherited. Thus, heredity plays a small part in many cases, but the adage, "Delinquents are made, not born," is generally true.

The Community. In some communities there is little or no delinquency. In others, it is virtually the way of life. Thus, it may be said that delinquency is made in the community. There are variations, but the typical delinquency-producing community is dirty and squalid, with crowded and uncomfortable housing. There is a general climate of frustration and discontent, anger and anxiety—more friction between neighbors and ethnic groups—more general hostility. Children have less adequate supervision, protection, and wholesome social and recreational outlets. They are in frequent contact with criminals and immoral characters of a variety of types who make a flashy appearance and whose activities offer a thrilling challenge to idle, bored, and hostile youth. While living this way, they see the attractive, affluent neighborhoods and the gaudy advertisements on television which are keyed to attract their buying power, and incite their desires. Frustration is great, hostility grows, tolerance is low; they strike out at the society which, by rationalization and projection, they feel has deprived them of what they ought to have. But not all; the majority of children in communities such as this do not become delinquents. The incidence of delinquent behavior is great in some affluent communities, but fewer of them reach court and are charged with delinquency.

The School. Most delinquents hate school. They are activists and chaff at the regimentation. They dislike academic work, fall behind, play hooky, and fall further behind. This increases conflict with parents and teachers and brings more jibes from fellow students. They don't fit. Low in patience and frustration-tolerance, they soon reach the boiling point, or the ennui-breaking point, and find themselves engaged in theft, burglary, or violent action of some kind. They want to drop out of school at the age of 15 or 16, get a job, make money, buy clothes and a car, have some "dough." But society says they must attend school until 18 or until they finish high school. Compulsory school attendance is a causative factor in many cases.

The Home. The frustrating home environment has been described in Chapter 6—the autocratic, rejecting parent and other deprivation conditions. If these deprivations are severe and begin at an early age, the usual consequence would be a neurotic, psychosomatic, or, under special circumstances, a psychopathic child. These conditions are generally not as severe in the early childhood of the average delinquent and begin in mid-childhood after the self is stronger and the character structure is more solidly built. The result is a delinquent, who is tougher and more outwardly hostile. The lack of emotional security and acceptance, lack of uniform discipline and parental concern, child-parent conflict, etc., continue into adolescence. Commonly added to these are a crowded and poorly furnished home usually avoided as much as possible, crime or immorality of parents or older siblings, and a home broken by divorce, desertion, death or a prison sentence. Recently the most rapid rise in delinquency is among children from more affluent homes where there is also frustration and deprivation of love, guidance, etc.

SOME RESEARCH FINDINGS

What makes the child a delinquent? In trying to find that answer, Barbara Wootton[9] (1959) made one of the most comprehensive and definitive studies of all significant research in the field that has been published to date. Her final summaries were based on 21 of the most thorough and reliable studies. She found wide variation among these as to the relative importance of each major causal factor. Regarding the broken home, for instance, the British studies rated it as important in 22 to 57 percent of the cases, while in the American studies the range was from 34 to 62 percent. In her final summary, she says:

> All in all, therefore, this collection of studies, although chosen for its comparative methodological merit, produces only the most meagre, and dubiously supported generalizations. On the whole, it seems that offenders come from relatively large families. Not infrequently (according to some investigators very frequently) other members of the delinquents' (variously defined) families have also been in trouble with the law. Offenders are unlikely to be regular church-goers, but the evidence as to whether club membership discourages delinquency is wildly contradictory. If they are of an age to be employed, they are likely to be classified as "poor" rather than "good" workers. Most of them come from the lower social classes, but again the evidence as to the extent to which they can be described as exceptionally poor is conflicting; nor is there any clear indication that their delinquency is associated with the employment of their mothers outside the home. . . . In their schooldays they are quite likely to have

[9] From Louise G. Howton, "Evaluating Juvenile Delinquency Research," *Mass Society in Crisis*, edited by Bernard Rosenberg, Israel Gerver and F. William Howton (New York: The Macmillan Company, 1964), p. 115. Used with permission.

> truanted from school, and perhaps an unusually large proportion of them come from homes in which at some (frequently unspecified) time both parents were not, for whatever reason, living together; yet even on these points, the findings of some inquirers are negative. And beyond this we cannot go!

In a previous publication (Roberts, 1958, pp. 32, 34), I have summarized several points of view based upon extensive research. Some of these are presented below.

The Gluecks, in their *Five Hundred Criminal Careers,* show that 84.8 percent of the cases studied have criminal relatives, 24.8 percent criminal parents, 39.6 percent a criminal sibling, and 18.8 percent had one or both parents and one or more siblings who were criminals . . . and Sullenger writes, "Many studies of the family life of delinquent children have revealed a high percentage of immoral backgrounds and delinquency within the immediate family." Healey, on the other hand, is supported by Reckless and Smith in finding that most delinquents are normal young persons with unfortunate environments and that juvenile delinquency cannot be attributed to personality type, age, sex, race, nationality, or to biological factors, and that it is the result of social factors such as the economic situation, size of family, broken homes, parent-child relations, social status, education and occupation, recreation facilities, neighborhood conditions, and school maladjustments; and that the juvenile delinquent is a normal child gone astray.

. . . Lindeman, while rejecting any inherited tendency toward crime, summarizes the matter by stating that the basic causes of crime are to be found in individual, psychological, mental and emotional defects on the one hand, and in the irregularities and malformations in our social institutions, legal practices, economic arrangements, and human relationships on the other.

SELF-PUNISHMENT

Karl Menninger (1956) presents the interesting theory that much delinquency and crime are closely related to suicide in cause. This particularly relates to the compulsive type of delinquent behavior where the victim is perpetually being caught and punished. Due chiefly to inadequate, or inadequately expressed love in his early childhood relationships, mainly with the family, the child grows up with resentment and aggressive feelings directed against his parents. These feelings are accompanied by guilt and cannot be expressed adequately against the parent. Thus, they become partly expressed against other persons (society) and partly against self in the form of aggressive delinquent behavior that cannot help but bring punishment upon the offender. Thus, unconsciously, by punishing himself he is destroying his position in society. His character is akin to the alcoholic, neurotic invalid, and others forms of partial suicide.

Menninger draws a clear distinction between the criminal who escapes punishment more often than not and whose criminal career is more or less a matter of free choice and those like the above whom he would designate as "neurotic criminals." Of such, he says: "Having yielded to their aggressive impulses, they are obliged to surrender in the end to the threats of their own consciences if not to the intimidations of the law. This leads them, then, to seek punishment, to allow themselves to be caught, to commit provocative offenses or even to "break into jail." (pp. 5–8, 203).

ALL ARE DIFFERENT

To grasp the complexity of causality in problem behavior, we may again draw an analogy from our alphabet and language. From these 26 letters, a million or more words have been composed. Now let us imagine that experimental psychologists could, by statistical analysis, factor out 26 specific factors that bear a causal relationship to delinquency. The different combinations of these 26 factors might well reach a million. Then, by adding different weights to certain of these specific factors (and they do carry different weights in different cases), this million of different causal patterns could be multiplied. The point I am trying to make is that the causes of delinquency are not the same in any two cases. Each delinquent child (or youth) has his own specific problems with their unique combination of factors. It has been my experience that nearly every one of them struggled with the problem from three to five years before getting in trouble with the law.

Our task, the community task, is to find the predelinquent during this period and help him solve his problem. With most, this can be done. In the small percentage of cases where psychopathic, compulsive-reaction, and sexual perversion characteristics are found, response to present methods of treatment is slow and general prognosis is poor. With increased understanding and improved methods, we may anticipate a great decrease in future delinquency and other psychosocial maladjustments.

Menninger no doubt is correct in his analysis of the motivation behind certain types of neurotic delinquent behavior, but we need not probe so deeply to observe the purpose (needs served) of most delinquents. In some cases, it is for kicks, to escape boredom. Some want the "things" of life that are so profusely advertised but which they have been unable or unwilling to earn. They take a calculated risk—not too realistically calculated, perhaps. Most are frustrated and angry young people who generalize and displace their hostility in a variety of directions as opportunity affords. There is prevalence of some parent-hate and self-hate, some unconscious motivation, but most of them know what they are doing and why. Their value system and self-discipline are not adequate. They know the chance they take, expect punishment if caught, and do not resent it too much if it is fair. Most of them are capable of assuming the responsibility for their conduct. They learned their motives, and they learned their mode of behavior. They can learn more acceptable motives and modes.

The findings of literally hundreds of extensive studies may be summarized in the general statement that "causes" spring from a cluster of factors inherent in family relationships, school and community conditions, and in the child's personal attributes (physical, intellectual, and temperamental); the relative weight and specific patterning of these are different in every case. The family cluster of factors is generally of greatest significance in that these contribute most to the child's basic values and attitudes, especially his attitude toward himself (self-image) which is most crucial.

LEARNING SUCCESS

Norman Tolman and Merle Smith,[10] in their extensive work at the Girl's Training School, Adrian, Michigan, found a low self-evaluation, negative self-image, to be a major characteristic of delinquent girls. They believe that their work with the girls lends support to the idea that to acquire and maintain a socially acceptable or appropriate self-concept is one of the best insulations against delinquency.

The training program at the school has been oriented toward consistently providing the circumstances wherein the girls could experience success. The philosophy is to accept the girl but to reject her substandard behavior. "However," they say, "attempts are made to see to it that more and more of the behavior becomes acceptable, so that eventually both the girl and her behavior meet with approval. This takes place in many subtle and seemingly incidental ways as staff freely supplies compliments in the day to day exchanges with residents. . . ."

Again they state: "The formula, reduced to its barest elements is this: once an individual has succeeded, the probabilities of future success are greatly increased. The award system that we utilize here at Girl's Training School is based upon the reality of reflecting success to the girls in a concrete manner; they must first meet a standard, and then be made aware that they have done so."

> It is probable that every member of the class is acquainted with one or more persons charged with delinquency. Let each make a short list of the personal characteristics of these delinquents and the causative factors as perceived. Compile and discuss these. Excellent material for class reports and discussion may be found in Rosenberg, Gerver and Howton (1964), especially selections by the Landers, Slochower, Durkheim, and Bell.

---

[10] From "Significant Alterations of Self-Concept and Defensiveness During Training School Residence," *Mental Hygiene*, Vol. 47, 1963, 279–286. Used with permission of publisher and authors.

WHY NOT DELINQUENT

Like many other people, Richard T. Sollenberger[11] became interested in why many children in economically depressed communities do not become delinquents. He made an intensive study of family life in New York's Chinatown, a community with almost no delinquency yet having all of the physical features of high incidence delinquency areas. He says:

> It was assumed that the low delinquency rate among the Chinese-Americans was due to their child rearing practices, their cultural values and their familial structure. Sixty-nine Chinese mothers were interviewed with the Sears, Maccoby and Levin schedule. In addition, the investigator participated in the daily life of Chinatown for seven weeks. From the interview responses, observation of familial relations and many discussions with people in the area, it would appear that the low delinquency rate, in spite of environmental variables which should favor such behavior, may be due to the following:
>
> 1. Through an abundance of nurturance and protection during early childhood, a reservoir of security and trust is built up, so that after the age of 6, when the rigid demands for conformity are expected, they will be accepted with a minimum of hostility.
>
> 2. From an early age, physical aggression is not only not encouraged but it is not tolerated.
>
> 3. The child comes from a close-knit, integrated family. He is reared in an atmosphere of mutual respect. Certain filial duties are expected of him and on the other hand, the parents accept responsibility for his proper behavior.
>
> 4. Within the family, and within the community, the child is continuously in contact with good models of behavior after whom he patterns his own behavior.

[11] From "Why No Juvenile Delinquency," Richard T. Sollenberger, an unpublished paper read at the American Psychological Association Convention in New York, September, 1966. Research supported by a N.I.M.H. grant. Published in February issue of the *Journal of Social Psychology*. Used with permission.

MENNINGER'S ANALYSIS OF DYSFUNCTION

We will end our discussion of the psychosocial disorders and introduce the next phase, restoration, with a long quotation from Karl Menninger.[12] He uses the terms "dyscontrol" and "dysorganization" to designate these disorders of varying degrees, and says:

> Increasing dysfunction, increasing dyscontrol, increasing dysorganization, can be identified empirically in a series of hierarchial levels, each one reflecting a stage of greater impairment of control and organization. . . .
>
> These clinical pictures (cases he described) of personality dysorganization and reorganization at various levels which appeared so clearly in the war cases can also be seen in the psychiatric phenomena of civilian life, though usually not so telescoped in their course. In the years that have passed since the war, we have had the opportunity to define the levels more carefully. It seems to us empirically that they are five in number.
>
> The *first* level or stage or degree of departure from the normal is that state of external and internal affairs which in common parlance is usually called "nervousness." It is a slight but definite impairment of smooth adaptive control, a slight but definite disturbance of organization, a slight but definite failure in coping.
>
> A *second* level or stage or degree of departure from the normal level to increased disorganization is one which in civilian life rarely results in resignation or hospitalization; it is that group of syndromes which harness individuals with the necessity for expensive compensatory living devices, tension-reducing devices. These are painful symptoms and sometimes pain the environment as much as the patient. In the last half-century they have been called "neuroses" and "neurotic syndromes," but these are not good names. The syndromes are thousands of years old.
>
> Our *third* stage of regression or dysorganization or dysequilibrium or dyscontrol is characterized by the escape of the

[12] From *The Vital Balance* by Karl Menninger. Copyright © 1963 by Karl Menninger, M.D. All Rights Reserved. Reprinted by permission of the Viking Press, Inc.

dangerous, destructive impulses, the control of which has caused the ego so much trouble. These are the outbursts, the attacks, the assaults, and the social offenses which result from a considerable degree of ego failure.

A *fourth* order of dyscontrol involves still more ego failure. Reality loyalty is abandoned completely or very largely; there is disruption of orderly thought as well as behavior; there are demoralization and confusion. These are the classical pictures of medieval psychiatry, the "lunacies" of our great-grandfathers, the "insanities" of our grandfathers, the "psychoses" of our fathers. We think it is time to abandon all these terms.

A *fifth* and penultimate stage is proposed, an extremity beyond "psychosis" in the obsolescent sense, the abandonment of the will to live. (pp. 162, 163).

An effective review might be conducted by a panel of students reading Chapters VIII, IX, X and XI of Menninger's book and discussing the points he makes in relation to the types of psychosocial disorders we have presented in Chapters 8 and 9.

Now, as an introduction to Chapter 10 and the interdisciplinary approach to treatment, we will cite more from Menninger. Of treatment, he says:

The public reads eagerly of new drugs to bring about a temporary serenity; some of us would be more interested in drugs that would evoke aspirations or spur a desire for learning or increase displeasures in wastefulness and self-preoccupation. We cannot be enthusiastic about chemical methods to produce a state of *sans souci*; what the world needs and what more human beings need, for their own mental health and that of their universe, is not to care less but to care more. For this we have no chemicals. There are no drugs "to keep the soul alert with noble discontent."

Drugs cannot inspire, encourage or comfort. "Only a person can heal a person," said Schilling two centuries ago. Perhaps this is only partially right, but it was a word spoken against mechanistic drug therapy long before ataractics were heard of. This is not to decry the use of drugs to relieve anxiety, but only to point out that just as relieving a sharp

> pain in the abdomen with morphine may mask the development of appendicitis, so the taking of sedative drugs often masks the development of dangerous pressure and retards steps toward its proper correction.
>
> The establishment or re-establishment of relationships with fellow human beings is the basic architecture of normal life; hence it is not only the index of recovery but one of the methods of recovery. To live, we say, is to love, and vice versa. If a patient is not frozen in his primary narcissism, or drowned in secondary narcissism which developed from his previous failures in attempting to establish and maintain love objects, he will continuously strive to find and touch persons and things about him. He will keep reaching out first a receiving and then a giving hand, making acquaintances and then friends, and finding more and more satisfactions and identifications. . . . (pp. 294–295).
>
> Psychiatry is a branch of medicine, but it is also—in its basic dependency—a branch of application of psychology, of sociology, of ethnology, of philosophy. It derives part of its structure from these sister sciences.
>
> In what is perhaps the most beautiful short essay ever written, a theologian and missionary listed three great and permanent goods: Faith, Hope, and Love. Of these, he declared, Love is the Greatest. . . .
>
> Today, after twenty centuries, this prescription is taken very seriously in psychiatry. We would even go so far as to say that it describes the basic philosophy of the psychiatrist. Faith, hope, and love are the three great intangibles in his effective function. (p. 358).

SUMMARY

Neurotic and psychosomatic symptoms overlap, especially in hypochondriasis and conversion reactions, but with certain marked differences. The mind-body relationship is more correlative than causative. Mental stress is conducive to illnesses with somatic disorders or dysfunction. Among the more common of these are migraine headaches, skin eruptions, gastrointestinal disturbances, respiratory ailments, and cardiovascular disturbances. The etiology of these and the psychological factors involved have much in common. Small differences in personality characteristics and ego- or self-strength largely determine which syndrome will develop. They are generally marked by a considerable amount of ambivalence and a near balance of motivation toward security and high accomplishment and thus much stress, but with less fixed defenses and repression than in the neuroses.

Alcoholism may be described as an illness but only in the sense that the neuroses are illnesses. The alcoholic may be thought of as a neurotic drinker, with a few psychotics included. He drinks to relieve his neurotic anxiety and conflict, but the side effects often lead to organic illness and social disaster. Treatment may be as varied as his neurotic (or psychotic) needs, with preliminary medical treatment to correct the organic side effects. Aversion (condition reflex) therapy has been an old form of treatment, with new conditioners giving new promise. Alcoholics Anonomous and certain church agencies provide a treatment program conducive to the experience of acceptance, love, and improvement of the self-image and self-strength.

Sexual deviation is a controversial social problem, marked especially by concern with homosexuality. What deviation is and who the deviants are (the incidence) are hard to ascertain. Feeling themselves to be a minority and looked upon with contempt, they are generally secretive and rarely request treatment. The etiology is still poorly understood. There is a widely held opinion that the central problem is in the child's inability to identify with either parent and fearing and rejecting the parent of the opposite sex and yearning for the parent of the same sex. This theory awaits confirmation.

Psychopathic behavior has been a puzzling phenomenon, and the term "psychopath" is a frequently used epithet. Though widely variant in specific type and degree, these persons are generally marked by a lack of conscience and social responsibility. The etiology is poorly understood, but a current concept attributes the central factor to childhood rationalization of love and that acceptance is of little value. This becomes a fixed defense, and he is unable to identify deeply with other people and establish a social conscience.

Juvenile delinquency is one of our greatest social concerns, and has many modes of expression. Youths of virtually every type are to be found in the delinquent population. Social immaturity, negative self-image, and low frustration-tolerance are common characteristics. Certain inherited temperamental traits may be conducive, but environmental deprivation and middle to late childhood conditioning appear to be the major determinants. Given understanding, acceptance, and help in experiencing success and forming a positive self-image, social re-education can be made highly successful.

GLOSSARY

Allergens. Substances that act as stimuli to produce allergic reactions.
Ambivalence. Contradictory and contrasting emotions or attitudes toward the same person or situation such as both love and hate.
Analgesic. A product (drug) that reduces pain, produces analgesia.
Ataractic. Drugs that lessen nervous tension, tranquilize.
Fetishism. Aberrant or deviant sexual gratification from objects associated with the opposite sex, e.g., gloves, shoes, hair, undergarments, etc.
Lesbianism. Female homosexuality, sometimes called sapphism from association with the ancient Greek poetess, Sappho.
Lesion. A rupture or break of organic tissue.
Lobotomy. A type of brain surgery to reduce neurotic guilt feelings. Certain nerves in the frontal lobe are severed.
Narcism (narcissism). Extreme self-admiration that impedes maturation. Sexual attraction toward oneself.
Oral dependence. In Psychoanalytic theory, a stage of development when pleasure and satisfaction center largely in the mouth (sucking, biting, etc.) and becomes fixed at that level, resulting in a continuing dependency on such source satisfactions; or, as in many cases regressing back to that level.
Psychogenic. Symptoms or traits that are psychological (mental) in origin, as generally contrasted with physical or physiological.
Sadomasochism. Aberrant and ambivalent sexual gratification from both inflicting and receiving punishment or pain with one or the other usually being dominant.
Somatic (-genic). Relating to the body. Organic or physical in origin.
Transvestism. The characteristic or trait of wearing garments of the opposite sex, i.e., cross-dressing; perhaps a mild or subdued form of fetishism.
Voyeurism. Pertaining to seeking sexual gratification from looking at sexual objects—the compulsive desire to see members of the opposite sex in the nude—"peeping Toms."

REFERENCES AND SUGGESTED READINGS

ARIETI, S. (ed), *American Handbook of Psychiatry,* New York: Basic Books, Inc., 1959.

BENNETT, I., *Delinquency and Neurotic Children: A Comparative Study with One Hundred Case Histories,* New York: Basic Books, Inc., 1960.

BIEBER, I. et al, *Homosexuality: A Psychoanalytic Study of Male Homosexuals,* New York: Basic Books, Inc., 1962.

CAMERON, NORMAN, *Personality Development and Psychopathology,* Boston: Houghton Mifflin Company, 1963.

CLINEBELL, HOWARD J. JR., *Understanding and Counseling the Alcoholic,* Nashville: Abingdon Press, 1956.

COLE, LUELLA (with Irma Hall), *Adolescent Psychology,* New York: Holt, Rinehart and Winston, Inc., 1964.

FRANKS, CYRIL M. (ed), *Conditioning Techniques in Clinical Practice and Research,* New York: Springer Publishing Co. Inc., 1964.

GRINKER, R. R., *Psychosomatic Research,* New York: W. W. Norton & Company, 1953.

KNAPP, P. H. and S. J. NEMETZ, "Personality variations in Bronchial Asthmatics," *Psychosom. Med.,* 19, 443–465.

KINSEY, ALFRED C., *Sexual Behavior in the Human Male,* Philadelphia, Pa.: W. B. Saunders Co., 1948.

———, *Sexual Behavior in the Human Female,* Philadelphia, Pa.: W. B. Saunders Co., 1953.

LORAND, S. and M. BALINT (eds), *Perversion: Psychodynamics and Therapy,* New York: Random House, 1956.

MENNINGER, KARL, *Man Against Himself,* New York: Harcourt, Brace & Co., 1956.

———, *The Vital Balance,* New York: The Viking Press, 1963.

MURPHY, GARDNER and ARTHUR J. BACHRACH, *An Outline of Abnormal Psychology* (rev. ed), New York: The Modern Library, Random House, 1954.

ROBERTS, GUY L., *Where Delinquency Begins,* Richmond: John Knox Press, 1958.

ROSENBERG, BERNARD, et al (eds), *Mass Society in Crisis,* New York: The Macmillan Company, 1964 (particularly the article by Louise G. Howton).

SELYE, HANS, *Stress of Life,* New York: McGraw-Hill Book Co., 1956.

STERN, PAUL J., *The Abnormal Person and His World,* Princeton, N.J.: D. Van Nostrand Co., Inc., 1964.

10

Restoring Mental Health

In the preceding chapters I have described, all too briefly in most instances, the frustrating circumstances and consequential behavior patterns by which people are designated as being mentally or socially "ill," and the behavior disorders which involve mental processes and interpersonal relations. Until some authoritative commission decides upon a more exact definition of these terms, they will continue to be used loosely and interchangeably. I prefer the term "behavior disorder," with behavior including mental and physiological processes in addition to physical action, or "psychosocial disorders." But "illness" is also commonly used.

The conditions of being either mentally or socially "ill" are widely prevalent in our society. It has been only in recent years that people have known where or to whom to go for help. Persons with religious, legal, or physical problems have had sources of professional help for many, many centuries. The twentieth century has attempted to supply professional treatment and care for the mentally ill, the sufferers of psychosocial disorders. Now, more people are no longer ashamed to seek help for a mental disorder and many know where to go for help. When the average layman hears or reads the term "mental illness," he immediately thinks of the psychiatrist, so to this discipline we will turn first.

Our concern in this chapter is with making the "sick," "not sick"; later, with making the "not sick," whole.

PSYCHIATRY

In the nineteenth century a few medical doctors began to study and "treat" the insane—those who had become alienated from the world of reality and from "respectable" society. These doctors were the alienists, the early psychiatrists. The psychiatrist is a medical doctor who may have specialized in neurology and abnormal psychology while in medical school and who did his internship in a mental hospital. Some work under the rubric of neuropsychiatrists and confine their practice largely to the diagnosis and treatment of organic psychoses and disorders which arise from malfunctioning nerves. The larger percentage, however, treat both organic and functional psychoses, the more serious neuroses, and other disorders described in the previous chapter. These psychiatrists may be divided roughly into two groups, which allow for a wide overlap. Some do little psychotherapy, and prefer to limit treatment largely to drugs, chemotherapy, and electroconvulsive therapy. They may recommend short-term follow-up psychotherapy by a clinical psychologist or psychiatric social worker. Others may use drugs and electric shock for emergency or crisis treatment, but they depend more on psychotherapy by a clinical psychologist or psychiatric social worker. Some psychiatrists may use drugs and electric shock for emergency or crisis treatment, but depend more on their own psychotherapy to effect a cure. Neo-Freudian psychoanalysis, in its several ramifications, seems to be the preferred theoretical and methodological approach of these, in the United States. Psychoanalysis has lost face in recent years in England. The psychoanalytic-psychiatric development in this country is due largely to the great influence of Dr. Adolf Meyer and the influx of many other continental European psychoanalysts to the United States immediately after World War I and during the rise of Hitler. There are indications, however, of a turning away from psychoanalysis in this country.

ENGLAND VS. AMERICA

Dr. William Sargant,[1] one of England's most prominent psychiatrists who has also taught and lectured in this country, wrote:

> The psychoanalytic dominance in the United States is a state of affairs which prevails in no other country in the world at the present time, except perhaps in Israel, where American psychiatric influences have been increasingly felt in recent years. In most other countries, a much more middle-of-the-road psychiatric viewpoint prevails, and this in turn, of course, greatly influences the treatment approaches to the mentally and neurotically ill. . . .
>
> . . . In England, for instance, we have had a very active Freudian school for more than forty years, but there are only about 250 Freudian analysts who practice this method alone, compared with 2500 other psychiatrists who are fully prepared to use and combine all methods likely to help any individual patient. It has generally been found over the years that psychoanalysis is a poor weapon to treat most forms of mental and even neurotic illness.
>
> Freud himself, when he came to England in his eighties, was still vainly insisting to his followers—some of whom had gone mad, he thought—that his methods were useful only in a limited number of cases of hysteria and obsessive neuroses. He was still insisting also that psychoanalysis was in the main a research tool, and of very limited value in treating many illnesses.

THE NEWER TREND

I have observed that recently, American psychiatrists are moving in the direction of chemotherapy. Improved methods of lobotomy and deep Insulin shock are used much more in England than in America; also electroshock and drugs, but not to such a degree. However, American psychiatrists are *now* turning more

[1] William Sargant, "Psychiatric Treatment: Here and In England," *The Atlantic Monthly*, 214:88–90 (1964). Copyright © 1964 by the Atlantic Monthly Company, Boston. Reprinted with permission.

to the tranquilizers and antidepressants in their treatment. Electroconvulsive therapy is widely used, especially in psychotic depression.

Psychoanalysts and other psychotherapists often state that drug and shock therapy are merely symptom-removers and that a cure requires insight into the dynamics and the building of ego-strength. There is some truth in their position. There are too many patients who have been treated in this manner and have had recurrences of their illness. The *self* does need to grow in strength and self-confidence in order for the frustrations and threats of real life not to appear as great and frightening. These critics tend to overlook two facts: (1) there is a set tendency in every person toward spontaneous recovery (health) and growth when the barriers are removed: (2) five or six weeks in a modern hospital with all the sympathy, understanding, and attention the patient receives gives the patient some sense of worth and "ego-strength," even though no formal psychotherapy is given. The drugs and/or "shocks" soften or break-up the old rigidly fixed mental processes, and give the opportunity for rebuilding more adequate mental structures. The attention, acceptance, etc., may provide the self with a new spark of self-confidence sufficient to carry him on to recovery, if his condition is not too serious and if external conditions are not too threatening.

> A student report and class discussion on chemotherapy, narcotherapy, and shock therapy may add interest at this point. See Appendix and Suggested Readings. Perhaps a panel discussion may be arranged.

PSYCHOANALYSIS

Both as a theoretical frame and a method of treatment, psychoanalysis was Freud's great contribution to man. Freud's was a brilliant, perceptive, and intuitive mind. His insights were profound. But most of his specific theories have been greatly modified by neo-Freudians. They have, however, clung to the framework of his more basic theories and to the main features of his analytic method. Freud was a true scientist who kept changing his theories with growing empirical evidence. His conceptual framework of psychosexual development—the oral, anal, phallic phases and his id, ego, super-ego constructs—with repression and the unconscious, are generally adhered to but with modified interpretations. In his early work with Dr. Charcot in Paris, Freud used hypnosis extensively, but later used it rarely, as he developed his free association technique, and finally the psychoanalytic method of *catharsis, free association, transference* (positive and negative), and *dream analysis.*

The full psychoanalytic treatment may require two to five sessions a week with the analyst and continue from two to eight years, and even more in some cases. For some people this becomes virtually a way of life. Rapport is established with the patient by the analyst's noncritical, fully accepting attitude and the patient's need for just such a person. The patient is seated in a relaxed position or is lying on a couch (the couch is less commonly used today) and is encouraged to talk freely. The patient pours out his (her) pentup feelings that have been suppressed or repressed. This is the *catharsis* phase, a mental purging; the patient *abreacts* (acts-off), something in the process of recall or re-experiencing. He is encouraged to give his memory and imagination free rein and relate anything that comes to his mind. In this *free association* technique, attention is paid to slips of speech, connection between words, literal and symbolic meanings, outer evidences of emotion, conscious and unconscious motives, etc. More repressed material is consciously recalled and insight attained as the weeks progress. *Dream analysis* is used in connection with free association. It is believed that the dreamer creates the dream as a manifest expression of repressed desires which are in condensed and symbolic form. Many of the symbols, allegedly, have universal meanings that are interpreted to the patient, while the latent meaning of other elements of the dream must be worked out by free association, since they are the personal and more or less unique constructions of the patient.

Resistance to the recall by some patients, of the most significant experiences and relations, is stubborn and does not yield to free association. In order to overcome this problem the analyst encourages or permits the establishment of a relationship called transference, which may be either positive or negative or may alternate between the two. The frustrated, unsatisfied and repressed love feeling of the patient, toward his (her) parent becomes transferred to the analyst. It may also be that the patient's repressed hostility toward his parent is transferred to the analyst. The analyst "works through" this transference relationship by helping his patient to see that such feelings are unwarranted from the viewpoint of the current situation, but rather reflect realistic feelings that were formerly attached to or directed against a significant person in childhood. With this insight the patient is able to recall and "abreact" the original relationship, is freed from the repression, and is able to build more adequate relationships.

LATER ANALYSTS

Most present-day psychoanalysts do follow the general Freudian procedure, with small procedural differences that are necessary to accommodate their much broader theoretical differences. One such "school" of analysts is frequently designated ego-analysts, of whom Anna Freud, Erik Erikson and David Rapaport are prominent representatives. For the antecedents of behavior disorders, they look to the broader base of the ego-functions rather than to the instinctual or id drive. Two prominent theorists and practitioners, Karen Horney and Harry Stack Sullivan, began their work as neo-Freudians but departed so far from Freud in theory that their methods also changed.

Freud himself considered psychoanalysis to be effective only with certain neurotic ailments, particularly conversion-hysteria and the obsessive-compulsive reactions. He did not think it could be used effectively with psychotics, since these patients could not invest sufficient libido in the doctor-patient relationship for transference and an effective working out of their problems. His followers have applied his system much more widely, to virtually all behavior disorders. There is much controversy over the effectiveness of psychoanalysis. At the present time many people feel that it yields too little positive change in character structure and behavior for the great cost in time and money which is involved.

Most psychoanalysts in the United States are medical doctors and thus psychiatrists. The ratio of lay analysts is higher in

Europe than in America. The lay psychoanalysts take a thorough course of training in psychoanalytic theory and are themselves psychoanalyzed. Thus, psychoanalysis stands astride the boundary between psychiatry and lay psychotherapy, with some analysts being psychiatrists and others lay psychotherapists.

CLINICAL PSYCHOLOGY

The majority of psychotherapists are clinical psychologists, but not all clinical psychologists are psychotherapists. The clinical psychologist is first of all a psychologist, who perhaps begins his work with a Master's Degree, but moves on to the PhD as soon as possible. His area of concentration is the study of personality, behavior, testing, and counseling techniques; he is usually required to serve an internship in a psychiatric clinic or hospital. He is not a medical doctor, and therefore, he is not a psychiatrist. A few have been psychoanalyzed and then practice as psychoanalysts. The clinical psychologist has a foundation in general psychology, but specializes in behavior problems, and testing and interviewing. Clinical psychology may be designated as applied abnormal psychology, yet it is broader in scope than abnormal or medical psychology. And it differs from counseling psychology since its concern is more with personality and behavior problems than with the more "normal" problems of marriage, occupation, etc.

GENERAL DUTIES

The clinical psychologist may work in a hospital, mental health or child guidance clinic, in a public school system as "school psychologist," or he may teach and practice therapy in college. Persons with neurotic or psychosomatic disturbances may seek his help, while psychotic (or suspected) and criminal cases (including juvenile) may be referred to him by the court, a physician, minister, school official, the family, or a social agency. He diagnoses psychosocial or behavior disorders and gives his psychological evaluation of the individual to the referral source. He studies a case history (medical and social) of the individual, conducts an exploratory interview (usually), and gives one or more diagnostic tests. The following is a shortened diagnostic report taken from my files.

Jimmie was referred for psychological evaluation because of generally poor and inconsistent school work, very short attention span, and "nervousness." He was 8 years old and in the second grade.

Interviews with his teacher and mother revealed the following characteristic behavior: speaks out in class, punches other children, does not seem to know how to work in peer groups, but works better alone if he accepts the task. On assigned tasks his "mind keeps wandering away"; he requires constant help, and when helped (by mother), whines and fidgets until she loses patience and "hollers" at him. Then he gets very nervous and upset, clenches his fists, grits his teeth, and pulls his hair. He is normally friendly and talkative with adults (especially when given attention). He is given to much fantasy, and is often bored at home and school.

The WISC shows high average mental ability. The Bender-Gestalt indicates perceptive distortions that could be due to brain damage or anxiety-produced selective perception.

He had a natural birth but was in a twisted position when delivered and his head was badly misshapen. At the age of two he had serious bronchial trouble and spent ten days in a hospital. Several allergies developed at about the age of four, and one foot became twisted, requiring corrective shoes. He had several head injuries but none appeared to be serious. His appetite was very poor in early childhood, and his mother had to feed him to get him to eat. . . .

Jimmie is a boy with much anxiety. Life became a great threat in early childhood. There is much mother dependency combined with the threat of its loss, which threat he has not learned to cope with. By wandering attention and fantasy flights, he ignores the reality that he fears. . . . In light of the Bender-Gestalt responses, his head injury, and the twisted foot condition, a thorough neurological examination is recommended, followed by short-term psychotherapy and professional advisement to the parents and teacher. The nature and origin of his anxiety should be more clearly determined, his self-sufficiency strengthened, and social maturation speeded up. . . . If he is given this special service, the prognosis is good.

VARIOUS SPECIALIZATIONS

Clinical psychologists specialize in certain areas of practice. Some choose marriage and family problems; some crime and delinquency; some serve chiefly as consultants to various personnel departments, schools, and social agencies; and some specialize in clinical research, perhaps combined with teaching. Some devote full time to diagnostic work, while others become full time psychotherapists. More engage in both diagnosis and therapy. Sundberg and Tyler (1962, p. 98) summarize clinical assessment as follows:

> Assessment can be seen as the way we go about understanding others; as the systematic development and communication of information about a person and his situation; as the description, prediction, and explanation of individual behavior in natural living situations, and as the process used for making decisions and for developing a working image or model. It is inevitable that there be some procedures for assessing patients in clinics and hospitals, although these may not be formal and obvious. In decision-making, both institutional and individual values enter into the evaluation of alternatives. The working image or model is a set of hypotheses about the person who is to be studied and about the situations that surround and affect him. The course of assessment can be broken down into a preparation stage, in which early information and the clinician's background of knowledge are used to make plans and decisions about how a case is to be investigated; an *input* stage, in which information is gathered by interviews, tests, and others procedures; an *information-processing* stage; and an output stage, in which decisions and conclusions are translated into reports and clinical actions. Referrals for assessment help determine its goals. . . .

The psychiatric social worker and the psychiatric nurse work with the psychiatrist and clinical psychologist as members of the diagnostic team. They also engage in limited psychotherapy, especially with children, and in group therapy.

The psychiatric social worker holds a master's degree in social work with a concentration in psychology. He (she) may interview the patient and his relatives when initially admitted to the hospital or clinic, write a "case history" of the patient, consult with the psychiatrist or therapist, and continue to work with the patient's family. He often plays a leading role in the rehabilitation of the patient when he is released from the hospital, by helping him to readjust to normal social and vocational life.

We now turn to the discipline and techniques developed almost entirely in this century for the treatment of functional disorders.

PSYCHOTHERAPY

Perhaps this topic should be introduced in its plural form, for there are many psychotherapies as practiced by psychiatrists, psychoanalysts, psychologists, social workers, and ministers. The term *psychotherapy* implies the healing or cure of psychic processes. This "cure" is attempted without recourse to drugs or any physical procedures. It is often referred to as "the talking cure." Two people are in confrontation and communication with each other, one seeking to bring about improvement in his behavior (psychic and social) by the help of the other. It involves the acquisition of self-knowledge and self-control, therefore, it is a form of education and re-education. It involves the *self*—two selves in a state of deep identity, one drawing strength from the other.

Ford and Urban[2] (pp. 3-5) emphasize the "behavioral change" function of psychotherapy and note that this has always been a concern of man in religion, education, philosophy and politics. They note that: "Brain washing, faith healing, and dianetics have all demonstrated some success in changing behavior." Then they strike the crucial note:

> Some behavior patterns, however, have consistently defied change attempted through the application of ordinary techniques. With the advent of individual verbal psychotherapy, a set of procedures for producing change in these as well as in other patterns became available, and it is now one of the most widely used approaches in attempting changes in some

[2] Donald Ford and Hugh Urban, *Systems of Psychotherapy* (New York: John Wiley & Sons, Inc., 1963). Used with permission.

kinds of behavior. The language used by various writers—psychotherapy attempts to make possible self-actualization or maturity; to reduce fears and restore higher mental processes; to bring the patient back to reality; to reduce anxiety and improve interpersonal communication—tends to obscure the fact that each is concerned with changing behavior in some fashion. Since psychotherapy's avowed purpose is to change behavior *selectively, it would seem that the development of sounder systems of psychotherapy* requires a study of the conditions under which specified behaviors will change in specified directions.

THE GOALS OF PSYCHOTHERAPY

Schneiders (1965, p. 480) lists the aims of psychotherapy as follows:

1. To relieve pent-up tensions that stem from feelings such as anxiety, guilt, hostility, or inferiority.
2. To resolve conflicts and frustrations.
3. To develop tolerance for frustration and stress.
4. To reduce (the need for) symptoms and defense mechanisms.
5. To increase self-esteem, self-acceptance, and security.
6. To increase capacity for developing interpersonal relationships.
7. Ventilation or expression of feelings (catharsis and abreaction).
8. To develop insight into personal motivations and psychological difficulties.
9. To increase personal integration, growth, and striving toward positive goals.

The psychotherapist does not consciously *aim* at accomplishing all of those o[illegible]tives in every case. With any individual case he may, with [illegible]nt, agree upon one, two, or three of these as specific ob[illegible] assuming that certain of the other goals will be a[illegible] process of therapy.

[illegible] PSY[illegible]HOT[illegible]APY

[illegible]he basic features of [illegible]alysis have been previously [illegible]nted. Broadly defined, psychoanalysis is a psychotherapy; [illegible]any analysts draw a sharp distinction between psychoanaly[illegible] psychotherapy in both their objective and method. Horney and others of neo-Freudian origin swung from a biological to a sociological frame of reference and became psychoanalytic psychotherapists in their practice. Some analysts contend that psychoanalysts and psychoanalytic psychotherapy are separable and distinct, based on distinct methods of working through resistance by means of transference and the degree of personal involvement between patient and analyst. The psychoanalyst serves much like a referee on the sideline directing the movement while the psychotherapist participates in the game interacting with the patient.

Hollender,[3] a psychoanalytic psychotherapist, discusses these arguments and discounts the differences. He recognized the differences in: (1) the psychobiological versus the psychosocial point of view; (2) the fostering of regression and transference; and (3) working through resistance. But, he said, "I am not sure if they are sufficiently distinctive or significant to justify the choice of a separate name." Concerning the interpersonal involvement of the analyst or therapist, he argues "*his conduct cannot properly be characterized as neutral.* No matter how he tries to behave, he remains to some extent a carrier of cultural values. . . . Unavoidably his outlook and values will be expressed, and they will be perceived by the patient. Since there is no way around this, I believe we should accept it as our base line and work from it. . . ." Horney[4] takes the same position on open and frank discussion of moral values.

Psychoanalytical psychotherapy, then, may be described as a system which uses the basic Freudian tools of free association and transference to deal with resistance and restore insight (self-knowledge) but in a modified form and with variable emphasis. This shift is due largely to a necessary accommodation to new findings in psychology, sociology, cultural anthropology, and education. Hollender (1965. pp. 12, 13) describes psychotherapy in terms of a hybrid discipline whose ancestors are medicine and education. He says:

> We can assume that when the mule is visited by his paternal relatives, they will be struck by his resemblance to the jackass; and his maternal relatives will comment on his resem-

---

[3] Marc H. Hollender, *The Practice of Psychoanalytic Psychotherapy* York: Grune & Stratton, Inc., 1965), p. 9. Used with permission.

[4] Karen Horney, *New Ways in Psychoanalysis* (New York: W.W. N[illegible] and Co., 1939), pp. 296–302.

> blance to the horse. They see what they are looking for; it is not a matter of inaccuracy but of incompleteness. . . . In the final analysis, it can be said that while the therapist functions like the physician and the teacher, he has developed a method that is unique, and distinctly his own.

STIMULUS-RESPONSE OR LEARNING PSYCHOTHERAPY

John Dollard and Neal Miller of Yale University are among the chief architects of this approach to psychotherapy. Wolpe has led in developing method. They are researchers and theoreticians more than practicians, and theirs is a hypothetical approach more than a method. The principal features have been utilized for years in the aversion treatment of alcoholics. A system of treatment is being developed experimentally which applies the classical and operant conditioning techniques (S-R procedures) to bring about behavior changes in certain types of psychosomatic and psychotic disorders.

Dollard and Miller[5] produced a synthesis of psychotherapy and education, interpreting psychotherapy as a learning process, looking at its "maternal ancestry." Beginning with a psychoanalytic orientation, they merged the basic principles of psychoanalysis with the Hullian learning theory.* Thus, psychotherapy became a system or procedure of motivated unlearning and relearning, with response conditioning by reinforcement and extinction. They enlarged the S-R formula to include the higher mental processes of thought and emotion, subjective responses (R) that may not be directly accessible to the observer. They are reputable scientists; they emphasize the need for extensive research to determine the extent to which these lower dimension learning principles, based largely on animal behavior, are valid when applied to behavior conditioning as in psychotherapy, and what kind of events and responses may be incorporated into the S and the R. These authors state:

---

[5] John Dollard and Neal Miller, *Personality and Psychotherapy* (New York: McGraw-Hill Book Co., 1950). Used with permission.

* Hull theorized that habit strength, degree of learning, increased only when followed by reinforcement, the reinforcer being any stimulus that reduces a drive, i.e., is experienced as pleasant or satisfying.

> If neurotic behavior is learned, it should be unlearned by some combination of the same principles by which it was taught. We believe this to be the case. Psychotherapy establishes a set of conditions by which neurotic habits may be unlearned and non-neurotic habits learned. Therefore, we view the therapist as a kind of teacher and the patient as a learner. . . .
>
> We believe that giving the solid, systematic basis of learning theory to the data of psychotherapy is a matter of importance. Application of these laws and the investigation of the new conditions of learning which psychotherapy involves should provide us with a rational foundation for practice in psychotherapy analogous to that provided by the science of bacteriology to treatment of contagious diseases. . . .
>
> If a neurosis is functional (i.e., a product of experience rather than of organic damage or instinct), it must be learned. If it is learned, it must be learned according to already known, experimentally verified laws of learning or according to new, and as yet undiscovered, laws of learning. In the former case, such laws, meticulously studied by investigators such as Pavlov, Thorndike, Hull, and their students, should make a material contribution to the understanding of the phenomenon. If new laws are involved, the attempt to study neuroses from the learning standpoint should help to reveal the gaps in our present knowledge and to suggest new principles which could be fruitfully submitted to investigation in the laboratory. . . . (pp. 7–9).

This approach holds much promise for short-term treatment and lends itself well to experimental research and thus technical improvement. It also lends itself to the same criticism made of chemotherapy in psychiatry: it removes symptoms without basic change in character structure. Its proponents would offer the same answer with respect to this criticism of chemotherapy (see p. 339), in addition to the argument that since these higher mental processes are learned in the same manner, the process of relearning need not stop until the basic attitude-value system is restructured. Its strong advocates will, of course, argue that when the symptoms are removed the neurosis is gone. Extensive research is in the process of altering maladaptive behavior by conditioned response learning. The student who is interested in more extensive study, might read Ford and Urban (1963, Chapters 7 and 8), Wolpe (1958), articles in the Appendix, or

Ullman and Krasner.[6] The latter authors write: "Behavior modification is in its early stages and is very definitely not complete. We look forward to improvement of present techniques, development of new ones, and applications to new subjects and behaviors. Behavior modification is as strong as the research and theories on which it rests. The increasing quantity and quality of both is the best insurance of the future of behavior modification." (p. 63).

CLIENT-CENTERED PSYCHOTHERAPY

Disciples turn guiding and enhancing principles into restricting and inhibiting dogmas. It has been so with disciples of the great founders of religion; it has been so in case of Freud; and it has been so with Carl Rogers and his disciples. Carl Rogers was the founder and exponent of what was first called nondirective, then later called client-centered, therapy. Rogers emphasized the method of client initiative and direction in the counseling interview; for him the technique is secondary, pliable, and must be naturalistic. His followers tended to make the method primary, rigid, and often artificial. Like Freud's, Rogers' theoretical formulations have been changing consistently with the accumulation of empirical evidence based on the extensive researching of his methods (Rogers 1942, 1951, and 1959). His orientation has followed the development of dynamic psychology and in recent years has moved toward a phenomenological and existential position, toward the still ambiguous psychology of the *self*. As a therapist he has been striving to develop a methodology consistent with his theoretical position.

It is of primary importance that the therapist see and understand stimulus situation (S) from the client's point of view, to perceive through his eyes (however subjectively colored), and to experience with the client his reactions, thoughts and feelings. In addition to this is the basic conviction that man's natural tendencies are good and self-fulfilling, and that they are directed toward self-actualization. He has the capacity and need-drive to move on toward full self-realization when an accepting, non-

[6] L. Krasner and L. P. Ullman, *Case Studies in Behavior Modification* (New York: Holt, Rinehart and Winston, Inc., 1965). Used with permission.

threatening climate is created. This simply means that the client-therapist relationship is fundamental, with warm empathy, mutual respect, trust, acceptance, and concern, i.e., love. In order to accomplish this, the therapist must reflect a natural spontaneity, wholeness, and freedom from defensive anxiety. His belief in and acceptance of the client must also be spontaneous and sincere. This is not a permissive, nor an impersonal objectivity, but a relationship of acceptance and trust. The client slowly gains self-trust, releases anxiety defenses and repression, attains insight, and can reorganize his behavior. The therapist's confidence in the client is reflected by the method of nondirected interview, by letting the client direct all conversation, perceiving that the therapist trusts him implicitly in his ability to work through his problem, thus the significance of the method. But technique is secondary to trust.

The subject seeks therapy because of strongly conscious anxiety or serious incongruity between his accepted self-concept (idealized self, perhaps) and his current self-appraisal. This incongruity tends to produce anxiety. There is little or no diagnosis or interpretation, since the client-centered therapists are not immediately concerned with etiology and causation. The client will gain the insight at the rate he is ready to accept it as anxiety and repression are released and self-trust and self-strength restored. Movement or progress is maintained by the therapist's accepting attitude and responses: "uh huh," "yes," "you were saying . . . ," or a reproduction of the client's expressed thought and feeling in paraphrase. The therapist is especially alert to the client's statements about himself (self-derogatory and self-accepting). Frequent use of the Q-sort test (Chapter 2, p. 42) is made, at the beginning, several weeks or months later, and at or near the end of the therapy period in order to measure changes in the self-concept. When the client is sufficient in his self-acceptance and positive in his self-concept, he can handle his other attitudes, emotions, etc., and is ready to face the outer world of reality. Therapy may then end.

Rogers[7] (pp. 221-223) summarizes the rationale behind client-centered therapy:

---

[7] Carl R. Rogers, *Client-Centered Therapy* (Boston: Houghton Mifflin Co., 1951). Used with permission.

> Behavior is caused, and the psychological cause of behavior is a certain perception, or a way of perceiving. The client is the only one who has the potentiality of knowing fully the dynamics of his perceptions and his knowledge. In order for behavior to change, a change in perception must be *experienced.* Intellectual knowledge cannot substitute for this. The constructive forces which bring about altered perception, reorganization of self, and relearning reside primarily in the client, and probably cannot come from outside. Therapy is basically the experiencing of the inadequacies in old ways of perceiving, the experiencing of new and more accurate and adequate perceptions, and the recognition of significant relationships between perceptions. In a very meaningful and accurate sense, therapy *is* diagnosis, and this diagnosis is a process which goes on in the experience of the client, rather than in the intellect of the clinician.
>
> In client-centered therapy we could say that the purpose of the therapist is to provide the conditions in which the client is able to make, to experience, and to accept the diagnosis of the psychogenic aspects of his maladjustment.

EXISTENTIAL ANALYSIS

Existentialism as a philosophy has been characterized as being a very ambiguous system or merely a point of view. This would apply equally to existential psychotherapy. The Swiss psychiatrist, Ludwig Binswanger, and several other Swiss, Dutch and German therapists began to apply these insights to their systems of psychotherapy and to modify them accordingly. It is not a system of psychotherapy but a number of psychotherapies related in point of view and goal and slowly drawing closer together in method. If we allow for the inadequacy of oversimplification, we may say that existential psychotherapy was born of a mixture of neo-Freudian psychoanalysis and phenomenological psychology infused with and transformed by philosophical existentialism. Rollo May, in America, is one of its exponents, and Carl Rogers stands very near in theoretical approach even though his method does not follow closely that of other existentialists, who find greater place for diagnosis and directed thinking.

No set system is laid down for therapist and client to follow. The required attitude of the therapist is similar to that as advocated by Rogers. Freedom is stressed; freedom to set one's own goals, to experience more fully, and to attain a fuller realization of selfhood. It finds room for organic, social, and spiritual dynamics, and emphasizes the human capacity to transcend one's organic nature and past conditioning and assume responsibility for more adequate behavior and enriched experience. It emphasizes values and the reorganization of behavior around a hierarchy of values which relate to the absolute. Client and therapist are in a state of mutual confrontation. Together they experience the clients perceptions and face alternate choices to be made on the basis of values. It is a relearning based on a *strengthened self* that can reappraise, re-evaluate and assume responsibility for reorganizing behavior on that basis, instead of conditioned response learning. Rollo May says[8] "it makes room for *will and decision*; it gets back of ego and super-ego structure to the *self* as the basis for and locus of autonomy; it finds a constructive function of anxiety and guilt (and neurosis); and it copes with the problem of future time."

"It" is not an appropriate term, since variation is too great, even in basic attitudes and approaches that come under the broad rubric of "existential." They are akin, but a family of individualists. It has been mentioned that some are strongly agnostic and secularistic and others are deeply religious; one group places the supreme source of value in man's being or becoming and the other group, in a supreme Being. There is widespread agreement that one of the chief causative factors in neurosis is confused values. The neurotic has no true sense of an absolute by which to order his values, thus making pseudo absolutes of less significant experiences. The other rather general agreement is that the greatest tension and anxiety springs from the experienced gap between the *is* and the *ought*, the image of oneself as he thinks he is and the experience, in those moments of special perceptivity, of the person he could and thus ought to be. This is the "great" experience of unworth with a vague dread of ultimate self-extinction. Therefore, the primary goal of existential psychotherapy is to guide the client into a true and fuller experience of his own self-hood, and the establishment of a truer and more realistic value system by which to guide his own growth *toward* the full expression of his potentiality.

---

[8] Rollo May, *Existential Psychology* (New York: Random House, Inc., 1961).

Adrian Van Kaam[9], who teaches and practices psychotherapy within the existential frame of reference, sees the core of psychotherapy in the human encounter and speaks of the client-therapist relationship as: "the fundamental attitude of authentic therapeutic care, which fosters in my client a personal looking for his own way in the world, his own destiny. The very trust which I give without limits to my client, revealed in my unconditioned therapeutic care, is in and by itself an appeal to the counselee to be concerned as I am concerned." (p. 30) To this he adds: "As we have seen, the authentic counselor wants to affirm the unique personality and the spontaneous initiative of his counselee; he wants him to grow in his own independent being. . . ." (p. 36) It is in this absolute acceptance and caring, which involves the whole of the other person regardless of his faults, that the client finds a new freedom to perceive himself and the world of others realistically and by which he may grow the self-strength to transcend former deterministic factors and become his own authentic self.

Van Kaam then adds: "If counseling, then, is a making free of the person and is an appeal to the freedom of my counselee, I could say also that counseling directs itself primarily to the will of the person." He warns that: "When I distort the authentic nature of the human will, I distort the whole of human life; for as we have seen, the will, the core of freedom, is the center of human existence." He points to certain misconceptions of "will" and says: "I do not have a will, but I *am* a will, or even better, I am a willing person. . . . Willing is thus an expression, a mode of being of myself as a whole interacting with the totality of my life situation. . . ." (pp. 70, 71).

In existential analysis we have a thorough-going existentialist therapy based on the deepest interpersonal involvement, love, commitment, freedom of choice, values, and responsibility.

LOGOTHERAPY

Logotherapy is one functional development of an existential approach. I shall present in brief form Viktor Frankl's therapeutic technique. It is not a system of psychotherapy but a supplemental

[9] Adrian Van Kaam, *The Art of Existential Counseling* (Wilkes-Barre, Pa.: Dimension Books, Inc., 1966). Used with permission.

procedure that may be used as a part of a more complete psychotherapy or the only needed therapy in certain cases.

Frankl is a neo-Freudian psychoanalytic psychiatrist, and a deeply religious man, who fused the psychoanalytic, phenomenologic, and existential into a systematic method of therapy. He found the roots of much neuroses in the conditions previously described and developed his own technique for leading his patients to a new realization of the meaning and purpose of *life* and a new purpose (value-goals) for their lives. Some portions of his point of view are expressed:

> If we present a man with a concept of man which is not true, we may well corrupt him. When we present man as an automation of reflexes, as a mind-machine, as a bundle of instincts, as a pawn of drives and reactions, as a mere product of instinct, heredity, and environment, we feed the nihilism to which modern man is, in any case, prone. . . .
>
> To our mind the situation is this: psychoanalysis to the contrary, psychic strivings can revolve about other than sexual matters; individual psychology* to the contrary, neurotic symptoms are not only a means to an end, but also are (primarily, at least) a direct expression of the most variegated psychic strivings. . . . We believe that individual psychology, finding status drives everywhere and under all conditions, has overlooked the fact that something like the striving for moral status exists; that a great many men can be activated by a more fundamental ambition than plain ordinary ambition; that there is a striving which, so to say, will not be content with earthly honors, but which longs for something far, far more, for an immortalizing of the self in some durable form.[10] (pp. XXI and 8).

REALITY THERAPY

This variant of psychotherapy has been developed chiefly during the past ten years, by Dr. William Glasser,[11] a psychiatrist. The rationale behind his method is somewhat as follows: virtually

* Theoretical Position.

[10] Viktor Frankl, *The Doctor and the Soul* (New York: Alfred A. Knopf, Inc., 1955. Used with permission.

[11] William Glasser, *Reality Therapy* (New York: Harper & Row, 1965). Used with permission.

all psychosocial problems stem from the inability to satisfy one's basic needs and the severity of the symptom reflects the degree of unfulfilled needs. All such persons, in one way or another, deny the reality of the world. Essential to the fulfillment of need is a deep involvement (identification) with one or more persons; the needs are of the nature of "the given," but we have to learn how to satisfy them; love and a sense of worth are the greatest needs. Regardless of circumstances, a satisfactory standard of behavior is essential to an adequate sense of worth; to satisfy need is a problem of the present, no matter what the past has been. The individual must assume the responsibility for his needs without depriving another. If he has not learned this in the past, he will learn this only through involvement with responsible fellow human beings.

In reality therapy there is no probing the unconscious and prolonged delving into childhood disturbances, trying to untangle dynamic factors. The therapist confronts the client with the present problem and its consequences, with only the experiences of the immediate past that are relevant. "It is your behavior." "It is your responsibility." "It is your choice." "You reap the benefit or suffer the consequences." "How realistic, how wise is this?" This blunt confrontation develops slowly, as the client-therapist relationship becomes strong enough to support it. Dr. Glasser says:

> Easy or difficult as its application may be in any particular case, the specialized learning situation which we call Reality Therapy, is made up of three separate but intimately interwoven procedures. First, there is the involvement; the therapist must become so involved with the patient that the patient can begin to face reality and see how his behavior is unrealistic. Second, the therapist must reject the behavior which is unrealistic but still accept the patient and maintain his involvement with him. Last, and necessary in varying degrees depending upon the patient, the therapist must teach the patient better ways to fulfill his needs within the confines of reality. (p. 21).

Glasser believes his method is more effective than most forms of psychotherapy in dealing with repeater delinquents, most neurotics, and many psychotics. And Dr. Mowrer[12] says, in reference to Glasser's work: "No one, at this point, is claiming that

[12] O. Hobart Mowrer, *The New Group Therapy* (Princeton, N.J.: D. Van Nostrand Co., 1964). Used with permission.

the evidence is definitive. But as a research psychologist I can attest that there is today much additional supporting data of a thoroughly empirical nature and that the premises of Reality Therapy are rapidly gaining credence in many quarters. Its promise for the future therefore seems very bright. . . ." (p. XXI).

ECLECTIC THERAPY

The adjective *eclectic* might best describe the majority of those who practice psychotherapy. Their practice consists of exactly what the term implies, techniques borrowed from a number of sources. The eclectic therapist may use one or more tests, welcome the findings of such tests, and use a full case history if available. He may be nondirective at certain stages, especially early in the procedure, and at other times he may use probing questions and explanations. He may pause at any point and give a special test, such as a word association or sentence completion projective type, to point up certain suspected problems or to stimulate interest, and he may engage in some dream interpretation. He is not all things to all men, but his system is somewhat more variable than the one-school type therapist.

BRIEF PSYCHOTHERAPY

I shall be very brief with this topic, and give the concise summary of Ford and Urban[13] and refer the reader to Suggested Readings at the end of the chapter and the report by Richard A. Levy in the Appendix, p. 614. Ford and Urban report.

> There is a growing emphasis on psychotherapy aimed at limited objectives. Sometimes the justification is economic, sometimes tactical in that longterm treatment is not feasible, and sometimes limited objectives are thought to be preferred. Whatever the reasons, there is increasing recognition that most individuals who seek psychotherapy participate for a limited number of sessions, and that there is no point in pretending that extensive psychotherapy is typical. . . . Brief

[13] Donald H. Ford and Hugh B. Urban, "Psychotherapy," *Annual Review of Psychology,* 18:333–372 (1967). Used with permission.

> psychotherapy emphasizes rapid rehabilitation of the person to acceptable levels of functioning in society. Efforts are directed toward mobilizing the patient's assets, with a focus on what's working for the patient, not just on what is wrong. The goals are circumscribed and more clearly specified. Efforts are made to restore the patient to performance of major social roles. A variety of techniques is used.
>
> These objectives reveal some common ground between "brief psychotherapists" and "behavior therapists." The latter group take a problem-oriented approach. They focus on limited portions of behavior. They try to make their analysis of the problem explicit and concrete and to choose some specific objective, some alternate behavior pattern, to be accomplished or developed. . . . (p. 342).

THE CASE FOR PSYCHOTHERAPY

In Chapters 8, 9, and 10, my hope has been to impart some significant information about the nature of man's functional disorders and their treatment and to impress the reader with the tremendous complexity of behavior disorders, their treatment, and how little we know *for sure*. The world of inner space is a greater realm for pioneer exploration than is the world of outer space. Only the border zones of the "mind" have been thoroughly surveyed; the vast hinterland still holds much mystery.

Most of us who think of ourselves as mental hygienists or psychotherapists would like to see the different psychotherapies become one psychotherapy with a sufficient variety of interrelated procedures, in order to cope with the varieties of manifested behavior disorders. The present trend is to search for commonality among them rather than to continue debating points of difference and relative merit. Let us now look at certain commonalities and kindred characteristics.

LEARNING IS INVOLVED

Behavior change is a goal and a process in all psychotherapies and this involves unlearning and new learning. By definition, the

S-R or conditioned reflex therapy is not true psychotherapy, words and person-to-person relationship being the tools of the latter, "the talking cure," while drugs and electric stimuli are used in many of the former to act as extinguishers. Since this is a method of treating psychic (behavior) disorders, it may be accepted as a psychotherapy. Many prefer the term *behavior therapy.* Regardless of definition, learning is involved in all psychotherapies, but there are different dimensions of learning. Stimulus-response or conditioned reflex learning is at the sensorimotor level where muscles and glands may be conditioned to change by repeated stimulation and accompanied by a reinforcer or extinguisher. Thus, the walls of the stomach may be "taught" to react aversively to alcohol and the walls of the bronchial tubes may "learn" not to chokingly contract in response to stimuli that formerly produced this reaction. Learning also takes place at a higher dimension, and involves the subject-self evaluating the stimulus situation. Instead of conditioning and unconditioning external stimuli, we now have two selves in empathic relation confronting problem (stimulus) situations together with one conditioned to fear, the other trusting. Repeatedly in this relationship, the fear-dominated self surrenders his fear, learns to perceive and evaluate differently both himself and the environment, and with new values learns new behavior. Normal classroom learning, and therapeutic learning both have room for varied specific techniques.

ONE-TO-ONE RELATION

All psychotherapies have a person-to-person confrontation. Many of the more orthodox psychoanalysts and behaviorism-oriented therapists, as are some clinical psychologists, hold to an impersonal, neutral client-therapist relationship; the trend is toward personal warmth, positive acceptance and concern, deep involvement and empathy, i.e., *love.* This is not only true with the Rogerian client-centered therapists and other existentialists, but also with the neo-Freudian psychoanalysts such as Karen Horney, Karl Menninger, Smiley Blanton, Izette deForest, and many others. The positive transference aspect of psychoanalytic technique can be worked through in the empathic relation. Negative transference would be unnecessary since the hostility and anxiety together are dispelled when deep empathy exists. Dr. Glasser, in his Reality Therapy, also stresses deep empathy or involvement. Acceptance, approval and love are strong reinforcers in S-R therapy.

A parallel situation prevails in the matter of values. The orthodox Freudians and behaviorists tended to ignore them or took a neutral stand. The growing trend is toward a deeper interpersonal relationship, where values confrontation becomes more prominent and more open to discussion. In empathy, two people are aware of each other's values. Open discussion clarifies them and reduces confusion. The trend is running this way, and there is room for differences in degree and detail.

DIRECTIVE-NONDIRECTIVE

There is wide variation in reference to techniques of movement, and how directive one can be. It is a directive-nondirective continuum, not a distinct dichotomy. No therapist is completely directive and none can be wholly nondirective. To be "client-centered" is basically a matter of attitude and in this the situation parallels that of the two preceding paragraphs. The various therapeutic "schools" are moving closer to each other. When empathy is established and the client fully understands the therapist's attitude toward and respect for himself, the client may be direct or indirect with his statements, may ask questions or interpret or explain; but he never imposes himself or his philosophy upon the other. They share freely. The nondirective appears to be preferable in the early stages; after which, a variety of techniques may be employed to maintain movement.

IMPORT OF CHILDHOOD

There is a wide variation in emphasis placed on the client's childhood conditioning and possible traumatic experiences, the time spent on etiology and dynamic development. The psychoanalytics give much time and significance to this, while Reality Therapy gives very little. The others range between and vary widely. That there is some value in knowledge of origin and development is recognized by all; but by utilizing certain techniques, its full conscious recovery and insight may not be necessary in most cases. This attitude seems to be growing, with the trend toward shorter periods of therapy. Recovery to memory of vast amounts of "repressed material" as emphasized in psychoanalysis was largely to make the patient aware of how irrational and inappropriate his anxiety-hostility-guilt complex and its defense mechanisms are so that he can cast them aside. In less severe cases. building self-confidence is sufficient for this; in the more severe cases with strongly fixed defenses, short-term chemo- or electroconvulsive therapy or conditioned reflex therapy may break up the defensive reactions.

A COMING TOGETHER

One might suggest a merging of therapeutic systems and procedures in this general fashion. When he is in a state of deep concern and/or desperation, the seriously malfunctioning individual seeks the psychotherapist's help. He is doubtful and defensive. The therapist responds with acceptance, understanding, trust, and concern. The first stage of empathy or identification is attained. With or without the aid of a full case history and diagnostic test report, the therapist perceives deeply established defenses and compulsive tendencies. After he has gained his client's confidence, he may recommend a short period of chemo-, electroconvulsive or conditioned-reflex therapy to break the compulsive habit or defense.

During the course of their meetings the psychotherapist continues his deeply involved (empathic) relationship with the patient, helping him develop a new self-strength, self-confidence, capacity to re-evaluate himself and outer reality, and with a renewed value system to redirect his behavior in a more realistic and creative manner. Thus, with five or six weeks of drug, electroconvulsive or conditioned-response therapy and five or six months of self-building psychotherapy, there could be accomplished what the older psychoanalysts attempted to do in five or six years, and then quite often failed. This self-growth objective, following short-term intensive treatment, may be attained in group therapy.

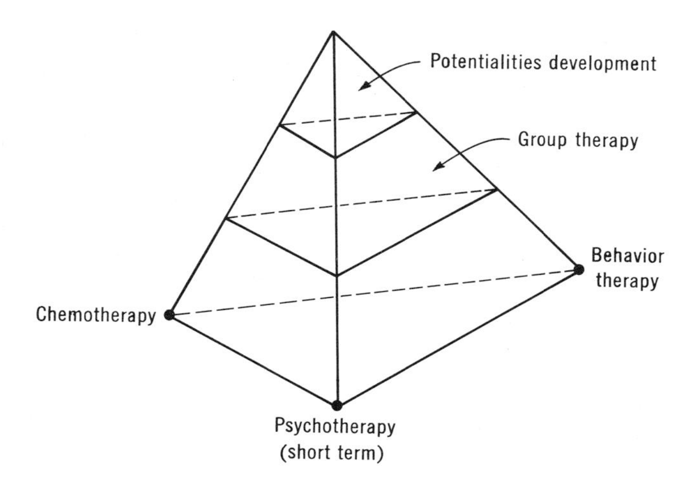

Figure 10. A schematic representation of a comprehensive treatment procedure utilizing complementary therapies. The patient may be given either one, two or three of the individual therapies conjointly. After a few weeks of these intensive therapies the more seriously disturbed would follow with an extended period of group therapy, then proceed with a potentialities development type of program. The less seriously ill may move directly from short-term individual therapy to potentialities development.

Psychotherapy can never become an exact science by the very nature of its subjective involvement. Much of the deeply shared experiences cannot be reduced to quanta and measured or definitively described. However, much profit can be derived from the scientific study of psychotherapy, formulating more specific procedural activities under more clearly defined circumstances. Experimental and clinical researchers need to work together in a greatly enlarged program, coordinating their work in researching specific aspects of enlarged behavior problems. Lack of scientific validation has been one of the legitimate criticisms of psychotherapy. Carl Rogers and his associates are among the most active psychotherapeutic researchers and are finding it very rewarding. Rogers writes[14] of research:

> Its major significance, it seems to me, is that a growing body of objectively verified knowledge of psychotherapy will bring about the gradual demise of "schools" of psychotherapy, including this one. As solid knowledge increases as to the conditions which facilitate therapeutic change, the nature of the therapeutic process, the conditions which block or inhibit therapy, the characteristic outcomes of therapy in terms of personality or behavioral change, then there will be less and less emphasis upon dogmatic and purely theoretical formulations. Differences of opinion, different procedures in therapy, different judgments as to outcome, will be put to empirical test rather than being simply a matter of debate or argument.

AN INTERDISCIPLINARY TASK

The current trend in psychotherapy, in making people whole, is not only toward integrating the different "psychotherapies" but also toward developing a new ecumenicity among the broader related disciplines. This is especially notable with psychiatry, sociology and religion whereby team effort has been found most helpful in dealing with problems rooted in external forces on the one hand and moral values on the other. We may recall or reread the Menninger quotation (p. 334): "Psychiatry is a branch of medicine, but it is also—in its basic dependency—a branch or application of psychology, of sociology, of ethnology, of philosophy." Then speaking of faith, hope, and love as the three great goods (values) given by a theologian, he added: "Today, after twenty centuries, this prescription is taken very seriously in psychiatry." Menninger has for many years advocated this interdisciplinary approach to psychosocial disorders in order to give what some have called "total push" programs.

Camilla Anderson,[15] a practicing psychiatrist for over thirty years, takes an even stronger stand on the team approach of psy-

---

[14] Carl R. Rogers, *On Becoming a Person* (Boston: Houghton Mifflin Co., 1961). Reprinted with permission.

[15] Permission to reprint granted by the Editor-in-Chief of the *Journal of the American Medical Women's Association,* excerpt from "The Pot and the Kettle," by Camilla M. Anderson, M.D., Vol. 18, pp. 293–298, April 1963.

chiatry and religion. She posits the theory that psychiatry or behavioral disorders spring from (1) structural or functional deficiences of the nervous system and (2) an unrealistic or false self-image, the nature of which can best be described as *grandiosity*. This latter, she feels, is very much a matter of religion and moral values, and that if religion will drop its empty cliches and put substance into its teachings, it has the solution to this basic problem. She thinks that psychiatry may help religion to do this and thus use its potential more effectively.

Thus, Anderson and Menninger emphasize changing professional attitudes, amalgamation of treatment procedures, and the utilization of people of various disciplines in helping the whole person to function more fully. This special concern, these "total push" activities, give the patient a new sense of self-worth and self-strength. This revitalized self, with its increased dynamics, can reorder its disorganized mental process and behavior patterns.

THE PATIENT'S REACTION

We shall close this section with a lengthy quotation from Dr. Carney Landis (1964, pp. 422, 428) who spent years collecting and studying the reports of mentally ill patients themselves, with relation to their condition and treatment. It should sharpen our impression of the need for further study and improved treatment.

> For the most part, anyone who attempts to do psychotherapy with mentally disturbed patients can only guess as to why he succeeds, and will almost never understand why he fails. From the autobiographical accounts, it does not seem that a knowledge of the source of the illness is particularly helpful to the recovery of the patient or the success of the therapist. What the patient most desires and appreciates is some evidence that the therapist has an emotional sympathy with his inner problems. The understanding of the physician need not be marked by any ready knowledge of the sources of the patient's turmoil or by any agreement with the patient's delusional convictions. It is enough for the patient to feel that the outsider appreciates the fact that he is suffering and stands by ready to render whatever assistance may be possible. One patient expressed his feeling in the following way.

"Meeting you made me feel like a traveler who's been lost in a land where no one speaks his language. Worst of all, the traveler doesn't even know where he should be going. He feels completely lost and helpless and alone. Then suddenly he meets a stranger who can speak English. Even if the stranger doesn't know the way to go, it feels so much better to be able to share the problem with someone, to have him understand how badly you feel. If you're not alone, you don't feel hopeless any more. Somehow it gives you life and a willingness to fight again."

. . . Patients obtain little direct help or self-enlightenment from any of the medical or pastoral psychotherapeutic procedures that are ordinarily followed, particularly during the acute phases of the disturbances. In fact, most patients are inclined to resent the psychotherapeutic efforts employed in most mental hospitals, saying that they are worthless and "cruel." They do appreciate "tender loving care," understanding, sympathy, and a modicum of praise. On the other hand, persons who suffer from the milder neuroses, "personality disorders," "troubled mind," or from certain obscure psychosomatic disorders, often do accept and seem to derive some benefit from a psychodynamically oriented treatment. This limited acceptance does not often characterize those who have suffered from a real psychotic disturbance. . . .

Why the simple fact of telling one's troubles to a sympathetic listener will ease the distressed mind, is a question that has been considered many times, but remains essentially unanswered. An attempt is made to clothe one's frightening, unreal, and bewildering experiences with words; that these words enable a discreet listener to understand one's suffering does, in part, make one's fears easier to bear and the turmoil easier to resist, and this remains as true today as it was in Burton's time. It is as though words can condense all the vague, chaotic feelings into a somewhat organized cognitive pattern; but, even so, the control and relief depends largely on the quality of the words employed. Words may heal, words may kill, but in either event the effect partakes of magic. The loving-listening, trusting-talking cure has much to recommend it, and much more needs to be learned about it.

Perhaps a student may want to read and report on Gertrud Schwing's little book, *A Way to the Soul of the Mentally Ill.*

SPECIAL TECHNIQUES AND APPLICATIONS OF PSYCHOTHERAPY

PSYCHODRAMA

As a therapeutic tool, psychodrama was developed largely by J. L. Moreno, who was perhaps influenced by the thinking of H. S. Sullivan whose system is sometimes referred to as relationship therapy. Sullivan chiefly emphasized restoring effective interpersonal relationships. Specific situations that are akin to certain of the patient's social problems are carefully set up by the client and therapist, the problems only, and not the manner in which they will be worked out in dramatic action. The therapist uses aides to play supporting roles while the patient is free to play his part spontaneously. Thus, it gives emotional release, brings insight similar to a projective test or play therapy with children, and provides exercises in interpersonal relations.

ROLE PLAYING

Role playing is of the same general nature as psychodrama but is less formal and usually involves only the client and therapist. The therapist plays the role of another significant person in the client's life. It may be used in working through the transference situation, or it may be a more easily managed substitute for transference. Its value is similar to that of psychodrama.

PLAY THERAPY

Play therapy is a device used by most child therapists, since play is the child's natural medium of expression and he is too young to "talk out" his problem. In a pleasant room alone with a pleasant person who seems to accept and love him, the child projects much of his anxiety and hostility into the dramatic action he devises with the toys and figures (both human and animal) that are given to him. His play is a modified psychodrama, since he gives roles to the figures. The roles he has these figures play, and the figures selected (father, mother, or child dolls), as well as his emotional response to them, tell the therapist the nature and source of the child's problem. The child obtains emotional release in the play itself, and gains some insight into his own problem as he talks with the therapist about the game, what and why these doll-figures are doing the things they are being made to do. Some therapists suggest other ways these doll-figures might act and the child learns better how to handle interpersonal relations. In an atmosphere of complete freedom and acceptance and love, the child gains in self-strength and a sense of worth.

Some child therapists are more specifically directive both in conversation and setting up the play situations, while others are more nondirective, permitting spontaneity and self-directed movement. Anna Freud, one of the developers of play therapy, used it as a substitute for much of the "free association," "dream analysis," and "interpretation," in adapting psychoanalytic therapy to children. But she used some of those techniques and was generally directive. Axline follows a more nondirective approach. In the case of a child who is more openly hostile and aggressive, directed play situation may reveal more quickly the objects and source of his hostility. But in cases where there is much more anxiety and repressed hostility, the less directed, more spontaneous play technique may be more rewarding.

Boris Levinson[17] has developed a new and promising type of play therapy which he calls "pet therapy." It has two interrelated aspects: (1) using a pet animal as a therapy instrument in the clinic and (2) the directed introduction of a pet into the child's home. He finds that the child can project into a live pet better than into an inanimate object. It is easier for the child to conceive of a pet as part of the family than it is for him to conceive a wooden doll or figure.

GROUP THERAPY

Group therapy has become popular during the past two decades. This is partly due to the increase in the scope of therapy and the fact that some problems are handled better in a group context than in a one-to-one relationship. Many institutions are

[17] Boris Levinson, "Pets: A Special Technique in Child Psychotherapy," *Mental Hygiene.* Vol. 48 (1964) 243–248. Used with permission.

now employing this procedure with nearly every type of psychotic, neurotic, psychosomatic and character disorder. Six to ten people, with somewhat similar problems, meet with a therapist once or twice a week in sessions of one to one-and-a-half hours in a pleasant, informal setting. As the meetings progress, the members not only identify with the therapist but also with each other, and each group creates its own special climate.

Free conversation and emotional expression are encouraged. Group members describe episodes, relationships with others, and their emotional reactions. Other group members reply with sympathy, support, or criticism and in turn, relate their similar experiences. The therapist's chief role is to maintain movement and be ready to deal with excess emotion when it occasionally breaks out. Sometimes he interprets, especially when asked, but usually in an indirect or suggestive manner. Sometimes role playing and/or psychodrama are employed. Thorpe[18] (p. 250) summarizes group therapy values as follows:

1. Transference of group members toward each other often is less intense and more readily understood and dealt with than when directed toward the therapist.
2. The authority figure is minimized, and there is greater "safety" for peers.
3. Basic or nuclear problems may be observed in others and desirable identifications made.
4. Familial interactions are more readily reproduced.
5. Members experience less guilt and uniqueness when a part of a group.
6. Techniques of self-examination can be established by example.
7. Reality roles may be observed and reviewed in the self and others.
8. Verbalizing or externalizing in a semiprotected or permissive group provides a bridge to greater communication and spontaneity in ordinary social relationships.

FAMILY THERAPY

The neonate of the types of therapies is family therapy, a very special type group therapy that the past decade has pro-

[18] Louis P. Thorpe, *The Pathology of Mental Health* (Second Edition). Copyright © 1960, The Ronald Press Company, N.Y.

duced. For several decades, marriage counselors have found it helpful to consult with other members of the family when working with a husband-wife problem. Therapists in child guidance clinics have long insisted on therapeutic work with the parent as well as with the child. These practices undoubtedly had some bearing on its inception, but family therapy as it is becoming known, grew out of new insights into and treatment of schizophrenia. It illustrates the principle that the whole is something other than merely the sum of its parts.

It has been known for a considerable number of years, that early childhood rejection and deprivation of love was a major factor in the etiology of mental illness. Then it was learned that most often the schizophenic's mother was both rejecting and dominatingly or indulgently overprotective while the father played a passive and inadequate role. It was learned that in therapeutic treatment of the schizophrenic, as the patient achieved progress and autonomy often other members of the family, especially a parent, began to show anxiety and subconsciously opposed the therapy.

Continued study seems to indicate that there is such strongly dependent interpersonal relationships and interlocking of pathogenic factors in the schizophrenic family, especially of the parents and the patient, that emotional balance (homeostasis) is maintained only as a group. In order for the others to maintain their defenses and precarious roles (parents chiefly and siblings to a lessed degree), one member must be the scapegoat. Researches in this special area speak of the "ego-mass" rather than individual egos in these families. The character structures of father, mother, and child are so interwoven as to be inseparable; and to effect important changes in one person requires working with all. These insights produced our present day family therapy. Zuk and Rubinstein write:[19]

> Techniques of family psychotherapy are still in a preliminary phase of development. The role of the therapist varies greatly. Midelfort, for example, advocates that the therapist behave like an auxiliary member of the family. It is important, in his opinion, that the therapist be of the same ethnic and religious origin as the family. Ackerman has suggested that the therapist assume the role of wise friend and counselor. Whitaker and

[19] In James L. Framo and Ivan Boszormenyi-Nagy (eds.), *Intensive Family Therapy* (New York: Harper & Row, 1965). Used with permission.

> other members of the Atlanta Psychiatric Clinic describe a role for the therapist in which he invites the patient into *his* fantasy life, thereby directing the flow of affect in greater degree than if the patient's fantasy life were focused on. . . . As Framo (1962) has aptly pointed out, the study of family treatment is still at the stage of hypothesis formation. Adequate methods to describe very complex processes are being sought. Adequate control of error has not yet been established. But despite these and other problems common to the early phase of development of any enterprize, family psychotherapy has rewarded its early exponents by exploring hitherto untapped levels in psychopathology. (pp. 24, 25).

COUNSELING

Psychological counseling is a professional service created to help people solve their problems of choice and behavior. How is it unlike psychotherapy? Generally the difference is in scope of training required, and in psychic depth of problems tackled. But the line of demarcation is hazy and the overlap is wide. Both the counselor and the therapist use diagnostic tests, both conduct interviews, both depend on rapport, and both deal with problems of choice and behavior change. Normal counseling, however, generally is limited to aptitudes, interests, motives, etc., which are readily accessible to consciousness and to academic, vocational, marital, and value choices which can be dealt with rationally. Counseling is usually of short-term duration and does not involve the deeper dynamics of behavior and more complex personality problems. *Generally* is the term of emphasis. One phases into the other and overlaps; psychotherapy is frequently called "depth counseling."

VOCATIONAL COUNSELING

This educational function is a post World War I development which received its big impetus during the industrial expansion of the 1920's and the popularization of psychology in industry and education. Vocational Guidance and the training of guidance counselors for secondary schools became a major educational movement. The public school counselor is usually a teacher with a Master's Degree which represents a concentration of courses in psychology, psychological testing, and occupational information. His major function is to help students with their academic and career problems. But since human problems do not confine themselves to neat little categories, he is also confronted with a variety of personality and social problems, which may involve emotional problems of considerable depth. The more serious of these he refers to a more specialized source. Some of the problems he works with directly.

The vocational counselor gives general aptitude (intelligence) tests, special aptitude tests, interest tests, and personality inventories to help the student form a realistic picture of himself. Then, if he is consulted, he helps the student apply that knowledge in working out a realistic pattern of life. Other counselors perform similar services in state rehabilitation services and federal-state employment offices.

MARRIAGE COUNSELING

In every metropolitan area the Yellow Pages of the telephone directory lists Family Service Agencies and Marriage Counseling Services. Some are publicly supported agencies; some are private agencies. Social case workers, clinical psychologists, and psychiatrists specialize in and practice marriage counseling, which includes premarital problems. Some states have Family Courts to handle divorce and child custody cases; some of these require attempted mediation before granting a divorce. These courts often employ marriage counselors as members of the court staff.

Husband-wife difficulties are many and varied; they usually center around one or another of some half dozen areas: finance or budget, in-law, child training, sex, religion, friends and social interests. Immaturity is the greatest single cause of marital malfunction, if it can be called single. Many marital problems can be solved by changes in a few attitudes and habits, which can be dealt with rationally in a few sessions; many others involve more rigidly fixed defense mechanisms and neurotic syndromes that require prolonged "depth counseling" or psychotherapy.

PASTORAL COUNSELING

From the dawn of civilization religious mediators have been chief counselors. In ancient times, from king to commoner, the priest or prophet was consulted on all matters of great concern, and often of minor concern. At the present time, more persons turn to the clergy with their problems than to any other one professional source. But the trend is downward, and there is greater selectivity of problem type. More people are turning to the specialist with their special problems. With the modern development in mental health and clinical psychology, the modern pastor (minister, priest, and rabbi) has added to his professional training a number of courses in these disciplines. Some religious leaders add to a thorough foundation in psychology a year of internship in a mental hospital or on the staff of a psychiatric clinic and specialize in pastoral counseling. The latter are psychotherapists working in a church context.

The pastor in nearly every parish, sooner or later, is confronted with nearly every type of human behavior problem. There are problems of grief and guilt, some normal and some neurotic; problems of moral turpitude, sincere ideals in losing conflicts with compulsive habits and unconscious needs; the alcoholic parent and delinquent child; the family torn with conflict but pridefully struggling to prevent divorce; all these and many more may be found among church-going families. Developing delinquencies, neuroses, and psychoses often confront the active pastor before they reach the psychotherapist. Some of these, the pastor himself, as counselor, must treat; others, he refers to the best source of professional treatment.

The busy pastor of a one-minister church usually allots several hours per week for these special problem cases. Some who specialize more fully in pastoral counseling may prefer the role of Associate Pastor in a larger church, where they can devote more time to marriage counseling and therapeutic work with their parish delinquents and neurotics. Others become staff members of special church agencies, mental hospitals, clinics, or prisons, and work as members of the therapeutic team. A few large churches have their own clinics with usually a part-time staff psychiatrist, a full-time social worker and a full-time pastor-counselor serving as a psychotherapist.

Most pastor counselors adhere to the existentialist point of view and lean toward a modified Rogerian client-centered and Viktor Frankl's logotherapy techniques. Most pastors are more goal conscious and less technique conscious. They identify deeply with their clients, share problems and experiences as fully as possible, discuss values and goals of life, relate relative values that operate in life's experiences with the great moral imperatives, and help establish a pattern of life that is fulfilling and transcending.

RECOVERY FROM MENTAL ILLNESS

We have been studying treatment in its many modes and varieties. Now what of the cure? Prognosis follows diagnosis, and methods are maintained or changed on the basis of probable cures. There is so much public interest focused on the psychosocial disorders, we want to know what the recovery chances are.

Harry Milt[20] of NAMH has summarized this topic so well I shall rest my case upon his evidence and prognosis which are being verified.

> *From the Neuroses*
> The chances of recovery from the neuroses are very good. Private psychiatrists and psychiatric clinics report that most of their neurotic patients show great improvement after treatment and that most of them are relieved of their most difficult symptoms and are able to lead much happier lives.
> *From the Psychoses*
> *Schizophrenia:* Not too many years ago, schizophrenia was considered all but hopeless. Today, hospitals which are able to give their patients adequate treatment, discharge two out of every three schizophrenic patients as improved or recovered within a year after their admission for treatment. Most patients who recover partially or totally from schizophrenia do so after only a few months of treatment.
> *Involutional psychosis:* This disease yields to treatment quite readily and about 7 out of every 10 patients treated improve considerably or recover entirely. In most cases, this change occurs after only a few weeks or months of treatment.

[20] Harry Milt, *Basic Facts About Mental Illness* (Fair Haven, N.J.: Scientific Aids Publication, 1959). Used with permission.

> *Manic-Depressive psychosis:* Hospital treatment has been very successful with this psychosis. In cases where it is effective, it serves to keep attacks farther apart, and in some cases eliminates them altogether. In many cases, where treatment has relieved this condition, the patient will need to continue under the watchful eye of his doctor, who will be on the lookout for the return of the symptoms and start treatment again if necessary.
>
> *The psychoses of Old Age:* Until recently, it has been felt that very little could be done for patients with old age psychoses—particularly those suffering from cerebral arteriosclerosis—because of the assumption that the brain has deteriorated. This point of view has changed considerably with the recent discovery that many of the patients suffering from old age psychosis do respond to treatment, some sufficiently to permit their return to home and community and even to holding a job.
>
> It should be remembered that these comments with regard to the chances and speed of improvement and recovery for the psychoses are in terms of the treatment methods which are available to science today. As these methods are improved, we may expect even better results.
>
> Under any circumstances, it has been definitely proven that the chances for improvement and recovery depend upon proper and early treatment. (pp. 29–30).

SUMMARY

The term, mental illness is still used to designate a wide range of behavior disorders. My preference is to think of these as *psychosocial disorders.* Their treatment requires a wide variety of procedures and disciplines. American psychiatry is roughly divided into two classes: those who limit themselves chiefly to chemo- and electroconvulsive therapy and those who prefer to practice psychoanalysis or psychotherapy. The trend is toward a greater dependence on drugs, with a renewed interest in improved methods of electroshock and lobotomy.

Modern psychoanalysis still employs basic Freudian theories and techniques, particularly free association, dream analysis, and transference, but with considerable variations and greater emphasis on social etiological factors. Psychoanalysis appears to be declining in popularity. The clinical psychologist is a specialist in behavior problems and is employed in mental hospitals and clinics, public school systems as school psychologist, and in colleges as teacher and researcher. Or he may engage in private practice. He may specialize in diagnostic testing or psychotherapy, or he may engage in both. The psychiatric social worker stands next in line with the psychiatrist and clinical psychologist, working with patients and their families and helping especially in social and occupational rehabilitation.

The general nature of psychotherapy is described as the "talking cure," two persons in a one-to-one confrontation. Among the commonly described psychotherapies are: psychoanalytic, stimulus-response (sometimes called conditioned reflex therapy or learning therapy), client-centered, existential, reality, eclectic, and short-term. Evidence points toward a coming together in theory and practice with greater emphasis on the client-therapist relationship, utilization of a variety of "methods," and more cooperation among professional workers of various disciplines. Special therapeutic techniques as psychodrama, role playing, play therapy, group therapy, and family therapy were described. Working with the whole family, or key members, as a dynamic unit is a new and promising procedure.

There is no sharp distinction between the psychotherapist and counselor. The latter usually has not had as much professional training in behavior dynamics and thus does not engage in long-term work with deeply disturbed persons, where there is much "repressed material."

Greater percentages of neurotics and psychotics are making relatively rapid recovery due mostly to early detection of symptoms and the newer methods of treatment.

GLOSSARY

Abreaction. Re-evaluating and expressing former emotion-laden experiences in free, uninhibited conversation—sometimes dramatic action—with one's therapist.

Catharsis. The unburdening of oneself, as above, from pent-up excess emotion, conflict, or mental stress—an expulsion.

Disulfiram. A light-grayish, almost tasteless drug used in the aversive treatment of alcoholism.

Rubric. Pertaining to being classified or categorized.

Transference. The passage or conveyance of an emotional attitude from a former significant person to the therapist.

REFERENCES AND SUGGESTED READINGS

BOSZORMENYI-NAGY, IVAN and JAMES L. FRAMO, (eds), *Intensive Family Therapy,* New York: Harper & Row, 1965.

CARUSO, IGOR A., *Existential Psychology,* New York: Herder and Herder, Inc., 1964.

DOLLARD, JOHN and NEAL MILLER, *Personality and Psychotherapy,* New York: McGraw-Hill, 1950.

FORD, DONALD and HUGH URBAN, *Systems of Psychotherapy,* New York: John Wiley & Sons, Inc., 1963.

———, "Psychotherapy," *Annual Review of Psychology.* Vol. 18 (1967), 333–372.

FRANKL, VIKTOR, *The Doctor and the Soul,* New York: Alfred A. Knopf, Inc., 1955.

FRANKS, CYRIL M. (ed), *Conditioning Techniques in Clinical Practice and Research,* New York: Springer Publishing Co., Inc., 1964.

FREUD, SIGMUND, *A General Introduction to Psychoanalysis,* Garden City, N.Y.: Garden City Pub. Co., Inc., 1943.

GLASSER, WILLIAM, *Reality Therapy,* New York: Harper & Row, 1965.

HOLLENDER, MARC H., *The Practice of Psychoanalytic Psychotherapy,* New York: Grune & Stratton, Inc., 1965.

HORNEY, KAREN, *New Ways in Psychoanalysis,* New York: W. W. Norton and Company, 1939.

KRASNER, L. and L. P. ULLMAN, *Case Studies in Behavior Modification,* New York: Holt, Rinehart and Winston, Inc., 1965.

LANDIS, CARNEY (Fred A. Mettler, ed), *Varieties of Psychopathological Experience,* New York: Holt, Rinehart and Winston, Inc., 1964.

MAY, ROLLO, *Existential Psychology,* New York: Random House, Inc., 1961.

MILT, HARRY, *Basic Facts about Mental Illness,* Fair Haven, N.J.: Science Aids Publication, 1959.

MOWER, O. HOBART, *The New Group Therapy,* Princeton, N.J.: D. Van Nostrand Co., Inc., 1964.

ROGERS, CARL R., *Client-Centered Therapy,* Boston: Houghton Mifflin Company, 1951.

———, *On Becoming a Person,* Boston: Houghton Mifflin Company, 1961.

SALTER, ANDREW, *Conditioned Reflex Therapy,* New York: Capricorn Books, 1949 and 1961.

SCHNEIDERS, A. A., *Personality Dynamics and Mental Health,* New York: Holt, Rinehart and Winston, Inc., 1965.

SCHWING, GERTRUD, *A Way to the Soul of the Mentally Ill,* New York: International Universities Press, Inc., 1954.
SUNDBERG, NORMAN D. and LEONA E. TYLER, *Clinical Psychology,* New York: Appleton-Century-Crofts, 1962.
THORPE, LOUIS P., *The Psychology of Mental Health,* New York: The Ronald Press, 1960.
VAN KAAM, ADRIAN, *The Art of Existential Counseling,* Wilkes-Barre, Pa.: Dimension Books, Inc., 1966.
WOLPE, J., *Psychotherapy by Reciprocal Inhibition,* Stanford, Calif.: Stanford Univ. Press, 1958.

11 The Community in Action: Through the School and Church

"Mother Society" is a phrase that well may attain a status of great significance next to that of "Father God." In a literal sense, society is the mother of its individual members. The biological mother creates the body of the baby; society creates the character structure of the man. There is, of course, a father whose genes contribute to the infant's physical structure, and there is the self that has something to do with character structure. Although they are not alone responsible, these two mothers play leading roles in the character and behavior development of their child: mother of the infant and mother of the adult.

MENTAL HEALTH IN THE SCHOOL

The home is the first and the greatest social force in the life of the individual. This influence has been discussed in earlier chapters. The school stands in second place, with the primary function of mental and social growth. Mental-social health is implicit, for growth does not take place without health. Functional disorder in the psychic and social life of the child is a functional failure of the school. In many cases these disorders have begun before the school is given custody of the child; but having adopted the youngster with the purpose of making him a capable and responsible member of society, the school has a greater responsibility than past performance has indicated. Our concern is with the school as an agency for the prevention and amelioration of mental and social disorders, and for growth in mental health.

THE PROBLEM

The mental problems of children were discussed briefly in Chapter 1. Hardly a day passes but that somewhere across the country a child, not yet or barely in his teens, murders a parent, a sibling, a playmate, or himself. There are many others involved in less violent but socially destructive behavior—child burglary, theft, prostitution, sex clubs, and narcotic users. Still worse are the withdrawn, anxiety ridden children who are month by month, year by year slipping into "mental illness," slipping away from a miserable world of reality. A dozen studies could be cited, covering several hundred schools and tens of thousands of pupils, which show between 10 and 20 percent of the elementary school children seriously maladjusted and another 20 to 40 percent poorly adjusted. Lack of adequate criteria for "adjustment" accounts for most of the wide range in findings.

Kaplan (1959, p. 58), after a review of several studies, says: "It appears safe to assume, then, that 25 percent of the children and youth in American schools and colleges are sufficiently maladjusted to require professional care or therapy." This would mean that there are now more than 12 million seriously disturbed children and youth in our schools. From this group will come most of our psychotics, neurotics, and delinquents, which are a minority of the total. The others will outgrow much of their trouble but continue to function at a lower performance and happiness level than they ought. The school can do much to prevent this.

Why hasn't it? Money! Yes, in part. The need has not been dramatized or the money would be forthcoming. *Tradition!* Predominant concern of the school has been with the academic and the intellectual. Broader objectives were formulated and discussed extensively in administrative circles, but implementation has been slow. It has been easy to rationalize the *lack of understanding* of the problem and what could be done in the schools. It sounds better to blame it on lack of money than on lack of the most judicious use of the money that is available.

But money has not been adequate. Teachers' salaries have been small and their classes large. Progress has been steady but very slow in adding specialists to the staff, e.g., counselors, social workers (visiting teachers), and school psychologists. Many schools have none of these and few, if any, are adequately staffed. Of greater importance, however, is the teachers' lack of basic training in child behavior and mental hygiene and their own lack of sound mental health. While the mental health of teachers is probably a little higher—the ratio admitted to mental hospitals slightly lower than that of the general population—it is not adequate in many cases considering their position of responsibility. On the basis of 11 major studies of teachers' emotional problems, Kaplan (1959, p. 66) concludes:

1. From 27–43 percent are unhappy, nervous, dissatisfied, and working under considerable strain.
2. From 17–49 percent may be classified as maladjusted, although not seriously disordered.
3. From 9–35 percent are probably in need of psychiatric care.

Then in summary, he adds: "While no exact data on maladjustment among teachers are available, research indicates that in 1957 there were at least 120,000 seriously maladjusted teachers in the nation's classrooms. A group almost twice this size could be described as being unduly nervous. Almost one-fourth of the teachers now employed are so unhappy that they would not again become teachers if they had a chance to start over." (p. 68).

These statistics are meant merely to be suggestive. They are out of date today and will be more so in another decade. Improvement has been made in salaries, working facilities, and insight into behavior problems. Our concern in the remainder of this section will be with what the school can and will be doing to promote mental-social health, high level psycho-social development.

THE TEACHER AND CLASSROOM

For many five-and-six-year-old children, entering school is like moving into a big and strange new world or like being adopted on a half-time basis by a big and frightening family. The school has adopted them, and the teacher becomes a parent surrogate, *in loco parentis*. For the well-adjusted child from the well-adjusted home, this change is not much of a threat, in fact, it is rather exciting and challenging. But for the emotionally disturbed child who has not been able to make a satisfactory adjustment at home, where the child-parent and sibling relationships are unsatisfying, the change is doubly difficult. He has a greater need and desire (conscious or subconscious) to identify and build satisfying relations than does the more adjusted child, but he has less ability to do this. There are many such children, as studies have indicated. These children try; they fail; they feel the more inferior; they become more hostile and aggressive or anxious and withdrawn. Their problems may be aggravated or helped, depending on the teacher.

Wholeness. The primary function of teaching has been, and may continue to be, to guide children in growth of knowledge and skills. But more recently, the function is seen as that of guiding the growth of the whole child toward wholeness of living, by helping him to actualize his potentials. The two functions, or points of view, are seen as being inseparable, since emotional balance and social adjustment are deeply interrelated with academic learning and that the skillfully performing "mind" must be a healthy "mind." The teachers of today and tomorrow—when better paid, better trained in child behavior, better screened with regard to their personalities—will do a better job in their parent surrogate role.

The child will find in this teacher a "parent" who understands him and his problems; who trusts him by giving him assignments and expecting satisfactory performance; who is firm but fair and always friendly and consistent; who helps him when he fails and encourages him to try again; who consistently wills his good (loves him). It may take considerable time for the hurt, suspicious child to become convinced of this, but it will come and he will be able to accept himself and his own worth. The understanding teacher will realize this and, in faith and good humor, she will withstand the testing period. She has the school counselor and/or school psychologist to confer with, for those few with whom she cannot cope.

Acceptance. By being warm and accepting and both directive and permissive in accord with occasion and individual need, the teacher sets a classroom climate that is nonthreatening. The child learns to feel secure, accepted, "at home." The teacher has at her disposal the facilities and resources to set up a large variety of learning activities. These can be so arranged and manipulated that every child can experience some success and the sense of worth from achievement. The child learns that he can find help when he fails and that he is accepted and trusted even when he fails, if he keeps trying. Before the child becomes of school age, his self-image is based largely on his parent's attitudes. Once he enters school he must re-evaluate himself on the basis of his own performance. The self-image or self-attitude is fluid at this period and the teacher can play a very significant role in helping the child remold it—a very important mental health function. The teacher can hug her pupils. They do not want an overly sentimental "sob sister" as a teacher. But they do like to swarm around her, at her desk. Others will sit over by the side of the room, withdrawn but longing to be up there with the group. For a child to identify emotionally with an adult and feel accepted and loved, there must be some hugs, some physical expression of love. We do not entirely outgrow it. Occasionally the teacher fills her arms with those about her and unobtrusively walks over to the little "wall flower" and gives her (or him) a special hug.

THE TEACHER AND PEER ACCEPTANCE

The peer group is the vital link between the family and society. The child who fails to identify with his peers and attain a sense of oneness with them will seldom adjust well in adult society. During the elementary and intermediate school years, the "we experience" should attain high development. These are the years in which deep and often permanent friendships are formed. "But he's my friend!" protested an eight-year-old boy to his mother who was severely criticizing a neighbor's child. The 20 to 30 percent, the disturbed children, find great difficulty in establishing satisfactory peer relationships. Their condition will not improve unless the teacher helps.

Children can be very inconsiderate and sometimes cruel, even the "nice" children. They have a limited value system and only a few criteria for accepting others into their groups: social class, friendly disposition, physical prowess and skill, social graces, and to a lesser extent academic ability. Many lack these qualifications and are the peer rejects; and most of these come from that big one-third who were already "disturbed," maladjusted children. They have not learned the social skills. They are not physically or intellectually capable of leadership; or if physically capable, because of previously formed hostilities they are bullies to be hated rather than stars to be admired. Many of them come from socially rejected homes. The elementary and intermediate school grades, when the child is from six to twelve, are the years in which most neuroses, psychosomatic illnesses, delinquencies, and other psychosocial disorder trends become fixed or may be changed.

Unique opportunity. The teacher's primary function is to teach, to direct learning, not to diagnose and treat emotionally disturbed, socially maladjusted children. But unobtrusively and with little extra time, she can do the latter. She does not have to be hasty. She has her 30 pupils, six or seven hours daily, 180 to 200 days for approximately 1200 hours. She observes them in free conversation and spontaneous play, in choosing associates for a project or team mates for a game. She observes the sad, anxious, withdrawn child, and the solicitous but rejected or half tolerated, and the aggressive and compulsively active. She records a dozen or more specific stimulus-response situations of each before making her appraisal.

Or, as a learning exercise, the teacher may assign short creative writing projects, e.g., anecdotes about certain suggested activities and relationships. Some of the topics may be quite specific: "What I fear most," "The experience that upset me most," "What I would do if. . . ." She may assign sentence completion exercises, both to grade the children in sentence construction and grammar and to use as a simple projective test. By these and other similar assignments, the teacher can learn much about each child's feelings of acceptance or rejection, anxiety and hostility. Some teachers have used "Question Box" or "Personal Problems Box" to obtain problems for open discussion. When the climate is right, the children are quite frank in revealing and discussing their problems.

Sociometry. Since peer acceptance is now recognized as being of great importance to the mental health and personal growth of a child, many teachers are using the more formal method of measuring the degree of acceptance-rejection or popularity termed sociometry. A normal size class is divided into two or three groups. Each group is given a list of questions which each member answers relative to the other members. Questions are framed in the form, "If you were to . . . whom would you choose?" The choice may be 1st, 2nd, and 3rd. Or the question may be in the negative form, "If . . . whom would you least want. . . . ?" With 10 or 15 such selections from each member of the group, the teacher can score the relative popularity of each child, the extent of his acceptance and rejection by his peers.

The teacher may then want to find out why certain ones are rejected. She gives a "Guess Who" test or game. Selecting several personality traits, both positive and negative, she frames each of them in a question: "Who is the neatest. . . ?" "Who is the quietest. . . ?" "Who is most like. . . ?" "Who does. . . ?" etc. A summary of the results of this test-game portrays peer group opinions, and shows why some are popular and others rejected.

The teacher can learn much about the emotional problems of her pupils during the school year. Since these procedures are repeated each year, progress or deterioration can be measured. Her work does not end with diagnosis but treatment. She has the confidence of the anxious and hostile, the rejected, and she can coach them in their adjustment efforts. Also, diplomatically and unobtrusively, she can single out a few of the more popular children and solicit their cooperation, helping them to be more accepting.

Children are really more tender than cruel and can be very considerate when they understand. The teacher can set up group activities and open doors to the formerly rejected. This has been done very effectively by some teachers in the form of short one-act skits prepared by the teacher and pupils. The value of acceptance and the hurt of rejection can be dramatized and experienced vicariously by all participants. After this, the popular and unpopular children have less difficulty identifying with each other.

THE TEACHER'S PERSONALITY

Professional training, general education and teaching technique is very important in the school room. But from the viewpoint of mental hygiene, the personality of the teacher is even more important. A PhD or M.D. or D.D. may be a person of eminence in his profession but a complete failure as a parent. The same may be true of the teacher in his (her) role as parent surrogate. School administrators have known this for years but have not been able to do much about it, because of the perennial teacher shortage and a general reluctance of teachers to submit to personality studies during their training period. This failure is being rapidly corrected, however, and the schools can soon expect a better screening of teachers on the basis of personality traits.

Many studies have been made of teachers in service relative to the effect of their personalities on pupil behavior. We have emphasized the *in loco parentis* role of the teacher, which is highly significant, but it is never quite the same as that of the "true" parent. Pupil-teacher rapport and identity should be strong and wholesome but not as complete as with the adequate parent. Affection may be expressed by the teacher, warmly and richly, but there remains a certain element of objectivity and reserve beyond that of the home. Nevertheless, from elementary school to high school, pupils rate their teacher's effectiveness largely on the basis of his understanding, sympathy, friendliness, good humor, etc., the teacher who cares, who is responsive to their interests and needs, with whom they can identify, admire, and love. The large majority of anxious-hostile, emotionally disturbed children who have teachers like this during their elementary and intermediate years will develop a stronger and healthier *self* which can order and direct more adequate academic and social behavior. Such teachers are not only contributing to the "mental" health of their pupils but to their intellectual and, later, vocational performances.

Laycock[1] studied teacher behavior and pupil response by actual classroom observation and described the results in case study form. A teacher who appeared to be poorly motivated, unimaginative, and repressed produced a classroom atmosphere he called "dead" in which the pupils worked quietly but listlessly and without enthusiasm. In another classroom where the teacher

[1] S.R. Laycock, "Effect of Teacher's Personality on the Behavior of Children," *Understanding the Child*, 19:50–55 (April 1950).

was an elderly man who was untidy, nervous, jittery, and highly critical and whose teaching was didactic and authoritarian, there was no class cooperation and the pupils appeared fearful, timid, insecure, and repressed. In a room where the teacher was young, pleasant, poised, and apparently well-adjusted but not "of the warm, out-going type," the atmosphere was calm but the pupils were listless and routine in manner of work. In still another case where the teacher was young and attractive and seemed to be "aware of the pupil's emotional, social, physical, and intellectual development," and where there was much pupil participation in cooperative activity, the climate was that of a busy, happy workshop with a strong "we" feeling.

In a study by Witty,[2] 33,000 pupils wrote letters describing "The Teacher Who Helped Me Most." The twelve most frequently described qualities were: (1) cooperative, democratic attitude; (2) kindliness and consideration for the individual; (3) patience; (4) wide interest; (5) good personal appearance and pleasing manner; (6) fairness and impartiality; (7) sense of humor; (8) good disposition and consistent behavior; (9) interest in pupils' problems; (10) flexibility; (11) use of recognition and praise; (12) unusual proficiency in teaching.

At the present, administrators can not fill all of their classrooms with teachers who possess all of these traits. But with advancing salaries and greatly increased numbers of young college people pursuing teaching careers, greater selectivity will be possible; and the school will play an increasing role in mental hygiene. Some pupils will always require special help even with the best of teaching. The schools are making steady progress in supplying these special services.

THE BEHAVIOR SPECIALISTS

Principal among the staff personnel with specialized training in behavior problems are the guidance-counselor, who works most frequently at the secondary level; the social worker (visiting

[2] P.A. Witty, "Evaluation of Studies of the Characteristics of the Effective Teacher," *Improving Educational Research*, American Educational Research Association, 1948, pp. 198–204.

teacher), who more often works at the elementary and intermediate levels; the speech therapist and school psychologist, who work throughout the school system. These specialists are available as consultants to help the classroom teacher understand and cope with the more seriously disturbed pupils. They also may conduct individual and/or group therapy with certain pupils. They have more direct access to the pupils' homes and may, in numerous cases, effect more satisfactory child-parent relations. The most seriously disturbed children may be beyond the reach of these school specialists but will be referred by them to a child guidance or psychiatric clinic for needed help.

SPECIAL SCHOOL PROJECTS IN MENTAL HYGIENE

Particularly during the past two decades many school systems have instituted a variety of forms of in-service training to help teachers and administrators make the school a more effective mental hygiene agency. Typical features of these are a one-semester, once-a-week course of training in child behavior and mental hygiene principles. These may be conducted by a visiting psychiatrist, clinical psychologist, or university professor. The program frequently includes illustrative films and follow-up discussions. Some school districts have visiting teams of specialists who conduct a concentrated one-week (evenings) seminar or an all-day workshop on Mental Hygiene in the school. Helpful literature is left with the teachers and, usually, some type of follow-up consultation service is made available. Kaplan (1959, pp. 89–99) describes several of these projects.

THE RYE PROJECT

The public schools of Rye, New York, have initiated a mental health program to introduce from kindergarten through the twelfth grade a series of experiences designed to increase understanding of self and others. This program involved (1) bimonthly seminars held with teachers and administrators of the high school and the two elementary schools; (2) weekly conferences with the guidance staff of the high school; (3) an experimental series of human relations classes in the schools; (4) a parent education program; and (5) a consultation service for parents and teachers who wished to discuss problems of individual children.

The bimonthly seminars were held after school on a voluntary basis. They consisted of lectures, films, and discussions related to child-behavior problems.

The high school guidance staff gave consultations and sought to formulate school policies on important issues in terms of good mental hygiene practices. Human relations classes were conducted in the fifth, eighth, and twelfth grades. In the fifth and eighth grades, instruction consisted of reading and discussing stories concerning good human relations, dramatization and discussion of prevailing problems, and the use of films and filmstrips. In the twelfth grade, human relations lessons were integrated in the social science course where emphasis was placed on student discussion of mental hygiene problems.

Parent education was conducted by a consultant who ran weekly classes entitled "Psychology of Family Relations." These classes were limited in size to 10 or 15 persons and met once a month in the homes of members of the group. Consultation service was also made available to parents and teachers wherever the problems of children could be solved without the use of psychotherapy. In the case of severe problems, children were referred to a child guidance clinic or to a private psychiatrist.

THE BULLIS PROJECT

This project originated in the schools of Delaware and New York, and has been used with over 200,000 children annually in about 21 states. The text for the course consists of three volumes entitled *Human Relations in the Classroom*, written by H. E. Bullis and E. E. O'Malley, and issued by the Delaware State Society for Mental Hygiene. These books provide the teacher with a discussion of basic mental hygiene principles, lesson outlines, and stimulus stories.

The procedure recommended to teachers is that the stimulus story be read to the children, and followed by a class discussion, and a conclusion. The stimulus story features the emotional problem scheduled for a particular lesson. Its purpose is to stimulate children to discuss the problems presented in the story, and to relate their personal experiences which parallel this problem. . . . Teachers require no special training to conduct human relations classes according to this plan. Consequently, the Bullis Project has gained widespread acceptance. However, some mental hygienists and educators criticize this approach as being too didactic and overly moralistic.

THE OJEMANN PROJECT

The University of Iowa is making an effort to integrate human relations education into the regular public school curriculum. This is a long-range human relations project which involves revising basic text materials and adding special units to existing courses, so that in grades one through twelve, children have before them recurring examples of typical behavior problems. Teachers are trained to encourage discussion of these problems whenever they arise in the normal course of class activity. . . .

The technique used in the primary grades is for the teacher to read descriptive narratives, or work out with the children skits or plays which deal with human relations problems. These narratives or skits portray a situation which involves some form of human interaction which the child can understand is developed. . . .

The intermediate and upper grades have special units which are developed to supplement the basic text material and adapt them to human relations instruction. At the seventh grade level, children have a series of units on "Guiding Our Own Development." In the community civics course, there is a unit called "Where Do People Get Their Different Ways of Behaving. . . ."

These projects illustrate a variety of experimental approaches to the problem of mental hygiene in the schools. They are constantly being revised and show much promise. My preference would be a program built along the lines of the Ojemann Project for the primary and intermediate grades. At the secondary level, however, I would prefer a program in which psychosocial health education is integrated with the physical education program in the school. This would entail a daily period of training in physical-social education (PSE). The social or psychosocial units would be taught by the school counselor or a teacher with special training in mental health. Various school clubs and extracurricular activities could be used for lab exercises in social behavior as the gym is used for physical exercises. Whatever patterns may crystallize out of all these experimental projects, and undoubtedly several will, the school seems destined to become the No. 1 agency for the prevention and early treatment of psychosocial disorders.

PROJECT RE-ED

Standing between the typical public school and child guidance or psychiatric clinic a special educational program known as Project Re-ED is developing for the re-education of emotionally disturbed children. I believe it will become an integral part of the school system. After five years of extensive study and planning, the project was launched in 1961 with one pilot school in Nashville, Tennessee and the other in Durham, North Carolina. It was instigated by George Peabody College for Teachers and supported by the States of Tennessee and North Carolina, with additional support by the National Institute of Mental Health. It was designed to meet three needs: "(1) the need for new sources of manpower, (2) the need for new ways of extending the effectiveness of highly trained mental health specialists, and (3) the need for new patterns of operation to ensure the fullest and most efficient utilization of all resources."[3]

THE PROGRAM

The program was planned on the basis of certain principles and assumptions stated as follows:

[3] From *Project ReED*, 1964, p. 7. A cooperative program of the States of Tennessee and North Carolina and George Peabody College for Teachers, supported by the National Institute of Mental Health under Grant MH-929, and by funds from the states and the College. Used with permission.

> Fully adequate programs for the re-education of emotionally disturbed children can be developed by (1) emphasizing selection of workers; (2) providing condensed, highly specific, functional training; and (3) backstopping the workers' day-by-day activities with a dependable system of consultation by top-level professional personnel.
>
> The model provided by education with its emphasis on health rather than on illness, on teaching rather than on treatment, on learning rather than on fundamental personality reorganization, on the present and future rather than on the past, on the operation of the total social system of which the child is a part rather than on intrapsychic processes exclusively, may provide an effective as well as feasible approach to the problems of a substantial number of emotionally disturbed children. (p. 10).

Programs in the two schools are similar but allow for flexibility. Forty children, ages 6 to 12, are taught in five groups of eight. Two teacher-counselors with student volunteers as aides, are responsible for each group on a 24-hour day basis, one by day and one by night. Other specialists in art, music, and physical education give assistance; professional consultants are available. The children remain at the school five days and spend the weekend at home. Formal school work, recreation, and camping are emphasized. Camping activities are purposeful and planned conjointly by teacher-counselors and pupils. The program is not offered as a substitute for individual psychiatric treatment but as a complementary service that should prevent many from needing psychiatry and hasten the return of others to normal school and community life. "It is seen as one unit in a complex of services that is needed for an optimum community program for disturbed children." (p. 13). The project directors state:

> The teacher-counselor is the central person in Project ReED. It is he who works with the children, at school, at play, at night, in camp, on trips to a museum, to a swimming pool, to a state park, to a concert. He is teacher and counselor and friend. He needs many skills: How to teach fourth grade arithmetic, how to help a child with a reading problem, how to manage a group of eight children in the evening after dinner, how to pitch a tent, pack a canoe, make a monkey-bridge, how to calm a child who has lost control of himself and comfort a child who is afraid or despairing, how to lead group

> singing, how to throw clay on a potter's wheel, how to operate a teaching machine, how to understand a psychiatrist, psychologist, or social worker, how to help a teacher plan for the return of a child, how to talk constructively with a distraught or distrustful or over dependent parent, how to do all this and many other things. . . . In the face of a demanding, draining life, he must be a person of inner richness, who is able to recreate himself from sources external to the job. Integrity in human relationships, equanimity of spirit, an abundance of sheer physical stamina, considerable trust in self, an ability to give and receive affection yet stand being hated day after day, a well of good humor, an affinity for joyousness, these are some of the requirements for being a teacher-counselor. (p. 16).

Purposes. The directors admit that these are traits that cannot be learned in a short period of teacher training but are a lifetime development. Thus, selection based on personality is of first importance. As to purpose, it is not to bring about a deep reorganization of the child's character but to make him functional, and permit the restorative process to continue. Their limited goals are sought by the following:

1. Restoring to the child some trust in adults, some competences to meet demands of family, school, and friends, some confidence in self, and some joy in the morrow.
2. Helping a child maintain normal progress in school, when possible and providing him with remedial work in reading, arithmetic, and other subjects as needed to arrest the downward trend in school achievement so often observed in disturbed children.
3. Mobilizing resources in the child's home community in the interest of the child, especially by giving assistance to his family.
4. Assisting the staff of the child's regular school to understand his problem and to make such reasonable adjustments in the school program as may be required to make possible an early and successful return of the child to his own school.
5. Helping the child to unlearn some specific habits that cause rejection by family, school, and friends, and to acquire some specific habits that make him more acceptable to the people who are important to his life.
6. Helping the child gain some cognitive control over his behavior by helping him identify specific goals and reviewing

each day as it is lived to identify sources of satisfaction and dissatisfaction and ways of behaving likely to bring more success to the next day.

7. Helping a child to achieve a sense of belonging in his home community, to perceive favorably and respond to the institutions provided by society to assist him in growing up: the schools, churches, libraries, health services, parks, museums, recreational areas, theaters, youth programs, and other similar agencies. (pp. 19, 20).

THE PENNSYLVANIA PROPOSAL

Mental health authorities recognize the need and value of close liaison with the school and Church. This is illustrated by the formulators of Pennsylvania's new *Comprehensive Mental Health Plan.*[4] They say:

> The following represents the spectrum of mental health services that should be available in the schools:
> a. development of mental health awareness on the part of school boards, executives, and teachers, and the community which supports the school system;
> b. development of liaison and communication with present facilities in the community or in adjacent communities, including psychiatric clinics, social work agencies and individual practitioners. . . .
> c. development of consultative resources for teachers and administrators;
> d. development of early identification and screening methods;
> e. development of resource teachers with special training within the school;
> f. development of mental health liaison personnel within the school;
> g. development of in-service staff training and development program;
> h. development of special classes for disturbed children based on local community readiness. . . .
>
> *The Church*
>
> 1) The various religious denominations should establish committees to study mental illness and the activation of such

[4] Clifford J. Bodarky (ed), *The Comprehensive Mental Health Plan,* The Governor's Advisory Committee, Commonwealth of Pennsylvania, December 1965.

committee work should be stimulated by the community mental health planning effort. Support is urged by both private and governmental sources for further study of the role of the clergyman in the area of prevention.

2) It is recommended that an interfaith committee be established at the State level, to provide for closer working relationship between religious leaders and mental health workers.
3) A multidisciplinary view of potential community mental health centers seems to be most appropriate. . . . Thus, the role of the church and synagogue would be primarily preventative and supportive, but with suitable qualified clergymen engaged in pastoral counseling in a setting where consultation and conference opportunity with other professionals in the allied health professions is readily available. Through such a setting, churches and synagogues would learn to do better what they have been doing. . . .
4) While interdisciplinary relationships between psychiatrists, the clergy, and others in allied health professions are to be encouraged, the necessity for discrete role-awareness and a clear identity on the part of each specialty, with its own discipline, is of fundamental importance.
5) It is urged that the proposed community mental health centers develop working relationships with existing pastoral training centers. . . .
6) The Department of Public Welfare should create the position of chaplain-consultant to the Department. . . .

MENTAL HEALTH IN RELIGION

Since mental health is multidimensional, involving wholeness of life, its attainment is multidisciplinary. Early in this book, mental hygiene was presented as a form of applied psychology. As a field of study, exploration, assembling and classifying information, and researching methods of treatment, the statement is basically true. But as an experience, a condition or state of being, its preservation, development, and restoration are consequences of all aspects of life. Any agency that profoundly influences man's thinking, his values and thus emotions, and his social relationships profoundly influences his mental health. I have shown how this is so with the family and the school. Now let us examine man's religion as a contributing agency.

Religion is another ambiguous term. Some argue that everybody is religious, that a man's religion consists of his highest values and how he relates to them, that atheism and communism are religions. I do not use the term quite as inclusively. In this discussion, religion means those specific activities, including mental processes, by which man attempts to relate himself to the eternal or spiritual realm or dimension of reality and which includes belief in some form of divine or eternal being. This is not offered as being adequately comprehensive or definitive, but merely as a statement of how the term is being used in this chapter. When I use the term Church, it refers to institutionalized religion of any branch whether Hindu, Muslim, Judaic, or Christian, or other. In small case, church is used to designate a local religious fellowship.

The mental health movement in America, beginning early in this century, has received wide-scale religious support from its inception. The old science-religion conflict which reached its apex in the nineteenth century, and though diminished had not died in the twentieth, flared out anew between religion on the one hand and psychiatry and psychology on the other. Relative to psychiatry, this was due largely to the religionists' reaction to Freud's exaggerated emphasis on sex and antireligious pronouncements,[5] to Freud's limited understanding of religion and the religionists' limited understanding of Freud. Relative to psychology, it was due largely to religion's reaction to extreme Watsonian behaviorism that ignored or denied a legitimate place for moral or spiritual values. We shall not be concerned with this conflict which, of course, had many facets and variants, but rather, with their realignment.

RAPPROCHEMENT

Not all early psychologists took a negative view of religion. William James' classic *Varieties of Religious Experience* has been

[5] Sigmund Freud, *The Future of an Illusion* (London: Liveright, 1927). Also New York: Doubleday (Anchor paperback).

widely quoted for decades. And Jung's classic statement has been quoted even more widely by modern religionists: "I have treated many hundreds of patients, the larger number being Protestants, a small number of Jews, and not more than five or six believing Catholics. Among all my patients in the second half of life . . . there has not been one whose problem in the last resort was not that of finding a religious outlook on life. It is safe to say that every one of them fell ill because he had lost that which the living religions of every age have given to their followers, and none of them have been really healed who did not regain his religious outlook."[6] A few of our American neo-Freudian psychiatrists maintained this same positive religious point of view, notably the Menninger brothers, who lectured extensively to church assemblies. Henry C. Link's *The Return to Religion* (1936) was a psychologist's call for rapprochement.

Two developments during the past three decades largely account for this rapprochement: (1) the invasion of theology, psychology, and psychiatry by existentialism with its emphasis on experience, being, fulfillment, and values; and (2) psychiatry's discovery of love as the great prophylactic and ameliorative force in mental hygiene. Since moral values and love have been chiefly the domain of religion for many centuries, (emphasized also in secular humanism) there has been a natural drawing together. Psychiatry and religion have become allies, seeking to clarify their common goals and to find the commonality and complementariness of their methods. But like allies, each maintains its autonomy and individual frame of reference; toward each other they are not free of tension, minor conflict, and perhaps some jealousy.

Since World War II, the togetherness movement has grown rapidly, religion and psychotherapy combining their resources in both preventative and curative services. Pastor counselors were assigned to mental hospitals as chaplains; psychiatrists and ministers jointly conducted forums and seminars on mental health; and numerous articles were written to point up their newly discovered kinship, their common objective to make people whole and their complementary methods. This cooperative venture may

[6] Carl G. Jung, *Modern Man in Search of a Soul* (New York: Harcourt, Brace & World, 1950), p. 264. Used with permission.

best be seen in the work of the Academy of Religion and Mental Health, founded in 1956, by representatives of the three major "Faiths" in America and the medical and social sciences. Its stated purposes are:

(1) to implement theological education with the findings of medicine, psychiatry and the social sciences in mental health. . . .
(2) to interpret for medical and theological education, the offices, rites and doctrines of organized religions in the light of relevant biological and sociological knowledge. . . .
(3) to illuminate issues, define attainable goals, develop work patterns, accumulate and exchange information, and stimulate research. . . .
(4) to affirm moral and spiritual values in man and the universe without any attempt to propagate doctrines, or to profane religious mysteries, or to resolve divergencies in religious thought, or to compromise medical and scientific differences. . . .
(5) to enlist participation within and between scientific disciplines and the ministry—not as an assembly for settlement or unification, but as a multidisciplinary approach that brings together workers in medicine, psychology, cultural anthropology, sociology and theology.[7]

Among the periodicals now being published that especially enhance this cooperative work is the Academy's own *Journal of Religion and Health*; also *Pastoral Psychology, The Journal for the Scientific Study of Religion*, and the *Catholic Psychological Record.*

RELIGION'S NEGATIVE CONTRIBUTIONS

Only the most radical religious advocates state that the practice of religion will assure mental health. The belief that the practice of religion is on the whole detrimental to mental health is a position that only the most orthodox Freudians and radical secularists now hold. But many mental hygienists find evidence

[7] From *About the Academy of Religion and Mental Health.* New York: Academy of Religion and Mental Health, 1956, pp. 1–3. Also in Thorpe, 1960, p. 510. Used with permission.

that there was some merit in Freud's criticism of religion. He felt that if religion *per se* is not a neurosis, it often aggravates neurotic conditions and that several neurotic and psychotic symptoms derive from the patient's religious life. It is frequently pointed out that ministers have become victims of mental illness, and the ratio of church members who enter mental hospitals is not much less, if any, than that of the general public. Thus, religion is no guarantee of mental health and may be a contributing factor in mental illness.

Guilt. The strongest charge against religion as a negative force in mental health is that by imposing rigid and often unrealistic moral standards and emphasis on eternal punishment, it fosters excess anxiety and guilt which are major components of mental illness. Morbid or pathological guilt is manifest in neurotic and psychotic depression; and the rigid, both protecting and crippling, defenses of the obsessive-compulsive and pathologically scrupulous types are measures to keep guilt repressed.

Many religionists agree with this charge, that it is true to some degree but not nearly so great as in the past. They argue that this is not an inherent weakness of religion *per se* but is due to its faulty application or mediation by some leaders just as some parents and teachers create faulty home and school climates. They also add that nonreligious practitioners are as prone to these morbid guilt symptoms as are religious patients, that these conditions are products or expressions of his illness rather than causes. Religion inadequately presented and inadequately practiced does often increase tension, anxiety, and guilt, but not when properly understood and practiced. In a discussion of religious neurotics, Schneiders says (1965, p. 431):

> . . . Pathological scrupulousness, which seems to be common among Catholic penitents, invariably involves three elements that are complexly intermingled—the moral, the religious, and the sexual. In such cases, one always finds a disordered conscience, an overdeveloped super-ego, sexual anxiety and confusion, unusual reduction of personal freedom, and a pathological attitude toward religious concepts and practices. The religious background is one of fear, repeated emphasis on the sinfulness of behavior, Jansenistic puritanism regarding sex, threat of hell and damnation, and ideas of an avenging God!

Obviously, this sort of religiosity is directly contrary to the religion of love, which characterizes true Christianity regardless of its denominational form.

Intolerance. Another way religion has been a negative factor in man's psychosocial behavior is its alleged tendency to promote intolerance, sectarianism, and an authoritarian type personality. History and common observation seem to support this accusation. The religionist will generally agree and say it is "all too true in the past," and also it "holds some truth today." He will point out that this is due to the faulty implementation of religion and that religion's gospel of love and brotherhood is the great bastion of tolerance and good will, of democratic personality, family, and social structure, and he will cite the role the leadership of the Church has played in Hitlerian Germany* and our civil rights war.

An Escape. A third basic charge against religion relative to mental-social health is that it fosters an escapist attitude, otherworldliness, "the opiate of the people." The accusation is true, for some people, and was more true in the past. The weak, the anxious, the security-motivated person is drawn to the Church. He finds security, and he finds a means of rationalizing his failure: "I could have succeeded if I had surrendered my standards, but I prefer a mansion in heaven to the luxuries of this world." Religion has been used to serve this need. However, the "defender of the faith" will argue that this is only half-true, and that religion offers the greatest challenge to effective, creative, sacrificial service that is known to man.

THE CHURCH'S CONTRIBUTION TO MENTAL HEALTH

Theologians and other high officials in the Church hasten to make clear that the Church (organized religion) is not primarily concerned with mental health and that mental health is not a

* It is stoutly maintained that the Church is the only institution that did not yield its opposition to the Nazi race philosophy, "blood purges," and general antidemocratic policies.

direct objective of religion but rather a consequence. The primary function of the Church, they would say, is to promote and enhance worship, to guide man in his need and efforts to transcend the material and biological aspects of reality and relate himself meaningfully and experientially to the spiritual and eternal realm of reality. In doing this, it satisfies man's highest need, the spiritual, and opens the way to his highest fulfillment or self-actualization. Man's deepest joy and soundest mental health is determined by the degree to which this is attained.

ANXIETY-GUILT

Many leaders in religion, particularly existentialists, see man alienating himself from the biological sphere where the animal is essentially at home because of his unique capacities. If he does not establish identity with the transcendent realm, he suffers primary anxiety, the dread of self-deterioration and annihilation, or eternal dread. This is the root anxiety that underlies most mental illness and which manifests itself in a variety of attachments and defenses. Jung was referring to this existential anxiety in his quotation but he did not adequately explain it. The recognition of this led Viktor Frankl into logotherapy, understanding its nature somewhat better. Preachers, especially in the past, have tried to bring the "sinner" into a full state of guilt-consciousness in order to motivate him to respond with repentence and faith and thus appropriate his divine inheritance. They called it being "under conviction," necessary to create a state of readiness or motivation. These ministers were over zealous and did not understand the dynamics involved. They often overdid the job or mistakenly applied it to all alike. The overly anxious, disturbed, incipiently neurotic or psychotic person found the dosage too heavy, and could not respond normally. He may have found it an aggravating factor in his developing neurosis or psychosis.

Modern day preachers are better grounded in psychology and are better equipped to handle this existential anxiety-guilt judiciously and realistically. They deal with it more on an individual than a mass basis, and vary their approach with the emotional state of the person. They work deliberately to bring that primary anxiety-guilt into consciousness while they extend the forgiveness, love, and acceptance of God to the repentent and trusting seeker. When the individual experiences divine forgiveness and acceptance, the anxiety is resolved and is replaced by a deep sense of eternal security, an at-homeness in the eternal realm, at-oneness with all humanity. By having his deepest security need met and by securing self-existence, the individual is free to expend himself in creative living, in the highest self-actualization. This, existential theologians say, is the Church's greatest contribution to mental health.

LOVE AND FAITH

It was mentioned previously that love was the great discovery of psychiatry in this generation, and that love and faith on the one hand and hostility (hate) and fear (anxiety) on the other are the "big four" attitudes that relate specifically to mental health. The child who grows to maturity in a climate of love and faith rarely develops mental illness or psychosocial disorders of a serious nature. But the child who grows to adulthood in a climate of hostility and anxiety is most likely to develop serious behavior disorders. A major factor in recovery is to help the patient build dominant attitudes of love and faith. Psychiatry has just discovered this, although the Church has advocated this theory for 3000 years. The psychiatric clinic is looking to the Church for an ally in order to find the best method of mediating love. Psychiatry can help religion in dealing with the anxiety-guilt dynamic.

THE FELLOWSHIP

Paul Maves[8] describes the group or community life of the Church in relation to mental health, by showing the need and nature of group life and the nature of the early Christian congregation as a *Koinonia* (a community of sacred love). He men-

[8] Paul B. Maves, *The Church and Mental Health* (New York: Charles Scribner's Sons, 1953), pp. 77–96. Used with permission.

tions the modern trend away from this close interdependent communal relationship, and then, in more recent years, the trend back and some of its implications. He says:

> First, every person who seeks membership in the Church will be related to a small, intimate, face-to-face group which will meet frequently over a period of time and in the spirit of *agape* for fellowship, study, worship, and service. . . . Perhaps the development of Christian nurture is one of the main contributions the Church can make to health.
>
> Second, these groups will be person- and need-centered rather than exclusively task-centered. . . . Within these groups they will find themselves respected as persons rather than as productive machines or centers of power, and they will find understanding, sympathy, and compassion. . . . (p. 94).

All social scientists emphasize the significance of the primary (face-to-face) group in character formation. It satisfies the need to be accepted, to belong, and to establish group identity. The modern Church has come to a new realization of its opportunity to meet this need. Thus, it not only teaches love but organizes its constituency into small fellowships for each age-group.

The members of these primary groups actively seek others, the neglected and rejected, and welcome them into the fellowship. Doubt, suspicion, and reserve (defense) slowly give way and the newcomer identifies deeply with the group; he experiences their acceptance and concern, and forms a new sense of his own worth. Soon he can "generalize" this new experience of faith and love and drop his defenses against society, since he is free to form more creative and satisfying social relationships.

This search for the social rejects, the disturbed and maladjusted individuals, has far to go before it is highly effective. Not all church members are free from their defenses and can be loving and accepting. Many church leaders, both lay and clergy, have much to learn about how to win the rejected and suspicious persons. Churches now aware of this need and their opportunity are working at it, and are making progress. Those who are already included in this program find that these fellowship groups serve an important prophylactic purpose. Under the leadership of a trained pastor-counselor, working with other community agencies, these church fellowships can be effective ameliorative agencies for the not too seriously maladjusted.

THE CHURCH AND THE HOME

The inadequacy of child-parent relationships in the home is found to be the chief source of psychosocial behavior disorders. If this climate is improved, this condition could be prevented. What is the role of the Church with relationship to the family? In a previous publication based largely on an intensive study of 150 delinquents which included various aspects of their family life, I made this observation. (Roberts, 1958, p. 79).

> The local church has a unique opportunity to reach and enrich the family relationships of problem homes. For, by and large, the parents of our problem children are not irreligious or antagonistic to the Church. The minister or church worker is a welcomed visitor in the vast majority of these homes. He does not have to wait until invited, but is free to visit any home, and he can tactfully bring the influence of his church to bear upon any problem discovered to exist there. Of the 150 inmates of schools for delinquents studied by the writer, approximately two-thirds came from homes where at least one parent was a church member. Slightly more than one-third claimed church membership for both parents, while nearly one-third were from homes where neither parent was a member of any church. Of these last, a sizable proportion reported occasional church attendance, by one or the other of their parents, though we may assume that the occasions were infrequent and the interests light. However, very few were aware of any conscious hostility toward the Church on the part of their parents, there were only five fathers and one mother, to be exact. The writer, visiting many of these homes, found little hostility but much confused thinking and shallow interest. . . .

Further investigation revealed that very few of these parents were active in the life of the church and that religion had a rather tenuous hold on them. The situation was similar with the delinquent children themselves, about 90 percent of whom had a strongly or moderately positive attitude toward religion and the Church but whose religious lives were characterized by being "ideationally strong but functionally weak. . . . Right ideas had been transmitted to their minds and had been accepted uncritically by them, but their concepts and convictions were shallow-rooted and their deep emotional drives left largely unaffected." (pp. 73, 74). These conditions prevail generally in the families of individuals with other types of serious psychosocial disorders.

Relative to the above family-church relationships, certain facts stand out that have a direct bearing on mental hygiene. First, the Church has direct access to the large majority of problem families. Second, while most of these families have a positive attitude toward religion, they are not functioning adequately in their religion as in other aspects of life. Third, the Church has not been meeting the needs of these families, by properly mediating a gospel of love to them, as well as it should and could. Fourth, the Church has become cognizant of its opportunity and past failures and is moving rapidly to make amends.

The Church, through its major divisions, now publishes magazines on family life and has boards or commissions which promote education for family living at the local level. Ministers are being trained in marriage counseling and are holding counseling sessions with their young people previous to marriage. These ministers are alert to marital problems that may arise among their parish families, and their services as marriage counselors are made available if they are desired. Many of these follow the marriage ceremony and baptism of infants with an individual pastor-parent service to help create a family climate of love and faith in which to rear their children. In other words, the modern church is trying to make its gospel of love operational within the family. It is trying to pull members of troubled families into its various fellowships where, as members of the church family, they can experience "family" acceptance and love. A booklet which was issued by one of our great churches, described a part of its service to families.[9]

> Believing that the family is the major school of Christian living, we try to encourage each family to be the church every day, in all its relationships. We visit each new mother, taking a rose to her and sharing with her a high inspiration and vision for her child. Young children are brought into the sanctuary

[9] A service manual issued by First Community Church, Columbus, Ohio.

to be consecrated to the Lord, and parents pledge themselves to bring their children up in the nurture and admonition of the Lord. We visit in their homes. We invite them to meet together to study how their vows may be faithfully fulfilled; study groups in all phases of guidance and leadership of children are provided for parents. Clinic sessions are held where help may be secured for special problem situations; we work with the school in the interest of special problem cases. We seek to work closely with the chief of police, the courts, all the special agencies. It is our purpose to hallow all their efforts.

. . . . . .

We seek to make every resource available for the guidance of Christian growth from the time of conception. When it is discovered that a child is having difficulty or is not making normal progress in his growth, we try to get all the adults who are sharing with him or her together. This includes the parents, the school and church leaders, the physician, and in very serious cases, the psychiatrist. If the child gets into difficulty with the law, then the chief of police joins in the conference. The purpose is not to rally against the child, but to bring all the understanding possible among those who live and share with him. If all of his adult friends have enough understanding, the solution of his problems becomes much easier. . . .

Our church feels that it is important to have a program of marriage education throughout the various ages. Young people should be helped to understand the home as an institution; they should see it as a part of God's plan. They need help in finding the greatest fulfillment with their present homes; there should be constant emphasis that will help them come to an understanding of dating from a Christian point of view, and to grow in a Christian rather than a Hollywood interpretation of love.

This church is doing a great service in prophylactic and ameliorative mental hygiene. But true greatness is rare, even among churches. While few churches are able to reach this high level of service, more and more churches are approximating this to an ever-increasing degree in their efforts to actualize their potential as a mental-social health building agency.

Thorpe (1960, p. 511) summarizes the contributions of organized religion to mental health as follows: "by (1) aiding the individual in understanding and achieving moral goals appropriate to his stage of development, (2) counseling aimed at better social relationships and the establishing of inner security and self-acceptance, (3) providing participative experiences in an understanding social environment, (4) strengthening marital ties and responsibility in family living, and (5) developing maturity and sound ethical values for healthy living and optimal growth."

Royce,[10] throughout his book, emphasized certain basic psychological needs which should be provided in a positive approach to the prevention of mental disorders. He then shows how religion meets these:

(a) *Security.* There is no more solid anchor than trust in Divine Proidence. Says William James, "the sovereign cure for worry is religious faith."

(b) *Self-esteem.* Feelings of inferiority and unworthiness plague so many of us. . . . Yet world-wide fame, even if attainable by all, would not give recognition as satisfying as the dignity which comes to one elevated to the supernatural life of Grace and made a partaker in the divine life.

(c) *Affection.* Religion is the ultimate, and for many the only, source of surety that one is loved. "God so loved the world" and "I have loved you with an everlasting love" recur through the Bible like the main theme of a great symphony. . . .

(d) *Achievement.* We are all ambitious. Yet success in worldy ways is possible to relatively few. Through religion, one can accomplish the one thing really worthwhile in any life, and be aided to realistic achievements in subordinate ways through cooperation in church activities, charitable groups, and the lay apostolate. . . .

(e) *Independence.* Religion furnishes means for emancipation from the group without loneliness. It gives the consolation of friendship with God and the means and motivation required to live one's own life. . . .

(f) *Submission.* To be subservient is often a necessity, but only through religion does one succeed in doing so without demeaning oneself. "Be obedient to Christ," advises St. Paul, and authority becomes at once meaningful and less irksome.

---

[10] James E. Royce, *Personality and Mental Health* (Milwaukee: The Bruce Publishing Co., 1964). pp. 294–297. Used with permission.

(g) *Self-knowledge.* Regular confession, with complete protection of secrecy and no check on one's honesty but a God who can't be fooled, is productive of a healthy acceptance on one's shortcomings without introspective brooding. Christian humility is not hypocritical self-deprecation, but realistic acknowledgement of one's place, one's assets and liabilities, one's dignity and dependence. Meditation, too, can be a great promoter of insight.

(h) *Knowledge of Reality.* As stated earlier, religion puts one in contact with more of reality. In addition, it meets one's quest for knowledge with certainties instead of doubt. . . . The meaning of life is no riddle to the religious person, however simple and uneducated.

(i) *Orientation Toward Future Goals.* This is commonly listed by psychologists as a mark of maturity. Obviously it reaches its highest perfection in religion, where man is oriented toward his ultimate goal.

(j) *Selflessness.* Emotional maturity demands that the egocentricity of the infant give way to a recognition that one is not the center around which the universe revolves. . . . Love of God and neighbor are the core of Christian living. . . .

(k) *Self-Control.* Clean living, sure guidance as to conduct, and stability amid the ups and downs of emotional moods are essential to both physical and mental health. . . . Religion gives moral principles with a backing which makes them easier to hang on to when the going is hard.

(l) Lastly, *Integration.* All of the above must be organized. Religion furnishes the only framework which guides the relationships of all in a harmonious whole with certain and adequate rewards.

To sustain this last point, Royce quotes several psychologists whose statements were based on empirical evidence. MacLeod (1952, p. 272) said:

> . . . What impresses us now about the religious man is his serenity, his courage, his loyalty, the firmness of his faith, his conviction that life has a deep meaning and that whatever happens to him as an individual is relatively unimportant compared with that which is greater than himself. Far from giving the impression of being a twisted person, this kind of religious man seems to have achieved something great in life, something that the rest of us would surely like to understand.

And he quotes Hadley Cantril (1950, p. 95) as saying:

> A survey made in the United States in 1946 found that nine out of every ten of those people who felt their lives were very happy were persons for whom religious beliefs were a consolation in times of trouble.

This is perhaps the first time in its long history that the Church has submitted itself to such soul-searching, such "agonizing reappraisal" of its task, as in this third quarter of the twentieth century. The Church is conducting experimental projects all over the world which are designed to restore its relevancy, to find new ways for effectual involvement at the "guts" level in modern society. This new attitude and approach is symbolized in a fundamental change of expression: from the Church as an "institution with a mission" to the "Church itself as mission." Typical of many manifestations of this new movement is the Ecumenical Institute of Chicago. Of its program the Rev. Phillip Mayfield wrote:[11]

> In many Churches through the research of the Ecumenical Institutes around the world, and particularly that one located in Chicago, attempts have been made to become the People of God in the twentieth century. In one Church, for example, seventeen people decided to take an intensive course in theology to get on top of the theological revolution of the last 500 years. In addition, they began an intensive study of the cultural revolution of our time covering such fields as science, sociology, history, art, psychology, philosophy, family life, and the national and world situation. Moreover they have been struggling to translate this wisdom into a meaningful image of the task in the world and in their local community. . . .
>
> If we can sense the urgency of the need for a new model of the Church and the world; if we are prepared to expend our lives in a massive re-imagining of the Church: if we can go out onto the point of history where the dangers are greatest, we will demonstrate that neither is God dead nor is the local congregation obsolete, and we will know that life *is* abundant and that *we* have died our deaths with intentionality and responsibility on behalf of all that has been and all that will be.

By way of implementation, the Ecumenical Institute has been sponsoring the Fifth City Project which is a 16-block ghetto of

[11] From *Newsletter*, Vol. III, No. 1, p. 4 (September 1966). Used with permission.

4300 people, 95 percent Negro. The stated aims are: "to equip the existing people to transform the existing community. It is committed to reforming from within, by educating the imagination, by equipping with tools and by developing prowess in corporate life and action. Every area of social existence—political, economic and cultural—is involved. All must be addressed and retooled in depth. The project presses on all fronts at once in a specific, clearly defined geosocial area. Specific human beings with specific human problems associated with particular human situations are participants in a design of metamorphosis."

The Institute works through trained cadres and conducts short and very intensive courses of training for the people of the area to carry out the above objectives. Training the imagination is the key to the educational program by imagining what a community could and should be and what can be done to change specific aspects of community living and produce a new image of oneself and his role. One aspect of the project is: "*A 13 week College* offers an intensive and comprehensive liberal arts education to culturally deprived young adults to enrich their skills and to open their opportunities toward creative citizenship in the urban world."

The Institute works along a half dozen other lines, all directed toward communities transforming themselves and in so doing alter the society. This newly "imagined" and created society will provide the milieu in which children will grow naturally into a state of mental-social health.

SUMMARY

Children spend more time at school than any other place except the home, and it is second only to the home in the psychosocial development of children. They bring their emotional problems to the school where, faced with new demands and frustrations, the problems may become aggravated. As a parent surrogate, the teacher may help to alleviate these emotional problems by creating a nonthreatening climate of acceptance and support in the classroom and by deliberate efforts to help her pupils attain peer group acceptance and experience successful performance.

In order to function more effectively as an agency for the prevention of psychosocial disorders and the promotion of its wholesome development, schools have been experimenting with a variety of programs. These include: (1) in-service training for teachers with follow-up professional consultation service; (2) various means of alerting parents to problems and treatment facilities and eliciting parent-teacher cooperation; and (3) both formal and informal training of the children in dealing with their emotional and social problems. Special experimental schools have been designed to provide diagnostic and remedial training for children too seriously "disturbed" for the regular school. Project ReED is one of these that shows much promise. Seriously disturbed children are accepted as boarding pupils, placed in classes of approximately eight; each group is given day and night service by specially selected and trained teacher-counselors. They help the children gain confidence in themselves and other people and mobilize their resources for wholesome performance.

Next to the school stands the church as a community agency that is most conducive to mental health. The very significant relation of love and values to mental health has prompted modern psychiatry to effect a rapprochement between religion and the behavioral sciences. The Academy of Religion and Mental Health stands as a symbol and practical manifestation of this new "togetherness." Although religion misapplied and malpracticed often aggravates emotional disturbances, religion properly expressed tends to increase faith in oneself and life, security and inner peace, transcendent living and self-actualization. The Church's special potentialities as an agency for mental health lie in: (1) its influence is brought to bear upon people virtually from the cradle to the grave; (2) it has freer access to the home than almost any other agency; (3) its strong emphasis on faith, love, and high values is a powerful motivation; (4) it has a most effective means of mediating love and acceptance through its small fellowship groups; (5) it has learned to handle the anxiety-guilt factor most realistically through its better trained ministers and (6) its pastors as counselors reach more emotionally disturbed people than any other one counseling agency.

GLOSSARY

Agape. A Greek term for love in its spiritual expression as opposed to Eros or erotic love. Also, the social "love-feast" of the early Christians.

In loco parentis. Latin, meaning in the place of a parent.

Jansenistic. Pertaining to Cornelius Jansen's doctrine of predestination, the irresistibility of divine grace and denial of free will.

Scrupulousness. An exacting, almost compulsive concern for doing the right or proper thing.

REFERENCES AND SUGGESTED READINGS

BONNEY, M. E., *Mental Health in Education,* Boston: Allyn and Bacon, Inc., 1960.

BULLIS, H. E., and E. E. O'MALLEY, *Human Relation in the Classroom,* Wilmington, Del.: State Society for Mental Hygiene, 1947, 1948, 1949. (Courses I, II, and III).

BUSH, R. N., *The Teacher-Pupil Relationship,* Englewood Cliffs, N.J.: Prentice-Hall, Inc., 1954.

JUNG, CARL G., *Modern Man in Search of a Soul,* New York: Harcourt, Brace, 1950.

KAPLAN, LOUIS, *Mental Health and Human Relations in Education,* New York: Harper & Row, 1959.

LAYCOCK, S. R., "Effect of Teacher's Personality on the Behavior of Children," *Understanding the Child,* 19: 50–55 (April, 1950).

MAVES, PAUL B., *The Church and Mental Health,* New York: Charles Scribner's Sons, 1953.

OJEMANN, RALPH J., *Personal Adjustment of Individual Children,* Washington: Nat. Educ. Assoc., 1962 (a pamphlet).

REDYL, F., and W. W. WALTENBERG, *Mental Hygiene in Teaching,* New York: Harcourt, Brace and Co., 1959.

ROBERTS, GUY L., *Where Delinquency Begins,* Richmond: John Knox Press, 1958.

ROYCE, JAMES E., *Personality and Mental Health,* Milwaukee: The Bruce Publishing Co., 1964.

SARRASON, S. B., *Anxiety in Elementary School Children,* New York: John Wiley & Sons, Inc., 1960.

SCHNEIDERS, A. A., *Personality Dynamics and Mental Health,* New York: Holt, Rinehart and Winston, Inc., 1965.

THORPE, LOUIS P., *The Psychology of Mental Health,* New York: The Ronald Press Company, 1960.

WITTY, P. A., "Evaluation of Studies of the Characteristics of the Effective Teacher," *Improving Educational Research,* American Educational Research Assoc. 1948, pp. 198–204.

12

The Community in Action: Through its Special Agencies

In 1963 the Community Mental Health Centers Act was passed by Congress and $150 million was appropriated to start building mental health centers. New hope was kindled in hundreds of communities which had been grappling with the problem of providing some degree of effective mental hygiene services to the lower socioeconomic classes, where the need was greatest and the services were virtually nonexistent. The few publicly supported clinics available to the poor were so over-worked and under-staffed, that applicants usually had to wait weeks for treatment. Most became discouraged and quit bothering to go. They struggled as best they could with their problems until circumstances produced a crisis and took the matter out of their hands. Then the community often had to act through its courts or put pressure on the family to commit the offender to a prison, a school for delinquents, or to a state hospital. Others "solved" their problems by means of dope, alcohol, or suicide.

HELP FOR ALL

Many social scientists, physicians, ministers, and educators had been aware of this great social problem for years. Hollingshead and Redlich (with their *Social Class and Mental Illness*, 1958) shocked others into the realization that treatment for psychosocial disorders was largely a social class service. Local communities were spurred by local chapters of the National Mental Health Association, PTA's, and Church commissions. They began to study their problems and check their resources, only to suffer frustration. There were too few trained professionals and the services were too expensive for the large majority of people. The 1963 Act gave new life to the movement. Great strides were predicted by mental hygienists for the years 1965-1975 in the building and staffing of mental health clinics, with staffing as the bigger problem. People become mentally ill in the community. It is here they must be healed; and it is here preventative measures must be established.

FEDERAL AND STATE SERVICES

The community is the arena in which the forces of mental health and illness are joined, for the community is society as experienced by the individual. Research findings indicate that removal from the community impedes recovery. However, the local community needs the help of the larger society as represented by the nation and state in the form of financial assistance, supervision, and sometimes initiation. In 1946, the National Mental Health Act was passed and funds were appropriated for the development of state and local programs. This act also made provision for the establishment of the National Institute of Mental Health, a division of the United States Public Health Service. By 1951, programs receiving federal support were operating in every state. But in many instances, little more than token services were being offered; or at best, relatively few people were being reached with effective treatment. This new Act came into being, with amendments in 1965 which authorized funds for staff salaries.

THE NATIONAL INSTITUTE OF MENTAL HEALTH

Much progress was made between these two Acts, largely under the stimulus of the National Institute of Mental Health

(NIMH). Several million dollars was appropriated each year for research programs, pilot projects, and community prevention and treatment services. Between 1955 and 1962, the number of persons treated in out-patient clinics doubled, from 379,000 to 741,000, and by 1960 approximately 600 general hospitals provided in-patient psychiatric service to 200,000 patients. Also, largely from these researches and pilot projects, two trends were initiated: (1) movement from the large state mental hospitals toward more treatment in local general hospitals; and (2) part-time care, some as day-patients and some as night-patients. With these may be added a third trend, the increase in short-term treatment. The result was a small but steady decline in the number of mental patients occupying hospital beds at any given time, yet an increase in the total patients treated.

In one of its own promotion folders, NIMH states its functions.

> The National Institute of Mental Health plans, directs, and coordinates the Public Health Service's national program for improvement of the mental health of the people of the United States through comprehensive and integrated programs to:
> 1. Assist in the development of State and community mental health services.
> 2. Support researches into the causes, prevention and treatment of mental illness.
> 3. Support the training of psychiatrists, psychologists, psychiatric social workers, psychiatric nurses and other mental health workers.
> 4. Support field and epidemiologic studies.
> 5. Perform clinical and basic research activities.
> 6. Collect and disseminate scientific information.

THE NATIONAL ASSOCIATION FOR MENTAL HEALTH

The NAMH is a national voluntary citizens' organization with several hundred local chapters through which it "carries on year-around programs to combat mental illness and help the emotionally disturbed and their families." Their program centers on:

Research. Support of important pilot and on-going studies on causes, treatment, and prevention.
Improved Hospital Care. Volunteer services giving personal aid and attention to the ill and their families. Stimulation of public pressure for psychiatric services in general hospitals and improved therapeutic programs in mental hospitals.
Aftercare and Rehabilitation. Initiation and sponsorship of social clubs, halfway houses, work training, reemployment, and other after-care programs for patients returning to the community from mental hospitals.
Childhood Mental Illness. Promotion of special diagnostic, treatment, and education services in public schools, in separate residential or day centers, in hospitals and in clinics.
Public Information and Education. Programs, films, and publications to reduce ignorance and fear and inform the public about treatment and rehabilitation facilities.
Community Mental Health Services. Mobilization of citizen action for comprehensive services in the community—within reach of everyone. These services are to cover every phase of care—from diagnosis through rehabilitation.

STATE LEVEL STRUCTURES AND SERVICES

In 1954, the National Governors' Conference on Mental Health adopted a 10-point program to serve as a general guide for the establishment of more effective state programs. These were rather general bases from which to develop specific programs and will not be quoted here. Many states reorganized and enlarged their services on the basis of these, and others are now (1967) in the process of reorganization to better coordinate their programs with the 1963 Federal Act.

In 1957, California passed the Short-Doyle Act for Community Mental Health Services. For the year 1964-65, 31 communities were carrying out approved Short-Doyle programs and receiving state aid to the extent of $19 million. A "community" by definition could be either a city or county or combination of cities and/or counties with a population of 50,000 or more. A community can receive financial support from the state, provided at least two of the following services are included in the program:

> 1. Psychiatric out-patient treatment.
> 2. Psychiatric in-patient treatment in a general hospital or in a psychiatric hospital affiliated with a general hospital.
> 3. Rehabilitation services for the psychiatrically disabled, to enable them to function at the best possible level socially, emotionally, vocationally, and physically.
> 4. Consultation by qualified mental health personnel to the professional staffs of public and private agencies and to individuals practicing privately in the community. . . .
> 5. Mental health information and education services to the public and to key professional groups, to build a broader understanding of mental health. . . .
>
> Patients pay what they are able for treatment services, but payments are not to exceed the cost of providing the services. . . . The Department of Mental Hygiene will advise on fee schedules, but each community establishes its own. No patient who needs treatment provided through this program can be denied services solely because of inability to pay. Services are provided those who voluntarily seek treatment and to those so ordered by the courts. All types of psychiatric disorders can be treated—mental illness, mental retardation, alcoholism, narcotics addiction, senility, character disorders.[1]

The various state structures that are formed to serve mental health needs, vary more in name or title than in services rendered. Some states established Departments of Mental Health (or Hygiene), with the chief executive officer holding cabinet rank. In others, mental health services are administered through a division of the Department of Health; while in another state the Department of Welfare is responsible for most of the services that relate most directly to mental health or psychosocial disorders. Departments of Education, through their educational rehabilitation divisions, came in for a share of mental health services. Since the 1963 Federal Act, the trend appears to be toward coordinating all mental health services under one department.

During the early 1960's, Georgia changed the name of its Department of Welfare to Department of Family Services with a semiautonomous Division of Children and Youth Services. This

---

[1] From a Department Brief, Sacramento: State of California, Dept. of Mental Hygiene 1966.

department directed a variety of services that would include virtually all preventative measures the public could take. Hospitals and specifically designated mental health clinics (treatment facilities) continued under Department of Health jurisdiction.

Pennsylvania officially adopted a new "Comprehensive Mental Health Plan" in 1966, titled the Office of Mental Health, and functions as a major division of the Department of Welfare. The organizational structure, however, is so comprehensive and its services so extensive, that the newly organized division carries responsibilities and renders services comparable with those states that now have full departments. The new structure calls for a special unit for Children's Services somewhat like the Georgia plan. Other special units are: (1) special programs (alcoholic and drug addiction, geriatrics, and correction and parole); (2) Clinical research; (3) Professional services; (4) Clinical training; (5) Research and planning; and (6) Public information.

COMMUNITY MENTAL HEALTH CENTERS

The Fact Sheet issued by NIMH states: "A center is not necessarily a new or separate building. It may be a wing added to a general hospital or to a clinic, or to another mental health facility in the community.

"Basically, the Mental Health Center is a program of mental health services in the community, in one or more facilities, under a unified system of care.

"The purpose of the Center is to provide a varied range of coordinated mental health services in the community.

"Through the Center's program, a patient will find the type of care he needs when he needs it, as close to his home as possible.

"Through the Center's program, the Community also strengthens its resources for prevention of the mental illness."

The Fact Sheet also states the services that must be provided in order to qualify for Federal funds:

1. *In-patient Care.* This unit offers treatment to patients needing 24-hour care.

2. *Out-patient Care.* This unit offers treatment programs for adults, children, and families.
3. *Partial Hospitalization.* This unit offers, at least, day care and treatment for patients able to return home evenings and weekends. Night care may also be provided for patients able to work, but in need of further care or without suitable home arrangements.
4. *Emergency Care.* Twenty-four hour emergency service is available in one of the three units named above.
5. *Consultation and Education.* The Center staff offers consultation and education to community agencies and professional personnel.

These are the required services. Other recommended services are:

1. *Diagnostic Service.* This service provides diagnostic evaluation, and may include recommendations for appropriate care.
2. *Rehabilitative Service.* This service includes both social and vocational rehabilitation. It offers, for those who need them, services such as prevocation testing, guidance counseling, and sometimes job placement.
3. *Precare and Aftercare.* This service provides screening of patients prior to hospital admission, and home visiting before and after hospitalization. Follow-up services for patients are available in out-patient clinics, or in foster homes or halfway houses.
4. *Training.* This program provides training for all types of mental health personnel.
5. *Research and Evaluation.* The Center may establish methods for evaluating the effectiveness of its program. It may also carry out research into mental illness, or cooperate with other agencies in research.

Among other pertinent facts stated by the Fact Sheet are:

"In the Center program, a patient can move easily from one type of treatment to another as his needs change. Treatment at any time will be appropriate to the course of his illness. This is called 'continuity of care.' It represents the most advanced psychiatric thinking and research concerning care of the mentally ill. It is the key concept of the mental health centers program.

"The word 'community' in regulations for Federal aid applies to areas of 'not less than 75,000 and not more than 200,000 persons.' "

LOCAL CLINICAL SERVICES

The Federal Government, therefore, has established a model, and the states and communities are tailoring their services to fit this model. Many communities, however, were already in business with clinical services that included some or all of the above elements, and these had taken on a variety of forms. It was mentioned earlier in this chapter that the trend is moving toward more short-term, intensive therapy in general hospitals and community clinics. Typical of one of the better programs, where the general hospital serves as the mental health center, is that of New York City's Lincoln Hospital and the Albert Einstein College of Medicine with which it is affiliated. Describing this program, Maya Pines[2] says:

> The plan is roughly analogous to a military medical scheme. At the front lines are neighborhood service centers (supported by a grant from the Poverty Program), which serve as first aid stations. Functioning as a kind of field hospital is the free mental health clinic at Lincoln Hospital. The base hospital—for those who cannot be treated on an ambulatory basis—remains a long ambulance ride away, in Jacobi Hospital, Albert Einstein's major teaching center. There the patient may be hospitalized for a short time, or sent on to a state institution for longer treatment. Eventually Lincoln expects to set up a "day hospital" of its own, in which psychiatric patients may spend the whole day, going home to their families only at night. But even without this service, it is believed that this program will cut in half the number of patients who actually need to be hospitalized.

USING NONPROFESSIONAL WORKERS

These neighborhood "first-aid stations" are staffed by local nonprofessional people who understand the problems and the

[2] Maya Pines, "The Coming Upheaval in Psychiatry," *Harper's Magazine*. Reprinted from the October 1965 issue by permission of the author. Copyright © 1965 by Harper's Magazine, Inc.

language of those who seek aid. The decor and general climate of these stations have a local flavor and tend to invite local confidence. The staff workers are understanding neighbors who have been given a short period of training and continuing in-service instruction. Much of their work is of a social welfare, homemaking, and referral nature, which frequently prevents more serious "breaks." They help talk out and work out the client's mental-emotional problems which, again, may prevent accumulation and a later breakdown. Pine's story continues:

> Regardless of the staff's background, "we all do the same thing here," Dr. Boyajian says, "with the exception of giving out medicines." Not only the psychiatrists, psychologists, and social workers, but also the nurses see patients. "Why not—pretty soon we'll let the aides do it." The nurses get on-the-job supervision, and also take part in seminars on group and family therapy. . . .
>
> Once a staff member has seen as much of a family as possible he discusses the case briefly with Dr. Boyajian and other members of the team—psychologist, social worker, or nurse—to decide on the next steps. . . .
>
> After the initial interview no more than six sessions of psychotherapy are allowed each patient or family. . . .
>
> He also pointed out that the traditional forms of psychotherapy would be of little use to the majority of troubled people in the area—people overwhelmed by unemployment, high infant mortality, juvenile delinquency, or other evils of slum life. For them, the most effective therapy may well be the kind of emergency treatment and practical assistance offered by the clinic and the service centers. Help given in a time of crisis may prevent the breakdown, which leaves no alternative but commitment to a state institution.
>
> For people who need further help after the crisis is past, and for patients recently discharged from state hospitals, the clinic runs two large groups—one Spanish, the other English speaking. Each group consists of about fifteen to twenty patients, and meets once a week with a psychiatrist and a nurse. These sessions are extremely informal—patients walk around, drink coffee, or even sew while taking part in the discussion. (p. 57).

This broad based program may be indicative of future metropolitian community developments.

A MODERN STATE HOSPITAL

The state mental hospital, however, is not being eliminated, but refashioned. The new state hospital in Fort Logan, Colorado opened in 1961 to serve the Denver Metropolitan area of 900,000 people. It focuses on short-term, intensive treatment, and provides facilities for some 3000 patients with a 400-bed capacity. "The treatment staff has achieved this by providing care of patients in halfway houses, night hospitals, evening hospitals, family-care homes, out-patient follow-up and day hospitals. Since this is the only State hospital facility for Denver's metropolitan area, approximately half the patients are originally admitted to the in-patient services, but are quickly transferred to the day hospital or another of the services available.

". . . There is a program for alcoholics, and plans call for in the future establishment of services for children and adolescents and a medical-surgical geriatric unit of 112 beds.

"The median length of a patient's stay is 100 days, and during Fort Logan's first 18 months of operation, readmissions were 70 percent of admissions."[3]

JOINT MUNICIPAL PROGRAM

The Kansas City (Missouri) Psychiatric Receiving Center is an example of an urban mental health center supported jointly by Federal, municipal and voluntary funds. It is operated by the Greater Kansas City Mental Health Foundation, a nonprofit organization which contracts with the city to supply mental health services to the indigent, as part of the general hospital system. The Foundation also provides diagnostic and treatment services to children and conducts an extensive training and research program. For example, police officers attend a 12-hour course on understanding the mentally ill and professional training is given to psychiatric residents and fellows, medical students, nurses, social workers and psychologists.

[3] This report and the three following were taken from *The Comprehensive Community Mental Health Center*, Public Health Service Publication No. 1137, April, 1964.

An important part of the service is the day hospital, which most patients use fewer than five days per week. This treatment program averages 22 days, spread over six weeks. In-patient care is designed to keep the ill functioning as normally as possible, even to washing and ironing their own clothing. In addition to an out-patient service which offers a wide variety of individual and group therapies, there is a medication clinic which offers brief interviews—from five to 30 minutes.

CHURCH AND COMMUNITY CENTER

Church and community joined hands in Elkhart, Indiana, a city of about 60,000 population, to build the Oaklawn Psychiatric Center, a nonprofit private center which emphasizes involvement of patients in community life. Chiefly a day hospital with a highly flexible program, it offers 24-hour-care in the Elkhart General Hospital and a community home program in which private families provide housing for out-of-town patients. There is a broad range of activities and a prevocational program at the Center, supplemented by the facilities of the local YMCA, YWCA and other recreational agencies. There is an out-patient program, children's study and treatment services, family therapy, 24-hour emergency service, diagnosis and evaluation, consultation to agencies, courts and schools, individual consultation to physicians and ministers, who also may be involved in the treatment process, and seminars and workshops for ministers.

The center is available to the entire community, but was originally projected as a service to members of the Mennonite Church in an area which offered little psychiatric service. Elkhart was chosen for the site after a survey because of the readiness of the community welfare agencies and schools for such a facility. The Church of the Brethren asked to join as an official sponsor, and Elkhart community leaders helped in developing plans.

RURAL AREA PROGRAM

Within a thirty-mile radius of Poughkeepsie, New York, most of the inhabitants live in small towns or rural areas. They, with the residents of Poughkeepsie itself, receive community based treatment for mental illness at the Dutchess County Unit of the Hudson River State Hospital.

As an example of the close relationship among individuals and agencies responsible for treatment in the community, the operation of the Dutchess County Unit of the hospital is significant because of the liaison which exists between the hospital and the Mental Health Board of the county. The psychiatrist who directs the unit at the hospital can integrate its program to the needs of the citizens, since he also holds the post of county mental health director and is therefore familiar with the comprehensive needs of the area.

From its inception, the unit staff set out to ascertain what proportion of the patients admitted there could be cared for by means other than full hospitalization, when a prediagnostic screening service was available. With the cooperation of the local medical society, the unit physicians agreed to see patients either in their homes, the hospital, or elsewhere in the community to determine whether or not hospitalization was necessary.

Further cooperation was forthcoming from the out-patient clinic operated by the County Mental Health Board, whose staff aided in determining the proper treatment for the individual patient—when admitted to one unit—in clinic, in day hospital, or in-patient service.

Under this arrangement, of the first 700 patients who received the prediagnostic screening, only 25 percent were admitted to the hospital for 24-hour care; 33 percent were admitted to the day hospital and 42 percent remained in the community.

The Dutchess County Unit, housed in its own building on the grounds of the State hospital, treats approximately 450 patients at any one time, and has achieved effective community treatment results, even though 35 percent of the patients are aged 65 or more.

SPECIAL CHILD TREATMENT

The NIMH Office of Biometry released figures showing that in the school population of several cities, 7 to 12 percent had emotional problems serious enough to need professional help. In 1963, about 23,000 youngsters under 18 received treatment in state and county mental hospitals, approximately 10,000 of whom were under 15. Also, of the nation's approximately 1,000 mental health clinics (1963), somewhat less than one-fourth were child guidance clinics. Only 32 percent of the 295,000 patients under 18 seen at out-patient clinics were treated.

Arrill and Braun[4] of the NIMH research services say:

> Of primary concern to NIMH are those community programs which accelerate the development of alternatives to hospitalization of emotionally disturbed and mentally ill youngsters; the use of nonpsychiatric physicians in treatment, and the use of therapeutic-educational techniques in residential settings, in child guidance clinics and in schools.
>
> The nursery school as a treatment resource for the emotionally disturbed preschooler is in an early stage of exploration. A project at the Putnam Children's Center in Boston is working with the antisocial or predelinquent preschooler. An earlier project at the Center reported the efficacy of using the nursery school alone as a treatment modality with children with less serious developmental problems. The East Bay Activity Center in Oakland, California and the University of North Carolina are exploring the potentials of group therapy with psychotic preschoolers. Psychiatric day care for disturbed children and adolescents is also receiving increased attention in many parts of the country.
>
> Superior (Wisconsin), and New Rochelle and Elmont (New York) are three communities which, with project grant support, have devised ways of helping seriously ill youngsters return to the normal classroom setting without removing them from their homes and environment. These public school systems are "teacher moms" to educate and treat severely emotionally disturbed children who cannot be handled in regular classrooms. The key to progress appears to be the one-to-one relationship with the child who is offered warmth and affection; for example, the "teacher-mom" holds the child on her lap when she thinks this is necessary. (pp. 21–23).

---

[4] Mildred B. Arrill and Samuel J. Braun, "Program for Emotionally Disturbed Children," Reprint from *Childhood Education*, September 1965, Association for Childhood Educ. Internat., Washington, D.C. Used with permission.

Project Re-ED, described in Chapter 11, is another of these special projects. These bode well for future treatment of emotionally disturbed children; but with these, there will remain the small percentage who are too seriously crippled for out-patient or therapeutic-educational treatment. For these children residential treatment is necessary.

RESIDENTIAL TREATMENT CENTERS

Few such centers designed and operated specifically for young children and adolescents exist, and they are expensive. But in view of the years of productive service that remain to the child successfully treated, the returns far exceed the cost. Bert Kruger Smith says (Sutherland and Smith, 1965, pp. 115-121): "What, exactly, is this residential treatment center? We have seen that it should be used for only the tiny percentage of children who cannot benefit from care while living at home, in a foster home, or in a nonmedical institution. . . . It is the 'evening children' who go to the residential treatment centers. They are the ones whose retreat has been so far or whose aggressions are so intense, that they cannot be reached through the channels of home or school or out-patient clinic. . . ." Smith quotes these treatment sources:

> . . . provides a therapeutically planned group living situation within which individual psychotherapeutic approaches are integrated. It offers the child support for growth, with individual psychiatric treatment according to individual needs, and provides appropriate facilities for schooling, recreation, and other activities. All these functions are typically carried out by personnel from the disciplines of psychiatry, psychology, nursing, education, and social work, and by other personnel. . . . (American Psychiatric Association, 1957, p. 2).
>
> But in our treatment efforts which try to embrace the child's total life, we have opportunities for insight into the workings of personality development that fall somewhere between what the artist and analyst can offer us. Because we live with the children twenty-four hours a day, we do not have to rely on symbolic substitutes for events that took place

> in the past to be able to understand what may have happened at that time. We can observe directly how those past experiences influence present behavior. But much more important is the fact that we observe and even participate in all activities which currently form the child's life. We see (and are often part of) the experience that brings about significant reactions. (Bettelheim, 1950, p. 67).
>
> The children treated there have often been discussed primarily in terms of unmet needs. They have been described as incorrigible, untreatable, have been ousted from public schools, and rejected by the neighborhood and community. Many of these cases have so baffled the ordinary attempts of psychiatric treatment that their diagnoses have been relegated to the catch-all nosological waste basket. They are labeled with obscure and nonverifiable organic defects, such as "constitutional psychopath." (Reid and Hagan, 1952).

HOSPITAL SERVICES INADEQUATE

It can easily be seen from these statements that the typical mental hospital is neither designed nor staffed to provide adequate treatment for such disturbed children. Smith further states: "Among the direct services which the National Organization for Mentally Ill Children suggests for the unified planning for emotionally disturbed children are: the development and extension of community-based out-patient day care, and residential treatment facilities for mentally ill children; publically subsidized 'halfway houses' for children not yet ready for or discharged from residential treatment centers which are under state hospitals or voluntary auspices; sheltered workshops, vocation guidance and placement services for the mentally ill adolescent and young adult, the assumption of responsibility by all 50 states in the Union for the public education for mentally ill children who can be maintained in the community; a local program to give parents daily relief from the burden of home care for mentally ill children in communities which have not yet developed adequate day treatment facilities; and early case finding and prevention of mental illness in children through a program of education and collaboration with general medicine, pediatrics, and people working in the field of early childhood education." (p. 121).

COMMUNITY CARE PREFERRED

In relation to all the above services, a spokesman for the U.S. Public Health Service says:[5]

> It is the idea of comprehensive treatment, provided in the community for all who need it, which becomes a new concept and a new challenge. Each community mental health center will provide the essential elements of comprehensive services. Patients will no longer be fitted into a treatment pattern, but rather the treatment will be individually tailored to the patient's needs, as he progresses from early diagnosis through a continuity of treatment and back to a productive life in his community, without the harmful effects of isolated institutional hospital residence.
>
> In a large, traditional mental hospital, even the most enlightened admission procedures submit frightened people to a series of events which cause them to ask not only "Where am I?" but also "Who am I?" at a time when they are least able to find their own answers to those basic questions.
>
> Community mental health centers, in contrast, can take the edge off the shock of that first day of treatment and go on from there to help the patient help himself. Because the center is situated in the patient's home community, his own family physician may continue to see him and to participate in his treatment. Since the comprehensive centers include several kinds of care and treatment, the patient can receive the sort of treatment he needs when he needs it, in surroundings which are familiar to him. And, because he never leaves his community, the patient need not return to it. . . .
>
> Some patients need not even give up their jobs during treatment. In some of the treatment programs, patients are absent from work for a period averaging anywhere from eight or nine days to a month, and this sick leave can be handled as it is for any other kind of medical care.
>
> For the mentally disturbed mother of a family, treatment in her community can mean the difference between the breakup of the family and the maintenance of its continuity since, in many instances, she will be able to continue to assume at least a part of her family responsibilities.

[5] Public Health Service Publication No. 1137, April 1964, pp. 5,6.

> Equally important is the fact that in addition to family physicians, the clergymen of the community, the lawyers, the health and welfare agency staffs, the public health nurses, the teachers and other guardians of mental health can consult with the center's professional staff to aid in serving individual patients about whom they share concern, as well as to add to their own knowledge of mental illness and mental health through formal and informal classes and meetings presented by the center's staff.

THE CLINIC STAFF

Since much paper work is required in a mental health clinic (community center or hospital), we can assume that the clinic has the necessary secretarial help. We are interested only in the professional or personal service staff. Clinical psychologists and psychiatric social workers do most of the actual personal service in most clinics. The psychologist tests, diagnoses, makes evaluation reports, and engages in individual or group therapy. The social worker prepares a case history when requested, deals especially with relationships between patient and family, employer, and community; and he (she) also may engage in therapy or individual and family counseling. The psychiatrist is at the top of the ladder. He makes final diagnosis, prescribes treatment, and generally supervises.

The number of these professionals maintained on the staff depends on the funds and case load. There are rarely enough of them. The very small clinic may have only a psychologist or psychiatric social worker with a psychiatrist available for occasional consultation. More often there would be found one or two psychologists, a psychiatric social worker, and a psychiatrist who may be on a full- or half-time basis. The large clinic (or Center) will have several of these professionals in addition to one or more nurses and one or more research specialists, which may include a statistician, a biochemist, and a sociologist. In the large mental health center the staff will also have special therapists: occupational therapists, physical therapists, recreational therapists, vocation counselors, and various aides and technicians.

In California, since the passage of the Short-Doyle Act in 1957, state supported local or community mental health clinics were integrated with the nearest state mental hospital. Thus, the hospital, with these other clinics or "centers," serves as a large community Mental Health Center in keeping with the Federal Act of 1963. Following is a short description of staff and functions in one of these. The normal patient population has been about 5200.

Facility. As a direct result of administrative and legislative action in 1965, Camarillo State Hospital is the regional center of an area which includes such facilities as the Los Angeles Mental Hygiene Clinic, the Los Angeles Day Treatment Center, and branch clinics in Los Angeles County. This reorganized catchment region is known as the South Coast Service Area. It is an implementation of the current philosophy that a maximum effort should be expended for the treatment of the patient in the local community and to shield him from the effects of institutionalization as much as possible. . . . Among the Hospital's considerable resources are the nationally outstanding Children's Division of 170 beds, an annex containing a Day Hospital and an After-Care Clinic, a proposed Adolescent Center of 150 beds, and a unique closed-circuit T.V. studio. . . .

Staff. There are 26 staff psychology positions at Camarillo State Hospital, two at Los Angeles Mental Hygiene Clinic and one at the Los Angeles Day Treatment Center. . . .

Program. The psychologist utilizes a variety of treatment modalities in his work, such as individual and group therapy, and takes an active part in maintaining a treatment milieu on the ward. In addition to these traditional services, the psychologist is encouraged to innovate and to experiment with new treatment techniques that will contribute either directly or indirectly to the improvement of the patient population. He also has ample opportunity to teach in a number of in-service training programs, and to serve as a psychology consultant, both within the hospital and for nearby community agencies; staff participation in the direction of community planning and demonstration is being given high priority. . . .

Another California hospital of similar size and service reported: The total full- and part-time staff consists of 20 psychiatrists, 29 physicians, 24 psychiatric residents, 20 psychologists,

33 social workers, 20 rehabiliation and occupational therapists, 129 registered nurses, 914 psychiatric technicians, and 310 positions in administration, dental laboratory, clerical, industrial and other areas.

NEW INSIGHTS AND METHODS

Community-psychiatry and -psychology are coming into focus with the new comprehensive community program. Services are being expanded to people of all social categories. This expansion program calls for new insights and methods in diagnosis and treatment, and for a greater breadth of training, with courses that include economics, sociology, local government, the humanities, and religion. Following are some of the highlights of the 1966 Convention of the American Psychiatric Association:[6]

> For the first time in history, the American Psychiatric Association staged a session called General Systems Theory (GST). . . . The concept of systems theory is a slippery one when it comes to human behavior, but, as one psychiatrist said, perhaps its appeal is that "it is so beautifully vague."
>
> Vague or not, systems theory has an impressive list of pioneers to its name such as Drs. Karl Menninger and Roy Grinker, and the movement is gaining considerable momentum.
>
> As it applies to society, GST is basically a change of focus, said Dr. William Gray of the Massachusetts General Hospital. Rather than focusing on one thing, as on an individual in psychoanalysis, it focuses on many things, particularly on the confrontation between those things.
>
> Each unit, whether it be a human being, a family, a newspaper, a chain of newspapers, a city, a nation, is a system (with subsystems). How these units interact when they come face to face is a test of how well or ill the system is. Therefore, the confrontation (or interface), if it is out of whack, is the thing needing adjustment.
>
> In a community center run with GST, said Dr. Frederick Duhl of Brookline, Mass., a man on his first visit would be questioned for medical, social, psychological and family data.

[6] From "New Job for Psychiatry," *Science News,* Vol. 89, No. 22 (May 29, 1966). Used with permission.

The goal would be to discover all of his disrupted interfaces then arrange integrated treatment. Perhaps the man would have to change his attitude to live in the society.

The dangers of community health centers, said Dr. Duhl, are that they may become fossilized, that treatment will not truly be transdisciplinary, and that psychiatrists, social workers, medical specialists, sociologists, will remain specialists, as they have been for the past century, resulting in fragmented services and sliced up citizens.

NEW DIAGNOSTIC METHODS

With respect to new and broadened diagnostic procedures, Dr. Robert Reiff[7] argues to the effect that while conventional diagnostic procedures (the clinical battery of tests) are valid for their conventional use, they provide descriptive statements about the psychodynamic factors that are at work within the individual. He feels that this is not adequate for the new comprehensive community service which is adding new dimensions and a new treatment technology, which moves out beyond the organic and psychodynamic factors, to a complex repertoire of behavioral and social factors in interaction. He says:

> . . . The focus is not so much on how the patient is *reacting* and what his defense mechanisms are, but on how he is *acting*, and what his coping mechanisms are. In this kind of a community mental health program, the traditional clinical battery is of little or no use in its traditional form. While the traditional battery is an excellent instrument for ascertaining or predicting how a patient will *react* to a situation, it can tell us little or nothing about how a patient will *act* in a particular situation. In place of the old questions such as: will he act out? will he withdraw? will he become depressed? . . . etc., we now have a whole host of new questions we need answers to about a particular patient in order to properly intervene, questions such as: can he hold a job? will he take his medicine regularly? . . . can he live up to group norms at work? etc. In planning community mental health intervention with its focus on rehabilitation rather than personality change, we need answers to

[7] From "The Usefulness of Diagnostic Tools in a Community Mental Health Setting," a paper read at the Annual Convention of the American Psychological Association, New York, September 1966. Used with permission.

> questions for which the traditional clinical battery was never intended. New instruments will have to be developed. . . . Social adjustment scales and coping behavior inventories may be the more appropriate tests for the future. . . .

CLOSE PSYCHIATRIC HOSPITALS

In a widely circulated interview, Dr. Werner Mendel[8] presented the challenging argument that most psychiatric hospitals could be closed both for economy and for the better treatment of patients, and that only the so-called "dangerous" be committed to hospitals, and that these are relatively few and difficult to determine. He said: "Our studies of 3,000 psychotic patients over a period of five years indicate that the shorter the hospital intervention, the more likely the patient is to function adequately outside the hospital.

"With new psychiatric drugs and techniques there simply are no catatonics, no severe cases that do not respond to treatment, except for those who have been in hospitals so many years that nothing can help them. Even these few cases should not be in mental institutions—they should be treated with drugs at home or in medical, not psychiatric, wards.

"We have found that taking a patient into a psychiatric hospital further complicates his disorganization and in no way prepares him for resuming his life in the community."

Dr. Mendel thinks that most patients have been admitted to mental hospitals as a convenience for physicians and for social reasons, if the patient is unable to find support in the community. If this support is given by a variety of agencies and counselors, very few would need hospitalization.

The diagnostic and treatment procedures suggested in these three reports mark goals toward which the community mental health services are directed.

> With new findings and procedures, changing programs, one session in the study of this chapter may be given to a panel discussion of 4 or 5

[8] From an AP news release published in many newspapers, April 1967. Used with permission.

principal features of community mental health services, supplementing the above material with the latest available. Consult your local NAMH chapter or write to NAMH or NIMH National Headquarters.

USING VOLUNTEERS

From their beginning, Churches have been manned very largely by volunteer workers. More recently, many other agencies have employed "volunteers" to help with administrative detail and clerical work, and the "gray ladies," as volunteer nurses aides, have proved their worth. The "volunteer" in the mental hospital or community mental health center is something else. She (mostly they are women) is proving her worth as a valuable member of the therapeutic team.

The state hospitals of Illinois have been making especially effective use of their "Ladies in Pink," their Volunteer Service Program (VSP) since the early 1950's. These volunteers work directly with patients, and under supervision they provide care, help to entertain, and engage in friendly visitation. They represent the community which the mental patient often dreads. Thus, they are intermediaries, mediating the community concern and love— "they needn't run away, the community wants them." Dr. Otto Bettag described this work as follows: "I have followed closely the work of the 5000 volunteers who came regularly to serve the 48,000 patients at our eleven state hospitals for the mentally ill and the two schools for the mentally deficient. The Volunteer Services Program is one of the latest aspects in modern psychiatric treatment. In Illinois, it has attracted outstanding civic, church, service and social organizations." (Roberts, 1958, p. 146).

THE WOODLAWN PROGRAM

One of the best descriptions of effective use of volunteers was written by Dr. Conte and Edith Liebes (Sutherland and Smith, 1965, Chapter 11) and will be condensed here. The place is Woodlawn Psychiatric Hospital, a relatively small hospital but high in quality, in Dallas, Texas. It is mostly a short-term treatment hospital and also operates as the teaching hospital for the University of Texas Southwestern Medical School.

Every person who is a member of the hospital staff—including the volunteer—is involved in the treatment of the patient. This implies that the volunteer is a therapist. She can be effective in her job if she can accept the patient and if she understands that his aggressiveness is not directed toward her. She also needs to possess enough self-understanding that she can control her own fear and hostility. . . .

The field of occupational therapy lends itself well to an understanding of the role of the Volunteer. Contrary to once popular belief, occupational therapy is not a time-filling procedure. Rather, it supplies the therapist with a tool (the actual making of something) through which she may establish an avenue to relationship with a given patient. While the finished product is not important, the relationship is!

This also is precisely the role of the volunteer. She performs many services in the hospital which are real, valued, and important; but by far her greatest function is that of providing an avenue of communication and relationship with the sick person whose illness reflects his difficulty in similar relationships in the past.

. . . The program at Woodlawn itself has developed some unique features. They are: (1) The method of selecting and orienting volunteers, (2) The utilization of volunteers as team members, and (3) The application of the volunteers' skills as research aides.

Volunteers seeking to serve at Woodlawn fell into three following groups:

A. Women who had acquired an interest in mental health and who were eager for community service.
B. Women who had mental health problems in their own families and had a specific need to discover more about case management and treatment.
C. Women who had experienced psychiatric hospitalization themselves and who seemed to feel that working with the mentally ill was evidence of their own newly found stability.

Research, vital in providing knowledge about mental illness, often has to be curtailed because of limited time which various staff members have. . . .

For example, in one study a physician interviewed a group of patients, each one for half an hour. Volunteers and staff members hidden behind one-way glass observed carefully all the patients, not knowing which were in the control group and the experimental. . . .

Interestingly enough, the volunteer rating sheets were almost identical with those of the observing staff members, which led the research team to believe that volunteer evaluations were as accurate as those of the professional judges. . . . As research aides, the volunteers may thus make possible the conducting of many studies which up to now have been ruled out because there was not enough staff time available. . . .

VOLUNTEER LAY-COUNSELORS

Another type of volunteer service that may well be of greater significance, especially associated with the newer comprehensive Community Mental Health Centers, is that of the volunteer lay-counselor. I have had a working acquaintance with several juvenile court programs where a well-supervised organization of volunteer counseling prevented many delinquent boys and girls from having to be committed to delinquency "schools." My previously stated observations are stated below. (Roberts, 1958, pp. 149, 150).

Except in cases of deeply fixed perversions, which are relatively few and seldom placed on probation, the deeply concerned lay-counselor, who serves as a volunteer with the court, is often the most effective worker in the social rehabilitation of the young offender—your problem child and mine. It is easier for him to establish rapport and empathy with the suspicious problem child. His is not a paid service or a professional duty, but is a service of love that is more likely to be accepted by the delinquent. He represents the concerned society, which offender, deep down inside, longs to be a part of and accepted by, not the dominating society symbolized by police and courts against which his resentment is directed. These lay counselors need not be professionally trained psychologists or case workers. They do not diagnose or prescribe, but establish a problem-solving relationship. They should be men and women with better than average education and and intelligence, who perhaps have some knowledge of psychology and a lot of understanding of kids; who are respected in their communities; whose experience will lend practical help in the circumstantial aspects of the child's problem; and who will take supervision and inservice training provided by the probation office. Church laymen, teachers, members of the various service clubs, AAUW,* and other community organizations can be enlisted by the local welfare associations as volunteer counselors in any community or county.

Furthermore, a parallel procedure can be developed with relation to mental illness. A sizable proportion of the patients now in mental hospitals could be treated successfully at home in their respective communities with the type of volunteer counseling service described above and the fellowship program described in Chapter 6. Like delinquency, mental illness is basically a failure in love. And, as was stated regarding delinquency, the cure is not solely a matter of accurate diagnosis and scientifically prescribed treatment. These have their place—perhaps an essential place in the more serious cases. However, while medication, shock therapy, and the professional service that only a psychiatrist can give are essential in many cases and helpful in others, it is now being widely recognized, even among psychiatrists themselves, that the essential cure lies in acceptance, love, the restored capacity to establish interpersonal relationships based on love. The community that has a system of winning these troubled souls into one or another of its little redeeming fellowships and provides a big brother, big sister counseling service motivated by love and supervised by competent professionals can increase the effectiveness of its limited psychiatric service thirtyfold or sixtyfold or a hundredfold.

The last statement was, of course, figurative; but it is literally true to a smaller degree. A decade later, it is a hopeful sign to see the trend moving rapidly in the direction or decentralization, and more local community, out-patient treatment, and greater use of volunteers in therapy. We can proceed much further in this direction.

---

* American Association of University Women.

THE BIG THREE

There are several organizations in the community that serve the cause of mental health in one way or another; the various business men's service clubs, labor unions and personnel departments, the PTA, the AAUW, Junior League, YMCA, YWCA, YMHA, Boys Club, Scouts, and especially the local chapters of NAMH. The three agencies with the greatest potential and responsibility are the School, the Church, and the Community Mental Health Center. A large number and variety of local churches or parishes, many schools, and several clinics will be found in each community. The combined and thoroughly integrated mental health services of these three institutions, through some type of interboard arrangement, will reduce the incidence of serious psychosocial disorders to a small fraction of their present level.

The school has virtually all children who are not defectives and already in the care of a special agency or clinic. By the time children reach school many have already developed more or less serious emotional and social problems. Others become seriously disturbed during their school years. The majority of these, however, are not so extreme that they can either be prevented or successfully treated by the school. This can be accomplished when school teachers are thoroughly oriented in mental hygiene, when the school is adequately staffed with supporting personnel (psychologist, counselor, speech therapist, etc.), and when in each metropolitan community or area a special school for the seriously disturbed child is provided. Therefore, the work of the school may be both prophylactic and ameliorative. It can greatly reduce the load that otherwise would fall on the Center.

The Church also has contact with a large majority of children even though that contact has been rather tenuous in many cases. The Church has a further advantage of having contact with these children from birth and of having the opportunity to establish a more intimate relationship with parents and the home. The Church of the past and present has fallen far short of actualizing its great mental health potential, which was always an indirect concern. But there are many indications that its leadership is more cognizant of this opportunity and responsibility now than it was in any past century, and is making rapid progress in this area.

Most of this chapter has been devoted to the Community Mental Health Center. We shall say in summary that it is the chief treatment agent for the more serious cases of psychosocial disorder, through its various special clinics and ameliorative activities for in-patients, out-patients, day-care and night-care patients, and special divisions for adults, youth, and young children. As schools and churches more fully actualize their mental health potentials, the Mental Health Center load will be greatly reduced. But there is no foreseeable future, not in many generations, at least, when they can be eliminated.

A 16-mm film entitled "Plan Ahead for Mental Health," prepared by the Nebraska Psychiatric Institute, suggests four lines of defense against mental illness: (1) teachers, clergymen, friends, etc.; (2) psychologists, probation officers, welfare department personnel, etc.; (3) the out-patient psychiatric clinic; and (4) the large psychiatric hospital (in-patient).

Figure 11 is a schematic representation of the community functioning in full capacity in prophylactic and ameliorative mental health service as the writer sees it. In the community, as defined by the Mental Health Act of 1963, several schools, several churches, and several hospitals, clinics and guidance agencies will be found. These agencies which are working together in a closely coordinated program comprise the base of the pyramid, the three corners of the triangle: the School, the Church, and the Mental Health Center. Our interest at this point is in the three-level hierarchy of therapeutic services these agencies may provide.

The first level is comprised of volunteer counselors of the type described on p. 437. The schools would provide several of these from their teaching and administrative staffs. The churches would also provide both clergy and lay members. Several others would be the "volunteers" working with probation office and various clinics. Altogether, the community could provide from one- to two- or three-hundred of these volunteer therapists, each working one or two "disturbed" persons, the less serious, of course.

The school psychologists, speech therapists, some of the more highly trained guidance counselors, and some of the pastor counselors have adequate professional training to serve at the

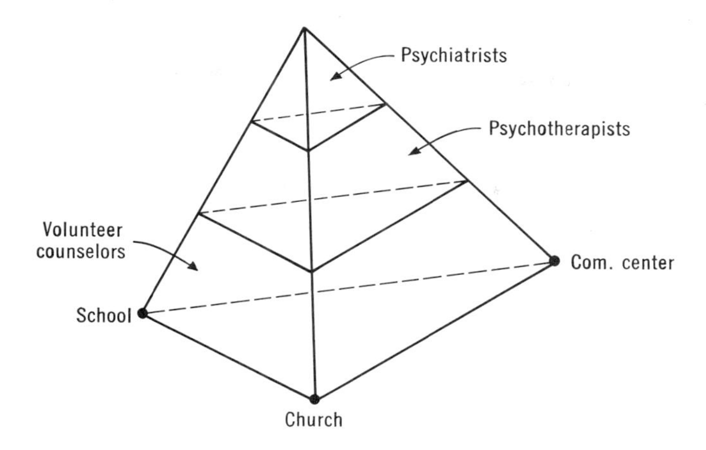

Figure 11. A schematic representation of the major health agencies and levels of service.

second level as psychotherapists. The majority at this level, however, would be the psychologists and psychiatric social workers who staff the various clinics. At the top would be the psychiatrists.

The Community Mental Health Director and his chief assistants, would coordinate, direct, and supervise this program. A working force of this order would catch most cases before their condition became too serious and help guide them back to effectual living, leaving fewer and fewer patients for the professional psychotherapists and psychiatrists.

MISCELLANEOUS PROJECTS

CAMPING

The value of the camping experience for wholesome character development has long been utilized by a variety of child and youth organizations. Camping has been mentioned as an important feature of the Re-ED project. It can, and in the future will, be used more extensively and effectively by training schools for delinquents. The Texas State Hospital system took a pioneering step in 1956, when it sent 180 mental patients at the rate of 60 a week to a camping project. During the first four summers, 505 patients from six hospitals participated. They began by spending one week in camp and slowly moved it up to three weeks. The following report is adopted from Glenn Ramsey (Sutherland and Smith, 1965, Chapter 14).

Some Operating Principles: (1) The staff recognizes that they carry the full responsibility for the over-all care and welfare of each patient; (2) To create a more democratic atmosphere and remove signs of hospital authority, the staff wears sports clothing instead of white uniforms; (3) Enhancement of the personal identity of patients is attempted by calling each one by name; (4) Freedom of choice is permitted in as many situations and activities as possible; (5) Freedom of communication between campers and staff is encouraged; (6) Social forces which make for conformity and adherence to camp rules are somehow generated; (7) The attitude of the staff is that campers can be trusted to care for themselves and fellow campers; (8) The campers are made to feel that they have a real part in determining the organization and functioning of the camp; (9) An easy family-like relationships is encouraged; (10) The staff and patients develop strong group restraints against unacceptable group behavior; (11) Mutual responsibility of one patient for another is fostered by a buddy system and other means; (12) The staff take the attitude that all patients are physically, mentally, and emotionally well enough to participate and to enjoy camping activities.

Selection. The selection of the patients for the camping program is the responsibility of the superintendent of each hospital. The state medical director has suggested that patients selected be those who are nearing the end of their hospitalization. These criteria would, in general, eliminate patients who are physically handicapped, suffering from gross brain damage, subject to seizures, mental defectives, or extremely disturbed individuals. In actual practice, however, some patients who were intellectually subnormal and others who were chronic long-term custodial cases were sent.

Activities. The range of activities offered to the patient-campers is exactly the same offered at this site to any other camping group. This includes hiking, fishing, swimming, handicrafts, nature study, field sports, small group cookouts in the hills, large group barbeques and fish fries, or simply sitting and enjoying the beauty and wonders of the natural setting. Free-choice activities fill two hours of each morning and afternoon. After the first few days, only a scattered few have not elected to join some group activity. In the evening, after-dinner programs include group singing, dancing, parties, camp talent shows, movies, insight games, and others. Special Sunday religious services are arranged by the staff and patients.

The basic assumption by the staff is that camping is fun for all, staff and campers alike. The genuine enthusiasm of the staff for each day's activities and events, sooner or later, enlists the active participation of practically all campers in most of each day's events.

Results have been highly satisfactory.

Mrs. Smith (Chapter 13) describes the Texas Camping Plan, and citing the results, says: "Herman might serve as an example of what the camping program can do for patients. In the hospital and when he first came to camp, he was mute and uncooperative. As he started fishing, he also began talking with the other campers. At the end of his week at camp, he was voted the 'Camper Who Has Improved the Most'. . . .

"Or take Linda, a former school teacher who had been in the hospital for eleven years, much of the time combative and confined to a back ward. Tranquilizing drugs had helped her, and she had improved to the point that she was nearly ready for discharge. However, she was still fearful when she arrived at camp. The first night, sitting around the camp fire, she sang a solo. From then on her progress was remarkable. . . .

"Perhaps the patients themselves can give the best evaluation of the camping program and its worth to them. . . ."

Here I feel like a person.

Here we can wisecrack, speak out our thoughts, be gay.

Never had I been more happy and having so much fun than being here . . .

The freedom of being out in the open I consider a real treat.

I feel as though I can go home (hospital) and when I ask the doctor to let me be released or furloughed, as he sees fit, I know I can make the kind of citizen this country needs. . . .

MOVIES AND TV

The field of mass media for communication and education has a direct bearing on psychological behavior. It is a field in which much research is needed to reveal specific ways in which it can be used effectively to promote mental health. Much has been written about the harmful effects of the "comic book" and the violent or sexy TV and movie films on child behavior. But there is little valid proof. They provide entertainment, and entertainment is generally beneficial. Certain studies that appear to be fairly valid indicate that adolescent dating practices have been modeled after screen practices, and cues or techniques for juvenile acts of violence have in some cases been traced to certain movies and TV programs. Whether these actually increase anxiety, hostility, dishonesty, sexual immorality or any other character disorder is not known.

That they have great potential for beneficial and harmful effects is generally believed. Educational TV and the teaching film can be used very effectively to dramatize psychological disorders and their cure. With growing Federal and State financial support and public concern for mental health, we may anticipate increased research and more effective use of these media.

SOCIOECONOMIC CLASS BARRIER

One of the serious problems in implementing the growing mental health concern is in establishing communication, understanding, and mutual trust between middle and lower socioeconomic classes. Most Americans do not like to think in terms of social classes, and most Americans like to think of themselves as middle class, upper middle class, middle middle class, and lower middle class, perhaps, but still middle class. There has developed in this century, a widening rift between a poverty class and an affluent class (most of us) such that two widely different subcultures have formed. The philosophy of mental health and nearly all of its functionnaires are middle class. Large numbers of those who need mental health services are of the lower socioeconomic class. If our schools, churches, and mental health centers, as well as our psychiatrists, psychotherapists, and counselors, are to effectively serve community needs, this rift must be bridged.

We have mentioned the Hollingshead-Redlich book that dealt with this problem. A more specific challenge has been raised by Gursslin, Hunt and Roach.[9] They state: "It is the conviction of the present writers that the phenomenon is not simply a result of an insufficiency of psychiatric facilities and trained professional workers (though neither of these is denied) or of simple ignorance of members of lower strata of society about the existence and value of psychiatric services. Rather, it is our thesis that the problem is rooted in the relationship between the American stratification system with its correlated value orientations, on the one hand, and the philosophic underpinnings of psychiatric practice, on the other. As a consequence, the bare problem posed by the work of the New Haven group and of others is in reality far more difficult to resolve than may initially appear." (p. 213).

TOWARD THE MORE SATISFYING COMMUNITY

The Church and Public School have been criticized for providing service geared chiefly to the middle class. Hollingshead and Redlich wrote their book and shocked behavioral scientists into the realization that our mental health facilities have been largely middle and upper class privileges. During the past decade, the general public became awakened to the realization that many community organizations were by and for the middle class. Not only through its churches and schools but also its many "service" and fraternal clubs, its professional sports, theaters, and many other activities which offered a rich variety of stimuli and experiences conducive to personal growth and self-actualization. But mostly it was the middle class that received the benefit. We had become middle

[9] Reprinted with permission of The Macmillan Company from *Sociology in Use* by Donald M. Valdes and D. G. Dean. © The Macmillan Company 1965. Chapter 24.

class communities. Then came the realization that in most of our communities there are sizable minorities (majorities in some) who are economically and culturally deprived and are thus stunted in their intellectual, emotional and spiritual growth.

OFFICE OF ECONOMIC OPPORTUNITY

This awakening brought sufficient pressure on Congress to pass the Economic Opportunity Act of 1964, commonly referred to as the Antipoverty Act. It established the Office of Economic Opportunity (OEO) of which President Johnson said,[10] ". . . The central problem is to protect and restore man's satisfaction in belonging to a community where he can find security and significance." In addition to several modes of direct financial assistance, some of the principle features are:

1. *The Job Corps*—provides residential centers for young men and women, 16 through 21, in a coordinated program of basic education, skill training and constructive work experience.
2. *The Work-Training Program*—provides full- or part-time work experience and training for youths, 16 through 21, enabling them to stay in or return to school, or increase employability.
3. *The Work-Study Program*—provides part-time employment of college students from low-income families, both on and off campus jobs, thus increasing opportunities for college attendance.
4. *Community Action Programs*—provides financial support for such typical projects as remedial reading, literacy instruction, job training, employment counseling, homemaker services, job development, vocational rehabilitation, health service, and many others as determined by local needs by local leaders. Federal assistance depends on the community's determination to (a) mobilize its own public and private resources, (b) develop programs of sufficient scope and size that promise to eliminate the causes of poverty, (c) involve the poor themselves in developing and operating the antipoverty attacks, and (d) administer and coordinate the community action programs through public or private nonprofit agencies, or a combination of these.

[10] State of the Union Message, 1965.

5. *VISTA* (Volunteers in Service to America)—provides an opportunity for those, 18 and over, to join the War on Poverty. They may work in various health and welfare agencies, in schools, community work in slum areas, on Indian reservations, or with migrants.
6. *Project Headstart*—a special community action program especially designed for culturally deprived (lower socioeconomic classes) preschool children. Its concern is to provide a learning climate of enriched stimuli to motivate these children and help them catch up with the more privileged, assuming that with this start more of them will continue on toward a high level development.

Discussing the topic, titled "Prospects for the Prevention of Mental Illness," Dr. Paul V. Lemkau says:[11]

> The discovery that has, in my estimation, done more to place preventative psychiatry on a firm ground than any other has been that showing the harm done to individuals by understimulation. This furnishes the theory upon which a great deal of the antipoverty program is based. . . .
>
> The implications for action are clear. We are at this time seeing action testing the theory on an unprecedented scale. The antipoverty program insofar as it relates to children is aimed at increasing the stimuli falling upon young children through prekindergarten exposure. For years such stalwart groups as the Child Study Association and, later, the adult education program in the schools have been trying to teach parents, in groups of ten or twenty, how to enrich their childrens lives. Now we are launched on a national program that will attempt not only to influence the parents, but the children as well—and not by tens and twenties, but by the hundreds of thousands. It is frightening to contemplate what will happen if the theory proves wrong! The terminology used in the antipoverty program is largely economic, but the theory is derived from mental hygiene. . . .
>
> So far I have discussed chiefly the prevention of damaging deprivation as a means of preventing some mental illnesses the decrease of which is considered to be of enormous importance to the nation. The coin has an obverse side, however. What has been discussed as *prevention* of illnesses can be

[11] From *Mental Hygiene,* Vol. 50, No. 2, pp. 172–179 (April 1966). Used with permission.

described equally well as an *increase* in mental health, and the program, as the promotion of mental health rather than the prevention of illnesses. . . .

Since this whole program is new and in a state of flux, any detailed description of activities would soon be out-of-date. This movement offers promise and may develop into a very significant community plan of action. I suggest that three or four short student reports on current developments; one covering points 1, 2 and 3 above; another on Community Action Programs, a third on Headstart, and possibly VISTA. Local offices or the federal Office of Economic Opportunity can provide ample material.

SUMMARY

The 1963 Community Mental Health Act gave a new thrust to the whole mental health movement. Funds were allocated and guide lines drawn for a comprehensive program that would reach into every community and every family with a diversity of agencies and treatment procedure. Among the services to be supplied by a Community Center are: (1) in-patient care; (2) out-patient care; (3) emergency care; (4) consultation and education; (5) diagnostic service; (6) rehabilitative service and (7) research.

Treatment trends run toward greater flexibility and diversification, short-term intensive therapy, and from the large mental or psychiatric hospital to the local general hospital and various outpatient clinics. The goal is to keep the patients in the community and as closely related to normal life as possible, by using a variety of agencies and personnel to lend ego-support and guidance. Of special concern is the establishment of treatment centers for children which have a climate and training program more like a home-school combination than a typical hospital ward, with "teacher-moms" and "teacher-counselors" providing most of the care.

In order to meet the broadened service demands of the comprehensive community center, new and more varied diagnostic and treatment procedures are needed, a trans- or multidisciplinary approach. The large corps of volunteer workers from all walks of life would offer a variety of "care" services, help entertain, engage in friendly visitation, and become effective members of the therapy team. They represent the community's concern for the patient and ease his fear of returning to the community. Treatment may be described at three levels: (1) the work of the lay counselor with problems of less serious dynamic disorders; (2) psychotherapy as engaged in by psychologists, psychiatric social workers and certain other professionals; and (3) full scale psychiatry. Conditioned reflex and other "learning" therapy may be placed at the second level.

Public concern has moved from that of preventing and treating mental illness to providing opportunities for the fuller psychosocial development of all. The Economic Opportunity Act was established in 1964 to offer enriched stimuli and growth conducing experiences to the culturally deprived families of the lowest socioeconomic classes. In addition to direct economic aid, the main service channels are: the Job-Corps, the Work-Training Program, the Work-Study Program, and a variety of Community Action Programs of which Project Headstart is of special interest.

GLOSSARY

Nosological. Pertaining to the systematic classification of diseases or characteristics of particular diseases.

Rapport. French—*en rapport*—in close accord. A state of mutual confidence, feeling at ease with, or harmony between counselor and client.

REFERENCES AND SUGGESTED READINGS

ARRILL, MILDRED B. and SAMUEL J. BRAUN, "Program for Emotionally Disturbed Children," *Childhood Education,* Sept., 1965.

BETTELHEIM, BRUNO, *Love is Not Enough,* Glencoe, Ill.: The Free Press, 1950.

HENRY, JULES, *Culture Against Man,* New York: Random House, 1963.

HOLLINGSHEAD, AUGUST and FREDERICK C. REDLICH, *Social Class and Mental Illness,* New York: John Wiley & Sons, Inc., 1958.

PINES, MAYA, "The Coming Upheaval in Psychiatry," *Harper's Magazine,* Vol. 231, (October 1965), 54–60.

REID, JOSEPH H. and HELEN R. HAGAN, "Residential Treatment of Emotionally Disturbed Children," New York: *Child Welfare*, League of America, 1952.

ROBERTS, GUY L., *Where Delinquency Begins*, Richmond: John Knox Press, 1958.

SUTHERLAND, ROBERT I. and BERT KRUGER SMITH, *Understanding Mental Health*, Princeton, N.J.: D. Van Nostrand Co., Inc., 1965.

VALDES, DONALD M. and D. G. DEAN, *Sociology in Use*, New York: The Macmillan Company, 1965.

13 | The Self-Actualizing Person

In this course we have moved from an examination of the human personality and potentiality to the study of man's needs and their satisfaction or frustration; through his psychic defenses and psychosocial failure when too frustrated; and to the types of corrective treatment needed and offered. We then explored the community which girded itself for effective prophylactic and ameliorative action and growth fulfillment. We are now ready to pick up the person who has been cured of his "illness" or who never became ill, and explore the high levels of psychosocial development, moving from the not-sick to the truly well level of life. How does man see himself at his best? What may he attain by way of functional health or wholeness? In this chapter we shall look at the individual in his knowing and experiencing best. The two remaining chapters will explore high psychosocial functioning and its relation to man's family-social and vocational living.

HUMAN DESTINY

THE ANCIENT CONCEPT

Confucius gave the ancient world his concepts of the "superman" long before Nietzche picked it up and propagated it and

Hitler applied it to the Germanic people. The "superman" of each of these had more depth than is portrayed in our modern comic strip Superman. The ancient Greeks set *excellence* as the supreme goal of life—to excel the normal or expected in war, statesmanship, athletics, intellectual or artistic attainment, or in some other significant accomplishment. They wrote songs, epic poems, legends and myths about their heroes—about those who attained the unusual, who excelled, whose activities expressed qualities and capacities that were beyond the norms by which people usually lived. They embroidered the deeds of their heroes, adding a few fanciful episodes for the sake of interest and art. Their concept of excellence often involved behavior traits that modern ethics would judge as being somewhat less than excellent. Nevertheless, these ancient Greeks recognized the high potential in man for excellence of life and anticipated its attainment in their poems and legends.

All the great religions have formulated concepts of what man ought to be which is in contrast with his typical behavior. This is notably true of our Judeo-Christian tradition which, for more than 3,000 years, has made high-level demands on human behavior; and has insisted that man has the high spiritual potential for such a life and is expected to attain it with divine aid. From the Ten Commandments, to the Sermon on the Mount, to the latest formulations of social ethics by modern religious philosophers or theologians, excellence in service and in quality of living has been the constant demand. The voice of "Thou shalt" and "Thou shalt not," though slightly muted by modern moral relativity, has not been silenced. And even though these commands and admonitions have been observed largely in their breach, in those moments of most lucid awareness man still expects this excellence, this something more of himself.

Through science man seeks perfect knowledge of and control over his physical world. Through aesthetics he seeks the perfect ideal in the fine arts. Through his religion, he seeks the perfect moral and spiritual life. (Well, now, he hedges a little at this point.) It is built into the structure of man to feel the need of and seek the attainment of this high excellence, this fullness of maturation, this complete self-actualization. It seems that perfection is the full maturation and expression of one's potentiality, maximum performance in accordance with one's endowments. At times, man becomes afraid of its implications and denies its possibility, but this is only at times. When man is most lucid, and most aware of self, he knows that there can be no other goal. It is the primary motive, the set of the self toward wholeness, the perfecting of his divine-human potentiality.

A MODERN VIEW

In his *Human Destiny*, adjudged by some reviewers as one of the most significant books of the twentieth century, Lecomte du Noüy re-examines the whole concept of evolution. He writes:[1]

> Man, with his present brain, does not represent the end of evolution, but only an intermediary stage between the past, heavily weighed down with memories of the beast, and the future, rich in higher promise. Such is human destiny. (p. 225).
>
> It is, therefore, that which is rarest in man, that which characterizes him specifically and differentiates him from the beast, which seems to have been the true reason for evolution. It is still through evolution that this character must improve and attain a state of perfection hardly conceivable today, but intuitively divined, and so powerfully felt that people have preferred the martyrdom of their bodies to the defilement of their ideals. . . . (p. 227).
>
> . . . Any man in his senses will realize that the cause of man's higher aspirations transcends our scientific concepts. Our rational activities must acknowledge this fact and give it a place in the pattern of our universe. We must recognize the reality of our unaccountable aspirations and the absolute value of the will to surpass ourselves. . . . (p. 233).
>
> The only goal of man should be the attainment of human dignity with all its implications. In other words, all his intellectual acquisitions, all the facilities which society puts at his disposal—schools, universities, libraries, laboratories; all those offered by religion; all the occasions given him to develop his own aptitudes, his work, his leisure must be considered by him as tools destined to improve his personality, his moral self, and to make it progress. . . . (p. 244).
>
> . . . If intelligence alone should rule, all the human traits of which we are proudest, the sense of duty, of liberty, of

[1] From *Human Destiny* by Lecomte du Noüy, Copyright 1947, New York. Used with permission of David McKay Company, Inc.

dignity, of the beauty of disinterested effort, would disappear little by little and fade out into oblivion, until civilization would vanish without even an afterglow. . . . It is the will to surpass oneself, the conviction that it can be done, and the certitude that such is the role of man in evolution which constitutes human law. (p. 253).

The goal of perfect psychosocial attainment as perceived by the founder of the great religions and by an eminent twentieth century biologist may appear to us to be far off. But this is the goal which man, in his most perceptive moments, continues to set for himself. It is to hasten the attainment of this goal that communities across the country are mobilizing their resources in building the newly conceived mental health centers, and churches and schools are submitting themselves to a painful reappraisal and redirection of their resources. They have accepted the du Noüy position that man is a major determiner of his own destiny (evolution) and they are determined to build the kind of communities which, in turn, will build better individuals, and continue the procedure until full mental health, full maturity or perfection, and full self-actualization is attained.

FROM YOUTH TO ADULTHOOD

THE STAGES

The first four of Erik Erikson's eight critical stages of personality or character formation, covering the childhood period, were briefly described in Chapter 6. We shall now examine the other four, since they feature maturation and fullness of growth. These are:

5. *Identity versus identity diffusion.* This coincides particularly with the first half of the adolescent period. Having attained sexual and near physical and intellectual maturity, the youth faces the impending necessity to take his place in the adult world—to identify with others on a different plane than in childhood. Finding himself, becoming himself, establishing self-identity is especialy important and particularly related to

this period. How well it is accomplished is greatly influenced, but not fully determined, by how well he surmounts these earlier stages. And how well he traverses the remainder of his course is especially influenced by this period.

6. *Intimacy versus self-absorption.* Having attained a satisfactory clarity of identity, thus role, in late adolescence and young adulthood, the individual is then confronted with the problem of intimacy versus self-absorption. The struggle for independence turns to the search for interdependence, a freely chosen intimacy and deep involvement. If identity is too diffuse, the individual may suffer too much anxiety to take the risks of deep involvement and choose isolation and self-absorption. What one's position is on this continuum greatly influences his social and vocational roles—the quality or character of productive love and productive work, in the view of Erich Fromm.
7. *Generativity versus stagnation.* By generativity, an admittedly awkward term, Erikson means the capacity to lose oneself, to give fully, in productive or creative vocational, avocational and social activities, the free release of one's talents in responsible work and interpersonal relations. This is the development of early to middle adulthood. Failure in this development stage leaves one at the other end of the continuum, in a state of sterile stagnation.
8. *Integrity versus despair and disgust.* This is final conflict or reorganization period associated with late middle and old age. With the bulk of productive life behind and declining usefulness and death ahead, one is faced with a reappraisal of life and a reorientation of oneself. It is a time of special need to "make sense" out of life and reaffirm one's essential selfhood, and on a somewhat different basis from that during his busily productive years. Having successfully passed through the preceding stages, there normally will be little difficulty at this last stage. Failing, one may succumb to a state of disgust with his present character and role and despair of the future.

The right ends of the four continuums, are the marks of the healthy self-actualizer, and portray the qualities of high-level psychosocial development. At the left are the maladjusted, growth-stunted individuals. Since there is a special break between Nos. 4 and 5, between childhood and adolescence, it is a new beginning and warrants special examination.

THE NEWLY GENERATIVE SELF

In reference to this developmental stage, Erikson (1965, pp. 435-37) says: ". . . . In their search for a new sense of continuity and sameness, some adolescents have to refight many of the crises of earlier years, and they are ever ready to install lasting idols and ideals as guardians of a final identity.

"The integration now taking place in the form of the ego identity is more than the sum of the childhood identifications. It is the inner capital accrued from all those experiences of each successive stage, when successful identification led to a successful alignment of the individual's *basic drives* with his *endowment* and his *opportunities*. In psychoanalysis we ascribe such successful alignments to 'ego synthesis'. . . .

"Ego identity, then, develops out of a gradual integration of all identification, but here, if anywhere, the whole has a different quality than the sum of its parts. Under favorable circumstances children have the nucleus of a separate identity in early life; often they must defend it against any pressure which would make them over-identify with one of their parents. . . ."

Let us extract from these short excerpts some apparent developmental facts and follow their implications a step further. We may especially note the adolescent's tendency to "refight" his earlier crises and the "ego synthesis" which in reality is self acting creatively upon its "childhood identifications" in its new orientation toward an adult world. This is done in order to form a new "integration" and self-identity (the psychoanalytic ego identity) which is more and of a different quality than the sum of its parts.

There is much subjectivity, much self-consciousness, much self-involvement in re-examining former identifications during this period. The purpose of refighting earlier crises is to prepare for adult-dimension identifications and involvements. Self is not merely the product of its past identifications but is especially generative* in the re-creation of a new identity and making new identifications on a new plane. Perhaps at no other period in personal

* I use the term generative in the literal sense of producing, giving forth, initiating actions.

development is the locus of behavior dynamics in the self as apparent as in this. At no other period is person more a subject, more an acting agent, as he struggles for a new self-identity and identification at a new level.

We have not made enough of this in our behavioral sciences and mental hygiene. This is the age, and stage, of the "new birth" of orthodox religion and a new birth in the more humanistic sense of being born into a new level of human identifications and relationships. And self is active, generative, searching, committing itself. How well or how poorly the young adolescent negotiated the earlier stages has a large influence on the generative or initiating strength of the self and on his success at this stage. But the past is not fully determinative. Under the worst of the earlier circumstances, the new identity may become a schizophrenic identity diffusion, but even in this, self is acting. If he is given the needed support and counsel, it need not be so. This developmental stage is a most opportune time to reset the course of life for the disordered individual. It is an equally opportune time for the "not-sick," the normal youngster, to be launched in speedy progress on the road to self-actualization.

FROM THE NORMAL TO THE TRANSCENDENT

THE WELL-ADJUSTED

Thorpe (1960, Chapter 10) gives a comprehensive survey of what several authorities have given as criteria of normal social adjustment and mental health.

> A "normal" person is said to be one who manifests no patterns of behavior symptomatic of mental disorder, who deals adequately with emotional conflicts, and who has the ability and capacity for useful and remunerative work. This criterion has been enlarged upon by Happock in the following words: "Two usable criteria of adjustment become immediately apparent: Health and earnings. . . . A related criterion is the percentage of time one is employed or unemployed. . . . After survival, we all seek to satisfy our other needs and wants. . . . Most of us

> spend more hours at work than we spend in any other single activity. Job satisfaction is thus an important aspect of total adjustment. . . . Here then are five criteria of adjustment with which we can start: health, earnings, percentage of time unemployed, satisfaction in human relations, job satisfaction. . . ."[2]
>
> A second definition offers a fourfold conception of normality or mental health, which includes (1) a *balance* between the demands of society and the desires of the individual, (2) *maturity,* or the absence of infantile and childish patterns, (3) *adequate functioning,* or the ability to surmount severe threats and frustrating situations, and (4) *compromise* between the desires of the individual and the demands of society. (p. 259).

Thorpe virtually equates the continuum of normality-abnormality with the continuum of maturity-immaturity, quotes several characteristics of immaturity, then gives his criteria of *optimum* mental health. These may be stated as: (1) adequate feelings of personal worth; (2) adequate feelings of security; (3) adequate feelings of self-confidence; (4) adequate understanding of self; (5) adequate understanding of others; (6) adequate emotional maturity; (7) adequate orientation and goals; (8) adequate integration of personality; (9) adequate vocational relationships, and (10) adequate basic harmony. (p. 262).

He follows with a discussion of development and maturity (p. 273): "A summary of these criteria by one author includes the following eight factors: (1) the integration of goals; (2) energetic problem solving; (3) insight; (4) tact; (5) productivity; (6) organizing ability; (7) spontaneity; and (8) problem-solving or goal-centeredness."[3]

LINKAGE TO REALITY

Many other writers have stated and described the qualities of emotional or psychological maturity. No two are quite the same,

---

[2] From *American Psychologist,* 1957, 12:232.

[3] From M. Brewster Smith et al, *Opinions and Personality* (New York: John Wiley & Sons, Inc., 1956), pp. 138–148. As quoted by Thorpe. Used with permission.

yet there is broad agreement among them. Overstreet[4] describes maturity in terms of linkages with the environment. He says: "A mature person is not one who has come to a certain level of achievement and stopped there. He is rather a *maturing* person—one whose *linkages with life* are constantly becoming stronger and richer because his attitudes are such as to encourage their growth rather than their stoppage. A mature person, for example, is not one who knows a large number of facts. Rather, he is one whose mental habits are such that he grows in knowledge and in the wise use of it. A mature person is not one who has built up a certain quota of human relationships—family, friends, acquaintances, fellow-workers—and is ready to call a halt, dismissing the rest of the human race as unimportant. Rather, he is a person who has learned how to operate well in a human environment so that he continues both to add new people to those whom he cares about and to discover new bases of fellowship with those already familiar." (p. 43).

In a summary statement Overstreet says: "In this chapter, we have indicated certain linkages so basic to our human growth that if they remain unformed, we remain fixated in our mental, emotional and social development: linkages of knowledge, responsibility, communication, mature sexuality, empathy, and philosophy. The fact that these have been separately and successively listed must not be interpreted to mean that they are independent of each other. . . .

"This then is the first basic fact about the linkage theory of maturity: it does not measure psychological maturity by any single, isolated trait in a person, but by a constellation of traits, by a total character structure.

"A second basic fact about the linkage theory must also be noted: It does not make maturity synonymous with *adjustment.* While it recognizes that an immature person who is also 'unadjusted' is in a miserable state and needs help, it recognizes no less that, given certain cultural conditions, the immature person is likely to effect a smoother 'adjustment' than is the mature person. He is not, however, because he can adjust himself, on that account a more genuinely fulfilled person. . . .

[4] Harry A. Overstreet, *The Mature Mind* (New York: W.W. Norton & Company, Inc., 1949), Chapter 2. Used with permission.

"The linkage theory, in brief, declares that it is no longer safe or sufficient to judge the immaturities and maturities of men by the average practices of any institution or any total culture. . . ." (pp. 73, 74).

EMPIRICAL FINDINGS

Heath[5] undertook an extensive empirical study of maturity, stating: "Reliance on authoritative wisdom, the humanistic tradition, public opinion, social adjustment, and psychopathological criteria did not advance our search to any great extent. Instead, biophysiological development theories offered greater promise. Our search suggested that the maturity concept could be located within a broadly conceived developmental theory about the major dimensions describing the maturing process. . . . (p. 34).

"We can now answer the question 'Who is a mature person?' with more confidence. He does seem to be a more stable person who masters disturbing information more efficiently; he is a more integrated and allocentrically* organized person, though he also is able to use regressive and autocentric types of thinking more effectively than the immature person. He may have more memories available to awareness, particularly those organized around his self-image which is more accurately symbolized. While his cognitions are less dominated by more primitive motives, it is still not clear just how autonomous he is of the influence of coercive external information. Our developmental theory seems to offer a reasonable description of the maturing person, though it may be incomplete. . . .

"As interesting as such findings are, they are only peripheral to the main aim of the book which was to demonstrate that a socially and psychologically important construct, such as maturity (or mental health), could be explored in depth with some objectivity and discipline. . . ." (pp. 340, 341).

> I would strongly recommend that a student report on this book, particularly Chapters 1 and 14 with enough additional material to reveal the method. Add to this, Bowman, 1965, pp. 262–286.

---

[5] Douglas H. Heath, *Explorations of Maturity* (New York: Appleton-Century-Crofts, Inc., 1965). Used with permission.

* See Glossary.

SELF-ACTUALIZERS

The term "self-actualization" is associated most directly with Abraham Maslow and his highly publicized studies of unusually high functioning persons and the "peak experiences" of "normal" people. Maslow prefers this term to mental health. It connotes "full-humanness," the highest level of healthfulness, the most complete psychosocial development and experience. He has described the chief characteristics of self-actualization in several books and articles, with slight variations. Following is an adaptation from these several sources:

1. Efficient perception of reality and comfortable relations with it.
2. Acceptance of self, others, and nature.
3. Spontaneity: thoughts, impulses, and inner life in general.
4. Problem centered: a purpose, goal, mission.
5. A quality of detachment: need for privacy.
6. Autonomy: independence of culture and environment.
7. Continuing freshness of appreciation: renewed interest and zest.
8. The mystic feeling or oceanic experience: limitless horizons.
9. Deep and profound interpersonal relations.
10. The feeling of identity, sympathy, and affection for mankind.
11. Democratic character structure.
12. Discrimination between means and ends.
13. Philosophical, unhostile sense of humor.
14. Creativity: in imagination and skills.
15. Resistance to enculturation: to conformity, ethnocentrism, etc.
16. At ease with certain imperfections.

These are not sharply definitive traits, but rather broad characteristics with overlapping traits. With additional study and more exact definition, these may be paired with their opposites at either end of a continuum; and as such, they mark degrees of self-actualization or maturity or perfection. Several psychologists have described the matter of maturity in this manner: movement along a continuum from one point to another, sometimes getting stuck (fixated) at any point along the way. Rogers (1961, Chapter 8) uses this approach in describing the processes by which the individual becomes "that self which one truly is"— in other words, self-actualization. Some of these movements are: (1) Away from facades, (2) Away from "oughts;" (3) Away from meeting expectations; (4) Away from pleasing others; (5) Toward self-direction; (6) Toward being process (fluid, free to change, free of defense); (7) Toward being complexity (free to experience and accept complex, even contradictory, feelings, attitudes, etc. without serious inner conflict); (8) Toward openness to experience; (9) Toward acceptance of others; (10) Toward trust of self.

Realizing that much of this is rather ambiguous, Rogers tried a different mode of description: "It seems to mean that the individual moves toward *being*, knowingly and acceptingly, the process which he inwardly and actually *is*. He moves away from being what he is not, from being a facade. He is not trying to be more than he is, with the attendant feelings of insecurity or bombastic defensiveness. He is not trying to be less than he is, with the attendant feelings of guilt or self-depreciation. He is increasingly listening to the deepest recesses of his physiological and emotional being, and finds himself increasingly willing to be, with greater accuracy and depth, that self which he most truly is. . . ." (pp. 175–176).

A careful analytic study would indicate that Rogers and Maslow are trying to describe the same general characteristics, with Maslow's description being the more complete. In both, we may see the movement beyond "normal," average adjustment or mental health, to a quality of *being* and *living* that transcends the norms.

PERSONAL TRANSCENDENCE

The uniqueness in man is portrayed by the individual's potential capacity of transcendence. Lecomte du Noüy, Scheler, May, Maslow, Rogers, and many others have recognized this capacity (and need) and have tried to deal scientifically and more definitively, with those unique human attributes that religious leaders have talked about for many centuries. Man as person, as a mature self, may transcend the deterministic forces of nature (instinctual drives, etc.), the norms established by social science, his past and present levels of behavior, and the expectations of himself and others. His attainment has no ceiling.

In one of his listings of self-actualization traits, Maslow (1962) mentions "transcendence of self." He admits that self-actualization at present is a relative achievement, and relatively low in most cases.

> This means for us that that which the person *is* and that which the person *could be* exist simultaneously for the psychologist, thereby resolving the dichotomy between Being and Becoming. Potentialities not only *will be* or could be; they also *are*. Self-actualization values as goals exist and are real even though not yet actualized. The human being is simultaneously that which he is and that which he yearns to be. (p. 151).
>
> If the various extant religions may be taken as expressions of human aspiration, i.e., what people would *like* to become if only they could, then we can see here too a validation of the affirmation that all people yearn toward self-actualization or tend toward it. This is so because our description of the actual characteristics of self-actualizing people parallels at many points the ideals urged by the religions, e.g., the transcendence of self, the fusion of the true, the good and the beautiful, contribution to others, wisdom, honesty and naturalness, the transcendence of selfish and personal motivations, the giving up of "lower" desires in favor of "higher" ones. . . . (p. 149).

FREEDOM AND TRANSCENDENCE

Sidney Jourard (In Otto, 1966, Chapter 25) makes his appeal for "a psychology of transcendent behavior" and states that it is long overdue. It would be a psychology that dealt adequately with man's capacity for freedom and transcending determiners of all kinds—of his optimal functioning. It would place the individual's intentionality, will or power of decision beside other major determiners, postulating that under most conditions man acquiesces to "forces" and "determiners," especially his socialization, but at times he has glimmerings of a *higher* way and feels upsurges of strength or accomplishes goals so atypical of him that even he is shocked. "Actually the study of transcendent functioning is a misnomer. Man doesn't transcend his real being: he transcends only someone's concept of his being, his own *concept* or that of an investigator. . . .

"Transcendent behavior, in contrast with habitual behavior, carries with it an element of surprise or unpredictability. In transcendent behavior, the person is literally "rising above" forces thought to be determinants, e.g., social pressure, habit, physical limitations such as blindness or lameness, all of which predispose some highly probable range of responses. . . . Transcendent behavior implies a release of latent potentialities, of capabilities to perceive, invent, create, achieve, endure or perform. In most people these capacities lie buried under the "crust" and inertia of habit, rigid role definitions and confining self-concepts. . . . He responds to situations in novel, unusual, valuable ways, and these ways depart from those which have been most typical of him up to the moment of transcendence. . . ." (p. 353).

Some of the factors involved in transcendence include a state of "letting be," in which the individual does not seek to steer, guide or direct each thought as it arises, but instead, he permits it to arise and be followed by whatever thought, image or memory comes next. Another is "*openness*" toward others, a trusting, free responsiveness and thus a fuller cognition and communication. There is also that which Jourard calls "*focusing and fascination*," the ability to become so fascinated with a topic, thing or person that the individual is given entirely to it in single-mindedness and unselfconsciousness. Again, there is the factor of "*commitment to some goal to which they assign high value*." And there is a diminution to self-doubt, *high self-confidence* with no fixed and limited concept of self. Finally, there is the factor of challenge: reality thus faced, rather than as a threat. Frequently for such persons the energy for transcendence is released by symbols, which somehow carry a deeper meaning than normal literal language. He concludes: "Since all of the classes of such behavior have occurred in some few people, the promise is implicit that they can occur in a large number of people more of the time. One of the aims of the field if personality hygiene, beyond that of preventing mental illness, should be to understand and master the conditions for transcendent behavior, so that ultimately the average personality will be not a mere noncandidate for a psychiatric hospital, but instead a being who can release his capacities for transcendent functioning as needed. Therapists of personality then would be not experts at restoring those with neurosis or psychosis to 'normal' levels of function, rather they would be more like those few inspired and inspiring teachers who are able to elicit transcendent performance from their students to the surprise and delight of all." (p. 370).

To accomplish the above, to provide the therapeutic aids and to create the community climate that is conducive to self-actualization and transcendent behavior are the new goals of community action through its churches, schools, and special clinics. These agencies are not groping entirely in the fog of theory, since several pilot projects have been conducted with sufficient success to establish a few guide lines. These will be described later, after we have explored the more significant areas of personal high-level functioning.

HEALTHY AND TRANSCENDENT COGNITION

The nature and quality of a person's beliefs may be symptomatic of his mental health and an important determinative factor in his level of attainment. Beliefs are based largely on cognition. Faulty beliefs are basically determined by false "knowledge." The paranoid has delusionary beliefs because his cognitive processes are faulty. He perceives cause-effect relations which are unreal. The prejudiced, ethnocentric or gullible person believes the untested opinions or superstitions of others, and accepts and acts on them as if they were true knowledge. The healthy-minded person is said to have "good contact with reality"—not only realistic object perception but realistic abstraction and interpretation.

PERCEPTION

Cognition includes the mental processes involved in becoming aware, in knowing. It begins with sensory experience, but sensation is chiefly physiological, the chemophysical reaction to a stimulus. Perception is the mental process of giving meaning to the sensation. It is no longer merely a sound or an image but rather a sound or image of some*thing*. The sensation may just happen to a person, but the person creates his perception. It becomes *his* knowledge, faulty or true, but the working of *his* mind.

Because perception is a two-way process with the person as subject acting on and reacting to the stimuli, it is selective in all cases. The question is that of degree. The person as subject-self gives meaning to the various elements of the stimulus situation. Some elements are ignored, others diminished, and some perceived as they really are, while still others are exaggerated. Thus, reality is usually distorted by the observing subject. The insecure, anxious, hostile, defensive—the emotionally disturbed—individual is prone to be more highly selective, according to his predominant needs. Thus he seriously distorts reality. Things, events, situations, the problems of life, and other people are not as he perceives them. Neither is he, in reality or in potentiality, the person he "sees" himself as being. All of this is associated with mental disorders which have been studied.

The truly "well" person with high-level mental health, the self-actualizer, who has learned to handle anxiety and hostility, who is confident, secure, and relatively free of defense mechanisms, distorts elements of the stimulus situation to a very small degree. Thus, his perceptions are relatively valid and reliable. He is said to have good contact with reality. The opinions, beliefs, motives, and behavior based on these perceptions are relatively true and realistic. He also perceives himself, his own behavior, accurately, realistically. Having a high degree of autonomy, self-confidence and maturity, he doesn't need to defend himself against a true cognition of himself. There is no need to create an exaggerated ideal "self-image" to camouflage a feared weak "self." ("Self" so used is, in reality, one's self-image or personality-image.) He can see and accept his strong points, because he has the strength and confidence to assume the responsibility that they would require of him. He can see and accept his imperfections because he is not afraid of being defeated, seriously crippled, or rejected for having them.

The "not-sick," the so-called "normal" person may be quite objectively accurate and nonselective in his perceptions. Yet, these so-called "realists" and "pragmatists," who may be well adapted individuals, may be falling short of the high-level, enriched perceptions that some are designating *transcendent.* Jourard says (In Otto, 1966):

> . . . "Desireless," or "undriven" cognition—when we simply open our eyes, ears, noses, taste buds, kinesthetic and organic receptors and let stimuli play upon them and impress them—seems to be the conditions for the enriched mode of perception. This mode of perception . . . adds new dimensions to experience or, rather, it permits new dimensions to happen.

> Colors are seen more vividly, and things, animals, people or scenes are perceived in their "suchness," in their concrete uniqueness, almost transfigured.
>
> Moments of such perception are experienced by people as unforgettable. In fact, when people recall the past with vivid imagery, the content of their recollection is almost always the moments when they let the world impress itself upon their senses without selection. They let the world disclose itself to them. When two people fall in love and are truly open and unguarded in their communication with one another, they come to see one another as unique, irreplaceable, quite *unlike* any other human being in the world—certainly not as mere representatives of the classes, men and women. And though it is true that "lovers" who are merely starved for companionship, are in fact somewhat "blind"—they see in the other only the means of satiating present appetites and hungers—it is also true that happy, fulfilled lovers see one another *and the world* more richly and more veridically. In this sense one can say that people who are in love, people who are open and spontaneous in relation to their loved ones, are *at that time* also more open to their own experiencing and more perceptive of the real world. Their senses all seem keener, and the world discloses itself more vividly to their eyes, ears, skin and olfactory lobes, to their experience. Such cognition, then, because it is rare and valued, may be called transcendent perception. (pp. 354–355).

Clinical study of peak experience and the few truly high-level self-actualizers affords much evidence that man has the natural capacity (potential and relatively undeveloped in most people) for a quality of cognition that bypasses the structured sensory apparatus, transcends his normal perceptions and gives a type of knowing that is very beneficial but as yet defies full explanation. This type of knowing is one characteristic of high-level health and self-actualization.

COGNITION OF BEING

Maslow (1962) thinks "Freud's greatest discovery is that *the* great cause of much psychological illness is the fear of knowledge of oneself—of one's emotions, impulses, memories, capacities, potentialities, of one's destiny. . . . To use Freudian language, incuriosity, learning difficulties, pseudostupidity can be a defense." (pp. 57, 62). Maslow explains how that resistance to self-knowledge defends self-esteem, then adds: "But there is another kind of truth we tend to evade. Not only do we hang on to our psychopathology, but also tend to evade personal growth because this, too, can bring another kind of fear, of awe, of feelings of weakness and inadequacy. And so we find another kind of resistance, a denying of our best side, of our talents, of our finest impulses, of our highest potentialities, of our creativeness. . . .

"And, if I may say it in a very condensed way, it is precisely the God-like in ourselves that we are ambivalent about, fascinated by and fearful of, motivated to and defensive against. . . . Every one of our great creators, our God-like people, has testified to the elements of courage that is needed in the lonely moment of creation, affirming something new. . . . Responsibility can be seen as a heavy burden and evaded as long as possible." (p. 58).

In his study of the truly high self-actualizers, however, Maslow has found a notable lack of this type of anxiety and resistance. Instead they revealed a freedom and readiness and capacity to know, accept, and express themselves to the degree "that sometimes they seem almost like a different breed of human beings." (p. 67). This quality of knowing, he calls *"B-cognition"* (cognition of being), contrasting it with mere adaptive cognition organized by the deficiency needs, which he calls *"D-cognition."* (see Chapter 3).

REALITY TESTING

Some people are more prone than others to credulity, prejudice, ethnocentric beliefs and attitudes. Immature, dependent, and defensive, they accept uncritically the opinions of others, especially others who are assumed authorities. They *select* the "authorities" to whom they listen, the authors whose works they read. They avoid the responsibility of having to appraise, judge, and decide for themselves. The mature, autonomous, healthy-minded person will read and listen to the arguments and opinions of people with different points of view. He will respect them on the basis of their reputation as scholars or persons of intellectual integrity but he will withhold his final opinion and is slow to accept or to reject.

In other words, the healthy-minded person welcomes ideas and information from others to supplement his own. He accepts them as possibly or probably factual, but not necessarily so. He tests them in the light of his own knowledge and experience and/or by the rules of logic, and finally seeks verification or contradiction by additional research. So-called authoritative opinions and beliefs are accepted hypothetically, but with a certain amount of reservation and open-mindedness until fuller verification is made.

This process is generally designated *reality-testing.* The individual seeks to eliminate the distortions of selective perception—of anxiety, self-doubt, rationalization, etc.—in order to objectively validate his cognitive processes. There are certain generally accepted but variously worded steps in the reality-testing of one's "beliefs" or tentative opinions, which are similar to the steps in testing hypothesis. They may be stated as follows: (1) state the opinion clearly and, so far as possible, operationally; (2) list all available supporting evidence; (3) list possibly contrary facts and interpretations; (4) check the logical consistency of this opinion with other valid beliefs in the same general field; and (5) if still uncertain, gather additional empirical evidence and replicate.

Parapsychologists have subjected psi experiences to extensive reality-testing. It would seem that the nonsensory awareness of the mystic could be reality-tested in some modified manner. It has been validated subjectively to the satisfaction of the religion-oriented person, but not objectively to the satisfaction of most scientists. This experience, having within it the qualities of wholeness, the timeless and the absolute, is, as Maslow would say, an "end-experience" rather than a "means experience" and needs no validation. Rather, its validity is intrinsic. The experiencer is immediately cognizant of its validity while in that state of experience. Paradoxically, there is both a diminution and enhancement of self in such experiences, and always an enrichment of interpersonal relations. Perhaps some degree of objective validation can be established on the basis of these effects.

The tendency to trust one's hunches, one's intuition, is sometimes contrasted with reality-testing; and high-level self-actualizing people generally trust and frequently follow their hunches. Usually, however, they depend on intuition, which is a major element in B-cognition, not as a substitute for reality-testing but as a supplement. They observe, test, and utilize empirical evidence to the limit, but they do not limit themselves to this objective and purely rational procedure. Since they have such high-level self-confidence, self-identity and the capacity to experience in wholes, their intuitive cognition is more generally reliable and its use more than normally realistic. The anxious self-doubting, self-alienated, defensive person who tends toward following hunches is not really utilizing intuition but wish-fulfillment. He uses this as a substitute for reality-testing and decision-making. It is not true intuitive cognition. His anxieties and defenses make true intuition virtually impossible.

CREATIVE THINKING AND EVALUATING

There is no sharp distinction to be found among the mental processes involved in cognition. The knowing, experiencing subject perceives an object or event as described above. He perceives specific elements and qualities with differences and similarities relative to one another and to their counterparts in other similar objects or events. This type or stage of perception is discrimination, generalization, and conceptualization. To perceive similarities and differences, one must depend on recall of past perceptions, re-cognition, and judge past experiences imaginatively. The object is perceived imaginatively as it (and its kind) has functioned previously and as it may function under new and varying circumstances. One must appraise and judge in order to perceive these similarities and differences. Therefore, perception is the basic element in memory, reflective or imaginative thinking, and judgment.

These processes are in constant change while knowing is growing, but they are basically similar. My point is that the conditions which distort perception, as described, impair the whole process (es) of learning and thinking. Maturity, autonomy, self-confidence, health-mindedness by contributing to the accuracy and efficiency of perception make the whole process (es) of knowing easier.

CREATIVE THINKING

Many experimental studies of the effect of mental set on problem solving have been made. Experimental groups who are trained to use certain fixed procedures in solving a given type of problem tend to follow the same procedures when given a new problem and freedom to use any procedure. Mental set is one strong characteristic of the psychologically disordered, while the healthy-minded, self-actualizer is noted for his freedom, spontaneity, flexibility, and creativity. We are not concerned here with the psychological distinction between creative and problem-solving thinking. The personal qualities which make for greater efficiency in one apply about equally to the other. Anxiety, inner tension, and self-doubt impede efficiency, while inner harmony and confidence facilitate it.

The very process of growth and self-actualization is creative, a finding of new avenues of expression and new goals of attainment. Therefore, healthy-minded growth and creativity are virtually synonymous. The characteristics of transcendence described also apply here. Creativity is transcendent. Exploration is an innate need-drive of all people. Imaginative or creative thinking is merely uninhibited mental exploration. Thus, all people are naturally creative, but their creativity may be inhibited by anxiety defenses and inner conflict. To be spontaneously creative indicates a facility of mental activity and thus healthy-mindedness.

Wallas (1921) gave four steps in creative thinking: *preparation, incubation, illumination, and verification.* These have been frequently quoted. The flashes of insight or sudden "inspirations" that often characterize the creative thinker, whether in science, art or religion, spring from a "reservoir" of previous learning. The creative thinker does not ignore research. Illumination may be designated as the end-result of a period of incubation. The thinker, who is actively directing the cognitive process in concentrated effort to solve a problem or create a new theory or a work of art, sets up strong resistance in the many neuron patterns of the brain in order to control his thinking. In doing this, the neuron clusters that may carry the answer are blocked. After hours of this concentrated effort, the thinker dismisses the problem and relaxes. He may turn to music, light fiction, a pleasant meal, or go to sleep. Suddenly the desired solution appears full-blown, with a pleasant satisfaction and sense of "that's it."

Our great creative thinkers have recorded many such instances; and the process is the same whether the answer comes while in a relaxed state of awakefulness or in a dream. When one is relaxed and not consciously thinking of the problem, the self continues to be motivated toward finding the solution (a self-set as it were). Then, with the resistance in the brain cortex greatly reduced, the right connections are made and the answer is conceptualized. Many creative, yet not-so-great thinkers, keep a note pad and pencil on the night table beside their beds for the purpose of recording ideas that appear after or during a short period of sleep. The incubation period is that time lapse between the period of concentrated thinking and the flash of insight. It may be a time period of several minutes or several days. The tension of self-set or need-drive remains although other interests have superseded it. Often it is merely a matter of permitting the resistance (from concentration) to relax, as when one suddenly recalls a name after he stopped trying to remember it. It is the ability to "let go," to "let be," and implies freedom from anxiety defenses. Sometimes the relaxed, apparently unrelated thinking that follows the concentrated effort, immediately or days later, provides the necessary cue or missing link. However, when the illumination comes, it is generally subjected to careful follow-up examination for verification, especially of detail.

This creative or transcendent thinking is a significant cognitive characteristic of the healthy-minded self-actualizer. It is he who is so free of repressions and defensive compulsions that he can give himself fully to self-directed, concentrated logical thought until he is mentally exhausted, and then permitted almost complete cortical relaxation or change to nondirected, free-flow reminiscence. In this change from the active to passive phase of the thinking cycle, there sometimes occurs the experience of "truth" from seemingly outside or beyond the realm of one's own experience which takes possession of him and uses his cognitive process to "spell itself out." The difference between this type of obsessive thinking and that of the neurotic obsessive character is that the passive respondent can break the "spell" and return to directed, logical thought at any time. He is free of repressive resistance areas and rigid defenses, and the "spelled-out" imagery or concepts are not distorted but are true to the wholeness of the passive thinker's experience of being and thus true to reality. The two preceding paragraphs present what we generally mean by intuitive cognition.

EVALUATING

The nature of values, the need of an adequate value system, and its significance for mental hygiene have been discussed in Chapter 5. Our concern at this point is with *evaluating* as a cognitive process that distinguishes the healthy-minded. A value may be defined as a conception of what is desired (positively or negatively) and which influences choice or decision. As a concept, values involve perception and appraisal. The significant factor is that the appraisal is of the thing, person or event in relationship with self, or self appraised in relation to these. In other words, a value is a concept of self-other in relationship; and that imagined relationship is experienced as being harmful or beneficial. Evaluating is the cognitive process of appraisal that involves self-in-relation—the appraisal of a cause-effect relationship relative to self. Thus, it carries affect (emotion), a sense of "ought." I ought to have this or I ought to escape this.

Since this is true, all that was said of selective perception applies to the process of evaluating. The defense-ridden person with psychosocial disorders in distorting perception also distorts his values and is unable to develop a realistic value system with a reliable hierarchy of significance. This reliable hierarchy attainment is a mark of mature, high-level, healthy-mindedness. The lack of such may be symptomatic of immaturity and psychosocial deficiency. Efficient perception, good contact with reality (including self, B-cognition) is the necessary prerequisites to an adequate value system. (See Chapter 5 for criteria.)

The experience of value reaches its ultimate in the "peak" or "mystical" experience which has end-value rather than means-value. Self and other are experienced in their wholeness and thus absolute character, together and yet detached, and free of dependency and utility. The value or worth of the other is experienced intrinsically, in and of itself, and not what it may do to or for oneself. Appraisal, in this instance, has become contemplation. Such experiences are always values as good, the value of being. Maslow has found in these peak experiences the following B-value elements or facets: Wholeness, perfection, contemplation, justice, aliveness, richness, simplicity, beauty, goodness, uniqueness, effortlessness, playfulness, truth/honesty (and reality), and self-sufficiency. (1962, p. 78).

HEALTHY EMOTIONAL BEHAVIOR

"How do you do?" is a popular salutation used by many people. It is not said as a question that demands an answer. Rather, it carries the implication, "I trust you are *feeling* well today. At least, say so. It will make me *feel* better." This dimension of personal experience—how one feels, the quality of his affect, his emotions—correlates so highly with one's state of mental health that the term emotional health is often used as a synonym. "Emotionally disturbed" has become the designation of the child who is mentally ill or psychosocially disordered. And the emotionally disturbed individual very often becomes physically ill. The nature and quality of an individual's emotions are so interwoven with all aspects of his life, that he cannot understand himself nor the personality of another without comprehensive knowledge of his pattern of emotional responses. What is emotional health, the emotional style of the high-level healthy-minded person?

In Chapter 3, I presented what I believe to be a practical working concept of emotion. Then, in several chapters, the negative emotions were seen in their etiological relationships to various defense mechanisms and psychosocial disorders, or as symptomatic expressions. It was stated that emotion is, primarily, the affective color tone of consciousness when self is central in one's concept, when the self-other relationship is being evaluated. A slightly different statement might be that emotion is the affect tone of the cognitive processes when self is a part of the cognitive image and there is considerable incongruence. It was also stated that emotion is, secondarily, a state of physiological excitement involving more than normal activity of the autonomic nervous system and endocrine glands, plus the consciousness (feelings) of some of these processes. Emotional behavior is emergency or optimal action in which these physiological and mental state preside as regulative instruments.

Jourard (1958, p. 87) says: "A person is said to display unhealthy emotionality when he does not respond emotionally as he is supposed or expected to, and when his emotionally-provoked behavior endangers his health, safety, his position, or anything else which he or society deems important." This gives us a fairly practical or applicable working definition of deviant or disordered emotional life. It centers on behavior. Emotion per se, as a quality or state of cognition, is not a something that can be immature or ill even though we frequently speak in terms of "emotional immaturity" or "emotional illness." Faulty or inappropriate emotional states are the consequence of faulty cognition—faulty perception, conceptualization, appraisal and evaluation—especially relative to oneself. Faulty cognition produces inappropriate emotions which, by acting as regulative instruments, help induce inappropriate or maladjustive behavior, psychosocial disorders. But our concern is with healthy emotionality—the pattern or style of emotional life that is characteristic of high-level healthy-mindedness or self-actualization.

In observing human behavior and its emotional overtones, one may look for the specific emotions expressed, the relative proportion of positive and negative emotions, the range of emotional scale, and the degree or strength of emotional ethos. The mature, highly healthy person has frequent experiences that are emotionally toned and of wide variety, and run the whole emotional scale or gamut. Emotions are essential to optimal response and add a qualitative richness to experience. The "abundant life" is richly emotional. The positive emotions far outweigh the negative ones in such a person's life, and his over-all mood is generally optimistic and happy or joyous.

CONSCIOUS OF ONE'S EMOTIONS

The psychoanalytical therapists emphasize repression and speak frequently of unconscious emotions. It seems to me that unconscious emotion is a contradiction in terms, and that this is another semantics problem. Emotion (feeling) is a state or quality of consciousness, i.e., color-toned conscious cognitive processes which are more than normally intense. To speak of unconscious emotion would seem to be equivalent to unconscious consciousness. But, turning away from semantics, we can readily admit that "repression" (anxiety resistance to perception and recall) prevents full and realistic cognition and re-cognition. If one blocks out parts of what one perceives of a present situation or of a past event, the distorted cognition or recognition causes inappropriate emotion and emotions that cannot be consciously associated with an appropriate objective cause. One may experience need conflict and its excess endocrine activity, the physiological correlates or secondary aspects of emotion, without being conscious of it; but it is highly doubtful that he can experience anxiety or fear, anger, shame, pleasure, affection, or joy unconsciously. These are qualities of consciousness. The healthy-minded self-actualizer is relatively free of anxiety and repression, is efficiently cognizant, and thus is fully conscious of what he is responding to emotionally. He is more fully aware of the appropriateness of his own emotionality.

APPROPRIATE RESPONSES

The autonomous, self-confident, healthy-minded person with little "selective" perception and good reality contact, is cognizant of himself and the outer world as they are. He is secure and confident, and his evaluations are realistic and reliable. The situation appears to be no more threatening or rewarding than it actually is. His consequential emotions are appropriate to the stimulus. A great frustration or threat, a great injustice or danger produces a powerful response of anger or fear. Thus, the righteous man may "rise up in mighty wrath" or his soul may "quake with great fear," but these causes are virtually of an infinite nature. The truly great frustrations and threats do not occur. Often, thus the truly healthy-minded individual seldom experiences strong anger or fear. The small frustrations and threats cause only ripples of annoyance. The healthy soldier in combat will normally experience fear. He faces constant and real threat and has no effective defense against 50-caliber machine gun bullets and exploding shells. However, his fear does not reach the point of panic. I have met a few soldiers who did not experience fear to any notable degree. They were not psychopaths, deficient in emotional capacity, but were young men of such strong religious faith that death itself was no serious threat. But they were few. The healthy-minded person is generally characterized by the quality of faith and goodwill that make ordinary fears and anger rare and of short duration, it is faith in and goodwill toward self, toward others, and toward life in general.

THE POSITIVE MOOD

The person of good mental health is no Pollyanna. His appraisals and evaluations of self and situations are realistic. He neither needs nor has any defense mechanism to hide the difficulties. His faith in himself and others, his problem-solving attitude, and his belief that all problems have solutions make for a general positive, optimistic attitude or mood. He is more often than otherwise happy or contented. He has learned to utilize community resources for enjoyable activities which stimulate positive emotional expression. He is generally more successful in work achievement and experiences the joyousness that he derives from a sense of worthy performance more frequently. His freedom from defenses enables him to identify more deeply with people and establish more satisfying and affectionate interpersonal relations.

WE FEELINGS

The healthy-minded person is sociable. He needs and enjoys solitude at times and can detach himself from others. He is no compulsive joiner. His deeper identity with others enables him to share their thoughts, problems, achievements, and feelings more fully. Thus, his emotional life is enriched by others. Injustices to them arouse anger in him, and their successes bring him joy. He *belongs* to his family, his community, his nation, the human race. That which enriches them, enriches him. If a neighbor wins a large prize in a contest or receives a big promotion, rather than feeling envious, he is happy with his neighbor. He also sorrows at his neighbor's loss. But this kind of sorrow is healthful and enriching if it is not too frequent and great. The neurotic person can not handle sorrow and is hurt by it. It is not the sorrow or grief that is morbid but, rather, the morbid (neurotic) person who mishandles sorrow, whose emotional response is inappropriate. The healthy-minded person shares generously in the joys and sorrows of others and is enriched by both.

CONTROLLED EXPRESSION

Healthy emotionality is seen in its mode of expression. The healthy-minded person, accurate in his perceptions and evaluations, is not prone to excess emotions and thus may express them freely, spontaneously and directly. Some people generate so much emotion that if they expressed it fully, they would be thought ridiculous or "crazy" by others. Fear of this often causes them to inhibit the emotional response. But he whose emotions are appropriate to the occasion and who is not afraid of what others may think is free to give direct expression to his feelings. And he is equally free to restrain himself and suppress the emotional response when its expression might offend a child, do someone an injury, or offend social custom. More emotion is inevitably aroused in this imperfect world than should be spontaneously and overtly expressed. Some suppression and displacement are essential. The healthy-minded person remains aware of the kind and degree of emotional suppression which he finds necessary, and he finds or creates harmless channels through which to displace his surplus negative emotions. He shows some restraint in his positive emotions, which is in accord with "good taste." However, in his overall emotional style, the self-actualizer shows much spontaneity and richness in emotional expression.

IMPROVING EMOTIONALITY

Do we inherit our emotional dispositions or are they acquired? Certain temperamental traits are inherited with tendencies to be a little more or less active, restless, and sensitive. But patterns of emotional behavior are learned. Thus, they can be changed. We may begin in the self-improvement of our emotional lives by seeking a clearer understanding of the nature of emotions and their role in life. High emotionality should be accepted and valued as highly as intelligence. When we appreciate this we may next try to discover exactly what stimulus situations evoke our various emotional responses. Are we really reacting to this person or thing with so much feeling, or is there some unseen factor which is partly responsible? From this we can turn to our various cognitive processes—forget our feelings and work on our perceptions, concepts, appraisals, evaluations, and recall. How selective and distorted are these? We put these to the reality-testing described above and as a part of this, the self-image (cognition or self) comes in for special attention.

Many "how-to-do-it" books have been written. Usually these are not very helpful manuals for self-guidance. The *self* that is strong enough to interpret such directions realistically and practice them effectively would already be the one who is doing a fairly good job controlling its responses. The weak self that feels seriously threatened, is defensive, and has developed serious behavior disorders, would need to be strengthened before making effective use of such "how-to-do-it" aids. However, the normally adjusted (the not-sick-not-well) person can enrich his emotionality by cultivating the cognitive qualities described and by joining a small "potential development" group to develop self-strength and its potentialities as described below. One does not attempt to directly cultivate "emotional maturity." Rather, he develops a mature self and transcendent cognition, and the effects of these are high-level emotionality and *appropriate* emotional behavior.

THE HEALTHY SELF

We continue to speak in terms of "mental" and "emotional" health and "mental" and "emotional" maturity, when we know full well that "mind" and "emotion" are not entities which can be well or ill, mature or immature. This manner of speaking is realistic and meaningful only in the indirect sense that the healthy person as acting subject, the healthy *self*, develops mental process and emotional states of a different character and quality than those of a weak unhealthy self. It is the self, the person as subject, the doer or behaver, who is conceived, is born, and grows; not as a mental construct, which may be mature or immature, strong or weak, healthy or sickly. The person as object (physical structure) may become defective by undernourishment, injury or disease and these defects impair the functioning of the individual. Spontaneous recovery may take place, or medical science may be needed to effect a cure. The person as subject (the self) may likewise become defective by undernourishment, injury or disease. Also, if not too seriously crippled, self may recover spontaneously; otherwise psychotherapy may be necessary. In the case of self, the undernourishment is chiefly the lack of love; the injury, those crippling traumatic experiences; the disease, those repressive, morbid, unwholesome family relationships as described in the etiology of schizophrenia.

At this point I refer the student to the last half of Chapter 3 for a review of self and its functioning. The conditions described in Chapters 7, 8 and 9 happen because self is too immature, weak or ill to face its environment in a realistic manner and to adequately structure its responses. The effective character traits, cognitive processes, and emotionality described above reflect the high level functioning of a strong, mature, healthy self. The weak, sickly self is defense-security motivated, and is afraid of responsibility and choice. Weak in generative drive, it is more reactive than active, and thus cannot order or control its own mental processes. Tensions grow, and disorders develop. The very weak self will need the self-reinforcement of a competent therapist (his acceptance, trust and love) before he can carry on and complete his behavior reconstruction. The previously stated characteristics of maturity and Maslow's qualities of the self-actualizer are the qualities of the strong, mature, healthy self which are reflected in behavior.

CLINICAL STUDIES OF HUMAN POTENTIALITY

Frequent reference has been made to Maslow's findings with respect to the characteristics of high-level self-actualizers and the more normal (average) persons in their peak experiences. Maslow's method of study was chiefly the personal interview and biographical anecdotes, analyzing the reports of his respondents and classifying the information he obtained. Taking his cue from the pioneer thinking of Maslow, Gardner Murphy, Erich Fromm, Carl Rogers, and the earlier hypothesis of William James that man is utilizing only ten percent of his potential, Herbert Otto, all during the 1960's, has been directing an extensive program in

Human Potentialities Research at the University of Utah. Similar studies are now in progress at other centers. The Utah studies include the following (Otto, 1966, p. 405).

1. To explore some of the dimensions of individual and family potential.
2. To build theory about factors and forces inimical to the development of human potential.
3. To devise means, methods and instruments to help individuals and families make better use of their potential.

A part of what is anticipated as the work progresses is: (1) an extension of the ability to communicate; (2) the development and amplification of sensory modalities; (3) increased availability of vast masses of stored date (memory); (4) marked increase in the range of affective functioning; (5) better understanding and application of motivation; (6) an expansion of the creative, intuitive and imaginative capacities.

These are not group therapy projects to make the sick "not-sick." They are classes or seminars for the "not-sick" who want to become high-level self-actualizers, utilizing their potentiality more efficiently. The format of the first session includes purpose reinterpreted and getting acquainted with the other members. The Depth Unfoldment Experience (DUE) Method has been developed of which, Dr. Otto says, "we can achieve a depth of interpersonal involvement and relationship in one session which formerly took us five or six group sessions to achieve." (p. 417). Then they discuss the concept of human potentialities and, with the aid of the "Otto Inventory of Personal Resources," assess their individual strengths and potentialities, and continue with the evaluation and development of methods designed to actualize potential. They seek the answers to "three core questions: (1) How can potential be actualized? (2) How much potential can be actualized? and (3) Which specific potential(s) should be actualized?" (p. 418). I shall now quote at length some of the findings:

> *There are strong indications that the marked resistance to the development and utilization of strength and potentialities which we have encountered as persistent phenomena is due to a deep-seated and powerful fear-guilt-anxiety cycle, as well as to inimical cultural forces.* The individual fears to develop

his strengths, as this would require both exercising leadership, "sticking his neck out," and, more fundamentally, would demand personality change and change in his basic habit and behavior patterns. Intimately linked with this fear is a deep sense of guilt. Such guilt stems from the individual's *awareness on a deep level* (although often partially conscious) *that he possesses specific resources, strengths and capacities which exist only as latent forces and are not being utilized.* The failure to develop and to utilize these resources leaves the individual with a lack of wholeness or lack of self-fulfillment, thereby generating pervasive guilt, which, in turn, is repressed. Anxiety, the third element, is seen as both flowing from this vicious cycle as well as contributing to it. Considerable psychic energy is bound up or invested in this process. Freeing this energy or redirecting it to more productive purposes, it is postulated, will enable the personality to move markedly in the direction of more optimal functioning. . . . (p. 419).

It is pointed out that certain fixed attitudes and feelings toward sex membership, death, and one's value structure and certain "pathogenic institutional forces" are inimical to more efficient use of potential, then these observations are made:

The average well-functioning individual has an exceedingly restricted self-perception of his personality strengths and a markedly limited perspective of his potentialities. . . .

The process of "taking inventory" of personality assets, strengths and resources is in itself experienced as strengthening by participants. . . .

There is some evidence that, in most individuals studied, deeply entrenched and ingrained habit systems, which dominate both behavior and perceptions and affect ideational processes, function to delimit spontaneity, creativity and the development of individual potential. . . .

There are indications that the achievement of an expanded self-conceit is directly linked to the ability to actualize potentialities. . . .

Finally, for man to be fully involved in the continuous act of self-creation he must have both the *vision* of his potentials and the courage to realize his possibilities. Unless he has that vision and hope, his courage may never develop. We are at a point of readiness for discarding an outmoded image of man and assuming a new image—the image of man's potentialities. (pp. 421–423).

> For more detailed information, I would suggest a classroom report and discussion on Potentialities Development, using Dr. Otto's material and later writings that undoubtedly will be forthcoming.

Other pilot projects have been and are being conducted in several research centers designed to enhance the growth and operation of our human potential. In this third quarter of the twentieth century, as never before, we have awakened to the need and possibility of making the mentally ill not-sick. We are not satisfied with that "halfway house." We are alert to the need and possibility of making the not-sick truly healthy minded—to help the "normal" become aware of their untapped and often undreamed of potentialities and transcend themselves in a more abundant living and creative service.

POTENTIAL IN OLD AGE

Erikson's last developmental or conflict stage, integrity vs. despair and disgust, carries the implication that the alternative need not be the latter. Integrity of selfhood, character, and performance may continue deep into the "aging years." During recent decades medical science has done much to prolong life. The next few decades may see behavioral science doing as much to prolong *living*. Comfortable existence is not enough. Inherent in advancing age are certain decreases in organic vitality and cellular efficiency, decreasing both physical and mental performance. Evidence is accumulating which indicates that sociologic and psychologic factors are the major determinants of the life shrinkage. Old people have been conditioned for decline, motivation drops or changes from growth- to security-oriented; therefore, there is both organic decline and functional shrinkage.

The opinion that old age brings a natural and inevitable decline of intelligence is being seriously challenged, especially in the findings of longitudinal studies.[6] London (1963) made a

[6] See reference to Robert W. Kleemeier's studies, *Gerontologist.* 3:18, (1963), and E.W. Busse, "The Aging Process and the Health of the Aged" *Frontiers in Medicine*, Seminar, Duke University, (November 15, 1963).

study of over 350 composers and conductors who lived during the past 1000 years. A relatively high percentage of these lived and worked well into their eighties and nineties. A new and promising field of research has evolved with the systematic study of such persons and other currently high-functioning old people. Sufficient evidence suggests that with the new freedom of retirement and re-examination of life's meanings, older people may make extensive and postive changes in their value system and personality. With this change comes a new release in potentiality, and a higher level of self-actualization.

Robert Kastenbaum[7] asks the question, "Is Old Age the End of Development?" He discusses four logical answers and reaches the following conclusion: "Thus, for some people, old age is the end of development in the sense that development has terminated, is all over with, is not part of the individual life plan and for other people, old age is the end of development in the Aristotelian sense: the end is that goal or final state toward which the entire process has been directed." (p. 69). The implication we may draw from this is that growth and self-actualization should terminate in a period of old age which may continue as a time of fruitful, satisfying living. The behavioral sciences, education, and religion are moving in the direction of making this possible for greater numbers of our senior citizens.

SUMMARY

Excellence of performance was the goal of the ancient Greeks, excellence in character has been a major goal of the religious, full self-actualization is seen by modern psychology as the supreme motive-goal of life. The late Lecomte du Noüy, eminent biologist, saw in all of this the goal of evolution. Man in his most lucid moments has always been aware of his high potentiality and has made high demands of himself, but more often he represses that awareness out of fear of the responsibility it entails. Erik Erikson has described the stages in the development of man's full character potential, maturity characterized by a firm self-identity, rich intimacy in interpersonal relations, rich and free generative capacity, and strong integrity of selfhood.

[7] Robert Kastenbaum (ed), *New Thoughts on Old Age* (New York: Springer Publishing Company, Inc., 1964), Chapter 4. Used with permission.

The movement in psychosocial development is from normal adjustment, of which several criteria are given, to high-level self-actualization and transcendent living. In the characteristics of maturity given by many writers, in Maslow's 16 qualities of the high self-actualizers, and in Jourard's description of transcendent living, we can see the same general state of personal attainment being described. It is a quality of life much above that of the normally well-adjusted individual.

Basic to this attainment is a healthy transcendent cognition, which means perceptions, generalization, evaluations, etc., that are free from anxiety defenses and selective distortion. There is good contact with reality and realistic appraisal, judgment, evaluation. Transcendent cognition, however, goes beyond this in a new dimension of perceptive vividness and qualitative uniqueness which gives the knowing experience end-value rather than a means of coping with a problem. It is described by Maslow as *cognition of being* (B-cognition), and these cognitive qualities culminate in creative thinking and true-to-self evaluation.

The more realistic and transcendent cognition of the high self-actualizer also culminates in more realistic or appropriate and enriched emotional states. His emotional states or moods are more than normally positive, although he is free to express great fear or anger when situations warrant it. Since he is mature and self-confident, great threats and frustrations are required to arouse his fear and anger, and these do not often occur. Since he is free of defenses, he identifies more deeply with other people and shares more fully in their emotional experiences.

From long habit we use the terms "mental" and "emotional" health, but it would be more exact to use the term "healthy self." In the self-actualizer, high-level psychosocial development, the self is mature, autonomous, strong and capable of generating, initiating, and directing the mental processes realistically and rewardingly. Clinical study of the self and its high potentialities, and how to more fully actualize them, is a new field of research, a psychological frontier. Several pilot projects of this type are now being conducted. Prominent among these is the work of Herbert Otto and his associates at the University of Utah. The recent research into the continuing self-actualization and release of potentialities deep into old age is another equally promising field of endeavor. With growing awareness of his hitherto unrecognized high potentiality, man begins to plan a lifetime program of training for self-actualization.

GLOSSARY

Allocentricism. A term used to define the sum of the differences in scale position of each of the thirty scales between the social self and independent judge ratings of the person's self. Theoretically, the person more allocentrically organized should be more centrally aware of the reactions of other persons to his own self than a person whose self-image was more subjectively organized.

Ethos. A cluster of the most distinguishing personality characteristics of an individual, a group, or a subculture—the prevailing and predominant character or "spirit" of a person or a people.

Psi experience. The hypothetical functional capacity for the various types of extrasensory perception as posited by parapsychology, including psychokinesis, e.g., physical changes induced by the mind such as objects being made to move, etc.

Veridically. Pertaining to accuracy or truthfulness.

REFERENCES AND SUGGESTED READINGS

BOWMAN, HENRY A., *Marriage for Moderns,* New York: McGraw-Hill Book Company, 1960, 1965.

ERIKSON, ERIK, "Identity Versus Identity Diffusion," *Readings in Child Development,* Paul Mussen et al. (eds) New York: Harper & Row Publishers, 1965.

———, *Childhood and Society,* New York: W. W. Norton & Co., Inc., 1950.

HEATH, DOUGLAS H., *Explorations of Maturity,* New York: Appleton-Century-Crofts, 1965.

JOURARD, SIDNEY, *Personal Adjustment,* New York: The Macmillan Company, 1958.

———, "Toward a Psychology of Transcendent Behavior," in *Explorations in Human Potentiality,* Herbert A. Otto (ed) Springfield, Ill.: Charles C. Thomas Publisher, 1966.

KASTENBAUM, ROBERT (ed), *New Thoughts on Old Age,* New York: Springer Publishing Co. Inc., 1964.

KENT, DONALD P., *Aging—Fact and Fancy,* U.S. Department of Health, Education and Welfare, Office of Aging, Washington: U.S. Government Printing Office, 1965.

LONDON, S. J., "The Ecology of Aging in Musicians," *Gerontologist,* 3:160–165 (1963).

MASLOW, A., *Toward a Psychology of Being,* Princeton, N.J.: D. Van Nostrand Co. Inc., 1962.
OTTO, HERBERT H. (ed), *Explorations in Human Potentiality,* Springfield, Ill.: Charles C. Thomas, Publisher, 1966.
OVERSTREET, HARRY A., *The Mature Mind,* New York: W. W. Norton & Co. Inc., 1949.
PRIESTLY, J. B., *Man and Time,* New York: Doubleday & Co. Inc., 1964.
RHINE, J. B., *New World of the Mind,* New York: William Sloane Assoc., 1953.
ROGERS, CARL R., *On Becoming a Person,* Boston: Houghton Mifflin Company, 1961.
THORPE, LOUIS P., *The Psychology of Mental Health,* New York: The Ronald Press Company, 1960.
WALLAS, G., *The Art of Thought,* New York: Harcourt, Brace & Co., 1921.

14

Healthy Social Living

The blurb on the front jacket of Dr. Blanton's *Love or Perish* (1956) says:[1] "Without love—in every form the collapse of life begins. From the simple drudgery of getting up in the morning, to the almost incredible disasters that lead into death itself, there is clear evidence that no man or woman can hope to survive in a life guided by hatred. The alternatives are, indeed, 'Love or Perish.'

"For without love, we lose the will to live. Our mental and physical vitality is impaired, our resistance is lowered, and we succumb to illnesses that often prove fatal. We may escape actual death, but what remains is a meager and barren existence, emotionally so impoverished that we can only be called half alive."

In his *Love Against Hate*, Dr. Karl Menninger says:[2] "When the scientist begins to talk about love, he is between Scylla and Charybdis. If he adheres rigidly to the conventional language and formulae of science, he will end in that same sterile futility that has long characterized science in its application to human social life. If, on the other hand, he abandons his scientific habits for a greater reliance upon intuitive truth, he risks verging upon the sentimental and the poetic. Sentiment and poetry are not necessarily antithetical to truth, but the scientist who uses poetic

---

[1] From *Love or Perish*, Copyright © 1955, 1956 by Smiley Blanton. Reprinted by permission of Simon & Schuster, Inc. and The World's Work Ltd.

[2] Karl Menninger, *Love Against Hate* (New York: Harcourt, Brace & Co., 1942).

terms is likely to be as discredited as a poet who uses scientific ones." (p. 260).

As Menninger states, this creates a dilemma for the scientist who is confronted with the phenomena of love and hate and who has something legitimate to say on these subjects, which, until recently, lay outside the sphere of scientific investigation. Regardless of this dilemma, the mental hygienist is working in an interdisciplinary field and must come to terms with *love* on the basis of scientific findings and nonscientific experience. For, at the roots of psychosocial disorders and high self-actualization, love is the central factor.

THE MEDICINE OF LOVE

I have repeatedly emphasized the need for love and its prophylactic and ameliorative role in relation to mental illness, and have pointed out that it was one of the great twentieth century discoveries of psychiatry. Dr. Blanton said:

> For more than forty years I have sat in my office and listened, while people of all ages and classes told me of their hopes and fears, their likes and dislikes, and of what they considered good or bad about themselves and the world around them. . . . As I look back over the long, full years, one truth emerges clearly in my mind, the universal need for love. Whether they think they do or not, all people want love.
>
> Modern psychiatry teaches us that we fall ill, emotionally and physically, if we do not use love in this way to guide and control our behavior. When we cannot give and receive love freely, we become easy prey to the dread emotions of fear and resentment, of anxiety and guilt. . . . Love's greatest glory lies in the fact that it alone provides the strength, protection and encouragement without which full growth is impossible. In every case, we must make the same decision between love and hate, and our ultimate success or failure will depend on the basic pattern we establish. Each act we perform from motives of love pours strength and health into the stream of life. Hate causes us to perish, sometimes in a series of little deaths, sometimes at once. If we preserve life in its fullest sense, we must choose the course of love. (1956, pp. 3, 12, 13, 14, 21 and 29).

Psychoanalyst Izette deForest[3] observes: "It may, therefore, be said that love and anger are the intrinsic fundamental emotions, and that it is on the basis of the conflict between these two forces and between their appropriate modifications that human beings form their characters. . . . Love must conquer hatred if the patient is to live a happy creative life. And this means living to his full capacity, undeterred by the blocking effects of destructive anger, envy, and jealousy. . . . (p. 79).

"As we well know, the act of loving stimulates one's whole being. The emotion of love vitalizes each physical and mental process. . . . There is no neurotic sufferer who is not to a large extent incapable of living at peace and in loving kindness with his fellow men. . . ." (pp. 125, 128).

The most dramatic utilization of love as a therapeutic force is exemplified by Gertrud Schwing, previously referred to. I shall close this section with the suggestion that if her little book has not been discussed in class, it should be at this time. I also suggest that the capacity of the therapist as a whole person to express love in its pure form of "motherliness" should be given attention.

THE CEMENT OF SOCIETY

Several books and many articles have been written during the past two decades about love as an aid to mental health. This, however, is not our major concern, for love finds its true function not as a means to anything but as an end in itself. Loves does not have a purpose, but it *is* a purpose—the goal of life, as stated in the language of the poet who wrote: "Ah sweet mystery of life, at last I've found thee!" To experience the love relationship in both its giving and receiving aspects fully and freely, maturely or perfectly, is the fullest self actualization. It is the goal of personal growth. And such interpersonal relationships wherein the love attitude completely dominates behavior, produces the perfectly mature society.

Communality. Erich Fromm, the social psychiatrist, has been fighting for communality of living, for a society that is con-

[3] Izette deForest, *The Leaven of Love,* (New York: Harper & Brothers Publishers, 1954). Used with permission.

ducive to true communion among its members, a society in which love rules. He has stated the two primary goals of life as being *productive work* and *productive love.* I would differ only slightly with Fromm at this point and make perfect (fully mature) love the supreme characteristic of self-actualization which, in turn, is expressed most fully in productive or creative work and interpersonal relations. The social scientist finds a special significance in the twofold admonition to love self and one's neighbor as himself. To truly love himself, the individual must find his true vocation, the work in which he can most fully express himself and receive the most complete satisfaction. To truly love others, the individual must identify fully with them, and must strive to find the field of work in which he can most fully satisfy the needs of others. In addition to this would be the interpersonal relationship of love as an end in itself.

Fromm stresses man's separateness and aloneness, having broken the symbiotic relationship with nature, and thus his absolute need of love as the voluntary achievement of inter-personal union. He says:[4] "Love is an activity, not a passive affect; it is a 'standing in,' not a 'falling for.' In the most general way, the active character of love can be described by stating that love is primarily *giving*, not receiving." (p. 22). He adds: "Beyond the element of giving, the active character of love becomes evident in the fact that it always implies certain basic elements, common to all forms of love. These are *care, responsibility, respect* and *knowledge. . . . Love is the active concern for the life and the growth of that which we love.*" (p. 26). Then he states: "Love is not primarily a relationship to a specific person; it is an *attitude, an orientation of character* which determines the relatedness of a person to the world as a whole, not toward one "object" of love. . . . The most fundamental kind of love, which underlies all types of love, is *brotherly love.* By this I mean the sense of responsibility, care, respect, knowledge of any other human being, the wish to further his life. . . . (pp. 46, 47).

Selfishness. Fromm compares different types of love and contrasts self-love with selfishness, saying: *"The affirmation of one's own life, happiness, growth, freedom is rooted in one's capa-*

[4] From *The Art of Loving* by Erich Fromm (Harper & Row, 1956). Reprinted by permission of Harper & Row, Publishers.

city to love, i.e., in care, respect, responsibility, and knowledge. If an individual is able to love productively, he loves himself too; if he can love *only* others, he cannot love at all. . . . *Selfishness and self-love, far from being identical, are actually opposites.* The selfish person does not love himself too much but too little; in fact he hates himself. . . . *It is true that selfish persons are incapable of loving others, but they are not capable of loving themselves either.*" (pp. 60, 61).

TO LOVE IS HUMAN

Animals may have the capacity to experience a rudimentary form of love. Certain feelings with elements akin to those in human love may be found in the herd and parent-offspring relationship. But love is a basic attitude, not an emotion. Two compounds may contain a common element yet be basically different. The animal is symbiotically united with "nature," and his inter-animal relationships and feelings are thus determined. Man stands aloof from "nature," detached, transcendent. Man identifies himself with his fellow man in a relationship of oneness, yet a oneness that enhances his individuality, his personality. This attitude and this capacity and this relationship are unique in man. Human love carries a quality and reaches a dimension utterly beyond the animal potential.

Goodwill. At the end of Chapter 3, I gave a brief description of love as being one of the highest capacities or potentialities of the self, and the three-dimension nature of love. Goodwill—to will the good of all people, family, friends, neighbors, enemies: this basic attitude or purpose is love. It implies freedom, choice, alternatives (ill-will or indifference). It requires, and is the chief characteristic of, a strong, mature, confident self, who is free of defenses and the anxiety-hostility-guilt complex. It is basic to mature, mutually enriching interpersonal relationships and is the binding force of society. Thus it is a high-level healthy-mindedness. It is fully mature psychosocial attainment. To will the good (love) of one's neighbor or enemy does not imply a feeling of affection. Rather, it is the mature attitude that one seeks to balance his own good with that of his neighborhood or society. It may in some cases mean punishment or incarceration of an obnoxious or criminal character, but the basic attitude is prophylactic and ameliorative, not merely punitive.

Affection. The mature person may love everybody in the sense of good will; but affection is for the relatively few, though it may include a sizable number of people in varying degrees. Love as affection is a bond of attraction with emotional overtones that grows as two people become involved, identify and share with each other. This occurs with members of the immediate family, near relatives and other companions with whom one is in frequent contact. The strength and richness of the affection depends on the frequency, depth, breadth, and quality of the shared experiences. Therefore, the degree of affection varies widely.

Conjugal. Although affection is limited to a relatively small number of people, close relatives and primary groups, every member of the group has affection for some other groups and all humanity may be cemented by affection which, with goodwill, provides the basis for a stable society and sound interpersonal relations. Love reaches its apex in the one-man-one-woman relationship of conjugal love. Here, identification, involvement, and sharing are complete—potentially, at least, and in ideal attainment. By choice, will (goodwill), the individual identifies and shares fully with his spouse permitting no other relationship to be so complete as to jeopardize that relationship. Thus, family life is stable; and with this, so with society.

Vulnerable. In one sense love is a terrible thing, and it is terrifying to many. Most people are afraid to love to the fullness of their potential. The lover is vulnerable, without defense. Empathy is complete when one has identified completely with another; and one experiences the fears, guilts, hurts, and betrayals of the other as if they were his own. They are his own. People never outgrow the need and desire (consciously or unconsciously) to receive love and to give love, but they may develop a fear of loving and thus block themselves from being loved. To love freely and fully is the mark of the mature self, a mature state of being, and it is expressed in mature, mutually enriching interpersonal relations and a stable society.

ACTIVE AND PASSIVE LOVE

Jourard (1958, Chapter 8) discusses "Love and Healthy Personality." Its essential elements may be gleaned from his summary statement:

> Loving-behavior is defined as any action undertaken by a person with the conscious aim of promoting the happiness and growth of the object. The loving person behaves in these ways toward his object freely, willingly, and with enjoyment.
>
> *Active* love refers to all occasions when a person behaves in loving fashion toward his object. *Passive* love refers to the process of accepting the loving behavior of another person.
>
> The motive which is most basic to loving behavior is the desire for the object's growth and happiness. *Identification* with the love-object is probably responsible for much of the emotion which a lover experiences; he feels the pleasures and pains of his object.
>
> People choose a love-object on the basis of many criteria, e.g., helplessness of the object, conformity of the object with the lover's ideals, the ability of the object to reciprocate love, etc. A *rational* choice of a love-object has been made when the person chooses someone whom he *can* love, and who can act in loving ways toward him. *Unhealthy object-choices* are likely to be made when the chooser is under the tension of very *strong needs*, when he *lacks self-knowledge*, and when he *lacks accurate knowledge of the personality and needs of the object.*
>
> Humans need *to be loved*, and they need *to love actively*, if they are to become and remain healthy personalities. Some of the factors which promote the ability to love actively include *rich gratification of needs* in the past, *affirmation of the value of love, high frustration-tolerance, self-love, a diversified personality-structure, a healthy self-structure, reality-contact, security, reasonable ideals* for the love-object, *emancipation from parental direction*, and *emancipation from inner-direction.* (p. 279).

By the last factor, Jourard means freedom from compulsive needs to conform, etc. On the whole, his treatment of the subject is comprehensive and satisfactory. But to move from a purely psychological to a broader point of view, love may be seen not only in its adjectival form, a type of behavior, but also in its noun-form, a relationship, a state of being—of being completely inter-related. Loving behavior is its manifestation, its expression. With respect to the "love-object," I prefer the term love-subject. The same thing may be either a subject or an object. The relationship determines the difference. Subjects act; objects only react. Love is a relationship of mutual action-reaction, giving and re-ceiving—subject-partners sharing in action or experience. Theo-retically, one may receive love and give none in return and thus be a love-object, but it is doubtful that this can be done without some loving action in return. This might be true in the parent-neonate relationship, but even here it is highly probable that the newly born child gives out with a small degree of love. Perhaps the more mature person in the partnership gives more love, and the immature member receives more than he gives, thus is both object and subject. But that is a moot question. It may be true that one cannot receive more love than he is able to give, thus much of the love of the mature partner is unaccepted, wasted. The issue is undecided. Nevertheless, the mature, mutually satisfying love rela-tionship is that of two subjects compounded. It is a *we* experience, not a *you* to *me*.

B-LOVE

Maslow (1962, pp. 39-41) contrasts D-love (deficiency-love, love-need, selfish love) with B-love (love for the being of another person, unneeding love, unselfish love), saying of the love-need: "Satisfaction of the need should cause it to disappear, which is to say that people who have stood in satisfying love relationships are precisely the people who should be *less* likely to give and to re-ceive love! But clinical study of healthier people, who have been love-need-satiated, show that although they need less to *receive* love, they are more able to *give* love. In this sense, they are more loving people." The contrast continues:

1. B-love is welcomed into consciousness, and is completely enjoyed . . . is nonpossessive . . . makes no trouble . . . is pleasure-giving.

2. It can never be sated . . . grows greater . . . is end rather than means.
3. The B-love experience is often described as being the same as, and having the same effects as the aesthetic experience or the mystic experience. . . .
4. The therapeutic and psychologic effects of experiencing B-love are very profound and widespread. . . .
5. B-love is, beyond the shadow of a doubt, a richer, "higher," more valuable subjective experience than D-love.
6. D-love *can* be gratified. The concept "gratification" hardly applies at all to admiration-love for another person's admiration-worthiness. . . .
7. In B-love there is a minimum of anxiety-hostility. . . . There *can,* of course, be anxiety-for-the-other. . . .
8. B-lovers are more independent of each other, more autonomous, less jealous or threatened, less needful . . . more altruistic, generous and fostering.
9. The truest, most penetrating perception of the other is made possible by B-love . . . non-love makes us blind.
10. Finally, I may say that B-love, in a profound but testable sense, creates the partner. It gives him a self-image . . . self-acceptance, a feeling of love-worthiness . . . which permits him to grow. . . .

It is the healthy-minded, self-actualizing person who can experience love in its "higher" modes as described and it is on the basis of such love that satisfying interpersonal relations are built and maintained. It is the cement of society. It gives to society that necessary ingredient which is most conducive to high self-actualization.

SEX AS INTERPERSONAL RELATION

In Chapter 4, sex was presented as a *social need,* rooted in the biological structure and physiological processes but functioning at the human level in its common modes of expression on the basis of learned values—the desire or drive more mental than physiological and the act more to satisfy social needs than biological. Sex is a social function, and hardly anything is more interpersonal. The mode of a person's sex life is a distinctive measure of his psychosocial development, and it has a vital bearing on the quality of his interpersonal relations.

The Freudian concept of sexual latency during middle childhood is only relatively true and not nearly to the degree that Freud believed. It varies widely with environmental conditions, stimuli situations, and other competing interests. However, adolescence is ushered in with the rapid, last stage maturation of sex organs and glands and the capacity to function sexually as an adult. There is a spurt of sex interest-need at this time, with physiological factors in the stimulus situations playing a relatively greater role than previously or later. But even at this time, one's training, his value system, and his imagination are the greater determiners of sex desire and behavior. One of the primary needs or problems of the adolescent period is to attain socio-sexual maturity based on the maturation of love, the predominant attitude of goodwill toward the many and rich affection for the several, on B-love.

SEXUAL EMANCIPATION

A current attitude or opinion held by many people argues that with modern contraceptives, particularly "the pill," societal involvement is reduced to the point of virtual non-existence. Thus, sex becomes purely an individual matter and the healthy way to express "love" or release tension when two persons agree that it is appropriate. The rising incidence of premarital pregnancies casts a shadow over the argument, but to use such counter-argument is to mask the important question. How may petting and sexual intercourse be used as a means to enrich interpersonal relations or psychosocial development?

Just how new is the so-called "new sexual freedom"? The news media have made much of it during the past decade, but reporters are often noted for exaggeration and distortion. The sensational adds to reader interest. Certainly, since World War I and the "Jazz Age" aftermath, this emancipation has been in progress. Advances in medical science and biochemistry, the "new psychology" with its emphasis on freedom of expression, a somewhat sudden admixture of values and mores by military personnel mingling with people of all cultures, the excess of emotion aroused by an endless succession of wars, the movies and the bold new emphasis on sex in entertainment and advertising, automobiles and motels—all these and other factors have combined to undermine the old controls or depressors of sexual behavior, namely, the fears of pregnancy, venereal disease, and social ostracism. In many ways this is good, for fear is stiffling to growth and is an unworthy control of social behavior.

Many college students with whom I have talked during the past decade, felt that organized religion too frequently has associated itself with warring governments and their war atrocities and with social institutions that impede personal growth. Thus they have rejected much of the morality sanctions of orthodox religion along with the mores of orthodox middle class society and are searching for their own means of validation. If the past decade has added a new element to the sex emancipation of the whole twentieth century, it is this search for meaning in their sexual experimentation. Does sex find its true significance in sheer tension release, in relaxation, in pleasure with no deep personal involvement or concern for the partner? Does sexual intercourse add meaningfulness to or validate a broader sharing relationship between two people of like interests and mutual liking, but dissociated from marriage and social responsibility?

Objective appraisal of this searching and experimentation reveals elements that are wholesome and some that appear extreme. To find the modes of sexual behavior that contribute most to the enrichment of interpersonal relations and self-actualization requires repeated re-evaluations and experimentation, for no other generation has yet found it. But is it rational or scientific to abandon all old guides, former hypotheses, in order to improve or correct? The old morality has not been good enough. The question seems to be whether this new experimentation will result in more fulfilling relationships now or whether a decline will occur for one or two generations before a new generation discovers the more satisfying way. For whether or not, or to what degree, we accept or reject middle class religious or secular orthodoxy, we are confronted with the life-demand to explore, learn, and create a better economy, a better government, a better art, a better religion, a better society, a better life.

If one could sincerely attain this freer or more promiscuous attitude through several years of mental conditioning, or for many generations as in many primitive societies, sexual intercourse would then be removed from the area of social responsibility and morality. There would be little or no anxiety-guilt tension and psychic ill effects. This would make the sexual response a simple hedonism—utilizing sexual stimuli to arouse tension for the pleasure of releasing the tension, making a physiological process and its emotional overtones an end rather than a means to a greater end. Clinical evidence indicates that there is a greater frequency of emotional disorder among young people who are sexually promiscuous than there is among those who abstain from premarital intercourse. This casts some doubt that this attitude can be deeply established, except by several generations of conditioning. If this were to become an eventuality, the question still remains: would it conduce or inhibit the highest psychosocial attainment?

The learning of values and conditioning of conscience were discussed in Chapter 5. I stated there that while the functioning of conscience is greatly influenced by internalizing social values, conscience itself is the inherent capacity and process of self-evaluation. With varying degrees of consciousness and frequency, there are moments of self-awareness when individuals experience themselves with approval or disapproval, as being worthy or unworthy, in accordance with their actual performance relative to its potentiality. This applies to man's vocational performance and the quality of his interpersonal relations. It underlies Fromm's dual goal thesis, e.g., productive work and productive love. It is the essential capacity and process by which we may account for man's unique control of his own destiny, his capacity to direct his own evolution. In this self-capacity lies the dynamic that prevents growth toward full self-actualization from stoppage and becoming fixed at the point of mere adaptation. It prevents *humans* from being satisfied with sex as a hedonistic personal matter and continues the challenge toward its becoming an instrument for expressing mature love that is family oriented and conducive to the highest quality of interpersonal relations.

Although we lack experimental proof of this theoretical position, I have found much clinical support from hundreds of sexual delinquents, normal college students, and couples in premarital counseling. Generally, it requires good rapport and two or three interviews before the individual is clearly aware of his own sexual attitudes or feels free to express them. In the light of this sincere researching by many students and my many years of observation, the following topic is presented as a hypothesis to be tested in the laboratory of social living and in the search for the most satisfying, self-fulfilling, and socially enriching sex life.

LOVE-SEX MATURATION

Degree. One of the basic functions of adolescent dating is to develop heterosexual love and social relations to the point of maturity in which sexual behavior is controlled by love (goodwill, affection, B-love). Sex becomes the physical expression of love. The adolescent who has grown up in a home where his love-needs were well satisfied and an adequate value system built—the healthy-minded, growth-motivated youth—can direct his sex responses on the basis of love maturation. Sex, as the physical expression of love, will be controlled and limited to the degree of actual love maturation—light petting, moderate petting, heavy petting, and sexual intercourse, the last stage only when love is fully mature and the couple has contracted (covenanted) to share life fully and permanently. The healthy-minded, self-actualizing adult (married) has disciplined himself to experience sex desire and engage in sexual intercourse only with his spouse—a one-man-one-woman relationship that is exclusive of others, for the full expression of a mature love which is mutually enriching. Willing the good of the other person, using the sexual response only as a channel for expressing a deep and mutual affection, and having a high appreciation and love for the *being* of the other person will prevent ever *using* him (her) to gratify pleasure desires or as an anxiety or hostility outlet.

In its biological origin, the sex drive or desire is not associated with love but is promiscuous in tendency. During a few years of adolescent dating, the association of sex with love only may be formed by insight and condition-response learning. Based on the youth's own value system and/or that of his family or peer group, his own approval and disapproval or that of family or peer group, provide the reinforcer and extinguisher. Thus, by late adolescence the individual's sex desires may be conditioned to full and free expression with the partner whom he loves maturely and has chosen for a life mate. Also, by the same learning processes, strong sex desire for others may be extinguished. Thus, sex in its full genital expression becomes the exclusive relationship of the couple who has covenanted to share life fully. This may well become the central emphasis in sex education for adolescents. As a hypothesis, this might be worth testing in experimental living.

D-Love. The immature, deprived, D-love individual cannot function at this high level in his love or sex life. In D-love there often are large elements of anxiety and hostility, and sex becomes a channel for expressing these rather than mature love. The other person becomes a thing used to satisfy one's immature desires rather than a subject with whom to share. It is a means-act instead of an end-experience that is of worth in itself. This type or level of sex-love becomes sated and seeks variety, tends toward promiscuity or frequent change of partners. It is detrimental to stable and richly satisfying family and other interpersonal relationships. It is irresponsible sex.

A large proportion of people are relatively immature in their sex-social relationships. During the past four or five decades there has been a moderate loosening of sex mores in the Western world, for reasons too numerous and complex to discuss here. But in the course of the past 2000 years, the trend has been (but slowly) toward greater control and mutual consideration, pointing toward the above hypothesis as the goal of the mature individual in a mature society. An intensive study of history and period literature appears to sustain this position. Much clinical evidence shows that premarital promiscuity and extramarital sex affairs are tension-producing, character-depressing, and conducive to family and social instability. This is revealed again and again in the empathic psychotherapeutic relationship. Promiscuity is not acceptable to mature society nor to the sex partners in the depths of their being. It is not an expression of B-love (love of being). It is selfish, irresponsible and often impersonal, using subjects as objects, dehumanizing. D-love may grow into B-love by experimental development and application of the above hypothesis.

HOW MUCH SEX? FREQUENCY AND ATTITUDE

We are not concerned here with statistics relative to sex attitudes and practice. As in any moral matter, there is a wide disparity between attitude, actual belief, and practice, thus value incongruence and tension. In this century, freedom to discuss sex has advanced far more than freedom of practice. In spite of the Kinsey studies and a few hundred others, there are still no highly valid measures of sex attitudes or practices. The statistics vary and often miss what is most significant in the practice. Henry A. Bowman, a long-time student of sexual-social problems, after quoting sexual intercourse incidence findings of numerous studies, says[5] (pp. 129–140):

> All studies of premarital intercourse up to date involve shortcomings of one sort or another, such as inadequate sampling, methodological errors, debatable interpretations, or time-relative validity (data gathered years ago). . . . Sexual intercourse is an integral part of life activity. . . . If one thinks at all about premarital intercourse, one cannot avoid relating it to other areas of interest and concern.
>
> There are several such broad areas: the nature of human life, the culture in which we live, and the objectives which the individual establishes for himself. In other words, if his attitude is to be critical and considered rather than uncritical and naive, whatever conclusion an individual reaches regarding premarital intercourse should be human-nature derived, culturally relative, and goal-oriented. . . .
>
> Hypothetical cases such as those mentioned above point up the pertinence of the issue: How and where is a line to be drawn between individual freedom and societal good? . . . Is premarital sexual intercourse entirely a matter of individual freedom and choice, or is there involved in it in some way a question of societal good? . . . Since sexual intercourse involves (or may) a third person, a child, as well as the couple, it has societal as well as personal implications. . . .
>
> Many present-day Americans, however, are working out a type of marriage somewhat new in history. It is new in its emphasis on interpersonal relationships and personal satisfaction, in the feelings and attitudes involved in assuming that love is its cornerstone, in its mutuality, in the degree of sharing anticipated, and in its expectation of sexual exclusiveness. Marriage is inextricably bound up as an integral part of the idealism of thoughtful people who want life to be meaningful. . . .

---

[5] Henry A. Bowman, *Marriage for Moderns* (New York: McGraw-Hill Book Co., 1965). Used with permission.

> If sexual exclusiveness is one of the expectations in this value system, it is clear that the kind of marriage we are discussing cannot be achieved if sexual intercourse is considered a casual experience of the moment, if it is disconnected from long-time goals and perspective. Sexual exclusiveness is not something that begins with the wedding. It is something that reflects an individual's point of view regarding the value system of marriage and the meaning of life. . . .
>
> Sharing loses its mutuality to the degree that one individual has an attitude of exploitation and uses another person for his own satisfaction alone. . . .

DEGREES OF LOVE AND SEX

In the preceding topics, I have attempted to point out the chief characteristics of mature sexual behavior that is most satisfying to society and the self. They serve to reiterate the concept of sex as the physical expression of love, and that sexual intercourse at the human level should be (is, in its higher intention) strictly family-oriented. Thus our concern is more with attitudes and degree of sexual expression than with statistics on sexual intercourse. From the simplest feeling of appreciation and approval through deepening stages of identification and affection to the covenanting of a full and completely shared life, the physical expression grows from the lightest caress to full genital union, symbolizing the merging of two selves into conjugal or familial oneness. Thus, sexual intercourse finds its *raison d'etre* in the double role of conceiving a child in a great act of love, and also as spouses and parents joining frequently in complete union (body, mind, and spirit) to enrich the love climate of the home for the child's (and parents') emotional nourishment. This would reflect the responsible sexual behavior of the mature, healthy-minded, self-actualizing person and conduce the highest quality interpersonal relations or social health.

Figures 12 and 13 are copies of two simple methods I developed and used for measuring the sex attitudes and practices of students. They were constructed on the principle of increased sexual intimacy with the growing maturation of love. Figure 12 shows the degree of sexual intimacy approved and/or prac-

A goodnight hug and kiss, but mild

Light petting—smooching but no body caresses

Moderate petting—body caresses but avoiding breasts and genitals

Heavy petting—including genital caresses

Sexual intercourse

						On first date
						Casual dating—after 1st date
						Going stady—not marriage-oriented
						Going steady—marriage-oriented
						When married only

Figure 12. Degrees of Intimacy Approved.

I would not voluntarily submit under any circumstances

I would seek to avoid it but may submit under strong pressure

I would engage in it but with some misgivings

I would engage in it quite freely

I believe the following percentage of (Sr. High) students indulge.

					On casual dates
					When going steady—not marriage-oriented
					When going steady—marriage-oriented
					When married only

Figure 13. The Role of Sexual Intercourse.

ticed at different stages of love maturation and interpersonal involvement. The same instrument may be used at one time to get actual beliefs and again to find the actual practices of the same group. Figure 13 may also be used twice with the same group to measure attitudes and practices relative to the role of sexual intercourse in life, under what circumstances or relationships it is appropriate. Column 5 is set off by a double line, since it is of a different category. The student is asked to estimate the percentage of his peers (senior high, college freshmen, etc.) who engage in sexual intercourse based on his observation and acquaintance.

I have not used these charts for statistical studies of large-scale samplings. Rather, they have been used with several classes as an aid in clarifying the student's own position in relation to his peer group. They were used anonymously and class averages were obtained. Results varied considerably from one class to another, but findings with respect to sexual intercourse fell within the range of several other studies. The big response clusters ran from upper left to lower right, a large minority of boys (over one-fourth) and a majority of girls (over 60 percent) limiting sexual intercourse to marriage, at least in attitude if not in practice. In each group the trend was clearly in the direction of greater sexual intimacy with growth or maturation of love. Estimates of sexual indulgence by peers varied greatly, indicating that young people do not know "what everybody else is doing."

RESPONSIBLE SEX

Premarital sexual relations fall into at least five general categories which reflect widely different attitudes and both personal and social consequences: (1) The all-out hedonist who is thoroughly promiscuous and indifferent to religious morals or social mores; (2) the person, more typically of the lower socio-economic class, whose value system is more permissive of overt expression of hostility and sex than is characteristic of our middle class society; (3) the social rebel in a reaction formation type of behavior that is contrary to generally accepted social standards, or perhaps trying to prove himself; (4) the individual who may have high moral standards but also a compulsive need for acceptance and love that finds symbolic or substitute expression in repetitious sex affairs; (5) the couple who is very much in love, perhaps engaged, but cannot get married for some time and whose premarital sexual relationship is monogamous.

Anthropological studies reveal a wide variation of approved sex behavior among people of different cultures, in what they demand and what they permit; but in every society studied, some regulations exist with respect to sex. It is rarely, if ever, considered a strictly private affair. Matters of legitimate name, inheritance, and family solidarity are social concerns. The individual's sex practices have a direct effect on his sex partner, his family, and his immediate community. Certain modes of expression may produce less complications and harm in some societies than in others. The customs of a primitive society need not be the same as in a complex industrial society. But the matter of personal or social ills is not our concern in this chapter. Rather, what mode of sex behavior may the individual develop that will contribute most fully to self-actualization and social solidarity. The mature responsible individual assumes a mature responsibility to himself and to society. His youthful independence yields to a higher order interdependence.

In the light of Bowman's extensive studies, my own years of observation and counseling, and the reports of numerous campus clinics, evidence indicates that the majority of students, consciously or unconsciously, are finding the true meaning of sex in the physical expression of love and to the degree of the maturation of love. There is a normal gap between attitudes and practice and much remains to be accomplished. With old and inadequate controls discarded, this new searching and experimentation, if reasonable and guided as effective research must be, may very well lead rapidly to more satisfying interpersonal relations.

HEALTHY SEXUAL BEHAVIOR

Let us close this section with certain summary statements by Jourard (1958, pp. 139, 140) on sexual behavior.

> *Healthy sexual behavior* is behavior which is effective in securing sexual gratification for the individual and accords with the social mores and the individuals self-structure.

> *Healthy sexual aims* include the giving and receiving of pleasure, the expression of affection for the partner, the conception of children. Examples of *unhealthy sexual aims* include reassurance, compensation for other frustrations, and the use of sexual behavior as a means of getting other valued objects.
>
> A person is said to display *healthy conditions for arousal* when he or she is sexually responsive to the typical forms of sexual stimulation, that is, stroking of erogenous zones, terms of endearment, etc. . . .
>
> *Healthy sexual behavior* is any kind of sexual activity which is mutually acceptable to the partners, and which achieves the various sexual aims. Many sorts of sexual behavior which would be viewed as perverse if they were an end in themselves are regarded as healthy and acceptable within the context of a healthy love relationship. . . .
>
> Some *signs of healthy sexuality* in a person include *accurate knowledge about sex*, an *accepting attitude toward sex*, and *the ability to integrate sexuality with the over-all value-system of the person*. . . .

I feel that in his chapter, "Healthy Sexual Behavior," Jourard has dealt comprehensively with the subject as accepted by most social scientists and the general concept of normal mental-social health. I would add that, in light of recent findings of marriage counselors and potential development studies, for sexual relations to be most satisfying and mutually enriching the pleasure aim should be secondary to its more significant end-purpose and the arousal largely limited to one's permanent love partner in a context of experienced love; and that the quality of mutual love and respect found in the most healthful and enriching relationship places certain limits on the kind of sexual activity chosen by the partners. I believe that Jourard would admit this amendment to his summary. It may be implied in the phrases "various sexual aims," "healthy love relationship," and "over-all value system."

HEALTHFUL FAMILY LIVING

Love and sex have been presented as the most completely interpersonal of all experiences, with love expressed genitally, and sex as the expression of mature love. I have taken the position that the most healthful, satisfying, fulfilling sexual love is family-oriented. Love reaches its greatest depth, perhaps, in the conjugal relation, but it is enriched and fulfilled in its parental expression. The love of a child, in its manifestation at least, is a dependency, receiving love. The love of husband and wife is an interdependent, mutually expressed love of equals. The love of a parent is a succoring, nourishing, giving love that demands no reward. It adds to self-actualization, to the process of becoming.

The Family is the oldest of all social institutions. Anthropologists, going back ten or twenty thousand years in their study of primitive man and his pattern of life, find that family life even then was a well-established institution. Mothers nursed, cradled, and sheltered their young. Fathers hunted, fought, and died to feed and protect their families. Tender affection grew to enrich instinctive care and the fierce passion of a primitive age. Shelf upon shelf of books and pamphlets describing the family and family living line the walls of every large library. Yet there is something about family living that eludes the mind and escapes the tomb of classification. It is alive, as mysterious as life itself. And it holds before us unexplored possibilities that we may anticipate but cannot comprehend.

Brothers fight; parents and children clash frequently. When one lives in intimate relationship, his ego desires come into conflict with the rights or desires of other members of the family. There is tension and conflict within the family. The individual members get on one another's nerves. But having learned to love each other as themselves, they forgive. They learn to balance justice and mercy—the strong and the tender responses of love. They learn to work together, play together, and worship together while holding different opinions and having occasional clashes which grow less severe and less frequent as they mature. Peace, happiness, and family solidarity become theirs. The capacities developed within the family become operative in the wider circles of social, economic, and international relations. Peace and a stable society are the results.

It is such that family living may be and often is in its better forms of expression. It provides the essential link between the individual and society. Parent-child and sibling relationships prepare the individual for essential and fulfilling interpersonal relations in an adult society. It is in the interpersonal relations of family living that one learns to identify with others, to trust and love, to fight and forgive and participate in social living. Since this is the case, the building of an adequate family relationship begins with the choice of a mate.

CHOOSING A MATE

In earlier times, and still in some countries, parents took care of this problem, saving the young people from much responsibility. In India where the custom of parents choosing marriage partners for their children is still in vogue, an American sociologist and family life specialist asked the students in several universities if they approved the custom. After some discussion, the majority voted in favor of the custom, saying that parents were more experienced and knowledgeable and could make the wiser choice. Perhaps our American young people will turn to the computer, a method frequently used in date selection.

Choice of a date and choice of a mate have certain elements in common but they are fundamentally different problems. Likewise, the qualities that make for a satisfying date and a satisfying mate are in some instances the same and in others quite different. Dates are usually chosen for temporary enjoyment and limited sharing—for recreation. Mates are usually chosen for permanent enrichment and complete sharing—for family life. Having fun together is a part of a satisfying marriage, but only a part. Too often date mates chosen on the narrow basis of recreational sharing continue to date and get married, only to find that the requirements of marriage open areas wherein their characteristics are too different for harmonious everyday living. Mate selection that offers assurance of a happy marriage also requires a broader and deeper knowledge, a thorough evaluation of many traits.

Three practical problems are involved in this matter of mate choice: (1) the opportunity to meet and date a variety of eligibles; (2) to be able to date each of several a sufficient number of times to really get acquainted; and (3) having sufficient self-knowledge and freedom from defenses to become involved with the other deeply enough to make a fair appraisal, which is subjective as well as objective. For the person who is inclined to face this problem as objectively or rationally as possible, Bowman suggests that one list the characteristics of: "1) The type of person one wants. . . . 2) The type of person one needs. . . . 3) The type of person one is likely to be able to get. . . ." (1965, p. 174). Practical!

Do opposites attract? Yes. There is a certain special interest, curiosity, even fascination in the person who is very different in appearance, cultural background, and mode of life. Sometimes very satisfactory marriages grow out of such unions, if both partners are very mature and adjustable. Two people do not become one simply because the clergyman pronounces them so. Any marriage requires a considerable amount of adjusting. If the differences are extensive, the adjusting is too much for many. The odds are in favor of the couple most alike in cultural background, basic attitudes, ideals; yes, and habits. They generally have more to share, more common interests, and less defenses against each other. However, if the couple have similar ideals and basic character traits, they may vary widely in their more superficial traits and interests and be complementary to each other.

Next in importance to commonality of basic interests and traits in the choice of a marriage partner is his (her) family background. Generally the person who grew up in a happy, well-adjusted family makes a better marriage partner than those who did not. In his classic study of 792 married couples, Terman[6] found the following background factors conducive to happy marriages: (1) happiness of parents; (2) childhood happiness; (3) lack of child-parent conflict; (4) fair and firm home discipline; (5) attachment to or identification with parents; (6) parental frankness about sex matters; and (7) a premarital attitude toward sex free of aversion and disgust.

KEYS TO HAPPY MARRIAGE

Most people want to be happy. I hope, however, it has been clear that no feeling or affect state should be sought as an end-goal. Rather, adequate, high-level functioning should be the aim; the

[6] Lewis M. Terman, *Psychological Factors in Marital Happiness* (New York: McGraw-Hill Book Co., 1938).

happiness will come as a consequence. Happiness, in turn, is a major criterion of adequate function. The happy marriage is one in which the partners have attained high quality relationships that are mutually enhancing. And since so much of a person's time is given to the family relationship, if it does not contribute to his fulfillment and happiness, his total life will be greatly depleted.

In spite of discouraging statistics (approximately 35 percent of our marriages end in divorce and another 30 to 40 percent are frustrating and dissatisfying) more than nine-tenths of our young people continue to marry. And most of them expect their marriages not only to endure but also to add to their happiness. As society grows more and more complex, greater demands and responsibilities fall upon the family; and as people become better educated and acquainted with life's potentialities, they demand more of their marriages. Marriage is no longer merely a biological and an economic partnership, to make a life and make a living. It is a partnership in living for the enhancement of life and personal growth. How can it be made such? What are the keys to happy marriage?

MATURE LOVE

Love is a basic attitude and qualitative state that carries emotional overtones; love is not a "thing" that can be mature or immature, yet we continue to use such phrases as "mature love" and "emotional immaturity." Such phrases designate the characteristic quality of love or emotion expressed by the mature or immature self. Although we contrast maturity and immaturity, they are relative, not dichotomous. Mature love is the quality and type of love responses that characterize the mature, self-actualizing person. Both this type of person and this type of love have been described. Mature love requires time to grow, is not instantaneous; involves the whole person(s), not chiefly physical attraction; has many facets of expression; is realistic and appropriate in affect and other response; is more fulfilling than frustrating even in disappointment; is outgoing and creative; is the attitude of sharing with a "we-feeling"; and grows richer with time. It is relatively free of jealousy and is exclusive in its genital mode of expression. It is the B-love described by Maslow.

The majority of marriage failures are due to immaturity of one or both partners. The immature lack self-confidence, fear their responsibilities, become defensive, jealous, suspicious; communication and sharing are impaired; doubts and distrust block affection; conflict destroys harmony and happiness. The persons who find the marriage relationships fulfilling and mutually satisfying choose mature partners or get help in attaining maturity soon after marriage.

COMPANIONSHIP AND SHARING

Next in importance to, and largely depending on, maturity, is the matter of companionship in many shared activities and responsibilities. This requires confidence in self and others, mutual trust, and common ideals, values, interests, purpose, etc.

Were he the epitome of masculinity and she the perfect "Miss America," and their romance exceeded that of Romeo and Juliet, it would not be enough for a satisfying marriage—else the Hollywood marriages would be the most successful and enduring. Robert Browning wrote: "Nay, love, you did give all I asked, I think—

> More than I merit, by many times.
> But had you—oh, with the same perfect brow
> And perfect eyes and more than perfect mouth . . .
> Had you with these, but brought a mind!
> Some women do so. Had the mouth then urged
> 'God and the glory! Never care for again!' . . .
> Had you given me a soul,
> We might have risen to Raphael, I and you."

Marriage is contracted on the basis of sexual differences. But marriage is solidified, held by multiple bonds of affection, on the basis of broad, deep and varied activities and responsibilities that are shared. This means likeness in many ways. It means a mutuality of interests, abilities, ideals, goals, and character traits. Many a couple are very much in love when they get married;

but because of too many differences, too little to share, they drift apart, live in different worlds, find greater satisfaction with others; and the marriage breaks. Similarity of social and family background, of intelligence, education, basic values and attitudes, and religion are conducive to broader and deeper sharing, more complete identity and richer love. The partners who make the most of the marriage relationship choose their mates accordingly. Or if they find themselves to be considerably different, they modify certain attitudes and interests sufficiently to become complementary rather than clashing, as both colors and personalities often are.

SEXUAL SATISFACTION

A number of years ago psychologists virtually equated marital compatibility with sexual compatibility and made sex satisfaction the primary factor in a satisfying marriage. Thus, the market was flooded with books on sex techniques, and many theorists advocated premarital sex experimentation to determine sexual adequacy. Later and more complete clinical evidence has discredited this earlier extremism. Love needs to be expressed physically (sexually) and it is enriched in marriage, but the sexual relationship is one of several modes of sharing life and only one of several keys to a happy marriage. Sexual maladjustment may and often does seriously cripple the marriage, but this is one of the easiest areas to correct. In most cases where it occurs, it is due to a more basic factor: immaturity, anxiety, guilt, and conflict in other relationships.

Mature, responsible sex life has been described. It is this type of relationship that characterizes the fulfilling, mutually enriching marriage. Those who find or make their marriage thus, choose their mates on the basis of the happy family background and wholesome attitude toward sex. With this, no premarital experimentation is necessary. The experimenting and adjusting that are necessary during the first year of marriage add to the enjoyment of discovery, and the knowledge that each is the only sex partner adds to the trust and depth of sharing which both may experience. Completeness of sharing is necessarily exclusive.

CHILDREN

Love reaches its most complete and richest expression as parental love, and personality cannot attain its fullest expression without the experience of parenthood. Having children is one of the two basic functions of human sex and is one of the major purposes of marriage. Children should not merely be had; they should be enjoyed and wanted. Their value lies not merely in tax deduction, nor in replenishing the human race, but in the enrichment of interpersonal relations, in the tenderizing of the human character. Everybody loves a baby, but it requires a mature parent to truly *care* for and *nourish* the child through his years of growth and to *enjoy* him. The frustrated and distraught parent who complains to his (her) child in a tone of martyrdom, "You don't appreciate how much I sacrifice for you," is correctly answered by the discerning reply, "Yes, but look how much joy I have given you."

There should be that sacrifice element in parental love, and its affect should be cancelled by the joy of the relationship and the "well-done" rearing practices. What the child-parent relationship should be and should not be has been covered extensively in Chapter 6 and with many later references. In the democratic family where each is fully accepted in his own right, where it's each for all and all for each, where love is adequately expressed in both its justice and mercy aspects, where discipline is firm but fair and both parents consistent and in agreement, where the children are given responsibility and pushed toward achievement but encouraged and helped (and loved) in failure, and where the family has fun together and worships together, there is fulfillment and happiness. The healthy-minded, psychosocially adequate couple plans their marriage accordingly. And if after medical and/or psychotherapeutic help they are unable to conceive and give birth, they will arrange for adoption. Even parenthood is more truly a psychosocial matter than a biological.

A VITAL RELIGIOUS FAITH

Some "mixed" marriages succeed admirably; and with the growing ecumenical attitude, the future will probably see more of them. But in the immediate past, the odds have been against marriages between persons from widely different religious fellowships, since they have not been as satisfying as marriage can and should be. Statistics are far from accurate, but they are ample to indicate that a much higher percentage of such marriages are broken by divorce, separation, or inner defense and conflict than those in which both partners have a similar religious orientation. Statistics also show that marriage failure is greater among those who have no active religious affiliation, whether from lack of interest or from choosing to ignore both religions in order to avoid conflict. They also reveal that there is generally greater stability and happiness in the families where religious faith is a vital factor in family life. It is not a matter of church affiliation which was discussed in connection with the family life of delinquents. It is where religious "belief" is sincere, deep, and realistic and where worship has become a regular, natural, spontaneous and meaningful experience.

I have contrasted faith and love with fear (anxiety) and hate (hostility) as the big four among the attitudes that conduce or inhibit growth, fulfillment, and self-actualization. Faith in God, in life, in oneself and in others tend to work together. One who experiences in worship some element of divine love enhances his own human love and sense of worth. Faith and love are *the* essential elements in the climate of the home. A vital religion enhances these. When husband and wife are joined by love to become one, the union is of body, mind, and soul (spirit)—the whole of both persons. For adequate sexual sharing, healthy and attractive bodies are necessary; for adequate cultural sharing, healthy and informed "minds" are necessary; for full self-sharing, healthy and well-developed spiritual attributes are essential. The couples which reach the highest quality of marital relationship chose mates with this in mind and/or, through faith and worship, share in a spiritual fellowship.

ECONOMIC SECURITY

How much money should a couple have to maintain a happy home? Need in this area of life is very relative. "To which she is accustomed," has been a thorny problem of many young husbands. Beyond a minimum subsistence level, material needs are secondary. They are acquired needs and their satisfaction is a matter of expectancy, conditioning, and habitual life-pattern. Extreme poverty is conducive to tension and anxiety and denies the family certain material things and pleasurable activities which normally enrich life. And excess wealth, judging from increased divorce rates at that economic level, seems to conduce marriage instability, e.g., the general pattern of life that the wealthy commonly follow. But there is a wide range of family income within which the specific amount has little direct effect on marital happiness.

Beyond the poverty level, the problem is more directly that of maturity and a similarity of attitudes. The mature person is adaptable and can accept with good grace, at least temporarily, a lower than accustomed economic status and can make it an interesting challenge. And where husband and wife have similar attitudes toward material things, a similar value system, they can avoid much conflict and share more fully in the solving of many economic problems. Matters of joint earnings, joint bank account (or separate), planned budget, decisions in buying, who pays bills, etc., pose numerous problems and compose a large area of potential conflict or harmonious sharing. Thus, it is an area in which a marriage may be wrecked or cemented and made more enjoyable. When the "tight-wad" marries the "spend-thrift," they are likely to have trouble. In cases of the very mature, this may be avoided by deliberately working out a balanced economic arrangement wherein the partners complement each other.

FAMILY RESOURCES DEVELOPMENT

In the preceding chapter, Herbert Otto's Personal Resource Development Project was briefly reviewed. Otto has conducted similar pilot projects with small groups of married couples to help families discover and utilize their strengths more effectively in more satisfying and creative intrafamily life. The purposes and goals are clearly defined at a preliminary meeting and during the first regular meeting. Otto says:[7] "During the first regular meeting the couples filled out a Family Strength Questionnaire designed

[7] Otto, Herbert A., "The Personal and Family Resource Development Programs—A Preliminary Report" Unpublished paper, 1962. Used with permission of author.

to explore what each family considered as strengths prior to the group experience. The Family Strength Inquiry was also marked together by each couple. Finally, each group member individually filled in a copy of the Elias Family Opinion Survey, a projective-type test designed to measure 'feelings of hominess or homelessness' of an individual toward his intrafamily relations." (p. 6). ". . . The Family Strength Inquiry lists sixteen areas of family strength. Each area lists five to six 'strength items.' For example, area IV *Giving Encouragement and Support* lists as item #3, 'Father, mother and children discussing in what ways they can give more encouragement to each other.' The family is asked to fill out the Inquiry *together* by marking one of three columns entitled 'this might strengthen our family (1) little, (2) some, (3) much.' The Family Strength Inquiry is essentially an educational device designed to help a family obtain an overview of some of the areas of strength and to help them determine particular areas of choice in which they wish to develop further strengths and family resources." (p. 3).

Otto states conclusions and findings:

1. A majority of the participants reported the strengthening of family relations. Families tended to engage in more activities together or communicated more fully and extensively than prior to the group experience.
2. This group, more than other groups, displayed a tendency toward "problem-centeredness." It was of interest to note that as members brought up personal and family problems, group members would usually point to the member's (specific and pertinent) strengths as a possible means of resolving the problem.
3. A deep feeling of interpersonal closeness was experienced by group members.

As a final conclusion he says: "On the basis of current findings and outcomes which have exceeded expectations, it can be concluded that a full-scale interdisciplinary research effort focusing on human potentialities could, within a relatively short number of years, result in a significant breakthrough. There is every indication that this research would make a major contribution to the broad range of preventative mental health programs and the field of public health/mental health." (p. 22).

With the churches, the PTA's, and other agencies sponsoring courses for married couples on family living; with increasing numbers of young people taking courses in preparation for marriage and seeking premarital counseling; and with such experimental projects as the above by which the resources for enriched family living may be more clearly perceived and fully developed, we have grounds for optimism concerning the psychosocial development of tomorrow's children. The higher level healthy-mindedness of their parents will be expressed in enriching family relationships that are satisfying and fulfilling for them and conducing growth of the self in their children.

THE FRIENDSHIP CIRCLE

In his "Generation of Zeros," Philip Wylie[8] has given us a thought provoking article. He described this "nothingness" trend in education, art, music, etc.—the evasion and shrinkage of responsibility and sense of self. He then turns to the point of our interest, saying:

> Another evidence of the self-reduction of mankind is non-involvement. The first instance to receive national attention concerned a horror in Kew Gardens, New York. There, a woman crawling in the lighted streets begging for help. No one came to help. No one even called the police—not even anonymously. Afterward investigators found 38 people who had watched the event—not one had made any effort to aid the women who was being slowly murdered.
>
> From many American cities, innumerable examples of exactly that sort of behavior have since been cited. And, always, those who could have aided but merely watched, explained that they "didn't want to become involved." Since, to remain human, humanity must be and remain *involved* with itself, such persons are subhuman, nothing people.

INVOLVEMENT IS ESSENTIAL

In the context of this book, I would place the people Wylie is describing in the category of the not-sick-not-well. Few, if any,

[8] Philip Wylie, "Generation of Zeros," *This Week* (Feb. 5, 1967). Copyright © 1967 by Philip Wylie.

of those 38 would have been diagnosed as being mentally ill, but as surely they behaved far short of their human potential and in a state of denial of true humanness—deficiency and security-motivated, not growth- and fulfillment-motivated. A strong healthy self requires deep friendships; and friendship is involvement.

Two adolescents begin dating and are soon "going steady." They engage in mutually enjoyable activities and become more meaningful and valuable to each other. Two selves become increasingly involved, interlocked, forming an empathic oneness. Affection grows; deep friendship is formed. It is love at the second level, as previously described, having moved from the good-will base to the interpersonal involvement that carries affection. It involves not only members of the immediate family but also other relatives and nonkin with whom one becomes deeply involved and shares in selfhood.

But true friendship is love, and love is vulnerable. Some of those with whom one is deeply involved will fail and hurt themselves, and in so doing will fail and hurt the friend who loves them. The immature, anxious, security-motivated person cannot take this chance. To avoid possible hurt or a heavy burden, he avoids deep involvement, true friendship or fellowship, and remains unsatisfied, unfulfilled, deficient in his humanness. It is the mature, self-confident, growth-motivated person who can give of himself in deep involvement with others, accept the risk, and in that involvement find satisfaction and fulfillment. A measure of one's self-actualization, one's healthy-mindedness, one's psychosocial development is found in the quality of one's friendships.

Self-disclosure. Freedom to become involved with others is indicated by one's freedom of self-disclosure in communication with others. Sidney Jourard has postulated the openness in disclosing oneself to others as a major variable in psychological wellness. For an empirical study of this trait or capacity, he developed the Self-Disclosure Questionnaire (1958 a). In this scale, 40 items of personal information are rated by the subject on total, partial, or no knowledge by certain persons—father, mother, same sex friend, opposite sex friend, and spouse. The score is computed for each related person on the basis of 2 points for total, 1 for partial, and 0 for no knowledge. Thus, a freedom of self-disclosure score may be obtained.

Jourard has found that emotionally disturbed, maladjusted persons are estranged from themselves and others. They lack the freedom to communicate themselves and their intimate experiences to others. Their interpersonal relations are characterized by impersonality, artificiality, play-acting, pretending. Their personalities tend to be masks. They are deficient in depth involvement and in true friendships.

What Jourard demonstrated empirically, Rollo May had previously discovered in his years of psychotherapy. He states (1953): "It may sound surprising when I say, on the basis of my own clinical practice as well as that of my psychological and psychiatric colleagues, that the chief problem of people in the middle decade of the twentieth century is *emptiness.* By that I mean not only that many people do not know what they want; they often do not have any clear idea of what they feel. . . ." (p. 14).

Accompanying this emptiness (inner vacuity) are large measures of loneliness and anxiety, a lack of self-identity. Many people try to fill the vacuum and drown the loneliness by compulsive partying and club-joining, but it gives little real help. Of such, May says: "He temporarily loses his loneliness; but it is at the price of giving up his existence as an identity in his own right. And he renounces the one thing which would get him constructively over the loneliness in the long run, namely, the developing of his own inner resources, strength, and sense of direction, and using this as a basis for meaningful relations with others. The 'stuffed men' are bound to become more lonely no matter how much they 'lean together'; hollow people do not have a base from which to learn to love." (p. 33).

True healthy-mindedness or high-level psychosocial development finds expression in a satisfying sense of self and self-worth and in deep interpersonal involvement, in satisfying friendships. And it is fostered by these.

GENERAL CHARACTERISTICS OF HEALTHY RELATIONSHIPS

In a summary statement, Jourard (1958, p. 226): says:

Healthy interpersonal relationships have seven main characteristics:

1. Each partner has an accurate concept of the other's personality.
2. Each partner likes more of the other's traits than he dislikes.
3. Each partner feels concern for the happiness and growth of the other.
4. Each partner acts in ways which will promote the growth and happiness of the other.
5. Each partner communicates fully with the other.
6. Each partner imposes reasonable demands and expectations on the other.
7. Each partner respects the right of the other to be self-determining.

Jourard especially emphasizes No. 5, *"full and honest communication,"* of which he says: "Thus, in a healthy relationship, each partner feels free to express his likes, dislikes, wants, wishes, feelings, impulses, and the other person feels free to react with like honesty to these. In such a relationship, there will be tears, laughter, sensuality, irritation and anger, fear, baby-like behavior, etc.

"The range of behavior, feelings, and wishes which will be brought out into the open is not arbitrarily limited. In fact, one gauge to the health of a relationship is the *breadth of the topics of conversation, the range of feelings which are openly expressed,* and *the range* of activities *which are shared.* In each case, the broader the range, the healthier the relationship." (p. 211).

> A report and class discussion based on Jourard's (1958) two chapters, "Healthy Interpersonal Behavior" and "Healthy Interpersonal Relationships," may be of interest and benefit at this point.

COMMUNION AND SELF-IDENTITY

Oliver and Barbara[9] are in agreement with May and Jourard, and with my thesis. In the Preface to their book, they state:

---

[9] Robert T. Oliver and Dominick A. Barbara, *The Healthy Mind in Communion and Communication,* 1962. Courtesy of Charles C. Thomas, Publisher, Springfield, Illinois.

> Communion, or warmly cordial relationship with those who are close to us, and community, a cooperative accord with the ideals and disciplines of the groups and institutions in which we live, are two of the values that are most meaningful to the living of a constructive life. Both of them depend to a high degree upon the maintenance of effective communication, just as communication, in turn, depends basically upon the realities of genuine communion and companionable community.
>
> We live, share, help, benefit, contribute, and receive most richly when we think, listen, and speak with an assured confidence in our own aims and substance and with a truly receptive appreciation for what we can learn and gain from others. Much of life is an attempt to establish a satisfactory personal identity, and much of it consists of findings (or at least of seeking) a bond of identification with our fellows.
>
> The first requirement is that what we *communicate* to others must satisfy our own deep-felt need to express the reality of our own thought and feelings, our own aspirations and needs. The second requirement is that what we *express* must be shaped with such considerateness that it truly conforms to and enhances the ideas and attitudes, the goals and the wishes of those with whom we are in immediate or remote communication. . . . The healthy mind is one that fulfills its own need to be itself to the fullest possible extent while also fulfilling its equal need to share the complexities, responsibilities, and rewards of companionship. (pp. V, VI).

True healthy-mindedness is reflected in the movement from independence to interdependence—from the "I" experience to the "we" experience—balancing ego-centricity with socio-centricity. And it is the person who is able to share richly, communicate freely, and identify deeply with another of kindred character who has the truest sense of self-identity and self-worth. The norm of satisfying, fulfilling living is to so communicate and express oneself as to conform to and enhance others. But there may be situations where the individual's self-needs and values are so different from those of the community in which he finds himself, that conformity would be too serious a compromise of selfhood. In such cases, the truly healthy-minded person maintains his independence even to the point of social ostracism. This, however, is the exception to the general rule. Highly autonomous, high self-actualizers, while they are never compulsive joiners, most commonly find at least a small community of persons with whom they can identify and communicate freely, forming meaningful, affectionate, creative relationships.

Oliver and Barbara go on to say: "There is no deeper need felt by individual's than the urgent yearning to understand ourselves. This is at the heart of the lonely wistfulness that marks a portion of the personality of small children, revealing itself in their repeated questioning: 'Mommy, what am I, where do I come from, why was I born?' It is the central fact in the unhappy rebelliousness of adolescence, as teenage youth struggles to free itself from adult dominance and to find a foundation of self-trust upon which to stand. It is a major factor in the restlessness that commonly afflicts men and women of middle age, as they wonder whether they have followed the right path in life or whether they may not have betrayed their better potentialities. . . .

"The search for identity—the wistful cry of 'Who am I? Where did I come from? Where am I going?' . . . is one aspect of the human personality, normal and universal. It is a part of the heritage we all have as rational creatures possessing the wonderful capacity to envisage in our minds a universe of possibilities far more extensive than the small niche within it which we are able to occupy. All of us have far more interests than we are able to pursue, far more abilities than we are able to develop, far more needs than we are able to satisfy. . . ." (pp. 42, 44).

THE WAY OF FELLOWSHIP

This cry for self-identity, for a fuller self-awareness, is the cry of a *self,* the cry of a person who, in the role of subject, is a whole, a universe, alone until he finds identity with another self. The way of selfhood is the way of fellowship, of brotherhood, of identifying with, loving and depth-communicating with his neighbor.

The child who is reared in a normal family will develop all the essential capacities for mere adjustment even though he is cut off from all other social contacts and relationships. And, as presented in a previous chapter, that deep affection which the family provides is essential for the development of qualities the child will need for wider social relationships. But to develop richness, fullness, and balance of personality, the child must engage in an ever-widening circle of social contacts with many and varied types of personalities in order to develop richness, fullness and balance of personality. Wholesome social adjustment depends on wholesome family living; the family as a healthful nursery of humanity depends on outside social contacts. If there were no fellowship beyond the immediate family, human personality would turn upon itself and decay in a quagmire of spiritual incest.

A mature and adequately expressed parental love is an absolute necessity in laying the emotional foundations for healthful character and personality growth. But more than that is needed. The growing person must experience and respond to the love of humanity as it is experienced one by one in an ever-widening circle of fellowship. Mother humanity (society) must take the place of one's biological mother as the giver of a mature sense of security and satisfaction. Each person is largely a product of two family lines that merged in the union of his parents. But each individual has potentialities that, in order to adequately develop and satisfy, require more than the family fellowship can provide. Shared experiences, in varying degrees of depth, with a variety of persons are necessary to develop a well-balanced personality and healthy self.

The truly healthy person becomes involved with other persons at the self-level; self with self in true fellowship. This chapter began with the discussion of love, so it ends; for love is the alpha and omega of adequate social living. But before ending a study of self-actualization through interpersonal relations, we ought to examine briefly what this means for old people.

DISENGAGEMENT OF THE AGING

Cumming and Henry[10] developed the "Disengagement Theory" to explain the general reduction in scope of life that is characteristic of old age. Though it allowed for a considerable amount of

[10] Elaine Cumming and William E. Henry, *Growing Old*, (New York: Basic Books, Inc., 1961).

individual variation, the theory is intended to apply to the aging process in all societies. The disengagement may begin in middle age with the grown children leaving the home, later retirement with the usual reduction of occupation and social roles, and the loss of age-level relatives and intimate friends by death. There is the inevitable lack of understanding and communication between the generations. Thus, disengagement is the mutual process of the individual withdrawing from society and society from the aging individual.

Children do mature and most of them do marry and leave the parental home, and spouses sometimes die young. Thus, a reduction in family life is inevitable for many older people. In many cases, a lowering of vitality plus certain cellular deficiencies and glandular changes will reduce the frequency of sexual intercourse. Now that geriatrics has become a very important social, economic, and political problem, it is being studied extensively by behavioral scientists. Slowly fantasies are being separated from facts. Consensus is moving toward the position that with the majority, (not all) sexual decline has been due more to sociologic and psychologic factors than to physiological. Allowing for a reasonable and normal decline in frequency of sexual intercourse as middle age moves into old age, it need not cease nor decline in quality. Freed of anxiety about pregnancy and of many responsibilities, there can be a freer and fuller coming together in covenant renewal, keeping at a high level the relationship which has grown through the years. The question is that of re-examination of the total marital relationship and re-evaluation of the role of sex in this relationship.

Also, with more leisure and less responsibilities, the elderly husband and wife are freer to cultivate numerous activities which they may share in mutually enjoyable experiences, thus making the most of the second key to happy marriage. And they still have their children even if they do not share the same house. The relationship has changed to adult interdependency instead of dependency-independency. Free of the responsibility the elderly may have a relationship that is more satisfying. Then, too, the number of children double when each takes unto himself (her-) a spouse. At last come the grandchildren and the family is soon quadrupled. The problem becomes once again that of re-examination and re-evaluation, as well as communication. Family life can be very satisfying for the oldsters, and it is being made so.

It is true that friends die or move to other locations when they retire. But the making of friends is a form of exploration and adventure that may continue as long as life. Spurred by Geronology Clubs, magazines published especially for older people, and the type of communal retirement homes now becoming numerous, there need be little decline in the enjoyment of friends until very late in life.

The disengagement theory is sound in principle to a certain degree and helps to explain some of the personality changes which have been generally characteristic of aging. But like many other theories, its empirical supports are based more on a periodic culture than on the inherent factors of the aging process itself. As our society reorients itself to cope with the matter of aging, the move will be from disengagement to re-engagement—a transition and, perhaps, a transcendence. Failure in old age (excepting organic) is largely the failure of youth and middle age. But, as was said of early adolescence in the previous chapter, it may be made a time of beginning again, if with the disengagement there is a re-examination and re-evaluation of life. This would give new motivation, new goals, new interests.

SUMMARY

The mid-twentieth century has been noted especially for its discovery of love as the great preventer and healer of mental illness. However, the love relationship is an end in itself, not a means. When so attained, health is a consequence. Love was presented as an all-encompassing attitude that embraces self and other selves; the opposite of selfishness which indicates immature defensiveness and inadequate love. Adequate love is a two-way involvement of subject-selves. But where one is immature as between parent and child, the one may give more and receive less while the other receives more and gives less.

My schema of love at three levels or stages was presented: (1) love as good-will, a basic attitude that may relate to all people; (2) love as affection, bonds of attraction for several people with whom much is shared; and (3) erotic or conjugal love which in maturity is exclusive, one-person centered. Maslow's B-love and D-love contrast was briefly reviewed with the latter more characteristic of the immature, defensive, deficiency-motivated person and more demanding and changeable. The immature defensive person often is unable to love because of fear of involvement and the vulnerability of love.

Sex was interpreted as the physical expression of love. As love matures, the physical expression increases from light petting, through heavy petting to full sexual intercourse. In its ideal and most satisfying expression, sexual intercourse is family-oriented and socially responsible since its twofold function is to create a child as an act of love and to help maintain an enriched climate of love for the emotional nourishment of the child. The mutual enrichment of the two selves who have contracted to share life completely is an important but secondary purpose.

The family was presented as an essential link between the individual and society and necessary for personal fulfillment. Since marriage involves the complete sharing of two lives, one's mate should be selected on the basis of common characteristics, mutual interests and capacities.

Six areas of marital adjustment or attainment were presented as the keys to happy marriage: mature love, sharing, sexual satisfaction, children, religion, and economic security. With increasing numbers of young people taking courses in marriage and seeking counseling, and with increasing numbers of married couples participating in projects such as Family Resources Development, we may anticipate increased stability and happiness in tomorrow's families.

Essential as the family relationship is, it is not enough for the development of a well-balanced personality and fullness of selfhood. The family circle should be broadened to encompass a variety of friends with whom one becomes involved and identifies with in varying depths. True self-awareness, self-identity, and sense of self-worth are seldom attained unless one is able to identify deeply in this subject-with-subject relationship.

The healthy-minded, psychosocially adequate person experiences and expresses love as good-will. affection, and in sexual intercourse that is socially responsible, family-oriented and mutually enriching. He chooses his mate on the basis of capacity to share and finds fulfillment in marriage, parenthood, and a circle of friends with whom he shares much.

GLOSSARY

Charybdis. A mythological monster dwelling in a whirlpool on the Sicilian coast, also the whirlpool.

Scylla. Another mythological monster (six-headed) who dwelt in a cave on the coast of Italy opposite the whirlpool.

These terms were frequent figurative expressions somewhat as we use "between the devil and the deep blue sea." To avoid one of these dangers would increase the threat of the other.

Symbiotic. Pertaining to a very close relationship, a living together—organic attachment as the fetus with the mother—or, more often, dissimilar organisms living in a mutually advantageous relationship.

REFERENCES AND SUGGESTED READINGS

BLANTON, SMILEY, *Love or Perish*, New York: Simon & Schuster, Inc., 1956.

BOWMAN, HENRY A., *Marriage for Moderns*, New York: McGraw-Hill Book Company, 1965.

CUMMING, ELAINE and WILLIAM E. HENRY, *Growing Old*, New York: Basic Books, Inc., 1961.

DE FOREST, IZETTE, *The Leaven of Love*, New York: Harper Brothers, Publishers, 1954.

FROMM, ERICH, *Man for Himself*, New York: Holt, Rinehart and Winston, Inc., 1947

———, *The Art of Loving*, New York: Harper & Row, Publishers, 1956.

JOURARD, SIDNEY M., *Personal Adjustment*, New York: The Macmillan Company, 1958.

———, "A Research Approach to Self Disclosure," *J. Abnorm. & Soc. Psychol.*, Vol. 56, No. 1, January 1958.

———, *The Transparent Self*, Princeton, N.J.: D. Van Nostrand Co., Inc., 1964.

KASTENBAUM, ROBERT, *New Thoughts on Old Age*, New York: Springer Publishing Co., Inc., 1964.

MASLOW, A., *Toward a Psychology of Being*, Princeton, N.J.: D. Van Nostrand Co., Inc., 1962.

MAY, ROLLO, *Man's Search for Himself*, New York: W. W. Norton and Co., Inc., 1953.

MENNINGER, KARL, *Love Against Hate*, New York: Harcourt, Brace & Co., 1942.

OLIVER, ROBERT T. and DOMINICK A. BARBARA, *The Healthy Mind in Communion and Communication*, Springfield, Ill.: Charles C. Thomas, Publishers, 1962.

OTTO, HERBERT (ed), *Explorations in Human Potentialities*, Springfield, Ill.: Charles C. Thomas, Publisher, 1966.
SCHWING, GERTRUD, *A Way to the Souls of the Mentally Ill*, New York: International Universities Press, 1954.
TERMAN, LEWIS M., *Psychological Factors in Marital Happiness*, New York: McGraw-Hill Book Company, 1938.

15 | The Healthy Vocational Life

THE CREATIVE PERSON

In his chapter "Personality," Erich Fromm[1] discusses the various nonproductive orientations of personality, then says: ". . . The productive orientation which I am going to discuss now points to the type of character in whom growth and the development of all his potentialities is the aim to which all other activities are subordinated.

"Generally the word 'productiveness' is associated with creativeness, particularly artistic creativeness. The real artist, indeed, is the most convincing representative of productiveness. But not all artists are productive; a conventional painting, e.g., may exhibit nothing more than the technical skill to reproduce the likeness of a person in photographic fashion on a canvas. But a person can experience, see, feel, and think productively without having the gift to create something visible or communicable. *Productiveness is an attitude which every human being is capable of, unless he is mentally and emotionally crippled.*" (p. 85).

Fromm discusses the "productive orientation" as a fundamental attitude and *mode of relatedness* which depends on a high degree of autonomy, inner freedom, and self-identity, and then says: "While it is true that man's productiveness can create

[1] From *Man For Himself* by Erich Fromm. Copyright 1947 by Erich Fromm. Reprinted by permission of Holt, Rinehart and Winston, Inc. and Routledge & Kegan Paul Ltd.

material things, works of art, and systems of thought, *by far the most important object of productiveness is man himself.*" (p. 91).

Fromm seems to be saying that the growth-motivated individual finds fulfillment, self-actualization, high-level psychosocial development in productive love and productive work. The former was the central theme of Chapter Fourteen; the latter provides a suitable take-off for this chapter. The matter of being or becoming is realized chiefly by the mode and quality of one's relatedness to other persons and to the world of work, his career, his vocation.

THE CREATIVE DILEMMA

As in the two preceding chapters, the present theme is high level psychosocial development—a high level of self-actualization that most of us have attained or will attain only to a moderate degree. We will discuss factors that relate to satisfaction in one's career and attitudes (motives) that conduce self-growth and self-satisfaction. We recognize the fact that the present economic climate and structure will present certain thwarting barriers, but this varies with the type of career chosen and the organization with which one is affiliated. Although business and industrial management appear to be showing increasing social responsibility and employee concern, profit is still the primary motive and efficient production and sales the primary concern. Thus the young person who sets the course of his vocational life accordingly may experience no little frustration and anxiety. Reality may demand a certain amount of compromise in favor of adaptation over true personal satisfaction and growth. The central problem is that of how much.

If we allow for minor changes which the human body may undergo in its natural development during the centuries ahead, general credence may be given to the contention that organic evolution attained its goal (thus ends) in man. "Nature" has developed the near-perfect brain and hand, and no longer needs to experiment with adaptive organs. With these, man can produce his own tools (mechanical and social) by which he can adapt to the environment and adapt the environment to his own creative purpose. Thus man effects his own growth (directs his evolution) in two ways: by changing his cultural environment which, in turn, changes the succeeding generation, and by the motives and quality of his work by which he changes the environment. In keeping with the central thesis of this book, the need is a function of capacity, it may be argued that creative or productive work is an inherent human need which marks a fundamental difference between man and animal. The latter is only adaptive, maintenance-motivated, with no creative capacity nor need to "work" in its human connotation. But man must create the cultural environment which is most conducive to his own growth; thus he finds meaningful, purposeful work a necessity. And in this need and its expression, he creates for himself a dilemma.

The social mechanisms which he creates, his institutions, grow big and become Frankensteins to enslave the mass of individuals and make pawns of them, forcing them to adapt to the mores of the institution and robbing them of much of their individual purposefulness and creativity. But the need-drive is never lost; it is only frustrated and suppressed periodically until a breakthrough occurs. One may trace through history this pendulum-swing from a relatively high degree of spontaneous and creative individual activity and influence with social fluidity and institutional change to a long static period of individual adaptation, security and maintenance motivation and institutional coercion or control.

There was the Hebrew-Greek period of roughly 1000 to 500 B.C. when the coercive rule of the nature cults and the family-clan rule of blood and revenge gave way to moral and rational law. This was followed by the Roman period of institutionalized coercion, chaos, and then an institutionalized Church. A new breakthrough of individualism and creativity came with the Renaissance to be followed by the rigid and coercive institutionalism of the late medieval period. Again the system was broken and the pendulum swung wide in the direction of free travel, trade, exploration, discovery, invention and social-economic change, and culminated in national and industrial freedom and purpose. Now this has reached its highest peak in big industrial combines, big labor combines, big educational combines, and bigger governments to control these other institutions, each with its rigid pattern of bureaucracy in which the individual is a cog or a pawn and "by the book" is standard operational procedure.

Caught in the mesh of struggle and conflict among these vast institutions, most people feel the futility of individual purpose and creative action. Only a few have the power and freedom to be truly creative self-actualizers. The climate of our day is such as to cause the individual to feel his impotence and the futility of creativity. The inducement toward adaptation, security motivation, and extrinsic satisfactions becomes strong. But this climate and system will change by the productive work of men within the system. And even in these periods of institutional rigidity and domination, individual purposefulness and creativity are never lost. They are only diminished, partly suppressed, hidden by the dominant mood, motive and institutional control. It is a matter of the relative amount of individual purposeful, creative work, growth motivation, and intrinsic work-activity satisfaction which is relatively low in one era and high in the other. The basic need and consequences to the individual are no different.

What, then, of the student who is in the process of choosing and/or preparing for his life work? It would seem to imply that his basic motive, purpose, goal-incentive must be growth and self-actualization via the intrinsic satisfaction and value of the work activities. It would also imply that he should develop as much self-strength, self-confidence, and frustration-tolerance as possible. Thus equipped, he can make the necessary compromises and adaptations, become a part of the system, but yet be able to detach himself from it and not become its victim. In this he may accept less than complete personal satisfaction and growth but would not be overwhelmed with anxiety nor surrender fully to the security motive and extrinsic reward incentive. For in this surrender, his growth toward self-actualization would be thwarted and his humanness diminished. In this context, we shall continue to explore the theme of personal growth through vocation.

In *The Accidental Century* (Penguin Books, 1966), Michael Harrington has given a challenging critique of our present social-economic era in problem and prospect. It is especially relevant to the above, and the class would benefit from a student report, especially Chapters 1, 8 and 9. This may be followed by a report based on selected parts from Levenstein (1962), with its equally challenging but complementary point of view. See Suggested Readings.

VOCATION, A WAY OF LIFE

Vocation is one of the basic orientations to life that makes for fullness of living. An excerpt previously published by me illustrates this point.[2]

Archibald Rutledge has told a very interesting story of a Negro boatman who took over the operation of a grimy old ferry boat that for many years had carried passengers back and forth across one of the many sluggish rivers along the Carolina coast. There was such a surprising transformation in the old boat! The decks were scrubbed spotless. The brass was so polished and the iron and steel so brightly painted that many a passenger who had known the boat before would make surprised comments of approval and ask the new captain the secret of the transformation. His answer to the questioners was, "I'se got a glory." He had a vocation, a mission, a service that he could render his fellow man and in which he rejoiced—a service into which he gave his best and which gave enrichment to his own life and to others. It gave him "a glory," and the shining boat was only a reflection of the glory that shone from within him. When a person has a true sense of vocation, he can say, "I'se got a glory."

When a young person investigates the many occupations of the world's workers—the broad fields of service—and then by means of aptitude tests and consultations with a counselor determines his abilities and interests and, after weighing advantages and disadvantages, makes his choice, he has merely chosen an occupation. Whether he has chosen wisely or foolishly, only time will tell. But when a purpose gets its hold on a man, something that seems to be more or other than just himself deciding, so that it is this one thing he must do, he has a vocation.

A vocation is a calling. And it has a glory about it. It is a call to a work that makes a difference—a creative work. If you do not do it, it will not be done. That makes a difference. It is to create something new under the sun—something new in human experience—for the enrichment of human experience. It may be a simple sort of service or creation, but it is yours. Only

[2] Guy L. Roberts, *The Way of Life* (New York: Comet Press, 1954).

you can do it. No one else is quite you. No one else can quite do it. A vocation is free creative service. It is free personality (self) accepting responsibility, the taking from experience and building into experience, consciously and freely, turning possibility into actuality. The words vocation and vocal stem from the same root. The deeps of life call to the deeps in man. It is the soul (self) of man from the depths of his true interests and abilities hearing and responding to the deep and true needs of the world. . . . (pp. 73–75).

VOCATION AND PERSONALITY

The point I was trying to make in a nontechnical description for young people was that having a true sense of vocation involves a deeper dimension of life than that of drifting or rationally working one's way into an occupation by which he earns a satisfactory income. It involves a high awarenesses of value, meaning and purpose in life, and a commitment to something of such significance that he can give himself wholly to it. It is a pattern of activity that most fully satisfies his growth needs, expresses his potential and meets a significant social need. The service value to others is experienced in vocation by the productive worker, giving him a sense of worth and the worthwhileness of his life—thus happiness. It is thus that an individual may lose himself in a certain career or institution in order to find himself.

The additional point being made was that such a mature, autonomous, committed self acting as a whole and upon the wholeness of human need, possesses the capacity for a measure of intuitive awareness which strikes a deeper dimension of cognition than sensory perception and rational thought. It does not negate these more common ways of knowing but may be used to supplement them in setting the general direction of one's life over a course in which the years ahead carry too many unknown factors to be solved by mathematical or logical formulas. It is not magic nor some "heavenly voice" but rather the person as a whole in attunement with life as a whole, an intuitive holistic awareness. It is an existential experience which may not be objectively validated. The validation is found in long years of richly satisfying living and high-level self-fulfillment. It is a mode of expression of man's high potential which vocational psychology is having to confront and of which the perceptive counselor is aware.

SOCIAL STATUS

Donald Super, prominent vocational psychologist for many years, discussing "Work and the Way of Life" says:[3]

> A popular writer and lecturer on work, Whiting Williams, once pointed up the central role of work in modern life by comparing methods of inquiring about and "placing" people in England and America. In the old countries, he pointed out, the inquiry: "Who is that man?" might elicit the reply: "He's a Percy from Northumberland," whereas in North America the reply would more likely be: "He's an engineer with the Standard Oil Company." The English reply enables the informed person to place Mr. Percy as a member of an old Norman family long established in a northern county. . . . The American reply conveys the information that Mr. Percy is a college graduate, of middle or upper middle class, working for a corporation with a national reputation; it tells nothing of his social origins, but it does place him socially in a manner which, in our culture, is most common and helpful. (pp. 17, 18).

Sociologists give much study and discussion to social strata and status. They find that the nature of a man's work, his occupation, is the most significant single criterion of social status in America. Work that reflects high-level talent and training is at the top category and includes the corporation executive, the scientist and the artist. This would, of course, include such high-level political positions as governors and congressmen. (There are not enough Presidents to form a social class.) The amount of income is an important criterion, and there are several others, but the nature and quality of a person's work is given greater weight in this country.

[3] From *The Psychology of Careers* by Donald E. Super (New York: Harper & Row, Publishers, Inc.). Copyright © 1957 by Donald E. Super. Reprinted by permission of Harper & Row, Publishers. Note particularly Chapter 2.

ONE'S STYLE OF LIVING

Super goes on to say that one's whole pattern of life is largely determined by his occupation. He describes the manner in which not only the worker's time and economic status are controlled by his employment but also how it determines much of the nature of his family and social life and many of his community roles. He summarizes: "Work and occupation play an important part in determining the social status, values, attitudes, and style of living of an individual. Important though some of these are as determinants of occupations, they, in turn, are in part determined by occupation. Occupation is not merely a means of earning a *livelihood,* but also *a way of life, a social role.*" (p. 35).

> Time may be well spent at this point on a thorough discussion of occupational influences on other aspects of life based on the two references above and/or personal interviews of workers by several members of the class. "Worker" is used here to include all types of employed people.

WHY DO PEOPLE WORK?

Let us avoid being facetious and answering that question with a "Yeah, Why?", for it is one of life's most significant questions. The obvious answer has been that one either works or starves: one works to make a living. But the obvious is seldom fully satisfactory. Why will a person tie himself to a particular pattern of work activities which require more than half of his conscious hours and influence most other aspects of his life? What satisfaction does a man (or woman) get from his "work"? The question *Why?* and the term *satisfaction* remind us of motivation, which we will discuss a little later in relation to vocational interests. Here we shall be less technical and explore some of the reasons people engage in certain occupations and some of the things they like and dislike. During the middle third of this century this has been a most widely studied subject.

RELATIONSHIP WITH OTHERS

Super discusses the matter of satisfaction and dissatisfaction first with respect to *recognition as a person, independence, fair treatment,* and *status,* saying:

> Much of modern living is anonymous. People live, travel, work, and play together in large numbers: the apartment dweller does not know who lives above him or below him, the worker driving to the factory does not know the driver of the car which tries to cut into the line of traffic ahead of him, the assistant bookkeeper does not know the clerk who sends him the forms from which he copies entries in his books or the other clerk to whom he sends them when they are entered. . . .
>
> This depersonalization is partly the product of the corporate nature of modern enterprise, in part due to the scope of present-day industrial and business activity, and it results also from the increasingly large concentration of people in a growing but settled country. It often makes the individual feel that he is lost in a large, complex, and impersonal machine. . . . The Hawthorne, Yankee City, and other such studies suggest that recognition as a person means preserving one's integrity. This, in turn, requires *independence, fair treatment,* and *opportunity for self-expression,* this last factor being, however, more one of work activity than of human relations.
>
> Just as relations with others must involve recognition of oneself as a person, as somewhat distinct and in some ways different from others, in order to be satisfying, so must they be such that the individual has some feeling of status. Prestige derived from status appears to be a need more of persons in higher level than in the lower level occupations. Occupational status is somewhat complex, for it involves a variety of relationships. . . .
>
> Thus, the nurse at work in the hospital is aware of the distance between herself and the physician; he expects to give orders, and she to take them. But, meeting in a social gathering where they are both strangers, they are aware of a good deal in common through their work with patients and in hospitals. When the nurse goes to a class reunion of her small-town high school, she and others are aware of her superior status as one

of the minority in her class who entered the professions. She is now superior to others, but subordinate, again, on returning to the physician's office. . . . Throughout all these contacts with others, however, the nurse is conscious of belonging to the profession of nursing, and to the larger family of public health occupations. . . .

A young assistant head of a department in a large organization brought out the feeling of status derived from his work: "It's fun being assistant department head. The other fellows come to me with their questions about things, and the boss and I talk over some of our problems. Now and then he will talk to me about something that's come down from higher up. It all gives me a feeling of being a part of something big and important, you know, I'm in the middle of things, and I see lots of wheels going around and things happening. Some of them work better because of what I am doing." (pp. 4–8).

WORK FOR ITS OWN SAKE

Man's work motives and his satisfactions and dissatisfactions in the work itself are of interest to all counselors and vocational psychologists. They are concerned about the nature of the activities, about self-expression and potential development through work activities; about their intrinsic value versus extrinsic reward, and about the still unresolved problem our economic system poses relative to these matters. We will see in this chapter and in later chapters, deep satisfaction is experienced in the nature of the work-activity. This is generally more apparent and of more direct concern at the professional and higher managerial levels, but it is becoming increasingly sought at all levels of employment. Growth and fulfillment, self-actualization, and psychosocial development by means of the work-activities are becoming of greater concern to many rather than the salary, pension plan, and other extrinsic factors.

This often means a variety of specific activities as opposed to a monotonous routine; but the variety must conform with the variety of one's potential capacities and his intrinsic interests. Or it may be value interests, more learned than inherent, that must be satisfied by the performance or the product. (The relationship of these interests will be discussed later.) The proprietor of a business or young business executive may leave one type of business to engage in another (product or firm) for either a fuller expression of himself through his work or because of his evaluation of the product. A teacher may change to a different school system or to another content-field for similar reasons. An example of this basic concern is the case of an electrical engineer I knew who, at the age of forty having a wife and two teenage children, left a well-paying position and spent a year at a university studying psychology. He then went into personnel work at a reduced but satisfactory salary because of the greater satisfaction he derived from working with people rather than with switch boards and dynamos. He valued the consequences as being of greater worth, believing that in some way it would add to his personal worth.

Every year thousands of workers change their employment for similar reasons. Lawyers and business executives leave lucrative positions to enter government service, education or the ministry for the intrinsic value and need-satisfaction of the work itself or the social value of its product. And this includes skilled operators in factories and white collar office people who turn to construction work, free lance carpentering or farming, not to make more money, or have more comfortable working conditions or more congenial surroundings, but for greater work satisfaction in building things, making things grow, seeing greater value in the product of their labor.

TO MAINTAIN LIFE

I spoke of the obviousness of people having to work to *make a living* which has been so widely stressed. Life must be maintained or else it cannot be fulfilled. The more elemental needs must be provided to free the individual for concern with the so-called higher need-goals. Super discusses this matter under the categories of absolute or "real income" (actual purchasing power) and relative level of income. He believes that most Americans are more concerned with the latter after their earnings afford a fair degree of comfort which indicates a status and competitive interest, both economic and psychological factors.

He noted, however, that as middle age approaches most blue collar and (but to a lesser extent) white collar workers become increasingly concerned with seniority and the reliability or regularity of their work, pension, etc., thus expressing predominantly security interests.

SECURITY AND GROWTH MOTIVATED

In his concluding remarks Super states: "Satisfying human relations, activities that satisfy carried on in conditions which are agreeable, and an assured livelihood, are three major desires which men seek to satisfy in work." (p. 14). Since each of these is compounded of several elements and our concern is with satisfaction, growth, and fulfillment in work, let us examine these in greater detail. Whether they are stated as likes, interests, desires, or needs, Super is speaking about fellowship or friendship, acceptance, recognition as a person of worth, independence, fair treatment, status, self-expression, values, interesting activities, variety, physical working conditions, income, and work security (dependability or stability). It might be informative to study these in relation to the motivation chart on p. 125. Some will fall clearly on the left, the security or maintenance side, others will fall on the right, the growth or self-actualization side, while still others will be found near the dividing line, straddling the fence, applicable in both directions. On the security side would be acceptance, physical working conditions, income and dependability of employment. On the growth side would be recognition as a person, independence, self-expression, and interesting activity. Fellowship, fair treatment, status, values, and variety may be found on either side but near the center.

VARIED AND STABLE

Any individual may be seeking to satisfy all the above desires and others through his occupation. But no two would be as concerned with each to the same degree. The exact pattern of interests and satisfaction-seeking is as varied as human personality.

Some are more alike than others, thus vocational interests or satisfaction-seeking can be typed with a fair degree of validity. The individual's pattern of relative abilities, interests, and value system have fairly well matured by late adolescence and will remain fairly stable throughout life. Unusual circumstances or experiences may, however, effect a marked change of interests or value-goals at any period in life. The person who is fully mature, autonomous, and chiefly growth-motivated will place greater value on and seek satisfaction in the occupations that provide interesting activities, self-expression, independence, recognition as a person, and/or service to others. On the other hand, he who has not matured adequately, who is more dependent, and who is basically security-motivated will value more highly and find more satisfaction in acceptance by other workers, physical and other working conditions, income and employment stability, fringe benefits. This person would be relatively satisfied in any of a large variety of *occupations,* perhaps never finding deep satisfaction in his work. The growth-oriented person must find his *vocation* within a narrower range of possibilities, experiencing a deeper satisfaction if he finds it (or it him?) and a greater dissatisfaction if he misses it.

In vocational guidance, the counselor directs the student toward greater self-awareness. By analysis of past performance, taking aptitude and interest tests, and talking with the counselor, the student becomes more clearly aware of his greatest potentials, his interest patterns, and his value system. He then studies certain specific occupations of several types to find the type of activities through which he can most fully express himself, experience challenge and growth, and perhaps best serve his community, state or nation. Many counselors with years of experience have found that, even with the best the above can produce, most students will be unable to set their life-course by the logical or rational handling of these empirical facts. As previously suggested, the years ahead carry too many unknown factors. Thus, the wise counselor encourages the mature student to trust his intuition, play his hunches, after obtaining and logically employing all possible empirical information. He supplements reason with faith (the nonstructured, nonsensory cognition of wholes), permitting the whole of himself to become attuned to the whole of life, intuitively grasping its meanings and purpose and demands.

SATISFACTION RESEARCH

Although presentation of work satisfaction in relation to general autonomy and motivation orientation finds some research support, much more is needed for greater clarification. Herzberg et al (1959) developed their Motivator-Hygiene Theory on the basis of certain findings which indicated that most workers found their greatest job satisfaction in such factors as the nature of the work itself, the responsibility it afforded, and opportunities for advancement. These job aspects were labeled "motivators" to draw attention to their ability to satisfy the individual's need for self-actualization in his work. On the other hand, a majority of workers expressed dissatisfaction more frequently with such factors as company policy, supervision, worker interpersonal matters, and general working conditions. These job aspects were labeled "hygiene" to represent the preventative role they play in regard to job dissatisfaction. In other words, the satisfaction-dissatisfaction matter involves more than merely the relative degree of certain factors. Relative to some, the worker may fail to be satisfied without being dissatisfied if these are deficient. Relative to others, he may be very dissatisfied if they are deficient but not especially satisfied when they are amply provided. Stated differently, both types of factors provide certain needs, either maintenance or growth, but only the motivators provide deep satisfaction.

Myers (1964) and Friedlander (1964) studied certain worker attitudes and conditions, and their findings lend some support to the Herzberg theory. But their studies were not replications of Herzberg's work and cannot be offered as sufficient support to warrant a distinction between work "motivators" and "hygienes." However it may be revised, the theory holds practical possibilities and warrants further research.

Halpern's study[4] of motivator and hygiene factors lends additional support to Herzberg, but only partial confirmation. Following is a brief summary of the Halpern study.

A sample of 101 men was located through the city directory,

[4] Gerald Halpern, "Relative Contributions of Motivator and Hygiene Factors to Overall Job Satisfaction," *J. Appl. Psychol.*, 1966, Vol. 50, No. 3, 198–200.

and each was contacted by telephone. Of the 101 contacted, 93 returned completed questionnaires. The average age of the selected subjects was 32.5 years, and had worked an average of 9.5 years. They had held an average of 3.9 jobs, and had an average of three years on each job.

Part of the questionnaire that the subjects completed asked them to rate various aspects of their best-liked job using the seven point graphic rating scales. Scales went from one, very dissatisfied through four, neutral, to seven, very satisfied.
The four motivator aspects were:

1. Opportunity for achievement—Opportunities to achieve something worthwhile, opportunities for successful accomplishments.
2. Work itself—The actual work performed.
3. Task responsibility—The amount of personal responsibility you were given for your own work.
4. Advancement—The opportunities for getting ahead, for being promoted.

The four hygiene aspects were:

5. Company policies—The procedures used by the company in conducting its business, as well as the company's attitude toward employees.
6. Supervision—The type of interpersonal relationships between yourself and your immediate superiors.
7. Interpersonal relationships—The social atmosphere of your work group, the kinds of feelings that existed between yourself and your fellow-workers.
8. Working conditions—Such things as the amount of work space available, lighting, temperature, equipment and so forth.

In addition, each subject rated his overall satisfaction with the job. Overall satisfaction was defined as the subjects feeling toward the job as a whole, taking into account both the favorable and unfavorable aspects of the total job.

Results. Two findings are readily apparent. First, Ss were equally well satisfied with both the motivator and the hygiene aspects of their job. There was no difference in their ratings of satisfaction with either the motivator or the hygiene factors.

Second, as predicted by the motivator-hygiene theory, the motivator factors contributed significantly more to overall satisfaction than did the hygiene factors. The average correlation between motivator job aspects and overall satisfaction was significantly higher than the average correlation between the hygiene aspects and overall job satisfaction.

These findings support the basic thesis of the motivator-hygiene theory of job satisfaction. In spite of the fact that Ss were equally satisfied with both aspects of their jobs, it is the motivators—the factors related to personal success in work and individual growth—that are primarily related to job satisfaction. In other words, there was little or no dissatisfaction with the extrinsic factors (hygiene aspects). Those conditions were quite acceptable. But true and deep satisfaction could be derived only from the intrinsic factors (motivator aspects).

Wernimont[5] challenges Herzberg's findings. He made an extensive study of what 50 accountants and 82 engineers reported as being most satisfying and dissatisfying in their job situations. He concludes: "In summary, satisfaction with the job can be due to higher levels of satisfaction with intrinsic factors, and dissatisfaction can be due to low levels of satisfaction with intrinsic factors. Extrinsic factors cause both satisfaction and dissatisfaction less readily than do the intrinsic factors, but individuals are more likely to *say* they have bad or dissatisfied feelings about these extrinsic factors. Measures of satisfaction with Salary and Working Conditions may show these two factors to be dissatisfiers, as Herzberg et al claim, but for very different reasons than those invoked in their interpretations. Two different sets of expectations were seen to be major determinants of how job-attitude factors effect overall job satisfaction." (p. 50).

It seems to me that Wernimont's study gave a little support to Herzberg et al and may have given more if he had used a larger number of subjects covering a wider range of occupations and that there is some validity to the motivator-hygiene theory but as in most human behavior, especially with subjective factors involved, sharply definitive categorizing is impossible.

---

[5] Paul F. Wernimont, "Intrinsic and Extrinsic Factors in Job Satisfaction," *J. Appl. Psychol.*, Vol. 50, No. 1, pp. 41–50.

> An interesting panel discussion of this topic may be presented, one student outlining the Herzberg theory and two others presenting supporting and contrary findings. See Suggested Readings at the end of this chapter; See also Appendix.

TREND TOWARD GREATER PERSONAL GROWTH

I have not engaged directly in any systematic occupational interest research, but I have discussed the matter of work interests and satisfactions with many students in psychology classes and individual counseling. Without statistical "proof," I have nevertheless formed certain conclusions: (1) a higher percentage of students in recent college generations value the nature and significance of the work activity above specific financial reward when compared with students of some 25 or 30 years ago; (2) the majority of students are seeking occupations that provide personal recognition, responsibility, independence, mobility, growth, etc., with a slight recent trend toward security, fringe benefits, etc.; (3) job sights are lowered (reality adaptation) by large numbers of students as they run into competitive difficulties with academically superior students, settling for what may be less personally satisfying but socially and economically least dissatisfying; (4) this trend continues during the early years of occupational adjustment after leaving school; (5) in spite of the fact that virtually all secondary schools and colleges have counseling services, relatively large numbers of students are seeking careers in the more highly publicized, even glamorized fields although their basic talents and interests may point toward a different type of work.

What are the implications of these observations? First, we need to improve our counseling services, and perhaps place less emphasis on certain so-called "glamorous" occupations. Second, we should institute in all systems of secondary and higher education some type of potentials development programs along lines previously mentioned, and reduce the need to compromise with reality on the basis of inadequate performance. Studies show a positive correlation between interests and performance ability but not as high as might be anticipated or desired. Perhaps the correlation between perceived interests and potential abilities might be much higher. Here is an area of applied psychology where much research is needed: how students may become more clearly aware of their basic interest pattern and how they may become more clearly aware of and free to express more efficiently their higher potentials. With this greater self-awareness and self-acceptance, the students' interest-ability correlation would be higher and they would have less difficulty finding their true vocation—the occupation that fits, is self-actualizing, and which contributes richly to their psychosocial development.

The third implication poses a more serious problem which involves our whole economic system, educational system, and government. With the rapidly expanding college population, the rapidly increasing percentage of college trained people, we are geared toward training too many "chiefs" and not enough "injuns." Too many who seek satisfaction at the professional or high management level must settle at the level of the technician. Too many who aim at becoming high-level technicians must settle for a semi-skilled occupation. Here is a problem for long-range planning by a competent study committee composed of statesmen, educators, other professionals, and industrialists. The efficiency, mental health, and general happiness of our citizenry could be much improved by this. The personal growth and self-satisfaction of many will depend on future changes at this point.

ROOM AT THE TOP?

The above observations which cover more than thirty years of counseling appear to be verified by Darley and Hagenah[6] who have analyzed several of the more significant work-satisfaction studies.

> In Super's study,[7] he notes that approximately 70 percent of his sample of employed men have never changed their occupational level. In a more detailed study by Davidson

[6] John G. Darley and Theda Hagenah, *Vocational Interest Measurement,* (Minneapolis: University of Minnesota Press, 1955). Used with permission.

[7] D. E. Super, "Occupational Level and Job Satisfaction," *J. Appl. Psychol.,* 1939, 23, 547–564.

and Anderson, summarized in Kuhlen and Thomson's book of readings (1952, pp. 456–464), a slightly higher degree of vertical mobility is found, possibly because their sample included a wider range of occupations than did Super's. Davidson and Anderson find that their "data as a whole suggest that the occupational pyramid possesses an institutional character, that its marked stratification is due in large measure to forces related to and emerging from the occupational status of fathers and family environments in which children are reared, and that these do not submit easily to other influences such as the school but tend to form certain patterns which become characteristic of the several occupational levels." In others words, people don't move up the occupational ladder as freely as the American dream indicates. Many able students are barred from higher education because of socioeconomic and cultural backgrounds of their parents. The labor market itself dispassionately shakes down its annual entrants from secondary schools to the various levels needed to maintain our total economy, regardless of the aspiration of the individual. (p. 7).

INCREASED PROFESSIONAL INTERESTS

The "barred from higher education" point is rapidly being nullified with Federal Government aid to students and the rapid growth in college opportunities. This enlarges the problem of the labor shakedown. Now and in the immediate future the problem becomes that of the labor market dispassionately shaking down its annual entrants from colleges, regardless of their high aspirations and expectations. This means greater frustration and forced accommodation with less personal growth and satisfaction. Darley and Hagenah continue:

A brief glance at the composition of the total civilian labor force will help to illustrate our concern with the relation between job satisfaction and job level. In his text on *The Sociology of Work,* Caplow (1954) presents a tabular analysis of this labor force based on recent census data. As counselors well know, the majority of young people aspire to specific jobs that are included in the first six* of the broad categories

* 1. Professional and semiprofessional
2. Farmers and farm managers
3. Proprietors, managers, etc.
4. Clerical and kindred workers
5. Salesmen and saleswomen
6. Craftsmen, foremen, etc.

shown in the table, with the heaviest concentration of claimed choices in the first and third groups. Only at such levels do students tend to say "*that* would be an interesting job." We, as adults, also tend to feel that the really "interesting" jobs are to be found only in the upper categories and that many workers are doomed to tasks requiring little training, repetitive and routine activities, and rather undemanding or unchallenging work assignments. If this interpretation of our beliefs is correct, then not more than 34,476,000 out of the 58,668,000 people in the civilian labor force,** or about 59 percent of workers, are in work that is perceived as "satisfying" in some vaguely defined way. And even here, we might wonder how "satisfying" would be many of the specific jobs in groups 2, 4, 5, and 6 of Table 1. . . .

In the various job satisfaction and morale studies, a crude division of responses appears to be related to the hierarchy of occupations. Respondents at lower occupational levels stress as sources of satisfaction economic factors, security, a chance to get ahead, a need for recognition as persons. Respondents at upper economic levels define satisfaction in terms of "interesting work," a chance to use their abilities, a chance to work independently at challenging tasks. For the former group, satisfaction derives from sources *external* to the work; for the latter group, satisfaction relates to internal feelings of accomplishment and involvement in work.

We may assume then that our highly productive economy has been created in such a way as to make many jobs essentially maintenance activities for workers, rather than intrinsically satisfying and absorbing ways of life. We know, as counselors, that the vocational dreams and aspirations of many of our students are doomed to go unrealized. We know that only a relatively small, though highly important, segment of our students will enter the high-status, high-income, and high challenge occupations. (pp. 7–10).

THE IMPLICATIONS

Perhaps it is time again to pause and examine the implications of the above more closely. Satisfaction is a rather subjective term with few objective criteria that allow for quantitative

** Figures based on 1950 census

description, yet nearly all workers are fairly cognizant of the degree of their own work satisfaction. It would seem that under the present circumstances, the majority of young people who leave school will fall far short of their anticipated, or aspired to, satisfactions and self-actualization in the occupations they will have to accept. If it is true, as many authorities believe, that one's *being* (becoming) depends, in large measure, on his *doing*, the majority of our students are doomed to face thwarting and crippling impediments to self-actualization or high level psycho-social development—our economic system seriously frustrating personal growth and fulfillment.

Failing to obtain occupational positions which provide the anticipated opportunities and personal satisfactions, many will be compelled by circumstances to lower their sights, surrender aspirations, cease to expect a great amount of personal need-satisfaction in their work, and in so doing they will cease to grow as persons. These turn from *intrinsic* to *extrinsic* rewards, from seeking personal growth and satisfaction to social and economic gain, relative freedom from circumstantial dissatisfactions, and suppressing or repressing personal dissatisfaction. Their work becomes a means of making a living, not an *end* or *goal* which is an intrinsic part of living. They become maintenance-security-pleasure motivated rather than growth-fulfillment-satisfaction motivated.

There is some research support for the above implications. Darley and Hagenah (1955) discuss an extensive study of the occupational satisfactions, dissatisfactions, and aspirations of 1100 men, and state: "Independence, self-expression, security, a chance to serve others, and interesting work were five of the most frequently chosen values. Power, fame, esteem, profit, and leadership were the five less frequently chosen. More important than these broad distinctions, however, are the relations of the choices to the occupational level of the respondent. Self-expression, independence, and interesting work were most frequently chosen by those in the upper occupational levels. Security and independence were most frequently chosen by those in the lower occupational levels. Thus, it appears that work means different things at different levels." (p. 165).

We may add that "independence" means different things to different people and that in the above, it probably meant economic rather than personal independence. We may also note that the persons who once aspired to the higher-level occupations and values lowered their values and satisfaction-seeking when they failed to make the upper levels. Darley[8] reviewed several studies and said: "It has been found that what people want out of life is related in some real degree to their occupational status. An occupational structure was postulated in which, at the upper end of the scale, intrinsic satisfactions can be found in work itself, and at the lower end of the scale, satisfactions were extrinsic to the work making up the job."

BECOME INVOLVED

The key to the problem appears to be in the reference by Darley and Hagenah to "involvement in work." As *involvement* is the key to "productive love" (Fromm), to true fellowship and satisfying interpersonal relationships, it is also the key to "productive work," to work that produces growth and self-actualization. Love is a relationship in which two selves are involved with each other at a deeply subjective level. The self of each, as acting-sharing subject, gives strength to and receives satisfaction from the other. So with a man and his work, if it is a true vocation in which the self of him is deeply involved. The man is then "in love" with his work. Its activities are so challenging and rewarding, offer such full expression of his highest potential, and carry so much social significance that the self is deeply involved with the activity, and is contributing something significant, something creative, through it; and the self receives vicariously the satisfaction experienced by others who benefit from his work. This is the manner in which a man may lose himself in order to find himself, may *become* through his *doing*. This fulfillment is experienced by a small segment of our population.

Commitment is closely related to *involvement,* and usually accompanies it. In true vocation, the worker is not only personally involved in his work activities, but also he is strongly com-

[8] In Wilbur L. Layton (ed), *The Strong Vocational Interest Blank: Research and Uses* (Minneapolis: University of Minnesota Press, 1960). Darley, p. 141. Used with permission.

mitted to his work and its accomplishments by it, similar to the lover who is committed to the one he loves. Crawford[9] calls attention to recent re-emphasis of this concept by both educators and counselors. He argues strongly the case for commitment, that it is more than a mere slogan and will bear scrutiny. "*Commitments are not partial or capricious.* You are or you aren't. . . . Note, for example, the intensity of its synonyms—pledge, covenant, and promise." He admits, however, that there are "*levels of commitment*" and that "*commitments may be changed*" and "*refined.*" Furthermore, "*levels of commitments imply that there is only one highest commitment,*" which, he thinks, "*is ethical or moral in nature*" and reaches the dimension of religion in its broader connotations. Then he adds: "*The nature of man is such that he needs a commitment.* But it is also true that *it is possible to have no commitment.* Man needs a sense of purpose. He needs to find meaning in life. His capacity for reasoned contemplation and his awareness of the future all serve to accentuate this need. . . ." (pp. 904–907).

I shall interpret commitment as the *set* of the self, a fixed motive based on one's ultimate or highest eschelon of values. Thus, it carries great meaning and purpose and is a strong interest-drive. When one strives to achieve top priority values, any significant measure of success would yield deep satisfaction.

TO INCREASE WORK SATISFACTION

What can the individual do in the face of such circumstances? Is he a victim of fate? Are the majority of students doomed to considerable frustration and dissatisfaction? Are we, as humans, so completely pre-determined by genetic factors and the conditioning forces of our culture that we (the majority) have no alternative but compromise and lower level adaptation? The answer is a resounding *No*! Every person is to a large degree conditioned by his genes and his training, and just how determining or compulsive those factors are varies widely from person to person. But it is my proposition that self as person-in-the-role-of-subject attains rela-

[9] Claud C. Crawford, "Commitment," *Pers & Guid. J.*, Vol. XLIV, No. 9.

tive independence, has the capacity to dissociate himself from his biological and social parentage, transcends "naturalistic determinism," and thus may create or choose from among alternatives. It is also my proposition that the old thesis of the self (or ego) and its personality being almost wholly determined by biological forces via instincts and the newer antithesis of these being almost wholly fashioned by environmental factors are both antiquated. They should be replaced by the new synthesis of a partially autonomous and transcendent self as acting subject, influenced but not wholly determined by the past and which, within limits, may create its own future. To bring out the implications of this, first let us examine certain basic propositions and a fundamental theory of occupational interest and choice.

VOCATIONAL DEVELOPMENT

After setting forth the basic facts and inferences, Super[10] organizes his material into a comprehensive theory of vocational development in the form of ten propositions:

1. People differ in their abilities, interests, and personalities.
2. They are qualified, by virtue of these characteristics, each for a number of occupations.
3. Each of these occupations requires a characteristic pattern of abilities, interests, and personality traits, with tolerances wide enough, however, to allow both some variety of occupations for each individual and some variety of individuals within each occupation.

. . .

7. Development through the life stages can be guided, partly by facilitating the process of maturation of abilities and interests and partly by aiding in reality testing and in the development of the self concept.
8. The process of vocational development is essentially that of developing and implementing a self concept; it is a compromise process in which the self concept is a product of the interaction of inherited aptitudes, neural and endocrine make-up, opportunity to play various roles, and evaluations

[10] Donald Super, "A Theory of Vocational Development," *Amer. Psychologist*, Vol. 8, 1953.

of the extent to which the results of role playing meet with the approval of superiors and fellows.

9. The process of compromise between individual and social factors, between self concept and reality, is one of role playing, whether the role is played in fantasy, in the counseling interview, or in real life activities such as school classes, clubs, part-time work, and entry jobs.
10. Work satisfactions and life satisfactions depend upon the extent to which the individual finds adequate outlets for his abilities, interests, personality traits and values; they depend upon his establishment in a type of work, a work situation, and a way of life in which he can play the kind of role which his growth and exploratory experiences have led him to consider congenial and appropriate. (pp. 158–161).

EGO STRENGTH AND INTEREST

In reporting his extension experimental study, Small[11] says in effect that more realistic occupational choices are made by well-adjusted boys than by boys who are poorly adjusted. The better-adjusted fantasy themselves as being deeply involved with the environment, whereas in their vocational responses the "disturbed" cases had fantasies of withdrawal from the environment and acting-out impulses. Small suggests that individuals of different ego strengths will show differences in the extent to which reality and fantasy determine their vocational choices, and thus a theory of vocational interest or choice determination must take account of ego strength. With this major factor held constant, he thinks that it would be possible to test the relative importance of a host of other personal, family and environmental factors.

And Super[12] sees interests as a product of inherited aptitudes and endocrine factors interacting with opportunity and social evaluation. He says: "Some of the things his associates do appeal to him and, through identification, he patterns his actions and his interests after them; but if not he must seek another identification and develop another self-concept and interest pattern. . . ."

---

[11] L. Small, "Personality Determinants of Vocational Choice," *Psychol. Monagr.*, (1953), 67, No. 1. (Whole No, 351) pp. 16, 17.

[12] From *Appraising Vocational Fitness* by Donald Super (Harper & Row, 1949). Used with permission.

AUTONOMY AND CHOICE

First, taking Small's findings, and substituting *self* for ego, what are the implications? Vocational interests are personality factors, reflections of the whole personality operating under given circumstances, and functions of the self. The strong, healthy, autonomous self deals with the past personality-conditioning factors (or personality traits derived from past conditioning) and present environmental factors differently, more realistically and effectively than does the weak, maladjusted self. This implies a certain freedom to choose between alternatives and fashion as well as be fashioned by outside forces. Thus, occupational choice is a function of the self, a mode of adaptations—the latter a continuation of choosing among alternatives—the relative freedom of choice and self-initiated, self-directed action depending on the strength and autonomy of the self. The dynamics of occupational choice and adjustment are to be found in the self which, in turn, has been conditioned but not necessarily controlled by genetic and environmental factors.

Next, looking back at Super's appraisal, we find him caught in the old thesis-antithesis dilemma of viewing interests as a product of inherited and environmental factors, rather than seeing them as the function of the self playing the mediating role. Through the years Super has done a great job in the field of vocational psychology; but in making this final synthesis, he could have produced a more comprehensive theory of vocational interest and choice. He implied that these are self-functions in his statement: "if he fits the pattern reasonably well, he remains in it, but if not, he must seek another identification. . . ." Here self is acting, choosing between alternatives. With logical consistency if not scientific proof, one may argue that vocational interests develop and choices are made as functions of a relatively autonomous, transcendent self acting on circumstantial factors as well as reacting to them. Thus, interests and choices are fluid, malleable, controllable; and so being, satisfaction is not *determined* by circumstances. It is only *influenced.* As an example, we may refer back to Frankl's statement (p. 116), ". . . to choose one's attitude on any given set of circumstances, to choose one's own way."

FLEXIBILITY AND SELF-DIRECTED CHANGE

We again refer to Super's 10 propositions, and find that the first three pertain to the wide variation and flexibility which is found when the detailed activities of any occupational group are examined and the equally wide variation and flexibility of specific interests and aptitudes the individual may possess. Thus, the strong self capable of acting creatively has much room to operate within most normal occupational situations, both in adjusting to and making changes within. The engineer, accountant, or sales manager may find one company frustrating but change to another and work out a relatively high degree of satisfaction. The dedicated teacher may find one school system very dissatisfying but in moving to another may find sufficient flexibility to create for herself satisfactory working conditions.

Points 4, 5, and 6 were omitted since they have no direct relation to the present theme and merely state that choice and adjustment are perpetual processes, that adjustment is continuing choice, and while one's occupation tends to stabilize after certain preliminary phases, its level is determined by ability and opportunity.

In point 7, "is determined by" should read is *conditioned* by which is a realistic and significant difference allowing for greater adjustment and satisfaction. Concerning points 7, 8 and 9, they are well said except as I previously stated, Super has not quite reached the new synthesis of behavior dynamics located in the self. It is the self that should be guided toward fuller maturation and autonomy. This done, self will have a realistic awareness of itself, confidence in itself, and choose its roles (also modifying them) in accord with its own approval rather than that of "superiors and fellows." As Small found in his sample of maladjusted cases, the weak, dependent self is incapable of creative adjustment, is determined by circumstances, and tends to "show fantasies of withdrawal from the environment, self-depreciation, and acting out of impulses."

And finally, in point 10, all that is necessary is to add to "finds adequate outlets" the phrase *"or is able to create."* This can be done, within limits, of course, by the strong, autonomous person who is an acting subject, not merely a reacting object.

RE-EVALUATION AND SATISFACTION

When the student is faced with an economic system that is highly organized and over specialized, what can he do to increase the probability of experiencing greater satisfaction in his work, to make it an intrinsic part of his living, a goal or end that is self-fulfilling, rather than merely a means of making a living? The answer is one of the key answers to mental health. For it is the person who has a true vocation who experiences the greatest self-fulfillment and psychosocial development. It is he who attains a high state of *being* through his *doing*.

One's first reaction may be that very little can be done for the assembly line worker and many machine operators. The man who spends day after day, month after month, doing nothing but making No. 10 screws could do little to make this job personally satisfying. He could go to another factory where he can make screws of different sizes and types. But the large majority of workers are not engaged in such highly specialized and narrow range of work activities, and the movement within industry itself has already begun to despecialize and reduce the deadening monotony of such narrow range activity. As a partial corrective measure, some companies take their assembly line and/or piece workers on conducted tours throughout the plant to see the other processes and the completed product.

Greater numbers of "average" students may participate in various types of "potential development" seminars as previously described, thereby learning to increase their performance ability and compete more favorably with the previously more brilliant students for occupations that offer challenge, variety, and opportunity for growth. But as this practice becomes a universal procedure, the whole level of performance and expectations is lifted, and the problem remains relatively the same, if not worse. This problem requires the long-range planning of government, business, and education as I have previously suggested. In the meantime, the problem is one which the individual must largely solve for himself.

Basic or core needs, interests, and thus satisfaction requirements, are fairly stable in the life of the mature person. But the mature, confident, creative person will not only find many or some specific activities and conditions in his work situation which he can change, but he will also be able to discover new meanings and values in the work or organization with which he is associated. Thus, he can change his specific interests and expectations and find increased satisfaction. The engineer or technician may find himself just one cog in a vast industrial complex and begin to experience the frustration of his own relative insignificance and the purposelessness of his life. Or he may identify more fully with the others of his team or department, or the entire company, and re-evaluate the significance of their service to society. Thus, vicariously he may experience a measure of satisfaction from being a valuable part of a big institution. This is an example of losing oneself in something big, in order to find himself growing bigger by his service therein.

However, at best there will be many people who are caught in occupations that afford very limited satisfactions. Most of these jobs require no more than 40 hours per week. This leaves an additional 20, 30, or 40 hours for avocational activities. The problem of the individual is to work out a pattern of work activities which offer outlets for his basic interests and abilities, which satisfy his basic needs. If he cannot find or build enough of these into his occupation then he builds them into his avocational activities for fun, growth and satisfaction. When one does not have a capacity-need satisfying *vocation*, he must have *avocation*.

WORK PROBLEMS OF THE AGING

The need to work, the problem of finding meaningful and satisfying employment, is not limited to youth. This problem becomes acute at the other end of the maturity scale, at the juncture between ripe middle age and old age. If Allport's functional autonomy concept of motivation is valid, the need for productive work may be greater at 65 years of age than at 20. Forty-five years of exercising acquired capacities for productive work may leave a powerful need-drive to continue.

So we raise the question: what of our senior citizens, the somewhat overly mature? The majority retire from their regular occupations either by choice or compulsion. They are again confronted with the problem of occupational choice, the constructive use of time and talent, how to continue in productive work. They turn to hobbies, from occupational activities to avocational interest. It is a part-time, a leisure-time activity. Our society does not provide enough of this to occupy the time of all retired but fit workers; and, as suggested, much "leisure-time" activity would lose its value in becoming "full time" work.

The aging, retired, person has a double problem with respect to his work-life. It has been maintained throughout this book, that need is inherent in capacity. Our retired worker with long established habits and skills of productive work finds these needs for continued expression frustrated either in part or full. Also, in adapting to his previous occupation and in attaining some satisfaction in it, he has endowed it with value, a work of worth by which he has experienced some sense of worth. Now, without this work, his sense of worth is reduced. Unless, and perhaps with the aid of society, he can reorganize his life and largely satisfy these capacity- and value-needs, the self of him will probably weaken from compromise with and surrender to circumstances. He will not be able to mobilize his inner forces to actively meet the stresses of life, will be depressed and unhappy (unsatisfied), and will be more prone to both physical and mental illnesses.

In most primitive societies old age carried distinction, respect, and prestige. The elders ruled the tribes. Later, the ruling "elders" were not chosen entirely on the basis of age. Today the emphasis is much more on the young or young-middle aged in both government and industrial administration, with colleges and churches often following suit. Society is rising to the challenge and, with the help of continuing education and geriatric programs and research, is developing means of not merely extending life and improving health but also making the autumn of life fuller and more satisfying. A chief factor in this is to find or create worthwhile work activities for the ever-increasing numbers of capable retired people. As they leave the work forces of business and industry, the so-called "production" employment, places are being found in the "service" fields. Many are unpaid volunteers or nominal-fee, part-time workers; many are finding significant and value-need satisfying positions in local government, public welfare work, hospitals, and various agencies of the rapidly, expanding community mental health programs. Some promise is shown by the increasing use of older people as teacher-aides. But the problem is far from being solved at present.

Not all older people retire. This is especially true in the higher administrative and professional positions. Senators, supreme court justices, prime ministers, and many business executives continue to work productively through their seventies and deep into their eighties. And artists like "Grandma" Moses or George Bernard Shaw may not be as rare as we think. The seeming trend is toward a deterioration of initiative, originality, and creativity with advancing age. But the loss of these is not inherent in the process of aging, except when it is due to organic deterioration that impedes mental functions. The more common problem is that of fixed habitual patterns inhibiting creativity rather than serious loss of potential. And this condition would respond to the type of creativity and potential development training programs described below. This is a great field waiting for exploration and development. As vocation or avocation, the varied arts offer an unmeasured field of useful and worth-giving employment for older people. With special training to release inhibitions of fixed habits and to increase perceptivity, a new dimension and zest for life can be opened to the many. Since originality and creativity are not limited to the arts, to the service fields may also be added many rejuvenated older people and those who have never lost their creativity.

Concluding a discussion of "Artistic expression in later life," Stephen Durkee (in Kastenbaum, 1964, p. 315) says: "Aged people in the year 2000 will be greatly different from those of the mid-twentieth century. This is a statement made hopefully and with the premise that the new American education now slowly emerging, including the contribution of adult education, will make learning a central life-time function, a natural part of daily life. The impact of this concept as a 'natural resource' of our nation is staggering to contemplate. Because of earlier retirement and longer life, it is possible to be retired for as long as 30 years, a period of time equal to the number of working years. The 30 years of retirement would not be lost in isolation and 'killing time,' but would provide the opportunity to revitalize interests that were perhaps set aside during the earning years, or to initiate new interests from the background of continuous learning that has occurred."

SELF AND ABILITY GROWTH PROGRAMS

I have been stressing the deficiency of work activities as a sufficient challenge to man's capacities, and need-satisfaction. Some people will challenge this, and argue that the greater problem is to find men big enough for available jobs. This may well be true at the professional and upper management level. But these will employ no more than 10 to 15 percent of job seekers. A much higher percentage of our young people are seeking and assuming to prepare for these higher status positions. The gap is widening as the ratio of college entrants increase. Nevertheless, there is widespread recognition that these upper level occupations do offer challenges and opportunities that are virtually unlimited and that they are much bigger than most of the men who assume to fill them. Business and education have begun to do something about this problem. Robert T. Golembiewski (in Otto, 1966, Chapter 33) describes some of these projects. He writes:

> Since there is no easy cataloguing of programs for developing human capabilities in organizations, attention below will be selective. That attention will be basically dual: on approaches to developing human capabilities that are established and burgeoning; and on approaches to developing human capabilities that are more or less "gleams in the eye" of many students of organizational phenomena. The former category includes: executive development; the stress on "creativity"; and sensitivity training. The latter focus of attention includes a variety of efforts aimed at fundamentally reorganizing work in ways that will at once require more of man while they permit man to self-actualize. . . .

CREATIVITY AND SENSITIVITY

Since emphasis on executive training is quite commonplace and many programs established, I shall pass that and quote Golembiewski on certain of the others. Our interest is in increased creativity in order to experience greater satisfaction from more productive work. Golembiewski says:

> Basically, creativity programs have as their objective the elimination of barriers to problem solving that do not inhere in the problem. The nonproblem barriers to problem solving may be found in: the techniques utilized; the person utilizing them; or the environment in which the application takes place. All creativity programs stress the first barrier, and many deal more or less directly with the second and third. . . .
>
> The claims and counter-claims in this area urge caution. At base, however, the results indicate that there are learnable or improvable component skills in creative problem solving, and some of the techniques which sharpen such skills have been isolated and can be transmitted. . . .
>
> Sensitivity training qua movement is a relatively new approach to increasing human capability, but it has its legions of advocates. The movement has an immediate history going back only to the late 1940's, but it is an object of interest in many areas (including productive organizations). . . .
>
> Sensitivity training helps develop the subtle relations of cognition and emotion in a living situation and often highlights the penalties of an undue emphasis upon either "knowing" or "feeling." Business concerns again have been the leaders in exploiting this new avenue to enhanced capabilities of their employees, but public agencies such as the Port of New York Authority and the Internal Revenue Service have supported laboratory training as a part of their total training effort. (pp. 511–515).

IMPROVING THE OCCUPATION

Various pilot projects have been conducted in an effort to restructure occupational activities and relationships along lines that are more appropriate to worker interest and growth. But the surface is only being scratched. With greater improvement in and application of such special training programs and changing structural relations within and among the occupations of large organizations, increasing numbers of people will find greater satisfaction and fulfillment in their work. As Golembiewski states in conclusion: ". . . This datum permits some optimism that organizations need not thrive upon, nor help create, the kind of developmentally crippled persons so often cited as the products of our organizational society. At one stage of our economic development, deep pessimism was perhaps as applicable a generalization as any. Increasingly, however, organizations cannot afford the awful convenience of stunted capabilities. Organizations will grow as their employees do and, perhaps for the first time in history, this generalization applies with some force at both high organizational levels and low." (p. 518).

> A half or whole class session might be given to a discussion of three or four of these enhancement projects, following short reports based on Golembiewski, Otto, Cooper et al., Samstad, Bradford et al. See Suggested Readings.

MOTIVATION, INTEREST AND SATISFACTION

In this last section it may be well to examine the nature of interests, their relation to motives and needs, drives and values, and how they are formed and may be changed. If the student desires to clarify his vocational interests, and perhaps learn to control or revise them in order to increase the satisfaction derived from his work, this knowledge will be helpful. It has been fairly well demonstrated that basic interest patterns are established by late adolescence and remain relatively stable thereafter. Throughout high school and college, every student is confronted with the problem of relating his interests to his abilities. His choice of and satisfaction in his life-work depend on this to a large degree.

Strong's Theory. If anyone understands vocational interests, it should be Edward K. Strong, Jr. Let us check briefly on some of his insights. He writes:[13]

> Experimentally an interest is a response of liking; an aversion is a response of disliking. . . .
>
> Interest is present when we are aware of an object or better still, when we are aware of our set or disposition toward the object. We like the object when we are prepared to react toward it; we dislike the object when we wish to let alone or get away from it. . . .
>
> Interest is an aspect of behavior, not an entity in itself. . . .

[13] Edward K. Strong, Jr., *Vocational Interests of Men and Women* (Palo Alto: Stanford University Press, 1943). Used with permission.

> Feeling, interest, want, and attitude all involve a physiological mechanism. Such mechanisms may be dormant or aroused. When aroused, certain overt behavior results and at the same time we are conscious of pleasantness, interest, satisfaction, belief, according to the type of response involved. The term dormant implies that the mechanism exists; and when it is aroused, action results in accordance with its structure. Thus, one may have an interest in collecting postage stamps without thinking of or reacting to it all the time; but when an appropriate stimulus comes along, one will tend to act in a positive direction toward such collection. (pp. 6–9).

Strong virtually equates interest and attitude, stating that with only slight rearrangement they may be measured by the same test. He argues that all interests are learned, acquired, but adds: "There are some interests, however, that come very close to being native, if they are not actually inherited, such as liking sugar and disliking quinine . . ."; then he "wonders how far it is possible to develop a given interest in all people. Can all be led to take an interest in mathematics, art, gardening, sewing, for example?" (pp. 12, 13). He gives several reasons why interest is an indeterminate indicator of achievement or success, but does indicate satisfaction; then he states a twofold hypothesis:

> First, if a student has sufficient interest to elect a college course, his grade in it will depend far more on his intelligence, industry, and previous preparation than on his interest. . . . Second, interest affects the situation in causing the student to elect what he is interested in and to avoid courses in which he is not interested. When a student discovers he has mistakenly elected a course in which he has little interest, he will finish it about as well as other courses but he will not elect further courses of a similar nature. . . .
>
> Interests may not correlate to any great degree with achievement over a short period of time and yet may correlate significantly when achievement involves performance over a considerable period of time. . . .
>
> . . . Interests supply something that is not disclosed by ability and achievement. They point to what the individual wants to do, they are reflections of what he considers satisfying. . . .
>
> Interest may be viewed as a single expression, such as "I like arithmetic" or "I am planning to be an engineer." Second, interest may be considered to be a general tendency

> toward a constellation of items, as when we state that a man has mechanical or scientific interests. Third, interest may be thought of as the total score on an interest inventory, as when he is said to have the interests of an engineer or lawyer or a high masculinity-femininity (MF) score. . . .
>
> The question remains, however, does such a score represent a general interest or merely a sum of many related specific interests? (pp. 18–20).

At a later time, Strong virtually equates interest and drive[14] saying that drive "has been defined as 'any intraorganic activity or condition which supplies stimulation for a particular type of behavior.' . . . Scores on the physician interest scale measure the amount or strength of this condition, this drive toward becoming a physician. It is a drive, just as lack of moisture in the body is a drive. The former causes one to work toward being a physician; the latter to seek water. Whether we call an interest score a measure of similarity of interests or a measure of drive toward a certain end, the practical result is the same; the scores of the interest test point to a desirable occupational solution by which one may reach the goal of earning a living." (p. 15). Then he says: "A drive represented by interest scores may be dormant because it is not appropriate to the man's dominant objective and/or because it is in conflict with other drives. A striking example of conflict between interests and values is that of a college student who possessed the typical interests of businessmen but objected strenuously to such a career, exclaiming, 'But I can't enter business; all business men are crooks.' Only after he had been brought to admit that his father, his uncle and several neighbors were businessmen and not crooks and so changed his attitude, was he ready to consider his interest scores." (p. 16).

RECAPITULATION

Strong has said that interest is present when one is "aware," and as being dormant in the mechanism of habit, skill, etc., the structured readiness (and capacity) to respond. Thus, indirectly, and later directly, he makes interests synonymous with both at-

[14] In Wilbur L. Layton (ed.), 1960, Chapter 1.

titudes or motives and drives, all of which are learned, with some reservations on this last point. Of course, they all come into conflict, partially canceling their effect. Successful performance depends less on interests than on other factors. As an "applied scientist," he has done a great work in dealing with interests operationally. The ambiguity of his theoretical or scientific explanation of interests is largely a problem of semantics.

As a first step in clarfying this issue and facilitating control of interests and satisfaction, I would distinguish more sharply between motives or attitudes and drives or interests. One may make certain fine distinctions between motives and attitudes, but at this state of usage it would be superfluous. In Chapter 4 motive was interpreted as including need-drive-goal, experienced as such when aroused from its dormant state. Both need and goal, the two poles of behavior dynamic like the positive and negative plates of a battery with drive as the current strength, are determined by one's evaluation of his condition and what is necessary for it. It was also argued that motive or attitude may exist as need in either a dormant or aroused state; but only when aroused would it be experienced as a drive toward a goal. Thus, I believe it would help clarify the issue, to think of interest as being equivalent to drive, or, better, the same as positive drive, and disinterest or dislike synonymous with negative drive or aversion. It is a conscious affect state that functions as a guide to choice of behavior—the intensity and qualitative state of consciousness. This, again, is a matter of semantics. But let us accept it tentatively and see where it leads us.

INTEREST DETERMINED BY CAPACITY AND BY VALUE

Let us refer for a moment to the thesis that need derives from capacity (potential ability) and capacity derives from structure. Certain basic structures and the scope of their maturation are inherited, while most, e.g., skills, habits, patterns of thought, etc., are acquired, with certain limitations placed upon these by inheritance. Thus, several broad basic needs are based on inherited potential and many more specific needs are based on acquired abilities. But even these "more specific" needs are compounded from many structure elements in their actual operation. Until aroused, these needs lie dormant as motives or attitudes, tendencies of structured capacities. When aroused they are experienced as drive (interest or disinterest, like or dislike) toward or away from a certain goal. The strength and quality of this drive or interest is determined partly by the actual existent capacity and partly by one's evaluation of his state or condition and his evaluation of what is most helpful.

The relationship between interest and ability begins to appear, and the reason for the low correlation between expressed interests and achievement, as well as the nature of conflicting interests. The case of Strong's student whose tested interests emphatically suggested a business career but who reacted negatively to the suggestion may be re-examined. This student has a relatively high capacity, innate and/or acquired, for a successful business career. When aroused by the proper stimulus, this need-capacity normally would have been experienced as a conscious interest or drive toward such goal. But the value system he had acquired placed a negative worth on business as a goal-occupation which was incongruent with and suppressed or inhibited (caused him to) his otherwise normal interest. When he was led to re-evaluate the facts, his value-derived interest (drive) became congruent with his capacity-derived interest and the inhibiting conflict cleared away.

The fact that most students or workers (the mature ones) do nearly as well at uninteresting courses or jobs as they do with those they enjoy is accounted for by these different types or sources of interest. The student may have a disinterest in the activities of the course due to his not having acquired the capacity-need structures; but since the course is a prerequisite to a college degree and a good grade in it is essential to his standing in his class, he places a high value on high achievement and thus experiences a value-interest. With this value interest dominating his capacity disinterest, he achieves successfully but with greater conflict and effort and less satisfaction.

The end of the matter is simply this: The person who would attain high level psychosocial development through his school career and life-work must be growth motivated, mature, and relatively autonomous. This means that he will be relatively free from selective perception and defenses and can evaluate himself and his various capacities and need states realistically. He will then form realistic goal-values that are arranged in a hierarchy that is highly congruent within itself, and by constantly re-evaluating specific tasks and goals in relation to long-term needs and goals, he will bring his value-interests into greater harmony (congruence) with his capacity-need-interests. Therefore, greater interest in one's work can be created and greater satisfaction derived from it. Year by year the less interesting activities can be reduced, and lead to a high degree of congruence between capacity derived interests and value derived interests: inner harmony, efficiency, creativity, satisfaction, joy, fulfillment—becoming by doing.

One finds or creates his vocation in harmony with himself, his personality; and he becomes, in turn, molded more like others who express their selfhood in similar vocations. More than in any other aspect of his life, except possibly his religion, man directs his own evolution through his work. And these, work and religion, may be inseparable. Did not a writer of the Scriptures say: "Show me your faith apart from your work, and I by my works will show you my faith"? (James 2:18). We may add to that: *and my love*. By these, *self* grows to *fullness of being*.

SUMMARY

Vocation has been presented as a basic way of life by which the growth-motivated, productive-oriented individual finds his fulfillment. Occupation and vocation were contrasted on the basis of the former being the type of work one enters largely by reason of social influences, circumstantial factors and a rational consideration of its opportunities and requirements and one's aptitude for the work. Occupation may or may not closely fit his personal needs and satisfactions. Vocation, on the other hand, may include these elements but also includes an intuitive awareness and is the occupation which *especially* fits the individual's capacities and needs and thus affords rich meaning and satisfaction. Donald Super's (1957) discussion of the great influence one's occupation has on his status, family and social activities and general style of life was reviewed.

Occupational interests and satisfactions sought have been presented in the two motivation or need categories described in Chapter 4, e.g., those that relate to maintenance needs and those that relate to growth needs. Certain studies were cited which tended to support this arrangement or gave comparable categories. Herzberg's *motivator-hygiene theory* was presented, as a similar but not identical interpretation of work satisfaction.

We observed the perennial problem of a disproportionate number of high school and college students who aspire to the upper level occupations. These young people begin with interests in the work activity, opportunity for self-expression, and personal growth. When they are faced with relative failure in the tough competition, they lower their aspirations, compromise with satisfaction expectations; and often their occupational interests swing from the growth to the security (maintenance) side of the need category chart.

The key to deep satisfaction and self-actualization in one's work seems to lie in the experiences of *involvement* and *commitment*. These characterize a true vocation in which the individual's capacity needs find relatively full expression in harmonious work activities. The worker is "in love" with his work, gives himself utterly to it and is enhanced by it. Super's 10 propositions were used as a take-off to show how the normal and mature individual may change his specific interests and specific occupational activities, re-evaluate the significance of his occupation, find new meaning in it, and increase his sense of worth and satisfaction.

Since a disproportionately large number of youth seek the high level jobs, many upper level positions demand more and offer more than the holders put into them. Consequently several large corporations, in some instances companies and universities together, are developing special training projects of the self-enhancement or potentials development type, e.g., creative thinking and sensitivity training. These are far from being perfected but they show a trend and much promise toward helping people identify more fully with their work activities, express themselves more freely and gain greater work satisfaction.

Interest is defined as being virtually synonymous with positive drive, and disinterest or dislike with negative drive; both are related to attitude as drive is to motive. As a drive, interest is partly determined by one's capacity needs and partly by his value-goals. This accounts for the sometimes low correlation between interests and abilities. Often there is incongruity within one's value system and between his value-goals and capacity-needs. This produces conflicting interests that may cancel each other.

The healthy, or health giving, vocational life is found by (and in) the mature, autonomous person who is relatively free from defense mechanisms, makes a realistic self-appraisal, and forms a realistic value system. His capacity-need interests and value interests are congruent, his abilities and interests correlate highly, he identifies fully with his work, and experiences fulfillment therein.

REFERENCES AND SUGGESTED READINGS

ARGYRIS, C., *Interpersonal Competence and Organizational Effectiveness,* Homewood, Ill.: Richard D. Irwin, Inc., 1962.

BERDIE, R. F., "Factors Related to Vocational Interests," *Psychol. Bull.* (1944) 41, 137–157.

———, "Range of Interests and Psychopathologies," *J. Clin. Psych.* (1946) 2, 161–166.

BLAI, B., JR., "An Occupational Study of Job Satisfaction and Need Satisfaction," *J. of Exper. Educ.* (1964), 32, 383–388.

BRADFORD, L. P., et al., *T-Group Theory and Laboratory Method,* New York: John Wiley & Sons, Inc., 1964.

CAPLOW, T., *The Sociology of Work,* Minneapolis: Univ. of Minn. Press, 1854.

CENTERS, RICHARD and DAPHNE BUGENTAL, "Intrinsic and Extrinsic Job Motivations among Different Segments of the Working Population," *J. Appl. Psych.,* V. 50, No. 3, 193–197.

COOPER, W. W. et al., *New Perspectives in Organization Research,* New York: John Wiley & Sons, Inc., 1964.

CRAWFORD, CLAUD C., "Commitment," *Pers. & Guid. J.* Vol. XLIV, No. 9, 904–909.

DARLEY, JOHN G. and THEDA HAGENAH, *Vocational Interest Measurement,* Minneapolis: Univ. of Minn. Press, 1955.

FRIEDLANDER, F., "Job Characteristics as Satisfiers and Dissatisfiers," *J. of Appl. Psych.* (1964), 48, 388–392.

FROMM, ERICH, *Man for Himself,* New York: Holt, Rinehart and Winston, Inc., 1947.

GOLEMBIEWSKI, R. T., *Men, Management, and Morality,* New York: McGraw-Hill Book Company, 1965.

———, "Innovation and Organization Structure," *Pers. Adm.* 27:3–5, 17–21.

HALPERN, GERALD, "Relative Contributions of Motivator and Hygiene Factors to Overall Job Satisfaction," *J. Appl. Psych.* (1966), Vol. 50, No. 3, 198–200.

HERZBERG, F., et al., *The Motivation to Work,* 2nd Ed. New York: John Wiley & Sons, Inc., 1959.

KASTENBAUM, ROBERT, *New Thoughts on Old Age,* New York: Springer Publishing Co., Inc., 1964.

KUHLEN, R. G. and G. C. THOMPSON (ed) *Psychological Studies of Human Development*, New York: Appleton-Century-Crofts, 1952.
LAYTON, WILBUR L. (ed), *The Strong Vocational Interest Blank: Research and Uses*, Minneapolis: Univ. of Minn. Press, 1960.
LEVENSTEIN, AARON, *Why People Work*, New York: Crowell-Collier, Inc., 1962.
LOFTIS, H. A., "Study of Commitment to Teaching," *J. of Home Ec.*, Vol. 56 (1964), 157–163.
MYERS, M. S., "Who are Your Motivated Workers?" *Harvard Bus. Rev.*, (1964), 42, 73–88.
OTTO, HERBERT (ed), *Explorations in Human Potentialities*, Springfield, Ill.: Charles C. Thomas, Publisher, 1966.
ROBERTS, GUY L., *The Way of Life*, New York: Comet Press, 1954.
STRONG, E. K., JR., *Vocational Interests of Men and Women*, Palo Alto: Stanford Univ. Press, 1943.
SUPER, DONALD, *The Psychology of Careers*, New York: Harper Brothers Publishers, 1957.
———, *Appraising Vocational Fitness*, New York: Harper Brothers Publishers, 1949.
———, "A Theory of Vocational Development," *Amer. Psychologist* (1953), 8, 185–190.
WERNIMONT, PAUL F., "Intrinsic and Extrinsic Factors in Job Satisfaction," *J. Appl. Psych.*, Vol. 50, No. 1, 41–50.

Appendix

PREFACE

The following selections are presented to provide special information which is relevant to psychosocial disorders and development, with particular reference to specific treatment. These should help to satisfy the larger interests of some students and provide selective discussion materials. The selection is not comprehensive, but it is illustrative of significant developments and procedures that are relatively new and promising, particularly conditioned response or behavior therapy and short-term psychotherapy. I have found that many of my students, tired of generalities, are quite interested in concrete specifics.

The LSD "trip" is of much interest to most students, and much has been written about its actual and potential harmful effects. Selection I is presented as one of the better pilot programs designed to explore its possible therapeutic value. Selection II is a short summary description of conditioned-reflex or conditioned-response learning which is rapidly being applied in behavior therapy. Selection III by White is one of the good, concise general descriptions of this newer therapy and is followed by four selections giving more detailed descriptions of specific applications. Selection VII by Adams has somewhat of a special interest due to the brief period of conditioning, the use of sensory deprivation as the conditioner, and its creating a readiness on the part of the patient to continue with prolonged psychotherapy.

In Selection VIII, Sculthorpe and Blumenthal describe a type of family relationship therapy that is gaining followers and proving to be quite significant in restoring the schizophrenic to normal family and social life, with the patient's role in the family constellation having been found to be a major factor in his developmental failure. In Selection IX, Beata Rank reveals 10 years of research findings on young children suffering "a typical development," the typical etiology, and the psychoanalytically-oriented treatment procedure of a famous clinic. Selections X and XI include descriptions of short-term psychotherapy as practiced in two very progressive clinics, the one of a more general nature and the other very specific.

While there is some controversy about specific aspects of the motivation-hygiene theory as presented by Herzberg and Hamlin and Buhler's basic life tendencies (Selections XII and XIII), the experimental work underlying these studies exemplify significant empirical work with motives and need satisfaction which are relevant to growth and self-actualization, especially as influenced by vocational, family and social life. The reader may find some helpful material for self-analysis and self-directed growth in these studies. Dukman's report (Selection XIV) on directed meditation illustrates one awkward but promising step toward a more realistic grappling with subjective experience and self-strengthening exercises. It is a frontier in psychosocial development that is calling for much more exploration.

Finally in Selection XV, White presents two comparative case studies showing different degrees of interpersonal competence—one more poised, self-confident, and self-assertive and the other more deferent, uncertain, and defensive. Both young men made good adjustments and could be termed "successful." But the reader may see in one a greater degree of self-actualization while in the other merely good adjustment. In this course interest should be given to this distinction.

Appendix

I. Psychedelic Therapy (Utilizing LSD) In the Treatment of the Alcoholic Patient

A Preliminary Report by Doctors A. A. Kurland, Sanford Unger, John Shaffer, Charles Savage, Sidney Wold and Robert Leily[*]

Introduction. That the administration of an effective dose of LSD will temporarily alter the functioning of the nervous system in unusual ways seems now to be an item of general information. However, the extent to which the period of drug action can be harnessed for therapeutic advantage has remained a complicated and unsettled issue.

Somewhat over two years ago, in view of both the treatment dilemma posed by the chronic alcoholic patient and then several extant reports of the drug's usefulness, we launched our own explanations with patients hospitalized in the Alcoholic Rehabilitation Unit of the Spring Grove State Hospital in Baltimore, Maryland.

From the very beginning, our approach to the use of this potent compound was marked by extreme respect. We started by implementing a treatment effort, called the psychedelic procedure, which consisted of approximately three weeks of intensive psychotherapy incorporating one, single high dose, highly-structured LSD session.

In the preliminary phase of this work, 69 male in-patients were treated as described, i.e., they received a time-limited course of psychotherapy which included one, and only one, LSD session. Our objectives were primarily research-oriented; namely, to increase understanding of LSD effects and to assess the safety and therapeutic poten-

---

[*] From a report issued by the Spring Grove State Hospital, Baltimore, Md. Adapted and used with permission. Later published in *Amer. J. Psychiat.* 123:10, April 1967.

tial of its use within a definitely time-limited treatment procedure, without regard for past history of personality pathology.

Rationale. Let us look first at the alcoholic patient and the treatment challenge he poses: The prodromal phase of this condition has been estimated to involve 10 to 12 years of heavy to excessive drinking. Apparently, quite diverse personality types—neurotic, psychopathic schizoid—are abnormally attracted to the effects of alcohol. The available evidence suggests that the common, underlying predisposition inheres in an inability, or at least lower-than-average capacity, to handle psychological stresses, tensions, and frustrations. In the early stages alcohol has even served a tranquilizing effect on tensions and anxiety. But eventually it becomes a dependent condition, with tissue tolerance increased and a whole take-over of the metabolism of the cell by alcohol. Alcohol consumption must be continued or maintained at levels associated with intoxication not because of psychological desire but because of physiological demand. A withdrawal syndrome (tremor, weakness, anxiety, nausea, vomiting, fever, etc.) seems easily to rival that associated with narcotics withdrawal.

As the condition becomes chronic, it carries in its wake a distinctive configuration of personality pathology which has been described and widely called 'alienation.' Tiebout (1951) has painted the picture as follows: "During the course of the alcoholic's illness, there develops a personality pattern with a characteristic negative, hostile coloring. Included in this pattern is a tendency to be: tense and depressed; oppressed with a sense of inferiority; weighted down by an over-powering sense of loneliness and isolation; egocentric; defiant; and walled off and dwelling, to a large extent, in a world apart from others."

The basic aim of the psychedelic procedures is to frontally assault the pathological process denoted by the term alienation: if possible, to break the patient loose from its hold, and to implant in its stead the seed of a new contact with himself and life. Long experience has indicated that unless and until there is a major re-orientation in the alcoholic patient's view of his own worth and his prospects, the return to alcohol is nearly invariable and rapid.

Method. All patients, as part of the process of integration and consolidation, are requested to write up a full report of the LSD day. Their reports contain references to "overwhelmingly beautiful" music, "most magnificant experience of my life," "of a wonderful experiencing of life," "of oneness in fellowship" and "to God."

Procedure. The therapeutic preparation leading up to the LSD session is brief and intensive. During the approximate two-week period, the patient is seen by the therapist nearly every day and for an average of 12 to 15 hours.

The nature of the therapeutic enterprise is outlined for the patient in the initial interview. Therapy generally begins with an examination of the patient's drinking history, his particular alcoholic course, and a detailed, largely didactic, explanation of the nature of the condition. Then, in a moderately directive fashion, the patient and therapist together begin to explore the patient's current personality difficulties and major problems. Once these have been preliminarily identified, and sufficient rapport has been established, the focus is turned to the origin and development of the patient's pathology, as the life history is exhaustively renewed in an attempt to develop insight into the dynamics of his case. An attempt is made throughout to clearly delineate and strengthen the "healthy" component of the patient's functioning. When the therapist judges (1) that his knowledge of the patient is sufficiently intimate, (2) that distorted and defensive ego functioning has been reduced, as well as "significant encounter," he then schedules the LSD session and proceeds to specific preparation for it.

The specific preparation, and in certain ways the literal rehearsal, for the LSD session, occurs on the day preceding it, and takes about one and one-half hours. The nature of the onset of the drug's effects, their course, and significance are outlined to the patient. He tries on the eyeshade and stereophonic headphones, and their functions are explained. The possibility and import of all potentially disruptive or alarming reactions are carefully reviewed and discussed; from incoordination, physical distress, fear (for instance 'of going crazy' or dying), to depression, paranoia, confusion, and so forth. Exactly what is expected of the patient is explicitly detailed (in so far as it is possible) along with the general format for the course of the day.

The conduct of the session itself has been more or less indicated, and we shall not pursue further description. There is no doubt that in our implementation of the psychedelic procedure, the patient is exposed to a heavy dose of tender, loving care. Occasionally, we have quipped that the function of LSD is to "potentiate love," and, in fact, this seems a not inaccurate characterization. It does most certainly appear that this dimension of the therapeutic contact constitutes a highly significant ingredient in the mobilization of psychedelic reactions.

The treatment process does appear to break patients loose from the grip of pathological functioning. Many patients manifesting relatively severe personality disturbances have shown significant benefit.

Concluding Remarks. It might be well to underscore that LSD, within the context of a treatment procedure as described herein, can apparently be used with relative safety. Actually, in the 69 cases under discussion, and in subsequent work with alcoholic patients, both clinical evaluation and psychometric test data agree that no patient has been harmed; on the other hand, the extent of benefit in some cases has seemed considerable. The seriousness of the LSD intervention, however, should never be underestimated, and it would appear evident that specialized experience and training are prerequisite to maximum safety and effective work with this agent.

In the sample reported, only 23 patients, or exactly one-third, had maintained abstinence up to the sixth month follow-up; and the informed guess is that a large number of these did not survive relapse past one year. It was in response to such experience, as well as other considerations, that we have been led to explore a more comprehensive program.

It has been said that the therapy seemed to be returning the patients to the human race. As Dr. John Buckman, of the Marlborough Day Hospital in London said, "the patients now were truly suitable and amenable to continuing psychotherapy." And he speculated, "what had been achieved might take a year or longer through conventional procedures, if, in fact, these patients could ever be effectively engaged in a therapeutic enterprise." In good part, we have come to share this view.

II. Conditioned Response or Association Learning

Learning and conditioning are virtually synonymous in the thinking of many behavioral scientists, depending on how narrowly or broadly the term conditioning is used. And there are differences at that point. But if we ignore for the present purpose those more complex and ill-defined mental processes involved in intuitive awareness, insight learning, and creative thinking, we may be in general agreement that all sensori-motor and most basic learning can best be described in terms of classical and operant conditioning. The organism that has "learned" a new response has been "conditioned" to act differently from its innate response.

CLASSICAL CONDITIONING

The Russian physiologist, Ivan Pavlov, gave to modern psychology the technique of measuring and concept of classical conditioning. After speculating on the matter of a dog's salivating at the sight of food when food was placed in its mouth, he hypothesized that the response was learned, i.e., conditioned. Then he devised his famous experiment which, with certain variations, has been replicated thousands of times. The stimulus of food particles on the tongue produced the "natural" response of saliva flow. Thus it was called the unconditioned response and the food particles the unconditioned stimulus. He set out to discover or demonstrate how other stimuli may induce salivation—how the dog may be made to salivate in response to other stimuli (sound, light, color, etc.), the conditioned stimuli to which the dog was conditioned to respond.

A frame structure and harness were designed by which the animal could be kept in a nearly motionless position on a table in a soundproof laboratory. The dog was placed in harness several times, until it could accept the position without agitation. Its cheek was perforated to expose the salivary glands and a capsule was attached to catch and measure the saliva. The laboratory was so constructed that the experimenter could observe the animal without himself being observed. By remote control he could drop powdered meat into a pan or bowl a few inches below the dog's mouth, which it had sufficient-head room to reach.

A small light that is placed a few feet in front of the dog is flashed on. The dog responds with slight random movements, but there is no salivation. After a few seconds[1] the meat powder is dropped into the pan. The hungry animal eats it and salivates copiously. The experimenter repeats the procedure several times, the light being followed by the meat to produce salivation. After several repetitions (trials), the dog begins to salivate in response to the light only; and with many trials, as copiously as originally to the meat. A conditioned response has been established. An unconditioned (natural) response has been associated with a new (conditioned) stimulus. Thus, conditioned response or association learning was demonstrated.

The animal's original response to the flashing light was random movement—the tendency to move in all directions. The presentation of the meat while this random tendency or set was in operation tended to associate the salivation response with the light stimulus, reinforcing this response to light rather than any of the other many random tendencies. Thus the meat offering is called the reinforcer or the reward. The learning or association order is from conditioned stimulus (CS), the signal, to unconditioned stimulus (US), the reinforcer, to the response that has become associated with the new signal which hitherto would not have elicited the response. This association between a conditioned stimulus and a response through repeated presentation and reinforcement by an unconditioned stimulus is referred to as classical conditioning. It typifies learning at the reflex or sensori-motor level.

By the same procedure, Pavlov's dogs were conditioned (learned) to salivate in response to color and sound signals. In the modern psychology laboratory many variations of the above experiment have been developed. A simple and commonly used experimental model, using students as subjects, is to condition the eye to blink in response to various signals by immediately following with a jet of dry air striking the eye. Many organic responses have been thus conditioned to respond to substitute stimuli. As mentioned in Chapter 10 and illustrated

[1] Later experimentation demonstrated that a 0.5 second interval between CS and US produced the best conditioning effect.

in following selections, this principle is being applied in practical methods of treating various types of behavior disorders and variously called "learning therapy" or "behavior therapy" or "conditioned response therapy."

In its therapeutic application, the above principle is usually applied in its reverse form. An undesired response is conditioned to disappear, become dissociated from a stimulus, by extinction instead of reinforcement. After a response has been thoroughly conditioned to automatically follow a certain stimulus (CS), if that stimulus is presented a great many times with no accompanying reinforcer, at least at intervals, the response tends to weaken and disappear—is extinguished. Or if pain in some form is applied in conjunction with or immediately following the stimulus, the extinction occurs more rapidly. Thus, dissociation of response with stimulus (unlearning) is induced by an extinguisher, just as association is induced by a reinforcer. In therapy, many devices are used as extinguishers to dissociate and eliminate the undesired response.

Other facts relating to classical conditioning such as generalization, discrimination, and spontaneous recovery of response need not be discussed here. Instead, let us examine the other basic type of conditioning.

OPERANT CONDITIONING

The process known as operant conditioning moves one step toward a higher dimension or a more complex type of learning or habit formation. It generally involves the organism as a whole rather than the simple reaction of an organic part. In classical conditioning, the experimenter manipulates the environment (stimulus situations) and the organism can do little more than react. In the other, the organism (animal or person) appears to act spontaneously, and emits or initiates response, on the environmental situation rather than merely react to a stimulus. Thus the organism "operates" on the environment to produce a certain effect, as when a dog learns by several trials to perform a "trick" in order to get his desired reward. The behavior of the organism is instrumental in producing the effect, thus this type of learning is sometimes called instrumental conditioning.

B. F. Skinner introduced both the concept of operant conditioning and its experimental demonstration. He constructed the apparatus commonly known as the "Skinner-box" to produce this type of learning in the laboratory. It is a box-like compartment, plain on the inside except on the one side to which is attached a protruding bar with a food dish beneath it and a small screen and light above it. The bar acts as a lever to release food pellets into the dish when manipulated by the animals and, of course, when the food magazine (outside) is attached.

Rats placed singly in the box and in varying stages of hunger will move about at random in varying degrees of activity, striking the bar at varying rates. The rate of movement generally increases with the degree of hunger. When the food magazine is attached and the hungry rat in his random movements presses the bar, he receives food as a reward (the reinforcer of that particular response). His operant behavior produces the desired effect. With repeated trials, the rat makes less random (erroneous) movements before pressing the bar and soon learns to go immediately to the bar and press it in order to feed himself. The animal has developed the habit of bar-pressing to obtain food when placed in a particular type of compartment. By a greater amount of movement and thus more frequent pressing the bar, the hungry animal (more highly "motivated") learns faster than the not-hungry one.

If the food magazine is removed and the hungry rat is repeatedly placed in the box, he presses the bar less and less frequently and finally ceases. The response has become extinguished, dissociated, unlearned. Failure to obtain food with the first two or three trials may incite more frequent and desperate bar-pressing, but the general effect is toward decline and extinction. Or if the animal is subjected to pain, as by a strong electric-shock, when he presses the bar, his efforts cease more rapidly. Thus the application of pain serves as an extinguisher.

Again, the experimenter may attach the food magazine when the light is on and detach it when the light is off. Under these conditions, the rat will learn to press the bar only when the light is turned on, ignoring it when the bulb is not lighted. He has learned to discriminate. As with classical conditioning, there are many other facts associated with operant conditioning (frequency and length of trials, regular vs. intermittent rewards, etc.) which do not concern us in this course. We are, however, interested in its application to therapy as presented in following selections. In such application the operant behavior of the individual determines the reward or punishment, the reinforcer or extinguisher. Both are used: one to extinguish undesired behavior and the other to reinforce the desired substitute response. Disapproval and blame or approval and praise may be used as social extinguishers or reinforcers to condition more acceptable behavior.

III. The Use of Learning Theory in the Psychological Treatment of Children

*by John Graham White, Ed. M.**

The following case study demonstrates that some forms of disordered behavior in chidren can be explained and treated according to well-established principles of learning, without any recourse to "psychodynamic" concepts and without any attempt to produce "insight" in the patient by means of verbal "interpretations" of behavior.

Case Study. A girl of five and a half was admitted to the hospital in consequence of her refusal to eat and also because she was suffering from what appeared at the time to be rheumatic pains.

Relevant History. The patient was the second of two girls who, by the disruption of war, had become her "father's baby" while her older sister, born while the father was away, was her "mother's baby." The father gave his baby lavish attention, played with her, and almost from the time she was born fed her. From infancy, when her father was nursing her, the patient "used to hold on to and play with his collar. She would never go to bed without his collar. . . . If she lost hold of the collar in the night she would call out and mother would find it for her."

Between the ages of three and four the child's appetite became capricious. She insisted on having her main meal at 6 o'clock, when the father came in from work. She would sit on his knee through the meal and he would feed her. When he was present the mother was

* From the *Journal of Clinical Psychology* (1959), 15, 227–229. Copyright 1959 by Journal of Clinical Psychology. Adapted and used with permission. (Also reprinted in Cyril M. Franks (ed), *Conditioning Techniques in Clinical Practice and Research.* New York: Springer Publishing Co., Inc., 1964.)

rejected; this younger child was the self-avowed rival of both her mother and her sister.

The father was the kind of person who would do anything to avoid "disagreeableness," such as violent scenes of any kind, and could easily be influenced by threat of this. The father would have to quiet the cries of the girl at bedtime, often by reading himself into exhaustion.

The father went to the hospital after a time for an illness that was to prove fatal. The patient (girl) could not see him at the time and clung to his collar at night. When her father returned home to die, the child wanted to spend all her time in his room. When he died, the mother told her that he had gone to "God's Hospital." The child expected that he would return.

Later that year (September) the mother started to go out to work, and the aunt used to give the patient her meals. The relatives resorted to fantastic antics to get her to eat but her appetite deteriorated gradually. In October she became ill with what was diagnosed as acute rheumatism. She was confined to bed for six weeks; and during this time her appetite deteriorated to the point where she was refusing all solid foods, and took only milk and fruit drinks. The family doctor himself tried to feed her with a spoon, but with no success. Once the child commented to her mother, "Dr. B says if I don't eat I'll never be a big girl. If I grow into a big girl my daddy won't recognize me, will he?"

Treatment. The immediate problem was formulated in terms of simple conditioning with father as the conditioned stimulus, upon which the conditioned response of eating had come to depend, reinforcement being supplied both by satisfaction of hunger, as well as by anxiety-reduction through sitting on the father's knee and being fed by him. The first steps, therefore, were to provide a substitute for the father and to arrange a series of experiences that might gradually approximate those obtained before the father's death. In other words, principles were to be used that involved both stimulus-substitution and the generalization continuum. The attempt was to be made to replace the father as conditioned stimulus, first by the psychologist and, later, by members of the child's own family, such as uncles, and the father's sister, and finally the mother. It was decided that the psychologist, a man, should undertake this part of the treatment, and in accordance with the theoretical formulation no "interpretations" were to be given to the child.

For the first week the psychologist saw the child every day for an hour and arranged a series of play sessions and tea parties in a large play house which was equipped with miniature furniture and paraphernalia such as cooking utensils, plates, and tea sets.

During the first session the child and psychologist attended to the various needs of dolls and only the dolls were fed. The next afternoon, the child ate a number of miniature biscuits and drank dolls' cups full of milk laced with a beverage to which her father had been partial. Doll play continued everyday that week with the child still refusing ward meals. At the weekend it was decided that the child should return home and in the future attend as an out-patient.

The weekend was spent partly at home and partly at the house of a paternal aunt and uncle. On Monday, mother reported that the patient had eaten a little solid food both at her aunt's and at home; and while the psychologist was having his coffee, the child asked for a cup, too. During the subsequent play sessions that week, larger cups were substituted for the dolls' cups and full sized biscuits introduced.

In the middle of the second week the mother reported that the child had eaten at a neighbor's house and that the child had told a neighbor who had called at her home, "I don't eat in this house. I won't eat for my mommy."

About a month after referral the mother reported that the child had for the first time inquired what there was for lunch and had eaten something of everything that was available.

During this period the play sessions had continued. The psychologist played the role of submissive father and catered to her whims, until one day, six weeks after the beginning treatment, when the child had him skipping for his tea while she beat time on a hammer-peg board, he made a note to introduce at an opportune moment a little more "reality" and a little less "pleasure" into the father-child relationship. When the patient refused to stay in the playroom while the psychologist had a talk with her mother, he terminated the interview and sent her home without the cup of coffee that had been promised her by the clinic secretary. When the child attended again, a period of retraining was started in which a different set of responses began to be rewarded, i.e., responses other than those of exploiting the relationship with the therapist. She began to do little useful jobs about the clinic, such as mending books, as well as playing. The child continued to eat better, now taking a regular breakfast, and even to say she was hungry; but after three months of treatment she suffered a set-back when the mother had to return to work. Her diet was again reduced to fluids; and she insisted on having a collar, this time an uncle's to go to sleep with. The relapse lasted, however, only three or four days.

. . . Five months after her referral to the Psychiatric Department, the child was showing interest in foods and developing special tastes;

and a month later her eating was no longer a cause for anxiety for her relatives. By this time the psychologist had managed to transfer a large part of the father's mantle on to two uncles, one of whom the patient described as her "No. 1 uncle," saying she loved him "nearly as much as Daddy."

After seven months, this phase of the treatment was concluded. For three years now the child has remained free of her symptoms. She has been healthy and fairly well-adjusted at home, at school with her play friends despite the death of her grandmother and more recently, her No. 1 uncle.

IV. Management of Nocturnal Enuresis by Conditioning Response

*by Thomas V. Geppert, M.D.**

Since only a minority of enuretic children have physical anomalies that hinder the control of urine, it seems that the major reason that enuresis appears is children have never been able to respond to the stimulation of a full bladder by awakening. With this fact known, the treatment proceeds:

Method of Treatment (Non-Aversive). The object of the treatment is to teach the enuretic to respond to nocturnal bladder tension by awakening rather than by urinating. This conditioned response is established with the aid of an automatic electric alarm device, which awakens the patient immediately each time micturition begins. Once this response pattern has been established, the patient tends to sleep for increasingly longer periods before awakening and eventually sleeps through the entire night.

The apparatus used operates on small, self-contained batteries. The alarm is contained in a small cabinet placed on a night stand near the head of the patient's bed. The patient sleeps directly on a moisture sensitive bed pad, which is connected to the alarm cabinet by an electric cord and plug. Whenever micturition begins, the first few drops of urine moistening the pad render it sufficiently conductive to permit the passage of an electrical current which, though feeble, is capable of setting off the alarm. Awakening in response to the alarm bell, the patient ceases voiding, silences the alarm by means of a switch, and goes to the bathroom to complete urination. Before the patient returns to bed, the

---

* From *The Journal of the American Medical Association,* May 30, 1953. Vol. 152, 381–383.

alarm is conditioned for reuse by a parent who replaces the wet pad with a dry one.

Since the treatment is carried out in the home, close supervision and cooperation of the parents was required. Parents were given the following instructions: (1) The patient must awaken immediately when the alarm sounds (if necessary someone must sleep by to awaken him). (2) The patient must be thoroughly awakened before he goes to the bathroom. Sleepwalking defeats the purpose of the experiment. The patient should turn the alarm off himself. (3) The patient should not be allowed to turn off the alarm and go back to sleep. (4) A sympathetic attitude by parents is necessary. (5) Use of a night light is recommended to eliminate confusion. (6) It is desirable for the patient to sleep naked from the waist down but the wearing of pajamas should be resumed during the last week that the alarm is in use, in order to return to normal conditions. (7) Ingestion of liquids should not be restricted. (8) The patient, or parent, must report to the physician weekly describing the process and reaction.

Results. In 38 (90.40 percent) of the 42 patients managed in this manner, enuresis was arrested. Five in whom treatment was successful reverted to the habit, but four of these promptly responded to a repetition of the treatment, the fifth is being treated similarly at this writing. Seventy-four percent of those treated successfully were eventually able to sleep through the night and 85 percent showed noticeable improvement in emotional stability and personality adjustment. Duration of therapy varied 4½ weeks. In seven patients enuresis had begun at the age of three or four years, but in all others it had persisted since birth. Seventy percent of the patients were males and 74 percent were in the five to ten years of age group.

The treatment broke down to four stages which varied in time length:

(1) Patient wets frequently, usually 2 or 3 times nightly—lasts usually less than a week with decreased frequencies of enuresis.
(2) Patient begins to awake without alarm but he still wets occasionally, thus setting off alarm—conditioned response beginning to appear; alarm decreases and dry nights increase.
(3) Patient no longer wets bed—may awake to go to bathroom or sleep entire night. The alarm does not operate, but the patient is aware of its presence.
(4) The patient is on his own; he tends to sleep for longer periods and, eventually, to sleep through the whole night.

Uncooperative parents are the chief cause of failure in this treatment. There is no evidence of symptom substitution.

V. Conditional Aversion to Alcohol

*by Ernest C. Miller, M.D., Anthony B. Dvorak, M.D. and Don W. Turner, B.S.**

PURPOSE

An attempt to create an aversion to alcohol using Pavlovian conditioning. The conditioned stimulus and alcohol is emphasized with the unconditioned stimulus (nausea and vomiting) which is induced by emetine hydrochloride or apamorphine. "The conditioned response is intense nausea at the taste, smell or even at the sight of alcohol."

The importance of timing and "reading" behavior and the variables of interpersonal factors are questions answered acceptably.

TREATMENT

The subjects were twenty whites who admittedly had a drinking problem and wanted to stop. They were chosen with no regard to distinctions "among psychiatric diagnostic categories except for the exclusion of obvious psychotic disorders." They were given physical examinations and were all in good physical health.

The subjects "were informed of the nature of the procedure" and received no adjuvant psychotherapy.

In a sound proof room, a table was set up with various alcoholic beverages, Vodka, whiskey, beer, wine, a two ounce jigger and a large

---

* From the *Journal of Studies on Alcohol,* Vol. 21 (1960), 424–431. Copyright 1960 by Journal of Studies on Alcohol. Adapted and used with permission.

paper cup for water for each man. Four chairs were placed around the table so that the patients could see each other.

New groups were started on Monday mornings at two-week intervals. For two weeks in groups of four they underwent continuous conditioning skipping Saturdays and Sundays.

Each man was required to fill his own water glass from his individual pitcher. It was necessary that the patient consume fairly large quantities of tepid water, in the amount of two liters during the session to potentiate emesis and also to obviate "dry heaves."

The patients entered the room, refrained from conversation, took their places around the table and were told to concentrate on the alcoholic beverages before them. Each patient drank two glasses of tepid water and then received a sub-deltoid injection of 12 to 14 minims of the emetine mixture.* Each of two therapists collected data such as amount of medication, and general behavioral observations.

Shortly after injection, the members of the group uncapped the liquid bottles, opened the beer and poured themselves a two ounce jigger of the beverage of their choice. At frequent intervals each man sniffed at his glass, and only when gagging began or when it seemed likely that the individual was about to vomit, was it suggested that he drink the liquor. The patients were encouraged to drink copious amounts of water between bouts of emesis and as many different beverages as possible were included in the pour-sniff-drink routine. Sessions lasted to 45 minutes, with the group kept until all doubt is dispelled from the mind of each participant that he cannot tolerate the alcohol.

The patients then wash out their glasses, cap the bottles, and rest for four hours in their rooms.

Prognosis. Of the 20 patients who underwent this technique, none failed to acquire an excellent conditioned aversion to all forms of alcohol which were presented to them.

Evidence that suggestion enhanced the emesis is indicated by the fact that 57 percent of the time, contagious vomiting occurred in two members of the group while individual isolated responses occurred only about 16 percent of the total period of emesis. There was no aversion to water as was feared might occur.

Of a followup on 10 of the men, five have remained abstinent, two have reverted to former drinking habits, and three have had brief lapses from 1 to 3 days of drinking, but stopped spontaneously.

---

* A sterile solution of emetine hydrochloride (1.25 gr. per cc), philocarpine hydrochloride (0.52 gr. per cc) and ephedrine sulphate (0.60 gr. per cc).

Those who did drink were able to do so only at the expense of strenuous effort at holding down the first drink. Thus we are reasonably assured that failure to establish a satisfactory conditioned aversion was not the fault. There is adequate Pavlovian conditioning established in a group setting. The external and internal influences were either inoperative or, if present without recognition, neutralized by the overwhelming element of suggestion. The interpersonal factor contributed to a solidarity feeling in the group and lends itself to further group therapy subsequent to conditioning.

VI. Systematic Desensitization with Phobic Schizophrenics

*by Richard C. Cowden and Leon I. Ford**

It has been shown that psychotic patients do respond to conditioning techniques and the benefits derived therefrom to generalize to other situations. If this could be applied to the "many patients who are confined to a mental hospital because of one primary phobic or obsessional symptom," the patients may be able to return to society. Admittedly, the patient would have to be able to attend to the therapeutic situation and be able to recognize and communicate to the therapist what is an anxiety-arousing stimulus. The authors, having demonstrated in a laboratory situation that schizophrenics do respond to systematic desensitization, "felt it necessary to attempt to use the technique with actual clinical symptoms." With a long-termed mental patient, who had well-structured encapsulated phobic reactions, diagnosed as paranoid schizophrenic, the experiment follows:

Case. The subject was a 27-year-old single, high school graduate who had served in the Marine Corps for three years. A survey of his clinical folder revealed that this patient began to withdraw and become more solitary toward the end of his military service. After a while he began hallucinating and had delusions of reference, persecution, etc.

He admitted himself to the hospital in 1956 and was diagnosed as schizophrenic reaction, paranoid type. He received a course of insulin coma treatments, with little sustained improvements, and has been treated with various tranquilizers since that time. He was seen in regular psychotherapy, off and on from 1957 to 1961, with little change shown on his part.

---

* From *The American Journal of Psychiatry,* (1962) V. 119, 241–245. Copyright 1962 by the Journal. Adapted and used with permission.

This patient was chosen for desensitization because he showed a clear cut phobic reaction of being unable to talk to other people without becoming extremely panicky and frightened.

His movement in the usual type of psychotherapy had been very slow. Primarily, he appeared to be passively resistive and at times negativistic. Rarely did he speak freely for a whole interview, and this happened only when he was feeling at his best. Discussing such things as familiar relations, anger, sex, etc. were quite traumatic to him. He would tremble, chain smoke, become tearful or block completely and claim that his mind was blank.

The symptom to be removed was his marked fear of talking to other people. Therapy lasted from October of 1960 until January of 1961 and covered 18 sessions.

Some of the items from the hierarchy relate to talking freely about: (2) a movie you saw; (3) your experience to an interested and sympathetic nurse; (11, 12) current event with someone you consider less intelligent and someone you consider more intelligent than you; (16, 17,18,19,20) your troubles to the ward nurse, a pretty girl in a restaurant, to your doctor, to your sister, and in group therapy; (22) your personal difficulties to your father, and (24) to your mother and father about your future plans or your lack of future plans.

The subject seemed to learn relaxation techniques quickly. However, his outside practice tended to be irregular. He preferred to practice while lying down, rather than while sitting up. He stated he was able to visualize the hierarchy scenes quite vividly. He refused to raise his hand if he felt disturbed; and he reported afterward that he thought he "would wait it out." The second presentation of the scene was not as disturbing. Fortunately, this was reported in the first desensitization session, so, thereafter, the experimenter watched for behavioral cues of disturbance—sharp intake of breaths, tensing of body, rapid breathing, swallowing, etc., and then stopped the visualization.

When he was about half way through the hierarchy, patients, ward personnel, and others who worked with the patient reported that he was more relaxed, friendly, and much more talkative. Auditory hallucinations had ceased entirely within a month or two after the last experimental session. They were unusual thoughts, vivid dreams which disturbed his sleep, and ideas of reference. He began going home on passes again. He became regular in his attendance and efficient in his work assignments. Cigarette smoking decreased. In regular therapy he talked freely and at length and was able to discuss things he had not mentioned in more than three years.

The patient reported that he still had some difficulty in talking in a very talkative group. However, on a pass early in May, he discussed with his mother and father the possibility of coming home to live with them when he was discharged from the hospital. This was a very unusual bit of behavior for this patient. However, the parents refused to accept him at home. He stated that he felt very disappointed and was somewhat depressed afterwards. So far, no adverse effects have become manifest, and the patient continues to be relatively talkative.

Discussion. This case might well be considered a successful demonstration of the desensitization therapy with schizophrenic subjects. However, due to the marked variability found in the schizophrenic population, it can be effective only with certain specific cases. This is reasonable since the term schizophrenic does not define a homogeneous population. Therefore, one should not expect a particular therapy to be effective with the entire population.

VII. A Case Utilizing Sensory Deprivation Procedures

*by Henry B. Adams**

Purpose. The writer of this study has been involved in an extensive research program, investigating the effects of sensory deprivation procedures on psychiatric patients who are exposed to mild conditioning of short duration. The results that emerged show that these procedures can serve a useful therapeutic purpose.

The procedures were intended to serve two aims. The first was to increase insight, self-awareness and self-acceptance and to reduce overall symptomatology. Effectiveness in achieving the first aim could be assessed by an analysis of changes in test-taking behavior before and after. The second attempt was to convince the patient of the advisability of more intensive individual psychotherapy on an out-patient basis. The degree of success in accomplishing the second aim could be determined quite easily by a later followup study inquiring whether the patient did in fact accept outpatient psychotherapy as a consequence of these procedures.

Procedure. The patient was a hospitalized 30-year-old white male veteran with the psychiatric diagnosis of (a) chronic anxiety reaction and (b) psychophysiological gastrointestinal reaction. He was selected in the same way as every other patient who acted as a subject. The selection criteria were that this patient was white, male, between the ages of 20 and 60, carried a functional psychiatric

---

* From Leonard P. Ullman and Leonard Krasner, *Case Studies in Behavior Modification* (New York: Holt, Rinehart and Winston, Inc.).

diagnosis, had no previous history or present evidence of organicity, and was not receiving tranquilizing drugs, insulin, or electric shock treatment.

The patient was administered the Minnesota Multiphasic Personality Inventory (MMPI) and the Interpersonal Check List (ICL), which were scored according to the multilevel system of interpersonal diagnosis.

On the basis of the scores on the tests, a written individual message was prepared for presentation during deprivation. The message also included an explanation of the ultimate aims, goals, and purposes of therapy. The message was tape-recorded by the therapist.

On the following day the patient received 3 hours of practical sensory deprivation and social isolation. He was placed on a bed in a quiet, comfortable air-conditioned room, and his eyes were covered, his ears plugged with glycerine-soaked cotton, and his eyes wrapped in gauze. After two hours the prerecorded tape message was presented to him through a bone-conductivity speaker that had been placed in the gauze wrapped around his head. At the end of three hours he was removed and returned to the ward where he resumed his usual daily schedule of activities.

On the third day, the MMPI and ICL were readministered to evaluate changes. In accordance with the research design, the patient was not interviewed again by his future therapist until after the past testing had been completed.

Results. The prerecorded tape message was aimed at reducing symptomatology and fostering realistic self-awareness. The test results showed generalized improvement after the message was presented to the patient. He had lower scores on all but one of the MMPI clinical scales when retested. These changes on the MMPI were accompanied by evidence of reduced defensiveness, faking, and repression. The multilevel measures revealed enhanced insight, more accurate self-perception, increased self-acceptance, and a reduction in the discrepancy between the patient's conscious ideals and his overt behavior. Covert preconscious attitudes of skepticism and distrust diminished, having been supplanted by a readiness to enter actively into a working relationship with a therapist. These changes on objectively scored tests could not have taken place unless presentation of the message under deprivation conditions had induced fundamental changes in the patient's basic attitudes and personality.

Long Range Follow-up and Appraisal. In evaluating the effectiveness in achieving the second aim, the patient's entire case history was reviewed thirty months after the date the message was presented. The case history indicated that as of the time of follow-up he had been admitted to the hospital as an inpatient six times during the preceding ten years. The patient was placed in sensory deprivation and presented with the message shortly before being discharged from his fifth admission.

Immediately after post-testing on the day following presentation of the message, the patient had his first regularly scheduled therapy session. His reaction to the message revealed that it had indeed produced a great effect on him. Presentation of the message under sensory deprivation, which maximized his receptiveness had served to exclude irrelevant topics and to focus all his attention on the most important problem areas at the outset of therapy.

When the case history was reviewed 14 months after termination of therapy, the patient had remained out of the hospital for the entire period since termination. By contrast he had been admitted to the hospital as an inpatient three times in 13 months before presentation of the message.

During previous admissions the patient had never received or indicated any particular interest in more than brief psychotherapy. But after he was placed in sensory deprivation and presented with the message individually prepared for him, he remained in psychotherapy for a full 16 months.

Since these procedures are simple, inexpensive, free of medical risks and hazards, and require little special equipment, staff, or hospital facilities for their use, there seem to be no significant contradictions to their use in facilitating therapeutic changes in any psychiatric setting.

VIII. Combined Patient-Relative Group Therapy—Schizophrenics

by William Sculthorpe and Irving J. Blumenthal[*]

PART I

Relatives Without Patients. Of primary concern in the treatment of the long-term patient is the encouragement and enhancement of family ties, so that hospitalization may not remove the patient entirely from the family structure. Of equal importance is the acceptance by the family of the patient's need for hospitalization and a constructive involvement of the family in the treatment regimen.

With this in mind, an attempt is made to bring relatives and patients together to facilitate understanding and thus further environmental adaption of the patient.

With Relatives Alone. The reactions of the relatives of schizophrenics are explored. In general these reactions were non-acceptance of overt symptoms, particularly incontinence and taciturnity, overprotective attitudes on the part of the family members, and projections of guilt and shame onto either the patient or ward personnel. Observation by ward personnel on visiting days appeared to confirm the retrogressive effects of such patient-relative relationships. For example, hyperactivity, resumption of incontinence or other regressed behavior sometimes occurred following visits from relatives.

Those selected for the original group of "relatives only" presented attitudes, all of which were in some way non-therapeutic for the patient or self-punitive. It was the intention (in addition to providing

---

[*] From *Mental Hygiene,* V. 49, 569–573 (1965). Adapted and used with permission.

orientation and education) to elicit feelings and reactions from the relatives about symptoms and behavior in order to discharge anxiety and tension to some degree.

The hope was that in this way some modification of negative attitudes could be effected either toward the patient or toward the treatment program, and that this might be reflected in better ward adjustment.

Sessions were held weekly for a period of six weeks. Attendance at these sessions varied between 2 and 6 relatives. They were not initially inclined to interact within the group but tended to look to the group leaders for answers to individual questions and for direct guidance concerning specific problems. Some members dropped out when the sessions failed to meet their expectations by not focusing narrowly on individual problems, or by not being concerned at that time with prognosis or discharge planning. When attendance dwindled to two relatives, the group sessions were terminated.

Taciturnity and stubbornness were of more concern to relatives than incontinence or behavior that might be related to psychosurgery. The most "directive" relatives were also the most hostile or defensive members in a group. Similar reactions were displayed in their relationships with ward personnel. Such relatives discontinued attendance at the group sessions quickly. Those who attended consistently were the relatives who were self-sacrificing or overprotective toward the patients.

Results. The results of the initial group meetings with relatives were minimal. Some signs of improvement in patients were short lived and the relatives who most needed help were the least receptive to what was offered. It appeared that mental illness with its chronic symptomatology had tended to crystallize certain reaction patterns in the relatives; patients and relatives had reached a certain emotional equilibrium, which was difficult to change. Relatives were most concerned with learning how to "manage" the patient with the least amount of difficulty or finding out how he might be completely cured, rather than gaining insight into the patient's behavior and their own reactions as well as the other implications of their interpersonal relationships.

PART II

Patients and Relatives. In including the patients in the therapy, it was felt that there would result more interest and cohesiveness in the group, while at the same time it might facilitate interaction between relatives and between relatives and patients. It was hoped the patients would derive some support from the group situation and the presence of the co-therapists and would feel freer to give expression to some of the feelings they were unable to convey directly to their relatives or to the therapist individually.

Procedure. Thirteen patients were selected for the second group, one year after the preceding study. Relatives from the previous study were included in the group. During the initial sessions of the second group, relatives who were defensive and overprotective continued to resent attending and confined their remarks to criticism of the program and ward personnel. Most relatives used the early session to raise questions related to individual patients, thus providing for more general interest. The relatives were also taken on a ward tour.

The patients were urged to contribute to the discussion and when they did, it appeared reassuring to the relatives. The hostile relatives became more constructive. Generally, it was sufficient for the co-therapists to start the sessions with a few opening remarks, and thereafter to enter in the conversation only when the relatives carried the discussion beyond the purpose of the meeting.

Result. A questionnaire submitted to the relatives following termination of the combined group sessions produced the following results.

General reactions to the group session were mixed. Five relatives said they would attend if the sessions were resumed. Four felt they had received some benefit from the sessions, most often in terms of being able to relieve their feelings. Only one observed a positive effect on a patient. Despite some negative comments by relatives about the sessions, all but one were interested in resuming essentially the same kind of group meetings.

A reduction of some negative attitudes on the part of the relatives, with a consequent lessening of the need to project negative feelings onto the ward personnel or patients, might well be of indirect benefit to the patients.

Comment. Rather hazy study of a good premise. The results are not clear but perhaps longitudinal follow-up will give more meaningful results.

IX. Intensive Study and Treatment of Preschool Children Who Show Marked Personality Deviations, or "Atypical Development," and Their Parents

*by Beata Rank**

INTRODUCTION

During the ten years of our study of severe personality disorders in young children we have gradually elaborated the concept of "atypical development." By this term we refer to those severe disturbances in early development which have been variously diagnosed as Heller's disease, childhood psychosis, childhood schizophrenia, autism, or mental defect. . . . While the specific clinical picture varies from child to child, the features common to all are a lack of contact with reality, little or no communication with others, and a lack of integration and uniformity in ego development.

ETIOLOGY

There has been a good deal of controversy in the literature regarding the etiology of these severe personality disturbances of childhood. Ideas have ranged from the predominantly hereditary or constitutional theories of Kallman and Bender, to the psychological theories of Despert, Kanner and others. We ourselves are convinced that hereditary and biological factors must play an important predisposing part, but are none the less impressed by the vital role of

---

* Adapted from Gerald Caplan (ed.), *Emotional Problems of Early Childhood,* Chapter 22. © 1955 by Basic Books, Inc., Publishers, New York. Used with permission of publisher and author.

post-natal psychological elements in the etiology or emergence of this disturbance. We make no attempt to evaluate the relative importance of these two groups of factors, and are keenly aware that they do not exist in isolation one from the other. Nevertheless, we have set ourselves the task of investigating the psychological aspects of the total problem, particularly the emotional climate in which the child's early object relationships develop and individuation takes place.

Current psychoanalytic theory states that the ego develops through the medium of identification with parental attitudes, and that gradually the early satisfactory relationships with significant figures in the child's environment lead over to the formation of object relationships and to the capacity for reality recognition and adaptation. It is through satisfactory object relationships that the child becomes progressively able to differentiate his image of self from that of the mother. For the process of individuation or ego identity to take place, it is necessary for the child from the earliest months of life to have a parent or parent figure who is sensitive to his needs and able to give him at least a minimal amount of consistent affection and support, thus contributing to his feeling of confidence in himself and in the world around him. Such a parent would encourage the child's need for freedom and exploration without relinquishing her responsibility to set appropriate limits to help him to give up his wish for immediate gratification. Only through this affectionate and flexible parent-child relationship is the child able to develop a central core of self or ego identity. Lacking this, there may be scattered achievements or pseudo-victory over the instinctual drives, but the ego remains so frail that any unfamiliar or difficult situation can disrupt its precarious balance. Hence the simultaneous study of both parents and child is the sine qua non for understanding a child's personality.

According to this central hypothesis we regard the following three factors as important in the etiology of atypical development in childhood:

1. Mother-Child Relationship
   a. There is a profound disturbance in the mother-child relationship during the child's first two years.
   b. The disturbance in the mother-child relationship antedates the appearance of atypical behavior in the child.
   c. All areas of emotional interchange in the mother-child relationship are highly ambivalent.
2. Father-Child Relationship
   a. For various reasons during the early years of this research project we focused on the study and treatment of the mothers and children. Our contacts with the fathers were not sufficiently

sustained to provide us with detailed information about them, although our early impressions led us to state that they were aloof and in many ways passive. Within the last few years we have had an opportunity to study more of these men and as a result have amplified our original assumption concerning the emotional climate leading to "atypical development" by adding the hypothesis that the father's personality plays an important role in the creation of this disturbance.

3. Traumata
   a. Physical Illnesses. What we have described above can be looked upon essentially as psychic trauma to the child produced by his emotional relationships during the first two years. Over and beyond this, we have found that many of these children have suffered an unusual number of respiratory and gastrointestinal illnesses during their infancy which may or may not be a somatic expression of their emotional disharmony. Since we are dealing with a highly complex series of intertwining factors, we suggest the possibility that these assaults on the child's body make him less able to withstand the emotional climate postulated above, and that secondarily they give rise to a new set of anxieties for the child; e.g., loss of body integrity.
   b. Specific Events. In a considerable percentage of cases we obtain a history of the outbreak of manifest symptomatology following specific traumatic events, i.e., separation from or loss of parent (or parent substitute), birth of a sibling. Although there is the possibility that parents are merely trying to relate the onset to a definite event, we feel that these specific events can act like the proverbial straw on the camel's back, and result in a massive breakdown in the child. Those most frequently reported have to do with a geographical separation from the parents; for example, parents going on vacation, child going to the hospital, mother going to the hospital to deliver another baby, or the loss of a significant figure, etc.

PSYCHODYNAMICS

As we focus on the development of the personality structure of the child which eventually results in the clinical picture of atypical behavior, we make the following dynamic and genetic reconstruction. The child's current symptoms are understood as the outward manifestations of his fragmented ego. We evolved this specific concept as a refinement of the more general one of "defective ego" since it seems to us to be a truer representation of the core of this disturbance. By this term, we refer to the clinically established fact that these children lack the capacity for integrations and that they demonstrate only single well-developed functions alongside the many other functions that are crippled or arrested. We can only understand the development of this type of ego structure in the contest of the emotional climate described in the section on etiology. Such an ego is the result of the infant's unsuccessful struggle to obtain vital satisfaction from his parents. When an infant is continuously thwarted or is raised in a milieu of rapidly alternating overgratification and needless frustration, when he is deprived of the mothering and sensory stimulation so necessary for his emotional and physical growth, he may develop anxiety which is expressed by fretfulness, sleeplessness, muscular tension, and excessive "demandingness." Sooner or later, he may give up his striving for gratification, because of the futility of his efforts; and thus he discovers his own helplessness and hopelessness. In the ensuing state of isolation and active exclusion of the disappointing outside world, the child will pursue only those self-circumscribed activities that provide him with narcissistic and autoerotic gratification without intrusion or interruption from the outside. The ego, now shattered by the struggle between the wish to obtain gratification from the parents and the desperate attempt to rescue at least fantasied and autoerotic gratification, may retreat into a fantasy world, which becomes his exclusive haven. Such an ego, though remaining frail, inactive, and depressed, will continue to show development of those functions which are the means of supplying him with narcissistic and autoerotic "pleasures." The coexistence of the paralyzed ego (which remains arrested, static and with minimal external contacts) with the development of single functions, leads to that disparity in the levels of development which is the *sine qua non* for the diagnosis of atypical development.

CLINICAL DESCRIPTION OF THE ATYPICAL CHILD

The following description of the atypical child is quoted from the paper, "Adaptation of the Psychoanalytic Technique for the Treatment of Young Children with Atypical Development" (1):

"As we have seen, each one of these children is an individual in his own right and represents his own entity. However, they show many definable similarities which together constitute the typical picture of this group of children.

"The most significant characteristic is that they are out of contact with reality and apparently without need for communication with others. They may or may not be in possession of speech, and language is used for purposes other than communication. Gestures are frequently seen, as well as stereotyped behavior, rituals, tics, grimaces, monotonously repeated mannerisms, appearing without external provocation but prompted from within. The quality of voice is peculiar. It varies from rasping, squawking, and hollow sounds to a melodious, normal-sounding child's voice. They use their eyes to detect or to explore some object intently. At persons they glance only fleetingly, looking through one as a rule rather than at one. Their eyes seem not to focus. Motor development is often above average; their grace and agility are frequently outstanding; or at the other end of the scale, they may show extreme awkwardness, stiffness, and rigidity. These children move either constantly, aimlessly (perpetual motion), or are so passive that they slide into their seats like lumps heavy to remove. Their play is mostly repetitious, compulsive; they do not derive from it real enjoyment but rather frequently excitement and at times sudden panic. Rocking in a rocking boat or moving cars, ritualistic touching, handling of mechanical gadgets, swinging, spinning, balancing objects or mouthing them are frequent activities, which in turn remove them even further from external contact. Except for play with water, which many of them enjoy, none of their playful activities resembles those of an average child. They are extremely finicky or eccentric eaters. Some accept only two or three items, always the same (usually bread). Others are gluttonous and devour tremendous quantities of food like an animal. Many drink enormous quantities of water, sometimes juice or milk. Their sleep, too, shows the same extremes. They either fall into a deep sleep, remaining immobile in the same spot from the moment they are put to bed to the moment of awakening, or they are restless wanderers, frequent visitors in their parents' bedroom. They are at first undoubtedly identified with inanimate objects (cars, radios, etc.) and in the next stage with animals (pigs, dogs, cats, lions, giraffes, etc.) before they are able to make an identification with the mother or 'mother-figure.' Each one of them has a special talent or ability. Whether it be music (this seems frequently to be the case), or an extraordinary ability to construct or build, or a special volubility or refinement of vocabulary, or whether it be simply their arcobatic agility, it amazes us and has a definite personal appeal regardless of what the specific characteristic indicates in the evaluation of the child's potentialities."

CLINICAL PICTURE OF THE MOTHER OF AN ATYPICAL CHILD

Again we quote from "Adaptation of the Psychoanalytic Technique for the Treatment of Young Children with Atypical Development" (1):

"On the surface these mothers may give the impression of being well-adjusted; not too rarely they are highly intellectual, prominent people. Close investigation reveals that the majority of them are immature and narcissistic with precarious social contact, akin to the type known as 'As If' described by Helene Deutsch, who have struggled heroically to build and maintain the image they have created of a fine woman, wife and mother. The nearer to perfection the success of their efforts, the stronger their belief in magic—their own magic (impenetrable defenses). In their background we find almost without exception an extremely strong but ambivalent bond to their own mothers, which resulted not in an identification which would lead to emancipation and maturity but in a hateful dependency. The urgency to flee this dependence, the need for an 'own' life and personality, even if only a vestige, makes it possible for them to enter matrimony rather early."

In spite of the outward appearance of self-assurance or worldliness, there is inner isolation. This type of mother tends to function on two levels: the surface level in contact with the outside world is a thin crust only, overlying a strong tendency to detachment. When this dual level of functioning is a constant way of living, it bespeaks a serious disturbance. This is illustrated in the case of Mrs. I. described below.

The picture which Mrs. I. had of herself, and which she successfully communicated to the world, was that of a well-educated, vigorous, charming young woman with many abilities and a host of satisfying interests. She had, in fact, obtained a graduate degree, and achieved success in her professional career. She had many friends, frequented the opera and theatre, and was extremely well-read. She exuded self-confidence and what we later learned to understand as a feeling of omnipotence.

The personality behind this facade was gradually revealed to us during the course of Mrs. I.'s therapy. We came to see her as a very isolated person who tries to combat her perception of her own emptiness and her tendency toward withdrawal by precipitating herself into constant activity and excitement. Her fantasy of omnipotence is one method by which she tries to ward off the dread loss of control over her own emotions (especially anger and sadness) and over her environment. As she becomes aware of her own detachment and the ease with which she tends to withdraw from any emotional involvement, she becomes more and more frightened and repeatedly erects again her old defense mechanisms to ward off impending depression. We then again see the strength of her denial and a new flurry of social and/or intellectual activity.

Mrs. I.'s description of her behavior with John during his first year provides us with a vivid picture of the emotional inconsistency in which he was reared. When she devoted herself exclusively to him, it was with her usual intensity and fervor. All too frequently, however, she was engrossed in the pursuit of her own pleasures and interests, leaving John completely out of the picture, diverting him to his bottle and unwittingly encouraging him to indulge in various autoerotic activities in substitution for her. As a toddler, he withdrew to a vacant room with his bottle whenever he became confused by the presence of too many people. While she gave John physical care she was emotionally detached from him as she dwelt in her preoccupation with external affairs. When John was twenty-two months old, Mrs. I. became pregnant with Carol, and withdrew even more completely from her son.

Surrounding herself with people, living in the midst of excitement and romances, she remains lonely and detached. She stoutly maintains her denial of the importance of a father in a family, tries very hard to exclude her own husband and on week-ends cannot bear the idea of sharing the children with him—either he or she must have complete care of one child. At the same time, she is forever seeking the fulfillment of her fantasy for a stable, dependable, devoted parent substitute. She, too, has the "one-track mind," cannot maintain an emotional contact with more than one person at a time and finds herself torn between her two children.

THERAPY

Since our main hypothesis is that the atypical child has suffered gross emotional deprivation and in self-defense has isolated himself from the unsatisfactory emotional environment, it becomes our first task in treatment to breach this isolation.

We try during the *first phase* of therapy to make restitution to the child for the frustrations of his past, which may still be operating in varying degrees in his current environment. We meet the child's needs at whatever level he presents himself, avoiding frustrations whenever possible and providing a maximum of gratification. Through the contact with the more understanding and emotionally consistent parent substitute the child slowly reaches out to the world around him. While the child may still be unable to cope with the postponement of his immediate wishes, he learns during this first phase of therapy to establish some contact with the outside world, to relinquish to some degree the primary process, to decrease the primacy of the pleasure principle, and to make some reality testing.

In the *second phase* of therapy it is the therapist's task to help the child make the necessary steps toward socialization. In learning to adjust to reality the child must develop the capacity to postpone immediate gratifications and to establish tender relationships with people. This implies a transformation of his inordinate demands and his passionate attachments into tender love and generally more mitigated expression of his libidinal and aggressive drives. Supportive and educational measures should play a prominent part in the therapy, to enable the child to modify his aggressive and libidinal drives by developing the capacity to play, to learn, and to be active. He learns, in short, to adopt the reality principle without completely relinquishing the pleasure principle.

X. Dynamic Psychotherapy in a Psychiatric Clinic

*by Peter E. Sefneas, M.D.**

In the Psychiatric Clinic of the Massachusetts General Hospital, short-term dynamic psychotherapy is offered to patients who, facing an emotional, critical situation in their lives, generally develop psychiatric symptoms, and who, after an initial evaluation, are found to have the strength of character and motivation to undergo such treatment. The observations of 50 patients who received short-term dynamic psychotherapy will be presented briefly.

The Patients. There were 11 males and 39 females, 23 were single and 27 married, ranging in age between 19 and 36 years; 28 were age 19 to 25, and 22 between 20 and 36. Occupations varied, but there were 24 students who studied in eight colleges and universities of the Greater Boston area. Housewives constituted the second largest group, and some had also been students who had recently married. Protestants outnumbered Catholics by a ratio of about 3 to 1. Nine patients were seen for four months, 14 for five months, and only one for a nine month period.

The criteria for evaluation and selection of the patients for the short-term dynamic psychotherapy were:

(1) The patient's life long ability to relate well to other individuals (in groups and individually), including the interviewing psychiatrist;
(2) The patient's ability to express emotion freely during the interview, and to specify for whom he had such feelings;
(3) The patient's motivation *for* psychotherapy;
(4) Above average intelligence;

---

* From Jules H. Masserman, (ed) *Current Psychiatric Therapies*. New York: Grune and Stratton, Vol. I (1966), pp. 168–174. Adapted and used with permission.

(5) A certain degree of flexibility, such as the patient's willingness to see not only his own, but also the other side of an emotional conflict;
(6) The ability of the patient to describe and specify his chief complaint as one of the following; anxiety, mild depression, phobia, and conversion.

Aims of Short-Term Therapy. The aims of such therapy involve the choice of and concentration on one of the predicted areas of emotional conflict and the avoidance of areas of conflict involving character problems. Early dependent needs, and problems with passivity, which create entanglements and lead to complications during treatment, is one especially avoided.

In short-term psychotherapy, the psychiatrist attempts to utilize systematically the patient's feelings for him in order to establish a therapeutic alliance, and to help the patient understand emotional conflicts underlying some of his symptoms. He also tries to show the patient that there is a connection between his present emotional feelings for the doctor and his neurotic feelings for other people in his past. New ways are then tried to solve past conflicts, and an effort is made to teach the patient to look into other areas of emotional difficulty. After sufficient progress the patient is trusted to carry on by himself.

It is hard to know exactly when to stop psychotherapy. The case of a young girl with spasms and weakness of her arm is an example. She gave a warning that termination was near when she said that she could recognize her anger for her mother, but did not want to discuss her dependence on her. She laughingly said, "You see, now I have my husband to depend on." She was right. An attempt to deal with her dependent needs would have unnecessarily prolonged the therapy.

Results. Follow-up interviews on 21 patients are summarized as follows:

(1) There was only moderate symptomatic relief. Some patients still had symptoms, but they felt better about them.
(2) More impressive was the description of the therapy as a new learning experience which helped the patients gain insight into their self and which aided them in interpersonal relations.
(3) There seemed to be a restoration of the patient's self-esteem.
(4) The psychotherapy helped the patients to deal successfully with the emotional crisis in their lives that previously they had been unable to overcome.
(5) There was also a change in the patient's original expectation of the treatment; that is, the exaggerated and unrealistic expectations of a miracle were abandoned.

Discussion. Who does well in short-term psychotherapy? A group of intelligent individuals, well-motivated to look into themselves, who have related well to people in the past, who relate well to their interviewers, and who have developed psychiatric symptoms, facing a critical situation in their lives, usually do well in short-term dynamic psychotherapy.

A "positive transference" is the main tool of short-term psychotherapy. "Transference" is defined as a normal emotional interaction between two people, having both conscious and unconscious aspects. The development of a positive transference is encouraged implicitly and subtly. The patient is helped to approach his emotional conflicts, to view his reactions, to tolerate his guilt and his shortcomings, and to learn to live with his ever demanding drives. He is also assisted to recognize his strengths of character, and to derive satisfaction out of his everyday life. He is even encouraged at times to identify with his therapist. Some patients may learn to use different, more successful psychological defense mechanisms to deal with their emotional conflicts. To assess such unconscious alteration is difficult, yet one should describe, as well as try to find new ways to evaluate, such dynamic changes.

Short-term dynamic psychotherapy based on systematic evaluation, observation, theoretical considerations and predictions of future course, with adequate follow-up, seems to be an approach helpful to the patient's needs and suitable for a psychiatric clinic population.

XI. How to Conduct 6-Session Crisis-Oriented Psychotherapy

*by Richard A. Levy, M.D.**

Community-based, crisis-oriented psychotherapy programs "with well-defined priorities in admission criteria and realistically limited treatment services, markedly diminish the need for state hospital or institutional services," according to Richard A. Levy, M.D., director of the mental health clinic, Maine Medical Center, Portland.

The need to develop new techniques to deal with large numbers of patients effectively—one of the frontiers of psychiatry today—led to establishment, three years ago, of the clinic's 6-session, crisis-oriented approach to community psychiatry. With this program, they obtained a "surprisingly high recovery rate in the light of both the severely disturbed patient population and severely limited treatment policy," said Dr. Levy. "Remarkably few people required institutionalization." Only 7 out of 500 patients treated during the first 14 months of the clinic's operation required commitment; 493 successfully completed the program. For nine who required readmission to the program for a second series, the subsequent crisis was rapidly resolved.

Serves Acutely Disturbed. The clinic is the only agency offering outpatient psychiatric services to adults in the greater Portland area of approximately 150,000 people. Professional staff consists of a full-time team of psychiatrist, psychologist and social worker, plus three volunteer psychiatrists, and a homemaker who spends three days at the home of the most severely disturbed patients when they begin their treatment. Freedom of communication between members of the treatment team is basic to the success of the program.

---

* From *Roche Report: Frontiers of Hospital Psychiatry*, Vol. 4, No. 9, 5 and 6 (May 1, 1967). Used with permission.

Because of the interest engendered by success, despite an "almost impossible task posed to community psychiatry in terms of caseload and available staff," Dr. Levy presented, at an American Psychiatric Association meeting, details on how to conduct 6-session, crisis-oriented psychotherapy. In a subsequent interview with *Roche Report,* Dr. Levy said that a session-by-session account of what the therapist does was requested by the audience hearing his paper at the 1965 APA meeting. "We hoped that this detailed presentation would offer specific guidelines to colleagues desirous of utilizing short-term therapy."

The techniques serve primarily to utilize available manpower effectively and to maintain the patient in his family in the community. "We have aimed this service at the patient who would normally be institutionalized," Dr. Levy told *Roche Report.*

Admission for treatment is limited to individuals who are severely disturbed (i.e., have acute psychoses, acute depressive reactions or severe anxiety reactions), are financially indigent, and who have lost ability to function in the family and on the job because of mental illness. "Any patient who needs attention urgently can be seen immediately," said Dr. Levy. "In this way, the clinic serves as a walk-in clinic, although the walk-in clinic patient is not usually as acutely disturbed as our patients. Our average patient and his family generally can and will wait three or four days before being seen, comforted in the knowledge that they have a definite appointment and something will be done."

Plan of Each Session. Each patient is limited to a total of six sessions, including the admission interview. The first session lasts 45 minutes, with subsequent interviews 30 minutes or less. The length of time between visits varies; "it is tailor-made for each patient." Although the average length of time between visits is one to two weeks, some patients have had three visits in one week, others, one visit every few weeks. If, after the six sessions, the patient is not sufficiently recovered to remain in the home and return to at least partial functional capacity, institutionalization is arranged. Follow-up visits for patients carried successfully through the program may occur in not less than a month.

At the *first visit,* the therapist states concretely that the purpose of the clinic visit is to help the patient avoid hospitalization, and that this is to be accomplished in a maximum of six visits. The patient's history is obtained with particular reference to uncovering factors that precipitated the current crisis, as well as similar past episodes. A supportive approach, actively embarked on, includes empathizing with the patient's plight (i.e., reflecting empathically upon his discomfort, confusion, chaos), enlisting the patient as an ally in the mutual effort toward resolving the crisis, and emphasizing the availability of the therapist and his intention of helping the patient. In addition, medication is often prescribed, and arrangements made for special services, such as homemaker or public health nurse visit, if required.

Concurrent with this first visit, the family is interviewed by the social worker who, during the session, phones the therapist to relate important history or current events; the therapist tells the social worker of planned treatment regarding medication, necessary environmental manipulation, date of next visit. The social worker then orients the family. A brief, cogent, readable record on the patient is prepared immediately following the visit, giving only essentials of history, mental status, diagnostic evaluation, and outline of treatment program.

The process of treatment sessions has a continuity, one session blending into those following, according to Dr. Levy. Each clinic day starts with a brief orientation conference with the social worker and psychotherapist covering all agency and family contacts of patients to be seen. Similarly, the clinic homemaker relates her experiences in direct patient care during the previous day. Thus, the staff is able to keep abreast of potentially explosive situations and avoid treating patients "in a vacuum."

At the *second session,* the therapist expresses directly to the patient his observation of improvement, with the specific aim of diminishing the patient's fear of mental disintegration, and reinforcing the supporting role of the clinic. The patient's personal concept of "going crazy" is explored and differentiation made between fantasy and action. Repetitious differentiation of thought and action has been found to be of particular importance for the very disturbed patient. The therapist can reflect his attitude in such statements as, "You feel yourself pulling together and gaining control," "Yes, you are recovering from your breakdown," "You and I know you have these murderous thoughts and fantasies but nothing has happened—they never go beyond thoughts."

Gaps in history are filled and a clearer picture developed of the patterns and process of the patient's illness. Current environmental status is evaluated. The need for further manipulation of the home situation is not based solely on the patient's impression, but also on the impression of the home situation as obtained by the social worker in this concurrent interview with a family member. A therapeutic platform for the remaining sessions, based on clarification of history and environment, is then established.

The psychiatrist delineates the patient's characteristic mode of response to relationships and events likely to trigger future crises and guides the patient toward recognition of these. This has been successfully accomplished by helping the patient recall trouble situations in terms of his feelings and physiologic responses, e.g., tightening of stomach, beating of heart, sensation that the "bottom has dropped out." In essence, an attempt is made to equip the patient with the ability to recognize and then express his feelings. The interview is terminated with reiteration of recognition of the patient's improvement and the therapist's optimism for the future.

The *third session* is initiated by reinforcing recognition of the patient's improvement and his ability to deal with his illness. The major work of this session is concerned with continuing to clarify the dynamic factors thought to contribute to the patient's illness, helping him recognize his patterns of disturbance, and teaching him to express his feelings. Emphasis is often shifted from precipitating factors to current life situation and related emotions. The patient's difficulty in handling these reactions is verbalized and a need to develop a plan of approach to conflictual situations stressed, both in the light of their destructive influence and in the rapid passing of treatment time. This sets the platform for teaching the patient alternate methods of handling difficult situations. No attempt is made to cover all major areas in the patient's life. Focus is on teaching him methods of coping with a particular, difficult situation. Questions on the approaching termination of therapy must be discussed in the light of the patient's ability to develop new techniques of learning to cope with his problems. Toward the end of this third session, the "patient is beginning to function on shaky legs," being concerned less with happenings and more with the future, Dr. Levy said.

Focus during the *fourth and subsequent sessions* is again upon a simple, repetitive, concrete statement to the effect that the patient has mastered his problem sufficiently to function, and is in the process of developing a plan of action to meet future stress. The patient has by now had an opportunity to practice his new techniques of coping. If the new techniques have failed, the failure is investigated. Anticipated stressful situations are rehearsed; such rehearsals are considered extremely important. One patient, for example, delighted in telling the therapist of a visit with her mother-in-law and of how she (the patient) had mastered her usual feelings of confusion and anger generated by such visits. Anticipating the visit, she had planned ahead, and rehearsed in a scene similar to those conducted in a previous clinic session, the events likely to take place—the things her mother-in-law would say, the involvement of the husband, how she (patient) would react, how she would like to respond, and what she would actually say and do. "The patient had apparently carried off the weekend beautifully and was luxuriating in the feeling of mastery," said Dr. Levy.

Because early life experiences of the majority of these acutely disturbed patients have often equipped them for defeat rather than successful resolution of life's daily problems; they have a great potential for mental disintegration. Therefore, "learning mastery of their comparatively simple family or life situation is a very important building block in shoring up a flimsy foundation." Maintenance of the bond between the clinic and these very fragile patients, even without actual interview, is very important. Therefore, to help sustain them, therapy is terminated with the understanding that the clinic is available if further crises occur. If necessary, a long-term follow-up appointment—in two, three or four months—may be given.

"I cannot emphasize sufficiently the importance of the team approach to short-term treatment of acute patients. Many families are themselves disturbed and must be treated by the social worker simultaneously with treatment of the patient by the psychotherapist. Without the social worker, the family support so essential to the success of therapy would not be available," Dr. Levy said.

XII. The Motivation-Hygiene Concept and Psychotherapy

by Frederick Herzberg and Roy M. Hamlin[*]

The motivation-hygiene concept grew out of a study of job attitudes. In that study engineers and accountants reported two kinds of experiences: a period in their professional career when their job satisfaction was very high, and a period when it was very low. They reported the factors which caused this satisfaction or dissatisfaction, their attitudes at the time and the effects on their adjustment.

In general, they talked about one set of factors leading to satisfaction, and a distinctly different set leading to dissatisfaction. The satisfaction or motivator factors included achievement responsibility, and goal-directed effort. The dissatisfaction or hygiene factors included supervision by others, interpersonal relations, working conditions, salary, and company policy and administrative practices.

The motivation-hygiene concept of job attitudes suggests that satisfaction on the job depends on task-oriented factors, whereas, dissatisfaction depends on context factors or surrounding conditions. The factors that lead to satisfaction do not influence dissatisfaction, and vice-versa. One set of factors is not the opposite of, or the absence of, the other set. Nor is one set primary to the other. Each of the factors serves different functions—one to avoid unpleasantness and the other to actualize the individual self.

The importance of the two distinct sets of factors to research in job satisfaction can hardly be overestimated. Traditional research in job attitudes has consistently emphasized the betterment of surrounding conditions, largely neglecting the self-actualization factors.

---

[*] From *Mental Hygiene,* V. 47, No. 3, 384–397 (July 1963). Adapted and used with permission of publisher and authors.

In a number of other studies, it has been shown that age, job tenure, place of work, and other demographic variables show no substantial effect on the above relationships.

Generalization of Theory to Broader Problems of Mental Health. The study brought out the following points: (1) It suggested a break with the tradition of a single continuum of mental illness to mental health and argued that we should properly think of each, i.e., mental illness and mental health as two distinct continua. It defined the mental illness continuum in terms of success with which individuals avoid unpleasantness in their life. The mental health continuum, in contrast, is defined in terms of the success with which an individual approaches psychological growth; (2) The mental illness factors described essentially the environment or extra-individual stimuli. Included in environmental factors are interpersonal relationships, such social-psychological influences as status, and the more tangible aspects of the physical environment. The mental health factors referred to occurrences which provide opportunity for self-actualization or psychological growth—task challenges, task achievements, responsibilities etc.; (3) The theory indicates that the environmental factors can only provide for the absence of mental illness and that they have no power to bring forth mentally healthy states; (4) The mental health factors serve primarily to promote mental health while having little effect in producing mental illness. No one is made sick by lack of growth potential, just as no one is made healthy by an abundance of hygiene factors; (5) While all organisms seek to satisfy both their approach-motivation needs, the mentally ill person seeks to achieve positive meaning in life via the hygiene factors.

This theory seems to suggest that psychotherapy has emphasized hygiene factors and mental illness. The motivator factors and mental health have been consistently neglected. It becomes apparent that therapy oriented toward the removal of unpleasantness coming from either environmental sources or interpsychic sources can achieve only a temporary non-illness state. The task of therapy is more fundamentally the correction of an inversion of motivation—specifically, the redirection of a person's goals for proper satisfaction away from the hygiene factors to the motivator factors.

It is not necessarily the achievement of psychological growth that is the primary goal of therapy, but the instilling within the patient of the desire to seek growth. It is the motivational change that is essential. If the desire for growth is there and the patient seeks his satisfaction from growth, an adverse hygiene will only have a noxious effect on him rather than the mental illness effect.

The mental illness stems from the combination of the noxiousness and the desire for happiness from the avoidance. If therapy can eliminate the latter, the seeking of happiness from avoidance of unpleasantness—it will serve first to vitiate the effects of unpleasantness and, secondly, it will bring the individual to a state whereby it becomes possible for him, given the chance, to become mentally healthy, as distinct from rising merely to the state of no mental illness.

Thus the primary goal is to bring about a motivational pattern which corresponds to the expectations that the two dimensional motivator-hygiene concept of mental health suggests, i.e., the satisfaction of the hygiene needs to serve only the avoidance, defensive, negative results. By reinforcing those factors which serve the avoidance-hygiene needs, we do not reinforce the growth-motivator needs.

Summary. Four principles for use in psychotherapy emerge: (1) The objective of therapy should be the reorientation of the individual's motivation to seek growth and not the alleviation of psychological stress; (2) Satisfaction from experiencing growth can arise only when there is opportunity to achieve on some task. It is a choice of a task-oriented approach in the face of difficulties over a difficulty-oriented approach in the face of a task; (3) The therapist must make absolutely clear the distinction between hygiene therapy and motivator therapy. The therapist cannot do the patient's behaving for him, but he can set, program, and manipulate the motivator factors—responsibility, effort, and sequence of achievement steps; (4) The therapist must avoid teaching or encouraging the patient's view of his illness as determined by forces beyond his control.

How these principles are formed into a specific technology of psychotherapy is the task and challenge for the mental health profession. The ingredients for the technology lie dispersed among all the current approaches, and perhaps what is required is not new methods, but a rebuilding of psychotherapy out of planks from the many structures that have proved architecturally unsound.

XIII. Some Empirical Approaches to the Study of Life's Basic Tendencies

*by Charlotte Buhler**

One of the most decisive and most difficult problems in the study of the basic tendencies of human life is the question of how the innumerable concrete goals that we pursue in our daily living tie up with the ultimate overall tendencies of our lives.

This is, of course, the question which Freud asked and tackled ingeniously at a time when we all considered it impossible to even approach at all. Psychoanalysis has in the half century of its existence, furthered an enormous wealth of material in answer to this question.

However, some of us felt it necessary to digress from the theoretical framework of psychoanalysis. The reason was that within it, it seemed impossible to explain certain phenomena of normal development satisfactorily. To these events belong the primary nature of creativity, of a positive reality, of some of our value orientation.

As for myself, I have, in several publications, given my reasons for the necessity of this digression. I also showed how, from all the available relevant information, I derived four basic tendencies of life which I called: *need-satisfaction, self-limiting adaptation, creative expansion, and upholding of the internal order.* The overall end-goal I called fulfillment in preference to self-realization, because the concept of fulfillment allows for different possible types of satisfying closure experiences.

Very briefly, need-satisfaction comprises essentially the area cov-

---

* In L. N. Solomon (ed),"A Symposium on Human Values." *J. Humanistic Psychol.* (1962), 2, 89–111. Adapted and used with permission. Dr. Buhler's work in this field. Later reports can be found in several Journals, in her *Life Goods Inventory: Manual and Scoring Devices* and her book, *The Human Course of Life in Its Goal Aspects* (in preparation).

ered by the psychoanalytic concept of discharge. It refers to more or less acute needs of any kind that call for satisfaction. *Self-limiting adaptation* is conceived of originating as a primary unconscious behavior that takes place to the degree that hindrances and demands are experienced as negative realities.

Also *creative expansion and upholding of the internal order* are conceived of as originating in primary unconscious processes in the infant. Creative expansion begins in the newborn's experimental movements and becomes a matter of conscious goal-setting and planning of accomplishments from about two or three years on, when the child begins to build playfully with blocks and when he begins to feel like a person equipped with the power to do and to *decide* things.

The concept of *upholding of the internal order* refers first of all to the internal organization and integration of processes which again starts on an unconscious level. On the secondary conscious level, this order-making becomes related to principles and values which we might call matters of *conscience,* in which *self-assessment* plays a role. This also begins at about two to three years of age.

My thesis is that in every individual all of these tendencies are in operation at all times, but to individually varying degrees and patterns, consciously as well as sub- and un-consciously. All of these tendencies are necessary for life and survival. Everybody needs to satisfy his needs; everybody has to adapt; every individual needs to produce or create in the widest sense of planned accomplishments; everybody has to uphold a certain degree of internal order in terms of integrated and coordinated functioning, and in terms of consideration of principles of conscience.

However, different individuals seem from the beginning—and with this I refer to infant observations on activity degrees and other primary differences—more inclined to steer themselves in one or the other of these directions. Environmental influences and experiences of life may enhance or also modify these inclinations. Directional patterns result in which more or less one-sided trends become sometimes temporarily *need-satisfiers.* They are first set on *happiness* in the sense of comfort, pleasure, love. The person who is primarily adaptive, always appears strongly impressed by the human being's inadequacy in the face of the overwhelming power of circmustances and of the surrounding world. These people's feelings about human frailty induce them to curtail their own wishes in the interest of *security* often in submitting to a hopefully protective *authority* of one kind or another.

The primarily *expansively creative* individual is, on the contrary, confident of his strength, of his ability to master circumstances and to improve and change the world to suit man's needs.

The individual who is primarily concerned with the *upholding of his internal order* seems mostly determined by the need for inner *harmony* and *peace of mind.* These he hopes to attain in pursuing certain *beliefs* and *values.* By means of these pursuits he tries to establish his own *worth.*

. . . . .

One more word about the *developmental* sequence of these four basic tendencies. As we said, all four are at all times in operation within the person, although with an individual emphasis on one or the other. Besides the individual emphasis we also find a *developmental* predominance at different stages of life. We can observe the *sequence* of an initial predominance of need-satisfying tendencies in the infant, followed by predominantly adaptive trends in childhood, this again is followed by the predominance of creative expansion in adolescence and adulthood and then by an emphasis on self-assessment in the interest of internal order in the climacteric years. After this, many individuals regress to the need-satisfying tendencies of infancy or to childhood's self-limitation, which retirement imposes on them, while others seem able to keep up their creative expansion.

I will now enumerate briefly the techniques which I tried and then dwell a little longer on my latest attempt which looks to me like the most hopeful one.

(1) I tried to obtain *biographical* and *autobiographical* data, comprehensive enough to interpret them in terms of conscious *self-determination.*

(2) I tried a Questionnaire about Goals. In setting it up, I was helped by two experts in the construction of questionnaires, Hermann Harvey and Raymond Corsini. But as we anticipated, we got only rather superficial constructs in spite of much precaution in our questions.

(3) I studied my *psychotherapy* records with respect to information they would yield on goals of patients. This is naturally the most fruitful technique as far as *depth material* is concerned.

(4) *Interviews* outside of psychotherapy situations are important, provided they can be carried on by a clinician and for a sufficiently long time, so as to lead below surface information. They also should preferably be *structured* to the degree that the basic tendencies come into the fore. On this method I plan to work still further.

(5) Following Paul Lazarsfeld's suggestion, I devised a questionnaire on *decisions.* This yields very interesting information, although it has all the shortcomings of spontaneous material. However, consider it worthwhile pursuing.

(6) The most promising in terms of systematic completeness and allowing for some degree of indirection is, however, a new question-

naire device which I conceived and tried only recently. It asks people to check off a list of suggested goals. The list of these was obtained in trying to envisage what the four basic tendencies would amount to in terms of *concrete objectives.* This, of course, involves some hypothesizing.

. . . . .

There are 16 values and fulfillments representing each of the four tendencies, altogether 64. They appear on the form in intermingled order. The subject is asked to check each of these goals in choosing from five possible categories. These are called: "essential," "important," "desirable," "not my concern," and "rejected."

The 64 goals are all socially more or less acceptable. I did not see any usefulness in putting down unacceptable goals, at least not as long as I am working with more or less normal people who function in society, who would not admit to socially unacceptable goals and who might even become suspicious of the whole check-list if they were asked such questions. This could, of course, still be changed if it seemed advisable.

Summarizing I should like to say, that among a number of different methods I tried to obtain empirical material on basic tendencies of life, this last questionnaire method appears to be the most promising. In conjunction with a clinically-oriented interview approach, I foresee in this questionnaire a useful new instrument for studying people's goal- and value-orientation in terms of basic tendencies of life.

PROGRESS REPORT ON THE EMPIRICAL APPROACH TO THE STUDY OF LIFE'S BASIC TENDENCIES

Since the preceding study was published in 1962, the questionnaire, now called *Life Goals Inventory,* has been developed to the point where it seems to be a usuable instrument.

The original questionnaire has been enlarged from 64 to 86 questions, and factor analysis studies of two samples have been conducted by Andrew L. Comrey and Richard S. Coleman, which result in a profile of the individual's professed goals, appear in the jointly authored *Life Goals Inventory Manual* (1964). The goal profile graphically represents the distribution of choices among twelve factors arranged in groups corresponding to the four basic tendencies. The 12 factors are: necessities of life; pleasure, love, and family; sex satisfaction; acceptance of limitations; submissiveness; avoidance of hardships; self-development; leadership, fame, and power; role in public life; moral values; social values; and having success.

Individual profiles indicating preferred versus less preferred or even rejected goals yield certain characteristic motivational patterns when subjected to analysis.

First, in comparing the profiles of relatively healthy individuals, we regularly find pronounced preferences expressed for "love and family," "moral values," and "social values." Depending upon the individual's potentials, there is strong or relatively strong belief in "self-development," adequate "acceptance of limitations," and an adequate belief in "having success." "Necessities of life," and "sex satisfaction" play a moderate to an important role.

The rest of the items, "submissiveness," "avoidance of hardships," "leadership," "role in public life," vary more widely in their distribution.

Second, in the healthy person's profile we do not find extreme scores. In fact, in cases of persons who live rather contented, unimpassioned lives, all scores cluster around the middle score (fifteenth percentile).

Third, the neurotic person, by contrast, tends to exhibit jagged profile patterns with extreme scores on demands as well as on limitations. There may be excessive expectations regarding success, self-development, leadership, or sex. There may be complete denial of self-limitations or excessive self-limitations and submissiveness. There may also be overemphasis on moral values or self-denial in terms of expecting very little satisfaction from life. Finally, there may be fear of sex expressed in very low scores.

Fourth, there are many incompatible scores in neurotic profiles. Extraordinary success may be hoped for without willingness to accept limitations or without interest in self-development. There may be profound submissiveness and yet the expectation of being a leader or disbelief in one's own success while aspiring to a role in public life.

XIV. Implications of Experimentally Induced Contemplative Meditation

by Arthur J. Dukman, M.D.[*]

This paper reports some results of a phenomenological investigation of meditation phenomena and attempts to explain the data and relate it to a broader context.

Procedure. In order to investigate the mystic experience, an experimental procedure was devised based on classical description of contemplative meditation. This procedure can be described as one of perceptual concentration. An initial short-term experiment study showed that very striking changes in the perception of the self and of objects were possible through the use of this procedure, and there were also indications that analogues to the classical mystic experience could be achieved as well.

The same procedure was then employed to study the effects of perceptual concentration over a longer period of time. The original experiment involved a total of 12 "concentration" sessions. It was hoped that four to six of the subjects could be studied over a total of 70 or more sessions.

The data with which this paper is concerned came primarily from two subjects, A and G, who completed the longest series of sessions. These subjects had the most intense and unusual experiences of the group, approximately in direct relationship to the number of sessions. In this connection it should be noted that vivid experiences seemed, on the one hand, to indicate a tolerance and compatibility with the procedure and, on the other hand, to motivate the subject to continue over a long period of time.

[*] From *The Journal of Nervous and Mental Diseases,* Vol. 142, No. 2 (1966), pp. 101–116. Adapted and used with permission.

Subject A was a 38 year-old psychiatric nurse who was undergoing psychoanalysis at the time of the experiment. Subject G was a 40 year-old housewife. Both subjects were personally known to the experimenter and were asked to participate in the experiment on the basis of their apparent intelligence, interest, and available time. Subject G was paid, Subject A was not. It seemed clear that money was not a crucial factor in their participation. There was evidence of neurotic conflicts (by history and the MMPI), but both subjects were functioning relatively normally in their environment.

The experiment was conducted in a comfortable, carpeted office—the lighting, colors, and atmosphere of which were subdued. The subject sat in an armchair about 10 feet from a medium blue vase which rested on a simple brown end table; the experimenter sat to one side and behind the subject at a desk on which there were two tape recorders. It was necessary to move to a different experimental room twice during the course of the experiment but the general atmosphere was maintained and the change did not seem to affect the phenomena reported by the subjects.

Contemplative meditation requires that the subject relinquish his customary mode of thinking and perceiving. Thoughts must be stopped, sounds and peripheral sensations put out of one's mind, and the contemplation of the meditative object be conducted in a nonanalytic, nonintellectual manner. This aim determined the composition of the instructions that were read by the experimenter to the subjects immediately preceding the first few sessions.

The same type of question was raised by both subjects. The principle difficulty encountered by the subjects was grasping the concept of "not thinking": to cease actively examining or thinking about the vase. The main problem that required additional explanation was the confusion about whether to try to block out all sensations arising during the session. They were told that insofar as the sensations were part of the experience of concentration rather than distraction or interference, they should accept them.

After a few initial sessions of 10 and 15 minutes of concentration, with cello music played as a background on the tape recorder, the concentration period was extended to 30 minutes and performed in silence. At the end of the designated time, the experimenter gave the signal "30 minutes" and the subject could stop or continue longer if she desired.

After the subjects had finished concentrating, the experimenter conducted an inquiry based on the following questions: (1) How did it go? (2) Describe the course of the session, etc. The remaining questions dealt with the time they could concentrate, thoughts, feelings, experience, and intent. The interview was flexible, designed to elicit whatever phenomena the subject had experienced and to follow up anything of interest to the experimenter. During the inquiry the experimenter endeavored to be as neutral as possible, but from time to time it was necessary to reinstruct the subjects in the procedure and to deal with the subject's anxiety when startling phenomena occurred. The inquiry lasted about 20 minutes and was tape recorded in its entirety.

Results and Discussion. In trying to understand the data that resulted from the experiment, a basic question was asked: What was the subject perceiving? The bulk of the percepts resulting from the experiment seemed readily explained in terms of such familiar concepts as after-images, phosphenes, stabilized retinal images, projection, and distortion. The data selected for discussion consists of perceptual phenomena whose explanation may require the construction of additional hypotheses.

The perceptual experiences were characterized by: (1) an unusual way of perceiving (e.g., light is felt; motion of the vase is felt but not seen—force envelops) although the usual perceptual routes are also employed; (2) the percepts are intensely real.

Suggestion by the experimenter in an overt sense was ruled out as a cause for the phenomena. However, some covert suggestion may have taken place. But suggestion seems to be ruled out by the fact that the phenomena were unexpected by the experimenter and thus he could not hint to what he wanted the subjects to see.

If you use Freud's definition of projection emphasizing its function of defense against the awareness of anxiety-provoking internal context, and apply it to the subject's experiences already stated, we see that the content of their perception did not consist of affect, motives, or ego-alien ideation but, rather, was composed of sensations referable to such qualities as force, light, and motion. Such sensory qualities do not lend themselves readily to explanations centered on defense against drives. The classical concept of "projection" does not seem to explain this experimentally obtained data.

Theory. To account more adequately for the experimental data, the process of sensory translation is postulated. Sensory translation is defined as the perception of psychic action (conflict, repression, problem solving, attentiveness, etc.) through the relatively unstructured sensations of light, color, movement, force, sound, smell, and taste. It refers to the experience of nonverbal, simple, concrete perceptual equivalents of psychic action. It comes into operation as a consequence of the altered cognitive mode brought about by the experimental instructions which focus on perceiving instead of thinking.

External Theory. De-automatization is an undoing of the automatization of apparatuses—both means and goal structures, directed toward the environment. It is, as it were, a shake-up which can be followed by an advance or a retreat in the level of organization. As automatization is the process by which the integration of the somatic systems involved in an action are automatized and with it the integration of the individual mental acts involved in it, then de-automatization is the undoing of automatization, presumably by reinstating actions and percepts with attention.

The experimental procedure produces a de-automatization of normal perceptual modes permitting the operation of sensory translation. At the same time a de-automatization of the reality function occurs such that the sense of reality normally bestowed on objects is now "transferred" to abstract psychical entities. As stated earlier, the experimental pressure away from abstract thought and towards pure perception fits the explanation.

Such a concept of de-automatization as a liberating process (liberated to experience in a new total stimulus array) leads to the hypothesis of perceptual expansion—the widening of perceptual intake to encompass "new" external stimuli, with a new perceptual route implied. Perceptual expansion is made possible by de-automatization of the selective gating and filtering processes that normally are in constant operation.

There is a developmental concept implicit in such a hypothesis, namely, that our earliest experience is probably one of being in more direct contact with numerous, vivid, primitively organized stimuli. As we mature, a learning process takes place in which stimuli and percepts are organized towards a high level of differentiation based on formal characteristics. This learning process not only takes place at the expense of the vividness and variability of sensory stimuli but possibly involves a loss of special perceptual functions other than those to which we are accustomed. There is evidence to support this concept.

To return to the data from the meditation experiment, it may be that the simpler perception of color, light, energy, force, and movement represents a shift of the "normal" perceptual processes to aspects of the stimulus array previously screened out, or it may be that these percepts are negotiated through the operation of new perceptual processes. In the course of the experiment, certain reports of A and G were very suggestive of this latter possibility. They seemed to be struggling to convey their perception of unfamiliar reality dimensions, difficult to verbalize exactly, requiring metaphors, and seemingly encountered in another realm so that they spoke of "coming back," "elsewhere," "the other place."

Conclusion. The evidence of scientific experience, thus far, is solidly behind the psychological theories that assume an internal origin of the "knowledge" or stimuli of unusual experiences. However, we cannot exclude the possibility that the classical mystic experience, LSD reactions, certain phases of acute psychosis and other unusual experiences represent conditions of special receptivity to external stimuli, ordinarily excluded or ignored in the normal state.

XV. Sense of Interpersonal Competence

by Robert W. White[*]

Every interaction with another person can be said to have an aspect of competence. Acts directed toward another are intended, consciously or unconsciously, to have an effect of some kind; the extent to which they produce this effect can be taken as the measure of competence. When interactions are casual, when we are merely "passing the time of day," the element of competence may be minimal, although even in such cases we are surprised if we produce no effect at all, not even an acknowledging grunt. When matters of importance are at stake, the aspect of competence is bound to be larger. . . .

In the main, competence is not the most distinctive feature of interpersonal behavior, and its significance is sometimes overlooked. If the transaction involves an important need, our attention is drawn to the gratification or frustration of that need, rather than to the background theme of effectiveness in dealing with people. Yet this background theme is always there, and we should always try to reckon with it. When a child wants to go to the circus but cannot persuade his parents to take him, he suffers a frustration of those urges that draw children to the circus—curiosity, excitement, adventure—and he may also be wounded by the revealed shortcoming of parental love, especially if it signifies that a sibling, taken to the circus the year before, is more warmly loved. But implicit in the whole situation is a setback to his sense of competence in dealing with his parents. He has failed to elicit their sympathetic interest in his heartfelt desires; he has failed

[*] From Robert W. White, *The Study of Lives,* pp. 72–93. Used with permission of publisher and author. Copyright © 1963, Atherton Press, New York.

to secure their cooperation in satisfying those desires. Along with his more direct frustrations, he has suffered a decrement of confidence in his ability to make himself effective in the human environment. . . .

We can detect the influence of sense of competence in the judgments we are constantly making, often half-consciously, about what we can and cannot do. . . . Past actions, successful and unsuccessful, have taught us the ranges of our effectiveness. Sense of competence is the result of cumulative learning, and it is ever at work influencing the next thrust of behavior. . . .

Although these thoughts may rank as self-evident truths with respect to dealing with the physical environment, the part played in the growth of personality by a sense of interpersonal competence has not been so clearly discerned. We shall examine it here by comparing two lives that afford a certain contrast, although neither can be considered to represent a pathological extreme.

CHATWELL AND MERRITT AS COLLEGE STUDENTS

Our subjects are two college students, 20 years of age, whom we shall call John Chatwell and Harold Merritt. They originally crossed the doorstep of the Harvard Psychological Clinic to serve as paid subjects in psychological experiments, but they were persuaded to expand this role by participating in extensive studies of personality, amounting in the end to more than 30 hours of interviews, tests, and experiments. Evidence will be presented concerning sense of interpersonal competence in each young man as revealed in this voluminous material. Then we shall look for the consequences later in life, for both men were studied a second time several years later, when they had become somewhat settled in their careers.

STYLES OF SPEECH

As a start, a special test to compare style of speech was administered to the two students. In general, Chatwell's was more "colorful, varied, emphatic, direct, active, . . . not so much to describe the external world and its relations as to express his own individuality and to impress the auditor." Merritt's speech was "complex, perseverative, thorough, uncoordinated, cautious, static, highly definitive, and stimulus-bound . . . seems to reflect a desire to avoid blame or disapproval."

RECOLLECTIONS OF HISTORY

During Chatwell's boyhood the family circle, which included the parents and a younger brother and sister, was the scene of much lively discussion and some quarreling. Both parents had scientific and other intellectual interests, and the father particularly enjoyed tossing out controversial problems for debate at the dinner table. Chatwell's mother, when interviewed, was a bit apologetic about the high-strung atmosphere of the home, but her eldest son looked back upon it with considerable satisfaction. He made it clear that the quarrels did not run deep: "I never remember an argument on any really important subject such as our education; it was generally on some never-proven point such as the question of who gained or lost the most in the World War." The picture that emerges is one of underlying secure solidarity, which gave the children a feeling of freedom to express and assert themselves. . . .

Merritt's account of his childhood was a little more somber. His middle-class parents were much involved in local civic affairs, and he recalled occasions when they would be out for the evening, when his older brother would also go out, leaving him alone and tearful in the house. He complained of "never having the real experience of a close family connection" and reported his envy of friends at whose houses he would find "their parents and brothers and sisters sitting in the front room and talking; this is an experience of which a greater part of my earlier life was deprived." He averred that his parents had never shown much sympathy for his troubles or excitement over his successes. "Everything is taken as a matter of course," he said, "I was never helped or admired."

If we turn to interactions with other children, we might conclude that Merritt had made a quicker start toward competence. Chatwell reported himself to have been a cry-baby at the start of school, whereas Merritt remembered at the age of six "inviting all my young friends to play in the yard with me." These sessions in the yard were marred by fits of temper on the part of the host: "I was stubborn and would get angry if they didn't agree to play my games or go where I wanted to go."

There was an interesting difference in the way the two young men described their relations with girls. As a sophomore, Chatwell wrote rhapsodically about the girl with whom he was then in love; as a senior, falling in love with the girl he ultimately married, he enlarged upon the relation developing between them without any particular emphasis on its physical aspect. To Merritt the sexual side was much more pre-occupying, though surrounded by embarrassment and guilt. Chronologically, Merritt might again be said to have made the quicker start; long before puberty he had been in a fist fight over a girl whom he wanted to kiss, whereas Chatwell at this age viewed girls with contempt. But Merritt's head start did not betoken fast progress. He was slow to attain confidence with girls. . . .

SELF-DESCRIPTIONS IN THE PRESENT

As sophomores, the subjects filled out a long questionnaire devised by Murray, consisting of highly specific items of behavior indicative of various needs. The following four needs, each represented by 10 items scattered through the questionnaire, are most relevant to a sense of interpersonal competence.

Dominance: to control one's human environment; to influence or direct the behavior of others.
Aggression: to overcome opposition forcefully; to attack, fight, injure; to belittle, censure, or ridicule maliciously.
Deference: to admire and support a superior; to praise, emulate, and yield eagerly to the influence of such a person.
Abasement: to submit passively to external force; to surrender; to accept injury, criticism, punishment, and belittlement.

Averaging the self-ratings given on the ten specific items in each case and using a scale of 0 to 5, we find our two subjects describing themselves as follows:

SUBJECT	DOMINANCE	AGGRESSION	DEFERENCE	ABASEMENT
Chatwell	3.8	3.6	2.7	1.2
Merritt	3.1	2.5	3.2	2.2

Merritt thus considers himself a shade more deferent than he is dominant and nearly as abasive as he is aggressive. Chatwell, on the other hand, puts himself decidedly high on both dominance and aggression, near the midpoint on deference, and very low on abasement—a picture of easy interpersonal self-confidence.

The same differences appear rather consistently throughout the interviews, especially in the subjects' allusions to their abilities. Questioned about leading and governing ability, Chatwell pronounced himself a good executive, who knew how to delegate authority, and said, "Responsibility in emergencies is my meat." Merritt could not recall taking an active part in an emergency. He felt that "as far as leading others is concerned, I can hold my own"; mentioned specific instances in which others had turned to him for advice; and replied to a question about his persuasive skill: "I think I can get my way—well, I mean, if my point is correct I can persuade others."

PLANS AND PROSPECTS

As sophomores, Chatwell and Merritt were both asked to write something about their self-estimates and expectations for the future. In the mantle of prophecy, Chatwell wrote as follows:

> I like people, and I think they like me. I get along well with people and can generally get them to do what I want—within reasonable limits, of course. I am well enough informed to be able to carry on a decent conversation with people from whom I may learn more, although I might never admit that to them. Unfortunately, perhaps, I think rather well of myself, although I realize my limitations. I know that there is some combination of things that I can do better than anyone else; I also know that there is no one of them that someone else cannot do better than I. I have a better than average mind, but I am also more lazy than the average. I have supreme confidence, if not in my skills, in my ability to figure out a way to get something done eventually.

Merritt's inspection of the crystal ball yielded a more guarded picture.

> I think that those whom I know have a favorable attitude toward me. I say this because there are very few people with whom I do not get along. I am treated well in my society—I can see that those of my associates who do not go to college respect me because I do. There are members of my family (whom I have heard speak of me) who say that I ought to be successful because I have a pleasing personality and can get along with people. As for my own estimate of myself, I might say that I do think that if upon graduation the opportunity presents itself, I can make a success of myself. That is, I feel that I have ambitions to graduate from one position to another, until, after ten years or so, I think I can be in a fairly "well-off" position. I think that in the right position, that is, one for which I am cut out, I would be a success, because I hold myself to be intelligent, willing to learn, willing to work hard for success and I think I can hold my own against any equal.

The curiously equivocal ending of the last phrase, possibly a slip, symbolizes beautifully the underlying in Merritt's sense of interpersonal competence.

Do our subjects possess the gift of prophecy? Fortunately, we can find out.

CHATWELL AND MERRITT A DECADE LATER

The military careers of our two subjects exhibit strikingly their difference in sense of interpersonal competence. Chatwell started lower in the military hierarchy but ended higher. He was challenged by competition with other men, and he lost no opportunity to advertise his skills and bring himself to the attention of his superiors. His confidence rose and his self-respect became firmer as a consequence of his success; we get less feeling of bravado as we find him constantly "delivering the goods." Merritt was unable to muster such impressive initiative. His first moves were nearly undone by an unwelcome hesitancy and deference. When the atmosphere included good companionship, he was content and functioned well, but he showed no inclination to push his career in any way that would imperil this source of security.

COURTSHIP AND MARRIAGE

Like so many of their contemporaries, both young men married during the course of their military service. Chatwell married the girl with whom he had fallen in love in the spring of his senior year, the fourth girl in whom he had had a serious interest. Merritt married the girl who had brought out his sexual interest during the spring of his sophomore year, the only girl to whom he was ever strongly drawn.

As a boy half way through college, fearing intercourse with its implication of being "hooked," Merritt had rather sternly broken off his relation with this girl and substituted less involving friendships. But the girl continued to be fond of him, and her parents, though possibly not his, had hoped that a match would occur. By a course of events which he could not clearly recall at the time of the second study, he drifted back into her company and became strongly aware of her hopes. She was tearfully present when he was seen off to the war, but he left without committing himself. His own decision took place one night at the Alaskan base, when there was strong rumor of enemy action with its inevitable choice between death and capture. In the midst of his anxiety he said to himself, "If I ever get out of here, I'll go back and marry her,"—as indeed he did on his next furlough.

Merritt's pattern of courtship reflects a weak sense of interpersonal competence with girls—a continuation of the bashfulness that troubled him in college. He took the first girl who gave him real physical satisfaction; and, overriding his reservations about their ultimate compatibility, he took her more because she wanted him than because he wanted her. He would be lucky if after such a slight search he found an ideal partner. In point of fact, the marriage has worked out, though not as a source of much ecstasy. . . . Apparently the marriage has reached an equilibrium.

Chatwell's final falling in love was the culmination of considerably more experience. As we have seen, he had already gone through the waxing and waning of three love affairs, and he had found his way from a rather abasive to a somewhat more dominant relation. But he by no means sought the competitive dominance that was so dear to him with respect to other men. His girl was lively and intelligent, a proper partner for his conversational talents, but she also provided a welcome sense of peace and security at the end of the day. He described himself as liking busy days but then wanting a place where he could take off his shoes. He was, in his own words, "sunk without firing a shot in about two months," and his only misgiving was that the feeling of security might be influencing him too strongly. His girl seemed to him to be "an ideal combination of intelligence, tenderness, and physical attractiveness." He kept after her, this time with no dying down of interest, for the year that was necessary to persuade her to become his wife; and he was both happy and proud when they were married.

He talked freely of disagreements over punishing the children and other common forms of domestic strife, but there was no bitterness or attempt at self-justification. One got the impression of a marriage in which deep devotion could easily absorb the frictions of domesticity.

FINDING A VOCATION

The occupational histories of Merritt and Chatwell illuminate with unusual clearness the problem of job satisfaction. For both of them, fitting the peg to the hole involved not only the gratifying employment of abilities but also the finding of a congenial pattern of human relations. At the time of the second study the positions they occupied seemed to be almost perfect expressions of the strength and pattern of their respective senses of interpersonal competence.

During the interval between graduation and military service, Merritt held a job from which he was fired and a second one in which he was successful. . . .

After the war he found a position in the New England office of a large financial corporation. At first he felt that he and other veterans had been put in the false position of supervising people who already knew their jobs. Then a high official came from the central office to look things over.

> The job of working with Mr. Driver was thrown to me, and I took an interest and got to work closely with him. He had the reputation of being the meanest so-and-so, but I found him upright. I never argued with him. A man who opposed him was fired after two months and I was put in the job, being made chief of one of the floors.

The people on that floor had wanted to promote one of their own men, so Merritt was "in a fairly tough spot, but to this day I don't have an enemy over the place." He continued to enjoy the support of Mr. Driver, who liked both his loyalty and his intelligence and who gave him opportunities for special training in new procedures. He could even have gone to the central office at higher pay, if he had not been disinclined to move away from friends and family connections. On the whole he was well-satisfied: "I think I've done pretty well for myself. Someone I think is important thinks I'm important, and that has given me a lot of confidence. That, in turn, lets me do a better job."

Merritt has found virtually the perfect way to utilize his interpersonal competence. His unusually strong deference allows him to become the servant of an overbearing, unpopular boss, and his uncertainties are dissolved by his being merely the instrument of company policy. At the same time, he manages to melt the antagonism of those below him through fair and considerate behavior fashioned by his need for their friendship. One must admire his skill in serving two masters. It is not easy, and he often finds himself under considerable tension. At the annual Christmas party, for instance, he must take a clear stand for company policy that no liquor be served and at the same time not spoil the festivities by noticing violations. But he manages well, and thus he fulfills his own prophecy that "in the right position, that is, one for which I am cut out, I would be a success."

Chatwell emerged from military service with the decision fairly well made that he would become a lawyer. He was presently in a position to choose between a large and a small firm, each of which would employ him as a law clerk while he pursued evening study. He made the choice that Merritt probably would not have made: the small firm, he believed, offered greater chances of advancement through independent achievement. Both then and later the work proved to be another instance of "duck soup." In the law classroom he argued the cases with tremendous zest, holding the floor and sometimes even clashing with the professor. In preparing briefs, he was strongly abetted by his excellent memory, wide range of information, and speed of learning, whatever technical matters the case might involve. The pattern of his enthusiasms, intense but short-lived, was no handicap in a business where each case had to be prepared rapidly but then put aside for an entirely different one. He was delighted with the combination of legal scholarship, new facts to be mastered, and "constant strife and argument to exact care and method from my disorderly soul." His seniors in the office accepted him as one of them and were, as he put it, "patient with me and kind to my ego, both when I failed and when I succeeded." His own summary varies but little from his sophomore prophecy:

> And so you see that I am very, very happy, busy as hell, with independence, a measure of security in a form in which I can accept it, a future with several broad avenues besides the attractive one I'm on, and plenty of problems—interesting problems, and none beyond my abilities.

In their military service, in their marriages, and in their jobs, Merritt and Chatwell exhibit the differences in sense of interpersonal competence that could be observed when they were in college. Although they had stripped away some of the illusions of that time of life, both had made gains in confidence and established self-esteem on a more solid basis. Both had been able to find and then to mold situations that went well with their needs and strengths in human relations.

Index

D

P

R

S